The Cost of Weaponized Government & Lawfare

Ken Pedeleose

Table of Contents

Case Id: 1-15101625741

Preface

I am writing this book to provide transparency into the Deep State, weaponized government, and lawfare link to the national debt. Meaning, that an estimated 30%-50% of the national debt could be attributed to the Deep State, weaponized government, and lawfare that have enabled a half century of systemic price gouging tactics against the U.S. Government and taxpayers.

The Deep State existence is normally seen as ambiguous, covert, and dismissed as vast conspiracy theory. In fact, the Deep State is real and traces back a half century to the Nixon administration of the 1970's. On or about 2003, there was a resurrection and improvement of Nixon's tactics, and the use of "Federal Machinery" (weaponization and lawfare of government resources) as administrative weapons, to conceal, and enable, government corruption.

I was a victim of the 2003 onslaught that remained systemic in my career. My career survived, but my reputation was damaged by a string of 13 repetitive retaliatory weaponized lawfare acts. I used that experience to gain insight to the Deep State operations, in some cases, documented minute-by-minute. I used the term "weapon", as in "weaponized government," as early as September 9, 2006. Prior to that, the weaponization was referred to as "Gestapo" tactics in formal complaints to Congress during September 8, 2005 and December 13, 2005. The tactic was later termed "lawfare."

In total, this book is a one-stop shop for reducing the national debt, price control, government efficiency, affordability, understanding the enabling of corruption, while providing transparency into the Deep State, weaponized government, and lawfare. This book is an evidentiary record that uses actual data starting in 1970 (Nixon Administration) up to 2023 capstone case. Many events that Congress is investigating, and society needs transparency on, can be explained by this book. Meaning, transparency into the Deep State herein opens transparency to many other areas normally thought as inaccessible.

Also documented in this book are remedies to drain the Government Swamp. Some of those remedies can start draining the Government Swamp in a matter of minutes. In all, this book explains the process to achieve the same amount of goods and services for government at a lower cost through technical analysis. Meaning, reset the government to efficiency.

Part of the remedy is attention to the cause, followed by definitive action. I designed this book as a one-stop shop to pass to Congress and the President for anyone that is concerned about the national debt, affordability, and reducing cost. If you are reading this please help. I can provide transparency to the problems and suggest a remedy. Getting Government to act against an entrenched Deep State needs wide public support.

<u>The Problem or The Solution</u>: The response to this book will show who wants resolution versus who is part of the problem and wants the Government Swamp expanded. The following is a summary index of understanding and takeaways from the evidence herein.

Evidentiary Record of Events - Now Contemporaneous

Contemporaneous Facts Defined: This book is based on actual data and information documented at the time of infraction and as events unfolded over half a century. This includes Government audits, Reports of Investigation, sworn statements, depositions, affidavits, emails, case file documents, news media reports, etc. The legal term for such data is "contemporaneous." Meaning, documented during infraction, and as events unfolded, not from memory alone. Some peripheral data was found on the internet or publicly known and accepted.

Every effort was made for exact quotes from data down to punctuation within the documents. Even misspelled words, poor grammar, vulgarities, and the like were copied from documents. However, as happens, there may be mistakes missed. But rest assured, the documents used to support this book are far more extensive, intense and incriminating than the quotes provided herein.

The original plan was a disclosure to Congress during 2009. However intense weaponization, lawfare and altered working conditions stalled the release. This allowed more data to be gathered over more decades to reach a half century milestone. Hence, the new disclosure to U.S. Congress, the President, and the public is this book which explains the following.

Index & Takeaways of Salient Facts in this Book

The Deep State, weaponization, and lawfare do exist and have left well documented trails to the highest levels of U.S. Government. Meaning, a contemporaneous, irrefragable, trail.

The Deep State genesis was during the Nixon Administration on or about January 5, 1970.

The Deep State, more than likely, tactically infiltrated National Security Intel community.

The reason the Pentagon cannot pass audits is explained herein.

The U.S. Legal and Judicial System decisions have vastly expanded the Government Swamp. The February 12, 2009 decision, explained herein Chapter 3, drastically increased the Government Swamp and stalled the originally planned 2009 Congressional disclosure.

Specific weaponization and lawfare tactics are outlined herein with supporting evidence.

The reason the F-22 Raptor and F-35 Lightning are the most expensive weapon systems ever built are explained herein.

Specific price gouging tactics (cost increases) are outlined herein.

About 30%-50% of national debt can be attributed to Deep State, weaponization, and lawfare.

Only the U.S President and U.S. Congress can eliminate the Deep State and drain the Government Swamp. Could be done is as little as 5 minutes. The introduction and executive summary follow to explain the aforesaid in greater detail.

Introduction & Executive Summary

I was a Department of Defense (DoD) employee from 1987 to 2020. My job description and duties would be related to the term Department of Government Efficiency (DOGE). DOGE efforts are nothing new in government. Only variation are the names used over the years.

I rose to the level of Subject Matter Expert (SME) and instructor for cost control for direct and indirect (overhead) cost of DoD defense contractors. I taught how to review DoD contractor price proposals for price gouging to make sure taxpayers were treated fairly and government money spent efficiently. I also worked on Congressional investigations, criminal investigations, a Federal Court case, news media support, etc. My resume in Chapter 1 explains in greater detail.

From 1994 to 2020, I worked at the Defense Contract Management Agency (DCMA) in the DoD. From 1994 to 2001 I witnessed an ethical deterioration that exposed the U.S. Government, public, and taxpayers to a high degree of criminal vulnerability, fraud, and public safety issues. I was in a unique data analysis position and was very disturbed by what I was seeing. Working conditions were altered from hostile work atmospheres and corruption was rampant. The only option was going public with a consolidated report to Congress and the President.

July 26, 2002 - Going Public to Protect the Public & Taxpayers

On July 26, 2002 I sent a 90 Page report to 57 Members of Congress, President George W. Bush, and Secretary of Defense Donald Rumsfeld titled "*Department of Defense Technical Report on Criminal Vulnerability and Fraud*". Two other colleagues cosigned the 90-page report. This report would rile the Deep State to engage in tactical weaponize government and lawfare.

Being public saved my career however the Deep State weaponized government and lawfare left my reputation in ruins. The evidence trail proves DCMA (my employer) is the quintessential, textbook, example of weaponized government and lawfare. DCMA tactically weaponized every aspect of administrative power and influence into focused lawfare against me.

One DCMA/Deep State tactic used electronic trails (emails) and other written materials to construct Falsified Trails (retaliations) against me. However, electronic trails have a huge flaw.

Electronic Trails Exposed the Deep State, Weaponized Government & Lawfare

The DCMA electronic trails traced to the highest levels of DoD. The tactical relaying of the emails (forwarding, etc.) left telling, chilling, and incriminating evidence of the retaliatory, weaponized, and lawfare campaign against me that I term Falsified Trails.

Falsified Trails were tactical and came in volleys of adverse personnel actions (lawfare) such as reprimands, suspensions, punitive training, threatening letters, and the like. At one point I was escorted off a Lockheed Martin facility by armed security guards ("Swatted") and had my name placed on a Lockheed Martin, Be On the Look Out (BOLO) list.

The weaponized, lawfare, volleys are likened to volleys of combat artillery shells to destroy enemy positions although volleys against me were adverse personnel actions. I meticulously kept and analyzed the volleys to show an "MRI" (Magnetic Resonance Imaging, of sorts) perspective on the Deep

State, weaponized government, and lawfare in daily operation, sometimes minute-by-minute. That "MRI" evidence forms the real-life experiences outlined in this book.

The point being, U.S. Government corruption, weaponization and lawfare traced to high levels.

Work atmospheres were hostile and altered to the point where the workforce lost sight of its mission. The evidence trail in this book proves this point by placing management behavior on full display. From there, evidence shows how the national debt is affected.

Half Century - Financial Effect of Weaponized Government & Lawfare

(30%-50% of National Debt)

In parallel to lawfare against me, I documented the monetary aspects of DoD corruption using pricing, financial, manufacturing, and quality assurance data, along with DoD Inspector General (DoD IG) audits, criminal investigations, depositions, General Accounting Office (GAO) reports, news media reports, etc. In short, data taken directly from the government "Swamp" to form a blueprint to understand how the weaponized government and lawfare effect the national debt.

The financial analysis result of weaponized government and lawfare was an estimated 30%-50% of the national debt, that was traced back over a half century from oversight organization corruption, weaponization, and lawfare that began in the Nixon Administration (Watergate). The Nixon administration proposed tactics against political foes were a watershed moment (genesis) of the modern weaponization and lawfare outlined in this book.

Oversight Organizations - Nixon/Watergate - Factored in Corruption

The following oversight organizations have contributed to weaponized government, lawfare, national debt, hostile workplace, altered working conditions, etc. Meaning, the following oversight organizations are institutionally not performing their intended mission and thus are contributors and enablers to the institutional aspects of corruption, weaponization, and lawfare.

Department of Justice (DOJ) & Assistant United States Attorney(s) (AUSA)

Department of Defense (DoD) & Department of Defense Inspector General (DoD IG)

National Security Agency (NSA)

Defense Contract Management Agency (DCMA)

Defense Contract Audit Agency (DCAA)

Office of Personnel Management (OPM)

Merit Systems Protection Board (MSPB)

Office of Special Counsel (OSC)

Equal Employment Opportunity Commission (EEOC)

Armed Services Board of Contract Appeals (ASBCA)

U.S. Court of Appeals for the Federal Circuit

Cerberus (Cover-up/Containment) Analogy – Repetitively Used by DCMA

Cerberus was the three headed hound of Hades that kept the dead from leaving and prevented the living from entering. The Cerberus counterpart in U.S. Government is OSC, MSPB, and OPM that contain and cover-up negative information from leaving government. Chapters 2 & 3 explain the Cerberus containment and cover-ups by OSC, MSPB and OPM in detail.

OSC, MSPB, and OPM are the "Federal Machinery" that resulted from Nixon's Watergate era. The evidence presented in this book shows that OSC, MSPB, and OPM, cover-up cases to stop transparency into the true depths of institutional corruption, Deep State, weaponized government, and lawfare. However, DCMA factored in and openly flaunted OSC, MSPB, and OPM cover-ups to provide a valuable looking glass into the propagation of weaponized government and lawfare.

Meaning, DCMA repetitively engaged in text book retaliation, weaponization, and lawfare. OSC, MSPB, and OPM (as needed), along with DOJ, repetitively came to the rescue of DCMA for cover-up. The result was multiple inventory lists of corruption, weaponization, lawfare, etc., documented herein that tied the U.S. Legal System to the "Swamp" and the national debt.

U.S. Legal & Judicial System Predictably Created The "Swamp"

Institutional corruption, weaponization, lawfare and the "Swamp" exists in the U.S Government because the U.S. Legal and judicial system is soft on crime, ineffective, and engage in cover-ups. OSC, MSPB, and OPM are a quasi-judicial subset of the U.S. Legal System that manipulate cases for failure. This manipulation traces to the U.S. Legal system. Meaning, the predictable cover-ups and manipulation created the "Swamp" and allow the "Swamp" to expand. DCMA used the predictable cover-ups, weaponization and lawfare repetitively after July 26, 2002.

Deep State Weaponization & Lawfare Engaged Repetitively 13 Times

After the July 26, 2002 report to Congress went public, DCMA quickly and repetitively engaged in Deep State retaliations. The first two retaliations started early 2003 and provided limited Deep State insight. However, subsequent retaliations and lawfare in 2005 were far more specific, detailed, and ominous. Most likely because I was the leader in a whistleblowing network and was labeled "*extremely effective*" by the DoD IG. Meaning, I was a threat to corruption.

By 2004 the whistleblowing network I led was the real deal threat to corruption. There were substantiated disclosures and strong Congressional support from Senator Charles Grassley. There was a multitude of news media articles related to my whistleblowing. Chapter 1, Resume, has the details. What I didn't know in 2004 was that the DoD IG was also a part of the covert Deep State effort against whistleblowers.

The DoD IG contingent to the Deep State covertly facilitated severing Congressional support for my network of whistleblowers and myself. The Appendices at the end of this book outline a short version of how this was accomplished using actual Deep State documentation that occurred in 2005. Chapter 3, Falsified Trail 3 of 13, has the complete details and is my flagship example.

On September 9, 2006 I sent an initial report to Congress titled *"Insider Cover-up Operations & Retaliatory Investigations In the Department of Defense"*. The report focused on the covert relationship of DCMA and DoD IG using weaponized investigations against whistleblowers. Follow-on information and investigations brought the Deep State, weaponization, and lawfare of DCMA and DoD IG into clear focus. Meaning, as of 2006 weaponized investigations existed and were reported on to Congress. There was a total of 13 Falsified Trails by 2015.

On/about January 10, 2023 the U.S. House Judiciary started a Select Subcommittee, chaired by Representative Jim Jordan, on the Weaponization of the Federal government. That subcommittee shows weaponization is an open topic of discussion in 2023. Meaning, the Subcommittee on the Weaponization of the Federal Government helps prove government weaponization does exist.

In fact, DCMA had used weaponization and lawfare about 20 years prior to House Select Committee on Weaponization, as this book shows. The weaponization with lawfare came in the form of tactical volleys of adverse personnel actions against me personally.

Weaponized Tactical Volleys Using 13 Falsified Trails - Started in 2003

The tactical volleys of adverse personnel actions included a reprimand, four suspensions without pay, punitive training, and multiple threatening letters. My security clearance was revoked although later reinstated when the weaponization and lawfare against me was explained. Chapter 3 has the details and expands on the case evidence used to restore my security clearance.

The tactical volleys summarized by 13 Falsified Trails (FT) as follows:

Volley [FT]	Year	Retaliatory Action	MSPB Case	Federal Case
1[FT(1,2)]	2003	Reprimand[1],"Swatted"	NA	NA
2[FT(3)]	2005	30 Day Suspension	AT-0752-06-0350-I&R-1	2009-3135[2,3]
3[FT(4,5,6)]	2009	1 Day Suspension	AT-1221-10-0662-W-1	2012-3027
3[FT(7,8,9,10)]	2009-2010	14 Day Suspension	AT-1221-14-0260- W-1	2015-3090
4[FT(11,12,13)]	2015	14 Day Suspension	System Too Corrupted	Corrupted

Note 1: Falsified Trail 1 was supposed to be investigated by DoD IG CRI (Civilian Reprisal Investigations) as whistleblower retaliation.

Note 2: Went to Supreme Court Case 09-780.

Note 3: Also went to Judicial Misconduct cases F-09-90008, F-09-90009, and F-09-90010.

DCMA weaponization and lawfare included electronic trails (emails). The main flaw of the electronic trails and documentation to build false cases against me is the fact that the planning and tactics were exposed in writing. In short, DCMA was *"Hoist by one's own petard."* Meaning, DCMA was caught in their own trap since the Falsified Trails were not naturally occurring and were planned out. Once caught DCMA relied on OSC, MSPB, OPM, DOJ and Court of Appeals to ensure the issues were covered up. Falsified Trail 3 is the flagship case.

The point is, the repetitive covert action by DCMA and the Deep State created a long index of names and a significant data trail that explained what later became known as weaponized government and lawfare. The index of names used in this book is as follows.

Volley 1 - Falsified Trails 1 & 2 Index of Names

(May 27, 2003 – August 14, 2003)

Colonel James Wright FT(1,2)	DCMA Commander, 4th Level Supervisor
Joe Caldwell FT(1)	DCMA 2nd Level Supervisor
Keith Ernst FT(1,3)	DCMA District East Director, then DCMA Director
Bruce Krasker FT(1,3)	DCMA Attorney
Charles (Ben) Chaffman FT(1,2)	DCMA Deputy Commander, 3rd Level Supervisor
Leigh Owens FT(1,3)	DCMA Attorney
Joe Cass FT(1)	DCMA Human Resources/Personnel
Sandra Shoemaker FT(1)	Lockheed Martin VP Integrated Company Operations
Dain Hancock FT(1)	Lockheed Martin President Aeronautical Sector
Marcia Farber FT(1)	Lockheed Martin Senior Manager, Marietta Site Account-
Roger Graham FT(1)	Lockheed Martin Attorney
Lee Rhyant FT(1)	Lockheed Martin Site Manager Marietta

Volley 2 - Falsified Trail 3 (Flagship Case) Index of Names

(October 18, 2005 – (Spanned June 21, 2005 – October 18, 2005))

Dan Meyer FT(3)	DoD IG Director Civilian Reprisal Investigations (CRI)
Colonel Nicole Plourde FT(3)	DCMA Commander
Uldric Fiore FT(3)	DoD IG Lead Attorney
Bruce Krasker FT(1,3)	DCMA Attorney
Leigh Owens FT(1,3)	DCMA Attorney
Stacy Scantlebury FT(3)	DCMA Chief, Special Processes, DCMA Atlanta
Keith Ernst FT(1,3)	DCMA Commander District East, then DCMA Director
Sallie Flavin FT(3)	DCMA Deputy Director
Steve Bogusz FT(3)	DCMA Deputy Director District East
Gill Bass FT(3)	DCMA Attorney
Charysse L. Alexander FT(3)	DOJ US Attorney Northern Dist. Atlanta
Gary Jencson FT(3)	DCMA Attorney
Donald Srail FT(3)	DCMA Attorney
S. Zimmit-Mack FT(3)	DCMA Attorney
Nicholas Retson FT(3)	DCMA Attorney
Henrietta Snow FT(3,10)	DCMA Deputy Commander
Leonard Trahan FT(3)	DoD IG Director, DoD IG Defense Hotline
Gentry Shellnut FT(3)	DOJ, US Attorney Supervisor
Thomas Gimble FT(3)	DoD IG, Principal Deputy, Acting DoD IG Director
Ray O'Connor FT(3)	DoD IG Attorney
Mark Boyll FT(3)	DoD IG Attorney
Michael Child FT(3)	DoD IG Attorney
Linda Springer FT(3)	Director Office of Personnel Management (OPM)

Kerry McTigue [FT(3)]	OPM Attorney
Steven Abow [FT(3)]	OPM Attorney
Becky Ronayne [FT(3)]	OPM Attorney-Advisor
Michael Hertz [FT(3)]	DOJ Deputy Assistant Attorney General
Jeanne Davidson [FT(3,4,5,6)]	DOJ Director
Todd Hughes [FT(3)]	DOJ Deputy Director
Michael O'Connel [FT(3)]	DOJ Trial Attorney
Tony West [FT(3,4,5,6)]	DOJ Assistant Attorney General

Volley 3 - Falsified Trail 4, 5, 6, 7, 8, 9, and 10 Index of Names

(March 3, 2009 – February 16, 2010)

Cleo Anderson [FT(4,5,6,7,8,9,10)]	DCMA Attorney
Nanette Nelson [FT(4,5,6,7,8,9,10)]	DCMA First Level Supervisor C-5 Engineering Team
Joe Tessier [FT(6,7,8,9,10)]	DCMA Second Level Supervisor C-5 Team
Lou Gentile [FT(10)]	DCMA C-5 Quality Assurance Supervisor
Colonel Casey Blake [(4)]	DCMA Commander
Henrietta Snow [FT(3,10)]	DCMA Deputy Commander, DCMA
Dorcas Smith [FT(10)]	DCMA Human Resources
Debra Mitchell [FT(10)]	DCMA Human Resources
Jeanne Davidson [FT(3,4,5,6)]	DOJ Director
Tony West [FT(3,4,5,6)]	DOJ Assistant Attorney General
Steven Gillingham [FT(4,5,6)]	DOJ Assistant Director
Christopher Bowen [FT(4,5,6)]	DOJ Trial Attorney
Benjamin Mizer [FT(7,8,9,10)]	DOJ Principal Deputy Assistant Attorney General
Robert Kirschman [FT(7,8,9,10)]	DOJ Director
Elizabeth Hosford [FT(7,8,9,10)]	DOJ Assistant Director
Joshua Kurland [FT(7,8,9,10)]	DOJ Trial Attorney

Volley 4 - Falsified Trails 11, 12, and 13 Index of Names

(March 10, 2015 – September 30, 2015)

Cleo Anderson [FT(11,12,13)]	DCMA Attorney
Mark Buckner [FT(11,13)]	DCMA Second Level Supervisor, Engineering Director
Myra Tate [FT(11)]	DCMA Third Level Supervisor, Deputy Commander
Isaiah Waindi [FT(12,13)]	DCMA First level Supervisor C-5 Team
Debbie Elwell [FT(12,13)]	DCMA Personnel Human Resources
Kimberly Turner [FT(13)]	DCMA FOIA
David Wray [FT(13)]	DCMA FOIA
Scott Faucet [FT(12,13)]	DCMA Investigator
Lt. General Wendy Massiello	DCMA Director
Captain Michael Murphy	DCMA Director East
Ray Burick	Lockheed Martin Vice President C-5 Program
Diane Stefani	Lockheed Martin Human Resources Director (Marietta)
Brad Kent	Lockheed Martin C-5 Manager
Ann Holland	Lockheed Martin Business/Finance
Denise Joyce	Lockheed Martin Pricing and Estimating

Common Ancestry with Other Events Linked to National Debt

With my observations and knowledge of institutional corruption, weaponized government, and lawfare, I am not surprised by the other events that have occurred in the U.S.

Those events include the Fat Leonard scandal, Boeing door blow out, Boeing guilty plea to defraud the U.S. for two fatal 737 MAX crashes, September 11, 2001 terrorist attacks, fall of Enron & WorldCom, Valerie Plame case, Pentagon failing audits, Minnesota fraud case, and many other such events. Meaning, my experiences are a subset of a bigger picture and more entrenched, institutional, problem in U.S. Government.

In short, a common ancestry linked via institutional corruption, weaponization, deteriorating ethics, lawfare, and oversight infrastructure failure with a connection to the national debt.

Encyclopedia of Weaponized Government & Lawfare

Chapter by Chapter Connection to National Debt & Government Swamp

The ancestry link to the national debt and expansion of the Government Swamp is built and supported Chapter by Chapter herein as an encyclopedia of linked events as follows.

Chapter 1: Whistleblowing and personal resume. Shows my efforts to support taxpayers, protect government interests' and results of my whistleblowing success.

Chapter 2: Shows the deterioration in oversight leading to expansion of Deep State, weaponized government and lawfare that interfered with efforts to protect U.S. government and taxpayer's interests. The origin and expansion of the Government Swamp.

Chapter 3: Shows the direct and repetitive retaliatory actions against me that interfered with me protecting taxpayers' interest and stopped me from increasing government efficiency. Most important, Chapter 3 shows specifically how and when the U.S. Legal and Judicial System expanded the Government Swamp of institutional corruption. In short, the evidence trails from weaponization to lawfare to expanding the Swamp.

Chapter 4: Outlines specifics of how I was intermittently able to protect taxpayer interests. Also explains in detail gross mismanagement and corruption that contributed to national debt.

Chapter 5: Capstone Case outlining my last whistleblowing disclosure. This is a recent example that traced up to 2024.

Chapter 6: The suggested remedy for the President and Congress to restore government efficiency and eliminate weaponized government and lawfare. This starts with the simple remedy of restorative justice for victims up to ensuring cost traceability and accountability.

This book is written and designed as an evidentiary trail, documenting the effects of weaponized government and lawfare from my many, multitasking, jobs as follows.

Evidentiary Trail – Encyclopedia & Cache of Evidence

While at DCMA I documented evidence of weaponized government, lawfare, and the Government Swamp from various perspectives that included.

1: My regular job which was related to DOGE. Protect taxpayers and government interests.

2: Whistleblowing to expose corruption, fraud, weaponization, etc.

3: Protect myself. Fight back weaponized retaliation and lawfare against me personally.

4: Assist other employees who were victims of weaponization, lawfare, etc.

5: SME instructor for Cost Control of Direct and Indirect Cost.

6: Supporting Congressional investigations, criminal investigations, court case, etc.

7: Working with news media.

I kept detailed notes as events unfolded which included reports to: Congress, investigators, news media, and in one case the President of the U.S. This was to ensure the proper dissemination of information. Those reports, notes, memoirs, data, etc., now form the foundation of this book and transform this book into an encyclopedia that shows the predictable weaponized government and lawfare tactics that trace to the national debt.

Weaponized government was predictable a quarter century ago. Meaning, on/about June 19, 2000 one DCMA commander, Colonel Sam Evans, refused to speak with me on a simple personnel issue stating:

"Mr. Pedeleose,

Feel free to go to whomever can resolve the issue for you. I do not need to review your package."

During 1998 Colonel Evans stated: *"Don't bother to call the Congress or the Senate they will do nothing for you"*.

This shows historical confidence in a system that fails. Past Congresses and past U.S. Presidents have resolved nothing. Falsified Trail 3 in Chapter 3 specifically shows how the U.S. Legal and Judicial System expanded the Government Swamp to the point where weaponized government and lawfare are publicly spoken and factored into daily, unethical, decisions. This book exposes weaponization and lawfare and provides a remedy to fix the corrupted system and national debt.

The U.S. taxpayers have a vested interest in remedying weaponized government, lawfare and the national debt. As such this book is made publicly available since the national debt that will cripple the U.S. economy to negatively affect health care, defense, infrastructure, etc., if the current trend continues. Meaning, will action be taken or will there be more useless rhetoric that expands the Government Swamp.

As the following shows, DCMA has weaponized every aspect of managerial power to contain and cover-up negative information from reaching the public.

DCMA - Entrenched and Integrated Weaponization and Lawfare

DCMA is the prime example of weaponized government and lawfare via a "tornado trail" of altered working conditions, "Swatting", chaos, and evidence. DCMA openly and repetitively flaunted weaponized government and lawfare including admissions to wrongdoing. The evidence in this book shows DCMA along with other DoD organizations and DoD contractors has weaponized the following to lawfare levels.

Weaponized Personnel Actions (Prime Weapon)	Falsified Trails 1-13
Weaponized Authority	Falsified Trails 1-13
Weaponized Attorneys, Attorney Client Privilege	Falsified Trails 1, 3-13
Weaponized Surrogates	Falsified Trails 1, 3-13
Weaponized Investigations & Coverups	Falsified Trails 2, 3 & 13
Weaponized Doctrine (Obey First, Grieve Later)	Falsified Trail 3
Weaponized Conflicts of Interest	Falsified Trails 3, 11, 13
Weaponized FOIA (Freedom of Information Act)	Falsified Trails 2 & 13
Weaponized Office Conflicts Between Employees	Falsified Trails 5 & 9
Weaponized Shunning	Falsified Trails 1, 3, 6, 8, 11
Weaponized Electronic Trails (Email Relays)	Falsified Trails 1, 3, 6, 11, 12, & 13
Weaponized Training	Falsified Trail 11 and 2011 attempt
Weaponized Human Resources/Labor Relations	Falsified Trails 3, 6, 10, 12, & 13
Weaponized Lockheed Martin Armed Guards	Falsified Trail 2 (Swatting)
Weaponized Lockheed Martin Human Resources	Falsified Trail 11
Weaponized Status & Access to Other Agencies	Falsified Trail 3
Weaponized Cover-ups by OSC, MSPB, OPM	Falsified Trails 3, 6, 10, 13 (Abandon Case)
Weaponized Kernels of Thought & Con Games	Falsified Trail 3 (Planting Ideas/Thoughts)
Weaponized Security Clearances	Chapter 3, Revoked Security Clearance
Weaponized Hostile & Abusive Workplace	Institutional & Overarching (Continuous)

The point being, DCMA flaunted the Deep State to the point of providing the planning and tactical documents for weaponized government and lawfare used against me. DCMA's exposure, embarrassment, and culpability is self-inflicted by DCMA.

There is no malice or ill will toward any individual or organization. There is only copious and detailed documentation that shows weaponization and lawfare do exist and have contributed to the national debt. National security is also at risk since voices such as mine are stifled via tactical retaliatory weaponization and lawfare. The Deep State are the specific individuals who tactically use weaponization and lawfare.

I was a high value target largely due to my successful resume where I was labeled “extremely effective”. Hence, a “perfect storm” of circumstances giving a unique insight to Deep State missions using weaponization and lawfare.

My detailed resume follows.

CHAPTER 1:
Resume - About the Author - Ken Pedeleose

College: Bachelor of Science in Industrial & Systems Engineering, 1983; Associate's Degree in Applied Science Mining (Mining Technology), 1980.

Military: Discharged Under Honorable Conditions, 1986, United States Army.

Government "Swamp" Experience: Spent 26½ years immersed within the "Swamp" of institutional corruption and tactical weaponized government, documenting corruption, retaliation, lawfare, price gouging, waste, fraud, and abuse of authority as it occurred against the interests of the U.S. Government, against others, and against me personally.

My total Federal Career spanned approximately 35½ years. My most noted expertise was analyzing and reversing price gouging and fraud against U.S. taxpayers.

Analyze and Reverse Price Gouging & Fraud Against Taxpayers

My primary job was analyzing Lockheed Martin price proposals for price gouging (over charges) and then reversing the price gouging to develop a negotiation position for the U.S. Government (DoD). The formal term was Technical Support to Negotiations (TSN) for direct cost elements. Indirect or overhead cost was known as Technical Support to Indirect (TSI).

Subject Matter Expert (SME) Designation 2017

Designated as Subject Matter Expert (SME) February 27, 2017: I was designated an SME on/about February 27, 2017, for my participation in developing a training course for Technical Support to Indirect Cost (TSI). However, it should be noted that I was used as an SME well before that time. TSI involves the analysis and evaluation of DoD contractor overhead costs/rates for accuracy. I later became a TSI instructor, traveling the U.S. in 2018.

Instructor/SME Technical Support to Negotiations (TSN): While developing the TSI course in 2017, I was called upon to be an instructor/SME for the TSN (direct cost analysis) course. TSN involves analysis of direct contract costs, as compared to TSI, which deals with indirect contract costs. I taught the TSN course across the U.S. and modified sections of the TSN course for accuracy.

1987 Version of DOGE

In 1987, I was hired by the DoD to analyze and make production improvements. This stemmed from a March 20, 1986, Department of the Navy Letter titled "*Industrial Engineering in Naval Shipyards*." The goal was cost savings of ten times my salary. This was an earlier analogy to the 2025 DOGE effort, although I was embedded within production operations at the Charleston Naval Shipyard (CNSY), Charleston, SC.

1994 Anti-Price Gouging on DoD Contracts

In 1994, my duties switched to DoD acquisition to make contract negotiation cases (Technical Support [TS]) for both direct and indirect (overhead) costs. I achieved ten times my salary savings on projects where my input was a major turning point, aside from contributing to a team effort on other projects.

My overarching resume is to analyze, investigate, and make cases to support a position for the public good (reverse price gouging). My focused experience on analyzing, investigating, and making cases made me an SME, where my reputation preceded me to assist with the following.

SME - Criminal Investigations

Assisted in Writing Criminal Subpoenas Against Lockheed Martin 2001: On/about early 2001 I assisted criminal investigators in writing criminal subpoenas against Lockheed Martin on C-5 potential false claims regarding spare parts. I had made the initial criminal disclosure on/about February 28, 2000, and followed through as an SME helping in the case on February 19, 2001.

Assisted in the Investigation of F-22 Tooling, September 2002 – December 2002: Supported AFOSI (Air Force Office of Special Investigation) and AUSA with Lockheed Martin F-22 Tool Operating System (TOS). The AUSA needed cost insight regarding rework on F-22 tooling due to poor vendor support. Early communications were on September 30, 2002 and October 23, 2002.

On/about December 2, 2002, I provided a basic pathway forward to assist in the case, although I was limited by the fact that by 1998, Lockheed Martin had degraded data and program analysis tracking. Notably, I was not on the F-22 program, confirming that my SME reputation preceded me.

SME - Congressional Investigations – Senator Charles Grassley

Congressional Witness, 18 USC 1505, April 26, 2004, and August 16, 2005: Senator Grassley named me in two letters, copies of which were sent to my then DCMA Director, BG General Darryl Scott. The first was dated April 26, 2004, stating in part: "*Mr. Pedeleose is continuing to assist the Finance Committee in its oversight investigation of spare parts overpricing on Air Force contracts.*" (See Appendix A1-4)

On August 16, 2005, Senator Grassley again named me in a letter regarding another employee (Henry Hagel) who was providing "*technical reports along with Mr. Pedeleose to Senator Charles E. Grassley to support continuing investigation of the C-130J including spare parts pricing and other financial aspects of Lockheed Martin and its products.*" (See Appendix A1-5)

SME - Congressional Investigations – Senator John McCain

Assisted DoD IG and Senator John McCain C-130J Program Cost Analysis June – July 2005: I assisted DoD IG and Senator McCain in the analysis of a Lockheed Martin July 7, 2005 response to Senator McCain's June 22, 2005 letter to Lockheed Martin Corporation. At issue was the C-130J cost and pricing data and the escalating C-130J costs. (See Appendix A1-10, A1-11)

SME – Federal Court Cases

Assisted Federal Court Case Honeywell vs U.S. July 11, 2006: On/about July 2006, I was contacted as a potential witness by Honeywell for deposition in a federal patent infringement case regarding Honeywell vs U.S. Government. I was selected for deposition by Honeywell.

The deposition was cancelled; however, I provided the U.S. Attorney data, including C130H model specifications for electronic components.

Congressional Staff Interview

Interviewed with the House Committee on Government Reform on or about January 30, 2006, for a committee support position. I would have technically supported the committee and not any particular member of Congress.

Engineer/Whistleblower History in the Department of Defense (DoD)

"Swamp" Immersion March 1994 – December 2020

My immersion into the "Swamp" of institutional corruption began on/about March 1994, when I began work at the Defense Contract Management Agency (DCMA) (then under Defense Logistics Agency [DLA]), overseeing the Lockheed Martin (Air Force Plant 6), Marietta, GA.

Within a few days of arrival, I heard stories of corruption and saw an office in disarray. I had no independent knowledge of allegations and took a wait-and-see attitude of documenting.

As time went on at DCMA, I gathered independent evidence, personal experiences, and drew independent conclusions that reinforced what I saw about DCMA management when I arrived.

I became an anonymous whistle-blower on/about June 12, 1998, with a disclosure to the DoD Hotline. That disclosure (69535) was closed partially substantiated and involved spare parts fraudulent pricing.

On/about February 28, 2000, I called criminal investigators into my office during a negotiation process to disclose the negotiation of contracts based on data known to be false and purposely overstated. That disclosure was substantiated and sent to the prosecution.

Beginning July 26, 2002, I became a public whistle-blower with my first written report to the U.S. Congress signed by two fellow DCMA employees and me. Substantiated disclosures and cover-ups within and from that report were identified and will be outlined shortly herein.

I authored multiple reports after the July 26, 2002 report, which outlined corruption, undermining audits, retaliation, falsification, cover-ups, and other similar topics that should not be found within any agency or organization, less to say documented in high volume.

Titles and dates of contemporaneous reports to Congress that I authored are as follows:

1. July 26, 2002: Department of Defense Technical Report on Criminal Vulnerability and Fraud (90 Pages)
2. March 8 2004: Department of Defense Technical Report on Criminal Vulnerability, Fraud, Price Gouging, & Reprisal (30 Pages)
3. May 16, 2005: Cover-up in the Department of Defense (52 Pages)
4. September 9, 2006: Insider Cover-up Operations & Retaliatory Investigations in the Department of Defense (35 Pages)
5. June 7, 2008: Corruption & Falsification in the Department of Defense (45 Pages)
6. August 31, 2013: Restoring Financial Accountability & Cost Savings in the Department of Defense (16 Pages)

Written reports to Congress represented only one aspect of my whistleblowing efforts to expose tactical, weaponized government and institutional corruption. The other portion was direct contact and access to potential remedies to identify and expose government corruption. The direct access is as follows.

Direct Access (Data, Criminal Investigators, Congress, & Pentagon)

Direct Access to Data: I had direct access to Lockheed Martin financial (Cost & Pricing) data, development data, financial tracking on system development (Earned Value Management System (EVMS)), manufacturing data, quality assurance data, aircraft flight test data, etc. This was data direct from the source, not second-hand or opinions.

My analysis of Lockheed Martin data revealed public safety issues, gross mismanagement, waste, fraud, and abuse, as well as cover-ups. From that point, I used direct access and communications to criminal investigators for remedy as the first step.

Direct Contact/Communications with DoD Criminal Investigators: Beginning on/about February 28, 2000, and continuing through December 2020 (retirement), I maintained direct communication with DoD criminal investigators, including Air Force Office of Special Investigations (AFOSI), and at times Defense Criminal Investigative Service (DCIS), mostly on a first-name basis.

I provided in-person inventory lists of disclosures, assistance in closing the loop on criminal cases, assistance with writing subpoenas, etc. Most communication was via email.

Criminal investigators provided an avenue to make criminal disclosures with some remedy. To up the remedy factor, I began direct access to members of Congress as follows.

Direct Contact Congressional Level: I had direct contact, primarily email with some faxing, with Senator Charles Grassley mainly via staffer Charlie Murphy and some with Bob Kerr. I also had direct contact with Senator John McCain via staffers Chris Paul and Shawn Grenier. Contact with Senator Grassley began on/about November 26, 2002 and continued to on/about September 15, 2008.

Contact with Senator McCain may have started on/about February 11, 2005, with cancellation cost on C-130J related to a Congress Daily article. Communications continued via email on April 11, 2005, and primarily during 2005 including June 23, 2005, regarding the C-130J aircraft.

Direct Contact/Communication with High-Level DoD/Pentagon Officials: I had direct (email/fax) contact and some phone contact with senior DoD officials, including then DoD IG Chief of Staff L. (Laura) Jean Lewis (2003-2004). I also had direct communication with then DoD IG Director Joseph Schmitz (2005). I had direct communication with Leonard Trahan, then Director Defense Hotline, which included a personal meeting on/about July 29-30, 2003. Meaning, I was well-connected and used those connections to gain great insight into weaponized government.

Mentor – Arthur Ernest (Ernie) Fitzgerald

My mentor and Pentagon contact was Arthur Ernest (Ernie) Fitzgerald, Management Systems Deputy, Office of the Assistant Secretary of the Air Force. On/about 1970 Fitzgerald was fired by then-President Richard Nixon, although he was later reinstated. Fitzgerald augmented my contact and insight to Senator Grassley via Charlie Murphy (staffer).

Ernie Fitzgerald provided valuable mentorship and insight to the Pentagon and DoD world of weaponized government since 1970 (half a century) and is included within this report.

Handlers - Project On Government Oversight (POGO)

I began work with POGO shortly after August 14, 2003, when I was walked out the gate by Lockheed Martin Armed guards (Falsified Trail 2, Chapter 3). POGO assisted with news media support, introductions to Congressional staffers, and was my "*handler in the non-profit world,*" as described on June 28, 2006.

Weapon Against Weaponized Government & Corruption

I was a weapon against weaponized government and institutional corruption. What this means is that I had direct access as follows:

- Direct access to criminal investigators
- Direct access to Congress
- Direct access to the Pentagon
- A nationally known whistle-blower, Ernie Fitzgerald, as my mentor
- My handlers, link to news media and Congress, were POGO

I used the direct access to make and substantiate allegations as follows.

Substantiated Allegations by Category

My substantiated allegations stemmed from my aforementioned direct access. Meaning, I used direct access to Congress and investigators for the public good to work within the existing system. I realized early on that I had to make the case upfront with the supporting data. Much like I prepared this book, which is following evidence and facts. Basically, make it easy for investigators. My substantiated allegations by category are as follows.

Substantiated Allegation 1 (Willful DCMA Act of Fraud)

<u>February 28, 2000 (C-5 Spare Parts, Negotiating Contracts on False Data)</u>: I made an in-person criminal disclosure regarding a potential false claim from Lockheed Martin to the U.S. Government. DCMA management was aware of the fraud and continued to negotiate regardless. Meaning, I was forced to call criminal investigators into the facility to stop the negotiation. My disclosure led to the following:

A. Criminal Report of Investigation ROI (December 19, 2001)
B. November 28, 2001, Criminal Vulnerability Report (CRV) #2002-01
C. Criminal Vulnerability Report (CRV) (January 10, 2002) cover memo

Attachment A to the Criminal Vulnerability Report (CRV) stated: "The investigation was declined for prosecution by AUSA Alexander, Criminal Division and AUSA Caldwell, Civil Division, Northern District of Georgia, and the following reasons were cited:

1. Government officials at DCMA-LM Aero (my office management) knew the proposal and termination claim contained inflated prices because of the inclusion of duplicative set up costs and the

government officials at DCMA-LM Aero negotiated the price proposal knowing the proposal to contain false information..."

In the statement above, only knowing the AUSA's last names, the following is notable:

Reputation Precedes Me (AUSA Caldwell): AUSA Caldwell worked in the DOJ Civil Division and was linked to my assistance on the F-22 tooling investigation in 2002, previously mentioned. Meaning, AUSA Caldwell knew I can make cases because my SME reputation precedes me.

DOJ Weaponized Against Me (AUSA Alexander): Regarding AUSA Alexander... If this is Charysse Alexander, then the AUSA would weaponize a DOJ letter against me on August 25, 2005 (Appendix A1-12). More to follow in the next few pages, and in Falsified Trail 3, Chapter 3.

The DOJ didn't prosecute Lockheed Martin for fraud; on the flip side, the DOJ was an accessory to retaliation against me. More will follow on DOJ participation in retaliation.

The following 3 items (Substantiated Allegations 2, 3, and 4) resulted from the July 26, 2002, report to Congress.

Substantiated Allegation 2 (Contract Negligence)

June 30, 2003, IG Report (Electronic Flight Instrument (EFI)) (D-2003-115): The DoD IG issued an audit report (D-2003-115) from a Hotline complaint I submitted in January 2001 that was revitalized in the July 26, 2002, report to Congress outlined previously in this resume.

The IG confirmed that a lack of DCMA and Program Office oversight led to more than 1,100 EFI failures in a 34-month period ending in October 2002, and grounded 16 C-130H aircraft. The DoD IG stated: "*DCMA oversight of contract administration was inadequate.*"

Substantiated Allegation 3 (Willful DoD IG Cover-up)

This substantiated allegation resulted from a Congressional investigation of DoD IG Audit D2004-054, where DoD IG tried to cover up Substantiated Allegation 1.

Substantiated Allegation 1 outlined a specific criminal case on C-5 spare parts with the following reports from November 28, 2001, to January 10, 2002.

A. Criminal Report of Investigation ROI (December 19, 2001),
B. November 28, 2001 Criminal Vulnerability Report (CRV) #2002-01,
C. Criminal Vulnerability Report (CRV) (January 10, 2002) cover memo.

However, on February 23, 2004, the DoD IG Audit Division issued audit report D-2004-054 titled "*Allegations of the Defense Contract Management Agency's Performance in Administering Selected Weapon Systems' Contracts*" which stated the DoD IG did not substantiate allegations on the C-5 spare parts. This clashed with existing criminal and criminal vulnerability reports that were issued a few years prior.

I had previewed an advance copy of the DoD IG report and spotted the cover-up. With this knowledge in hand, I immediately notified Senator Grassley via Charlie Murphy. The Chief of Staff of the DoD IG, L. Jean Lewis, was directly informed of criminal vulnerability on February 17, 2004, nearly a week before the February 23, 2004 DoD IG report was made public. Regardless, the DoD IG issued the falsified report.

Senator Grassley Investigation: On March 10, 2004, at 10:30 AM, Senator Grassley's office (staffer Charlie Murphy) contacted John Crane (DoD IG Congressional Liaison) and L. Jean Lewis, stating: "*The DCIS report addressed spare parts that were procured based on cost and pricing data that was known to be false and purposely overstated.*" Charlie Murphy went on to state (regarding DoD IG report D-2004-054):

"*…the IG provides a status report on negotiations – in progress – on one of the parts covered by the DCIS report. That particular section of the IG's report is therefore based on false information. The auditors' analysis – as it pertains to that part – is based on false information. The prices cited in that section of the report are based on false information. That issue should have been resolved in that section of the report.*"

On March 19, 2004, Charlie Murphy sent me an email indicating he (Murphy) had a meeting with the DoD IG audit group. Charlie Murphy indicated that the:

"*DoD IG audit report is tainted. The write-up on page 5 on the C-5 engine bracket contains false information. They knew that, and failed to address and resolve that problem.*"

The point is, the DOJ refused to prosecute fraud. Second, the DoD IG deliberately issued an audit report with false information on February 23, 2004. Third, L. Jean Lewis was directly informed of fraud in front of a Congressional staffer on February 17, 2004, nearly a week before the February 23, 2004 DoD IG report was made public, and did nothing. The bottom line? The cover-up at DoD IG and my direct access helped uncover that fact.

Senator Grassley wrote a two-page scathing letter to Joseph Schmitz the following day (February 24, 2004) (Appendix A1-1), which included rebukes about DCMA and DCAA, stating in part:

"*Your auditors close with this warning: "DCMA and DCAA [Defense Contract Audit Agency] need to maintain vigilance until the price for the remaining parts is negotiated." In my mind, Mr. Schmitz, that conclusion is truly weak. Those two entities have a long-standing reputation for turning a blind eye to contractor rip offs. They are not known for being vicious junk yard dogs when it comes to protecting taxpayers' money. Please don't depend on them to be vigilant. I am depending on you to watchdog them.*"

Buried Statement: The DoD IG never retracted the February 23, 2004, report, but later issued a buried statement on Page 17 of the C-130J audit on July 23, 2004 (Substantiated Allegation 4) that stated in part.

"*IG DoD Report No. D-2004-054, "Allegations of the Defense Contract Management Agency's Performance in Administering Selected Weapon Systems' Contracts," February 23, 2004. The report included an allegation that the Government paid an excessive price for a C-5 aircraft bracket. This allegation was not substantiated because a final price for this part had not been negotiated. However, a related Defense Criminal Investigative Service report (report cited below) found that cost or pricing data in the proposal that included this part was based on false information.*"

"Defense Criminal Investigative Service, Criminal Vulnerability Report No. 2002-01, November 28, 2001. The report discussed the lack of appropriate controls and contract requirements in the procurement of spare parts for the C-5 aircraft, which were based on cost and pricing data that were known to be false and purposely overstated. The report recommended that the Defense Supply Center, Richmond, Virginia, and the Defense Contract Management Agency, Marietta, Georgia, review procedures and controls and implement appropriate action to ensure that future contracts are negotiated based on current, accurate, and complete cost and pricing data."

Having this direct access provided some clarity; however, the clarity was buried. This demonstrates that I can expose government cover-ups at the highest levels. The biggest cover-up I ever exposed was the C-130J, as follows.

Substantiated Allegation 4 (Willful Act - Accept Defective Equipment)

July 23, 2004 (DoD IG Report on C-130J, (D-2004-102)): The DoD IG issued a report on the C-130J stating: "We substantiated the allegation that the C-130J aircraft does not meet contract specifications and therefore cannot perform its operational mission. The Air Force conditionally accepted 50 C-130J aircraft at a cost of $2.6 billion even though none of the aircraft met commercial contract specifications or operational requirements."

The Air Force and DCMA knowingly accepted defective military equipment that did not meet operational requirements, indicating that government efficiency and national security are not motivating factors.

On April 5, 2000, I made a disclosure to DCIS regarding the "substantial and specific danger to public health or safety" of the C-130J. This went nowhere until I went public on July 26, 2002.

Denial by Marvin Sambur: At the end of the July 23, 2004 report were Air Force comments on the draft version of the July 23, 2004 report (March 25, 2004). Marvin Sambur (Assistant Secretary of the Air Force [Acquisition]) responded on April 29, 2004, stating: "The Air Force takes issue with all of the DoD IG findings and recommendations."

March 15, 2004 – Claim Victory: L. Jean Lewis (then DoD IG Chief of Staff) stated that I had the "right to claim victory as a whistleblower" if the C-130J allegation was substantiated. The C-130J allegation was substantiated and gave me high public notoriety. It also caused Falsified Trail 3, which will be explained in Chapter 3.

ABC News & Sambur Resignation: On November 17, 2004, I was on ABC News with members of the Air Force outlining how the Air Force could not use the C-130J aircraft because the C-130J was not operationally ready, even though the Air Force and DCMA accepted the C-130Js. Marvin Sambur resigned that same day (November 17, 2004).

Substantiated Allegation 5 (Checkmate Allegation - Deception)

June 21, 2006 DoD IG Report (D-2006-093): The July 23, 2004 DoD IG Report on the C-130J (D-2004-102) eventually proposed the cancellation of the C-130J program. To keep the C-130J, the Air Force falsified cancellation costs. DoD IG "*substantiated the allegation that the C-130J termination cost estimate was unsupported, and that had the estimate been valid, there was a potential for an Antideficiency Act violation.*"

<u>Checkmate Allegation Via Signed Contract</u>: This allegation was checkmate in all directions. What it showed was that the Air Force stated C-130J cancellation costs were $1 billion, when, in fact, the C-130J cancellation ceiling costs in 2005 (when the allegation was made) were $439.7 million per the signed contract. So, if the C-130J cancellation was indeed $ 1 billion, then the government would be in an anti-deficiency position, obligating more money than allowed by Congress. I win on that point.

If there was no anti-deficiency, then the $1billion cancellation cost was a lie and ruse to keep the C-130J. I win on that point since the contract cancellation ceiling costs were well under $1 billion. The C-130J was not cancelled and was later deemed non-commercial. Regardless, I won either way on the allegation, and the C-130J commercial contract aspect was later reversed.

In summary, providing a well-supported disclosure to investigators for my allegations, with the supporting data upfront making the case, provided a good number of substantiated allegations. However, it also made me a target for the Deep State by being categorized as "*extremely effective*" for a government whistleblower. This was my highest honor as follows.

Highest Honor & Praise – Weaponized & Tactical DoD IG Division Civilian Reprisal Investigations (CRI)

<u>Lawfare, Weaponized & Tactical Division at DoD IG Over Me</u>: On/about January 26, 2004, DoD IG activated CRI based on my "*experience.*" Meaning, CRI was created over me (Ken Pedeleose). CRI was the centerpiece and embodiment of lawfare and weaponized government. CRI was the perfect Deep State operation that had access to DoD IG, DoD Agencies, Congressional staffers, whistle-blowers, and whistle-blower supporters like POGO.

<u>June 28, 2006</u>: The then-CRI Director was Daniel P. Meyer, who stated his (Meyer) "*position was actually escalated and staffed because of that meeting,*" meaning a July 2003 meeting regarding Falsified Trail 1 in Chapter 3. Meyer also stated my (Pedeleose) "*experience that led to the creation*" of his (Meyer) office.

Dan Meyer was a one-man lawfare weaponized DoD IG Division (CRI) created over me personally. Meyer was the centerpiece of Falsified Trail 3 and demonstrated how tactical con games were run and managed against Congress, serving as both the catalyst and textbook example of lawfare. Had it not been for Dan Meyer, this book and the transparency into the Deep State would not be possible. Appendix A1-2 shows how on March 19, 2004 Dan Meyer labeled me "*extremely effective.*" That came about as follows.

<u>March 19, 2004 - Extremely Effective</u>: After about 2 months of knowing me, Meyer rated me "*extremely effective*" based on my interactions with Senator Grassley via Charlie Murphy in exposing a DoD IG cover-up of criminal findings on the Lockheed Martin C5 Program (Substantiated Allegation 3). Meyer's mention of "*extremely effective*" seemed both praise and targeting based on events that followed in Falsified Trail 3.

This followed a scathing letter from Senator Grassley to then DoD IG Director Joseph Schmitz on February 24, 2004 (Appendix A1-1).

CRI Ruse: By April 22, 2004 (about three months after Meyer contacted me), it was evident CRI was a ruse. By 2005, CRI proved a weaponized surreptitious Confidence (Con) Game, severing my rapport with Senator Grassley and ruining my reputation. CRI was an effective weapon; however, CRI left a tornado trail of evidence easy to follow, as Chapter 3, Falsified Trail 3, will show.

Double Con Game: Evidence shows DCMA (my then employer) was running a con game on Dan Meyer that would "*drop the dime*" on the DoD IG proving CRI was a weaponized DoD IG Division. Chapter 3, Falsified Trail 3, has greater details. My being extremely effective desperately caused at least two con games to emerge, which enhances my resume for the public good.

Con games were only one prong of attack against me. The other prong was the cover-up of facts report.

CRI Poor Quality Report – Avoid Garnering "National Attention"

June 5, 2008 - Meyer Poor Quality Report: One IG investigation indicated Dan Meyer (CRI) was "*far from finishing his* (Meyer) *final report due to poor quality in the writing.*" The IG report further stated Meyer's report was: "*not even susceptible to reasonable editing. He* (Meyer) *wasn't anywhere near closure two to three years into this investigation.*" "*So [the DoD complainant]* (Pedeleose) *claiming there was a conflict involving Dan was his 'get out of jail free' card.*"

Dan Meyer wasn't interested in being a whistle-blower advocate but rather in damaging me. Falsified Trail 3 in Chapter 3 leaves no doubt in this matter. I already had a major whistle-blower win outlined in Falsified Trail 2, Chapter 3, where I was walked out the gate by Lockheed Martin armed guards under false charges and prevailed without litigation. Meaning, Meyer was handed a winning case.

On August 10, 2005, Meyer admitted his (Meyer) report may "*garner national attention.*" (Appendix A1-9). It is notable that Dan Meyer was so close to DCMA on the retaliation against me that the DCMA used the August 10, 2005 email from Meyer (Appendix A1-9) as evidence against me (Stamped "EXHIBIT 3") to the MSPB in Falsified Trail 3.

The point is, Meyer believed my case would "*garner national attention*" and made efforts to derail that case. Meaning, I was a high-value target for resume purposes. That was supported by my case being briefed up to Under Secretary of Defense.

Acting Deputy Secretary of Defense Gordon England – The "Pentagon Flank"

September 12, 2005: Further praise came when the Acting Deputy Secretary of Defense Gordon England was briefed on my case by then commander Colonel Nicole Plourde. Per Dan Meyer, a week prior to September 12, 2005, my then commander, Plourde, "*had Gordon England down last week, so she is shoring up the Pentagon flank.*" (Appendix A1-13)

Meaning, I garnered Pentagon attention from the then Acting Deputy Secretary of Defense, which is noteworthy for my resume, as it seemed there was a large gathering of senior officials forming against me. The Index of Names for Falsified Trail 3 had approximately 29 names of which about 20 were

Government attorneys and about 7 at the Command and Directors Level. So, it is not surprising that one attorney was "*flying in*" over me.

Regional Counsel "Flying In" Over "Emails from Mr. Pedeleose"

August 8, 2005 - "Flying In": The DoD IG lead attorney, Uldric Fiore, contacted then DoD IG Director Joseph Schmitz and other DoD IG Principal Deputies, in an email titled "*Emails from Mr. Pedeleose*" indicating "*Boston Regional Counsel*" will be "*flying in on Wed.*" (Appendix A1-8)

This was part of Falsified Trail 3, where the DCMA lead attorney (believed to be Bruce Krasker), "*Boston Regional Counsel,*" was "*flying in*" over me personally. The meeting date was August 10, 2005. This unprecedented meeting flowed into the following unprecedented communication over "*one employee, Ken Pedeleose.*"

AUSA – "One Employee, Ken Pedeleose"

August 25, 2005: DCMA attorneys Leigh Owens, Gill Bass, and AUSA Charysse Alexander (DOJ) participated in special communications regarding me personally, where Alexander stated in part, "*one employee, Ken Pedeleose,*" was mentioned in communication. (Appendix A1-12)

This communication followed from the aforementioned August 10, 2005, meeting at DoD IG Headquarters (HQ) over me, where the Boston Regional Counsel was "*flying in.*" This was one cornerstone of Falsified Trail 3, in Chapter 3. The point is, my resume has grown to show more focus on me, meaning "*one employee, Ken Pedeleose.*"

The aforementioned events in 2005 were part of a high-level effort to bring about my demise as an extremely effective whistle-blower. However, prior to that time, there was lower-level travel around the country, which centered on me as follows.

DoD IG Hotline Director Visit

July 29-30, 2003: This unprecedented visit/trip over me occurred in 2003, led by the then-DoD IG Hotline Director, Leonard Trahan, and two DoD IG investigators. This visit/trip followed Falsified Trail 1 (reprimand) in Chapter 3.

The unprecedented visit served only to deliver a veiled warning to me, stating: "*You're their leader. They follow you. You're attracting a lot of attention to yourself.*" Meaning, I was a leader in the whistle-blower world; others were following, and I was garnering attention. Which was true since even prior to that, I prompted another visit several months earlier in 2002 as follows.

Misdirected Fax – DCMA Investigator Visit – Pulled Personnel Files

October 22, 2002 & November 6, 2002 Kenneth Leisure Private Fax & Visit: Kenneth Leisure was a DCMA investigator involved after the July 26, 2002 90 Page report was sent to Congress, President Bush, and Secretary of Defense Rumsfeld. Leisure first engaged in a private fax sent to DCMA attorney Leigh Owens.

Leisure typed the wrong number, and by chance, the fax ended up at a local Marietta, GA company, who then notified me based on my contact information on the faxed letter, which was from me to President Bush. I then called Leigh Owens.

From there, Kenneth Leisure had a special visit to my facility on November 6, 2002, to meet with the cosigners, including me, of the July 26, 2002 90 Page report to report to Congress. In prior communications, Leisure informed me that upon receiving a copy of the July 26, 2002 report to Congress, Leisure pulled the files of those who cosigned the document. This shows that my actions and efforts caused movement by senior officials that I was previously unaware of.

Ernie Fitzgerald Category of Whistleblowers - Shunning & Email Relays

Shunning is an act of aggression, avoidance, and dislike. Falsified Trails 1, 3, 6, 8, 11 included shunning as a weapon. In Falsified Trail 3, my emails to senior officials were ignored to the point where MSPB judges noticed them. Falsified Trail 3 lasted all summer (June – October 2005).

For management officials to avoid and shun me shows that I had honor and worried those whom I accused of malfeasance. I garnered attention. Dan Meyer once told me I was in the category of Ernie Fitzgerald whistle-blowers. Meaning what I did would not be quickly forgotten.

<u>No Words or No Explanation Email Relays</u>: DCMA senior officials and attorneys forwarded/relayed emails with no words or no detailed explanations. In Falsified Trail 1, this occurred on May 29, 2003, at 9:15 AM. In Falsified Trail 3, this happened on August 4, 2005, 2:01 PM (Appendix A2-2), August 5, 2005, 8:08 AM (Appendix A2-2), August 8, 2005, 1:09 PM (Appendix A2-3), and August 8, 2005, 1:10 PM (Appendix A2-4). This suggests I drove management to engage in detailed planning behind the scenes to discredit me. Lockheed Martin also took notice and engaged against me as follows.

Lockheed Martin Vice President & Human Resources Director

Falsified Trail 11

<u>November 17, 2014</u>: In Falsified Trail 11, a Lockheed Martin Vice President (VP), Ray Burick, sent the following email to my then second-level supervisor.

Mark,

Good Morning.

If possible, I would like to get together with you this week for a discussion regarding a personal matter. Diane Stefani (Marietta Site HR Director) will attend with me.

Would like to meet as soon as convenient. Is there a good day/time for you Mark.

Thanks,

Ray

I now had Lockheed Martin's attention and concern at the VP level in an open and blatant act against me that was put in writing, topped off with the Lockheed Martin HR Director. However, this was just one blatant effort in writing. There were prior efforts, which are as follows.

Lockheed Martin's Involvement in Falsified Trails 1 & 2

<u>Falsified Trail 1</u>: May 29, 2003 - An email trail leading to entrapment by Sandra Shoemaker, VP Integrated Company Operations. Falsified Trail 1 in Chapter 3 explains further.

Falsified Trail 2: Lockheed Martin armed guards personally escorted me off the facility and searched my vehicle on August 14, 2003, under false charges that I physically threatened someone at the facility. This would be considered "Swatted," and I was aware that a call to 911 may also have been placed. Falsified Trail 2 in Chapter 3 has further details.

Private Discussions

Denise Joyce (Lockheed Martin Pricing and Estimating Manager): At about 11:20 AM on May 22, 2013, I discussed a complaint with Mark Buckner from Lockheed Martin manager Denise Joyce. Denise Joyce was stonewalling my inquiries regarding my inquiries about Lockheed Martin estimating system problems.

When asked exactly what Denise Joyce complained about, Buckner stated on May 31, 2013: "*I have concluded that Ms. Joyce's discussions with me will remain private*."

The point is, Lockheed Martin is in the facts of cases and complaints. I attribute this to being successful and related to my trail of substantiated allegations that drove Lockheed Martin to my management to silence me. However, one large issue remains as follows for Lockheed Martin.

Lockheed Martin - Be On the Look Out (BOLO) for Pedeleose

September 15, 2003: After I was escorted off the facility by Lockheed Martin armed guards on August 14, 2003, Lockheed Martin (Falsified Trail 2, Chapter 3) issued a BOLO against me as if I was a criminal. Lockheed Martin security (Daniel Cain) refused to provide the BOLO on September 15, 2003, stating:

"*Per our Legal, I will not provide a copy of the BOLO.*"

Lockheed Martin would have openly displayed the BOLO, probably at entrances to the Lockheed Martin facility; however, they would not share it with me. This is concerning and shows a guilty conscience. The BOLO was about me, and I should have been given a copy.

Nevertheless, my demise exceeded Lockheed Martin's involvement and would later become a "trophy" that the DoD IG was "*happy to discuss*."

Trophy & "Happy to Discuss"

September 16, 2005: In Falsified Trail 3, one DoD IG Associate General Counsel (possibly Ray O'Connor) stated he would be "*happy to discuss*" disciplinary action against me (Pedeleose) "*at the appropriate time.*" DoD IG was "*happy*" to contribute to my demise, meaning I must have shaken up DoD at some very high levels. (See Appendix A1-14)

Trophy: On January 23, 2006, DCMA Attorney Bruce Krasker emailed DoD IG attorney Uldric Fiore, (Appendix A3-2) Subject "*KP*" stating:

"*Ric We delivered the Decision to Suspend for 30 days today to Mr. Pedeleose. He was out last week so we reissued it with a new effective date, Jan 25. He refused to sign and we so noted.*"

The updates on Falsified Trail 3, and the trophy, were on display and passed around.

This is notable because a Freedom of Information Act (FOIA) request included an email sent to Uldric Fiore by DCMA on January 18, 2006, 9:38 AM (Appendix A3-1), and then printed by Fiore. The Attachment was titled "*KP.pdf,*" which was the 30-day suspension letter dated January 17, 2006 (the day prior).

Senior-level DoD executives were invigorated to participate in my demise. The 30-Day Suspension was a trophy. Updates were provided until the 30-Day Suspension was delivered and in effect. DCMA may also have tracked and forwarded the OSC letter closing my case.

The point is, my success garnered the attention of the DoD IG and DoD at high levels.

However, my success was also documented in news media articles, which doubled as a peripheral support for this book. The biggest catapult to my success was Falsified Trail 2 the walk out the gate by Lockheed Martin armed guards as follows.

Lockheed Martin Armed Guards (Falsified Trail 2) – "Swatted"

News Media Catapult

The infamous and retaliatory escort out the gate by Lockheed Martin armed guards in Marietta, GA, catapulted me to national attention. There was not one piece of evidence, even after a lengthy investigation, that warranted my removal from the facility, let alone removal by Lockheed Martin's armed guards. News media articles are as follows, centering on Lockheed Martin armed guards.

August 15, 2003 – Hearst Newspapers: "*Government Whistleblower Booted from Lockheed Facility*" By Eric Rosenberg. This story was written in one day following my removal from the Lockheed Martin facility. I was told on August 25, 2003, that the article ran in the following papers.

- Baltimore Sun
- San Antonio Express News
- Caspar, Wyoming
- Arizona Star
- Victoria, Texas Advocate
- Monterey County Herald, CA
- Montreal Gazette
- Akron, Ohio Beacon Journal

I was told that when the story went out the Atlanta Journal-Constitution was on the newswire recipients. I received a call the evening of August 15, 2003, maybe within an hour or so after Hearst Newspaper went public, and agreed to an interview with the Atlanta Journal-Constitution. The news articles are as follows:

August 24, 2003 – The Atlanta Journal-Constitution: "*U.S. auditor at Lockheed suspended*" "*U.S. auditor says Lockheed overcharged government*" By Dave Hirschman.

August 28, 2003 – The Atlanta Journal-Constitution: "*Pentagon to join Lockheed case*" By Dave Hirschman. This was an update to the case after the story changed on my removal for allegedly physically threatening someone to the new story of my unusual demeanor.

August 28, 2003 - Peripheral Evidence Story: The Atlanta-Journal Constitution ran an article stating "Lockheed settles with feds," agreeing to "*pay $37.9 million to settle government allegations that it inflated costs on four Air Force contracts*." This supports my case as well.

August 28, 2003 – Hearst Newspapers: "*Pentagon Probing Action Taken Against Whistleblower*" By Eric Rosenberg.

August 30, 2003 – The Atlanta Journal-Constitution: "*Suspended federal auditor to return to Lockheed job*" By Dave Hirschman.

I was out of my job for 3 weeks. I was granted a few days of administrative leave (September 4th and 5th, 2003) to recover from the emotional trauma. The return-to-work conference was on/about September 3, 2003, and I returned to work on September 8, 2003. However, the damage was done to me and to Laura Jean Lewis as follows.

L. (Laura) Jean Lewis (Whitewater Background) Publicly Exposed

September 16, 2003 – Media Whores Online (MWO): The Lockheed Martin armed guard escort from the Lockheed Martin facility (Falsified Trail 2) was linked to the circumstantial exodus of L. Jean Lewis, then DoD IG Chief of Staff in 2003. The flurry of news media attention caused L. Jean Lewis to be exposed after I was asked who I associated with. I did not know who L. Jean Lewis was at the time.

One of the first articles came from MWO, which may have been a media watchdog that operated from on/about 2000 to 2004. MWO may have read an early article from Michael Isikoff that was later published in Newsweek Magazine on September 22, 2003. MWO administratively skewered L. Jean Lewis, stating in part.

"Notorious Whitewater Wingnut Hired by Defense Department" "Rabid Winger to Oversee Department that Audits Pentagon Contracts"

The point is, I did not know who L. Jean Lewis was, and only in interviews, after I was walked out the gate by Lockheed Martin armed guards, did I release Lewis's name. From there, the rest is history, and I was blamed by the DoD IG for L. Jean Lewis being exposed.

September 22, 2003 – Newsweek Magazine: The Periscope section of Newsweek ran a small article on L. Jean Lewis titled *"Pentagon Defense's Whitewater Hire."* That article, about 1/5 of a page, was one of many to follow.

The resume relevance is, I spoke with high-level personnel and was connected. My information brought demise to others by what I was exposing. Meaning, Falsified Trail 2, in part, is related to the exodus (exposing) of L. Jean Lewis from the DoD IG perspective. Dan Meyer (CRI) informed me of this fact, as I had upset some at the DoD IG. However, the walk of the gate by Lockheed Martin armed guards spurred a series of articles well beyond L. Jean Lewis.

Series of News Articles – Federal Times

("Blind Trust: Whose Watching DoD Contractors? April 5 – 19, 2004 Series")

The first spinoff of the infamous escort, out the gate by Lockheed Martin, armed guards, got the attention of Federal Times magazine. The original focus was a story about me. As the information flowed, the single story about me grew into a series of stories as follows:

April 5, 2004 - Federal Times: "*The Dark Side of Acquisition Reform*" "*Diminished oversight leads to overpricing*" By David Phinney. This story occupied most of the cover page with intros to stories on April 12 & 19, 2004. This series of articles grew from my story.

April 5, 2004 - Federal Times: "*Aircraft's costs soar despite reforms.*" This story is about the Lockheed Martin C-130J and is also written by David Phinney.

April 5, 2004 – Federal Times: "Commentary Perspective and Analysis, Editorial, "*Acquisition Reform*" "*The importance of auditors*" This flowed from the main story on Page 1.

April 5, 2004 – Federal Times: "*For the Record*" Senator Grassley quote from the February 24, 2004 scathing letter to Joseph Schmitz (Substantiated Allegation 3) where Senator Grassley stated regarding DCMA and DCAA:

"*Those two entities have a long-standing reputation for turning a blind eye to contractor rip offs. They are not known for being vicious junk yard dogs when it comes to protecting taxpayers' money.*"

This ties to the circumstantial exodus of Joseph Schmitz (June 15, 2005) and ties to the September 3, 2005 article by David Phinney titled "*More to Pentagon's Top Watchdog Resigning.*"

April 5, 2004 – Defense News: "*The Dark Side of Acquisition Reform*" "*Less Oversight Leads to Rising Costs*" By David Phinney. Essentially the same story, Federal Times wrote, occupying a smaller portion of the front page.

April 12, 2004 – Federal Times: "*Undermining the auditors 'Collaborative arrangement' lets DoD contractors slide*" by David Phinney. A story about how those who complain about defense contractors are removed.

April 12, 2004 – Federal Times: "*A case of reprisal?*" By David Phinney. Follow-on to the cover story of undermining auditors and how I was walked out the gate by Lockheed Martin armed guards.

April 12, 2004 – Defense News: "*U.S. C-130's Costs Soar Despite Reforms*" By David Phinney. A follow-on story from Federal Times April 5, 2004, regarding the C-130J.

April 19, 2004 – Federal Times: "*Defense's revolving door*" "*When managers join contractors, good oversight takes a hit, auditors say*" By David Phinney. Regarding DoD managers who go to work for defense contractors.

April 19, 2004 – Federal Times: "*For the Record*" Fellow colleague quote related to article on Page 1 regarding "*Defense's revolving door*" stating:

"*I was supposed to turn in fraud situations and then the commanding officer, who has authority over these things, jumps to the other side. If they are worried about their job future, then they have one big conflict.*"

April 5, 2004 – Federal Times: "Commentary Perspective and Analysis, Editorial, "*DoD's Revolving Door*" '*Oversight, not ethics rules, needs repair.*' This flowed from the main story on Page 1.

The articles flowing from my case show that DoD malfeasance is widespread. In mid-2004, I interviewed with CBS News 60 Minutes' Ira Rosen and an associate producer. I was told there would be no interviews for my story because the story kept "morphing" out, meaning that, like Federal Times articles, there is not just one isolated story. That's why I did this book. Corruption is institutional and not discrete or isolated. However, there were separate stories over the years.

News Media Appearances – Separate Stories

The next spinoff from Federal Times was ABC News, who took the place of 60 Minutes in doing a story on the Lockheed Martin C-130J.

November 17, 2004 – ABC News: "*C-130J Military Transport Planes Deemed Unfit for War*" Subtitle: "*U.S. Government Plans to Spend Billions for More Aircraft Despite Concerns*" by John Cochran, Peter Jennings. At the end of the news segment, Peter Jennings stated:

"*Another example of why whistleblowers in government are important.*"

November 21, 2004 – Los Angeles Times: "*Defense Audits Kept Behind Closed Doors*" Subtitle: "*Examinations of military purchases rarely face public scrutiny. Officials value confidentially, but critics worry about waste and fraud,*" by Paul Pringle.

February 11, 2005 – Congress Daily: "*Foes of transport plane call Air Force cost estimates exaggerated*" by Amy Klamper. My name was not mentioned in this article; however, it was a spinoff of my assistance to Senator McCain's staff. Specifically, the purported cancellation cost for the C-130J was reported as $ 1 billion. However, the cancellation section in the C-130J contract, which I advised Senator McCain's staff of, started at $438.7 million, dropped to $383.3 million in 2006, $347.3 million in 2007, and reached $0 in 2008. This was part of Substantiated Allegation 5 previously mentioned.

March 24, 2005 – New York Times: "*The Flawed Plane Congress Loves*" Subtitle: "*Rumsfeld Fights to Kill Program for Cargo Jet That Can't Fly Its Missions*" by Leslie Wayne. This was a spinoff of my assistance to Senator McCain's staff.

June 1, 2005 – Dow Jones Newswire: "*Whistleblower challenges Pentagon Stance on C-130J Costs*" by Rebecca Christie. This was a spinoff of my direct disclosure, regarding C-130J cancellation costs, to DoD IG Joseph Schmitz on May 12, 2005. Schmitz responded to me on May 13, 2005, stating that one of his Deputies was overseeing a review of my allegations. This started Substantiated Allegation 5.

I followed up with the May 16, 2005 report to Congress titled, "*Cover-up in the Department of Defense*" that same day – May 16, 2005. It is also notable that Falsified Trail 3 directly involved the DoD IG in a confidence game against Senator Grassley. Meaning, the DoD IG was in the facts of the case.

July 6, 2005 – New House News: "*Whistleblower, 78, Still Battling Air Force*" by Mary Orndorff. This article was about Ernie Fitzgerald, although I did provide commentary. During 2005, both Fitzgerald and I were targets of DoD retaliation.

November 9, 2005 – Washington Post: "*Government Engineer Faces Suspension in Leak Inquiry*" by Charles R. Babcock. The suspension in the Washington Post article was Falsified Trail 3. Notably, the 30-day suspension coincided with the evisceration of Ernie Fitzgerald's duties.

Desperation & Eliminate Transparency: The takeaway is, my whistleblowing peaked in 2005 with multiple news articles, which explains why Falsified Trail 3, that also happened in 2005, is my Flagship case. Meaning, the Deep State and military-industrial complex were desperate to discredit me and eviscerate Ernie Fitzgeralds duties at any cost to avoid transparency into the Government Swamp. The timing evidence shows this was a national retaliatory tactic as follows.

Fitzgerald's Evisceration of Duties & Pedeleose 30-Day Suspension

National Retaliatory Events One Day Apart

Evisceration of Duties (October 17, 2005) & 30-Day Suspension (October 18, 2005): Ernie Fitzgerald (my mentor) in an October 17, 2005 Time Magazine Article stated "*his job has been eviscerated.*" On October 18, 2005 (following) I was given a 30day suspension (Falsified Trail 3).

The close proximity of Fitzgerald's eviscerated position and my 30-day suspension add peripheral support to DoD organized and tactical retaliations. Meaning, I was swept up in an organized national retaliatory event against high profile persons which included the following.

Valerie Plame: On the same page in Time Magazine, as the Fitzgerald article, was a short article on CIA operative Valerie Plame titled "Rove Redux" and how Plame's identity was leaked to the news media. This timing suggests there was a linkage between retaliations of high-profile government persons. Chapter 2 explains the linkages and Deep State tactics that trace to the Nixon administration, that were resurrected and perfected by the Bush Administration. Hence, it is not surprising that a media blackout on my case also occurred.

Media Blackout

January 24, 2006 – Raw Story: "*Whistleblower suspended by Pentagon oversight committee*" original story by Eric Rosenberg posted by "Fintan" January 25, 2006. The 30-day suspension caused news media support to wane off so the new story was "*Media Blackout*" on my case.

Meaning, the DoD efforts to execute my reputation began to take hold. I still had some following news media coverage however my core public support dropped off showing the institutional corruption took hold.

Other News Media Support

April 2008 – Psychology Today: "*Personality Overhaul*" "*Build Courage, Passion, Joy, and Optimism*" By Kathleen McGowan. This article was about making personality changes in life and I was the example of courage coming forward with fraud allegations.

August 10, 2009 – POGO: "*Whistleblowers Still Being Left as Road Kill*" By Bryan Rahija. Despite overwhelming evidence in my favor, I lost my case and fell into national trend of whistle-blowers left as "*road kill.*"

August 10, 2009 – Truthout: "*Anti-Whistleblower Track Record Continues*" By Nick Schwellenbach. This is a similar story as the previous story written by Byran Rahija.

2013 – Brave New Foundation: "*War on Whistleblowers*" A Robert Greenwald Film. I appeared in the Bonus Section > Extended Interviews > Whistle-blowers. The Washington Post stated about the film:

"*The stories about the government's aggressive moves against federal employees who worked to uphold the finest traditions of public service are chilling and deserve the notice and outrage the film hopes to generate.*"

My segment was about 5 minutes in length including a description of the "*Bounty*" on my head.

August 10, 2015 – Law 360: "*Fed. Circ. Upholds DoD Agency Suspension of Whistleblower*" By Jacob Fischer. Articles such as this sway public opinion without the public knowing the true facts and depth of judicial corruption that flows from institutional corruption (the "Swamp"). Relevance is, the Government Swamp would not exist without U.S. Legal System and Judicial System corruption.

The impact of my whistleblowing did have a tremor effect in DoD if not the effect of "throwing some senior DoD officials under the bus" via circumstantial exodus as follows.

Circumstantial Exodus of Senior DoD Officials

Exodus 1: L. (Laura) Jean Lewis (Then DoD IG Chief of Staff)

L. Jean Lewis was the first circumstantial exodus caused by the "tremors" and turmoil from my whistleblowing. The timeline is as follows.

February 14, 2003: Charlie Murphy of Senator Grassley's staff states he was: "*...working with Jean Lewis to bring her into this loop. She is the Chief of Staff in the DOD IG's office. She is a former whistleblower. And I want to trust her. She is trying to change the culture in that office. She wants to work with whistleblowers and is creating a new framework for doing it.*"

Falsified Trail 3 will show that Lewis's "*framework*" was a Deep State operation against whistleblowers where I was the first target. This explains why Jean Lewis was elusive.

June 16, 2003, 6:53 AM: L. Jean Lewis remained elusive, so I asked my other DoD IG contacts for Lewis's contact information. Within an hour, I received a mailing address, FAX number, phone number, and email. I brought Lewis into conversations, not knowing her true background.

August 14, 2003: I was walked out the gate by Lockheed Martin armed guards at about 4 PM.

August 15, 2003: Hearst Newspapers ran my story "*Government Whistleblower Booted from Lockheed Facility,*" which catapulted me into the national spotlight.

Week of August 18, 2003: I received a flurry of calls from people wanting to help and asking who I had dealt with. I mentioned "Jean Lewis." An online query produced no results for "Jean Lewis." However, the query "L. Jean Lewis" produced a vast amount of negative information exposing L. Jean Lewis as a main political figure in the Whitewater investigation of the Clintons during the 1990s. A political figure in the DoD IG raised concerns. The news media pounced on L. Jean Lewis with the following examples.

Newsweek September 22, 2003: "*Pentagon Defense's Whitewater Hire*"

Media Whores Online on/about September 16, 2003: "*Notorious Whitewater Wingnut Hired by Defense Department!*"

These are only a few of the negative stories regarding L. Jean Lewis that have been traced to me and ultimately caused by the infamous August 14, 2003, walk out by the Lockheed Martin armed guards.

March 11, 2004: L. Jean Lewis stated in an email: "*Please note that I will be leaving the agency in the next 30 days and that Mr. Meyer should remain your ongoing point of contact.*"

L. Jean Lewis was the first circumstantial exodus caused by the turmoil of my whistleblowing. Most notable is that L. Jean Lewis brought on Dan Meyer, who became the centerpiece of the con game against Senator Grassley and was the target of the DCMA con game in Falsified Trail 3 (Double Con Game). Meyer did indicate to me that I was blamed for the exposure of L. Jean Lewis. Meyer was correct; however, the August 14, 2003 walk out the gate (Falsified Trail 2) was the real cause.

Exodus 2: Colonel James Wright (Then DCMA LM Commander)

Colonel Wright was my fourth-level supervisor and arrived on or about August 9, 2001. Exodus timeline to my whistleblowing success is as follows:

March 25, 2004: Advance copies of my Substantiated Allegation 4 were sent out March 25, 2004. Substantiated Allegation 4 (DoD IG Report on C-130J, (D-2004-102) was dated July 23, 2004 was a major negative mark on Colonel Wright, who was the commander of my DCMA office overseeing the C-130J.

July 9, 2004: Colonel Wright stated: "*Col Nicole Plourde and I will have our CoC* (Change of Command) *7 Oct 04.*"

July 23, 2004 (DoD IG Report on C-130J, (D-2004-102)): The DoD IG issued a report on the C-130J stating: *"We substantiated the allegation that the C-130J aircraft does not meet contract specifications and therefore cannot perform its operational mission. The Air Force conditionally accepted 50 C-130J aircraft at a cost of $2.6 billion even though none of the aircraft met commercial contract specifications or operational requirements."*

Colonel Wright's exodus was circumstantial to my Substantiated Allegation 4. The rumor of the revocation of Colonel Wright's one-year extension would indicate that Colonel Wright was forced out. More concerning is the fact that Colonel Plourde would (not a rumor) decimate the whistleblowing capability in our office that led to substantiated allegations.

Most shocking is the fact that Dan Meyer was aware Colonel Plourde (June 28, 2006) had a "*reputation within the Air Force of being brought in to fix problem shops.*" Relevance to my resume is Colonel Plourde played a central role (no rumor) in administrative decimating the whistleblowing effort in my office, and in combination with Dan Meyer, severed my ties with Senator Grassley.

Hit Job Relevance: The exodus of Colonel Wright and the entrance of Colonel Plourde show an Air Force hit job on me and those who associated with me. Falsified Trail 3 brings out this fact in extreme detail. Plourde (my fourth-level supervisor) was the Air Force surrogate who came after me personally. The exodus of Colonel Wright's Deputy Commander (Chaffman) and the entrance of Plourde's Deputy Commander (Snow) rounded out an extremely vicious ensemble as follows.

Exodus 3: Charles Ben Chaffman (Then DCMA LM Deputy Commander)

August 24, 2004: Charles Ben Chaffman was my third-level supervisor and had the same circumstantial exodus as Colonel Wright, tied to Substantiated Allegation 4 (DoD IG Report on C-130J, (D-2004-102) dated July 23, 2004. Chaffman announced he was leaving August 24, 2004. Chaffman indicated he was moving to a position to improve "*the Agency's Product Assurance support to customers in the Systems Design and Development phase of the program life cycle.*"

Chaffman's replacement was Henrietta Snow, who rounded out the ensemble with Colonel Plourde in removing whistle-blowers. That was no rumor, it was a fact with an evidence trail.

<u>Exodus 4</u>: Marvin R. Sambur (Assistant Secretary of the Air Force)

<u>November 17, 2004</u>: Marvin Sambur's circumstantial exodus was also tied to Substantiated Allegation 4 (DoD IG Report on C-130J, (D-2004-102) dated July 23, 2004. On April 29, 2004, Marvin Sambur responded to the DoD IG advance comment request dated March 25, 2004. Sambur defiantly stated:

"*The Air Force takes issue with all of the DoD IG findings and recommendations.*"

Marvin Sambur announced his resignation on November 17, 2004, which is the same day I was on ABC News on a segment titled "*C-130J Military Transport Planes Deemed Unfit for War.*" The segment included Colonel Guy Walsh, commander of the Maryland National Guard's 175th Wing, who stated safety is a concern.

<u>Exodus 5</u>: Joseph Schmitz (DoD IG Director)

<u>June 15, 2005</u>: Joseph Schmitz's circumstantial exodus was tied to Substantiated Allegation 3. A September 3, 2005 news article titled "*More to Pentagon's Top Watchdog Resigning*" by David Phinney describes how "*Relations between Grassley and Schmitz began getting rocky in February 2003* (should be February 2004)" further stating "*Pedeleose had found that Lockheed Martin purposefully used false information to justify excessive prices for airplane parts on the C-5.*"

The September 3, 2005 news article ties to the scathing letter Senator Grassley wrote to Schmitz on February 24, 2004 (Substantiated Allegation 3). Phinney used quotes from the February 24, 2004 letter in an April 5, 2004 article in Federal Times previously mentioned. Senator Grassley's February 24, 2004 scathing letter to Schmitz is shortly before David Phinney of Federal Times issued a series of articles in April 2004 based on my experiences and the fraud I uncovered.

To expand on "*Relations between Grassley and Schmitz began getting rocky,*" I copied Charlie Murphy (Senator Grassley's staffer) and Joseph Schmitz on the same email on August 4, 2005, at 8:16 AM during Falsified Trail 3.

Six minutes later (August 4, 2005, 8:24 AM), Joseph Schmitz sent an internal email to Thomas Gimble (DoD IG Principal Deputy), Richard Race (Deputy Inspector General, Investigations), and other senior IG persons, including Uldric Fiore, stating:

"*Tom: Why am I getting this email (along with Charlie Murphy)? /Joe/*"

Race responded back 9:28 AM August 4, 2004: "*Dan, Plse c the IG's note. U have this con. Plse advise Tom as FA.*"

Meyer responded back at 9:34 AM in part recommending to "*set the IG's Outlook software to delete*" my (Pedeleose) emails on arrival.

Gimble responds August 4, 2005 at 11:19 AM, stating: "*I think the IG wants remain in the loop as long as someone is working the issues.*"

The point being, I caused a stir within DoD IG, and the senior levels of DoD IG knew who I was. This was peripheral evidence for Schmitz's circumstantial exodus. The next was Uldric Fiore.

<u>Exodus 6</u>: Uldric Fiore (Lead DoD IG Attorney)

<u>June 5, 2008, IG Investigation Report Fiore, Uldric</u>: Uldric Fiore's circumstantial exodus was linked to an IG investigation report with Case Title "*Fiore, Uldric*" dated June 5, 2008, stating:

"*Our investigation also revealed that Fiore's conduct and involvement regarding the DoD OIG complainant* (Pedeleose) *may have compromised the independence of the DoD OIG, creating an appearance of the loss of impartiality.*" (Appendix A3-4)

Fiore's attendance at an August 10, 2005, tactical meeting was only one part of how Fiore worked against me in Falsified Trail 3. Fiore kept in contact with DCMA well past my 30-day suspension (Falsified Trail 3). The other IG investigation, Fiore had the distinction of being in, was June 28, 2006. So, I had two resume-worthy IG investigations supporting my case and allegations.

On September 15, 2008, I discovered Fiore was no longer at DoD IG. I emailed Charlie Murphy of Senator Grassley's staff to gather more information. Charlie Murphy stated September 15, 2008:

"*You are right. Fiore is gone. Kicklighter* (then DoD IG) *gave him the boot as he departed, but we do not know why. He didn't tell us. We can make some guesses. I will also tell you that the questions regarding Fiore go way beyond your case. That's all I will say for now.*" (Appendix A3-5)

Fiore's circumstantial exodus corresponded to the June 5, 2008 IG report, which was mostly about me (the "complainant" in the report) and the critical findings against Fiore by name. The June 5, 2008 IG report on Fiore also outlined a DoD IG retraction letter by Thomas Gimble that lends insight to remedy issues of government maleficence.

Thomas Gimble - Retraction Letter DoD IG – Embarrassment Remedy

The June 5, 2008, IG report outlined how Thomas Gimble, then the DoD IG Principal Deputy, was forced to issue a retraction letter to me by then-DoD IG Director Claude Kicklighter. I forced the situation by not allowing the DoD IG to cover up the August 10, 2005, tactical meeting (part of Falsified Trail 3).

The June 5, 2008 IG report stated the retraction letter was a "*result of [the DoD complainant's] relentless requests for information...*" I was the "DoD complainant." The IG report gave a sample of the "Thirty Fourth Request" purported to be part of the "relentless" requests. From memory, there were over 50 requests sent nearly every workday by a combination of fax and email.

The DoD IG lived up to expectations with no clear response, and Gimble later issued a retraction letter. Claud Kicklighter ordered the retraction letter because Gimble sent the original letter in response to Kicklighter. Kicklighter found out and got upset. John Crane, DoD IG Director of the Office of Communications and Congressional Liaison, assisted Gimble. John Crane stated in the June 5, 2008 IG report, regarding the retraction letter:

"*Should he* (Gimble) *have been upset? That's up to Tom Gimble, that he felt humiliated by it, that he felt that it made him look bad, that he felt it would give [the DoD complainant] extra ammunition.*"

"*And he* (Gimble) *said that he* (Gimble) *would rather retire than to sign a retraction letter. And I said, 'Once again, that's a matter that you need to raise with General Kicklighter.'*"

"Shock Therapy" & Humiliated: Gimble was right, the retraction letter was "*extra ammunition*" in the fight against institutional corruption and maleficence. The "*ammunition*" was Gimble being "*humiliated*," "*made him look bad*" and Gimble "*would rather retire than to sign a retraction letter*."

"Shock Therapy" to The Government Swamp: Forcing the reversal of weaponization, lawfare, corruption, maleficence, etc., is an easy and quick start to drain the Government Swamp. The retraction was the administrative "shock therapy" that will help drive resolution, and as such, is a part of my resume. The other significant reversal was my revoked and reinstated security clearance.

Revoked & Reinstated Security Clearance

The DoD dredged up every minute negative piece of evidence against me, beginning with the Army (where I was given an Honorable discharge), and combined it with the 13 Falsified Trails of Chapter 3 to revoke my security clearance. I had my security clearance reinstated by explaining why the charges were based on retaliation. Chapter 3 explains this in detail.

The point being, the DoD added to my resume with the most blatant retaliatory act of malice against me, and I still survived. This just goes to prove that I was extremely effective and can prove that I did well in the DoD. The following is a summary of my early days in the DoD and cost savings.

Engineer Charleston Naval Shipyard (CNSY) - Gridlock Examples

CNSY (1987-1994): On April 2, 1987, I started work at CNSY as an Industrial Engineer (IE) to cut the overhaul cost of Naval Ships and Nuclear Submarines. I was hired as part of a March 20, 1986, Department of the Navy memo (5240 Ser 0704/68) titled "*Industrial Engineering in Naval Shipyards*." The goal was for Naval Shipyards to hire Industrial Engineers with savings of 10X salary. Meaning, I was value-added and saved DoD money. This was an early analogy to the DOGE.

My main job and reason for being hired was cost reduction and method improvement, although I did have other duties. I was highly respected and referred to as a "*super engineer*" on May 22, 1992 handwritten on a May 15, 1992 memo. My project savings achieved/projected are as follows.

Verifiable Savings May 15, 1992: $217,150 on abrasive grit and lead ballast loading aboard submarines.

Projected Savings January 8, 1990: $118,925 for Submarine SWLIN (System Work Line Item Number) 534A01 (Rescue, Salvage, & Survival System) for replacement strategy versus repair on smaller needle valves.

- Total Savings would be $217,150+$118,925=$336,075.
- Total CNSY estimated salary (1987-1994) was approximately $265,000.
- I achieved about 1.3X salary ($336,075/$265,000=1.3 rounded)

Major Awards May 15, 1992: Winner 1992 NAVSEA (Naval Sea Systems Command) IE of the Year. Nominated for the 1990 NAVSEA IE of the Year Award, January 12, 1990.

Symposium Papers April 22, 1991, June 1991: Presented papers at NAVSEA symposiums, most notably in the area of SWLIN review as part of the Naval Industrial Improvement Program at that time. This was another early analogy to the DOGE.

Ruination & Gridlock Strategy

(Forecast, Prepare, Project Execution to Success)

Ruination and gridlock at CNSY resulted from intransigent management and ill-advised production practices unrelated to corruption, unlike DCMA where corruption and incompetence was apparent upon arrival in 1994. In anticipation of a predictable production disaster at CNSY, I would prepare a response plan of my own volition, and then wait until production was in gridlock. There was no other way. Gridlock and ruination were the only things intransigent management understood.

Meaning, I was forced to wait for the disaster, and then when reality overcame intransigence, I would present the plan and complete the project successfully. Two such projects are as follows:

December 20, 1991- Lead Ballast Handling: The Navy hired accountants to try and cut costs. One project was the lead ballast loading and unloading for submarine overhaul. The accountants noticed a cost of \$10,000 - \$15,090 to make hull cuts and decided to delete hull cuts during overhaul. This was a forecast for disaster since hull cuts are a massive time saver, as well as limiting lead (carcinogen) contact for workers.

To prepare for inevitable ruination and production gridlock, I kept the hull cut plan at the ready. There was nothing I could do except wait for production gridlock.

As forecasted, the deletion of hull cuts drove production to ruination and gridlock. I was called in and reinstated the hull cuts and saved \$72,150. The premise is: Accountant's approach spends \$87,240 to save \$15,090 (hull cut cost). I spent \$15,090 and saved \$72,150.

I have a strong ability to forecast ruination and gridlock; Prepare a response plan; And then successfully execute the plan. Lead ballast is only one of my successes.

March 21, 1991 - Abrasive Grit Clogging Dry Dock Drains: Abrasive grit (for paint removal on submarines and ships) clogged dry dock drainage systems, impeding the drydocking of a submarine.

Management notes stated: "*Pedeleose has been working this for some time.*" The phrase "*working this for some time*" was my forecasting ruination and having a plan of action ready.

The initial plan for standard dry grit collection was presented May 1, 1990, with the next signature being May 4, 1990. The project stalled until ruination on March 21, 1991, which may have been for the best since the prepared plan would not have had the capability as the final solution (Vacuum Trucks) to go beneath the dry docks and vacuum wet/submerged grit. Meaning, it was known for some time that wet grit beneath the dry dock was an issue, aside from collecting dry grit, which was the initial project.

Vacuum Truck: I had already started researching more powerful vacuums (vacuum trucks) for wet, submerged grit, aside from the issues encountered in 1990 for dry grit. Both centered on vacuums, one was more powerful than the other. My prepared plan of action was to use truck-mounted diesel vacuums to remove spent grit (sand-like substance) from drydock drains.

The trucks were powerful enough to sit atop the drydock and vacuum grit/sand underneath the dry dock, in the drains, with about a 50-foot vertical lift. Shipyard scuba divers (with possible Navy SEAL experience) were used in many cases to complete the project.

The combination of lead ballast and abrasive grit removal was a contributor to my winning the 1992 NAVSEA Industrial Engineer of the Year award on May 15, 1992.

April 30, 1993 – Purchase Equipment: The grit removal process was such a success that I was provided funds to purchase a truck mounted vacuum unit for the shipyard. I wrote the contract specifications and saw the project through completion. The vacuum truck was so well built with a heavy chassis and axles that vacuuming projects aside from routine abrasive grit may have been used. Meaning, abrasive grit weighing more than standard abrasive paint removal grit.

CNSY was the best job I ever had. Unfortunately, CNSY was targeted for Base Realignment and Closure (BRAC) on/about 1993. I was placed on a DoD Stopper List for displaced employees and was provided a job at Defense Contract Management Agency (DCMA) (then a part of Defense Logistics Agency (DLA)) in Marietta, GA, assigned to the Lockheed Martin facility. Unbeknownst to me, this was an immersion into the "Swamp." Prior to CNSY was my Army experience.

Army – Negligence Diagnosing Health Issues

My time in the Army was short (1984-1986). I originally entered Officer Candidate School (OCS). Unbeknownst to me, I had a lung condition prior to entering the Army. I was never good at physical exercise and always thought it was due to a lack of trying. I did have some improvement, but not enough to meet Army physical training standards. I deteriorated over time.

On/about 1985, I went on sick call at the urging of my superiors to get checked out. I was placed on a treadmill to do a breathing test and nearly collapsed. The test could not be performed because I was so out of breath. The person running the test may not even have been a doctor and stated the problem was in my mind, although they gave me breathing medications. The medications did not help. Over time, I was harassed and eventually began to shut down on issues to the point of conflicts with superiors. It was not my fault I had health issues. I could not overcome these issues.

In 1986, I was given an honorable discharge.

While at CNSY, I went to training and medical exams to enter nuclear radiation areas of submarines if projects warranted. Within minutes, my medical exam found the lung condition. Other doctors over the years recognized the same issue.

Relevance is, the Army was negligent in health care, and it caused me problems. Had I been properly diagnosed, as I was at CNSY, things would have worked differently. Aside from my circumstances, I understood that the Army at that time had retention issues, so it is unknown how those issues played into my case from the Army's perspective. The Army was my first experience with incompetence related to negligent medical diagnosis.

Personal Financial Loss from Government Swamp Retaliation

My estimated financial loss from weaponized government, lawfare, and retaliation is $22,241. This includes lost salary, mailing and some copying costs for cases, legal expenses, and lost benefits. This does not include lost interest, loss of promotions, other copying costs, and office supplies over the years. The total loss to taxpayers would be a conservative estimate of 30%-50% of the national debt which would be in the trillions of dollars. More than likely, the entire national deficit may be attributed to institutional corruption, weaponization, and lawfare of the Government Swamp.

I was lucky because some employees lost a lot more. Taxpayer loss is much greater and is leading the U.S. toward ruination and gridlock. I approached whistleblowing tactically by staying public, which kept management off balance, although they remained aggressive. I handled the majority of litigating my own cases and used my experience to help others. The litigated cases provided me greater insight into institutional corruption, weaponization and lawfare.

Pro Se Litigation Experience, Helping Others, Radical Case Reversals

My ability and training to research production operations, analyze complex technical data across a wide spectrum, lay out a logical path to remedy and/or negotiation positions, and prepare coherent logic-based reports laid a good foundation for litigation and modest wins at litigation.

Notes are made on violent reversals of judges to conceal institutional corruption. Also note, aside from Falsified Trail 2, the other wins were against trained attorneys, sometimes working in teams. Examples are as follows.

<u>Falsified Trail 2 Removed by Armed Guards and BOLO Issued August 14, 2003)</u>: Armed guards of Lockheed Martin dramatically escorted off the Lockheed Martin facility, and a BOLO was posted at the entrance to the Lockheed Martin facility. On September 8, 2003, the decision was radically reversed, and I had full facility access reinstated.

<u>EEO Case Retaliation (September 30, 2005)</u>: I assisted a fellow employee in litigating an EEO case. It was determined that DCMA retaliated against the employee. The employee was given a cash award. Proves at the very least that DCMA does retaliate against its employees.

<u>EEO Case Retaliation (August 9, 2006)</u>: I litigated my EEO case (Pro Se) and had a finding where DCMA retaliated against me. Proves DCMA has sustained retaliatory motives.

Relevance is, I successfully litigated two cases proving that DCMA retaliates against its employees.

<u>EEO Case Settlement (July 26, 2007) (Half Credit)</u>: I was the "first responder" for an employee terminated from Federal Service in 2005. This was part of Falsified Trail 3. I assembled the case file and worked the issue to the point of a live hearing. The employee retained an attorney who took the case to a settlement. Based on office conversations, DCMA cashed in the office travel budget to settle the case.

<u>MSPB Falsified Trail 3 (June 14, 2006, October 24, 2007, February 12, 2009)</u>: Falsified Trail 3 took radical reversals substantiating MSPB's lack of quasi-judicial integrity. MSPB's first ruling on June 14, 2006, was solidly against me, restating DCMA's position and ignoring evidence.

The second ruling on October 24, 2007, was solidly <u>in my favor,</u> referring to my commander, Colonel Plourde, as "*disingenuous*" among a multitude of other findings. This ruling followed evidence where DCMA stipulated to my sworn deposition testimony and response to charges, agreeing that whistle-blower retaliation had occurred.

The third ruling, on February 12, 2009, vacated the October 24, 2007 decision and reverted to restating DCMA's case, thereby covering up critical and overwhelming evidence and expanding the Government Swamp. This was necessary because Falsified Trail 3 traced into the Pentagon, via Uldric Fiore, and would be considered the "Rosetta Stone" for deciphering retaliation from high-level DoD officials. That "Rosetta Stone" deciphering now translates further to MSPB in cover-ups and will be discussed in detail in Chapter 3 of this book.

<u>MSPB Falsified Trail 6 (December 14, 2010, September 30, 2011)</u>: Falsified Trail 6 took the same type of radical reversal as did Falsified Trail 3. Specifically, on December 14, 2010, the MSPB initial decision ruled in my favor in what was another case of textbook whistle-blower retaliation.

On September 30, 2011, the full MSPB again reversed against overwhelming evidence in my favor to grant DCMA a win, further covering up retaliation. As in Falsified Trail 3, the DOJ had multiple attorneys sign on to the falsified case, prompting the Federal Court to rule against me.

I presented winnable cases with irrefutable evidence, forcing the U.S. Legal and Judicial System to make capricious cases and rulings that provide objective evidence to question U.S. Legal and Judicial System integrity.

<u>Pro Se Coach and Representing Other Employees</u>: I assisted other employees as a pro se, non-attorney (behind-the-scenes), coach by explaining processes, timelines, and what is needed to make cases, and as a representative at times. I had mixed results, although the cases support allegations of institutionally corrupted government. Meaning, the information from those cases was used to support allegations of maleficence made herein.

Regardless, of the overwhelming weaponization, lawfare, and institutional corruption I was able to save the U.S. Government some money, and overall meet the savings goal of at least 10 times my salary over my entire government career combined (1987-2020). Those savings claimed were on projects where I was the main catalyst, not including other projects where I was a contributor to a team. Those total savings, which were actually 12 times my salary, are as follows.

Career Savings (12 Times Salary) Despite Deep State Retaliations

(Weaponization & Lawfare Enabled 30% - 50% Price Gouging Average)

The following are my savings where my involvement made a difference. Meaning, had I not been there the savings may not have been achieved. Keeping in mind, I participated in many more projects than the following and was obstructed from achieving even more savings.

Year	Savings	Part #	Summary Title
January 8, 1990	$118,925	1	SWLIN 534A01 (Rescue, Salvage, Survival)
May 15, 1992	$217,150	1	Grit Removal & Lead Ballast Loading
February 23, 2000	$2,254,963	4	Single Item Purchase (79%-80% Over)
August 12, 2016	$13,467,811	4	Price Gouging Elaborate Math (31% Over)
September 7, 2018	$12,324,092	4	Price Gouging Elaborate Math (31% Over)
November 18, 2011	$584,610	4	Material Estimating Glitch
	$28,967,551		

My career salary (1984 – 2020) was approximately $2.41 million calculated from online Social Security records.

Total Career Savings: $28,967,551/$2,408,930 = <u>12 Times</u> Entire Federal Salary 1984 – 2020.

As a note, I was asked for by name on July 5, 2017, for the September 7, 2018 savings.

Other Calculated Savings, Independent Research and Development (IRAD) & Potential Savings

Year	Savings	Part #	Summary Title
March 18, 1999	$140,468	4	C-130J Cargo Handling (IRAD)
March 18, 1999	$311,925	4	C-130J Propeller (IRAD)
March 18, 1999	$6,822,939	4	C-27J IRAD Foreign Offset
December 10, 2003	$1,061,975	4	Global Air Traffic Management – C-130J
August 31, 2000	-	4	23.9% - 38.5% Overhead Rate Overestimating
August 16, 2007	-	4	24%-69% Judgement Overestimating
July 23, 2013	-	4	Up to 12X Cost of Air Force Work
July 27, 2016	-	4	49%-60% Factor Overestimating – F-35

The point is, the Deep State retaliations, weaponization, and lawfare enabled 30% - 50% overestimating (price gouging) as an average. This was enabled from, casual ("foot-in-the-aisle") interference, to outright blatant obstruction and cover-ups of waste, fraud, abuse, and gross mismanagement issues. The 30%-50% conservative estimate would be from the past percentages from the "Summary Title" in the previous charts where the low was 23.9% to the high which was 80%.

Why Didn't I Leave?

The question may be asked…Why didn't I just leave and seek employment elsewhere? First, it's doubtful that the "grass would be greener" anywhere else, meaning that everywhere has its own issues, internal politics, despotic managers, corruption, cronyism, and the like. Second, I had the hope that things would improve with the next DCMA commander and/or the next DCMA Director. That never happened at DCMA. Things stayed the same or got worse.

Mainly, I appreciated my job because shortly after I graduated from high school and entered college, there was a major economic downturn in my area. My original plan was mining and mining engineering. The coal industry in my area was nearly shut down, causing high unemployment. So, in effect, I promised myself that when I got a good job, I wouldn't quit even if I didn't like the job.

Resume Conclusion & Relevance

My resume explains my positive attributes, successes, and how I was labeled "*extremely effective*" and a "*super engineer*." What was positive to me was negative to others, such as the DoD, DCMA, and DoD IG, among others. I worked for the efficiency of the Federal Service. I was an early analogy to the DOGE.

My success was DoD management's reasons to execute my reputation. DoD would call out the gambit of institutionalized corrupted government against me including the Deep State, weaponization, and lawfare. I documented what transpired and now have a book that extends beyond cost savings, questioning the U.S. Legal and Judicial System in an effort to fix a broken government.

If there is concern about questioning the U.S. Legal and Judicial System, and questioning management integrity, then the U.S. Legal and Judicial System and management should not have provided an objective evidence trail and reasons to objectively question the U.S. Legal and Judicial System and management integrity.

Trying to find the end of institutional corruption and tactical weaponized government is like trying to find the end of the universe. This book is a start. Chapter 2 follows…

CHAPTER 2:
Resume - About the Deep State & Government Swamp

Military-Industrial Complex "In Bed" With DoD Contractors: President Dwight Eisenhower (January 17, 1961) stated in his farewell address to the nation:

"This conjunction of an immense military establishment and a large arms industry is new in the American experience... We must guard against the acquisition of unwarranted influence, whether sought or unsought, by the military-industrial complex. The potential for the disastrous rise of misplaced power exist and will persist."

The military-industrial complex is a source of significant revenue and power that has become corrupted over time. I challenged that corruption and had my personal and professional reputation attacked. The process of executing my reputation (Explained in Chapter 3) completes the loop on understanding tactical weaponized government. Chapter 4 shows the cost to U.S. taxpayers.

In 2002, I befriended the first known public whistleblower, Arthur Ernest "Ernie" Fitzgerald. Fitzgerald became my mentor and helped me understand the true basis of tactical weaponized government, starting with the Nixon Administration.

Nixon Administration – Tactical Weaponization of Government Blueprint

The Nixon administration provided the blueprint for modern tactical weaponization of government. The tactical weaponization began with Ernie Fitzgerald and President Nixon a half-century ago.

Half Century (50-Year) Starting Point: Ernie Fitzgerald was a Pentagon Senior Executive Service employee with the title, Management Systems Deputy, Assistant Secretary of the Air Force for Financial Management and Comptroller. In 1968, Fitzgerald testified before Congress regarding a $2.3 billion cost overrun on the Lockheed C-5A aircraft program. This related to the military- industrial complex (money & manufacturing) and not the military warfighters.

Industrial Complex (Acquisition, Money) vs Military Warfighters: Fitzgerald made the first known public exposure of the "*military-industrial complex.*" The important distinction is the word "industrial," which refers to military acquisition related to finances and contracts. This marked Fitzgerald as a whistleblower and a target since money was involved. Money equates to power, and money transfers are traceable.

Adverse Personnel Action Followed: On November 4, 1969, Fitzgerald was given a 60-day notice that he would be terminated from Government. On January 5, 1970, Fitzgerald was ultimately terminated by then-Defense Secretary Melvin Laird. It appeared that Defense Secretary Laird fired Fitzgerald; however, the Nixon Watergate tapes told the true story.

Nixon Fired Fitzgerald – Laird was the Surrogate: On January 31, 1973, Nixon commented to presidential aide Charles W. Colson: "*This guy that was fired, I'd mark it in the news summary. That's how that happened. I said get rid of that son of a bitch.*" Hence, Nixon ordered Fitzgerald fired, and Laird (surrogate) carried out the termination, insulating Nixon. Nixon was insulated until he spoke to Colson.

Nixon's firing of Fitzgerald was the improvised genesis of the tactical weaponization of government. A watershed moment. The more wholesale and widespread Nixon tactics for the enemies list evolved into tactical "Federal Machinery" and "Insulation" for corruption.

Nixon Enemies List & Federal Machinery

August 16, 1971 - Nixon Enemies List & Federal Machinery (Insulation): John Dean (White House Counsel for President Nixon) issued a cover memo outlining "*available federal machinery to screw our political enemies*." Dean described a "*project coordinator*" to oversee the process. This process centered on the Nixon Enemies List.

The Nixon Enemies List outlined how a "project coordinator" would "*have access to and the full support of the top officials of the agency or department in proceeding to deal with the individual.*"

What Nixon Planned versus Actuality: One important note is the distinction between what Nixon planned to do versus how Nixon's ideas were corruptly inbred-upon and used over the years. Meaning, what actually happened versus what was planned.

In short, the recorded history via the internet of the Nixon "Enemies List" was to harass opponents ("enemies") with "Federal Machinery" such as tax audits, litigation, prosecution, etc. As explained by John Dean, "*how we can use the available federal machinery to screw our political enemies*."

Documented Example of Weaponized Government

Watergate ultimately stopped Nixon, although Nixon's ideas evolved and "inbred" in different forms, with upgrades and enhancements. This book uses me as the example (Chapter 3) of what Nixon's ideas evolved into. Chapter 2 herein outlines the operational framework of Nixon's ideas leading up to 2001.

One tactical idea of the Nixon Administration, which forms a cornerstone of retaliation in my book herein (primarily Chapter 3), was termed the Malek Manual, which gained control through personnel actions. Currently enhanced and explained as weaponization and lawfare.

Nixon's Malek Manual – Stealthy Removal of Employees

"Malek Manual" - Tactical Control Through Personnel Actions: The Nixon administration recognized that absolute control of government was achieved through personnel actions. As such, Nixon's Personnel Chief, Fred Malek, developed the infamous "*Malek Manual*" (1972), which was a plan to "*skirt around*" adverse action proceedings in a legal manner against career Federal employees. Basically, skirt the law and insulate management. Fred Malek was special assistant to President Nixon from 1970 to 1973.

April 22, 2003 "The President and the Executive Branch by Joel D. Aberbach): The Nixon Administration message (copied from documents provided by Ernie Fitzgerald) was: "*You cannot achieve management, policy or program control unless you have established political control.*" For Nixon, political control meant removing Fitzgerald, who had attempted to protect Federal interests. My situation mirrors Fitzgerald's, which is why I included this information.

Basically: "*Career employees...can only be dismissed or otherwise punished for direct disobedience of lawful orders, actions which are tantamount to the commission of a crime, and well documented and provable incompetence.*"

Meaning, the Malek Manual was a conglomeration of harassment tactics to force Federal employees from Federal Service who were trying to protect U.S. Government interests.

<u>Malek Stealthy Replacement Tactics & Insulation</u>: Malek proposed stealthy replacement tactics on the civilian workforce and insulation of the management staff. The following was copied from Wikipedia, November 15, 2018, regarding Fred Malek:

"*In the first Nixon administration, Malek designed and directed the "Responsiveness Program," a strategy to replace civil servants with Nixon supporters and to steer government resources to benefit Nixon's 1972 re-election...In advocating the plan, Malek wrote of "substantial risks" to politicizing the Executive Branch and expressed concern that the plan would "undoubtedly backfire" if made public; therefore he recommended that "to minimize any links to the President, there should be no directions on this project in writing.*"

This would appear as the first use of surrogates to insulate management. Additionally, and as important, is the aspect that no directions on the project be in writing. However, the Malek Manual did have some documentation as follows.

<u>Malek Manual Force Out Tactics</u>: The Wikipedia report on Malek (November 15, 2018) outlined tactics against the civilian workforce to drive out undesirables who challenge management. Some of the tactics were designed to be used on individuals and others to control entire offices. The following was copied from the internet.

1: <u>Frontal Assault (Individual)</u>: Straightforward verbal attack and ensure no witnesses.

2: <u>Transfer (Individual)</u>: Transfer employee to location that employee will not accept.

3: <u>Traveling Salesman (Individual)</u>: Force travel and employee quits on their own.

4: <u>Layering Technique (Organization)</u>: Loyal management layer over disloyal employees.

5: <u>Shifting Responsibilities (Organization)</u>: Create parallel organization rendering duties of undesirables meaningless.

6: <u>New Activity (Wholesale)</u>: Transfer undesirables to meaningless positions.

The relevance is that Fred Malek proposed stealth tactics to force out civil servants while unethically insulating management. Management used a series of Falsified Trails in Volleys over the years to attempt to drive me out. I had no doubt what was happening and took the opportunity to further expose management, as this book shows.

Aside from the Falsified Trails against me, management heavily used the Malek layering scheme.

Malek Layering Technique (Cronyism) is DoD Institutional 2nd Level Upward

The Malek "Layering Technique" is cronyism. Cronyism is so extensive that I can say second-level supervisors and above are of no value in the DoD. The ethics of first-level supervisors are evaluated on a case-by-case basis. Meaning, my interactions with second-level supervisors and above indicate that ethics are at best zero, sometimes even negative (corrupt). That Malek tactic has inbred over 50 years. This book provides examples of what Malek tactics evolved into.

The aforementioned comments are based on Chapters 3 and 4 of this book, which are my observations, experiences, and documentation spanning 26 ½ years. Chapter 2 provides the boilerplate and genesis of weaponized government and lawfare that expand the Government Swamp and explain how the Government Swamp was formed.

Variations on Themes: The tactical weaponization of government utilizes buzzwords such as "Malek Manual," "Deep State," "Federal Machinery," and "Enemies List," among others. The buzzwords are an intermix chamber of variations on themes such as tactical retaliation, abuse of authority, coercion, bullying, etc. Nothing new, just repackaged and relabeled ideas currently termed weaponized government and lawfare.

Malek Manual will Re-emerge 2005: The Malek Manual will re-emerge in 2005 in this book and will be further detailed in Chapter 3. The Malek Manual weaponized tactics will be a major part of the cases for Ernie Fitzgerald and me. For now, the 1970 timeline continues. Corruption rose to the point where Fitzgerald wrote books.

"The High Priests of Waste" by A. Ernest Fitzgerald - 1972

In 1972, Ernie Fitzgerald wrote a book titled "*The High Priest of Waste.*" The forward of the book, copied in part below, sounds like my experience.

"*I was part of the arms-buying process for most of twenty years. As an Industrial Engineer, I had opportunities to see stupendous waste at first hand and sometimes to document it. While this concerned me greatly, I also saw an opportunity. The folklore about the inevitability of waste notwithstanding, I knew how to eliminate much of it, and so did many other people I worked with over the years.*"

I am an Industrial Engineer with decades of experience in addressing DoD waste, fraud, abuse, and gross mismanagement. The most difficult part for me was having to confront DoD management, which was intent on tarnishing my reputation and trying to force me from government. That is why I kept contemporaneous documents. I saw the cliff (financial ruination/debt) the U.S. is headed for. I saw the cover-ups firsthand. I didn't read the books of others to tell my story. However, the other documentation complements my story and accounts herein as peripheral supporting evidence.

Extrapolating National Debt: The most important part of Fitzgerald's book, "*The High Priests of Waste,*" is that it was written in 1972, over half a century ago. Meaning, DoD at least was wasting money as of that date. This supports allegations herein that a sizable portion, if not all, of the national debt may have been avoidable and dates back to the 1970s. The next notable event of the 1970s was the pardon of President Nixon.

President Ford Pardoned Nixon – Nixon's Ideas Remained and Used Eternal

Nixon resigned the presidency on August 9, 1974. On September 8, 1974, President Gerald Ford pardoned Nixon, allowing Nixon's ideas to be improved upon, relabeled, exemplified, and embodied in the 1978 Civil Service Reform Act (CSRA), soon to be discussed.

The point is, even though Nixon left the presidency, the ideas of Nixon and Malek still remained without remedy or oversight to stop any reemergence. The 1978 CSRA became the enhanced and direct embodiment of Nixon and Malek's ideas, which I have termed "Cerberus." Meaning, to contain negative information from leaving the government and discredit the messenger who releases or exposes negative information.

1978 Civil Service Reform Act ("Cerberus" Analogy) OSC, MSPB, OPM

Watershed Moment to Enable Weaponization & Lawfare

Weaponized "Federal Machinery": The Nixon dream of a perfect tactical weapon and "Federal Machinery" to control the government was embodied in the 1978 CSRA. The 1978 CSRA exemplified Nixon's proposed agenda and ideas in reality and operational perfection. The reality and working practice of OSC, MSPB, and OPM are not what appear on paper. The "Cerberus" analogy explains what OSC, MSPB, and OPM really do, which is to serve as an administrative "Garbage Disposal" and a weaponized "Federal Machinery."

OSC, MSPB, OPM - "Cerberus" Analogy: Cerberus in mythology was the three-headed hound of Hades that kept the dead from leaving and ensured those who entered never left. The modern "Cerberus" analogy used to cover up and enable institutional corruption, weaponization, and lawfare is the 1978 CSRA.

The 1978 CSRA established MSPB, OSC (once part of MSPB), and OPM. The 1978 CSRA was partly in response to Watergate. However, the evidence in Chapter 3 of this book, along with extensive peripheral evidence in the following paragraphs, clearly proves that OSC, MSPB, and OPM are the total package embodiment of a weaponized government and enablers of institutional corruption. MSPB is comically labeled "Quasi-Judicial."

Relevance is that OSC, MSPB, and OPM will engage in major cover-ups of institutional government corruption, weaponization and lawfare as outlined in Chapter 3. Meaning, OSC, MSPB, and, if needed, OPM capriciously cover up findings of whistleblower retaliation and violations of 18 USC 1505. Meaning, a "garbage disposal" that contains and grinds up anything ethical.

Falsified Trail 3 is the Rosetta Stone for deciphering weaponized government and covers the "Cerberus" trifecta of OSC, MSPB, and OPM, as there is a lot to conceal that traces directly to the highest levels of DoD. The rest of this book also helps decipher weaponized government and lawfare as well as the negative financial effects of weaponized government and lawfare.

Nevertheless, as time progressed, Nixon's ideas enhanced and enabled corruption. OSC, MSPB, and OPM provided valuable cover. Meaning, corruption grew, and so did non-profit organizations that report on corruption, as follows.

Non-Profit – Full-Time Employment Exposing Corruption

Corruption in the USG grew to the point where reporting on corruption was full-time employment. The Government Accountability Project (GAP) was formed in/about 1977. Project On Government Oversight (POGO) was formed in/about 1981. The National Whistleblower Center was formed on/about 1988. The Center for Public Integrity was formed in/about March 1989.

The point is that non-profit organizations have a full-time staff that reports on government corruption. This is peripheral evidence supporting the fact of institutional government corruption that is covered-up by weaponization and lawfare. Corruption was at the point where Ernie Fitzgerald wrote another book on DoD corruption.

"The Pentagonists" by A. Ernest Fitzgerald - 1989

About 17 years after Ernie Fitzgerald wrote his first book, "The High Priest of Waste," Fitzgerald wrote another book titled "The Pentagonists." The front cover had the subtitle:

"*An insider's view of waste, mismanagement, and fraud in defense spending*"

The historical data point is… Fitzgerald's first book, The High Priest of Waste, was written in 1972. The second book by Fitzgerald ("The Pentagonists") was 17 years later in 1989. This book, which is about 36 years after 1989, is presented herein. The point being, a half-century plus (since 1970) of documented waste, fraud, abuse, and gross mismanagement. It is plausible that all of the national debt is attributed to waste, fraud, abuse, and gross mismanagement. It also explains why management has worked extensively to silence and discredit me, and to prevent Fitzgerald from working with Congress, as follows.

Tactical Pentagon & DoD Level Interference Against Ernie Fitzgerald

On May 4, 1988, Ernie Fitzgerald made a memo for record, on Department of the Air Force letterhead, regarding a discussion between a DCMA employee (Reggie "Reg" Andrews) and Brad Allison, Executive Vice President of Lockheed-Georgia Co. Allison, according to Reg Andrews said that Richard E. Carver, Asst Secretary of the Air Force (Manpower & Reserve Affairs) had recently visited the management of Lockheed-Georgia.

"*He said Mr. Carver bragged that "they" had finally gotten Fitzgerald under control. They did this, he said, by putting Fitzgerald under a general who was charged with "keeping Fitzgerald busy" and "not letting him work with Congress.*"

The May 4, 1988, memo by Fitzgerald is an example of collaboration in the military-industrial complex (DoD officials) and DoD contractor Lockheed Martin. Hence, the "Federal Machinery" was augmented by collaborative DoD and contractor efforts to stifle whistleblowers.

My resume (Chapter 1) outlines how DCMA has had "private" conversations with Lockheed Martin officials, such as Vice President Ray Burick and another Lockheed Martin management official, Denise Joyce. A Lockheed Martin Human Resources director (Diane Stefani) was invited into conversations with DCMA against me by Ray Burick, a Lockheed Martin Vice President. That is one parallel I have with Fitzgerald. Fear is another.

Fear to Force Silence

Evolving Amoral Behavior of Using Fear as a Stifling Force

Fitzgerald's book "The Pentagonists" includes a conversation from a Lockheed employee, Henry Durham. On August 1, 2003, Fitzgerald sent me that page, which stated in part.

"*When it became known that I might go outside with the problem, Mr. Paul Frech, the director of manufacturing, was sent to Chattanooga to see me. [Our] conversation was predictably short. The first thing he said was, "Do you know what happened to Ernie Fitzgerald, who went to Washington with some Lockheed problems?" When I said I didn't, Frech said, "He's now chief shit-house inspector for the Civil Service Commission and will never be able to get a good job as long as he lives.""* "[Erwin Kroll, "The Education of Henry Durham," reprinted from The Progressive, 1972]."

Ernie Fitzgerald was pilloried as a public example of what happens when DoD corruption was exposed. Chapter 3 of this book reveals how I was targeted by 13 Falsified Trails to divert attention from the real DoD corruption. However, corruption can be contained only so long.

In 2002, there was a major influx of public and private events that were documented. The following is a brief list that proves the effects of corruption will eventually come to the surface.

2002 – Institutional Corruption Broaches the Surface

2002 was a busy year for corruption, with scandals emerging to the surface. Meaning, corruption came to the surface in 2002; however, that corruption had begun years earlier. The 2002 events are as follows.

The Whistleblowers

Time Magazine December 30, 2002/January 6, 2003 – Persons of the Year: Cynthia Cooper of WorldCom, Coleen Rowley of the FBI, and Sherron Watkins of Enron were Time Magazines Persons of the Year. The specifics of each case (WorldCom, Enron, and the September 11, 2001 terrorist attacks) are now a part of history. It would have been better if the whistleblowers had been heard prior to the events.

The Time Magazine article on Coleen Rowley indicated in part "*the FBI head-quarters is mired in mediocrity*"; there is an "*unevenness in competency among head-quarters personnel*" and; how "*Rowley's memo charges that FBI officials "glossed over" how much they knew about the possibility of an attack.*"

After this string of incidents with Enron, WorldCom, and the September 11, 2001, terrorist attacks, I honestly thought Congress would take concrete, definitive action to ensure that such things wouldn't happen again. I was wrong. There was a brief flare-up in congressional action, followed by a return to the status quo and steady-state corruption covered-up by weaponization and lawfare.

Additionally, in 2002, I authored the first report I presented to Congress.

90 Page - Report to Congress

July 26, 2002: By 2001, I had all I could stand of DoD corruption, cover-ups, and negligence. I began preparing a formal report to Congress. It took time to write because DoD corruption was very deep. I was experienced in preparing reports and had access to Lockheed Martin's financial information and data, including direct & indirect/overhead costs, pricing reports, quality assurance information, test reports, and the like. I had the data and analysis aspect covered.

The other half of the plan was multifaceted, utilizing existing avenues for remedy and to root out corruption, negligence, discrimination, and fraud, among other issues, that were present in the DoD. Those avenues included the DoD IG, EEOC, OSC, MSPB, and the news media, among others. At the time I did not know the true depth of Government corruption. I would soon find out.

The plan had success as my resume (Chapter 1) has shown. As the harassment unfolded, I continued to document and eventually found that the DoD had a lot of allies and organizations supporting cover-ups. Among these were OSC, MSPB, and OPM, which will be discussed shortly.

My contemporaneous documentation assembled a story that would be negligent of me not to tell. My strategy forced the DoD and DCMA to take the long way around to retaliate against me with an elaborate trail of weaponization and lawfare. DoD IG used confidence games against Senator Grassley (my main congressional supporter) and me to damage my reputation. That will be discussed in Chapter 3.

Another DCMA employee, Doug Kinan, unbeknown to me at the time, issued an affidavit about a week after July 26, 2002.

Doug Kinan Affidavit

August 2, 2002: Doug Kinan was a direct witness to DCMA's amoral acts and provided an affidavit as documentation. I was contacted by Kinan when Falsified Trail 2, August 14, 2003 (walk out the gate by Lockheed Martin armed guards), went public, and Kinan was made aware of my name.

Kinan's affidavit included a DCMA attorney quote and other info as follows:

"We (the Legal Directorate) can do anything we want. It's called gaming. We can deny, we can delay...dismiss. We can manipulate the system anyway we want."

Kinan further stated: "*Other evasive manipulations are silence or when required to explain their conduct, the Legal Directorate declares the claim of "attorney work product or "attorney privilege.""*" I have experienced this weaponized-lawfare tactic as well.

Kinan stated DCMA accused him of "*armed robbery*," "*rough background*," "*threatened*" officials, and "*may become violent*."

By no coincidence, DCMA and higher DoD used the same weaponized playbook of alleged and unsupported violence accusations against me.

The DCMA Alleged Violence Playbook for Retaliation

My case was a duplicate of Doug Kinan's, as Chapter 3 herein shows. Meaning, DCMA and DoD use false and unsupported violence and behavior allegations. The following are some brief examples.

May 12, 2005 – Diving for Body Armor: False allegations included people in my office allegedly "*diving for body armor*" because of me (May 12, 2005). I went and spoke with the employees near me, and no one knew where the "*diving for body armor*" comment came from.

November 18, 2003 – Pulling Employees Along by the Arm: In this false allegation, Ben Chaffman (then Deputy Commander) testified in a sworn statement that he was "*working behind closed doors*" and then saw me "*become incensed and proceeded to the command suit literally pulling Ms. Davis* (then Union President) *along by the arm.*"

The first issue is that Chaffman was "behind closed doors," meaning Chaffman could not have seen me do anything. Second, knowing the office configuration, Chaffman couldn't see me allegedly pulling Ms. Davis by the arm even if the door was open.

Third, Ms. Davis testified on September 15, 2005, to questions asked by me as follows.

"During that time, from the time he (Chaffman) *told you until the time we went to his office, did I at any time ever physically touch you?"* Davis testified: "*No*"

"Did I ever physically take you by the arm and pull you into Mr. Chaffman's office?"

Davis testified: *"Absolutely not."*

"Did my hand at any time ever touch any part of your body?" Davis testified: *"No"*

The point is that circumstantial evidence and direct testimony prove that Chaffman made false allegations. This also happens at the DoD level, as follows.

August 16, 2005 – Lunging at DoD IG Hotline Director: This involved then Director of the DoD IG Hotline Leonard Trahan. I discovered and documented the remark about me allegedly lunging at Trahan on August 16, 2005. This false "lunging" incident was also part of a June 28, 2006, IG investigation, where Trahan provided no evidence that I lunged at him (Trahan). It took me from 2003 to 2005 to first hear about the lunging incident. Others thought Trahan's comment was "unprofessional," as documented in the August 16, 2005, email by Dan Meyer.

Trahan's sworn testimony was me leaving the interview room before the interview was over. I did leave only after the DoD IG investigators became verbally abusive. Probably because I was in the early stages of exposing the DoD IG for what it really was, based on Trahan, who stated the following on June 28, 2006, regarding the OIG (Office of Inspector General).

"Since 2003 this defense hotline has come under scrutiny more than any other activity within the OIG (Office of Inspector General)*."* Trahan used the acronym "MPRI." The MPRI audit of the DoD IG, apparently requested by Senator Grassley, was also issued in 2002 as follows.

Military Professional Resources Incorporated (MPRI) – DoD IG Corruption

April 21, 2002, MPRI on DoD IG: The DoD IG was so corrupted that a private company known as MPRI was tasked to do a study on the DoD IG. The MPRI report stated in part:

"The tasking to make an assessment of the Department of Defense Inspector General (IG DoD) organization originated at the time that the current IG DoD was being considered for confirmation by the Senate Armed Services Committee. Mr. Joseph E. Schmitz concluded that if his nomination was approved he would ask for an independent assessment by an outside team and that he would provide the results to the Committee."

The following are sample quotes from the MPRI report.

"*The first and overriding issue in OIG DoD is the quality of leadership, particularly at the Senior Executive Service (SES) and senior GS 15 level. No member of the team has seen an organization, civil or military, manned by so many talented people, so ill served by its senior leadership. This level of management displays all of the malignant attributes attributed to entrenched bureaucracy. Much of this assessment and the supporting findings is a direct result of deficient leadership.*"

"*A pervasive system of cronyism drives promotions, work assignments, and performance awards. Potential whistleblowers are deterred with reprisal and the message is ignored.*"

"*As a general observation, senior OIG DoD leaders have displayed by their actions an arrogance of leadership and have placed their personal aspirations and goals above OIG DoD's mission accomplishments. A buddy system or "who you know" permeates the agency in both facts and in perception. OIG DoD personnel view senior managers, with few exceptions, as being entrenched and intractable. It is believed that reprisal or retaliation could result if the party line is not followed.*"

"*The culture of the OIG DoD has been, and continues to be, hostile to internal whistleblowers. All too often, OIG employees who have endeavored to identify mismanagement or violations of law have been punished by their chain of command.*"

"*A final concern about work product voiced by OAIG Auditing employees is that audit report findings and recommendations are sometimes diluted or killed all together for questionable reasons.*"

"*Personnel appeared "beaten down," junior auditors reported that they were not productively employed, and there were numerous complaints about a "good old boy" system of favoritism that was often linked to participation on an OAIG Auditing softball team. Many rank and file employees felt that cronyism impacted jobs and promotions, team assignments, and bonus awards.*"

"*In other cases, employees who are at odds with management are assigned to Program Directors known to have abrasive styles of management in the hope that such a hostile working environment will drive the employees to resign from the OIG DoD. Senior officials even admitted to once having had "Turkey Farms" which grouped disliked employees onto the same teams. In short, the perception that employee assignments by senior management are tainted by favoritism (e.g., based on softball teams and car pools) only serves to undercut confidence in the leadership of the organization. The Assessment Team uncovered enough evidence to conclude that this perception has a strong grounding in reality.*"

"*Management's past practice has been to silence the messenger and ignore the message. Past alleged reprisals included the planting of evidence designed to jeopardize security clearances, poor performance appraisals, forgone promotions, and distasteful assignments.*"

"*Even more disturbing were acts of retaliation by OIG DoD management against individual employees who were perceived to be whistleblowers or otherwise assisting the Assessment Team.*"

"*It came as a shock then, when Assessment Team members heard comments about the OIG DoD Deputy General Counsel's Office such as; "they're worthless," "they fight us rather than help us," "Once it goes up to Headquarters, you're screwed!" These comments come disproportionately from DCIS agents in the field. They expressed extreme frustration at the turn around time on subpoenas and requests for consensual monitoring. While a certain natural tension between police and prosecuting attorneys may be at work in this relationship, the agents' complaints do seem to have merit.*"

The MPRI investigation on the DoD IG sounds like a duplicate of DCMA, most notably in the areas of cronyism, abusive working environments, retaliation, etc. Cronyism, abusive working environments, retaliation, etc., are performed at DCMA as if the managers very lives depend on these amoral activities. Largely because some management careers could come to end if the story is told and Congress or the President objectively moves toward resolution.

OSC & MSPB Discredited April 21, 2002 – Restrictive (Enabling) Interpretations

DoD IG Administrative Model – CRI (Con Game) 2003

OSC & MSPB Discredited: The MPRI report also made another finding about OSC and MSPB.

"*The OIG DoD also should develop an administrative model for resolving whistleblower reprisal complaints on an informal basis. An informal binding arbitration process would avoid the adverse publicity, cost and delay inherent to litigation. This approach also would provide OIG DoD employees with an alternative to the U.S. Merit Systems Protection Board ("MSPB") and the Office of Special Counsel ("OSC"). These forums have become increasingly discredited as a viable source of legal relief for aggrieved whistleblowers. Few whistleblowers now prevail before the MSPB because the governing statute, the Whistleblower Protection Act, has been steadily eroded by restrictive interpretations that make it most difficult to sustain a winning case.*"

The administrative model will be discussed first, as it actually evolved into a con game.

DoD IG Administrative Model – Civilian Reprisal Investigations (CRI) – Con Game: My resume described the DoD IG's "administrative model," called CRI, which started in 2003 and went online in January 2004. Dan Meyer was the CRI Director.

CRI was developed over me. Dan Meyer testified (June 28, 2006).

"*So not only did he* (Pedeleose) *have a reprisal complaint before us but it was pretty much his experience that had lead to the creation of my, my office.*"

CRI would be the "framework" to enable whistleblower retaliations.

The L. Jean Lewis "Framework" for Whistleblowers

February 14, 2003: Charlie Murphy of Senator Grassley's staff indicated Jean Lewis was developing a "*framework*" for working with whistleblowers. That "*framework*" evolved into CRI. CRI was the centerpiece of Falsified Trail 3 (Chapter 3) and was a con game against Senator Charles Grassley. Meyer left a substantial electronic "pile of paper" trail in his wake. OSC, MSPB, and OPM would cover up for Dan Meyer and DCMA. Meaning, CRI may have been a well-planned con from the start.

CRI, OSC, MSPB, and OPM left irrefutable evidence trails that went beyond discredited. The "*restrictive interpretations*" were a "slippery slope" that enabled corruption and further retaliation. The overwhelming evidence suggests the "*restrictive interpretations*" cover-up wrongdoing. This shows that case law is part of a tool used by a weaponized government to water down the law and enable further corruption.

As noted earlier, OSC, MSPB, and OPM were born from the Nixon Watergate era and the 1978 CSRA. Jean Lewis was involved in the Whitewater investigations against the Clintons. My observations and documentation show OSC and MSPB rig whistleblower cases for failure. That is why I applied the "Cerberus" analogy to OSC and MSPB along with OPM. The reality version example will be made clear in Chapter 3, with particular reference to Falsified Trail 3.

DoD IG Does Not Support Whistleblowers

MPRI also noted on April 21, 2002, how the DoD IG does not support whistleblowers.

"The OIG DoD does not appear to devote significant resources towards the protection of civilian DoD whistleblowers outside of the OIG. Although the OIG DoD Hotline takes in whistleblower complaints regarding waste, fraud, or abuse, no policy or procedures exist for following up to ensure that ensuing retaliation is documented, much less prevented or stopped in progress. This approach detaches the message from the messenger, and thereby discourages whistleblowing by leaving the employee at risk after making the protected disclosure. When asked what recourse was available to civilian DoD employees who were punished for reporting waste, fraud and abuse, OIG DoD officials would often shrug and respond that legal remedies could be sought through the MSPB and the OSC. No acknowledgement was made of the aforementioned legal obstacles facing whistleblowers who use those forums to seek legal redress for injuries caused by management retaliation. In short, the OIG DoD is not encouraging the intake of a valuable source of information, whistleblower complaints, which it is authorized to investigate under Section 7 of the IG Act of 1978 (as amended)."

When DoD IG "shrug and respond that legal remedies could be sought through the MSPB and the OSC" the DoD IG is well aware that MSPB and OSC are discredited and basically an administrative "garbage disposal" for whistleblower cases.

As MSPB and OSC were labeled discredited, and CRI was formed, Nixon's ideas reappeared.

Nixon's Malek Manual Re-Surfaces Under Bush Administration

April 22, 2003 (Malek Manual Re-Surfaces): By 2003, the Bush Administration took a page from the Nixon era Malek Manual. One article was titled:

"Uncle Sam Really Does Need You. The United States Government has a serious people problem. But it can be fixed" By Nicholas Thompson, Understanding Government (April 22, 2003). The article states in part:

"But under Donald Rumsfeld the department has been digging in its heels, taking a cue from a Nixon underling named Fred Malek who wrote a 600-page manual for placing political appointees in the civil service."

"The result is that high-level civil servants don't move up, and their former positions don't open."

"The politicians always go after the civilians, but this administration is going much deeper into the bureaucracy," says another Republican senior official, who, like most everyone else in the Department, asked to be quoted without identification for fear of political reprisals."

Nixon's ideas and the Malek Manual were never defeated or forgotten. Malek's ideas and tactics were nothing special; they were merely organized in one place to illustrate how to achieve nefarious goals. Political appointees would more resemble cronies. The ever-present fear of reprisal is always present and active, as identified in "fear of political reprisals."

Less than a year later, the Bush Administration gutted protections for DoD workers as follows.

National Security Personnel System (NSPS) – Gut Civil Service Protections

November 25, 2003: "Defense Guts Civil Service Protections" January/February 2004 By AFGE (American Federation of Government Employees) in The Government Standard.

The front-page article stated, *"With the simple stroke of a pen, Defense Secretary Donald Rumsfeld acquired unprecedented and unimaginable powers to hire, fire, demote and promote 720,000 civilian defense workers at will."* This was guised as the NSPS.

The front page further stated: *"This system was designed to strip civil service protections from public workers-not to improve security...This administration repeatedly raised the red, white and blue to justify their actions when, in hindsight, it has become so clear that the only color they really care about is green."*

2003 Retaliatory Preparation: The 2003 preparation for retaliatory onslaught starts with the Nicholas Thompson (April 22, 2003) article on Fred Malek. Then came the NSPS part on November 25, 2003. Both resemble Nixon's plans and ideas. President Bush just used NSPS as a cover story. From there, the Bush plan went to the (parallel) 3rd part with the OSC branch of the "Cerberus" analogy. That involved Scott Bloch (OSC Director) with support from Linda Springer (then OPM Director).

Linda Springer and Gordon England (then Acting Deputy Secretary of Defense) were part of Falsified Trail 3 and gave testimony on September 20, 2006 at a Senate Committee on Homeland Security supporting NSPS that gutted civil service law. Meaning, the Deep State weaponization expanded.

OSC Director (Scott Bloch) - OPM Director (Linda Springer)

December 12, 2003 (OSC Director Scott Bloch): Scott Bloch was a political appointee for President George W. Bush with a statutory term from December 12, 2003, to December 11, 2008. Bloch came on after the Bush Administration took a page from the Nixon era (Malek manual) and implemented NSPS. With no surprise, Bloch left a wide trail of destruction, which included my case starting with Falsified Trail 3 which was a weaponized-lawfare retaliatory investigation.

Articles and Wikipedia entries on Scott Bloch indicate that on May 6, 2008, Federal Bureau of Investigation (FBI) agents raided Bloch's offices due to allegations of obstruction of justice. On April 27, 2010, Bloch pleaded guilty to a misdemeanor criminal conviction by having computer systems wiped.

The story leading up to those points is as follows, and includes an October 17, 2005, OPM letter to a law firm that made allegations against Scott Bloch. The evidence trail is as follows.

March 22, 2005 – Government Accountability Project (GAP): "*Federal Workers Who Sought Help from U.S. Special Counsel Scott Bloc.*" This article stated:

"*The controversy began when Bloch abruptly announced reassignment of twelve attorneys and investigators from Washington, D.C. headquarters to field offices, including a new field office in Detroit, Michigan. The reorganization targeted employees who were either whistleblowers or suspected of being whistleblowers.*"

"*Recently, GAP has also learned that some 1000 cases and whistleblowing disclosures have been dumped without investigation by the OSC, often without even calling the whistleblower. This is an emergency, because plans to gut due process appeal rights at the Merit Systems Protection Board mean aggrieved federal workers will have nowhere to turn except the Special Counsel.*"

Relevance is that OSC was discredited before 2005, along with MSPB. The actions of Scott Bloch solidified OSC as being discredited and provided insight into the weaponization of government and lawfare.

Predictable OSC Discreditation Factored In: June 2005 to October 2005 was the enactment of Falsified Trail 3 against me. So, as of March 22, 2005, DCMA and DoD IG knew I was vulnerable, and they (DCMA and DoD IG) were safe. Meaning, Falsified Trail 3 was essentially a foregone conclusion because the U.S. Government had already been proven to be weaponized before Falsified Trail 3. Cover-ups were predictable. The "Cerberus" analogy would prove to contain negative information.

June 28, 2005 (OPM Director Linda Springer): Linda Springer was appointed OPM Director on June 28, 2005, with a term to August 13, 2008. OPM played a critical role, as personnel actions were at the center of Bush's plan. Linda Springer (OPM) would form the 3rd part of the "Cerberus" analogy on November 28, 2007, covering up for Scott Bloch and Falsified Trail 3. Chapter 3 explains that in detail.

The following is the evidence trail on Linda Springer (OPM), who is allegedly investigating Scott Bloch.

OPM Allegedly Investigating Scott Bloch October 17, 2005: The date of October 17, 2005, for the OPM investigation of Scott Bloch coincides with the October 17, 2005 issue of Time Magazine, which outlined how Ernie Fitzgerald's position was eviscerated, along with a brief article on Valerie

Plame and Carl Rove. The following day (October 18, 2005), I was given a proposed 30-day suspension in Falsified Trail 3.

Meaning, OPM was part of the problem. On the surface, OPM seemed honest. Behind the scenes, OPM would cover for Scott Bloch. Falsified Trail 3 in Chapter 3 explains this fact. The point being, Linda Springer's investigation of Bloch was a cover that began on October 17, 2005, as follows.

From: OPM, Office of Inspector General, Washington, DC.

To: Debra S. Katz, Esquire, Bernabei and Katz, PLLC, Washington, DC 20009

"*Dear Ms. Katz:*

I am writing to advise you that Inspector General Patrick E. McFarland, U.S. Office of Personnel Management, has been asked by Clay Johnson III, Chair, President's Council on Integrity and efficiency to investigate the allegations contained in your March 3, 2005 letter concerning Mr. Scott Bloch, Special Counsel, U.S. Office of Special Counsel. I am requesting that you provide me with an additional copy of this letter, attachments and all documents related to this matter. Special Agent in Charge (SAIC) Jill Maroney from our Office of Investigations is available to collect these documents."

Signed: Patricia A. Marshall, Special Counsel to Inspector General.

Scott Bloch was OSC at the time Falsified Trail 3 was in work. When I submitted Falsified Trail 3 to OSC, Scott Bloch was under investigation. More disturbing is that Clay Johnson III, President's Council on Integrity and Efficiency (PCIE), farmed out an investigation against Bloch to OPM. Meaning, a problem (OPM) was investigating a parallel problem, OSC, where both OPM and OSC were part of the "Cerberus" cover-up analogy. (OSC, MSPB, and OPM are the same "family").

Apparently, PCIE lacked jurisdiction because the allegations did not concern an Inspector General or the staff of an Inspector General.

PCIE was useless: On November 1, 2006, I received an NSA response to my PCIE complaint about DoD IG that was incoherent, useless, and vitriolic. Falsified Trail 3 has more details.

October 20, 2005 – News From OPM: OPM issued a public news release regarding the investigation of Scott Bloch, concluding:

"*Inspector General McFarland has agreed to promptly conduct a thorough investigation and report his findings along with recommended remedial actions, if appropriate, to OPM Director Linda M. Springer and Deputy U.S. Special Counsel Jim Renne.*"

OPM issued a public statement, making it appear as though an investigation of Scott Bloch was underway, and name-dropping Linda M. Springer in the article for legitimacy and status. From there, Scott Bloch openly engaged in intimidation.

February 16, 2007 – Washington Post: "*Special Counsel Accused of Intimidation in Probe.*" By Elizabeth Williamson. This article stated in part:

"*The 16-month investigation has been beset by delays, accusations and counter-accusations. The latest problem began two weeks ago, when Bloch's deputy sent staffers a memo asking them to inform*

OSC higher-ups when investigators contact them. Further, the memo read, employees should meet with investigators in the office, in a special conference room. Some employees cried foul, saying the recommendations made them afraid to be interviewed in the probe.

This week Public Employees for Environmental Responsibility, the Project on Government Oversight, the Government Accountability Project and Human Rights Campaign and a lawyer for the OSC employees protested in a letter to legislators and to Clay Johnson III, the Office of Personnel Management and Budget deputy who ordered the OSC probe.

The OSC's memo, the group said, "was only the latest in a series of actions by Bloch to obstruct" the investigation. "Other actions have included suggestions that all witnesses interviewed... provide Bloch with affidavits what they had been asked and how they responded."

The article stated that Bloch would not comment on an ongoing investigation, but Bloch has cooperated with the investigation. The article stated that new procedures will be implemented to conduct employee interviews.

Scott Bloch's blatant antics confirmed OSC as a branch of the "Cerberus" analogy, which contains information negative to the government. It takes a lot to close the loop and convince disinterested observers of the alleged con games and cover-ups presented herein. Linda Springer would close that loop on November 28, 2007, and bring OPM directly in as the 3rd part of the "Cerberus" analogy.

Linda Springer Confirmed OPM "Cerberus" Analogy – Closed the Loop

Cover-up of Textbook Retaliation Case (Weaponization): Since 2002, OSC and MSPB have been labeled as discredited. OPM was not yet in the "Cerberus" analogy. Linda Springer put up a good front in investigating OSC Scott Bloch. Linda Springer appeared as a hero for the public good. However, on October 24, 2007, Linda Springer was handed a textbook whistleblower retaliation case that had been covered up by OSC and later won at MSPB in Washington. Meaning, Linda Springer needed to cover-up textbook retaliation against me, confirmed on October 24, 2007.

On November 28, 2007, Linda Springer confirmed OPM in the "Cerberus" analogy, stating in part.

"This is notice that the Office of Personnel Management (OPM) is exercising its statutory right under5U.S.C. §7703(d)to request reconsideration of the Board's decision in the case cited below. 1am of the opinion that the Board erred in interpreting a civil service law, rule, or regulation affecting personnel management and that the Board's decision will have a substantial impact on civil service law, rule, regulation, or policy directive."

"Kenneth M Pedeleose v. Department of Defense"

"Docket No. AT-0752-06-0350-I-1, October 24, 2007"

My MSPB case (Falsified Trail 3) was irrefutable, with MSPB confirming 19 reasons to rule in my favor. Falsified Trail 3 in Chapter 3 explains further. The death nell was a May 10, 2006, no rebuttal letter by DCMA that literally admitted to whistleblower retaliation. The case had irrefutable evidence of whistleblower retaliation. Linda Springer couldn't state what was wrong with the MSPB decision and generally stated:

"*that the Board erred in interpreting a civil service law, rule, or regulation affecting personnel management and that the Board's decision will have a substantial impact on civil service law, rule, regulation, or policy directive.*"

Springer's plan was seemingly to "throw everything at the wall and see what sticks" or "run it up the flagpole and see who salutes." Knowing that MSPB was a fellow "Cerberus" cover-up analogy to OPM, along with OSC, Springer stood a good chance of success. The following sample quotes from the MSPB on October 24, 2007, demonstrate the corruption within DCMA and the impact of my case.

"*Both parties submitted the entire transcript of the appellant's deposition into the record. For that reason, the Board has credited the deposition testimony as it would a stipulation by the parties. We find it noteworthy that both parties submitted many of the same documents into the record.*"

Both parties using the <u>same documents</u> means DCMA stipulated (admitted) to retaliation by placing my sworn deposition, taken by 2 DCMA attorneys in person, and other documents onto the MSPB record <u>without</u> rebuttal. DCMA defeated DCMA's case. Linda Springer had that to contend with.

<u>No-Rebuttal Letter May 10, 2006</u>: MSPB was boxed in because DCMA issued a formal no-rebuttal letter on May 10, 2006, stipulating to my sworn deposition taken by DCMA and my Response to Charges. Linda Springer helped overturn a case where DCMA admitted to retaliation and where the commander, Colonel Nicole Plourde, was labeled as disingenuous as follows.

"*...there is no evidence that Plourde or Scantlebury informed the appellant of the steps that the agency had taken to coordinate the two investigations. This failure contrasts with the fact that Scantlebury, with Plourde's knowledge, informed the appellant of the actions that the agency had taken to consult with the U.S. Attorney. Further, this failure appears disingenuous against the backdrop of the appellant's repeated statements of concern to Plourde and Scantlebury about the potential conflict with the IG's investigation. By not conveying the IG's views to the appellant, Plourde and Scantlebury essentially cut off the means by which the appellant could have complied with their investigation and orders without fearing interference with the IG's investigation.*

Under the circumstances of this case, we find that the agency failed to prove its charges."

Linda Springer covered up, documented, and admitted to disingenuous management behavior by using OPM legal resources to overturn a well-supported, irrefutable MSPB decision. From there, MSPB identified Colonel Plourde's "shifting reasons" as follows.

"Plourde's motive to retaliate is also inferred from the shifting reasons that she gave to conduct the investigation. On one hand she said that there was no basis for the rumors and the investigation was because the rumors were having a negative effect on employee morale. Yet, as we quoted above, in her affidavit, Plourde stated "I was concerned that one of my supervisors was inappropriately discussing confidential management information with subordinates and that this conduct was feeding rumors that certain employees were targeted to be fired.""

"Plourde was also well aware of the appellant's contribution to Congressional investigations into the C-130J program, investigations which resulted in a report calling for the termination of the C-130J, the program that she was charged with administering. The appellant's participation in those investigations was widely known at DCMA. The IG had cautioned Owens in an e-mail that Senators Grassley and McCain were interested in the issues the appellant was perceived as advancing."

<u>Watershed Moment for Weaponized Government</u>: OPM was part of the 1978 CSRA along with OSC and MSPB. Meaning, the trifecta of OSC, MSPB, and OPM forms the "Cerberus" (three-headed) team that covers up and enables wrongdoing by government managers. The strength of my case, and overwhelming evidence, allows no other explanation. OPM created a watershed moment to enable and expand weaponized government and lawfare to a new level.

In all, Falsified Trail 3 was a textbook irrefutable case of weaponized government and lawfare in one concise package. Linda Springer, OPM attorneys, and MSPB covered-up irrefutable facts that would later enable and further weaponized government and lawfare. Chapter 3 shows this in detail and from there the traceability to national debt from weaponized government and lawfare is made.

For Falsified Trail 3, the DOJ and Federal Court of Appeals completed the cover-up.

<u>DOJ & Federal Court of Appeals Completes Cover-up</u>: MSPB issued a capricious decision on Falsified Trail 3 on February 12, 2009, simply reversing the October 24, 2007 MSPB decision. DOJ and the Federal Court of Appeals rubberstamped MSPB's February 12, 2009, capricious decision (Falsified Trail 3), completing the cover-up. Congress was aware that DOJ and Federal Court of Appeals were also problematic as follows.

DOJ & Federal Court of Appeals – I Met the Irrefragable Proof Standard

On September 9, 2006, I wrote to Congress about the events of the 2005 weaponized investigation (Falsified Trail 3). On November 1, 2006, Congressman Todd Platts responded and stated that he has "*heard many stories*" such as mine and is pushing for further whistleblower protections.

Congressman Platts stated: "*As you are aware, I introduced House of Representative Bill 1317 (H.R. 1317), the Federal Employee Protection of Disclosures Act, to strengthen inadequate protections currently afforded federal whistleblowers.*"

"*... it is important to review the legislative history in the area of whistleblower protections for federal employees. As a result of findings the civil service protections of the time were inadequate, Congress and the first Bush Administration enacted into law the Whistleblower Protection Act (WP A) of 1989, which expressly stated that "any" protected disclosure of waste, fraud, and abuse by a federal employee is covered by the law. Unfortunately, as interpreted by the Merit Systems Protection Board*

(MSPB) and the Federal Circuit Court (which has monopoly jurisdiction over whistleblower appeals), loopholes began to develop in the WPA. Accordingly, Congress strengthened the law in 1994. It is noteworthy that the report accompanying the WPA amendments of 1994 expressed great frustration with the way the WPA was being interpreted."

"*Unfortunately, we are once again largely back to where we started. Since the 1994 amendments, 101 whistleblower cases have come before the Federal Circuit Court. However, only one whistleblower has prevailed. Among the reasons are a number of decisions which have continued to create exceptions to the law, including decisions stating than an employee is not protected by the WPA if: the employee directs criticism to other witnesses or a supervisor in an attempt to start the process of challenging misconduct, or, the information disclosed was done in the course of the employee's ordinary job duties; or, the information "disclosed" has already been raised by someone else.*

In addition, the Federal Circuit has stated that—for a federal employee to "reasonably believe" there is evidence of waste, fraud, and abuse, as required by law—he or she must overcome with "irrefragable proof" the presumption that the agency was acting in good faith. This is an unheard of legal standard, defined in the dictionary as "impossible to refute." In other words, the Agency pretty much has to admit to waste, fraud, or abuse"

My case met the "*irrefragable proof*" standard. My resume shows that, at the time I was retaliated against, I had multiple substantiated disclosures. The October 24, 2007 MSPB decision acknowledged "*The IG had cautioned Owens in an e-mail that Senators Grassley and McCain were interested in the issues the appellant was perceived as advancing.*" DCMA was directly informed that I was a whistleblower and knew the same regardless.

Falsified Trail 3, in Chapter 3 shows the irrefragable evidence in detail. In total, Chapter 3 shows how weaponized government and lawfare is conducted to cover-up whistleblower cases and contain negative information on institutional corruption from leaving government and informing the public. Hence, the reason for this book and the half century of evidence used to inform the public. The "Federal Graveyard of Whistleblower Cases" adds further evidence.

Federal Graveyard of Whistleblower Cases

April 1, 2008 Project on Government Oversight: "*The Federal Graveyard of Whistleblower Cases.*" From POGO's Blog. The article stated in part.

"*Out of the 186 whistle-blower cases that came before it [the Federal Court] from October 1994 to Feb. 14, 2008, this employee* (Teresa Chambers, United States Park Police) *victory was only the third time that the court has ruled for the whistle-blower.*"

Specifically, there were 3 Federal Court wins according to the April 1, 2008, article. Two of the wins were Teresa Chambers and Carol Czarkowski. Could not find the third win.

The point is, the odds of sustaining a winning case are remote. If a case is determined in favor of the whistleblower, the next step is to see how far the case traces to senior management. Cases that do not involve high-level management may be candidates for straightforward decisions. In my case, the retaliation reached the highest level of the DoD. Meaning, Pentagon level was not an easy decision and will more than likely be covered up.

Ernie Fitzgerald spent 35 years battling the Pentagon, and to my understanding, had to maintain an attorney for the majority of the 35 years.

Ernie Fitzgerald - Thirty-Five (35) Years Battling Pentagon

(Mercenary vs Political Relevance & Rigging Cases)

Ernie Fitzgerald informed me he (Fitzgerald) spent 35 years (1970 - 2005) confronting fraud and corruption within the DoD and battled the Pentagon/DoD all the time. Fitzgerald protected U.S.G. and taxpayer interests and was the continual target of Pentagon/DoD wrath.

I protected taxpayer and U.S.G. interests and experienced the same wrath as Fitzgerald from the "Federal Machinery," a product of the Nixon era. The 35-year timespan Fitzgerald spent battling the Pentagon was more than likely a mercenary vs political retaliation.

Mercenary, not Political: Ernie Fitzgerald's 35-year span battling the Pentagon/DoD crossed many political administrations, meaning the 35 years of strife were not politically based. From memory, Fitzgerald worked with all members of Congress regardless of political affiliation.

This supports the fact that retaliation is mercenary-based versus party-based. Meaning an effort to contain any negative information from leaving government which further enables institutional corruption.

Rigging Cases: Whichever political party is in office takes control of the "Federal Machinery" (Mercenaries) and has the advantage of the "Cerberus" analogy of OSC, MSPB, and OPM, who rig the cases well prior to any DOJ or Federal Judicial involvement. By the time the cases reach the DOJ and Federal Court level, the "interpretations," if not outright cover-ups, at the earlier stages have already taken hold. Meaning, cases are rigged for failure.

The next section progresses beyond the judicial corruption and lawfare involving OSC, MSPB, OPM, and outlines the problems at DCAA. Meaning, weaponized government, lawfare, and the "Cerberus" cover-ups enable further corruption to the institutional level with altered working conditions.

DCAA (Defense Contract Audit Agency) Problems

Altered Work Conditions - Oversight Deterioration

November 12, 2003 – DCAA Altered Working Papers: I could only find 2 of 4 pages of the DoD IG letter attachment to Senator Grassley, signed by Joseph Schmitz, stating in part.

"Inspector General, Department of Defense

Review of Alteration of Working Paper at Defense Contract

Audit Agency (DCAA) New York Branch Office"

"Allegation: DCAA auditors, including high level management, spent thousands of hours fabricating audit working papers for audits that had been completed in order to pass a peer review that wasted Government resources and was in violation of the Government Auditing Standards and the principles of JER 12-50la. The allegation is partially substantiated.

Conclusion: DCAA auditors and technical specialists spent 1,139 hours re-doing working papers and updating files in advance of a DCAA internal quality assurance review. However, this did not include any time spent by the administrative staff, audit supervisors, branch manager, or RAM (Regional Audit Manager) because the DCAA policy for time charging only provides for the auditors to charge audit assignment numbers direct."

"Allegation: High-level DCAA management knew about the matter and did not take appropriate action, in violation of the principles of Executive Order, "Principles of Ethical Conduct for Government Officers and Employees," Part I and Section 3 of Chapter 12 of the JER, "Code of Ethics for Government Service." This allegation is partially substantiated.

Conclusion: This is partially correct. One high-level manager (Regional Audit Manager - GS 15) directed that the working papers be altered."

Even though only 2 of 4 pages on the attachment were found, the cover page of the November 12, 2003 letter to Senator Grassley confirmed disciplinary action was taken, stated in part as follows.

"As of the date of your facsimile, DCAA had already identified the altered working papers, conducted an internal review of the office, and proposed disciplinary and administrative actions to address the matter. Although we determined that the DCAA review substantially addressed all the known issues and proposed appropriate disciplinary action, our review uncovered additional information. On October 6, 2003, we provided the results of our review to the Regional Director, Northeastern Region, DCAA, and recommended that the Regional Director consider conducting an additional review in light of this new information. As a result, the Regional Director re-opened the prior review and estimates completing all necessary actions by December 1, 2003."

DCAA is a problematic entity, as is DCMA. On February 24, 2004, Senator Grassley stated in a letter to Joseph Schmitz regarding DCMA and DCAA: *"Those two entities have a long-standing reputation for turning a blind eye to contractor rip offs."*

The negative story on DCAA continues as follows to July 22, 2008.

DCAA Intimidation & Abusive Work Environment

July 22, 2008 GAO-08-857: The U.S. Government Accountability Office (GAO) issued a report titled: "*Allegations That Certain Audits at Three Locations Did Not Met Professional Standards Were Substantiated.*" The report stated in part.

"*GAO substantiated the allegations. Although DCAA policy states that its audits are performed according to GAGAS* (Generally Accepted Government Auditing Standards)*, GAO found numerous examples where DCAA failed to comply with GAGAS. For example, contractor officials and the DOD contracting community improperly influenced the audit scope, conclusions, and opinions of three audits—a serious independence issue. At two DCAA locations, GAO found evidence that (1) working papers did not support reported opinions, (2) DCAA supervisors dropped findings and changed audit opinions without adequate evidence for their changes, and (3) sufficient audit work was not performed to support audit opinions and conclusions. GAO also substantiated allegations of inadequate supervision of certain audits at a third DCAA location.*"

Hence, DCAA issues continued from November 12, 2003, to July 22, 2008. The GAO report had multiple mentions of the word "abusive." Samples as follows:

"*Moreover, during GAO's investigation, DCAA managers took actions against staff at two locations, attempting to intimidate auditors, prevent them from speaking with investigators, and creating a generally abusive work environment.*"

"*During our investigation, we noted a pattern of frequent management actions that served to intimidate the auditors and create an abusive environment at locations 1 and 2. As a result, some auditors were hesitant to speak to us. We performed our investigation from June 2006 through July 2008 in compliance with the standards for investigations prescribed by the President's Council for Integrity and Efficiency.*"

"*Our review of the documentation and interviews with numerous current and former auditors, supervisors, and managers concluded that they set an authoritative and abusive tone in which several auditors told us they preferred to speak with us on a confidential basis without their management or supervisors present. A few auditors were hesitant to speak with us even on a confidential basis.*"

"*We learned of reassignments of auditors and were told of verbal admonishments and threats of disciplinary action against auditors who raised questions about management guidance or who spoke with or contacted GAO, contracting officers, or investigators within DOD without prior management approval. As a result, at least two DCAA auditors have filed complaints as whistleblowers with the Office of Special Counsel.*"

DCAA's abusive work environments flow from weaponized government and a lack of corrective action. DCMA is similar to DCAA, although DCMA issues threats in writing and takes illicit action, as Chapter 3 shows. DCAA issues were further noted in a follow-on DoD IG study as follows.

DoD IG Follow-Up Review (D-2009-6-009)

August 31, 2009: The DoD IG issued a follow-up review to the GAO audit number GAO-08-857. The DoD IG audit report was titled:

"*Defense Contract Audit Agency Audit Work Deficiencies and Abusive Work Environment Identified by the Government Accountability Office*"

The DoD IG report had the following findings, stated in part.

"*Employee concerns with (1) time pressures, (2) uncompensated overtime, (3) changes to audit results and opinions, and (4) unprofessional behavior created a work environment not conducive to performing quality audits. Additionally, we found a flawed audit may have allowed a contractor to recover $271 million in unallowable costs (Case 2). DCAA provided ineffective audit advice and services to a contracting officer (Case 3). DCAA has insufficient evidence to support a contractor's participation in the direct bill program (Case 4). Seventeen of 18 forward pricing audits did not comply with standards (Case 8). DCAA did not adequately qualify the audit results on a compensation system (Case 9). DCAA had insufficient evidence to support a purchasing system audit opinion (Case 10). DCAA did not have sufficient basis for dropping four findings (Case 11). DCAA did not report a contractor's uncompensated overtime practice and increased the risk of cost mischarging (Case 12).*"

"*DCAA concurred with 22 of 24 recommendations, concurred in principle on 1 recommendation, and reserved comment on 1 recommendation.*" Appeared that DCAA agreed that DCAA has problems.

The DoD IG "*could not find consistent criterion or definitions for what conditions reflect a "generally abusive" work environment. Nonetheless, some employees may have considered the work environment conditions to be abusive.*" This demonstrates negligence by the DoD IG, as an abusive work environment contributed to the issues the DoD IG was investigating at DCAA. Meaning altered working conditions.

Problems at DCAA traced to December 2019 and are included in the capstone case Chapter 5, further showing that DCAA abusive work environments trace to the national debt and altering reports.

Altered Working Conditions: This book focuses on abusive or hostile work environments that alter working conditions. DCAA changed working conditions, causing problems that were later discussed by DCAA employees. The GAO documented instances where DCAA auditors were hesitant to speak with the GAO. DCMA, however, alters working conditions and threatens, typically in writing, through electronic or written trails.

At the beginning of Chapter 2, there was a quote stating:

"*Do you know what happened to Ernie Fitzgerald, who went to Washington with some Lockheed problems?" When I said I didn't, Frech said, "He's now chief shit-house inspector for the Civil Service Commission and will never be able to get a good job as long as he lives.*"" "[Erwin Kroll, "The Education of Henry Durham," reprinted from The Progressive, 1972]."

Hence, nothing changed from 1972 to 2009. DCMA runs in parallel to DoD's abusive and hostile work environments via cultivating depression, stress, anxiety, and fear as follows.

Cultivating Depression, Stress, Anxiety, & Fear

This section provides some examples of the psychological effects of altered, abusive, weaponized, and hostile working conditions in DoD and DCMA. My arrival at DCMA is outlined first.

1994 Hostile Workplace on Arrival

In/about mid-March 1994, I arrived at DCMA in Marietta, GA. The office seemed a hostile workplace with multiple discord. There was pending litigation, and one EEO case seemed to be an office legend. The employees were expanding the union to confront management. I didn't know enough to draw conclusions, so I stayed out of the fray. I kept detailed notes that are now contemporaneous. The notes, document trail, and evidence would confirm that the employees were correct.

DCMA is the Intersection of Politics & Money – The "Swamp"

DCMA is a contracting organization at the intersection of politics, money, and finances, which is the core of the military-industrial complex and the "Swamp." I saw the organization from the ground level, as an employee, and from the military-industrial complex perspective. I had access to financial data, quality assurance data, manufacturing/production data, test data, contracting data, cost proposals, direct & overhead rates, and the like. I was uniquely positioned to witness and report on facts versus pressure for cover-ups.

I was a gatherer of data and facts. A report writer and a "watch dog" for taxpayer interests. I was part of the early version DOGE embedded at a contractor facility, Lockheed Martin, in Marietta, GA.

The following sample statements run in parallel with issues in this book. Meaning this section (Chapter 2) is for peripheral support of allegations to follow. The first is the 1994 meeting notes.

"Road to Hell"

<u>August 19, 1994</u>: There was a one-page staff meeting notes that concluded in part as follows.

"*Reorganization: Nobody down here knows nothing. Don't think about it. We'll know when it's time to know. It's just a matter of time. The road to hell is paved with good intentions. You get more flies with honey than vinegar. That's all!*"

This was a small omen to things that followed. The following are peripheral, sample hostile workplace comments over the years that I documented. Meaning, the peripheral office climate (odds and ends) that help reinforce the growth and effects of weaponized government and lawfare.

Abrupt Resignation

<u>Prior to June 26, 1997</u>: I am aware of an employee who abruptly resigned from the office prior to June 26, 1997. The employee had a very specialized set of skills, and, to my understanding, was prior military. The employee just up and walked out of the office.

The documentation of June 26, 1997 stated the employee suffered "*mentally/physically*" with a "*loss of sleep, diabetes, problems with his wife (from taking this home) etc.*"

While going to the commander to issue the resignation letter, the employee stopped by my desk and spoke with me. The employee was so disgusted with his supervisor that he just walked out.

Crappy Weapon Systems

April 7, 1998: The following is an email discussion that involved the aforesaid abrupt resignation. The comments in part are as follows.

"*It's really pathetic that DCMC* (prior name of DCMA) *can't do a better job of keeping quality folks around. I do think the problem is DoD-wide.*"

"*I do believe a lot of what is going on there will ultimately result in DoD getting basically crappy weapons systems.*"

About 6 years and 3 months later, Substantiated Allegation 4 (July 23, 2004 (DoD IG Report on C-130J, D-2004-102) stated in part: *"We substantiated the allegation that the C-130J aircraft does not meet contract specifications and therefore cannot perform its operational mission. The Air Force conditionally accepted 50 C-130J aircraft at a cost of $2.6 billion even though none of the aircraft met commercial contract specifications or operational requirements."*

Lack of Trust

August 23, 1999 – July 11, 2019: The lack of trust was continuous in my 26 ½ years at DCMA. On August 23, 1999, a PowerPoint presentation stated in part.

"*Lack of Trust among Employees*" and "*Cliques and Favoritism*"

The same issues emerged on July 11, 2019, about 20 years later, stating in part.

"*Increase trust and respect between employees and supervisors"*

"Improve employee and supervisor morale"

"Improve relationships between employees and supervisors"

"Employees and supervisors mutually understand expectations clearly"

"Increase team productivity"

"Improve employee morale"

Meaning, nothing changed in nearly 20 years, from 1999 to 2019, even among different people with different management. This helps prove the institutional corruption aspect.

Scathing Employee Surveys

January 20, 2000: DCMA was under DLA (Defense Logistics Agency) at this time and before. The employee survey forms were scathing. Sample comments are as follows.

"The "good-old-boy" syndrome prevails. If you dare disagree you are out. So no one will risk telling the emperor his backside is showing."

"DLA's plan to increasingly rely on contractor self-oversight to control quality will eventually prove to be a colossal failure."

"Too much reward for good old boy and kissing up to management."

"Morale is low to zero due to many factors"

"There have been internal promotions that have sent out the message; it's okay to lie and cheat within DCMC...More than several years ago, two personas performed copulation in the office and were caught but no disciplinary action was taken."

"There is a general feeling of mistrust and disclaim for senior leadership in this organization."

The comments were not isolated, as the following shows in the next year.

The State of DCMA Engineering

February 15, 2001: The following is from a DCMA engineer who left after 19 ½ years. The exact date is unknown; however, February 15, 2001, appeared in the document. Comments in part are.

"*As I leave my position here after 19 ½ years, I would like to discuss the current state of the Engineering profession in DCMA.*"

"*But many, including myself, have failed miserably to find a value-added yardstick for DCMA.*"

"*DCMA doesn't want us to query our own customers about what specifically they like or would want improved!*"

"*What I see as I leave this Command, and I know it exists elsewhere, is a very low level of morale.*"

"*But sadder is the fact that over 15 better-qualified applicants did not even apply. They had no desire to fight the battles necessary to keep engineering staffing levels, fight unproductive metrics, have responsibility without authority, or rally engineers into a high morale group.*"

"*I am, therefore, writing this out of concern for other DCMA engineers and as a way to see if other engineers are behind these sentiments. If it turns out that I am alone in wanting to bring this out in the open, then very likely, nothing will come of this letter.*"

Closing Envelope for Corrective Action: In my case, I hope something comes from this book as the envelop for corrective action on the national debt that traces to weaponized government and lawfare is closing. Meaning, the time to ruination from national debt must be addressed sooner rather than later since past personnel actions have left the government at a loss for a workforce that understands how efficient government should work.

Too Many Personnel Actions – Promotion Panels Compromised

March 26, 2001: A selection panel for the "F-22 Administrative Contracting Officer (ACO)" noted that *"one of the other members on the selection board wanted to solicit information from an outside individual."* This action prompted the individual to call the DCMA attorney Leigh Owens, who stated there are *"several grievances/personnel actions at this facility. The intent being, we have too many adverse personnel actions already."* Meaning, internal resolution is unlikely since personnel actions were weaponized to the point of pervasive cronyism and acquiescence. Further meaning the existing workforce has lost sight of the efficiency and ethics mission.

On November 29, 2010, and August 18, 2003, there were rumors management officials ignored selection panels anyway further compounding issues. These will be discussed in this Chapter. Nevertheless, my chances for promotion were small as follows.

Chances for Promotions Are Small

March 27, 2001: By 2001, I was labeled a whistleblower. I documented where my 2nd-level supervisor told me that my (Pedeleose) "*chances for promotion are small.*" I documented where other employees had their position descriptions written such that they graded out at a higher grade. On March 7, 2001, Joe Cass, Human Resources Director for DCMA District East, responded to non-competitive promotions, stating in part: "*both individuals had previously held positions at the level to which they were recently repromoted. This allows management to make non-competitive promotions if they so desire.*"

Meaning, performance does not matter; it only matters if the employee "held" the position.

Administrative Judges (AJs) Compromised

June 7, 2001: The following are examples of EEO judges' adverse mentality.

"*The perceived and/or actual relationship between some AJs and the management of some agencies is too close and cozy in many instances, which give the complainant(s) some very serious concerns.*"

"*A number of complainants and employment lawyers have violently complained that the AJs frequently restrict the scope, and framing of some individual complaints, thereby limiting the chances of winning.*"

"*One of the more frequent complaints/allegations involves the wide scope of defense allowed the agencies, while simultaneously limiting the scope of the discovery, refusing complainant witnesses, and refusing to allow the usage of relevant documentation in the investigative process, by the complainant.*"

"*A number of complainants alleged that they and their representative were subjected to inhumane and disrespectful treatment by AJs.*"

EEOC is almost as bad as OSC, MSPB, and OPM. However, EEOC is more discreet in appearance.

"Unprecedented" Dissatisfaction

April 18, 2002: Joe Cass, Human Resources Director for DCMA District East, contacted my commander, Colonel James Wright, and Deputy Commander Ben Chaffman about surveys taken in my office. Joe Cass seemed surprised, stating in part.

"*I am very concerned by the Customer Survey Reports that you recently provided to me from a number of your employees at DCMA L/M Marietta. While it is normal to see some level of dissatisfaction in these Survey Forms, since interests and concerns vary among employees, the general level of dissatisfaction in this case is unprecedented. Much of the dissatisfaction seems to come from the perceived failure of my staff to answer questions or addresss matters of concern that have been raised. I personally view this as extremely serious and of much greater concern than situations where customers are unhappy with responses provided to them.*"

Joe Cass (March 7, 2001) agreed with non-competitive promotions simply because employees had held the position in the past, and then was surprised when employees gave unprecedentedly dissatisfied reviews on customer surveys.

Furthermore, DCMA Human Resources would train supervisors and managers to fire employees. Volley 1 (Falsified Trails 1 & 2) in Chapter 3 of this book identifies this fact with actual evidence from the electronic trail tactics to build cases. Meaning, the rumors were supported by actual documented practices.

In other words, Joe Cass (DCMA HQ, in particular) and local DCMA management were the cause of the "*unprecedented*" dissatisfaction. About 6 months later, more negative data emerged.

"Law of Unintended Consequences"

October 19, 2002: Keith Ernst (DCMA Director East) proved the reason for "*unprecedented*" dissatisfaction by the typical DCMA deniability argument regarding an EEO case that was lost.

Keith Ernst stated in part as follows.

"*Law of Unintended Consequences: We received an EEO decision this week from OFO* (Office of Federal Operations) *that was not in the agencies favor. While there may not have been any discrimination, a series of events occurred that could be (and were) interpreted as discrimination. I would ask that any personnel decision (even the cancellation of a JOA* (Job Offer Announcement)*) be evaluated very carefully to impacts to individuals who may have a pending EEO complaint or where action was just completed and reprisal may be a concern.*"

Keith Ernst was a centerpiece of DCMA weaponized retaliation. Ernst would cheer Falsified Trail 1 in writing on May 29, 2003, and Ernst would play a key role in Falsified Trail 3, which was, in part, a con game against Senator Grassley and a wholesale whistleblower retaliation in 2005.

Racial discrimination resurfaced in 2003, indicating that Keith Ernst, as the director, failed to take corrective action.

Racial Discrimination

July 8, 2003: This case involved an employee who was denied a $500 award. The case began on September 5, 2000, and was decided on June 12, 2003. The employee prevailed on a claim of race discrimination. The posting order stated in part.

"*The facility was found to have discriminated against an employee based on her race when she was not awarded a performance award.*"

The point is, Keith Ernst (DCMA Director) still did nothing to resolve issues. Less than a year after the last event (October 19, 2002), DCMA had a confirmed case of discrimination. In parallel to this is Falsified Trails 1 & 3 that will be outlined in Chapter 3, where Keith Ernst was involved. The following continues the trend.

Climate Review – Labor Management Strife

April 16, 2004: A Climate Review at my facility confirmed serious issues and problems. Keith Ernst was still Director. The issues and problems were so serious and embarrassing that only a summary of findings was distributed to the local workforce. The findings stated in part include.

Losing Sight of DCMA Mission: *"The strife which characterizes labor management relations at DCMA-LMM permeates many, if not most, of the interactions at that facility. In this climate, many employees asserted that the organization has lost sight of its mission..."*

That mission was to protect government interests. The new mission manipulates the system, covers up problems, weaponizes resources, uses lawfare, and eliminates/discredits witnesses.

Lost Credibility, Distrust, & Suspicion: *"Opportunities for positive communication are lost, late, piecemeal, or begrudging and as such, met with distrust and suspicion."*

"For agency credibility, the employees need to believe that the organization is telling the truth. Employees have many resources available to them and can quickly identify when the explanations they have received "just don't add up." The consistent feedback suggests that employees do not believe that agency management "walks the talk."

Conflict Management: "*Issues that remain unresolved fester and lead to poor morale and performance, turnover, and eventually litigation. All are present at DCMA-LMM.*"

The point is that nothing was resolved at DCMA, even though Keith Ernst was the DCMA Director during multiple occurrences over several years. Meaning, the problems start at the top in senior management, not at the employee level. Things were so bad at DCMA that a series of news media articles were published.

News Media Series

In the same month (April 2004) the climate review was released, a series of news media articles from Federal Times was issued. Keith Ernst was still the DCMA Director over my office. The following article series focused on the overall corrupt state of DoD and how prices were soaring.

April 5, 2004 - Federal Times: "*The Dark Side of Acquisition Reform*" "*Diminished oversight leads to overpricing*" By David Phinney.

April 5, 2004 - Federal Times: "*Aircraft's costs soar despite reforms*" By David Phinney.

April 5, 2004 – Federal Times: "*Acquisition Reform*" "*The importance of auditors*" Editorial.

April 5, 2004 – Federal Times: "*For the Record*" Senator Grassley quote from the February 24, 2004, scathing letter to Joseph Schmitz (Substantiated Allegation 3), stating in part.

"*Those two entities have a long-standing reputation for turning a blind eye to contractor rip offs. They are not known for being vicious junk yard dogs when it comes to protecting taxpayers' money.*"

April 5, 2004 – Defense News: "*The Dark Side of Acquisition Reform*" "*Less Oversight Leads to Rising Costs*" By David Phinney. Duplicate story as in Federal Times, although less prominent on the front page.

April 12, 2004 – Federal Times: "*Undermining the auditors*" "'*Collaborative arrangement' lets DoD contractors slide*" by David Phinney.

April 12, 2004 – Federal Times: "*A case of reprisal?*" By David Phinney.

April 12, 2004 – Defense News: "*U.S. C-130's Costs Soar Despite Reforms*" By David Phinney. A follow-on story from Federal Times, April 5, 2004, regarding the C-130J.

April 19, 2004 – Federal Times: "*Defense's revolving door*" "*When managers join contractors, good oversight takes a hit, auditors say*" By David Phinney.

April 19, 2004 – Federal Times: "*For the Record*" Fellow colleague quote related to article on Page 1 regarding "*Defense's revolving door*" stating:

"*I was supposed to turn in fraud situations and then the commanding officer, who has authority over these things, jumps to the other side. If they are worried about their job future, then they have one big conflict.*"

April 19, 2004 – Federal Times: "Commentary Perspective and Analysis, Editorial, "*DoD's Revolving Door*" "*Oversight, not ethics rules, needs repair*".

The point being, problems were so bad that a series of articles was needed to explain the problems. Similar to this book where multiple chapters were needed to explain the origins and effects of weaponized government, lawfare and "Cerberus" style cover-ups that are linked to the national debt. The evidence has risen to the point of encyclopedia length, irrefutable, proof.

Following the Climate Review and Federal Times series of articles was Substantiated Allegation 4.

Substantiated Allegation 4

July 23, 2004: Substantiated Allegation 4 (C-130J) was the precursor to Falsified Trail 3 in Chapter 3 in 2005. This involved the C-130J, and I was the whistleblower who wrote the report that confirmed the C-130J's problems. Keith Ernst was still the DCMA Director East over my office. Meaning, Ernst did nothing to resolve the C-130J debacle, although Ernst would take a direct leadership role to bring about my demise in Falsified Trail 3.

Falsified Trail 3

June - October 2005: DCMA and DoD IG weaponized an investigation against me and a con game against Senator Grassley. Chapter 3 explains further. The point is, Ernst had a participatory role in Falsified Trail 3. Ernst was well aware of the problems that DCMA had. Ernst would focus efforts on me with a weaponized investigation that Keith Ernst would sign. This implies that, at the very least, since 2002, Keith Ernst was aware of the problems and did nothing to resolve them, instead engaging in retaliation for the issues. Especially in Falsified Trail 1 (Chapter 3), where Keith Ernst cheered on retaliation. This may explain why DCMA was one of the worst places to work.

DCMA Worst Place to Work 2005

A 2005 study by the Institute for the Study of Public Policy Implementation, School of Public Affairs, ranked DCMA above 143 with a score of less than 60 for places to work. Meaning, DCMA was among the worst places to work, along with the Bureau of Prisons/Federal Prison System. Still, nothing has been done to improve DCMA that I was aware of or witnessed, which helps explain the following.

Employees Fearing Retaliation

June 16, 2005 - Pleading the 5th: It was documented that if the employee *"was subpoenaed about her source, she would "take the fifth." I didn't have the heart to tell her that she can only take the fifth when it comes to self-incrimination."* This was a part of Falsified Trail 3.

Comments I heard personally over the years include

Bury their "*head in the sand*"; (Circa on/about 2017)

Just "*Do what the boss says*"; (Circa on/about 2006)

Only want to hear "*pleasantries*"; (Circa on/about late 1990s)

"*Pray*" themselves into the office; (Circa on/about 2005)

Management won't mess with 2 employees because of all the "*stuff*" they (the 2 employees) have on management.

How could I (Pedeleose) "*stand this place* (DCMA)" all those years? Meaning, a hostile workplace silences and scares employees.

"Gun Slinger"

July 26, 2005: Falsified Trail 2 was a retaliation where DCMA alleged that I physically threatened someone at my facility. The charge was investigated and proven false. However, on July 25, 2005, one employee at a meeting referred to me as a "gun slinger". A Memo for the Record was done on July 26, 2005. In other words, I was falsely accused in Falsified Trail 2 however my reputation was still damaged even though I was cleared of any charges or allegations.

Falsify Records

December 9, 2005: I made a criminal disclosure based on a call received by a person representing a company in dispute with DCMA. On December 8, 2005, the caller made it seem that DCMA "*created or altered documents that put the contract in the government favor when it should have been in the contractor's favor.*" That was the gist of what was said. This further confirms that DCMA's reputation and evidence go beyond my observations and my documentation of DCMA.

Weaponized Investigations - Weaponized Attorneys – Weaponized Status

June 20, 2006: The centerpiece of Falsified Trail 3, and Falsified Trails in general, are found in the DCMA Legal Directorate briefing with the following quotes regarding the role of DCMA attorneys.

"Ultimate Multitasked Legal Machine"

"These are the legal Hotshot Crew"

"Pull Irons [an butts] out of Fires"

"Direct Liaison With DoD IG, All Investigative Agencies, US Attorneys, and Debarring Officials"

The point is that the DCMA legal directorate has a direct participatory role in the weaponized government and lawfare. Falsified Trail 3 is the clearest documented example, as evidenced by electronic trails and admissions. Falsified Trail 3 demonstrated how DCMA attorneys leveraged access to the DoD IG and U.S. Attorneys to enhance a weaponized investigation (Falsified Trail 3) for the purpose of retaliation.

At this point, June 20, 2006, is a placeholder for what is to follow, so it doesn't seem like much. However, in Falsified Trail 3, the aforementioned phrases will mean a lot more. Similar to the August 2, 2002, affidavit by Doug Kinan (former DCMA employee).

Kinan's affidavit included a DCMA attorney quote and other info as follows:

"We (the Legal Directorate) can do anything we want. It's called gaming. We can deny, we can delay…dismiss. We can manipulate the system anyway we want."

Kinan further stated: "*Other evasive manipulations are silence or when required to explain their conduct, the Legal Directorate declares the claim of "attorney work product or "attorney privilege.""*" I have experienced this tactic as well.

DCMA weaponized attorneys and weaponized attorney access to DoD IG and U.S. Attorneys. From there, fear set in the workforce, as evidenced in the same DCMA legal briefing, which altered working conditions.

Altered Working Conditions – Fear of Retaliation

June 20, 2006: DCMA legal directorate posted a briefing that included the following quotes from DCMA personnel.

"*You ask me if I'd report Fraud? I'd rather place my thumb on a concrete slab and strike it with a 5 pound hammer!"*

"*Whistleblowers are not protected, despite the law*"

"*Very few whistleblowers make out very well even with all the supposed protections*"

"*Management too cozy with contractor. Will take action against employee so as not to lose potential job with contractor*"

"*I was told to drop it by the District and my supervisor*"

"*Only when placed on the defensive does management spring into action to protect itself*"

"*The higher in the chain, the more ferociously they try to stop reporting. From what I can see they look upon it as embarrassment to the agency, and a stumbling block to their careers.*"

"*Our management mandates that we go through the Chain of Command*"

"*Employee is blamed first*"

"*I'm not sure if I will pursue this. It may be best to just let it be. I don't want to lose my job.*"

"*First line supervision does not want fraud reported unless it goes through the Chain of Command first! What is the point of having an anonymous means if you have to tell people who will filter or advise you not to do it to begin with?*"

"*Forced to get the product out the door. No support from management or Buying Commands and the contractors know this all too well.*"

"*Encouraged to "team, not tattle'"*"

The point is, DCMA has installed fear in their employees. Meaning, fear is a weapon. If it can be weaponized, DCMA will weaponize it.

The aforementioned comments demonstrate that the workforce has taken notice and how working conditions have been altered.

Stop Shaking Hands

December 14, 2006: Colonel Plourde, my then Commander (4th Level Supervisor) was a central figure in Falsified Trail 3 and filed a 30-Day suspension against me. At a holiday luncheon, Plourde grabbed my hand and started shaking it. I believed it was an attempt to goad me or provoke more actions to enhance retaliation. In response, I filed an EEO harassment complaint that forced Plourde to stop shaking hands with me.

I recall a similar situation where Joe Tessier (then a 2nd-level supervisor) said hello to me. Tessier was a major player in creating a hostile work environment for me during Volley 3 of retaliation (Falsified Trails 4 through 10, March 2009 to February 2010). I had to file a complaint to stop Joe Tessier from saying hello to me.

Meaning, working conditions were altered to the point where I was forced to file complaints to separate myself from management for simple issues. As the following shows, DCMA has no respect for any employee outside of cronies.

Dispensable Partner

June 20, 2007: A fellow employee indicated she was awake at night about a term in our office relating to "*dispensable partner*." This was a morbid reversal of the term indispensable partner where employees are appreciated.

I do remember the term "*dispensable partner*" being used by DCMA management. I took the term "*dispensable partner*" in stride as a typical DCMA hostile workplace. The other employee did not and was notably upset.

Another employee overheard the conversation and asked in an agitated way, "*"What did you just say?" "What did you just say?"*." The agitated employee left without incident. However, others were disturbed and made memos for the record to the supervisor. That led to the following.

Altering Evidence

July 9, 2007: Apparently, the employee who was agitated on June 20, 2007, made a complaint to DCMA HQ. This brought in DCMA attorneys. The gist is that the employee who wrote the memo for the record against the agitated employee somehow favored the agitated employee. From there, it seemed that DCMA was asking, if not hinting, to alter memos for the record to favor management position.

The point is that DCMA falsifies or alters evidence. I did not follow up and do not know what became of the situation.

The next incident documented was the mishandling of nuclear weapons that happened outside of DCMA authority.

Nuclear Weapons Mishandled

July 22, 2008: One concern of the hostile work atmosphere in DoD was a nuclear incident. A report by the Associated Press confirmed it did happen, as the following states in part.

"*If confirmed, Donley and Schwartz would replace former secretary Michael Wynne and chief of staff Gen. Michael Moseley, fired together in June in an unprecedented decapitation of Air Force leadership that Defense Secretary Robert Gates said was to hold the men accountable for a decade-long decline in the way the service handles the nation's nuclear arsenal.*

Gates said his decision was based mainly on the damning conclusions of an internal report on the mistaken shipment to Taiwan of four Air Force fusing devices for ballistic missile nuclear warheads. And he linked the underlying causes of that slip-up to the August incident in which a B-52 bomber was mistakenly armed with six nuclear warheads and flown across the nation without anyone realizing it."

The nuclear incident aligns with the theme of this book, where system integrity is unraveling. I even remember a conversation about the year 2000 or a little earlier, where one manager asked me if I felt that DCMA is "*unraveling.*"

Retaliation Complaint

February 2, 2009: One employee came to me and asked me to review a complaint against Henrietta Snow (Deputy Commander). The employee email to me stated in part as follows.

"*Ken,*

I want to send the following to Col Blake. Take a look and comment please.

This serves to formally request your action/intervention into unfair and unethical treatment I've received from Ms Henrietta Snow. I believe I am being retaliated against for reasons I'd rather not state in this communication. Ms Snow has damaged my reputation with my peers, the Customer, and the Contractor by her actions. I will site only two prior occasions in this communication."

The employee stated lengthy reasons and concluded by stating to Colonel Blake (then Commander).

"*Request you take actions to ensure Ms Snow cease her retaliatory conduct towards myself and that Ms Snow is aware of the gravity of her actions as it relates to my working relationship with my peers, the Customer, and the Contractor. I am available to discuss this communication with you at your convenience.*"

It is unknown if the employee ever made the complaint; however, the complaint is documented and suggests that management staff was out of control. Shortly after this incident, DCMA management issued a volley of Falsified Trails as follows.

Volley 3 – Falsified Trails 4, 5, 6, 7, 8, 9, & 10

March 3, 2009 – February 16, 2010: DCMA escalated administrative attacks (retaliation against me). The focus was destroying me as a part of the workforce. Chapter 3 explains further.

Lockheed Martin Profits Too High

February 4, 2010: While the DCMA was focusing on forcing out whistleblowers, the financial problems continued to grow. I made a disclosure on February 4, 2010, stating that the Forward Pricing Rate Agreement (FPRA) was too high, and as such, the government had to withdraw in a formal letter dated December 18, 2009. I was told this was due to Lockheed Martin making excessive profits.

DCMA decimated their technical workforce to the point of collapse thus enabling high profits (price gouging) to contractors. Chapter 4 expands upon this in greater detail

DCMA and DCAA Issues

May 7, 2010: The hostile work environment had spread and deteriorated to the point where a formal letter had to be issued to try to establish some semblance of order. The Directors of DCMA and DCAA co-signed a letter stating, in part.

"*We are working together very closely to overcome the challenges often mentioned in various forums about the strained relationship between DCMA and DCAA. We do not accept the notion that the workforces of our Agencies are unable to work professionally together to accomplish the Department's business.*"

There was a noticeable deterioration of the workforce to the point where Directors had to give the appearance of order. This helps confirm altered work environments. In fact, DCMA and DCAA were like organizations, as noted by Senator Grassley, who stated in part on February 24, 2004: "*Those two entities have a long-standing reputation for turning a blind eye to contractor rip offs.*" So, DCMA and DCAA were largely on the same page after all, as this book shows.

Mis-drill Holes

August 23, 2010, back to January 31, 2002: The issue came up in 2010 that Lockheed Martin had a hard time drilling holes. I reminded those involved that the issue actually went back to 2002. Meaning, problems continue over several years.

I also recall an incident where the C-130J NESA Window (heated windshield) had problems dating back to 2004, which were again mentioned in late 2019. The DCMA placed new employees reviewing the engineering who did not have the history to know the issues were systemic over the years.

Promotion Panel Write-Ins

November 29, 2010: I was told Joe Tessier (my 2nd-level supervisor in Volley 3 of retaliation) had his name written in on promotion panel recommendations. My Memo for the Record stated in part.

"The panel did not recommend Tessier for promotion. Specifically, Joe Tessier was hired in this organization as a GS-12. When he applied for a promotion he was not on the list of recommended persons from the selection panel. Apparently Henrietta Snow wrote in Tessier's name."

This was actually the second incident. The first was on August 18, 2003, where a person named "Joe" (more than likely Joe Tessier) did not have a promotion panel recommendation. The point is, Tessier wreaked havoc and obstructed, especially with me. DCMA wanted Tessier in management as part of a bigger plan. That plan, is what this book is about. Tessier was a small part.

C-5 Modernization Program Problems – Trailer to Capstone Case $131 Million

March 15, 2011: By this time, Lockheed Martin and DCMA had unraveled significantly to the point where major problems had to be openly discussed. Meaning, while DCMA and DoD focused largely on executing my reputation and ridding DoD of whistleblowers, actual work issues emerged. The following is from a March 11, 2011, Memorandum that was attached to a March 15, 2011, email. The memorandum stated in part, regarding C-5 Modernization Program (Reliability Enhancement and Re-engining Program) Low-Rate Initial Production (LRIP).

"MEMORANDUM FOR: DCMA LMM Senior Leadership Team (SL T), C-5 Program

Offices at Air Force Materiel Command (WR-ALC/GRS, ASC/WLS), and Logistics and

Requirements Directorates at Air Mobility Command (AMC/A4 and AMC/A5)"

"SUBJECT: Minutes of Government Only Meeting between AFMC, AMC, and DCMA"

"DATE OF MEETING: 14 February 2011"

"PURPOSE: To determine the way-ahead for successful execution of the C-5M LRIP Modification program by discussing significant issues impacting the ability to execute Contract Administration Services. The topics of discussion included LRIP Statement of Work (SOW), Clause Hl06 Rapid Repair and Response (R3), Foreign Object Debris (FOD) inspection requirements, 781 write-ups, AFMC 202, Mandatory Program Guidance, Use of C-5A versus C-5M technical orders, and Timely Response to Contract Deficiency Reports (CDR)/DD Form 1716. Action items were generated and assigned to responsible parties along with milestone dates for completion."

There were about 8 pages of problems and Action Items. The problems were too numerous to mention or summarize other than the aforesaid "Purpose" of meeting section.

In the end, the U.S. Government had to pay an additional $131 million due to Lockheed Martin's poor performance. Chapter 5 of this book (Capstone Case) focuses on what the problems developed into, which is a Claim proposal. This ties weaponized government and lawfare to the national debt with an actual case study that followed from the aftermath of weaponized government and lawfare. Meaning, cover-ups versus corrective action to resolve problems.

Employee Forced Move

<u>October 2, 2012</u>: A union official sent the following e-mail to me regarding a forced move by management, stating in part.

"*Ken, the move is under a shroud of unknown reasons, however I believe Snow and Commander had a big hand in it because of my representation of an employee complaint against management on an EEO complaint that made it out of the CMO* (Contract Management Office, my office) *to HQ is the real reason for the move. Grievance filed through Union waiting response from HQ.*"

That employee, who was a union official, later retired, as the following shows.

"Turned My Stomach"

<u>May 16, 2013</u>: The aforementioned employee, who was forced to move, sent me an email stating.

"*Yes, I decided to retire after 46 years, this agency turned my stomach. Please feel free to mention any EEO complaint to HQ. I can't mention the individual name but I will say he is no longer working at Marietta.*" Hence, another example of a hostile workplace.

Union Representatives Fear Hostile Workplace & Fear Retaliation

<u>August 26, 2013 & September 9, 2013 – Fear of Management Retaliation</u>: I assisted an employee in an EEO case and received some shocking comments regarding fear of management retaliation. The first comments below were stated on August 26, 2013, and stated in part as follows.

"I am a union representative, but if someone on my team had a concern/problem, I would refer the employee to other union representatives because we had the same supervisor."

"*I directed her to go the union. I personally didn't want to be involved.*"

"*I personally didn't want to be involved because Complainant and I had the same supervisor and at times were on the same team.*"

"I have been working for the government for 27 years and do not wish to be involved in this matter. Our team is not a hostile work environment. I also don't recall dates."

The point is, even a union representative fears retaliation. The employee (complainant), not the union official stated in part:

"*The coworker told me that they did not want any involvement because they feared possibly being terminated for speaking out.*" The employee wrote a rebuttal to the supervisor, instead of filing a grievance, because the union suggested not to file a grievance, because the supervisor and management "*would try to find a reason to terminate me* (the employee) *if I went against them. I was very confused by that statement and did not know how to respond.*"

The point being, DCMA has a reputation for retaliation and installing fear in employees. Even union officials fear DCMA management.

"Not a Wise Thing to Do"

September 9, 2013: A witness, in the aforesaid case, regarding challenging the supervisor about abusive remarks, stated in part. "*...this was not a wise thing to do.*"

The point is, in a hostile workplace like DCMA, employees will not be candid or open. That's why this book is so detailed like an encyclopedia. DCMA, and DoD for that matter, are textbook hostile workplaces where hostility is celebrated and position of authority are weaponized along with lawfare. Sometimes, employees may even threaten to call the police.

"Call the Police"

April 8, 2014 EEO Complaint (Dated July 7, 2014): Another DCMA employee "*contacted the commander and threatened to call the police.*" This was documented in an EEO complaint I assisted with. The complaint alleged "*Hostile Work Environment/Harassment.*"

On May 9, 2014, the "*call the police*" comment was used against the employee when the employee's supervisor issued the employee a "*Mandatory Employee Assistance Program Referral.*" Basically, the employee was forced into mandatory counseling.

I would believe this to be a weaponized retaliatory move because during Falsified Trail 1 there was a similar threat made to me. Meaning, my second-level supervisor threatened to send me to anger management. This follows from weaponized training outlined on January 20, 2011 (Chapter 3), where training was weaponized against me.

The trend continued on the same EEO case on July 8, 2014, where the following comments were alleged made by the supervisor as follows.

"*might find some dead bodies floating in the river*";

"*Yeah, cause I will have to string her up*"

"*an employee and some certain African woman*"

"*at least they did not have to wear a bullet proof vest to work every day*"

The point is that there is a trend of hostility across DCMA offices, as well as a plethora of litigation involving unrelated employees across the office spectrum. Meaning, there is too much of a trend to allege that it is all made up.

Employees came to me with problems, and I have noticed that my problems are the same as those of other employee problems. Meaning variations on themes.

When the data was assembled, it showed an irrefragable trend of a hostile and abusive workplace covered up over the decades. Meaning, there is too much to easily dismiss.

That is why it is very handy for DCMA to have DCMA investigate DCMA and clear DCMA of problems, as the following shows.

DCMA IG – Corruption Circles

May 16, 2018: DCMA in 2017 started their own IG division so DCMA could investigate DCMA. This was efficient in the hostile workplace to contain negative information. The trend of DoD IG farming out investigations was spoken of on May 16, 2018, in an open article to DCMA employees about the new DCMA IG, stating in part:

"*The DoD IG just returns the referral to us* (DCMA) *as either an information referral or an action referral.*"

The article went on to state that in the last four years, only one of DCMAs allegations was investigated by the DoD IG.

The point is, allegations against DCMA are sent back to DCMA for DCMA to investigate DCMA. Meaning, circular self-contained corruption scandal inbreeds upon itself. It should also be noted that DCMA has had investigators for many years. It's just that the investigators are now formalized in an IG capacity.

Falsified Trail 13 is the perfect example. DCMA investigated DCMA against my allegations and DCMA found my allegations unsubstantiated and conveniently closed the investigation. When I attempted to obtain a clean, unredacted, FOIA report of what happened, I was denied.

Meaning, I submitted the FOIA in August 2015, and as of the date of this book, I have not received a clean FOIA that is not heavily redacted. Furthermore, this shows that DCMA also controls the FOIA process. Falsified Trail 13, in Chapter 3 has the details.

That DCMA mentality is probably why DCMA has to bribe employees to fill out survey forms.

Bribe to Fill Out Surveys

July 1, 2019: The DCMA workforce was so passive that by 2019, there had to be bribes to get employees to fill out the Federal Employee Viewpoint Survey (FEVS). One for my team (designated as ALEA) stated:

"If you're interested in 59 minutes time off, please complete the FEVS survey. If we as a team (ALEA) get to 70% participation, we'll each get 59 minutes. Look for your specific email from OPM since the link is specific to you."

Meaning, employees had to be bribed to fill out surveys. There may also be some fear since I remember one comment on/about 2005 or 2006 where one employee was afraid to fill out the survey because of the electronic link (email) back to the employee.

The aforementioned are just some samples of high points for the resume of the Deep State and the Government Swamp… The conclusion of this Chapter follows.

Half Century – Expanding & Enabling the Government Swamp

Documented Behavior & Mentality of the Hostile Workplace

The majority of Chapter 2, and for the most part, this book, is comprised of the words, comments, and behavior of others, which is the foundation of institutional corruption in government along with weaponization and lawfare that expand and enable the Government Swamp. Not my words. I draw conclusions based on what others have stated in the past and what has happened to me personally. Information that is now contemporaneous. Meaning, documented as events occurred and not from distant memories written down in the present day. A half century collection.

There are too many corroborated data points to believe the issues are isolated or discrete. Meaning, the number of data points from different individuals, over half a century, across a wide spectrum reveals systemic and institutionalized problems within the U.S. Government.

Summarizing the issues is nearly impossible. In 2004, 60 Minutes told me that my case keeps morphing out. Meaning, expanding issues past what the public can understand in what should be a simplified story. That is because of adverse systemic and institutionalized issues that exist. Finding the end of corruption in government is like trying to find the end of the universe. I don't think I'm even close to the information in this book. However, this book is a start and does suggest remedy.

The hostile work environments do have an effect on the government workforce. I am a witness and a victim all in one. Any conclusions herein are based on the words/actions of others, mentality, and behavior. The data points and evidence speak for themselves.

Chapter 3 that follows shows the operational, documented in detail, version of weaponized government and lawfare in practice. Some documentation is provided in minute-by-minute email trails. DCMA provided the direct evidence of weaponization and lawfare with any "blanks" (uncertainties) being filled in by investigations, sworn statements, etc. Falsified Trail 3 is the flagship case of weaponized government and lawfare, with the remaining Falsified Trails following the same pattern. The notable point is the improvements from Nixon to 2003.

1970-2003: Improved Electronic Weapons – Wider & Deeper Swamp

The electronics of the Nixon Administration were tapes for recording. Limited range, large, and bulky. Nixon's ideas had not spread and were not perfected in 1970. Watergate stopped Nixon.

By 2003, when weaponization and lawfare were used against me, the circumstances had changed. Just about everyone had computers outfitted with emails. The emails became weaponized electronic trails used in lawfare. The Government Swamp grew and inbred to a combination of a fiefdom and a crime syndicate. The oversight was no longer for the public good but for the good of the military-industrial complex. The disastrous rise of power had begun. I challenged the military-industrial complex on July 26, 2002 with a 90-Page report exposing corruption. I discovered the depth of the Government Swamp by May 2003. I was not a nuisance whistleblower.

CHAPTER 3

Deep State Weaponization & Lawfare in Action

Introduction to Whistleblowing – Nuisance Vs Impact

The Falsified Trails against me were attributed to my on-target and damaging allegations to the "Belly of the Beast" (heart of the problem). I had access to Lockheed Martin cost and pricing data, manufacturing data, overhead cost data, direct cost data, aircraft test data, manufacturing/production data, etc. I was well-experienced in technical reports and data analysis. I was on target, had impact, and got attention. That is why I experienced exceptional wrath versus being a nuisance.

Nuisance Whistleblowing versus Impact Whistleblowing: Prior whistleblowers who wrote to Congress in a limited way caused a mild, temporary stir lasting about 6 months or so, and eventually were forgotten. Management may be strengthened by a weaker whistleblower, who might simply claim a vast conspiracy theory, downplay issues, or suggest that employees are "fanning flames."

Widescale Deeper Impact Whistleblowing: I was not a normal whistleblower. I had the skills for making cases. I was hired by the DoD in 1987 to analyze and make cases for production improvement as part of a March 20, 1986, Department of the Navy memo to hire Industrial engineers in Naval shipyards. In 1994, I moved into cost analysis to develop negotiation positions on Air Force aircraft (mainly C-130, C-5), new production, spare parts, modernization, etc. This facilitated a seamless transition to the whistleblower role.

The following are examples of nuisance whistleblowing that become "stale" after 6 months.

Nuisance Whistleblowing Congressional Disclosure – 1996 Example

December 4, 1996 FOIA with January 22, 1996 Data Date: Three DCMA employees in my office wrote to Congressman Newt Gingrich and Senator Sam Nunn. Documentation shows the complaint as follows (DoD Control Number: 95-L681863-96011, August 15, 1996):

"*Complainants expressed concern for quality and safety of C-130 aircraft produced at Lockheed Martin Aerospace Systems (LMAS), Marietta, GA. Complaint alleged improper procedures were followed by LMAS engineering and a government member of the Senior Material Review Board in handling non-conforming materials pertaining to improperly machined C-130 nose wheel landing gear trunnion.*"

At the time, the three employees were considered nuisances. Regarding nonconforming parts, I do not believe the current workforce has anywhere near the hands-on experience that the three engineers who made the Congressional disclosure had. Meaning, that new disclosures (nuisance or not) will be limited due to weaponized government, lawfare and deteriorating oversight conditions.

For example, one of the three employees who made the Congressional disclosure was a DER (Designated Engineering Representative) for the Federal Aviation Administration (FAA), meaning the person can approve or recommend approval on behalf of the FAA. Hence, even though the employees were considered nuisances, specialized engineering skills were involved. This goes to the public safety aspect of this book.

Anonymous Complaint - June 12, 1998 Example

DoD IG Hotline Disclosure 69535 June 12, 1998 – Closed Partially Substantiated: I made a hotline disclosure regarding Lockheed Martin providing false prices (price gouging) for C-5 aircraft parts. The case was closed as partially substantiated, but it later evolved into a criminal complaint due to inaction on the initial complaint.

During a team meeting, possibly on or before November 1998, Colonel Evans (my then Commander) made an unsolicited remark to the effect, "*Don 't bother to call the Congress or the Senate these people will do nothing for you*". I asked Colonel Evans if he meant the C-130J or the C-5 PDM, and he responded with the C-5.

The point is, the Hotline disclosure was considered a nuisance. This later evolved into a criminal complaint as follows:

Local Criminal Complaint – February 28, 2000 – Not a Team Player

Follow-on to Disclosure 69535 – Criminal Complaint February 28, 2000: On/about February 28, 2000, I called criminal investigators into my office during one negotiation process to disclose what was negotiating contracts on data known to be false and purposely overstated. That disclosure was substantiated and sent to the prosecution. This was a follow-on to case 69535, previously mentioned, where the corruption never ended, and the case was closed as partially substantiated.

However, after the February 28, 2000, criminal disclosure, I was criticized for not being a "*team player*". The interesting part is what happened before the disclosure and 6 months after the disclosure. The timeline follows the "*team player*" remark written on my performance appraisals.

Performance Appraisal August 12, 1998: The term "*team player*" was handwritten on my performance appraisal. No whistleblowing had occurred by me as yet.

Performance Appraisal July 27, 1999: The term "*Team player.*" was handwritten on my performance appraisal. No whistleblowing had occurred by me as yet.

Performance Appraisal July 26, 2000 Post Whistleblowing: After whistleblowing on February 28, 2000, my then supervisor (Walt Walker) wrote on my performance appraisal:

"*Needs improvement in the area of Teaming & Teamwork*".

This was apparently related to anonymous complaints about my "attitude" by fellow employees and a Lockheed Martin official. The only known issue was whistleblowing on February 28, 2000. The point is, "*Teaming & Teamwork*" are not related to "attitude" complaints, and followed the whistleblowing, which was well known in the office since I openly called in criminal investigators.

However, the situation subsided after about 6 months.

Performance Appraisal January 10, 2001 - Supervisor Confused: At my next performance appraisal, Walt Walker was confused. I documented the following in a memo for record after the fact from handwritten notes.

"*Mr. Walker was proceeding smoothly through my performance appraisal (reviewing the mid term appraisal as he went along) when he came upon the statement indicating, Needs improvement in the area of teaming and teamwork. He was confused as to why he made the remark. At this time I offered to refresh his memory, and did just that.*

I indicated that there were anonymous complaints made by both the contractor and office employees about my attitude. (I deliberately mentioned the contractor because I was only somewhat sure as to what he indicated regarding the contractor during my midterm performance appraisal on July 26, 2000.) At that time I began to pump him for information.

I indicated that I could guess who complained on the government side of the house. However, I was confused who could have done it with regards to the contractor. I began thinking out loud and mentioning names as I went. I said that it could not have been Andy Cozzolino due to the fact he was retired at the time. I mentioned Dick Reeves, and also said that he was retired. Then I indicated that the only remaining individual was Brenda Cleveland, however I had no ill words exchanged with her.

At that time Mr. Walker indicated that it was the individual who was not retired. (This left Brenda Cleveland, essentially the individual from LMAC (Lockheed Martin) *who was responsible for me making the February 28, 2000 call to the OSI.) As the conversation progressed Mr. Walker indicated that the complaints were against me, <u>and others</u>. Mr. Walker did emphasize, <u>and others</u>.*"

The point is, Walt Walker had forgotten why he wrote the remark, "*Needs improvement in the area of Teaming & Teamwork*".

On January 10, 2001 (less than a year after my disclosure), Walt Walker wrote on my performance appraisal: "*Certainly an asset to the team*" among other positive comments, such as me performing at an "*exceptional*" level. The end point is that the whistleblowing on February 28, 2000, was forgotten because it was considered nuisance or low-level whistleblowing.

However, the inaction on corruption continued. Meaning, my management acquiesced to fraud and corruption. I noted that the in-person disclosure I made on the C-130J on April 5, 2000 (outlined in Chapter 4 of this book) went nowhere, and the investigator was frustrated. I decided to run a test on the DoD IG.

I summarized the following test disclosure in the July 26, 2002, report to Congress.

DoD IG Test Disclosure to Prove DoD IG Ineptness & Corruption

January 27, 2001 (DoD IG Complaint 79529): I emailed a written complaint to the DoD IG Hotline outlining four initial accusations and one follow-on accusation. The accusations involved Contracting Officers being rotated at the time Lockheed Martin was going into production on the F-22, and a follow-on contract was being negotiated for the C-130J. (Note: The e-mail/disclosure stated date January 27, 2001, while the July 26, 2002 Congressional Report stated January 28, 2001. January 28, 2001, was a misprint.)

I provided complete contact information, including my name (no aliases), work and home phone numbers, and e-mail address. The original and follow-on accusations include:

(1) Failure to issue CAR to keep Lockheed Martin off the Contractor Alerts List. (Loss of Integrity)

(2) Supervisors having the ability to override/rewrite employee inputs into RAMP (Risk Assessment and Management Program).

(3) Exclusive meetings.

(4) Stonewalling General Accounting Office (GAO) auditors.

(5) Rotation of Contracting Officers during contract critical negotiations (March 14, 2001)

The complaint was assigned case number 79529. I was never contacted for additional information prior to July 26, 2002, and gave up even asking for status updates. This proves the theory of inept investigations, or more specifically, a lack of concern or integrity. One update is outlined as follows.

April 5, 2001 Case 79529 Update: I documented an update to Case 79529 to a criminal investigator (April 5, 2001) and forwarded it to Senator Boxer's staff on October 21, 2003. The complaint is copied as follows.

"*Below is my compalint and additional information I submitted on case 79529. (That was the case where I explained how Corrective Action Requests (CARs) are being covered up at this facility, along with other things.) Well in any good investment one should expect dividends, interest, capital gains, etc. This project (cover-up) was no exception.*

Yesterday and today (4/4/01 and 4/5/01) I attended a British Standards Institute (BSI) audit of LMAC. Basically LMAC has to be recertified in ISO 9000 periodically. During the management briefing (4/4/01) LMAC (Ms. Janet Nash) presented to BSI (Mr. Peter Tilford) that they had received no Level Ill CARs this year. A truly outstanding event, in my opinion.

CONGRATULATIONS ARE IN ORDER, and believe it or not, I kept my mouth shut the entire time."

The point is, the situation was worsening with DoD IG inaction. CARs were issued in Draft form (not documented) to cover up for Lockheed Martin's problems. Lockheed Martin took advantage of this benefit and was recertified in ISO 9000. If I had spoken up, I would have been rebuked and retaliated against, making me look bad. Year after year, no definitive action is taken.

I expected the DoD IG would cover up case 79529. In parallel to the January 27, 2001, disclosure, I prepared a Congressional report that would awaken the Deep State.

Awaken the Deep State

July 26, 2002 – 90 Page Congressional Report: The July 26, 2002, Congressional Report was titled: "*Department of Defense Technical Report on Criminal Vulnerability and Fraud*". I wrote the report with two other signatories.

The report was sent to 57 members of Congress with copies to President Bush and Secretary of Defense Donald Rumsfeld. The mailings went in groups beginning on July 26, 2002, and went through August 9, 2002. The July 26, 2002, report was the catalyst for Falsified Trails to follow. Meaning, I awakened the Deep State that would deploy weaponization and lawfare against me.

DoD and DCMA were well aware of what happened with the July 26, 2002, report to Congress, and there was a time link to the Falsified Trails against me. The DoD defense grid was pierced.

The first retaliation was documented in my September 16, 2003 deposition to the DoD IG, testifying to what I was told after DCMA received the July 26, 2002 report to Congress.

Knowledge of Disclosure, Pull Personnel Files, & Pedeleose "Killing People"

September 16, 2003 Deposition: For Falsified Trail 2, I did a deposition with the DoD IG that included the events surrounding the July 26, 2002, report to Congress, focusing on what I was told at the time in 2002 and 2003 and what DCMA knew about the report. My testimony focused on conversations with Kenneth W. Leisure, Program Manager, Criminal Investigations and Hotline, Defense Contract Management Agency (DCMA-DSS).

I testified to the following in part on September 16, 2003, regarding the July 26, 2002, report and how the other two signatories and I met with Kenneth Leisure.

"*We met with Kenneth Leisure, okay, and Kenneth Leisure came down . And he was kind of a little bit loudmouthed about this, okay, and he knew that report better than I did. I had written that technical report, the July 26, 2002 report, and this guy knew this thing better than I did. He refreshed my memory on several areas and led me in there, okay.*

And the bottom line is one of the things he said was they put this thing out for comments up there at Headquarters."

Relevance is that the July 26, 2002, report to Congress was circulated at DCMA HQ for comments. Unknown how many read the report. DCMA attorney Leigh Owens also had knowledge of the July 26, 2002, report as follows.

"*But Ms. Lee* (Should be "Leigh") *Owens said that they did have it* (July 26, 2002 report) *up there a month-and-a-half prior to October the 22nd, 2002.*"

The date of the October 22, 2002 report will be relevant a few paragraphs from now, where I discovered (by a misdialed fax) that DCMA had the report.

"*Mr. Leisure indicated that -- he said, okay, "What are we going to do with this?" and he says, "Do you think I ought to go down there and talk to these people?" And apparently Sally Flaven said, "Yeah, that ' s a good idea. Why don't you go down there and talk to them."*"

Sally Flaven, the then DCMA Deputy Director, played a critical retaliatory role in Falsified Trail 3, as did then DCMA Director Keith Ernst. Keith Ernst also made incriminating and retaliatory comments in Falsified Trail 1 that will be discussed later. I further testified,

"*And one of the other comments that came back when they -- was is Ken Pedeleose capable of killing people*"

I was never told who made the "*killing people*" comment, and I was shocked by it. Especially since there were 3 signatories on the report. This focus on "*one employee, Ken Pedeleose*" (as discussed in Falsified Trail 3 and my resume [Chapter 1]) played a critical role in the retaliation.

My September 16, 2003 deposition is now contemporaneous and supported by the subsequent events and peripheral evidence. The most notable is the misdirected Fax of October 22, 2002.

Misdirected Fax from "Tom Selleck" (Kenneth Leisure)

October 22, 2002: An employee at a local Marietta, GA company called me about a Fax that came in. The Fax was from "Tom Selleck" to "Ms. Owens" and "Ms. Bass". The fax included a letter to President Bush with my contact information (phone numbers and home address). I didn't know who "Tom Selleck" was, but I did know Owens and Bass, who were local DCMA attorneys.

The caller was disturbed and shaken by the letter I sent to President Bush, which stated in part.

"*The problems began with fraud and ethics violations that should have been resolved at low levels and were not. These problems are now embedding themselves into reprisal and adverse personnel actions that increase criminal vulnerability and fraud on the taxpayers, while compromising national security and integrity.*"

"*We are asking for your assistance with the issues and violations outlined in the enclosed report. However, the fraud and ethics violations and reprisal against whistleblowers are a matter of deeper concern that may require specific legislation, remedy, or enforcement of existing laws.*"

"*Thus far we have contained the information surrounding the problem, however have sent copies to various members of the Congress, Senate, and Secretary of Defense Rumsfeld. As you will see in the report, the DoD Chain of Command is disinterested and lethargic towards resolution.*"

Standard Conversation: The aforesaid comments on the letter to President Bush, and a similar letter to Congress, were standard feelings and standard conversations since corruption is integrated into daily DoD operations.

What to Do with the Fax: The caller asked what should be done with the misdirected Fax. I informed the caller to immediately fax me what was sent to them. Then, mail the misdirected printed Fax to my home address. The caller complied and sent the Fax in a company envelope.

Contacting Leigh Owens: When I received the misdirected Fax from the local company, I called Leigh Owens and asked if she had lost anything. I identified the Fax to her and Bass from "Tom Selleck". Leigh Owens said she wondered what happened to that Fax.

Owens said "Tom Selleck" is really a nickname given to DCMA investigator Kenneth Leisure.

About a week after I spoke with Leigh Owens, I received a call from Kenneth Leisure.

October 30, 2002 – Meet With Kenneth Leisure: I received a call from Kenneth Leisure and immediately contacted the co-signers to the July 26, 2002 report, stating in part.

"*I just got a call from DCMA headquarters (Mr. Kenneth Leisure). He said he wants to meet regarding the 90 page complaint sent to our friends. I told him that we are a group and I will have both of you there. The tentative date (he said he needs to get his travel orders in order) is either the 6th or 13th of November. He said that this will be a first contact of sorts. Depending on the day is depending on the fact that the counsel (Owens and Bass) or the acting commander (Mr. Chaffman) will be able to attend.*

He indicated that he wanted to meet as soon as he can."

November 4, 2002 – Meeting Set: Kenneth Leisure stated in an e-mail.

"*This should hopefully confirm our meeting on Wednesday, 6 Nov 02. I have been advised that the DCMA Atlanta Commander's Conference Room has been reserved for us. At the present time I should be arriving in Atlanta @ about 09:00, and arrive at DCMA Atlanta shortly thereafter. I will telephone you upon my arrival. I would assume that we could meet @ 13:00 hours, it will give me time to get settled and for you to have lunch. Any questions please get with me via email. I will be in and out of the office, so I will check e-mail and voice mail throughout the day.*"

DCMA Management Well Aware: We did meet with Kenneth Leisure. It was also obvious that DCMA HQ was well aware of the July 26, 2002 report, as evidenced by my conversations with Leisure.

Retaliation Followed: The management's timely knowledge of the July 26, 2002, report to Congress corresponded with the subsequent adverse actions. This means management reacted, and tactical retaliations began. This was the start of weaponization and lawfare. The first action was to pull the personnel files of those employees involved in the July 26, 2002 report to Congress.

Pulled Personnel Files/Folders of Whistleblowers

I was told in my first conversation with Kenneth Leisure that the personnel files/folders of the signatories (whistleblowers) on the July 26, 2002, report were pulled. That was one prong of the retaliation pattern. Much like the comment about me (Pedeleose) "*killing people*".

DCMA Well Aware of DoD IG Schedule & Coordination

January 9, 2003 – DCMA Knows DoD IG Schedule: Kenneth Leisure confirmed the following.

"*Mr. Pedeleose:*

After my return from Atlanta in Nov 2002, among other things, coordination was made with the DoDIG Internal Review. They advised DCMA that because of pertinent information you provided and information obtained from their own initial inquiry, their office had initiated inquiries and dispatched audit teams to Wright Patterson AFB, the Defense Supply Center Richmond and Lockheed Martin-Atlanta. I have been in contact with the DoDIG Internal Review on a bi-weekly basis. As of January 6, 2003, I was advised that the audit inquiries were still on-going with a expected completion date of February 2003. DCMA will respond and take whatever action is deemed appropriate, once the DoDIG completes their inquiries and provides DCMA with their results."

This was a precursor to Falsified Trails and lawfare, meaning the whistleblowing was on target, and I became a target.

Ernie Fitzgerald's Visit to Marietta, GA

The information on the following data points (March 12-13, 2003) was copied from the May 16, 2005, report to Congress titled "*Cover-up in the Department of Defense*".

<u>March 12, 2003 - Ernest Fitzgerald Visit</u>: Ernie Fitzgerald visited the Marietta, GA facility and met with Colonel James Wright (Commander), Charles (Ben) Chaffman (Deputy Commander), and signatories on the July 26, 2002 report to Congress. The July 26, 2002, report was mentioned, along with a discussion on how Mr. Fitzgerald would be reviewing cost control techniques at the Lockheed Martin facility in Marietta, GA.

The day after Fitzgerald's visit, the DoD IG visited Lockheed Martin's local executive office spaces.

DoD IG On-Site Visit

<u>March 13, 2003 (Supporting Information)</u>: On or about this date, IG auditors Thomas Bartoszek and Mary Hoover visited Marietta, GA. I provided nearly <u>800 pages</u> of supporting information for the C-5 PDM, along with a summary highlighting salient points. The summary and supporting data were <u>page numbered</u> for easy reference. The intended visits were discussed on October 21, 2002. Meaning, I met the DoD IG off-site prior to the facility visit.

<u>October 21, 2002 – DoD IG In Brief</u>: On October 18, 2002, I made note to one signatory on the July 26, 2002 report that we would be meeting with DCIS. From memory, this was the date we met offsite with the DoD IG, actually at the DCIS building, regarding the upcoming audits from the July 26, 2002 report. I stated.

"*Our meeting with the DCIS will be 1400 hours on Monday October 21, 2002.*"

During the October 21, 2002, meeting, I remembered that DoD IG auditors indicated C-130J users were approaching C-130 user conferences and stating, to the effect, "What are they giving us" with regards to the C-130J that was not mission capable. This supported the whistleblower allegations.

DoD IG Formal Announcement Letter to DoD

October 30, 2002 DOD IG Announcement Letter: The DoD IG issued an announcement letter, as a result of the July 26, 2002, report to Congress, titled:

"*Audit of Allegations of the Defense Contract Management Agency's Performance In Administering Selected Weapon Systems Contracts (Project No. D2003AB-0017)*"

The letter was sent to the DoD Agencies below.

Under Secretary of Defense for Acquisition, Technology, and Logistics

Assistant Secretary of the Air Force (Financial Management and Comptroller)

Director, Defense Contract Management Agency

Director, Defense Contract Audit Agency

Chief, National Guard Bureau

The letter stated in part:

"*The primary audit locations will be the Office of the Director, Defense Contract Management Agency; Wainer Robbins-Air Logistics Center, Wright Patterson Air Force Base; and other Government organizations involved with the C-130, F-22, and C-5 aircrafts that may be identified during the audit.*"

The October 30, 2002, DoD IG letter was forwarded to my team on November 5, 2002, by my team supervisor, so it was well known on my team. Possibly the entire office.

November 5, 2002 – DoD IG Site Visits: DoD IG auditor Tom Bartoszek stated to me.

"*Ken as you can see with the annoucement memo I have decided that there is sufficient information to warrent a full audit of the allegations made. The audit will take some time and we will be at different locations because of the players involved I have a staff or 6 people working the issues We may not be back there until sometime in December. Talk soon*"

Impact & Knowledge of Whistleblowing – Not A Nuisance Disclosure

The relevance is that the July 26, 2002 report to Congress got attention, was known by management, caused movement, and was not a nuisance disclosure.

As the leader of the whistleblowers and author of the July 26, 2002, report to Congress, I was now a target of the Deep State. Weaponization and lawfare did follow. Those who signed would be considered nuisances. I was in the category of Ernie Fitzgerald, who made an impact through whistleblowing. I also caused an impact.

Dan Meyer (mentioned in Chapter 1/Resume and key figure in Falsified Trail 3) informed me that my whistleblowing would be in the category of Ernie Fitzgerald. That is why I provided my resume and the aforesaid information on the July 26, 2002, Congressional report and the attention it garnered. I made an impression at the heart of the problem that caused the 13 Falsified Trails. I became a target. DoD and DCMA made their intentions clear in effecting my demise.

The following Falsified Trails integrate management's own words using e-mails, sworn statements, letters, Memorandums, etc. The documents are contemporaneous, taken at the time of management involvement in, and creation of, the 13 Falsified Trails.

Memoranda of records were also done at the time near the Falsified trails. Meaning, documents are contemporaneous.

Falsified Trail 1 is first.

Falsified Trail 1: July 9, 2003 Reprimand via Entrapment & Ambush

The following are DCMA and Lockheed Martin management officials of Falsified Trail 1. Some officials were also key players in Falsified Trails (FT) 2 & 3.

Colonel James Wright FT(1,2)	DCMA Commander, 4th Level Supervisor
Joe Caldwell FT(1)	DCMA 2nd Level Supervisor
Keith Ernst FT(1,3)	DCMA District East Director, then DCMA Director
Bruce Krasker FT(1,3)	DCMA Attorney
Charles (Ben) Chaffman FT(1,2)	DCMA Deputy Commander, 3rd Level Supervisor
Leigh Owens FT(1,3)	DCMA Attorney
Joe Cass FT(1)	DCMA Human Resources/Personnel
Sandra Shoemaker FT(1)	Lockheed Martin VP Integrated Company Operations
Dain Hancock FT(1)	Lockheed Martin President Aeronautical Sector
Marcia Farber FT(1)	Lockheed Martin Senior Manager, Marietta Site Account-
Roger Graham FT(1)	Lockheed Martin Attorney
Lee Rhyant FT(1)	Lockheed Martin Site Manager Marietta

Falsified Trail 1 Timeline

Cost Mischarging - Independent Research & Development (IRAD) Evaluation: In early 2003, DCAA (Defense Contract Audit Agency) contacted me to evaluate an IRAD project. The law allows DoD contractors to charge certain research and development costs to overhead for the overall benefit of the U.S.G. IRAD has specific criteria that must be followed, including that IRAD not be part of an existing contract. DCAA requested the IRAD review to ensure the IRAD project covered no existing Lockheed Martin contracts.

Concurrent with Whistleblowing: The IRAD review occurred in parallel with the DoD IG auditing Lockheed Martin for my allegations outlined in the July 26, 2002, Congressional disclosure.

Joe Caldwell Held Request: DCAA sent a request to Joe Caldwell for me to do a review on the IRAD project known as GATM (Global Air Traffic Management). When Caldwell didn't respond, DCAA contacted me. I informed the auditor that I had not received the request and asked them to send it directly to me, copying Caldwell. The DCAA auditor agreed.

May 1, 2003 – May 7, 2003 – GATM IRAD Information Request: When I received the DCAA request to review GATM IRAD, I contacted Lockheed Martin (Lisa Stephens) on May 1, 2003, to gather data on the GATM IRAD project and determine if it was related to any existing Lockheed Martin contracts. There was instant resistance. I was told on May 5, 2003, that I would have to sign a "non-disclosure" agreement to review the data, which I refused to do. Lisa Stephens stated in part.

"Lockheed Martin Corporate Policy requires execution of a Non-Disclosure Agreement prior to release of proprietary information to a third party."

The relevance is that I have worked at DCMA since around March 1994 and have never had to sign or been asked to sign non-disclosure agreements. This was a first. I also wasn't a third party. The only "third party" would be criminal investigators if this were a cost mischarging issue.

May 6, 2003, 7:07 AM– Contact DCMA Legal: I contacted DCMA Legal, Leigh Owens, and Gill Bass for a legal position on Lockheed Martin's demand to sign a non-disclosure agreement. I copied Lockheed Martin employees Marcia Farber, Lisa Stephens, and others, stating in part.

"*Ms. Owens or Ms. Bass: Please provide your legal perspective on LMAC request that I sign a non-disclosure agreement on the issues mentioned below. Additionally, I believe that it is inappropriate of Lockheed Martin to even ask me such a question. I handle proprietary data on a routine basis and have no desire to disclose it to another company. I question Lockheeds current motives in forcing me to now suddenly sign documentation, and your continual reluctance to release information that is routine in nature involving your charging of projects to overehead accounts.*"

"*If I find that LMAC has acted in an inappropriate manner in charging Independent Research & Development funds I will refer the matter to the proper investigation and fraud remedies regardless of any non-disclosure statement I sign.*"

That request was also documented in a May 27, 2003, e-mail from Leigh Owens, which stated in part.

"*Please remember that my initial involvement in this matter was at your request. On May 6 you requested my opinion relative to LMM's demand that you execute a non-disclosure agreement. As a result of your questions, I contacted Roger Graham to discuss my recommendation that you decline LMM's request.*"

I did not trust Leigh Owens. However, I was forced to work with Leigh Owens as a DCMA Attorney. So, at this point, Lockheed Martin Legal was also notified.

May 6, 2003 9:08 AM – Owens Response: Leigh Owens responded to me, stating in part.

"*It has long been our policy not to sign such disclosure statements. If we have a right of access to the materials under the terms of our contract with Lockheed, then access needs to be provided. The reason that we do not sign these types of agreements is that there are numerous statutes and regulations that prohibit our release of proprietary and trade secret information. DCMA employees are obligated by law to comply with these statutes, and so we have generally not seen any reason to execute a further nondisclosure agreements.*"

May 6, 2003, 9:16 AM – May 7, 2003: I forwarded the DCMA legal opinion to Lockheed Martin about 8 minutes after I received it. About 24 hours later, on May 7, 2003, at 9:35 AM, Lisa Stephens responded and asked in part.

"*Ken, our legal office wants to know the names and agency affiliation of all persons who would review the technical proprietary information, as well as the purpose of their review. Please provide this information to me, and I will convey it to Legal.*"

I responded on May 7, 2003, 10:19 AM, stating in part:

"I will be the primary one who reviews the information. Ms. Judi Klein (DCAA) may also review some of it. If I ever suspect fraud or contract mischarging (on any document I have in my possession, proprietary or not) I will refer fraud remedies and/or DoD IG.

For the record I am offended by the tone of your e-mails and the inference that I may send proprietary information to a competitor company. I routinely handle LMAC proprietary data and have never sent it to a competitor company."

The relevance is that Lockheed Martin remained intransigent in providing data. Before 2003, I would rate the facility where I worked as a hostile workplace, which explains the July 26, 2002, report to Congress. Working conditions were altered and deteriorated to the point documented herein. Meaning, working conditions became worse after July 26, 2002.

On May 8, 2003, Marcia Farber entered the e-mail chain and copied Joe Caldwell. This was the start of Falsified Trail 1.

<u>May 8, 2003 – Complaint to Joe Caldwell</u>: From May 1, 2003, to May 7, 2003, my Lockheed Martin point of contact was Lisa Stephens, although others were copied on the e-mail trail, including Lockheed Martin employee Marcia Farber. Even DCMA Legal representatives Leigh Owens and Gill Bass were on some communications, including those with DCAA.

On May 8, 2003, Marcia Farber interceded in the e-mail trail and copied Joe Caldwell regarding my request to review the GATM IRAD. Marcia Farber stated in part.

"Frankly, I consider your remarks insulting and unprofessional and resent your accusations.

The Company requires that Lockheed Martin proprietary Information be controlled and we are simply following the process required to insure it is controlled. This is a Company requirement that you have evidently taken personally."

Relevance is, I worked at the Lockheed Martin facility since 1994 and was never denied proprietary information in this fashion. This was the first resistance I have seen. Also, when Lockheed Martin is in trouble, Lockheed Martin contacts the DCMA management for assistance. Here, Marcia Farber contacted Joe Caldwell. I responded in kind to Lockheed Martin senior management in Fort Worth, Dain Hancock.

It is noteworthy that the email communications exhibited hostile overtones. It is also noteworthy that management really didn't care. Venting in internal emails kept external venting to a minimum. That's because the facility had deteriorated to that degree. Meaning, altered working conditions.

There was a long weekend, so I responded on May 12, 2003.

Contact Lockheed Martin Senior Management (Dain Hancock) at Ft. Worth

May 12, 2003 – Email to Dain Hancock: I contacted Dain Hancock to set the record straight regarding the actions of Lockheed Martin employees towards me and to correct the inaccurate information sent to Joe Caldwell. Email distribution included:

Lockheed Martin Personnel: Dain Hancock, Marcia Farber, Lee Rhyant, David Glidewell, Kim Herrington, Rick Elliott, Lisa Stephens.

DCMA Management/Legal Personnel: DCMA Agency Director General Edward Harrington, Keith Ernst (DCMA District East Director), Sallie Flavin (DCMA Deputy Director), Colonel James Wright, Ben Chaffman, Joe Caldwell, Phillip Perry (1st Level Supervisor), Leigh Owens, Gill Bass. (DCAA Auditor was also copied)

I stated in part.

"*Below you will find an e-mail where Ms. Marsha Farber (Lockheed Martin Aeronautics Company (LMAC) employee at Marietta, Ga.) contacted my management regarding my remarks, which she interpreted, as insulting and unprofessional. These remarks by Ms. Farber are a misrepresentation of the truth and will lead to inflame an already sensitive situation between Defense Contract Management Agency (DCMA) and myself. I will provide the correct facts below leading up to these events and will then request information on what you plan on doing to correct the situation with Ms. Farber.*

I was requested by the Defense Contract Audit Agency (DCAA) to do a review on an Independent Research & Development (IRAD) project involving Global Air Traffic Management (GATM). The controversy began when LMAC provided information on the development and testing of the C-130J mission Computer versus GATM. I was requested by DCAA to provide a technical analysis on the situation. Since the C-130J is a commercial venture already under contract and the C-130J Mission computer is part of that commercial venture, I was suspicious of contract mis-charging."

"*When Ms. Farber contacted Mr. Caldwell (DCMA Marietta, GA, Operations Manager) she opens a sensitive area of conflict between DCMA management and myself. Ms. Farber presented inaccurate information and made me out to be the villain on unprofessional conduct.*"

May 12, 2003 Hancock Changes Distribution: Dain Hancock responded to my May 12, 2003 e-mail and changed the distribution to include Lee Rhyant, Ross Reynolds, Sandra Shoemaker, Jay Brozost, John McCarthy, James Wright, and Thomas Heiserman. Dain Hancock stated.

"*Mr. Pedeleose,*

Thank you for your email of this morning. I appreciate the input, and I am disappointed to see that this situation has apparently deteriorated to the point that you felt compelled to write to me. I apologize that resolution did not come much sooner and much easier.

I have requested Ms. Sandra Shoemaker (VP of Integrated Company Operations) to immediately get personally engaged and bring this issue to a satisfactory resolution. She should be in contact with you shortly."

Management Silence/Shunning (16 Days)

From May 12, 2003, until May 27, 2003, DCMA and Lockheed Martin senior management were silent. I had communications with DCMA Legal (Leigh Owens and Gill Bass) regarding Lockheed Martin; however, I was surprised that Sandra Shoemaker never contacted me.

Non-Management Communications

Exclusive Meeting (Coordination) with Colonel Wright: Leigh Owens, May 27, 2003, 8:51 AM e-mail, among other issues, documented a private meeting on May 16, 2003, as follows.

"*As I have previously advised you, my May 16 meeting with Mr. Graham and Col. Wright was at Mr. Graham's request.*"

Shun Me – Talk with Lockheed Martin: The exclusive meeting between Leigh Owens, Roger Graham, and Colonel Wright is typical practice. This means going to the Colonel when Lockheed Martin is in trouble and limiting witnesses. Most importantly, I am shunned while DCMA management meets with Lockheed Martin. No management conversation with me and no effort to resolve the situation. Only inflame the situation via silence and shunning (altered work conditions).

Re-Contact Lockheed Martin – Dain Hancock & Sandra Shoemaker

May 21, 2003 7:07 AM: With my management staff in shunning mode (altered work conditions), I contacted Dain Hancock and Sandra Shoemaker again for assistance, stating in part.

"*I would like to begin working with you on a permanent resolution of issues. My main request is that you please have your local company attorney Mr. Roger Ghram (I am not sure of the spelling of his name) begin working with me versus using Ms. Leigh Owens (DCMA Attorney) as a liaison. The reason for my request stems from the fact that there is a lot of turmoil within DCMA that has continually caused me to elevate issues far past what I should have. I have been sickened by these events however that is the DCMA pattern of practice: All Issues Are Elevated for Resolution. This. pattern has left me exposed to reprisal actions and a hostile work environment.*

Beginning immediately (until I get the internal situation resolved), and with specific matters regarding LMAC (especially stubborn employees), I would like the opportunity to resolve the issues within house versus continually elevating issues that can be resolved at low levels."

This email caused Colonel Wright to plan a tactical ambush.

Colonel Wright Shuns Me - Coordinates Tactical Ambush Behind the Scenes

Electronic trail shows Colonel Wright was the catalyst in a tactical ambush versus resolving the situation or even trying to talk to me. Meaning, shunning was a weapon to inflame the situation. Evidence trail is as follows.

May 21, 2003 9:21 AM – Shoemaker Forwards Email: Joe Caldwell provided a partial e-mail trail where Sandra Shoemaker forwarded my May 21, 2003 e-mail to Lee Rhyant and Jay Brozost (unknown who Brozost is). Lee Rhyant forwarded to Wilma Walker (unknown) stating: "*Please forward to the Colonel*". Wilma Walker forwarded the e-mail to Colonel Wright minutes later.

The relevance is that Dain Hancock or Sandra Shoemaker had no intention of resolving issues. My May 21, 2003 e-mail was sent at 7:07 AM and was relayed three times before being sent to Colonel Wright at 9:04 AM the same day, less than 2 hours later.

Colonel Wright started the coordination of the tactical ambush (Falsified Trail 1) about 10 minutes after he received the e-mail from Wilma Walker. Colonel Wright/DCMA continued shunning me.

May 22, 2003 9:14 AM Colonel Wright Gathers Ideas & Coordinates: Colonel Wright e-mailed Ben Chaffman, Leigh Owens, Bruce Krasker, and Joe Cass stating:

"*Mr. Pedeleose continues to go around management and is going direct to President of the company and of course the DoD/IG. Any advice in dealing with this. Open to any ideas, here in Marietta.*"

The relevance is that Colonel Wright coordinated efforts against me, showed no concern for fraud, made no effort to resolve or calm issues, continued shunning me, and sarcastically mentioned the DoD IG. Colonel Wright's behavior is typical of DCMA, contributing to this book and my continual need to write to Congress. Colonel Wright's e-mail distribution was tactical as follows.

Bruce Krasker & Leigh Owens: Colonel Wright copying Bruce Krasker and Leigh Owens was a precursor to tactical retaliation (weaponization and lawfare). This is based on the foresight of Falsified Trail 3, where Bruce Krasker, Leigh Owens, and Dan Meyer would engage in a detailed, multitiered con game against Senator Charles Grassley, erasing any doubt and confirming that weaponized government and lawfare does exist.

May 23, 2003 10:01 AM Chaffman to Caldwell: Chaffman e-mails Caldwell and states, "*I am still looking for e-mail with earlier direction.*" It is unknown what is meant by this exchange.

The relevance is that during the silence, something was being planned behind my back. However, I did have contact with Leigh Owens and acknowledged that I was basically giving up on the situation.

May 27, 2003 9:16 AM – Altered Work Conditions – Weaponized Legal: The morning of May 27, 2003, I had given up on Dain Hancock, Sandra Shoemaker, and DCMA management. I also had no confidence in DCMA legal since it was weaponized in favor of management, thus altering working conditions. I sent an e-mail to Leigh Owens stating in part.

"*I will work through you regarding the information needed from LMAC. If they do not respond this week I will contact you so that you may contact LMAC/Roger Gram.*"

"*Remaining issues are the fact that Mr. Hancock indicated that Ms. Shoemaker would get with me. Obviously she has not.*"

"*Regarding me talking with you I would prefer that as a last resort. You consider it your position to defend management and others (LMAC) against DCMA employees versus avoiding conflicts to begin with. I believe that your job should be to advise management on how to stay out of trouble versus only defending them when they get in trouble.*"

"*If at all possible lets resolve this by e-mails. You have been giving me further anxiety by your vigorous defense of management when they trash employees careers. Allowing the exclusive meeting between Roger Gram and Colonel Wright on May 16, 2003 further caused me to lose faith in you. (My mind is made up on this issue.)*"

"*Translation, your giving me headaches and stomachaches. I consider you as the enemy although I am forced to work with you due to your position as legal counsel.*"

The May 16, 2003, private meeting between Owens, Graham, and Wright was concerning. Regardless, I abdicated the process to Leigh Owens. However, the tactical ambush was underway.

Tactical Weaponized Letter of Direction (LOD) After 16 Days of Shunning

May 27, 2003 (3 PM): Joe Caldwell gave me a written LOD after about 16 days of first contact with Lockheed Martin. This insulated DCMA from reprisal actions and, most importantly, stopped the need for shunning. Shifted the blame to me like I was at fault. Caldwell stated in part.

"*I have been provided with a copy of your May 21 2003 e-mail to Ms Sandra Shoemaker and Mr. Dain Hancock of Lockheed Martin and your 12 May e-mail to Mr. Hancock. As you should already know, all communications with the company's senior Executive leadership, including Messrs. Hancock and Rhyant, must be coordinated with DCMA Lockheed Martin Marietta management. This Command's managers must be aware of and involved in any issue significant enough to require the attention and involvement of the company's senior management officials. Likewise, all communications with Lockheed Martin attorneys must be through our legal channels, e.g. Ms. Owens. You are directed to coordinate any and all communications with company senior leadership with Col Wright, Mr. Chaffman, or myse lf, and any and all communications with company attorneys with Ms. Owens prior to issuance.*"

Caldwell handwrote on the LOD: "*Hand Delivered – Employee Refused to Sign 5/27/03 – 3PM*"

The point is, rather than talk with me to resolve the issue, I was silenced. However, DCMA and Caldwell left a trail that shows efficiency or concern is not the issue.

DCMA – No Concern for Efficiency of the Service or Contractor Oversight

Shunned & Singled Out: Joe Caldwell was copied on the May 12, 2003, e-mail to Dain Hancock, as well as my entire chain of command up to DCMA Directors Ernst and Harrington. No one mentioned the communication or the DCMA policy regarding communications with Lockheed Martin senior officials. I was clearly tactically shunned and singled out.

Legal Writing Tone – Weaponized Document: The LOD had a legal tone that Joe Caldwell would not have used. More than likely, Leigh Owens or a DCMA attorney wrote the letter because Joe Caldwell had a lethargic demeanor, which places Caldwell into the category of a surrogate.

DCMA Management Doesn't Care: At the time the retaliatory weaponized LOD was written, one of my substantiated allegations (June 30, 2003) was sent out in draft copy on May 23, 2003. DCMA Executive Director, Contractor Management Operations, Robert W. Schmitt, concurred that;

"*DCMA did not comply with FAR 44.304* (Federal Acquisition Regulation) *and it's internal policy regarding Contractor Purchasing System Review (CPSR). A purchasing system review has not been performed since August of 1998 and the ACO does not have a surveillance plan to monitor the contractor's oversight of its' subcontractor.*"

The June 30, 2003, substantiated allegation stated: "*DCMA oversight of contract administration for the EFI on the C-130H aircraft was inadequate.*"

The November 28, 2001, Criminal Vulnerability Report (CRV) #2002-01, with Criminal Vulnerability Report (CRV) (January 10, 2002) cover memo, stated in Attachment A in part.

"*1. Government officials at DCMA-LM Aero* (my office management) *knew the proposal and termination claim contained inflated prices because of the inclusion of duplicative set up costs and the government officials at DCMA-LM Aero negotiated the price proposal knowing the proposal to contain false information...*"

The aforesaid and my substantiated disclosures in Chapter 1 show that DCMA has zero concern for ethics and zero concern for proper contract administration. The LOD was a weapon that insulated DCMA and shifted attention to the charade of a personnel action that singled me out. The LOD had no legitimate reason other than a weapon used in lawfare. Knowing this, I began gathering evidence to prove DCMA management was retaliating against me and covering up for Lockheed Martin. That documentation traced directly back to Colonel Wright, who was cheered on by Keith Ernst.

Joe Caldwell's Memory Versus Electronic Trail

<u>May 28, 2003 – Memorandum of Record for Case 87535</u>: Case 87535 may have been an early version of a reprisal case started over me. Nevertheless, within Case 87535, I documented what Joe Caldwell said regarding the May 27, 2003 LOD. The statement of interest is as follows.

"*I asked Mr. Caldwell which member of management told him to write me up and he could not remember.*

The key point is that electronic trails provide better documentation than Caldwell's memory. Meaning, the electronic trail confirms Colonel Wright as the coordinator behind the scenes in the weaponized entrapment/ambush (lawfare). The date of May 27, 2003, is the pivot point.

Electronic Trail Relay for Entrapment & Ambush Leads to Colonel Wright

<u>May 27, 2003 Entrapment/Ambush - 3 ½ Hours Later</u>: On May 27, 2003 (<u>6:30 PM</u>), Sandra Shoemaker responded to an e-mail that I sent to her <u>6 days</u> earlier on May 21, 2003, stating in part.

"*Regarding your e-mail message to Mr. Hancock and me dated 21 May, please be advised that Mr. Roger Graham is a Lockheed Martin attorney assigned at Marietta who represents the legal interests of the Lockheed Martin Corporation, and thus he cannot serve as your personal liaison for DCMA matters replacing Ms. Leigh Owens, the DCMA Counsel at Marietta. Mr. Graham. can engage in a dialogue with DCMA attorneys in an effort to facilitate resolution of issues, but I am advised that the standards of professional conduct applicable to attorneys would not permit him to engage in liaison activities directly with you.*"

Shoemaker's e-mail, received <u>3 ½ hours</u> after I initially got a LOD, reeks of manipulation and tactical collusion between DCMA and Lockheed Martin. However, there was no positive proof.

Notably, a Lockheed Martin attorney did engage with Colonel Wright, with Leigh Owens present, as to what happened on May 16, 2003, per Leigh Owens' May 27, 2003 e-mail stating that the:

"*May 16 meeting with Mr. Graham and Col. Wright was at Mr. Graham's request.*"

The relevance is that Lockheed Martin attorneys engage with DCMA management, not just DCMA attorneys, which puts Sandra Shoemaker's comments in question.

One question that arises is why Colonel Wright and Leigh Owens met privately with Roger Graham. Why wasn't Joe Caldwell present? Why didn't Colonel Wright or Leigh Owens give a readout or synopsis of the meeting to anyone to resolve the situation? Why was I shunned and my first level supervisor excluded? The answers can be found as follows.

<u>Electronic Trail Relay</u>: The lack of candor in the Wright, Owens, Graham, May 16, 2003, meeting confirms the shunning and maleficence aspects documented in this book. The electronic trail relay (like baseball relay throws) proves this point.

<u>May 28, 2003 1:05 PM</u>: I responded to Sandra Shoemaker's e-mail and honestly was not even considering the LOD not to contact Lockheed Martin senior management since Sandra Shoemaker <u>contacted me</u>. I <u>did not</u> initiate the conversation and asked nothing from Shoemaker, stating in part:

"*The issue of data is being resolved, although very slowly. In Mr. Hancock's message to me on Monday, May 12,2003 6:00 PM Mr. Hancock indicated that "I have requested Ms. Sandra Shoemaker (VP of Integrated Company Operations) to immediately get personally engaged and bring this issue to a satisfactory resolution. She should be in contact with you shortly.*""

"*I have obviously taken this remark out of context since the only contact was your company Attorney (Mr. Graham) contacting Ms. Owens and then meeting with my commanding officer Colonel Wright.*"

"*I consider LMAC as a partner in the reprisal against me.*"

Relevance is, Sandra Showmaker <u>contacted me</u> via electronic trail (e-mail) immediately after Joe Caldwell issued the LOD. This would suggest some type of prior tactical coordination. The following day, Colonel Wright admitted to coordination.

Colonel Wright Admits to Tactical "Coordination"

<u>May 28, 2003 2:18 PM (Joe Caldwell – Front Person)</u>: I complained to Colonel Wright and Ben Chaffman about the actions of Joe Caldwell's LOD. I stated in part.

"*Mr. Caldwell could not remember which member of management directed/encouraged him to take this action.*" Thus, Caldwell didn't deny that the coordination came from higher management.

I asked Colonel Wright and Ben Chaffman the following specific question.

"*Very respectfully: Did either of you direct/encourage Mr. Caldwell to write the Letter of Direction?*" Colonel Wright later responded as follows.

May 28, 2003 4:14 PM (Coordinated Management Decision): Colonel Wright responded to my May 28, 2003 2:18 PM e-mail stating: "*Ken this was a coordinated management decision that I directed Mr Caldwell to take.*" Colonel Wright copied Joe Caldwell on the e-mail.

Colonel Wright took responsibility in writing. Coordination would explain the future tactical timing of emails and the way emails (electronic trails) were relayed quickly. Meaning, the next day, Lockheed Martin would directly communicate with Colonel Wright, as the subsequent electronic evidence and relays show.

Sandra Shoemaker Electronically Relays Directly to Colonel Wright

May 29, 2003 7:34 AM Coordinated Entrapment/Ambush Complete: Sandra Shoemaker relayed (forwarded) my response to her May 27, 2003 e-mail directly to Colonel Wright, stating;

"*Col. Wright,*

I am attaching the last communiqué I received from Mr. Pedeleose.

Sandra"

The noticeable point is the old electronic relay versus the new tactical electronic relay.

Old Electronic Relay: Sandra Shoemaker's old electronic relay of May 21, 2003, 9:21 AM went to Lee Rhyant and Jay Brozost (unknown who Brozost is). Lee Rhyant relayed/forwarded to Wilma Walker (unknown) on May 22, 2003, 8:54 AM, stating: "*Please forward to the Colonel*". Wilma Walker relayed the e-mail to Colonel Wright about 10 minutes later.

New Tactical Electronic Relay: Shoemaker's new relay on May 29, 2003, 7:34 AM went directly to Colonel Wright and only copied Lee Rhyant.

Three Times to Colonel Wright: Lockheed Martin went directly to Colonel Wright 3 times. The first was May 16, 2003, with Roger Graham. The second was May 21, 2003. And the third was May 29, 2003. This suggests Colonel Wright was a tactical focal point of coordination. However, Colonel Wright would prove the focal point via another electronic email relay as follows.

Colonel Wright's No Words or Instructions Electronic Trail "Relay"

May 29, 2003, 9:15 AM: Colonel Wright relayed/forwarded Shoemaker's May 29, 2003, e-mail to Leigh Owens, Ben Chaffman, and Joe Caldwell with no words or instructions. This indicated prior plans and tactical coordination (conspiracy), which reeks of ambush and entrapment. Like a Relay in baseball to take out a runner. Something trained for as was the next relay.

Colonel Wright's "Ditto" Email Relay – DCMA Director's Level Retaliation

May 29, 2003, 7:34 AM: By late May 2003, working conditions were altered and hostile. I felt like a punching bag with the retaliatory LOD, shunning, and no resolution to my concerns. I sent an e-mail to Colonel Wright and Dain Hancock, copied to Sandra Shoemaker, Joe Caldwell, and Ben Chaffman, stating in part:

"The actions of Ms. Marsha Farber have caused a serious rift in my relationship with LMAC and DCMA management. I consider the Letter of Direction as a reprisal action against me caused by the actions of Ms. Marsha Farber. This is unacceptable and directly affects my career, health, and chances for advancement. To resolve this situation I request the following:

1: DCMA to rescind the Letter of Direction

2: If the Letter of Direction is in my personnel file it will be removed immediately and destroyed.

3: No further adverse action against me by Lockheed Martin Aeronautics Company or DCMA

4: An apology from Ms. Marsha Farber or Lockheed Martin Aeronautics Company

This incident is at the point that it can be resolved. I will include it as part of my reprisal case that now includes LMAC. It is not my fault that LMAC is non-responsive and cannot maintain records or audit trails for their finances."

The relevance is that the DCMA's hostile work environment, chaos, and shunning had an effect. Meaning, the hostile work environment, chaos and shunning were tactical weapons. Colonel Wright again took advantage and relayed more electronic communication.

May 29, 2003 3:34 PM- The "Ditto" E-mail: Colonel Wright took my e-mail sent at 7:34 AM and relayed it to Joe Cass and Bruce Krasker, and copied Keith Ernst (DCMA East Director) and Steven Bogus (DCMA Deputy Director). Colonel Wright stated only the word "Ditto". This would imply that Cass, Krasker, Ernst, and Bogusz were in on the tactical plot. Meaning, why didn't Colonel Wright send to Joe Caldwell? Why send so high in the chain of command? It's because I was a high value target. My resume in Chapter 1 proves as much.

The word "Ditto" implies two of the same things. Meaning, Colonel Wright relayed my other e-mail sent directly to Colonel Wright by Sandra Shoemaker. Something was planned in advance.

Keith Ernst would cheer on the retaliation in an email (electronic trail).

Keith Ernst (DCMA Director) Cheers Retaliation – The Trophy

May 29, 2003 5:42 PM: Keith Ernst replied to Colonel Wright, stating:

"*Jim, Thanks for keeping me up-to-date on this. Hope Mr. Pedeleose figures out that he needs to abide by the rules and not blame everything on retaliation. R/Keith*"

The retaliation (weaponized entrapment/ambush) was cheered on by a DCMA Director. It's like a coach telling the team "Good job," where Keith Ernst was aware of the trap. Keith Ernst played a major role in Falsified Trail 3, as would Steven Bogus, Bruce Krasker, and Leigh Owens.

Wright relayed Ernst's comments like a trophy to Joe Caldwell and Ben Chaffman the following day, with the phrase "*FYI*" (For Your Information), because Wright was the coordinator.

Colonel Wright's "Actions" During DoD IG Visit

May 29, 2003: I learned Joe Caldwell was planning disciplinary action against me and contacted the union representative. I copied Colonel Wright on May 29, 2003, at 3:43 PM, copying DCMA senior management, including Ben Chaffman, Keith Ernst, Edward Harrington (then DCMA Director), Sallie Flavin (then DCMA Deputy Director), Leigh Owens, and union officials, to state.

"*Mr. Joe Caldwell will be giving me disciplinary action this monday (possibly) we need to set a time frame when you are available.*

Mr. Caldwell is acting on orders and coordination from Colonel Wright. His actions are reprisal due to the fact that a LMAC employee called him and gave information about me that was false. This also has roots in past fraud issues."

Colonel Wright responded back to all on distribution May 29, 2003, at 4:00 PM, stating:

"*Ken, again your off-base. My actions have nothing to do with reprisal nor past fraud issue. As you well know the DoD/I G has been visiting us this week, and we will take the appropriate action necessary when we receive their findings/recommendation. The issue here is your failure to comply with your Letter of Direction regarding communication with LM management and, again using the chain of command.*"

Colonel Wright took responsibility for the entrapment/ambush against me by stating "*My* (Colonel Wright) *actions*". This was the second time Wright mentioned the DoD IG. The first was May 22, 2003 stating "*of course the DoD/IG*". Wright admitted the DoD IG was visiting the same week I was scheduled to be reprimanded.

Reprimanded for Insubordination By the Surrogate Joe Caldwell

July 9, 2003 – Reprimand: Joe Caldwell was the management surrogate who reprimanded me. The reprimand by Joe Caldwell to me stated in part.

"*This is to notify you that I have decided to reprimand you for your offense of insubordination. This action is taken in accordance with DCMA One Book Chapter 15.6.3.3.6, Maintaining Discipline.*"

"*You were issued a Notice of Proposed Reprimand dated 3 June 2003, and delivered to you on that date. You replied to that notice in writing on 9 June 2003 with follow-up clarification requested and provided on 12 June 2003. The following comments are made concerning your reply:*

a) Your reply confirmed that you contacted Senior Lockheed Martin executives without prior coordination in direct violation of my May 27, 2003 letter of direction to you.

b) Your reply provides no indication of apology, remorse or understanding that your actions were inappropriate."

"*After consideration of your reply, your past record and review of the Douglas factors, I have decided that the charge of insubordination is fully supported by the facts and warrants this reprimand.*"

"*You may bring any questions about this action or your grievance rights to me and I will explain any points that are not clear to you. If you desire to discuss the procedural aspects of this action, your grievance rights, or review pertinent regulations, you may call Mr. Derek Kushmerek, Human Resource Specialist in the Human Resources Directorate...*"

July 10, 2003 9:40 AM: I contacted Derek Kushmerek and copied my entire DCMA chain of command up to DCMA Directors Keith Ernst and General Edward Harrington. Stating in part.

"*Mr. Kushmerek,*

I just received a reprimand from Mr. Joseph Caldwell (Operations Manager) that was part of a concerted effort involving Colonel James Wright (Commanding Officer) who indicated that this was part of a coordinated management decision that he directed Mr. Caldwell to take. I have included my chain of command on this e-mail as notification that there were deleberate efforts against me (concerted actions) to damage my career."

After the email to Kushmerek, Colonel Wright drastically changed the story.

Colonel Wright Changes Story to Blame Surrogate (Joe Caldwell)

July 11, 2003 10:32 AM: Colonel Wright waited over 24 hours to respond, stating in part:

"*Ken, for the record, no one on my management staff is taking any action to damage your career. We are trying to work all issues at the lowest level. Any action that we have taken has been with the goal of making you a more productive member of the organization. I did not direct Mr Caldwell to take this action- - -it was Mr Caldwell's decision that he then coordinated with me and the management staff. Your career is in your own hands.*"

Colonel Wright drastically changed position from taking responsibility on May 28, 2003 for "*coordinated*" decisions and May 29, 2003 for "*actions*".

Wright had direct communications with Lockheed Martin on May 16, 2003 (Roger Graham), May 22, 2003 (Lee Rhyant/Wilma Walker), and May 29, 2003 (Sandra Shoemaker).

On May 29, 2003, Colonel Wright sent an email with no words and another email containing the word "Ditto" to DCMA senior leadership, implying prior knowledge and coordination of concerted plans.

Colonel Wright mentioned the DoD IG in e-mails on May 22, 2003 and on May 29, 2003.

Keith Ernst even cheered on the entrapment/ambush on May 29, 2003. (The Trophy)

The bottom line is Colonel Wright was responsible, and Joe Caldwell was the surrogate.

Conclusion is as follows...

Conclusion – Nightmares, Shunning, No Resolution, Relay Emails, Retaliation

Evidence shows Colonel Wright coordinated Falsified Trail 1. Colonel Wright's actions followed a pattern of action and reaction to me trying to resolve government corruption and malfeasance. The first action was Nightmares where DCMA and Colonel Wright were caught with their "pants down". Nightmares started as follows.

Nightmare 1 - July 26, 2002 Report to Congress: Colonel Wrights retaliatory actions followed the July 26, 2002, 90 Page report sent to 57 members of Congress, President Bush and Secretary of Defense Rumsfeld. This report was well known at DCMA HQ level and Colonel Wright either knew or should have known.

Around the time of September 24, 2002 Myra Tate (a co-worker at the time) also informed me that whatever I was doing was shaking up management. This was most likely due to the July 26, 2002, 90 Page report to Congress that did make it back to DCMA Headquarters (Senior Management).

Nightmare 2 - October 30, 2002 DOD IG Announcement Letter: The DoD IG announcement letter for the items being investigated by the DoD IG, as a result of the July 26, 2002 report to Congress, was titled: "*Audit of Allegations of the Defense Contract Management Agency's Performance In Administering Selected Weapon Systems Contracts (Project No. D2003AB-0017)*". A copy of the letter was sent to DCMA.

Colonel Wright was directly responsible for the C-130, F-22, and C-5 programs at my facility.

Nightmare 3 - March 12, 2003 - Ernest Fitzgerald Visit: Ernie Fitzgerald visited the Marietta, GA facility and met with Colonel Wright and Ben Chaffman and all signatories on the July 26, 2002 report to Congress. Involvement of Senator Grassley's office may also have been mentioned.

Fitzgerald was definitely a nightmare for Colonel Wright since I was now aligned with possibly the highest rated whistleblower in DoD and military-industrial complex history. My observations were that Colonel Wright was stunned, almost speechless during the meeting. Fitzgerald once stated Colonel Wright looked as if he was "*hit in the head with a wet corn cob*". Meaning, hit in the head with a heavy weighted object and left stunned.

Nightmare 4 - March 13, 2003 – DoD IG On-Site Visit: On or about this date IG auditors Thomas Bartoszek and Mary Hoover visited Marietta, GA. The intended visits were discussed on October 21, 2002. I remember a courtesy visit to the command suite where Colonel Wright resides.

Nightmare 5 – May 29, 2003 – DoD IG Visit: Colonel Wright stated in an e-mail to me:

"*As you well know the DoD/I G has been visiting us this week, and we will take the appropriate action necessary when we receive their findings/recommendation.*"

The 5 nightmares confirm Colonel Wright was well informed of my whistleblowing.

Keith Ernst (DCMA director) was also well informed of my whistleblowing and cheered on retaliation on May 29, 2003, stating to Colonel Wright:

"*Jim, Thanks for keeping me up-to-date on this. Hope Mr. Pedeleose figures out that he needs to abide by the rules and not blame everything on retaliation. R/Keith*"

Shunning & No Resolution: A major part of Falsified Trail 1 is the weaponized shunning and no response to issues. Any professional management staff would resolve issues quickly through communication. The issues at play in Falsified Trail 1 occupied the majority of May 2003. Meaning, I was shunned for days and weeks for issues that could have been resolved in a day, if not minutes.

Relay Emails: The most objective part of Falsified Trail 1 was the way emails were relayed between Colonel Wright, Lockheed Martin, and DCMA senior management. One email had no words or instructions. This objectively proved that a tactical concerted action was at play, most notably, following the shunning and no response to resolve issues/conflicts.

The end result was that Falsified Trail 1 worked smoothly for DCMA. I was defenseless.

However, Falsified Trail 2 did not have the same happy, trophy, ending for Colonel Wright, Ben Chaffman and DCMA.

Trying to "Swat" me backfired very badly and was a watershed moment that catapulted my whistle-blowing efforts to a national level.

Falsified Trail 2: August 14, 2003 Swatting Tactic by Armed Guards

Falsified Trail 2 was brute force only, falsified charges, and suborning perjury. In current terms, this equates to being "Swatted" (calling in law enforcement on falsified charges). Colonel Wright and Ben Chaffman were the primary perpetrators, with Lockheed Martin armed guards assisting. The evidence trail starts with Nightmare 6, which was Substantiated Allegation 2 in my resume.

Nightmare 6 - June 30, 2003 IG Report (Electronic Flight Instrument (EFI)) (D-2003-115): This was Substantiated Allegation 2 from a DoD Hotline complaint I submitted in January 2001 that was revitalized in the July 26, 2002, report to Congress. The IG confirmed that the lack of DCMA and Program Office oversight led to more than 1,100 EFI failures over a 34-month period ending in October 2002, resulting in the grounding of 16 C-130H aircraft. The DoD IG stated: "*DCMA oversight of contract administration was inadequate.*"

The relevance is that the July 26, 2002, report to Congress was being substantiated, causing another nightmare for DCMA. However, DCMA was presented a target of opportunity for Falsified Trail 2.

Target of Opportunity – Lockheed Martin Shooting, Meridian, Mississippi

July 8, 2003: Douglas Williams, a Lockheed Martin employee at Meridian, Mississippi, engaged in an office shooting. This incident was a weaponized target of opportunity for DCMA to cover for whistleblower retaliation against me. Basically, seize the moment, ride the wave to victory, grasp public sentiment, and be a hero. Shortly after July 8, 2003, rumors emerged about potential firings that would eventually prove true.

Targeted to be Fired – Special Visits – "Hit Lists"

July 10, 2003: There was a memorandum of record that one of the co-signers to the July 26, 2002, report to Congress, Henry Hagel, "*was being targeted by management to be FIRED. A couple of weeks ago management & supervisor's had attended a human resources "Supervisory training" (June 23-27, 2003) course.*" Even though this was a "rumor," it shows that a conversation was taking place to fire individuals. This rumor was again repeated a few days later with variations.

July 18, 2003 – More Employees Targeted to be Fired: About a week after the first Memo for Record, another employee came forward with information about other potential firings. A memo of record was done by two employees this time, stating in part.

"*He said that management was going to fire one employee to "set an example." Management and supervisor's attended a one-week course from human resources "Supervisor's Training" (June 23-27 2003) course. At this course management and supervisor's learned techniques on how "to fire employees.*" My name was one of four employees targeted to be fired.

The memorandum of record specifically stated: "*one technique was to use the computer e mail trail of establishing a negative trend of objective evidence to fire employees.*" This explains why Colonel Wright brought in Joe Cass on his May 22, 2003, e-mail for Falsified Trail 1. Joe Cass was in the DCMA Human Resources office that was tactically training supervisors to fire employees.

Tactical Training to Fire Employees

November 19, 2003: The July 18, 2003 Memo for Record was mentioned in litigation, and a sworn statement was completed. The sworn statement stated in part.

"*In June 2003, supervisors at DCMA LMM attended a supervisory management training course in personnel management. Afterwards, someone who had attended the course stated to me that he expected more from the course, rather than just teaching supervisors how to fire employees and deal with difficult employees.*"

The individual making the sworn statement commented on the July 18, 2003 Memo for Record stated that he read the "*memorandum of our conversation, and agree to much of what he stated. However, no one has ever stated to me that management has a "hit list" and were specifically setting up him, Mr. Pedeleose, or any other employee to be fired.*

The rumors of firing employees were confirmed by two sources and a sworn statement. The term "hit list" was used to categorize the malicious, weaponized, plot to fire employees. The malicious plot was forwarded to the DoD IG, as was the July 9, 2003, reprimand (Falsified Trail 1).

Special DoD IG Visit

July 29-30, 2003: The July 9, 2003, reprimand and the July 10 & 18, 2003 memo for records got the attention of Jean Lewis (then DoD IG Chief of Staff). Jean Lewis sent Leonard Trahan (Director DoD Hotline), David Brothers (Investigator), and Vincent Stewart (Investigator) to visit the signatories of the July 26, 2003, report to Congress, along with local DCMA management.

The initial meeting was scheduled on the afternoon of July 29, 2003, at about 1400 hours. There was concern when no one was seen other than Colonel Wright escorting an unknown individual.

At about 14:30 hours, Colonel Wright's secretary informed my colleagues and me to go to a conference room upstairs, where Colonel Wright, Ben Chaffman, and Leigh Owens were already in a meeting with the visiting IG team. Again, DCMA Legal attorneys were protecting management.

Trahan went into a long-winded speech about the new Rumsfeld (overhauled) DoD personnel system, NSPS. Trahan indicated that most whistleblowers choose to remain anonymous; however, we choose to sign our names and send them out to the world. Trahan also made reference to Ernie Fitzgerald with the inference that what happened to him (Fitzgerald) will never happen again.

Following the meeting, Trahan indicated he wanted to talk to me for a few seconds off to the side. When alone, Trahan stated to me: "*You're their leader. They follow you. You're attracting a lot of attention to yourself*". The inference was that attention was being garnered for my allegations.

July 30, 2003: Trahan and his investigators did nothing to resolve the collusive actions by DCMA management. I was berated by one member of the IG team (Vincent Stewart) while the other investigator, and Trahan, watched.

No Name Business Card: At one point, a member of Trahan's team (Stewart) gave a business card that did not have a name and included the simple address of the Pentagon, Washington, DC. When I complained that I needed a specific location, David Brothers provided a specific address.

The IG visit served no other purpose than to in-brief and out-brief Colonel Wright.

July 31, 2003 – Sold Out E-mail Jean Lewis: The following day, an email was sent to Jean Lewis, with a copy to Ernie Fitzgerald and Senator Grassley's office, expressing how whistleblowers had been "sold out" by this visit. Ernie Fitzgerald faxed the e-mail back with comments from his book "The Pentagonists" with a conversation from a Lockheed employee, Henry Durham, stating:

"*When it became known that I might go outside with the problem, Mr. Paul Frech, the director of manufacturing, was sent to Chattanooga to see me. [Our] conversation was predictably short. The first thing he said was, "Do you know what happened to Ernie Fitzgerald, who went to Washington with some Lockheed problems?" When I said I didn't, Frech said, "He's now chief shit-house inspector for the Civil Service Commission and will never be able to get a good job as long as he lives".*" "[Erwin Kroll, "The Education of Henry Durham," reprinted from The Progressive, 1972]."

The Pentagonists was written in 1989, and the following shows that nothing has changed since then.

"Swatted" - Walked Out the Gate by Lockheed Martin Armed Guards

August 14, 2003: The rumors of potential firings to *"set an example"* were proven true. I was escorted off the Lockheed Martin facility by Lockheed Martin's armed guards. I did a lengthy memo for record; however, the following are salient points.

August 14, 2003 Morning: At about 8:30 AM, I was in the command suite with Ben Chaffman. This was to support statements in a pending EEO case. I met with Ben Chaffman and there was no indication of anything wrong and left about 11:30 AM. No incidents took place. All was well, so I went to lunch and then returned to my office on South campus. My office was about 2 miles from Chaffman's office, which was at North Campus.

The afternoon was also uneventful, and I handled administrative tasks and my job.

August 14, 2003 Afternoon: At about 3:00 PM, I was summoned to the command suite by Ben Chaffman through my then supervisor. I called Ben Chaffman, who stated, *"follow my direction"*. I proceeded to the command suite around 3:30 and discovered that my badge wouldn't open the security gates. I was eventually let in by another employee. The next step was being "Swatted".

"Swatted" & Escorted off the Facility - Retaliation Enacted

August 14, 2003: I arrived at Command Suite, and Colonel Wright and Ben Chaffman were in Colonel Wright's office. I was directed to hand over my facility access badges and informed that I would be escorted off the facility. I was also told that an investigator would be in contact with me. At some point when I was facing Colonel Wright and Ben Chaffman the room had filled behind me with Lockheed Martin Armed Guards and other personnel. I asked the Lockheed Guards if I was under arrest, and they stated that I was not.

From there, 4 Lockheed Martin Armed Guards escorted me out the door. Then two Lockheed Martin armed guards split off, and two-armed guards (Captain David Abels (Badge 554669) and Rick Bissel) remained with me until I reached my vehicle.

I was never told what I was charged with. I cooperated with the guards who searched my vehicle and seized my vehicle facility access placard. The following is the "Swatting" inventory list.

"Swatting" Personnel and 911 Call: I was aware of the following on August 14, 2003.

1. Started with 4 Lockheed Martin armed guards, later reduced to 2.

2. Air Force Criminal Investigator (OSI) Bob Bournival was present.

3. DCMA supervisor at the time Frank Carey was present.

4. Colonel Wright was physically shaken and could barely stand up, much like a scared child.

August 18, 2003: I later discovered other things, some of which were documented in an August 18, 2003 memo for record by another employee of a conversation with Colonel Wright, including.

5. Call to Cobb County 911 for assistance.

6. Two Cobb County Police vehicles originally responded and may have left prior to my arrival or were hidden; I'm not sure.

7. Two Lockheed Martin Security vehicles.

8. The sheriff's car was seen driving on a back road. Probably to surround the scene (my guess).

9. Lockheed Martin issued a Be On the Look Out (BOLO) for me personally with my photo.

10. "Going Postal": The August 18, 2003, Memo for Record Stated in Part:

"Col Wright stated that it was his responsibility to provide for the safety of the DCMA members here and that if he thought someone was going to go "Postal" then, he would be have to do something about it. I must have given the impression that I didn't understand (I actually couldn't understand the phrase he used "Going Postal", right away) and he repeated the phrase three times that I clearly remember."

Colonel Wright never mentioned my name. However, I was the only person escorted off the facility. "Going Postal" is a term used for someone on a shooting rampage, like the Lockheed Martin person at Meridian, Mississippi. This was the retaliation pretext to falsified charges against me.

Wright and Chaffman combined whistleblower retaliation with "Swatting". An administrative shock & awe scenario that would later be proven a total farce, even involving suborning perjury. However, Nightmare 7 would happen within the hour. This started a watershed moment.

Nightmare 7 – News Media Within the Hour - Phone Went Silent

News Media Attention Spread & Stayed Engaged

August 14, 2003 4:30 PM – 5 PM (Approximate): I immediately went home and tried to call Senator Grassley's office to relay news of the retaliation. I had two numbers in my automatic dialer that had the 202-area code. One was for Senator Grassley's staff, and the other was for a reporter from Hearst News, Eric Rosenberg. I chose one number, hoping it was Senator Grassley's staff.

I chose the wrong number, and Eric Rosenberg answered. I apologized for the wrong number, and Rosenberg asked what was going on. I informed Rosenberg of what had happened, and Rosenberg asked if I would like him to make some calls. I agreed.

I gave Rosenberg the names of Dain Hancock and Sandra Showmaker from Lockheed Martin, as well as Colonel Wright and Ben Chaffman. Chaffman was called first.

Rosenberg called Chaffman's home phone number within the same hour I was escorted off the facility. Chaffman answered, and Rosenberg informed Chaffman that a story was being written, and asked if he (Chaffman) had any comments. At that point, Rosenberg stated the phone "went silent" or "there was silence", I forget which phrase. Chaffman then indicated to call DCMA public relations. This started Nightmare 7 for Chaffman, Wright, DCMA, and L. Jean Lewis.

August 15, 2003 – Writing the Story: The following day, Eric Rosenberg wrote the story. The story centered on my overcharging allegations against Lockheed Martin and included interviews with other whistleblowers at the facility. At the end of the day on August 15, 2003, Rosenberg read me the story and put it out on the news wire. The story had the title "*Government Whistleblower Booted From Lockheed Facility.*"

Ann Jensis-Dale (DCMA spokeswoman) denied that I was expelled for reprisal and indicated the following DCMA cover story:

"*…the action was in direct response to allegations that Pedeleose had physically threatened someone at the facility.*"

"We took immediate action", she said. "We had reason to believe that we were going to have a safety-in-the-work place issue. For the safety of DCMA employees as well as for Ken, that decision was made" to remove him from the premises".

No specifics were ever provided by DCMA on the alleged "*safety-in- the-work place issue*". DCMA falsified the entire situation and that will become evident shortly.

Story Catapulted and Spread Nationally: Rosenberg stated that the Atlanta Journal-Constitution was on the news wire and may give me a call. Rosenberg was correct. About an hour or so later, I received a call from the Atlanta Journal-Constitution, who said they had a great story that came across the news wire and wanted to do a story too. I agreed.

The story spread across the country. Meaning, Lockheed Martin armed guards catapulted me to the national stage. From there, Nightmare 8 came on the scene.

Nightmare 8 – Suborn Perjury & Refusal to Make False Sworn Statement

DCMA now had to perform on a national stage, unlike Falsified Trail 1 (reprimand), which was internally contained. The news media was not going away, and the story had attention since DCMA was now "out for blood" in the administrative sense.

August 19, 2003, Changing the Story & Suborn Perjury: DCMA quickly changed the story from me physically threatening someone to my *"unusual behavior and/or comments"* and *"trips to a firing range"*. Nevertheless, DCMA tried to suborn perjury from other employees. The following focus was placed on Myra Tate, a fellow employee at that time.

August 26, 2003: The first piece of evidence came from the local AFGE union president, who documented that "*Mr. Chaffman was trying to get Ms. Tate and others to say that they had been threatened by Mr. Pedeleose*". This was suborning perjury. When I eventually returned to the office, I was told by employees that they had been asked to make false statements against me.

The memo for record by the then Union President further stated: "*When Ken arrived in the front office, the Colonel stood directly behind Ben Chaffman and would not come from behind him. He was visibly shaking and his hands were trembling.*" I also witnessed Colonel Wright.

Colonel Wright was trembling because Wright was "Swatting" me (retaliation) and not because Wright was afraid of me. There was a room full of people, including Lockheed Martin armed guards.

I also noticed Colonel Wright was highly nervous when meeting Ernie Fitzgerald on March 12, 2003. Fitzgerald stated Colonel Wright looked like he was "*hit in the head with a wet corn cob.*"

However, there was further information on management training to fire employees.

Tactical Training to Fire Employees – 1st Hand Experience, Not Rumor

August 26, 2003: The then Union President prepared a Memorandum for Record (MFR) that stated the following in part related to management training to fire employees.

"*I told Mr. Pedeleose that I had a conversation with Ms. Myra Tate whereby she discussed recent supervisory/management training she had taken along with Mr. Kenneth Pates, Ms. Henrietta Snow and Mr. Jerry Andrews. I told Mr. Pedeleose, per Ms. Tate, the consultants actually held a class wherein they gave instruction to government management personnel on "how to" fire government personnel. I told Mr. Pedeleose that per Ms. Tate, both Henry Hagel and I were the subjects of much discussion between the instructors and members of the group to include Ms. Snow and Mr. Andrews. I told Mr. Pedeleose that per Ms. Tate, the instructor's gave specific instructions on the steps management should take to "push" an employee or cause an employee to take action that could lead to a firing. I told Mr. Pedeleose that per Ms. Tate, there were specific references to the local union president (meaning me) and Mr. Hagel (not identified by name) and our perceived behaviors as troublemakers and difficult employees.*"

Falsified Trail 1 is 1st hand experience and usage of tactics. Meaning, while the August 26, 2003, July 10, 2003, and July 18, 2003 MFRs are hearsay, Falsified Trail 1 shows tactics in a real-world usage. Shunning was the tactic to "push" me to failure. Myra Tate provided more 1st hand info.

"Pacing" Allegation & Suborning Perjury – 1st Hand Information

October 27-28, 2003 – Pacing Allegation: I called and spoke with Myra Tate directly on October 27, 2003, and made a Memo for Record on October 28, 2003, to the DoD IG, stating in part:

"*I called Myra Tate yesterday and asked if she had been interviewed when the DCMA investigator was here back in August 2003 asking questions about my demeanor and if I had ever physically threatened anyone. Myra Tate indicated that the investigator had only asked her one question which was Did she (Myra Tate) ever see Ken Pedeleose pacing in front of the building. She indicated that that was not what she said and the investigator ended the interview right there.*

Myra Tate told me yesterday afternoon that her remark was that I (Ken Pedeleose) was seen walking to my car (actually a pickup truck). Myra Tate also indicated that Mr. Ben Chaffman was very disturbed with her (Myra Tate) when she would not say that I (Ken Pedeleose) was pacing in front of the building. That is how weak and nonexistent management's case was against me. Management built their case on me allegedly pacing in front a building. This proves a level of desperation.

Myra briefly spoke of another conversation with another DCMA employee where it seemed that DCMA managers were trying to get others to say I threatened them. Myra told me that she indicated to the other employee (no name was given) to say specifically if I (Ken Pedeleose) had actually physically threatened them. The other employee just indicated that I Ken Pedeleose was just (to the effect) upset."

Relevance is that Falsified Trail 2 was a complete lie, planned to "set an example" with fanfare, drama, and an audience at the Lockheed Martin executive building and command suite in Marietta, GA, then known as the B-2 Building (North Campus). I worked at the L-10 Building (South Campus) about 1-2 miles away. Meaning I was summoned to a bigger audience.

Even mundane allegations of "*pacing*" failed. Pacing was probably mentioned during another office shooting, which would allow a racist dovetailing with Falsified Trail 2 as follows.

Racist Dovetail to Meridian Shootings

I wondered why Chaffman focused on Myra Tate and other employees to make false statements against me. I had no issues with Myra Tate and other employees. However, the answer was found regarding Douglas Williams, who perpetrated the July 8, 2003, shooting at Lockheed Martin's Meridian, Mississippi, facility. A Wikipedia article stated in part.

"*Five of the six killed in the incident were black...Given the nature of the attack and Williams' long-known history of racially-motivated threatening behavior, the incident was described by some at the time as the worst hate crime against African-Americans since the civil rights movement.*"

Relevance is, Myra Tate was black, and the other employees who told me that Chaffman wanted employees to make false statements were also black employees. Simply put, race was the dovetail between Falsified Trail 2 and Douglas Williams, who targeted "*Coworkers, particularly African Americans*" with the motive "*Anti-black racism*".

Return to the Facility Conference

September 3, 2003: On/about August 28/29, 2003, Ben Chaffman called me at home and asked me if I wanted to return to work. I said yes. Chaffman indicated that prior to my return, there would be a conference between management and me, moderated by a private company later identified as AVS Consulting, LLC, by Dr. Anthony Stone of AVS, and titled "*Return to Work and Work Circumstances Expectations*" and categorized as a "*Non-Binding Document of Understanding*".

Conference attendees included two union officials representing me, Dr. Anthony Stone, Colonel Wright, Ben Chaffman, and me. I never understood the need for AVS Consulting. However, I played along and was glad the ordeal was nearing an end.

At one point in the conference, Colonel Wright wanted me to sign a document that guaranteed office safety. I indicated I would not sign it, meaning there was no need to do so when I did nothing wrong. Colonel Wright retracted his statement, so I returned the document, and a general document was written up with non-binding expectations for each side.

I returned to work on September 8, 2003.

Conclusion of Volley 1 (Falsified Trails 1 & 2)

The news media put an end to Volley 1 retaliations against me. Falsified Trail 1 (July 9, 2003) and Falsified Trail 2 (August 14, 2003) were in a quick sequence against me, slightly over a month apart.

Falsified Trail 2 was designed as a quick "kill shot" to end my career. The shock of news media involvement quickly turned the tables, and I was asked to return to the facility.

September 30, 2003 - DCMA "Witch Hunt" Investigation Final Report: The DCMA investigation of Falsified Trail 2 was a "witch hunt" to find any wrongdoing by me, even after the investigation was closed after one question to Myra Tate. The "witch hunt" investigation stated in part.

"*The investigation was initiated based on a perception of a threat of violence allegedly made by PEDELEOSE.*"

"*PEDELEOSE did not make any direct threats towards anyone, but his unusual behavior had concerned the DCMA LM Marietta Command.*"

"*This investigation failed to substantiate or develop any pertinent information, which would indicate that PEDELEOSE threatened anyone in any manner. Based on the information contained in this memorandum this investigation will be administratively CLOSED and no COMMAND ACTION is required.*"

Relevance is that DCMA used DCMA investigators to cover up the real origins of Falsified Trail 2 (August 14, 2003). Meaning, the DCMA investigators never investigated why the charges against me were false. There was no investigation into retaliation. Only investigating on what management stated. I also recall no investigation statements from Ben Chaffman or Colonel Wright who perpetrated the entire event. There was a big shift in allegations from me physically threatening someone, to unusual demeanor, that was never investigated. I would call that a cover-up.

DCMA investigators would also play a cover-up role in Volley 4 (Falsified Trails 11, 12 & 13). After that, DCMA would formalize a DCMA IG that worked at the DCMA directors' level on May 16, 2018.

Meaning, DCMA investigators can investigate DCMA and clear DCMA of any wrongdoing. A very convenient and necessary relationship knowing the maleficence of DCMA.

The short story is, DCMA investigates DCMA as part of weaponized investigation cover-ups and retaliation. Falsified Trail 2 was a cover-up investigation.

Had Falsified Trail 2 not happened, this book would not be possible.

There were collateral damage and fallout from Falsified Trail 2, as follows, along with the developing of a covert "*framework*" for dealing with whistleblowers.

Collateral Fall-out & Aftermath from Falsified Trail 2

September 11, 2003 - BOLO: I tried to get a copy of the BOLO issued for me on August 14, 2003. Colonel Wright was involved and forwarded a message from Lockheed Martin Security, Daniel Cain, who stated: "*Per our legal, I will not provide a copy of the BOLO*".

Lockheed Martin did not deny the BOLO existed. Lockheed Martin would not provide the BOLO, indicating that a BOLO was issued for me. Hence, another cover-up.

News Media Catapult: Falsified Trail 2 catapulted my news media exposure. If Colonel Wright and Ben Chaffman hadn't had Lockheed Martin walk me out the gate under false charges, my story and whistleblowing would have stopped after the July 26, 2002, 90-page report to Congress. My resume in Chapter 1 has the full range of my news media contacts, thanks to Wright and Chaffman.

Nightmare 9 came next for Luara Jean Lewis, who was political during the 1990s.

Nightmare 9: L. Jean Lewis Exposed – Circumstantial Exodus

September 22, 2003: Around the week of August 18, 2003, my news media catapult took hold and expanded from Hearst News and the Atlanta Journal-Constitution. One question involved who I was working with as a whistleblower. I identified Ernie Fitzgerald, those on Senator Grassley's staff, and I mentioned Jean Lewis.

The name "Jean Lewis" led to no known results or resume, especially for someone who was the Chief of Staff at the DoD IG. I was asked how Jean Lewis's e-mail read. I responded, "L. Jean Lewis". Adding the "L" brought up Lewis's real background. From there, a swarm surrounded Lewis. The first article was from Newsweek magazine, September 22, 2003, titled "*Pentagon Defense's Whitewater Hire*".

L. Jean Lewis was actually Laura Jean Lewis, who was political during the 90s and involved with the Whitewater Investigation against the Clintons while Lewis was part of the Resolution Trust Corporation. The exposure of L. Jean Lewis went public through the news media, eventually leading to the circumstantial exodus of L. Jean Lewis in 2004, as stated in my resume (Chapter 1).

I was blamed for the exposure of Jean Lewis and was later told by Dan Meyer that it upset some at the DoD IG who liked Jean Lewis. I did not know Jean Lewis's resume prior to August 2003. This explains why I had to ask my other DoD IG contacts for Lewis's contact information on June 16, 2003, after Charlie Murphy said Lewis wanted to help. Meaning, Lewis feared exposure.

It would appear that Lewis was political in the 1990's with the Whitewater investigations of the Clintons. This could be a watershed moment (turning point) similar to Nixon tactics in Chapter 2 regarding weaponization and lawfare in politics. Most notably since it was L. Jean Lewis who brought on Dan Meyer who was a key figure in Falsified Trail 3. Meaning, Dan Meyer held a key role in weaponization of government that Nixon would have loved to have had. Hence, there is the appearance that Lewis was expanding weaponization and lawfare at the DoD IG via Dan Meyer.

This was probably the "*framework*" for working with whistleblowers, that Charlie Murphy of Senator Grassley's staff spoke of in the introduction to Jean Lewis (February 14, 2003).

That covert "*framework*" use by Dan Meyer in Falsified Trail 3 gave great transparency to the Deep State. So, in effect the covert "*framework*" backfired. Dan Meyer informed me that a cover story was floated that Jean Lewis left the DoD IG because Lewis needed an operation. The DoD IG knew I exposed Lewis, which plays into Falsified Trail 3, where the DoD IG contributed to a weaponized investigation and lawfare. However, more fallout occurred from Falsified Trail 2 with future seeds of weaponization and lawfare being identified similar to Dan Meyer as follows.

Joe Tessier – 2nd Level Supervisor – Falsified Trails 4 thru 10

Joe Tessier was my then 2nd-level supervisor and key player in Falsified Trails 4 thru 10 (2009-2010). Tessier actually started on me in 2008, shortly after his arrival. Management went to great lengths to get Tessier promoted, as the following shows.

August 18, 2003 - No Promotion Panel Rating: A person named "Joe", apparently Joe Tessier, was the end of the August 18, 2003 memo for record of Falsified Trail 2, which stated in part.

"*...an outside person was hired for the C-130J job promotion even though he was not suppose to be on the list. He said "Joe?" I said "Yes, Joe!" I told him that according to Mr. Chaffman at a Navy Team meeting, he said only the top three names were submitted. According to my sources [Union] the person that was hired (Joe) didn't even have a rating. He told me to talk to Ben about that issue. I submitted e-mail request to talk to Ben Chaffman that same day.*"

Only the name "Joe" was mentioned; however, for local DCMA Quality Assurance (QA), Joe Tessier was the only "Joe" that came to mind regarding management. However, more data surfaced.

December 13, 2007 "Backstabbers": Hearing Joe Tessier would be C-5 Team Group Chief, one employee openly stated with Henrietta Snow (then Deputy Commander, 3rd Level Supervisor) and others present: *"I informed Ms. Snow that the C5 team will not tolerate "backstabbers".* The remark was documented in a sworn statement on July 28, 2010.

November 29, 2010: I was further informed that Henrietta Snow wrote in Joe Tessier's name on a promotion panel recommendation. I made a memo for record stating in part.

"*...Henrietta Snow wrote Joe Tessier's name on a selection panel recommendation. The panel did not recommend Tessier for promotion. Specifically, Joe Tessier was hired in this organization as a GS-12. When he applied for a promotion he was not on the list of recommended persons from the selection panel. Apparently Henrietta Snow wrote in Tessier's name.*"

The point is, Tessier's observed and documented behavior aligned with the rumors that preceded Tessier. Meaning, Tessier lived up to his reputation. From 2008 to 2010, there was an administrative "run & shoot" battle with Joe Tessier and Nanette Nelson (1st level supervisor). Tessier and Nelson worked in sync with obstruction and lawfare. The evidence trail follows after Falsified Trail 3.

The following expands on Dan Meyer (CRI) as a weapon developed over me and used against me. Meyer was also fallout from Falsified Trails 1 & 2, 2003 timeline. Meyer was an associate of L. Jean Lewis and was instrumental in Falsified Trail 3. Meyer was supposed to be a whistleblower advocate at the DoD IG. Meyer proved anything but an advocate.

Dan Meyer - CRI (Civilian Reprisal Investigations)

Dan Meyer's position as CRI is interlocked between Falsified Trails 1 and 2 as follows.

June 28, 2006 - CRI Genesis - Investigation & Sworn Statement: Dan Meyer testified that his position began as the result of an August 2003 DoD IG site visit to my facility by Trahan with investigators. Meyer misspoke since the meeting was July 29-30, 2003. Meyer stated in part.

"*We had gone down there on a site visit in August 2003, prior to me showing up, and this idea of kind of counseling and advising investigate at the same time had not done as well because we ended up I think, kind of distancing both sides, we kind of, kind of stepped in it.*"

"*...my position was actually escalated and staffed because of that meeting.*"

Meyer also stated my (Pedeleose) "*experience that led to the creation*" of his (Meyer) office.

The end result of the July 29-30, 2003, meeting was contemporaneously documented as follows.

July 31, 2003: I sent an email titled "*Sold Out*" to describe what the DoD IG team (Leonard Trahan and his two investigators) did on the July 29-30, 2003 meeting/visit, stating in part:

"*It now is confirmed that the DoD Transformation will be the managerial weapon of mass destruction to ensure that whistleblowers are not heard and with hast removed from government service or positions of responsibility.*

Colonel Wright has been allowed to openly spit in the face of integrity and obviously his superiors agree with his actions."

August 5, 2003: Jean Lewis responded with platitudes, stating in part.

"*First, on behalf of the Inspector General of the Department of Defense, I want to thank each of you for meeting and cooperating with the OIG Team members during their visit to the DCMA-Marrietta site last week. Second, earlier today I received an extensive briefing from Len Trahan, Vincent Stewart and David Brothers on their impressions of the on-site visit. Please let me assure you that the OIG's involvement and concern with your situation did not end with the on-site visit and that we intend to remain actively engaged in this endeavor, conducting a further review into matters you have raised...*

Again, thanks for receiving the IG Team in the best spirit of "Southern Hospitality", and we look forward to communicating with you in the near future."

The July 29-30, 2003, DoD IG visit was a sham. Knowing Dan Meyer's position as CRI was formed at the time of the July 29-30, 2003 visit confirms why Meyer was the hub of weaponized retaliation in Falsified Trail 3. It was unknown what Meyer's role was as CRI.

Unknown What Dan Meyer's Role Was

June 28, 2006: Another member of the DoD IG (Henry Shelley) testified that it was unknown what Dan Meyer's role as CRI would be, stating in part.

"*...when Dan Meyer came on, came on board it was, it was never clearly in my mind, never clearly defined what his role was going to be and so I envisioned at some point there would be these issues, you know, when you, you know, calls himself a coach, calls himself an advocate...*"

"*...I was involved in some of the discussion at the office, certainly we had a problem identifying or, or clarifying Dan Meyer's role, what was his role when he was brought in here by Jean Lewis and, and Schmitz, the former IG was a little bit unclear and I'm not sure it's been totally clarified...I do remember actually offering an opinion at some point there was some questions about confidentially...there's no privilege.*"

No Privilege & Multiple Con Games: Falsified Trail 3 shows confidentially and privilege did not matter since CRI was a con game on Senator Grassley via Charlie Murphy. Simultaneously, DCMA ran a con game on Dan Meyer. Falsified Trail 3, Chapter 3 has more details.

Henry Shelley's mention of Dan Meyer as a "coach" was also confirmed by Dan Meyer.

Daniel Meyer Arrival – "Coach" – Disappointment in 4 Months

January 26, 2004 CRI Launched - January 28, 2004 Arrive: CRI was launched on/about January 26, 2004, during the tenure of Jean Lewis. Dan Meyer came on board on/about January 28, 2004.

February 12, 2004: The first email from Dan Meyer to me stated: "*Got a brief from Melissa and David last week. Ready to take up your remaining issues. Send me you phone number-when is a good time to call.*" Melissa and David (DoD IG investigators) did my deposition on September 16, 2003 for Falsified Trail 1 and 2.

As a side note, the MPRI report of April 21, 2002, suggested an administrative model for DoD IG to help whistleblowers. Unfortunately, the administrative model (CRI) ("*framework*") was weaponized against whistleblowers rather than to help whistleblowers.

Meyer/CRI Director Covered 660,000 People – No Staff: Meyer's office was envisioned by Jean Lewis to have a staff of eight persons, including two audit employees, two military reprisal employees, and two investigators of senior officials. As of May 23, 2006, Meyer had four volunteer law clerks. This was concerning since Meyer was covering 660,000 employees essentially by himself.

Meyer Multiple Cases: To my understanding, Meyer interacted with NSA whistleblowers. Meyer even told me he had an advisory role with the Abu Ghraib incident after the fact. Meaning, Dan Meyer's interactions went beyond my case. Dan Meyer was in the loop on my whistleblowing and acknowledged I was "*extremely effective*".

February 24, 2004: During February 2004, I worked with Charlie Murphy of Senator Grassley's staff on what would develop into Substantiated Allegation 3. (DoD IG cover-up of criminal findings on the Lockheed Martin C5 Program.) This was mentioned in my resume, Chapter 1.

Senator Grassley sent a letter to DoD Inspector General Joseph Schmitz criticizing the report (No. D-2004-054) for not mentioning previous criminal findings known to DoD IG. Senator Grassley took particular exception to one weak statement in the IG report, which stated in part:

"DCMA and DCAA [Defense Contract Audit Agency] need to maintain vigilance until the price of the remaining parts is negotiated."

Senator Grassley further stated: *"Those two entities* (DCMA & DCAA) *have a long- standing reputation for turning a blind eye to contractor rip offs. They are not known for being vicious junk yard dogs when it comes to protecting taxpayers' money."* (Appendix A1-1)

Relevance is that I gained credibility as a whistleblower, adding to my extensive case against DCMA. I had Senator Grassley in my corner, which Dan Meyer should have appreciated. I would be labeled "*extremely effective*" by Dan Meyer. (Appendix A1-2)

<u>March 19, 2004 – "Extremely Effective"</u>: Jean Lewis forwarded Dan Meyer an e-mail on March 19, 2004, 9:52 AM, where Charlie Murphy stated in part:

"*Ken, I met with the DOD IG audit group on Wednesday. I walked them thru the problem from our perspective, focusing of course on the DCIS documents. My bottom line: the DOD IG audit report is tainted. The write up on page 5 on the C-5 engine bracket contains false information. They knew that, and failed to address and resolve that problem.*" (Appendix A1-2)

Dan Meyer sent me an e-mail one minute later on March 19, 2004, 9:53 AM stating:

"*I have to admit, Ken, that you are extremely effective -- I have never seen Congressional staff this active on an intake.*

Working away on your case,

Dan"

Relevance is that Dan Meyer knew I was an effective whistleblower, and I was in direct contact with Senator Grassley's staff (Charlie Murphy). Dan Meyer was also aware of the retaliations of 2003, termed Volley 1 (Falsified Trails 1 & 2). I had already won at Falsified Trail 2. The point being, Dan Meyer was handed a textbook case of whistleblower retaliation. However, it was notable and concerning that Dan Meyer did not engage DCMA as the following shows.

Dan Meyer Refused to Engage – Meyer the "Coach"

<u>April 22, 2004 – CRI/Meyer Ruse</u>: About three months after Meyer contacted me, it was evident that Dan Meyer (CRI) was a ruse. I contacted Meyer, stating in part. (Appendix A1-3)

"*I won't single you out as DoD is largely at fault, however you are calling this thing like a "fight" commentator looking to see who scores the "knockout punch" on the other. I blame the DoD climate for this. That is why I changed my tactics from a back alley brawl to an open, in the news media issue*".

"*That way the world can see how DoD reacts and supports fraud and let's the little guy take up the fight for the big shots like Rumsfeld and Schmitz who should be taking the side of what is right. Instead everyone is looking to see "who wins", and who inflicts the most pain and misery on the other. Like the Roman games, gladiators, run the gauntlet, etc.*"

Meyer responded as follows: (Appendix A1-3)

"More like a 'referee' Ken, or better yet a coach aiding competing athletes. I'll be bold here an tell you I think our former COS (L. Jean Lewis, Chief of Staff) *came close to compromising our role in your case. She was too emotionally involved, perhaps due to her own issues in Whitewater. The IG act requires me to be independent and neutral like a referee – if you have been fouled under the court rules – Title 5 I'll blow the whistle and recommend penalties.*

This doesn't mean I don't understand the pressure you are under. Mt whistle blowing led to two 30 million dollar lawsuits, took me 15 years to resolve them."

The relevance is that Meyer lost my trust. At best, I considered Meyer worthless. Meyer may have been affected by the torment of being a whistleblower. I remember Meyer saying that he was glad he didn't get any money from a book that was written, apparently about his whistleblowing.

Meyer also brought up Whitewater, which was political for Jean Lewis, meaning politics was in the mix. I continued conversing with Meyer so as not to alienate Meyer, Senator Grassley, and Charlie Murphy. I expected nothing from Meyer, but anything I got was more than I expected.

It was obvious that with Meyer's prior whistleblowing and Jean Lewis in Whitewater, there were existing issues and politics at play. However, Meyer's inaction continued.

<u>July 19, 2004 – Meyer Still Inactive</u>: A fellow employee (Henry Hagel) and I contacted Dan Meyer again to inquire about any progress in engaging DCMA. Dan Meyer was proving useless at best. The following comments were an extension of the "Don't Write It Down – Cover-up" training, July 13-15, 2004, by DCMA. The comments in part are as follows:

"All management does is sit back and do nothing or deny allegations.

Please inform us of your mission, progress to date, etc. regarding my/our issues in Marietta. The longer the issues go on the more they will favor management."

"Since you have taken over in your current DOD/IG position [Whistleblower Advocate] nothing seems to get resolved. Do you intend to resolve issue(s) or just "file them in a way which will move the issue forward." It is probably about time that real issues started getting resolved up the chain of command or are you just filling these issue(s) in a paper basket and just biding your time."

Knowing Dan Meyer was useless, I participated in other actions to expose DoD corruption.

April 2004 Parallel News Media to Expose Military-Industrial Complex

April 2004 was very active against the military-industrial complex. The actions did not prompt a retaliatory response because the military-industrial complex's "armor" was not pierced, and the Deep State wasn't fully engaged as yet. The backlash of Falsified Trail 2 failure had paused the weaponization and lawfare. So, the news media continued. A brief summary is as follows.

The first was the Federal Times series of articles, in part, as follows.

<u>April 5, 2004</u>: "*The Dark Side of Acquisition Reform*". The article centered on me (Pedeleose).

<u>April 12, 2004</u>: "*Undermining the Auditors: 'Collaborative Arrangement' Let's DoD Contractors Slide*". Centered DCMA retaliating against DCMA employees who expose fraud.

April 12, 2004: "*A Case of Reprisal*" Article centered on me as a whistleblower.

There were about 11 stories and articles between Federal Times and Defense news in April 2004 and two stories during November 2004 (Chapter 1 has the complete list). The Climate Review was next in April 2004. Meaning, a lot of negative issues emerged against DCMA on or about April 2004.

DCMA Losing Sight of DCMA Mission

April 16, 2004: On February 9, 2004 a Climate Review Report was requested on my office. The report confirmed issues and problems so serious and embarrassing that only a summary of findings was distributed to the local workforce. The summary stated in part.

"The strife which characterizes labor management relations at DCMA-LMM permeates many, if not most, of the interactions at that facility. In this climate, many employees asserted that the organization has lost sight of its mission..."

"For agency credibility, the employees need to believe that the organization is telling the truth. Employees have many resources available to them and can quickly identify when the explanations they have received "just don't add up". The consistent feedback suggests that employees do not believe that agency management "walks the talk."

"*Issues that remain unresolved fester and lead to poor morale and performance, turnover, and eventually litigation. All are present at DCMA-LMM.*"

This activity prompted Senator Grassley to issue me a protection letter as follows.

Senator Grassley Protection Letter

April 26, 2004: By 2004, I was a nationally recognized whistleblower at a corrupt organization. I was a target. Senator Grassley wrote a protection letter and sent it to the then DCMA Director Brigadier General (BG) Darryl Scott, warning that Federal law prohibits retaliation (18 USC 1505).

Relevance is that April 2004 was an action-packed month; however, it did not pierce the "armor" or arrogance of the military-industrial complex. Nightmare 10 did pierce the "Armor" and arrogance and awakened the Deep State into "Out for Blood" action.

Nightmare 10 – Pierced "Armor" of the Military-Industrial Complex

July 23, 2004 (DoD IG Report on C-130J, (D-2004-102)): The DoD IG stated in part.

"We substantiated the allegation that the C-130J aircraft does not meet contract specifications and therefore cannot perform its operational mission. The Air Force conditionally accepted 50 C-130J aircraft at a cost of $2.6 billion even though none of the aircraft met commercial contract specifications or operational requirements."

I was the whistleblower who challenged the C-130J, and on March 15, 2004, Jean Lewis stated I had the "*right to claim victory as a whistleblower*" if the C-130J allegation was substantiated. The C-130J allegation was substantiated and gave me high public notoriety. The point being, the military-industrial complex went "out for blood" against my career. I was no longer a nuisance. The first move was the exodus of those ineffective against me.

Circumstantial Exodus of the Ineffective

Colonel Wright met circumstantial exodus as a result of Substantiated Allegation 4 as follows.

July 9, 2004: Colonel Wright stated, "*Col Nicole Plourde and I will have our CoC* (Change of Command) *7 Oct 04.*" Colonel Wright was my 4th-level supervisor. I heard a rumor that Colonel Wright had a one-year extension in hand and that the extension was revoked.

August 24, 2004: Ben Chaffman was my third-level supervisor. Chaffman announced he was leaving on August 24, 2004. Chaffman indicated he was moving to another DCMA position to improve "*the Agency's Product Assurance support to customers in the Systems Design and Development phase of the program life cycle*".

November 17, 2004: While not in my chain of command, Marvin Sambur (Assistant Secretary of the Air Force) announced his resignation on November 17, 2004, which is the same day I was on ABC News on a segment titled "*C-130J Military Transport Planes Deemed Unfit for War*".

Relevance is a notable exodus surrounding Substantiated Allegation 4, which comfortably suggests the exodus was due to my whistleblowing. The more vicious management was assigned as follows.

Henrietta Snow (Deputy Commander) – 3rd Level Supervisor

In late 2004, Henrietta Snow replaced Ben Chaffman as Deputy Commander in my office, serving as the 3rd-level supervisor. Snow proved far more vicious than Chaffman ever could be. Henrietta Snow would go directly to terminations in Falsified Trail 3 (Volley 2), which began in early 2005. However, Henrietta Snow did not act alone.

Colonel Nicole Plourde (Commander) – 4th Level Supervisor

October 7, 2004: Colonel Wright was replaced by Colonel Plourde on/about October 7, 2004, as announced in a July 9, 2004 e-mail. Plourde had a reputation as outlined in a June 28, 2006, investigation, where Dan Meyer stated in part:

"*she has a reputation within the Air Force of being brought in to fix problem shops.*"

Plourde's "reputation" was cryptic. However, Plourde's actions, conduct, and behavior needed no interpretation. Plourde systematically dismantled the whistleblowing in my office, damaging my reputation and severing my working relationship with Senator Grassley. However, the momentum and fallout from my whistleblowing continued despite new management.

Momentum & Fallout Following Substantiated Allegation 4

January 10, 2005 – Cancel C-130J Program: A letter was written by Senator Saxby Chambliss and signed by 23 other Senators stating in part: "*We understand that the Department of Defense is proposing the termination of the C-130J multiyear procurement contract beginning in FY2006.*"

Relevance is that Substantiated Allegation 4 got real, meaning it's not just a nuisance. I later worked with Senator McCain and the news media on the exaggerated $1 billion cancellation cost for the C-130J. Meaning, I boxed in the military-industrial complex from falsifying C-130J cancellation costs.

June 1, 2005 – Dow Jones Newswire: "*Whistleblower challenges Pentagon Stance on C-130J Costs*" Rebecca Christie. This was a spinoff disclosure, regarding C-130J cancellation costs, to DoD IG Joseph Schmitz on May 12, 2005. Schmitz responded to me on May 13, 2005, stating one of his Deputies is overseeing a review of my allegations. This started Substantiated Allegation 5 and the Dow Jones Newswire story.

From there, I forwarded the May 16, 2005, report titled "*Cover-up in the Department of Defense*" to Schmitz and Senator Grassley. I may also have sent a copy to Senator McCain. This supported the investigation into falsified C-130J cancellation costs that would become Substantiated Allegation 5.

At this point I became even a higher value target.

The point is, I was actively engaged in public whistleblowing in May–June 2005. In that time, Colonel Plourde and Henrietta Snow were engaged in warm-up retaliations for easier whistleblower targets in my office. The warmup retaliations did not invoke, or need, the full Deep State as yet. Simply put, go after the vulnerable targets (whistleblowers) that are not heavily protected.

Warmup Weaponized Retaliatory Terminations

Colonel Plourde and Henrietta Snow first engaged against vulnerable employees or soft targets. This was the first stage to rid my office of whistleblowers. The local union president that assisted me in Falsified Trail 2 was first.

Weaponized Retaliatory Termination 1

February 16, 2005: Henrietta Snow issued a Notice of Proposed Removal (Termination of Employment) for the then-union president. The first reason cited was a leave restriction letter in May 2003. This was the same timeframe when the retaliations began against me in Falsified Trail 1, and when management officials were being trained to tactically terminate employees using techniques to push them to failure. This insulated management and concealed motives.

Perceived failure in my office is due to the hostile workplace and altered working conditions. I adjusted to the situation; however, the union president and others did not adjust as well. Over the years, some employees would permanently leave the office with little or no notice. Just walk out. My outlet and comfort zone were the news media and conversations with criminal investigators.

Adding to the controversy is the fact that Henrietta Snow, the third-level supervisor, jumped two supervisor levels to initiate a proposed termination soon after being installed as Deputy Commander. Meaning, little time was being wasted in the retaliations.

March 9-10, 2005: The union president provided a response to the proposed removal (termination) on March 9, 2005, with some brief corrections on March 10, 2005, for typographical and grammatical errors. The gist of the union president's response mentioned a 25+ year career with references to medical conditions. Emotional effects of the hostile workplace were also mentioned.

The following excerpt from the response confirms the hostile workplace in my office caused by Ben Chaffman. The union president stated in part.

"*When Ben Chaffman arrived, it was the beginning of the end. Chaffman arrived in this office and began to steam roll right over the union, the employees and anyone else he chose to. When I arrived in this office employee morale was low. With the arrival of Chaffman it worsened. Colonel Wright made a critical mistake after the arrival of Ben Chaffman. He gave Ben Chaffman complete autonomy to work all labor/management issues. He refused to meet with me. When it became apparent that my relationship with Chaffman was going to be a tumultous one, Colonel Wright refused to intervene and calm the situation. Things got so bad employees complained that the union and management were taking pot shots at one another in a series of email messages. Any attempt to work any issue at the lowest possible level did not exist.*"

Ben Chaffman arrived in our office on/about October 29, 2001 (Per July 26, 2002 Report). It took Chaffman about one day to erode what was left of employee morale. The first action was to revoke DCMA parking passes and let Lockheed Martin occupy government spaces. Chaffman's arrival intensified the hostile workplace in my office. Chaffman seemed to bask in the office chaos. The point is, Chaffman created an environment where employees could fail and insulated management. This doubled as cover for Lockheed Martin that was failing as early as 1998 and price gouging taxpayers.

April 15, 2005 – Notice of Decision to Remove: Colonel Plourde issued a formal letter to remove the union president, rubber-stamping what Henrietta Snow proposed and Ben Chaffman caused.

Relevance is, Plourde, Snow, and Chaffman had sadistic tendencies and left a trail of destruction, a hostile workplace, and altered work conditions. Plourde, Snow, and Chaffman were void of emotion. A fellow employee told me prior to the arrival of Ben Chaffman that I (Pedeleose) "*Don't know this guy* (Chaffman)". The June 28, 2006 statement, where Colonel Plourde "*...has the reputation within the Air Force of being brought in to fix problem shops*" is another example where reputations preceded management officials.

The union president, three other employees, and I signed the second report to Congress on March 8, 2004. By then, it was obvious management wanted turmoil in the office. Employees who engage in protected activity (whistleblowing, EEO cases) were the main targets of the hostile workplace. DCMA was confident in any retaliation due to the well-known bias at OSC and MSPB in Chapter 2.

Unhinged Behavior - Confidence in a System That Fails – Cerberus Analogy

On May 20, 2010, the union president shared accounts of being bullied and bullying by the MSPB judge, stating in part. "*The bullying occurred before the hearing that I waived and I complained very early in my case to the Supervisory ALJ* (Administrative Law Judge)." The union president waived the live hearing and went for a Hearing on Written Records, meaning documents and sworn statements only. This helped avoid the chaos from an unhinged MSPB hearing.

I also used the Hearing on Written Records strategy due to the unhinged and chaotic nature of MSPB judges. At one point, I experienced paralysis due to intense MSPB judge bullying.

October 19, 2010 - Psychologically Pummeled to Physical Paralyses: In a September 29, 2010 e-mail (regarding Falsified Trail 4, 5, and 6, first segment of Volley 3) there was a MSPB mediation scheduled for on/about 0930 AM of October 19, 2010. Hope for resolution turned to paralysis.

When I met with the MSPB mediation judge, I was psychologically pummeled to physical paralysis. The MSPB judge was so unhinged and unstable that I could barely walk. My legs were paralyzed from the trauma. I was stunned. I staggered from the mediation to the parking lot and eventually recovered to be able to drive home.

The point is, DCMA was confident in any retaliatory acts because the Cerberus analogy of OSC, MSPB, and OPM's ability to derail (rig) cases for failure would contain negative information about management. Meaning, confidence in a system that fails. The union president's 2005 experience with MSPB trained me on how to proceed with cases at MSPB.

The October 19, 2010, incident confirms the fact that MSPB is an enamoring "lovefest" between the Agency and MSPB judges. MSPB is a Kangaroo Court on the best day. MSPB was an unhinged, bullying, and biased organization against Federal employees that drives, and enables, other bullying and unhinged tactics. The point is, DCMA capitalized on, and factored in, that well known MSPB ("Cerberus Analogy") trait. Colonel Plourde also exhibited an unhinged management style and a hostile workplace demeanor in 2005.

Colonel Plourde's Hostile Workplace & Chaos

April 21, 2005: One example of office chaos from Colonel Plourde and Henrietta Snow in 2005 was a supervisor who misdirected a very disturbing email stating.

"Henrietta,

It is 0400 am here and my email may have been a little too emotional. I do apologize I guess our Commanders style of management will take some getting used to. At least hearme out before you decide things. If you are meeting with david Haines I thought you needed to know what has took place. I might need a few days of leave next week to shake some of this. It is a little upsetting."

The supervisor who wrote the e-mail was on the C-130J Team. The terminated union president was on the C-130 Team. The employee fired in Retaliatory Termination 2 (to follow) was on the C-130 Team. David Hanes was a Lockheed Martin employee (possible C-130J management). Meaning, the main focus of Plourde and Snow was the C-130J. This focus led to Retaliatory Termination 2.

Weaponized Retaliatory Termination 2 via US Mail – Insane Innuendo Reasons

June 14, 2005 – "Verbal Lashing" of a DCMA Engineer: The next DCMA employee terminated was also on the C-130J team as an engineer. The employee was critical of the C-130J to the point of receiving a "*verbal lashing*" from a military officer associated with DCMA management. The history included the following.

July 29, 2004 – DCMA Director General Scott Briefing: When it was clear that the DoD IG report on the C-130J (Substantiated Allegation 4, July 23, 2004) was going to materialize, the DCMA Directors asked for a briefing. (Remember the draft report was issued March 25, 2004, so DCMA knew what was coming.) Based on actual management reactions and behavior, the briefing aimed to identify those responsible for the negative report and those who continue to raise issues.

The employee terminated in Retaliatory Termination 2 made the following comments, stated in part on July 29, 2004.

"*Obviously, being new, I am limited in scope and in depth to that I am able to comment on. However, based on approximately twelve years of industry engineering experience, and on my brief observations here working on the C130J, I offer the following:*

Being a Fixed Cost contract, DCMA Engineering appears to have been limited in involvement compared to other Cost Plus contracts I've worked on. There appears to be an extremely low accountability on the contractors (LM Aero) side for implementing "Best Engineering Practices" or in some cases, "responsible" engineering. A strong noticeable DCMA Engineering "Hands Off' attitude exists on behalf of LM Aero.

As an Engineer, I personally do not prescribe to the "Shade Tree" Mechanics approach to making Engineering Changes on aircraft since it is clearly different, with much higher risks, than an automobile. If a car mechanic fixes the wrong problem and your car breaks down, chances are good the car can be safely towed back into the shop for another "quick fix". With an airplane, LM Aero engineers need to have a high degree of certainty that they know the root cause of a problem before recommending a solution. Also, LM Aero engineers should have a clear understanding of the scope of the problem as well as the solution. It appears, however, this is not always the case and DCMA Engineering is expected by LM Aero to stand on the side lines without questions, comments and/or recommendations."

The relevance is that the DCMA engineer, who would soon be terminated, quickly saw the true picture of DCMA. The engineer continued to question Lockheed Martin regarding defects on the C-130J well into 2005, leading to a "verbal lashing" that would follow termination.

2nd Weaponized Termination Starts – Known by Other Employees

June 16, 2005: Employees knew the 2nd termination would take place prior to the employee knowing. Termination documents were mailed to the employee's home while the employee was out sick. Henry Hagel (fellow whistleblower) sent an e-mail to Dan Meyer stating in part that there was a "*strong indication*" the employee would be fired.

June 16, 2005 – Memo for Record by Terminated Union President: The 2nd termination had a detailed account of events by employees who worked close to Plourde and Snow. The memo for record documented events about Plourde several days earlier than June 16, 2005.

Documenting Colonel Plourde's Comments, Actions, & Demeanor: The June 16, 2005, Memo for Record stated the Colonel and Henrietta had a meeting about the employee's status and "*she was told that the Colonel said "just get rid or her, just get rid of her, she's a probationary employee"*." The relevance is that Colonel Plourde's documented unhinged style is leading to office chaos.

The employee stated the Colonel and Henrietta wanted the employee fired, not the supervisor. The supervisor went to the union and "*asked what he could do?*" to protect the employee. This was the same supervisor who put out the April 21, 2005, misdirected e-mail. The union then contacted the union president (who was terminated) for advice. Plourde was now in the facts of cases.

Several days after the employee shared the above with the terminated union president, she phoned or visited the terminated union president at home, expressing great concern about the employee's termination and asking her to call the employee. The relevance is that the termination, planned for a while, was causing a shake-up in the office and with the supervisor. The memo for the record mentioned other employees targeted for termination and explained how the employee relaying the information wanted to remain anonymous, stating in part.

"I said "LaNorma when the subpoena's start to flow and people are sworn under oath, they will have to tell what they know. I said that is the problem with the agency, the management personnel are messy with their personnel actions, lack professionalism and people are always running their mouth until its time for someone to take a stand". At this point LaNorma stated to me that if she was subpoenaed about her source, she would "take the fifth". I didn't have the heart to tell her that she can only take the fifth when it comes to self-incrimination."

Relevance is that Colonel Plourde's comments, actions, and demeanor were documented, albeit it was hearsay. I heard other employees say Plourde would state she (Plourde) "didn't have a problem firing anybody". What followed wasn't a rumor. The employee was terminated.

Employee Terminated Via Mail

June 14, 2005: The termination Memorandum was dated June 14, 2005, and mailed to the employee. The employee received the letter on/about June 16, 2005. The reason for termination, signed by Henrietta Snow, was as follows in part:

"*You are hereby informed that you. are being separated from your position of Electrical Engineer (0855), effective June 14, 2005, in accordance with 5 CFR 315.804. You will be paid for the balance of this work day.*

The reason for your separation is a lack of interpersonal skills to include your inability to effectively work with people; your inability to apply judgment outside of the realm of basic knowledge; your inability to apply filters in situations where diverse and sensitive issues exist; your erratic and unpredictable behavior; and your inability to have open, meaningful and candid dialog with your customers and the contractor."

Relevance is that Henrietta Snow was the employee's 3rd level supervisor. The 1st level supervisor went to the union to save the employee from termination (per the June 16, 2005, Memo for Record).

Other employees knew of the termination in advance, although the specific reasons were unknown. I was asked by the employee for assistance since I was experienced in DCMA retaliation tactics and how to move cases to litigation. I did assist the employee.

June 16, 2005 – Request for Support Documents: I asked Colonel Plourde and Henrietta Snow for supporting data on the employee's termination at/about 4:45 PM. I was acting on the employee's behalf. Plourde and Snow stated that no supporting data would be provided.

I documented these facts to Dan Meyer in a June 20, 2005, e-mail regarding the termination. I was the employee's EEO representative and continued to pressure for supporting documents. Shortly after June 16, 2005, I received the specific termination reasons, which were bizarre and represented insanity, desperation and arrogance.

Bizarre & Insane Termination Reasons

July 7, 2005 Affidavit: After I received the termination documents, I prepared a detailed affidavit for Dan Meyer. Plourde and Snow's erratic, insane, and retaliatory actions had to be made known.

Meaning, the termination reasons were innuendo and not performance-based.

One termination reason was "*took a LM Aero bicycle without permission*". The bicycles were used at the flightline to get around. The employee thought the bicycles were government property and only barrowed the bicycle.

Another reason for termination was that the employee called a fellow employee a "*whiner*".

The most insane termination reason was when the employee "*drank from a Sparkling Cider bottle at the Christmas luncheon. Even though it was non-alcoholic this event prompted some to ask me* (1st Level Supervisor) *if she had a drinking problem. I asked her about it and she said she was thirsty. I told her that her action could be misinterpreted and she has to be aware of that.*"

The relevance is that DCMA management provided gift bottles of non-alcoholic sparkling cider to DCMA employees at the 2004 Christmas luncheon. Employees were allegedly distressed by the fact that the employee did not use a glass to drink from. Hence, DCMA was a hero for employees in distress caused by an employee who didn't use a glass to drink from.

First & Second Level Supervisors Learned Termination via Rumor

Sworn Statements - 1st & 2nd Level Supervisors: Sworn statements prior to the EEOC hearing indicated the 1st and 2nd level supervisors were not involved in the termination. Henrietta Snow knew the termination of the second employee was not valid. Testimony in part is as follows.

April 3, 2006 – 2nd Level Supervisor (Contract Operations Group Chief): Stated in part.

The 2nd level supervisor rated the terminated engineer's skills as "*Above average*". The 2nd level supervisor stated: "*I have taught engineering at college level, and have supervised and mentored military engineers for 17 years.*"

The 2nd level supervisor rated the terminated engineer's interpersonal skills as "*Average.*" The 2nd level supervisor had "*Eight years serving in a contractor oversight capacity requiring tactful teaming between government and contractor personnel.*"

"I was informed of the command section decision to terminate after it was already made. I do not recall whether I was informed before or after her first line supervisor."

"To my knowledge, the decision to terminate was made at the command section level. I was not advised or consulted."

"I am aware he (male military officer) *scolded her for the procedures issue. He did speak to me and stated he was upset and that he gave her a verbal lashing."*

The relevance is that the 2nd-level supervisor was neither advised nor consulted in the second retaliatory termination. The termination was handled at the 3rd (command) level of management.

April 7, 2006 – 1st Level Supervisor, C-130J Engineering Team: The 1st level supervisor stated the following in part.

"She was an employee working under my supervision. I have known Complainant since she started at DCMA-LMM in June 2004."

"I was not involved in the decision to remove Complainant during her probationary period. Ms. Snow took the action but I provided performance input. I provided written documentation of counseling and complaints from contractors, customers, and team associates."

"I did not terminate her."

"Complainant informed me someone knew she was going to be terminated. I was not at the meeting where the decision to terminate her was made. Myra Tate (another supervisor) told me on May 17,2005, that a decision had been made to terminate one of my employees. I called Lt. Col .Jones that same day, and he told me that Complainant was going to be terminated. Sometime after May 17, 2005, Ms. Snow told me she was going to remove Complainant."

Private Notes Provided After Termination & Threatened by Henrietta Snow

April 7, 2006: The private notes for recall were provided after the decision to terminate.

"As to the notes I made, they were a record of events I kept for recall. It was not until after the decision was made to terminate Complainant that these notes were shown to Ms. Snow. Ms. Snow was the only other person to see these notes before they were released to Complainant after she had been given the three page summary I wrote for Ms. Snow in early June 2005."

It is notable that the alleged notes were shown to Ms. Snow after the decision to terminate. The termination was unsubstantiated from the onset, and the supervisor was threatened as follows.

"I had been threatened by Ms. Snow with disciplinary action depending upon the outcome of this EEO investigation. Her words were "it looks like the Agency will be taking a hit on this case, and Ms. VanDerbeck may get her job back and receive compensation." She said if that's the case, she would have to take some kind of disciplinary action against me. Therefore, I hired a personal attorney, and she was unavailable on that day."

The termination was based on such insane reasons that the case was settled before the first level supervisor could testify at the hearing. There was also reason to believe that documents were falsified after the fact.

Documents Potentially Falsified After the Fact & Altered Email

April 21, 2006: A witness testified that the week Henrietta Snow dated and mailed the termination letter for the second retaliatory termination, the supervisor was traveling. The following week on return, the supervisor "*spent most of three days of that week (at least 2/3's) in Ms Henrietta Snow's office writing at the table. The door was open so I saw him at the table nearly every time I made a trip to that area.*"

The relevance is that there is a circumstantial question about when the supervisor's notes in the second retaliatory termination were made. Doubtful that the issue can be resolved. However, one issue of altered documents is obvious and was actually printed by Henrietta Snow.

May 10, 2005 – February 20, 2007 – Altered E-mail: DCMA provided a statement on the official record from the military officer who administered the "verbal lashing". That statement was dated February 20, 2007, and mentioned an e-mail sent to Henrietta Snow. I had assembled the EEO case file and could not remember an email from the military officer.

Upon detailed examination there was an e-mail printed by Henrietta Snow that was clearly altered. There was no send date and the title had been altered to make it appear that the employee had apologized. The date of the e-mail within the altered e-mail was May 10, 2005.

Relevance is that the military officer was a target of the EEO case due to the "verbal lashing" and was not interviewed in the EEO investigation. The military officer gave a sworn statement afterward and mentioned a forwarded e-mail to Henrietta Snow, likely sent immediately after May 10, 2005. That e-mail was more than likely the altered e-mail. The 1st level supervisor stated, "*Sometime after May 17, 2005, Ms. Snow told me she was going to remove Complainant*".

The point is, Henrietta Snow was protecting the military officer who did the "verbal lashing". The termination and the "verbal lashing" were both over the C-130J. The issue is now academic because the case was so insane that DCMA was forced to settle and cashed in the office travel budget.

Insane Case Innuendo Drives Settlement – Cash In Office Travel Budget

July 26, 2007: I led the assembly of the EEO case file and drove the case to an EEOC hearing. I went to EEOC since MSPB was too corrupt. The employee later retained a law firm in representation, and I briefed the attorney on the case. I was complimented on pushing the case to that point.

I later heard DCMA was so bizarre during the EEOC hearing that the judge suggested DCMA consider a settlement. DCMA did settle. I later overheard an employee say travel was canceled because the office travel budget was cashed in to settle the second retaliatory termination. The employee mentioned the name of the terminated employee. The settlement may have been large.

There was another instance related to the second retaliatory termination that gave more insight into the weaponized government between Dan Meyer and DCMA. By this time, Falsified Trail 3 had begun and there was some indication of Deep State involvement. Meaning that Dan Meyer was awakened as a "sleeper" in the Deep State against me.

Dan Meyer Tactical "Brightlines" – Information Leaks About Colonel Plourde

June 21-22, 2005: My July 7, 2005 affidavit to Dan Meyer included supporting data for the weaponized investigation by Keith Ernst and Colonel Plourde (Falsified Trail 3), where Plourde was desperately trying to find out who was leaking information about Plourde's tactics. On the evening of June 22, 2005, I documented where an employee…

"*…indicated to me that Colonel Plourde was trying to find the "leak". This implies that Colonel Plourde is interested in who made the information "leak" that warned employees were going to be fired.*"

The Other Leak: There was actually another information leak where an employee, who should not have known the DoD IG was involved, did, in fact, know. The employee emailed me on June 21, 2005, and stated that her situation *"has been turned over to the IG"*. I was a little confused and forwarded the e-mail to Dan Meyer for clarification. Meyer responded on June 22, 2005, stating.

Prior to the termination, I gave Leigh Owens a heads up regarding the difference between probationary employees, and probationary employees who had disclosed to the IG. She may have advised management to proceed accordingly, based on her legal opinion. I wanted to make sure they understood where the brightlines were.

Relevance is that Dan Meyer didn't answer the question asked; however, he made it clear that he tactically advised Leigh Owens on the second retaliatory (warmup) termination. This was the first cryptic data point of Deep State involvement. No vector could be drawn until October 18, 2005, which was Falsified Trail 3. In Falsified Trail 3 Dan Meyer would emerge as a major operative in the Deep State retaliation against me. There was significant evidence of that fact thanks to DCMA who ran a con on Dan Meyer in desperation to ruin my reputation.

Warmup Retaliations Complete – Now Retaliate Against the Fortified Targets

Deep State is Engaged in Force

The two warm-up retaliatory terminations of the soft targets were complete. Now it was time for the harder, more fortified targets (Henry Hagel and me) that were publicly known and linked to Senator Grassley. This was a Deep State operation that involved private tactical meetings; A con game on Senator Grassley via his staffer Charlie Murphy by Dan Meyer; A con game on Dan Meyer by DCMA; And flying across country on airplanes. There was an impressive entourage of attorneys and senior leadership persons.

20 Government Attorneys & 7 Senior U.S. Government Leadership

There were overall about 20 Government Attorneys and 7 Director and Command senior leaders involved in Falsified Trail 3. This included Keith Ernst who was involved at the DCMA HQ level and who had a part in Falsified Trail 1. This was an all-out, no holds barred, effort.

In Falsified Trail 3, DCMA had to thread a tight needle due to the involvement of Senator Grassley. Meaning, the Deep State had to work tactically in sync. Like a sniper scoping in on a human target with tactical adjustments for accuracy. A weaponized investigation provided the perfect insulation and cover story (pretext).

Falsified Trail 3: October 18, 2005 30-Day Suspension-Weaponized Investigation

Falsified Trail 3 (Volley 2) spanned the summer of 2005 and was tactically sighted in much like a sniper on a target against "*one employee, Ken Pedeleose*". Adjustments were made as needed since Falsified Trail 3 was a retaliatory and falsified work in progress that traced into the Pentagon (DoD Level) with the following index of names in rough order of culpability and associated surrogates.

Dan Meyer FT(3)	DoD IG Director Civilian Reprisal Investigations (CRI)
Colonel Nicole Plourde FT(3)	DCMA Commander
Uldric Fiore FT(3)	DoD IG Lead Attorney
Bruce Krasker FT(1,3)	DCMA Attorney
Leigh Owens FT(1,3)	DCMA Attorney
Stacy Scantlebury FT(3)	DCMA Chief, Special Processes, DCMA Atlanta
Keith Ernst FT(1,3)	DCMA Commander District East, then DCMA Director
Sallie Flavin FT(3)	DCMA Deputy Director
Steve Bogusz FT(3)	DCMA Deputy Director District East
Gill Bass FT(3)	DCMA Attorney
Charysse L. Alexander FT(3)	DOJ US Attorney Northern Dist. Atlanta
Gary Jencson FT(3)	DCMA Attorney
Donald Srail FT(3)	DCMA Attorney
S. Zimmit-Mack FT(3)	DCMA Attorney
Nicholas Retson FT(3)	DCMA Attorney
Henrietta Snow FT(3,10)	DCMA Deputy Commander
Leonard Trahan FT(3)	DoD IG Director, DoD IG Defense Hotline
Gentry Shellnut FT(3)	DOJ, US Attorney Supervisor
Thomas Gimble FT(3)	DoD IG, Principal Deputy, Acting DoD IG Director
Ray O'Connor FT(3)	DoD IG Attorney
Mark Boyll FT(3)	DoD IG Attorney
Michael Child FT(3)	DoD IG Attorney
Linda Springer FT(3)	Director Office of Personnel Management (OPM)
Kerry McTigue FT(3)	OPM Attorney
Steven Abow FT(3)	OPM Attorney
Becky Ronayne FT(3)	OPM Attorney-Advisor
Michael Hertz FT(3)	DOJ Deputy Assistant Attorney General
Jeanne Davidson FT(3,4,5,6)	DOJ Director
Todd Hughes FT(3)	DOJ Deputy Director
Michael O'Connel FT(3)	DOJ Trial Attorney
Tony West FT(3,4,5,6)	DOJ Assistant Attorney General

Tactical Weaponized Investigation, Lawfare & Tactical Insulation

The tactical weaponized investigation was a perfect Deep State tool for insulation and camouflage to retaliate against a well-connected, well-established, publicly known whistleblower.

However, the tactics were complicated and widespread, involving a con game against Senator Charles Grassley and staffer Charlie Murphy, and they relied on the last-minute element of surprise. After that, there was the hope that the Cerberus analogy of corruption at OSC, MSPB, and OSC would cover up the act, along with DOJ corruption. This was an ambitious plan that left a tornado trail of evidence. The key to the retaliation was Dan Meyer.

Dan Meyer (CRI) Network Hub for Tactical Retaliation

Direct Unfettered Private Tactical Weaponized Access

I originally relegated Meyer as zero value in my case. I was badly mistaken. Meyer proved to be a great detriment to me and an asset to tactical whistleblower retaliation. Meyer was a Director at the DoD IG with direct unfettered private weaponized access to the following:

1: Senator Grassley Staff (Charlie Murphy): Meyer interacted, as I did, with the staff of Senator Grassley, including Senate staffer Charlie Murphy. This was direct, unfettered Congressional access.

2: DoD IG Staff: Meyer was a CRI Director at DoD IG with direct unfettered access to DoD IG.

3: DCMA Attorneys: Meyer interacted (direct unfettered access) with DCMA attorneys on cases because DCMA attorneys responded to allegations against DCMA/Agency.

4: Whistleblowers: Meyer (CRI) was the gathering point for whistleblowers by virtue of being CRI (alleged whistleblower advocate). Meyer had direct, unfettered access to whistleblowers.

5: Whistleblower Supporters & Handlers: Meyer also had direct, unfettered access to whistleblower supporters and handlers such as POGO (Project on Government Oversight).

Weaponized Attorneys: DoD/DCMA/DoD IG attorneys were weapons in and of themselves to create falsified cases because attorneys can scope what a judge would want to see. Basically, falsify a case, frame-ups, and set-ups.

The retaliation tactic of Falsified Trail 3 was an investigation that specifically targeted me while driving other whistleblowers out of Federal Service. Access by Meyer was the key. In short, the investigation itself was a weapon that insulated management.

The following shows the tactical weaponized investigation without behind-the-scenes facts. Meaning, the investigation (pretext) was conducted by Colonel Plourde using Stacy Scantlebury, who just showed up with no credentials and no authority.

Tactical Weaponized Retaliatory Investigation – No Behind-the-Scenes Facts

<u>June 21, 2005 – Retaliatory Command Investigation</u>: Colonel Plourde initiated a haphazard retaliatory "Command Investigation" into an unspecified personnel incident, which stated.

"MEMORANDUM FOR: Ms. Stacy Scantlebury

FROM: DCMA Lockheed Martin Marietta Commander

SUBJECT: Command Investigation into a personnel incident reported by DCMA employee on 20 Jun 05.

1. *This appoints, you to inquire into the subject incident.*
2. *Report facts in letter form by 24 Jun 2005, unless an extension is requested. Ensure facts made are appropriately characterized.*
3. *Consult with DCMA Legal Counsel prior to the investigation*
4. *This appointment order authorizes you all necessary assistance from members of1he DCMA HQs in executing this tasking. Access to records germane to this investigation and clerical assistance will be provided."*

By June 21, 2005, it was obvious that Colonel Plourde and Henrietta Snow were on a mission to rid the office of whistleblowers. The 1st and 2nd level supervisors and other employees were spreading information from Plourde's arrogant office rants about firing people, not to mention those who were actually fired. Plourde's unhinged behavior caused conversation and concern across the office. The initial evidence of tactical weaponized investigation began with Stacy Scantlebury. Scantlebury was a DCMA office manager from another DCMA office nearby.

Stacy Scantlebury First Contact with Weaponized Investigation

<u>June 22, 2005, 1:15 PM</u>: My first encounter with Stacy Scantlebury was a phone conversation before for lunch. Scantlebury's demeanor was concerning. I asked Scantlebury if she was an investigator, and she essentially said no. After lunch, I met with Scantlebury. I refused to give answers because Scantlebury didn't act like a normal investigator. I then went to meet with Colonel Plourde the same day. I immediately documented my concerns as follows.

Documented & Complained to DCMA Directors About Scantlebury & Plourde

<u>June 22, 2005 6:03 PM</u>: I documented the encounters with Scantlebury and Plourde in an e-mail to DCMA Director East Keith Ernst and DCMA Director Major General (MG) Darryl Scott copy to Union President Roy Rogers, Dan Meyer, Colonel Plourde, Henrietta Snow, Leigh Owens, Sallie Flavin (DCMA Deputy Director), and Steven Bogusz (DCMA Deputy Director). The subject of the e-mail was. *"Illegal Order by Colonel Plourde, Abuse of Authority, Threatening a Federal Witness, and Witness Tampering"* I stated in part to the DCMA Directors.

"Today at about 1315 hours Myself and Mr. Roy Rogers (Then Union President) *went to speak with a person who Colonel Plourde allegedly requested to investigate an incident about people being targeted to be fired in our office. (This was a good rumor since an employee was actually fired last week by Ms. Henrietta Snow.)"*

"The individual's name doing the investigation was Ms. Stacy S. Scantlebury who was the Chief, of Special Processes at the DCMA Atlanta Office. When I asked Ms. Scantlebury if she was an investigator she stated no and indicated that Colonel Plourde had directed the study with a written letter. When I asked Ms. Scantlebury if she was taking sworn affidavits Ms. Scantlebury indicated she was not. When I asked for a copy of the letter from Colonel Plourde that Directed the Investigation, Ms. Scantlebury indicated that I could not have it. Ms. Scantlebury indicated that she is not a licensed investigator."

"Mr. Rogers and myself then when to talk to Colonel Plourde and Ms. Leigh Owens in Colonel Plourde's office for a prescheduled meeting. The discussion began by either Colonel Plourde or Ms. Owens indicating that I was a problem in that they cannot figure out if I was a union representative, and EEO representative, or a whistleblower."

"Colonel Plourde's actions are circumventing the DoD IG investigation by conducting her own investigation and using her authority to threaten employees with disciplinary action (Letters of Direction) if they do not participate in Colonel Plourde's investigation. If I were to provide the information to Ms. Scantlebury it would likely compromise ongoing and future IG investigations by trained investigators versus Ms. Scantlebury who is not an investigator."

Plourde issued me a Letter of Direction on June 22, 2005, directing me to talk to Scantlebury. I refused and instead sent the aforesaid e-mail. Regarding my roles as a union representative, an EEO representative, or a whistleblower, I can say I was all three since all three are protected activities and an offshoot of the DCMA hostile workplace and altered working conditions. My wide and systemic participation and data gathering in these activities made this book possible.

Scantlebury, Friend of Henrietta Snow & Surrogate

April 25, 2007: My inquiries regarding "Who is Stacy Scantlebury?" revealed that Scantlebury was not an investigator but a personal friend and colleague of Henrietta Snow, who recently fired two employees in our office. A 2007 email titled "*Stacy Scantlebury's Luncheon*" stated in part:

"Stacy has taken a job as the TAG (Technical Assessment Group) *Chief in Huntsville. Her luncheon is next Thursday, May 3rd, 11:15. Cheesecake Factory at Cumberland. Since she worked with lots of people over there, especially Henrietta, she suggested that I write you concerning the luncheon. Could you please canvas people as to whom would be interested in going to the luncheon?"*

Relevance is, Scantlebury was not independent and was a friend of Henrietta Snow for years, so I heard. Scantlebury also worked in the same building as Leigh Owens. The tactical weaponized investigation proved Scantlebury was a surrogate used by Keith Ernst.

Keith Ernst Appoints Scantlebury AR 15-6 (Army) Investigative Officer

Leak Investigation of a False Office Rumor

June 23, 2005: Ernst immediately shunned me (ignored my June 22, 2005 email) and quickly appointed Scantlebury an AR 15-6 (Army) investigative officer. Keith Ernst's memorandum stated.

"SUBJECT: APPOINTMENT AS AR15-6 INVESTIGATING OFFICER"

"You are hereby authorized to conduct an independent investigation into a personnel matter at DCMA Lockheed Martin Marietta which occurred on Friday, June 17th 2005 and was reported to Col Nicole Plourde on Monday, June 20th 2005.

You are to limit your investigation to the matter above and not to follow additional lines of inquiry.

You are authorized to gather sworn statements using the format in the attached document. You are not to make any factual findings or conclusions based on the evidence gathered. AR 15-6 is to serve as a guide and is enclosed.

Ms. Leigh Owens, Counsel, DCMA Atlanta will serve as your legal advisor for this investigation."

Keith Ernst cheered on Falsified Trail 1, and now Ernst was directly involved in Falsified Trail 3. Keith Ernst also appeared in Chapter 2. Meaning, Keith Ernst showed no concern for efficiency of the Federal Service. I first saw the June 23, 2005, Memorandum signed by Keith Ernst on/about October 21, 2005. Meaning, Ernst was in the background at that point. I continued confronting Scantlebury as follows.

Stacy Scantlebury – "No Need to Know This Information"

June 23, 2005, 10:25 AM: I again complained to DCMA Directors Keith Ernst and MG Darryl Scott, copy to Meyer, Plourde, Snow, Owens, Flavin, Bogusz, and Scantlebury, that Plourde was continuing her retaliatory acts. In this case, Plourde/DCMA tried to tactically shift from a whistleblowing matter to a union/labor relations matter. I wrote the following e-mail, stating in part.

"Mr. Ernst,

Colonel Plourde is continuing her reprisal actions and I have not heard from you regarding her hostile attitude toward Mr. Hagel and myself. Per past practice the DCMA lawyers are directly involved in the matter firmly on the side of management. The facts are:

First, this is not a union matter that I have presented to the DoD Civilian Reprisal Investigations (CRI) Mr. Dan Meyer it is a whistleblower matter..."

"The information given to CRI was comprehensive and for the record directly mentioned DCMA management officials by name, in some cases. This was given to Civilian Reprisal Investigations (CRI) in support of an active investigation. Now DCMA management is trying to extract information from the whistleblowers who submitted the information. I consider this as illegal and abuse of authority by Colonel Plourde."

"Since the information provided to CRI is a whistleblower matter and not a union or employee matter, I will ask that Colonel Plourde and/or her designated representative directly address any questions to Mr. Dan Meyer (CRI)... Mr. Meyer is also on distribution for this e-mail."

Relevance is that Dan Meyer was copied on the e-mail with Meyer's contact information. The DCMA Directors shunned me; however, Scantlebury responded to me only 2 minutes later, stating.

"I respectfully request that you not include me on e-mail messages such as this. I really have no need to know this information."

The DCMA Directors, Plourde and Scantlebury, were specifically informed that this was a whistleblower matter and provided with specific contact information for Dan Meyer. I was shunned by management and Scantlebury didn't want to hear facts.

<u>Original Weaponized Investigation Faded Away</u>: The original weaponized investigation faded away and then reappeared about 42 days later in a far more tactical and ominous way as follows.

"Sighting In" (Adjusting) the Weaponized Investigation to Lawfare

Ominous Kalkines Warning

August 2, 2005: DCMA "sighted in" (adjusted) the weaponized investigation to a lawfare level with a far more tactical, threatening and ominous tone as follows. Scantlebury (surrogate) stated in part.

"I have been appointed by Mr. Ernst, Director of DCMAE, as an Investigative Officer."

"Pursuant to the rule set forth in Kalkines v. United States, 473 F.2d 1391 (Ct. Cl. 1973), the United States Attorney for the District of Atlanta has authorized me to communicate to you that you will not be subject to a criminal proceeding for any response(s) that you may give, except for providing a false answer. I will provide you with the "Kalkines" Rights and Obligations Notification form at the beginning of the interview. This Notification removes the right to remain silent for fear of criminal prosecution. However, the Notification Form advises that you may be subject to administrative penalties imposed by the Agency for a failure or refusal to respond, or lack of candor in the response. You may be removed from federal service if you do not fully, completely and accurately respond to my questions. Additionally, you may be disciplined for any misconduct revealed by your responses."

This was the exact point where government weaponization incorporated the lawfare aspect.

August 2, 2005, 3:01 PM – Notified Scantlebury of DoD IG: I responded to Scantlebury's ominous email and copied Joseph Schmitz (DoD IG), DCMA Directors (Ernst & MG Scott), Bogusz, and Plourde. I stated in part,

"I consider this as reprisal against me. I am also suspicious that you did not include Mr. Ernst on your letter.

The DoD IG already has an investigation in this area and I have already provided the information I have to them."

Scantlebury responded only to me at 4:03 PM, reiterating her position. I then responded…

August 2, 2005 4:33 PM: I expanded the e-mail distribution to Scantlebury to include Dan Meyer, Joseph Schmitz, DCMA Directors (Ernst and Scott), Bogusz, Plourde, and Flavin, stating in part:

Ms. Scantlebury,

"Please provide me the name of ""the United States Attorney for the District of Atlanta"" that you spoke with in regards to this matter (as mentioned in your letter below)?"

"Why do you continue to respond to only me when I have the DoD IG on distribution and other members of senior management?"

"Mr. Ernst,

If this this a legitimate issue for you why don't you inform DCIS (Defense Criminal Investigative Service) *of your concerns and have them or the DoD IG do an investigation? (I have already sent my concerns to the DoD IG.)"*

Systematically Shunned: I was systematically shunned by all DCMA management levels. Probably because Scantlebury was a surrogate in a weaponized investigation that was now elevated to the lawfare level for my demise.

Stacy Scantlebury was a Surrogate – Leigh Owens was the Local Mastermind

August 3, 2005, 4:01 PM: I sent a lengthy e-mail to Scantlebury, with a copy to Dan Meyer and the employees who were targeted by Colonel Plourde. I informed Scantlebury that I "*also need to meet with the United States attorney*" referenced by Scantlebury in the ominous e-mail.

August 4, 2005 1:42 PM: Scantlebury forwarded my August 3, 2005 e-mail to Leigh Owens, only stating:

"FYI

Stacy S. Scantlebury"

Leigh Owens was an attorney who would know the specifics of lawfare. Scantlebury was a surrogate with no answers. Personal meetings would solidify this fact.

Personal Meetings with Scantlebury

September 12, 2005: Henry Hagel and I met with Scantlebury and gave her written statements, protection letters from Senator Grassley, and informed her of the following.

"In addition to retaliation which is a violation of 18USC 1505, I believe that the investigation is also a violation of the AR 15-6 Regulation which states Item 3b: Informal procedures are not intended to provide a hearing for persons who may have an interest in the subject of the investigation.

There is an obvious interest that DCMA has in the investigation since there have been ongoing accusations against DCMA on a wide spectrum involving retaliation. Additionally, ongoing litigation and lawful investigations would be compromised if I participate in your investigation.

At this time-I must regretfully decline to participate in your investigation. I have turned over information to the DoD IG and will continue to support lawful and duly authorized investigations."

There was continued shunning and no response to the concerns. Other employees experienced and documented the same attitude from Stacy Scantlebury as follows.

Other Employees Were Intimidated & Given No Valid Answers to Concerns

August 4, 2005: Another employee, targeted to be fired, made the grave mistake of approaching Colonel Plourde. The employee made a Memorandum for Record, stating in part.

"On Wednesday August 3rd 2005, I sent an e-mail to Col. Plourde outlining some of my concerns to subject myself for Ms. Scantlebury's interview in view of the serious and extremely pertinent questions raised by Mr. Pedeleose and Mr. Hagel regarding Ms. Scantlebury's upcoming interview. Col. Plourde didn't answer my e-mail, but instead called Mr. Pates (2nd Level Supervisor) *to take me personally to her office."*

"I asked Ms. Scantlebury whether she had any legal backgrounds and she said no. I brought to Ms. Scantlebury's attention some of the serious and legitimate concerns raised by Mr. Pedeleose and Mr. Hagel surrounding this interview and I mentioned her that I am also very concerned on the legitimacy and legal implications of the subject interview. Ms. Scantlebury reiterated the fact that she has absolutely no legal backgrounds and has no valid answers to any of the concerns and that made me very uncomfortable with the subject interview."

This further confirms, even absent behind-the-scenes evidence, that Scantlebury was the surrogate in a tactical weaponized investigation that had moved into the lawfare stage. This was from general interactions with Scantlebury. As time progressed, investigations and FOIAs helped bring the DCMA tactical weaponized investigation and lawfare into focus.

Meaning, there was a massive behind-the-scenes tactical operation at play that explains why DCMA Directors and management at all levels were shunning me and how the weaponized investigation was intensifying with a more ominous and threatening lawfare tone.

Deep State Transparency: In short, transparency into the Deep State was coming into focus as the following shows. The Deep State transparency was achieved several months to years after the fact from investigations, FOIAs, legal case filings, depositions, and the like. That information was integrated into the following timeline to prove the Deep State does exist.

Tactical Weaponized Retaliatory Investigation – With Behind-the-Scenes Facts

Deep State Transparency on the Ominous Kalkines Warning - Lawfare

The prior section examined the tactical weaponized investigation without considering behind-the-scenes facts. Meaning, circumstantial evidence. The following is the tactical weaponized retaliatory investigation with behind-the-scenes facts. Meaning, direct evidence and Deep State transparency.

August 2005 Parallel Paths: The evidence begins on August 10, 2005, with a special in-person meeting between DCMA and the DoD IG concerning the tactical weaponized investigation, with Scantlebury as the surrogate. DCMA had already issued the ominous email on August 2, 2005, with the Kalkines threat; however, further refinement was needed to ensure the tactical investigation was successful with the lawfare enhancement. This was the Deep State tactics at work.

Tactically Sight-In (Sniper) Weaponized Investigation to Lawfare

The events of August 2005 are best described in the June 5, 2008, IG investigation of Uldric Fiore (Lead DoD IG Attorney), who attended the August 10, 2005, meeting along with Dan Meyer, DCMA attorney Bruce Krasker, and other DoD IG attorneys/management. The June 5, 2008, IG report was lengthy and stated in part:

"When we asked [one of the Associate General Counsels] about the September 16, 2005 e-mail, he explained that it was in reference to the discussion about the Kalkines warning that they had at the August 10, 2005 meeting. [He] said he had provided similar advice to other DoD agencies that he considered clients of the OIG. [He] said he never had a meeting similar to the August 10, 2005 meeting; however, he said, "I didn't think it was totally out of the ordinary, though, given the fact that we also were conducting a Hotline and reprisal investigations, and we wanted to ensure that we kept them separate and apart to assure our independence under the IG Act."

The Kalkines Warning was tactical and designed to instill fear by name-dropping of the Assistant United States Attorney (AUSA). However, the Kalkines warning was not enough. Tactically, DCMA needed a declination letter from the AUSA to make Kalkin's warning more lethal and ensure the lawfare retaliation was successful. The Deep State provided the necessary tactics.

Tactically Obtain AUSA Declination Letter for Maximum Lawfare Effect

The June 5, 2008, IG investigation report went on to state the tactics used to obtain a declination letter from AUSA. Meaning, DoD IG was teaming and scheming alongside DCMA as follows.

"[The Associate General Counsel] said he recalled talking to [another Associate General Counsel] on one or two occasions about DCMA's authority to investigate and the adverse action letter for [the DoD complainant]. [He] said he conducted research after the August 2005 meeting and helped DCMA identify and articulate its authority in an appointment letter for the DCMA investigator.

[He] also recalled speaking with [another Associate General Counsel] after he had received a declination from the Assistant U.S. Attorney; [the Associate General Counsel said he advised him to get the declination in writing if DCMA was intending to take adverse action."

DoD IG attorneys tactically articulated letters that falsified DCMA authority with the eventual purpose of "*adverse action*" against me, even though DCMA did not have authority to investigate. Meaning, DCMA was using AR 15-6, an Army instruction, not applicable to DCMA. This is aside from the fact that DCMA was in a gross conflict of interest with DCMA investigating DCMA. Then, DCMA divided into teams to ensure an effective weaponized lawfare effort.

DCMA Director & Attorney Teaming with Documentation & Email Relays

The top-tier scheming team, for Falsified Trail 3 was DCMA and the DoD IG. Sub teams included: Keith Ernst and Sallie Flavin; DCMA attorneys Leigh Owens and Gill Bass; Leigh Owens and Stacy Scantlebury; and, Leigh Owens, Stephanie Zimmt-Mack and Bruce Krasker. The Owens and Bass team are first.

Leigh Owens & Gill Bass Team to Tactically Sight-in Kalkines for Lawfare

"One Employee, Ken Pedeleose"

August 16, 2005 – False Statement to AUSA: About 2 weeks after August 2, 2005, (Kalkines Warning) was issued, Leigh Owens sent a letter to AUSA Charysse Alexander stating:

"This is to confirm that you were telephonically contacted by the undersigned and Ms. Gill Bass on or about July 19, 2005. Ms. Bass and I explained that DCMA was conducting an inquiry into the circumstances under which one of DCMA-Lockheed Martin Marietta's employees had been advised that she was on a "hit list", and was being targeted by agency management for termination. We indicated that several of our employees, including, Mr. Kenneth Pedeleose, had declined to cooperate with the inquiry.

You advised that no federal criminal statute appeared to be implicated in the situation described, that you were declining prosecution on anything related to this situation, and the Kalkines notice was appropriate in this situation. You have subsequently advised Ms. Bass that it is the practice of your office to conduct such coordination orally.

We would appreciate receiving a written confirmation of our conversation.

Thank you for your assistance in this matter."

Leigh Owens and Gill Bass abused their direct lawfare access and tried to con the AUSA. Charysse Alexander responded back on August 25, 2005, as follows.

August 25, 2005 – "One Employee, Ken Pedeleose": Charysse Alexander responded to Owens as follows. (Appendix A1-12)

"*Re: Administrative Matter*

Dear Ms. Owens:

I received your letter of August 16, 2005, attached hereto, In which you requested written confirmation of my previous oral opinion on whether our office would pursue criminal prosecution of a particular matter. On July 19, 2005 you and Gill Bass described a matter to me that involved one employee, Ken Pedeleose, allegedly advising another employee that she was about to be fired. You asked whether the United States Attorney's Office would consider such a matter for criminal prosecution. I advised that we would not, and that in my opinion, it was appropriate to use the Kalkines warnings in the administrative investigation. If the facts as described above vary in substance from my summary, please advise me immediately, as my conclusions could change.

Leigh Owens and Gill Bass focused on "*one employee, Ken Pedeleose.*" Meaning that Leigh Owens tried to con Charysse Alexander. I was singled out with lawfare.

Name-Dropping, Perjury Trap: The DCMA weaponized lawfare investigation used the DOJ as a name-dropping, perjury trap, and intimidation scam. The DOJ letter was a perfect weapon for intimidation and insulation. It had a Fax stamp from "*U.S. Attorney's Office*".

The DOJ letter had the DOJ emblem and the words "*U.S. Department of Justice*", "*United States Attorney*", "*Northern District of Georgia*". The signature block had the names "*David E Nahmias United States Attorney*" and "*Charysse L. Alexander Chief, Public Corruption & Government Fraud*". The point is, DCMA and DoD IG went to an extreme length to target me specifically.

While Owens and Bass worked the AUSA (DOJ) another DCMA team, Keith Ernst and Sallie Flavin worked the weaponized lawfare investigation from the DCMA Headquarters (HQ) level.

Keith Ernst & Sallie Flavin Team Tactically Sight-in Weaponized Investigation

August 18, 2005, Flavin Tactically Sights-in Weaponized Employment "Oaths": Sallie Flavin's contribution to the tactical weaponized lawfare investigation teams was sworn statements. Meaning, DCMA had no authority to run investigations let alone take sworn statements. So, Sallie Flavin issued a "*Memorandum for DCMA District Directors/Commander*" with the subject "*Delegation of Authority to administer Oaths*". Sallie Flavin's August 18, 2005, memorandum included the following section.

"E1.1.1.3. Administer oaths of office to those entering the Executive Branch of the Federal Government or any other oath required by law in connection with employment therein, in accordance with 5 U.S.C. 2903, and designate in writing, as may be necessary, officers and employees of the DCMA to perform this function."

Flavin used the employment oath, designed to protect the U.S. Constitution, not the oath to take sworn statements. This was bizarre and flattering because I had caused a DCMA Deputy Director, via signature on a formal document, to be openly part of a Deep State tactical retaliation and lawfare. The next day, Keith Ernst used Flavin's Memorandum in the tactical weaponized lawfare investigation.

August 19, 2005 – Keith Ernst Tactical Sight-in Weaponized AR 15-6 Investigation: The following day, Keith Ernst vastly improved his original June 23, 2005 appointment letter for Stacy Scantlebury as an AR 15-6 Investigative Officer. This was Ernst's part of the retaliation team.

Ernst incorporated Flavin's August 18, 2005, Memorandum for the sworn statements; added the Kalkines warning; and continued Scantlebury as an AR 15-6 (Army) Investigative Office. Ernst's August 19, 2005, Memorandum appointing Scantlebury as AR 15-6 (Army) Investigative officer was sighted-in for ultimate retaliation and lawfare. The overall flattery is serialized as follows.

Seven Flattering Events of the Deep State in Action Over Me (Pedeleose)

The first was the DoD IG Division of CRI (Dan Meyer) position created over me (Chapter 1, my resume). The second was Charysse Alexander, confirming Owens and Bass spoke of "*One Employee, Ken Pedeleose*" (August 25, 2005). The Third was Flavin tactically sighting in the employment oath against me.

The fourth was Keith Ernst's bizarre and enhanced use of AR 15-6 (Army Regulation) using Flavin's employment oath along with the Kalkines Warning specifically targeting Henry Hagel and me. The fifth is the time frame which lasted the summer of 2005 (June 21, 2005 to August 19, 2005) to adjust a tactical retaliation to lawfare. The sixth is Colonel Plourde, who, again on September 8, 2005, tactically issued another more specific retaliatory Letter of Direction stating the following.

"MEMORANDUM FOR: Mr. Ken Pedeleose

FROM: Commander, DCMA Lockheed Martin Marietta

SUBJECT: Letter of Direction related to Command Inquiry conducted by Stacy Scantlebury

Mr. Pedeleose,

You are hereby directed to be present on 12 September 2005 at 09:30 a.m. at the DCMA Lockheed Martin Marietta Command Suite (old TAG Office) in Building B-2.

In addition, you are directed to meet with Ms Stacy Scantlebury for her interview of you and to fully cooperate and answer all questions posed by Ms. Scantlebury as part of her inquiry."

Synchronized Lawfare: The seventh flattering, retaliatory lawfare event, was the overall, cumulative, collaborative efforts of Owens, Bass, Ernst, Flavin, and Plourde who worked with precision, in sync, specifically targeting me.

However, the centerpiece was actually the one-man team (retaliation hub), closed loop of Dan Meyer. Meyer's efforts enhanced the retaliation, and Meyer even became a focus of the Leigh Owens, Stephanie Zimmt-Mack, Bruce Krasker Team. Meaning, while Meyer was running con games, Meyer was the focus of a con by the Owens-Mack-Krasker Team. Dan Meyer follows…

Dan Meyer - Hub & One-Man Closed Loop

Weaponized Direct Access Within DoD & Outside DoD

Meyer was the direct access hub of retaliatory activity. Meyer had direct access to whistleblowers; direct access to Congress (Senator Grassley via Charlie Murphy); direct access to DoD Agencies; direct access to the DoD IG; and Direct access to whistleblower supporters like POGO.

Dan Meyer was a one-man closed loop. Meaning Meyer had no staff and no investigators to farm work out to. Meyer was the DoD IG Director for 660,000 DoD employees, a position specifically created for me, as outlined in my resume (Chapter 1). Dan Meyer's emails (electronic trails) tell the best story of how Dan Meyer operated in the Deep State lawfare scheme against me.

Dan Meyer Electronic E-mail Trail to Con Me (Pedeleose)

The following electronic information trail, along with the DCMA-stipulated sworn statements, is as follows. Meaning, Dan Meyer's con game against me.

June 30, 2005 2:19 PM: I e-mailed Meyer, indicating that Scantlebury is not quitting, and I expected that Colonel Plourde would take disciplinary action. Meyer responded and copied Charlie Murphy, stating: "*Will incorporate it, Ken.*" Implying Meyer would add it to my case against DCMA. So, in this case, Dan Meyer is supposedly my friend.

This e-mail was a result of Scantlebury allegedly "*Wrapping Up*" her weaponized investigation into *"the events surrounding a "rumor" of employees being targeted for termination of employment by members of management at DCMA Lockheed Martin Marietta."*

August 4, 2005 8:51 AM: Meyer stated (on weaponized investigation): "*Our attorneys are meeting on this right now – started 0830. I* (Meyer) *have routed the non-reprisal complaint alleging criminal activities. You can also take that to your local office of the FBI, if you want to.*"

August 9, 2005 11:39 AM: Meyer indicated the DoD IG was questioning the alleged investigation. Meyer stated:

"*We are meeting tomorrow at 2PM; Leigh Owens has told me that Stanglebury* [sic] *will not proceed until our attorneys have taken a crack at this situation.*

Generally what you are asking for is "stay" authority, which I have not been given. OSC is the only entity with stay authority right now; I am willing to make this my first request, if it comes to that."

Dan Meyer appears to be my friend in this communication; however, Dan Meyer responded to me only. The original e-mail was addressed to DoD IG Joseph Schmitz, with copies to Dan Meyer, Henry Hagel, and DoD IG members I was assisting on Senator McCain's investigation (Joe Bucsko and Henry KleinKnecht of the DoD IG), along with Rudy Noordhuisen, possibly associated with Senator Grassley's investigation, in my Resume Chapter 1. I informed Schmitz in part.

Mr. Schmitz,

I must inform you that Management Officials of the Defense Contract Management Agency (DCMA) are in the process of actively impeding the due and proper administration of law and are tampering with witnesses (Mr. Henry Hagel and Myself). In short, Mr. Hagel arid I have been threatened by DCMA management to the point where management actions have significantly interfered with support to IG investigations and Senate Investigations. DCMA Management officials have also threatened/pressured other DCMA employees whom lam associated with.

The e-mail to Schmitz was longer and was based on Scantlebury's ominous August 2, 2005 11:15 AM e-mail to me that included Kalkin's warning. However, as of August 3, 2005, Meyer had a parallel clandestine email trail with DCMA supporting the DCMA investigation. Meaning, Meyer was working behind my back (duplicity) as follows.

Dan Meyer Parallel Con to Me (Duplicity) - Clears Questions for DCMA

August 3, 2005 4:27 PM: Leigh Owens e-mailed Dan Meyer, only stating in part.

"Please find attached a list of the questions Ms. Scantlebury intends to ask Messrs Hagel and Pedeleose when they are interviewed. The agency would, of course, ask follow on questions logically arising from the responses provided. In the interest of moving this matter forward, I think it would be more efficient to have your office review the questions and give us some guidance on the appropriate scope of our inquiry on the front end of the process." (Appendix A2-4)

Relevance is that the email has no Subject stated and Stacy Scantlebury is not copied on it.

August 3, 2005 4:38 PM "Pedeleose Matter, Next Stage": Dan Meyer e-mails DoD IG attorneys Mark Boyll and Michael S Child and adds the Subject "Pedeleose Matter, Next Stage". The attachment is titled "ScantleburyQuestions.doc". Meyer states.

"Is there a reason why I should not go down this route? See DCMA's request below."

August 3, 2005 4:51 PM: Meyer,13 minutes later, e-mails Mark Boyll, Michael Child copy to Richard Race with Subject "*DCMA Questions with my thoughts – Pedeleose/Hagel cases*" stating.

"Attached are the questions sent by DCMA; I have added in red font the questions I am would be concerned about – as in having an impact on my investigation".

Relevance is, I am an open topic at DoD IG. Meaning, I am well known. Also, Leigh Owens stated openly to Meyer that "*The agency would, of course, ask follow on questions logically arising from the responses provided.*" Meaning, it doesn't matter what is cleared, DCMA will ask what they want anyway. The e-mail trail reappeared on September 6, 2005.

September 6, 2005, 9:35 AM - Krasker to OConnor & OConnor to Meyer: The email trail took up over a month later between DCMA Bruce Krasker and DoD IG Ray OConnor. Krasker emailed OConnor at 7:53 AM and then OConnor emailed Meyer at 8:02 AM, stating in part.

"FYI: If you have any concerns with the questions, please respond to Bruce directly, with an info to me. I did not identify any problems with the proposed questions, from our perspective.

Please let me know if I can be of further assistance.

Thanks Dan

Ray"

At 9:35 AM, Meyer e-mails Ray OConnor and Bruce Krasker a copy to Leigh Owens, stating in part.

"Bruce, thanks for narrowing these questions; on their face, I see no conflict between my investigation and DCMA's. I will be in Georgia this weekend, with Monday at the facility."

One salient point is, Dan Meyer tried to partition himself in the lawfare effort with "top cover" concealment by spreading blame to others. Meyer would speak of this later as follows.

Clandestine Trap – Surprise Evidence - "Top Cover" for Meyer

Scantlebury provided a copy of the questions to me in a letter, with the DCMA address blotted out; however, there was no indication that the questions had been cleared by Dan Meyer or that Dan Meyer was involved in any way. The first time I saw or heard of questions being cleared was on/about April 3, 2006. I was denied access to the allegedly cleared questions even after the suspension was proposed on October 18, 2005.

Dan Meyer best explained the delay from August 3, 2005 to September 6, 2005 on July 27, 2007 where Meyer stated: "*I had no contact with DCMA Boston, except through OGC. That is why I was invited to Ric's meeting with them, because OGC was 'providing me top cover"*.

Meaning, Meyer partitioned himself from culpability via "*top cover*" by other DoD IG officials. The email trails exposed Meyer. DCMA stipulated on May 10, 2006 (No Rebuttal Letter) Meyer had no idea if the DCMA weaponized investigation was legal as follows.

Dan Meyer Verbal Statements - Stipulated to in March 29, 2006 Deposition

<u>Dan Meyer Has "No Idea"</u>: In 2005, I asked Meyer about the legality of the DCMA weaponized AR 15-6 investigation, stating: "*Dan, is what they're doing over here lawful? Is this a lawful investigation?*" *He* (Meyer) *said*, "*We* (DoD IG) *have absolutely no idea. We* (DoD IG) *have never seen this before.*" DCMA stipulated (agreed) to this conversation on May 10, 2006.

<u>Dan Meyer stated, "DCMA was Told to Quit</u>: DCMA stipulated (agreed to) the following.

"*At one point to my knowledge, DCMA was told to quit what they were doing until a such time they justified that this was like a lawful investigation. In other words, the Inspector General's Office had been involved at that point in time.*"

<u>Dan Meyer "Head Scratching"</u>: Regarding DCMA "implicit authority" for the AR 15-6 weaponized investigation, Meyer stated to me: "*We know there's going to be some head scratching on that one.*" DCMA stipulated this as well on the MSPB official record.

Hence, Dan Meyer led me to believe the DCMA investigation was unlawful. Meyer later told me a DCMA attorney, possibly Gary Jencson, wanted to depose him. Meyer's voice to me was shaky.

On June 28, 2006 Henry Shelley stated in part, Dan Meyer was "*really, really worried about that*". Meaning an MSPB hearing. There was a hearing on written records, including sworn statements and depositions. Meyer didn't testify and was *"really, really worried"*, probably due to the following.

Dan Meyer - Parallel Con Part 1 – Story to Senior DoD IG

"Let Some Steam Out of This Situation"

August 4, 2005 8:16 AM: I e-mailed Dan Meyer, Joseph Schmitz, and Charlie Murphy with the title "*Need Help and Request for Criminal Investigations Against DCMA*". Schmitz forwarded my email at 8:24 AM to Thomas Gimble and copied DoD IG senior people, including Richard Race, John Crane (DoD IG Congressional Liaison), Uldric Fiore, and Mark Boyll, stating:

"Tom: Why am I getting this e-mail (along with Charlie Murphy)? /Joe/"

August 4, 2005 9:28 AM: Race responded to all and copied in Dan Meyer, stating: *"Dan, Plse c the IG's note. U have this con. Plse advise Tom as FA."*

August 4, 2005 9:35 AM: Meyer responded, explaining some background of the tactical weaponized investigation, and went on to state:

"Do you want to set the IG's Outlook software to delete them upon arrival? They will still come to me.

Murphy is getting the e-mails because Senator Grassley issued a whistleblower protection letter to Ken Pedeleose last year; Murphy has been handling this case since 2003.

I am traveling to Atlanta on September 12th to try to let some steam out of this situation."

August 4, 2005 11:19 AM: Gimble responds to Meyer, only stating: *"I think the IG wants remain in the loop as long as someone is working the issues"*. Relevance is, Dan Meyer conned DoD IG senior leadership about taking "*steam out of this situation*" while Meyer added steam in parallel, that same morning, as follows.

Dan Meyer Leaves No Doubt – Parallel Con Part 2 – Story to Me (Pedeleose)

Add Steam - Planting a "Kernel" of Thought About Unlawful DCMA Investigation

This e-mail trail is profound and incriminating. Meyer has me question Scantlebury's credentials, turning me against the weaponized investigation. Meyer then, behind the scenes, supports the weaponized investigation. This finale con took under 2 hours (8:51 AM to 10:48 AM on August 4, 2005). The initial e-mail was sent on August 2, 2005, 8:16 AM.

August 4, 2005 8:16 AM: I sent an e-mail to Meyer, Joseph Schmitz, and Charlie Murphy with the title "*Need Help and Request for Criminal Investigations Against DCMA*". The e-mail was a rehash of what I have been stating all along regarding the DCMA tactical weaponized AR-15-6 investigation by Ernst, Plourde, and Scantlebury. Meyer used this e-mail to start the finale con game less than an hour later as follows.

August 4, 2005 8:51 AM: Meyer e-mailed me only stating:

"*Our attorneys are meeting on this right now – started 0830. I* (Meyer) *have routed the non-reprisal complaint alleging criminal activities. You can also take that to your local office of the FBI, if you want to.*" Here, Meyer leads me to believe he is on my side.

August 4, 2005 8:53 AM: Meyer states: "*Ask Scantlebury for the letter of authority adopting AR 15-6 as the standard for investigations within DCMA. Odd that they did not cite the Air Force regulation.*" Meyer turns me against the alleged investigation and continues as follows.

August 4, 2005 8:55 AM: Meyer joined in another conversation with Charlie Murphy, Henry Hagel, and me regarding a protection letter for Hagel where Meyer stated:

"Charlie - a letter with Henry's name would be a good idea; his contribution over the past 18 months should also be highlighted. Henry, you might want to do a draft for Charlie using Ken's letter." Meyer then continued conning me as follows.

August 4, 2005 8:57 AM: Meyer e-mailed me stating: "*Plourde is Air Force, right? or Army. What about you and Henry – are you DCMA employees (my hunch), or Army civilian employees detailed to DCMA? Our attorneys are intrigued as to why AR 15-6 is being cited.*"

August 4, 2005 9:55 AM: Meyer e-mailed me stating: "*And ask her* (Scantlebury) *for the organizing Air Force or Department of Defense regulations for Colonel Plourde's office, giving Colonel Plourde the authority to authorize an administrative investigation.*"

By this stage, I am opposed to the alleged investigation and am actively forwarding questions to Scantlebury. Then Meyer goes behind my back in true duplicity fashion.

Dan Meyer Parallel Con Part 3 – Story to DCMA & DoD IG Officials

Enable DCMA Weaponized AR 15-6 (Army) Investigation

Dan Meyer Goes Behind My Back Supporting DCMA: Meyer (less than an hour later) goes behind my back and e-mails Leigh Owens (DCMA) and other DoD IG officials, supporting the DCMA's alleged investigation as follows. (Appendix A1-7)

August 4, 2005 10:48 AM: Meyer e-mails Leigh Owens and copies DoD IG officials (Thomas Gimble, Mark Boyll, and John Crane), stating: "*I'd like your input on this, my goal being to enable the Colonel as much as possible in an AR 15-6 investigation. Our attorneys came up with three options, less appealing to more appealing:*"

"(1) Give you my concerns with five of Stacy's questions, and ask that they not be used in the AR 15-6 investigation. I am not a fan of this option, because if I were Stacy I would consider these five questions essential. But on CRI's side of the coin, those five questions may endanger a source in the VanDerbeck case."

In Option 1, Meyer knows DCMA's investigation would clearly interfere with Meyer's case on the second terminated employee. Option 2 by Meyer is even more incriminating.

"(2) Second idea, OIG DoD could initiate an investigation of Mr. Pedeleose's non-reprisal allegations that an unlawful termination plan (the so-called "hit list") was being implemented. We would then ask DCMA to not proceed in deference to our investigation. I think this is a little heavy handed."

In Option 2, Meyer clearly knows that allegations/information of unlawful terminations exist, so any investigation by DCMA should be ruled out.

Additionally, Leigh Owens (DCMA attorney) was the primary "To" recipient on the e-mail, and, as such, should have stopped the investigation at that point; however, she did not. Meaning, Leigh Owens was an active participant in alleged unethical activity, including whistleblower retaliation, lawfare, and a violation of 18 USC 1505. Meyer's third option was still more incriminating.

(3) Third idea, using my recent NSA work as a model. The Colonel could request a Joint Investigation. I could deputize Stacy (for lack of a better word) and she could report to me, the findings could be run through OIG DoD, and DCMA would benefit from the neutrality and impartiality of an IG. We could bring DCMA's IG into the equation as well. Mark did recommend that we establish the reporting protocol up front

Option 3 to "*deputize Stacy*" was an instant administrative "death sentence," knowing that Senator Grassley, via Charlie Murphy, had high hopes that Dan Meyer would change DoD IG culture. It is also concerning that Dan Meyer mentioned recent work with NSA as a model. Meaning, Meyer may have ran the same unethical cons on NSA as happened to me thus jeopardizing the intel community. It seems Meyer's influence and antics may have went past NSA per the following.

Director of Whistleblowing & Transparency: On/about February 8, 2011 I discovered Dan Meyer may have occupied the position of Congressional Liaison of DoD IG as Director of Whistleblowing & Transparency. Meyer may have provided counsel and advice to DoD IG and DoD Agencies on how to handle whistleblowers. This was very disturbing since Chapter 3 of this book, Falsified Trail 3 outlines specifically how Dan Meyer handled my case.

Also, during August 5, 2010 I kept some contact with Charlie Murphy regarding DoD IG and reports of impropriety. Murphy provided little assistance or comfort that issues would ever be resolved or at the least made transparent. Hence the best option after decades of stagnation and worsening government ethics I opted to write this book. Because I had a lot more to talk about Dan Meyer, using Dan Meyer's own words. Meaning, the conclusion in Dan Meyer's August 4, 2005 email proves a con game against Congress as follows.

Dan Meyer - Tactical "External Credibility" for Weaponized Investigations

Meyer closes the August 4, 2005 10:48 AM e-mail by stating. (Appendix A1-7)

"*Given Senators McCain and Grassley's interest in this case, this may provide a way for the IG community to aid the Colonel and provide external credibility which will be desirable as events move out of Georgia and up towards Washington. Something to mull over.*

Get back to me when you get into the office."

This is a crystal-clear, no-doubt con game by Dan Meyer. Meaning, Meyer and DoD IG would enable Colonel Plourde to finish me off with a weaponized investigation and lawfare. This is so clear that Dan Meyer admitted in a sworn statement on June 28, 2006 that:

"*On this issue of authority I will take credit whether he's* (Pedeleose) *giving it to me or not for putting the kernel of that thought in his head, and that it that I said to him when he came to me and said they want to interview me and I said when the investigator shows up you should ask them for their credentials and their authority to do the investigation.*"

The tactic was to thwart Congressional investigations by using the DoD IG's alleged credibility to cloak retaliation and weaponize investigations. However, this was not the first time Dan Meyer sought to thwart Congressional investigations. The e-mail trail went back to March 22, 2005, as follows.

Dan Meyer – Tactically "Well-Situated" Against Congress

March 22, 2005 "Well-Situated": Dan Meyer used *"external credibility"* of the DoD IG against Senator Grassley and Senator McCain, stating. (Appendix A1-6)

"Ken Pedeleose is drafting a third Congressional to McCain, this one regarding the F-22 Raptor. This document lies at the heart of his disclosure.

He is also teaming with Doug Kinan, so I am forwarding this also to Len (Leonard Trahan, DoD IG Hotline Director) *so that we can make sure we are well-situated should Congressional 3 go to Grassley (hence Murphy), as well.*

There are no additional reprisal allegations to this; I am now midstream in the depositions of Lockheed and DCMA management in the reprisal complaint CRI inherited from MRI/COS (Military Reprisal Investigations, COS is possibly Chief of Staff L. Jean Lewis).

As in all cases, my goal is to separate the source's thoughts on "disclosure" from the "reprisal", so as to leave appropriate authorities such as Audit, DCIS, etc. free to do their work in deciding whether specific and credible information exists to prompt further investigation.

Getting the whistleblower to "let go" the issue is the hardest part of the interaction,"

Meyer knew conning Senator Grassley went through "Murphy" (Charlie Murphy, Senator Grassley's staffer). Being "*well-situated*" was tactical. However, Dan Meyer was incorrect about the "let go" aspect. I actually "let go" of the whistleblowing prior to Falsified Trail 2, when I was escorted out of the facility by Lockheed Martin armed guards on August 14, 2003. Falsified Trail 2 rekindled and vastly expanded my whistleblowing. Had Falsified Trail 2 not happened, my whistleblowing would have ended.

Regardless, the March 22, 2005, e-mail was a little ambiguous. Fortunately, Dan Meyer continued the electronic email trails to show the real con game against Senator Grassley, "hence Murphy".

Dan Meyer – Tactical "Liaison" Against Congress

August 10, 2005 1:27 PM: Dan Meyer e-mailed Leigh Owens and tactically warned:

"*Though it is perhaps beyond my portfolio, be careful of the Congressional end of this case – which has been quiet for a while. Grassley and McCain are interested in the issues Pedeleose is perceived as advancing, so you may want to make sure your liaison is in the loop when the Colonel's investigation goes ahead.*" (Appendix A1-9)

The tactical use of a liaison would allow DCMA access to con Senator Grassley via Charlie Murphy the same way Meyer would con Senator Grassley via Charlie Murphy. Meaning, direct access has weaponized value, as Dan Meyer has demonstrated, and will continue to do so shortly. Meyer also stated.

"On the Pedeleose case, our attorneys are meeting with the DCMA Acting General Counsel today at 2PM; the Director of the Hotline and I will sit in; sorry this has taken so long, but I think they will have some solution by the end of the day." (Appendix A1-9)

Here, Meyer is a DCMA ally. Probably because my case would "garner national attention".

Dan Meyer – Tactically Avoid Garnering National Attention

August 10, 2005 1:27 PM "Garner National Attention": Meyer further stated to Owens in part.

"I think I can share with you that of the 21 alleged reprisals, I am down to looking at 1 – that is 1, Leigh...I am more concerned about thoroughness at this point, as I think this report may garner national attention." (Appendix A1-9)

Relevance is that Meyer was reviewing Falsified Trails 1 & 2 in 2003, which were textbook cases of retaliation and abuse of authority. Falsified Trail 2 did garner national attention and catapulted my popularity and my ability to expose Government corruption. I prevailed on Falsified Trail 2 by keeping my job. No more investigation by Meyer was needed.

The next email trail is an extension of Parallel Con 2 that was previously mentioned. This is where Dan Meyer's direct access to Congress (Charlie Murphy) pays off.

Dan Meyer – Tactical Duplicity in Whistleblower Protection

August 4, 2005 8:29 AM - Grassley Protection Letter: A fellow whistleblower (Henry Hagel), who cosigned congressional reports and assisted me in whistleblowing, was also targeted in the DCMA tactical weaponized investigation. Hagel sent an e-mail on August 4, 2005, at 8:29 AM to Charlie Murphy requesting a protection letter, stating in part:

"I sincerely believe that I am vulnerable and that my DCMA management staff is planning shortly to fire me from government service. Two individuals on the C-130J team have already been fired. Your letter would be helpful and greatly appreciated."

August 4, 2005 8:55 AM: Dan Meyer responded to Hagel, Murphy, and me at 8:55 AM, stating.

"Charlie - a letter with Henry's name would be a good idea; his contribution over the past 18 months should also be highlighted. Henry, you might want to do a draft for Charlie using Ken's letter."

August 4, 2005 1:09 PM: Meyer e-mailed Leigh Owens, stating, in part.

"Senator Grassley is probably going to weigh in on Henry Hagel's case; not sure whether the letter is going to Schmitz or to DCMA" (Appendix A2-1)

This was tactical duplicity via direct congressional access. Meaning, Meyer appeared to be a whistleblower advocate to Congress and whistleblowers, then went behind the scenes to support those retaliating against whistleblowers.

It was clear to DCMA that Dan Meyer's duplicity was an asset enhanced by DCMA's direct access to Dan Meyer, meaning Dan Meyer's obvious duplicity meant Dan Meyer assumed all risks. Since the tactics were emails (electronic trails), DCMA could easily use Meyer's duplicity in the electronic trails (emails) as "Stay Out of Jail Cards" as follows.

DCMA's "Stay Out of Jail Cards" – Dan Meyer Assumes All Risk

DCMA Con on Dan Meyer by "Relaying" Meyer's Emails (Appendix A2)

August 4, 2005 1:10 PM – (Appendix A2-1): The previous August 4, 2005 1:09 PM email was forwarded directly (Relayed) to Bruce Krasker and another DCMA attorney, Stephanie Zimmt-Mack, 1 minute later at 1:10 PM on August 4, 2005, only saying "*FYI*". Leigh Owens provided the initial relay. The 1-minute delay signifies a DCMA con on Dan Meyer. A one-minute delay was too long. DCMA did improve as follows.

August 4, 2005 2:01 PM – (Appendix A2-2): Less than an hour later, on August 4, 2005, at 2:01 PM, Dan Meyer emailed Leigh Owens stating in part:

"Mr. Pedeleose used to send these directly to the DoD Hotline; I have been routinely hitting "Forward" to the Hotline, without reading the emails. The Hotline will handle his non-reprisal complaint alleging violations of federal merit system principles according to its protocol. I am still not convinced this is not an outgrowth of his union duties and responsibilities, hence the desire to find a way to parse it away from the VanDerBeck complaint and its investigation.
Your observation about appearances is very important,"

Leigh Owens immediately, at 2:01 PM (the same minute), forwarded (Relayed) the e-mail to Stephanie Zimmt-Mack with no explanation of the reason for forwarding. This implies the con was in full swing, and Zimmt-Mack was a willing part. The following day, on August 5, 2005, at 8:08 AM, Zimmt-Mack forwarded the e-mail to Bruce Krasker, again with no words or explanation. Proving this was a working con against Meyer, with Krasker as the mastermind, using relayed emails from Leigh Owens who had gained Meyer's trust.

However, the con against Meyer as the "Stay Out of Jail Cards" was taken back to August 3, 2005. Meaning that the quick email relay plan was taking shape and being improved.

Genesis of the DCMA "Stay Out of Jail Cards" Con Against Dan Meyer

August 3, 2005 11:27 AM (Appendix A2-3): Meyer stated to Owens he "*urged Pedeleose and Hagel to cooperate*". Owens forwarded this e-mail to Bruce Krasker without words or explanations 5 days later on August 8, 2005 1:09 PM. This implies the day the overall con was being sighted in on Dan Meyer. The next email, sent one minute later by Owens to Krasker, eliminates any doubt.

August 3, 2005 4:27 PM (Appendix A2-4): Owens emails Meyer and starts the email trail about allegedly clearing questions. In this case, Meyer has not responded. Five days later, on August 8, 2005, at 1:10 PM, Owens forwards the email to Krasker with no words or explanation.

Quick Email Relays with No Words: The quick relay of Owen's emails at 1:09 PM & 1:10 PM on August 8, 2005 with no words or explanations proves a con was at play against Dan Meyer, and DCMA was sighting in the tactical weaponized investigation via conning Meyer. Albeit Meyer set himself up for the con.

Bruce Krasker would hold the emails as surprise evidence until March 31, 2006, when they were released internally to Gary Jencson from 3:53 PM to 3:58 PM, after my deposition of March 29, 2006.

I first saw the relayed emails on or about April 6, 2006. Appendix A2 to this book shows the actual emails being relayed up to Bruce Krasker by Leigh Owens.

This was used as tactical surprise evidence against me at MSPB, while being a con against Dan Meyer. It was Meyer's duplicity that enabled the con against Dan Meyer.

Meyer was very active on August 4, 2005, with a flurry of the aforesaid e-mails (electronic trails) that turned me against the DCMA weaponized investigation while appearing to be an ally of DCMA. However, Uldric Fiore knew the dangers of electronic communications outside the DoD IG and was personally providing tactical advice to Joseph Schmitz and other DoD IG members.

Uldric Fiore – Tactical - "Need Not Respond/Acknowledge E-mails"

August 8, 2005 (Appendix A1-8): Fiore sent an e-mail to Joseph Schmitz, Richard Race, and Thomas Gimble with the subject "E-mails from Mr. Pedeleose," tactically warning the DoD IG Joseph Schmitz personally about responding to emails. Fiore stated.

Sir -

Fully concur that you need not respond/acknowledge e-mails (same rational as with-(Name Redacted)

Not responding or acknowledging my emails was a weaponized shunning tactic. However, there were private tactical meetings announced in the same email with DCMA attorneys.

DCMA's Acting GC (probably Chip Retson General Counsel (GC)) *called in and asked to meet with us with the Boston Regional Counsel* (Probably Bruce Krasker) *who will be flying in on Wed. We (including) Dan Meyer will meet with them Wed. afternoon.*

Relevance is that meetings cannot be traced like emails (electronic trails), which explains a personal meeting and the "*Boston Regional Counsel who will be flying in*". Fiore admitted in a sworn statement on June 28, 2006, that Retson was a "*former Army colleague many years ago*" who requested the August 10, 2005, meeting Meyer would later regret attending.

Meyer stated on July 27, 2007, to DoD IG personnel, "*In retrospect. I should have left you all alone with Krasker.*" (Appendix A1-15)

In retrospect, Dan Meyer caused Dan Meyer's problems by conning me and Senator Grassley via Charlie Murphy as follows.

Dan Meyer Focuses Con on Senator Grassley via Charlie Murphy

Weaponized Direct & Unfettered Access to Congress

September 12, 2005 5:43 PM (Appendix A1-13): Dan Meyer communicated differently to Charlie Murphy than to me. Meaning, Meyer fed another story to Charlie Murphy, stating:

"*Just got out of the Lockheed facility. Contrary to my advice, Ken and Henry have given DCMA your letters, and invoked them to say they don't have to cooperate with the administrative investigation into wrongful employment practices. I think they are both on thin ice – Bruce K is calling you to ask what they are suppose to do with the letters. I am on record having coordinated their questions under the IG act (requiring agencies to not interfere with our investigations). They limited the timeframe involved, and struck questions not related to Ms. Gerry Sands* [sic] *who was allegedly targeted for wrongful removal.*

Plourde also had Gordon England down last week, so she is shoring up the Pentagon flank."

The con against Senator Grassley via Murphy is analyzed in the following sections.

<u>Kernel of Thought</u>: As previously shown, on the morning of August 4, 2005, Meyer turned me against the retaliatory, weaponized investigation. On June 28, 2006, Meyer admitted, under oath, to putting a "*kernel of that thought*" in my head, that the weaponized investigation was unlawful.

<u>Coordinating Questions – Surprise Evidence Tactic</u>: Meyer told Murphy that the questions were coordinated. However, Meyer never told me that questions were coordinated. I first learned of alleged coordination on October 18, 2005, when Colonel Plourde proposed a 30-Day suspension, and entered the surprise statement, "*This command coordinated the scope of our investigation with the DoD IG to assure that it did not conflict with their ongoing inquiries.*"

Dan Meyer would stonewall me and refuse to answer any questions on alleged coordination. Meyer referred me to Uldric Fiore, who also refused to answer questions. More will follow on this soon.

<u>Name Dropping Tactic</u>: Meyer named dropped Gordon England (then DoD Acting Deputy Secretary of Defense) to Charlie Murphy, adding the external credibility of the "*Pentagon flank*".

<u>Insulate via "Administrative Investigation"</u>: The switch to "*administrative investigation*" was tactical and provided insulation by diverting attention from whistleblowing. The investigation was a retaliatory weapon itself, and, as shown, Meyer was in the facts of the case by September 2005.

Dan Meyer also conned Charlie Murphy on the phrase "*They limited the timeframe involved*" for the weaponized investigation. This was very tactical as follows.

Tactical Start Date of Weaponized Investigation – Questioning Intelligence

During the Discovery (Interrogatories) at MSPB (April 3, 2006), I asked DCMA the following:

"The questions posed to me by Ms. Stacy Scantlebury indicated that her questions were from a period of time from March 18,2005. What was the significance of the date March 18, 2005?"

DCMA responded as follows:

"Response: This date was suggested by the DoD IG so that the agency investigation did not cover a period of time that was relevant in a DoD IG investigation."

This was a clear ruse tactic, meaning the alleged investigation started on March 18, 2005; however, all questions were related to the summer of 2005 (June – August 2005), which was highly relevant to an IG investigation. This tactic questions the intelligence and makes a fool of whoever believes it. Meaning, DCMA could have its start date from July 4, 1776 —the fall of the Roman Empire — or the War of 1812. All questions were related to the summer of 2005, and that was clear.

Dan Meyer's tactics did work on Charlie Murphy as follows.

Dan Meyer Successfully Cons Charlie Murphy to Withdraw Support

September 15, 2005 9:40 AM (Appendix A1-13): I desperately tried to reason with Charlie Murphy and went to the length of calling Charlie Murphy at home to explain my position. Murphy instead responded to Dan Meyer's aforesaid September 12, 2005, 5:43 PM email stating:

"Ken is calling me at home which honks me off. Ernie must have given him my home number. He is spinning-out of control. I can tell. He is getting nutty. I want him to work this with you. You have to look at it and make a determination. I am not telling you what to do or looking for some particular outcome. You just have to figure out what's right - all things considered. I am not convinced this guy has a solid case. Let me know how you want to proceed, charlie"

September 15, 2005 10:34 AM (Appendix A1-13): Dan Meyer responds to Murphy, stating:

"*I have been working on a solution with Dina Rasor, my fear is that Ken will cook off before I can bring the resources together. Fitzgerald is willing to bring him in to his shop.*"

Dina Rasor, per Dan Meyer (June 28, 2006), was my "*handler in the non-profit world*" (POGO). Dina Rasor and Ernie Fitzgerald were trying to get me a position at the Pentagon working for Ernie Fitzgerald, since, per what Dan Meyer told me, some Pentagon officials were getting "*long in the tooth*". Meaning, I was good at my job and relatively young, so I could help out with Pentagon personnel who were ready to retire.

At one point, Dina Rasor tried to help me with Senator Grassley by going to another staffer for Senator Grassley to honor Senator Grassley's April 26, 2004, protection letter to me. I forget the staffer's name, but I believe it was a lady. Charlie Murphy intercepted the request and basically let the DoD IG and DCMA retaliate against me. I was now abandoned. Dan Meyer knew it since there were other communications from Charlie Murphy as follows.

Abandoned by Senator Grassley via Charlie Murphy – Support is Gone

September 12, 2005 8:57 AM: Charlie Murphy emails me with copy to Dan Meyer stating.

"*Ken, I expect you to work with Dan. You need to rely on him and trust him. I do - completely. If you cannot do that, then I cannot help you. Dan is our first line of defense against whistleblower retaliation, Charlie*"

September 15, 2005 9:45 AM: Charlie Murphy emails me with copy to Dan Meyer stating.

"*Ken, I will not say it again. I want you to work with Dan. We must make that office work. Dan is looking at your problem. When he knows what to do and what is right and best in your case, he and I will discuss it. Until then, you have to back off and stop calling me at home. I did not give you my home number. It is not listed in the phone book. Thanks Charlie*"

Relevance is, Dan Meyer saw Murphy's responses to me and knew Senator Grassley abandoned me. Dan Meyer would later admit to acting on Senator Grassley's abandonment as follows.

Tactical Green-Light – Congressional Interest not Following

July 27, 2007: Dan Meyer sent an e-mail to DoD IG officials that included the following comment regarding Senator Grassley, via Charlie Murphy. (Appendix A1-15)

"*As of August 2005, KP was going to MSPB, we had found no reprisal into the allegations we were looking into, and the Congressional interest was not following KP into his labor activities (which is what led to the August meeting).*"

Dan Meyer successfully conned Charlie Murphy into abandoning me, thus green-lighting and enabling the tactical, weaponized investigation, at which point DoD IG was "happy" to discuss disciplinary action. Meaning, the con by Dan Meyer on Charlie Murphy worked.

Trophy – "Happy to Discuss" Charges Against Pedeleose

September 16, 2005 (Appendix A1-14): DoD IG Associate General Counsel stated (e-mail), copy to Fiore that:

"*... we discussed possible charges against the individual and whether a charge for failure to cooperate should be considered. I'd be happy to discuss that with you at the appropriate time.*"

DoD IG is overall "*happy*" to assist in retaliation against me (a whistleblower). This was the result of the successful con on Charlie Murphy (Senator Grassley staff) by Dan Meyer.

Congressional Abandonment Greenlights Weaponized Investigation

Proof of a Weaponized Lawfare Trap with Covert Alleged Coordination

September 20, 2005 9:28 AM: Stacy Scantlebury continued the tactical, weaponized investigation by sending another threatening email, warning of disciplinary action. I forwarded Scantlebury's email to DCMA senior management, including DCMA Director General Darryl Scott, Keith Ernst, Steve Bogusz, Sallie Flavin, Colonel Plourde, Henrietta Snow, Dan Meyer, and the DoD IG Hotline on September 20, 2005 11:02 AM, stating in part:

"I have been continually harassed by Ms. Scantlebury and Colonel Plourde since June 22, 2005. Even Ms. Flavin and Mr. Ernst have been involved in the harassment.

I do consider the e-mail below by Ms. Scantlebury to be a direct threat against me and direct interference with lawful investigations."

"I consider this as no coincidence that Ms. Scantlebury's recent harassement and threats coincide with visits of the Inspector General's office. The last incident involved a Letter of Direction from Colonel Plourde to meet with Ms. Scantlebury on the exact day that Mr. Dan Meyer (DoD IG Civilian Reprisal Investigations) was to be visiting the facility.

Now that the DoD IG is here investigating the May 12, 2005 e-mail I sent to DoD IG regarding Anti Deficiency, misrepresentation of cost, misappropriation of Funds on the C-130J. The timing is too close to be a casual coincidence."

"At this time I must regretfully decline to participate in your investigation. I have turned over information to the DoD IG and will continue to support lawful and duly authorized investigations."

"At this point there are efforts to directly impede lawful investigations. I believe that Ms. Scantlebury's timing is no accident.

I have contacted the DoD IG regarding this matter and copied the Hotline on this e-mail.

I will decline the interview with Ms. Scantlebury as the issues have been forwarded to the DoD IG."

Proof of Covert Trap - Silently Cleared Questions: No one responded to indicate any coordination between DCMA and DoD IG, most notably after the alleged coordination on September 6, 2005, at 9:35 AM to clear questions, as previously stated. And most notably, after I specifically mentioned and copied Dan Meyer on the e-mail. This confirmed a tactical trap that Meyer enabled.

The pressure from the weaponized retaliatory investigation directly forced out, under duress, Henry Hagel from Federal Service as follows.

Forced Out Under Duress – Hostile Workplace Alters Working Conditions

September 20, 2005 2:54 PM: Henry Hagel responded to "All" on my September 20, 2005 11:02 AM email, stating, in part, to DCMA Director MG Darryl Scott.

"You and your DCMA Management staff [Mr. Ernst, Ms. Flavin, Col Plourde, Ms. Snow, Ms. Owens & Ms. Bass] have finally succeeded in "forcing" me to retire from the Federal Government under "duress." This action is not of my own choosing since I was planning to retire on January 3, 2006. The stress and aggravation that I am being placed under is not worth staying or coming to work in this DCMA organization."

"General Scott I am extremely tired of the continual intimidation, harassment, turmoil and threats by your DCMA Management Staff. This will be my last communication with you as DCMA employee. Please do not respond since you have "never responded" as the DCMA Commander to my previous e-mails."

Relevance is, one whistleblower down (Hagel) and one whistleblower remaining (Pedeleose). However, Plourde had a loose end with a retirement under duress.

September 20, 2005 4:46 PM – Plourde Denies Duress: Colonel Plourde sent a private e-mail to Henry Hagel, with an obvious Blind Copy to Leigh Owens, basically stating that Hagel's retirement under duress was "*completely voluntary*".

Leigh Owens forwarded the e-mail chain to Dan Meyer, on September 20, 2005, 5:09 PM, stating only: "*This is Col. Plourde's response to Mr. Hagel's message.*"

Dan Meyer responded back on September 20, 2005, 5:32 PM, appearing as a DCMA ally, stating:

"I have been firm with them on the obligation to cooperate with lawful investigations."

This was Meyer's tactical catchall cover statement since Dan Meyer put the "*kernel of that thought*" (Per June 28, 2006 testimony), the weaponized investigation was unlawful as of August 4, 2005. Meaning, Meyer keyed in on the word "lawful" while Meyer deliberately led me to believe that the weaponized DCMA investigation was unlawful.

Leigh Owens forwarded Dan Meyer's e-mail to Colonel Plourde on September 20, 2005, 6:42 PM.

Plourde and DCMA used Dan Meyer's email to justify the weaponized investigation in support of a 30-Day suspension against me, meaning the September 20, 2005 email chain was part of the MSPB Discovery received on April 3, 2006, after my deposition on March 29, 2006.

So, as of September 20, 2005, I was the only remaining target. This prompted a new DCMA tactic that Meyer definitely did not like and could derail the entire weaponized investigation as follows.

Final Weaponized Tactic – Tell Pedeleose of Coordination

September 28, 2005 8:44 AM: Leigh Owens emailed Dan Meyer and asked if it was appropriate to inform me that DCMA and DoD IG *"cleared the questions to be asked with the IG to assure no conflict with you ongoing investigation?"*

September 28, 2005 1:52 PM: Dan Meyer relayed the e-mail from Leigh Owens to another DoD IG member (name blotted out) and asked.

"*help us out; can we do this-is it appropriate—and what can we cite in the way of authority.*"

Relevance is that the alleged DCMA and DoD IG coordination started on/about August 3, 2005. Now, on September 28, 2005, after 1 ½ months of alleged coordination, Meyer asks, "*what can we cite in the way of authority.*" All this after Dan Meyer delivered different stories to Senator Grassley via Murphy and me, and the August 10, 2005, tactical meeting between DCMA and DoD IG.

October 5, 2005 9:04 AM "Inform Mr. Pedeleose": A member of the DoD IG emailed Dan Meyer and DCMA (name blotted out), stating in part.

"Coordination of investigative efforts is commonplace based on the inherent authority of various agencies and commands to investigate allegations of wrongdoing. DCMA has provided Mr. Pedeleose with the bases for their exercise of its investigative authority and obviously CRI has authority to investigate allegations of reprisal pursuant to the WPA (Whistleblower Protection Act) *and the IG Act of 1978, as amended.*

I see no reason why DCMA cannot inform Mr. Pedeleose that coordination of efforts continues, to avoid prejudicing either investigative effort."

The main point is, DCMA never provided specific authority to investigate. DCMA indicated that inherent authority was used. Regardless, 1 ½ hours later, the coordination came to a halt as follows.

October 5, 2005 10:37 AM – Last Coordination Email: Dan Meyer emailed a member of the DoD IG (name blotted out) and copied DCMA (name blotted out) and Leonard Trahan about 1 ½ hours later, stating.

"*I have informed our Hotline that any reprisal allegations emanating from the alleged unlawful investigation by DCMA should be forwarded to OSC. I will continue to work on Mr. Pedeleose's matters relating to contractor waste, fraud and abuse, but this sidebar into labor relations properly belongs with the Special Counsel. It is outside the discretionary priorities of my office established by the IG. Mr. Pedeleose will get the same protection at OSC he enjoys here.*"

Relevance is that something negative happened on October 5, 2005, between 9:04 AM and 10:37 AM. One reason may be that DCMA never provided me any authority to run investigations. Another likely cause was from the fact that Meyer was running a con on Senator Grassley via Charlie Murphy, and Meyer had misled me as well. Meaning, Meyer was stuck with an incriminating electronic trail of evidence. An electronic trail that makes Falsified Trail 3 the flagship case of this book.

Informing me of the alleged coordination would have exceeded a "can of worms" and been more like a "bushel basket of rattlesnakes" because Charlie Murphy placed hope in Dan Meyer.

Simply put, DCMA played with fire while Dan Meyer played with a volcano in the con games being run on Charlie Murphy and me. Regardless, I was never told of the alleged coordination prior to the proposed 30-Day suspension of October 18, 2005. The timeline shows that the alleged coordination between DCMA and the DoD IG abruptly ended on October 5, 2005, as follows.

October 5, 2005 Culmination of DCMA Con Game on DoD IG

<u>April 3, 2006 MSPB Discovery Information</u>: During the Discovery at MSPB, for Falsified Trail 3, DCMA was asked the following (Interrogatory) question.

"Please list the DCMA officials (employees, legal counsel, managers, etc.) by first and last name that allegedly made contact with the Department of Defense Inspector Generals Office (DoD IG) regarding the investigation done by Ms. Stacy Scantlebury. Do this from the dates of June 20,2005 - January 20,2006. Include the dates of contact with the DoD 1G and the members of DCMA that made contact with the DoD IG?"

DCMA responded as follows:

1. Ms. Leigh Owens, August 3, 4, 10, 12, 15, 17, 2005, September 6, 7, 12, 16, 20, 28, 2005, October 5, 2005
2. Col. Plourde, September 12, 2005
3. Bruce Krasker, August 10, 17, 19, 2005, September 6, 2005
4. Nicholas Retson, August 10, 2005

October 5, 2005, was the last date on which DCMA and DoD IG communicated regarding the tactical weaponized investigation. DCMA had the "Stay Out of Jail Cards" (emails) Meyer provided to Leigh Owens and relayed to the mastermind Bruce Krasker. Meaning, Meyer outlived his usefulness, and DCMA had the electronic trail necessary to retaliate against me. The next step was to ambush me with the proposed 30-day suspension, lawfare, in a national hostile whistleblower climate.

Proposed 30-Day Suspension Ambush – October 18, 2005

Extension of National Climate of Weaponization

<u>National Anti-Whistleblower Climate Enabling</u>: Falsified Trail 3 (DCMA's tactical, weaponized investigation) occurred during a period of national tactics against whistleblowers. Meaning, DCMA rode a wave of national corruption. The 30-Day suspension I would receive on October 18, 2005, was preceded by anti-whistleblower actions against my mentor, Ernie Fitzgerald, as follows.

<u>October 17, 2005 – Fitzgerald's Job is Eviscerated</u>: Ernie Fitzgerald (my mentor), in an October 17, 2005 Time Magazine Article, stated "*his job has been eviscerated*". Fitzgerald informed me in 2005 that he was being harassed, and that there was a meeting at the White House to put him down. Fitzgerald informed me that the Pentagon/DoD had harassed him for 35 years, 1970-2005. Fitzgerald retired in early 2006.

<u>Valerie Plame</u>: On the same page in Time Magazine as the Fitzgerald article was a short article about CIA operative Valerie Plame and how her identity was leaked to the news media.

Relevance is that the close proximity of Fitzgerald's eviscerated position and my 30-day suspension add peripheral support to DoD's organized and tactical retaliations. The fact that Fitzgerald and Plame were on the same page in Time Magazine adds credence to the fact that what happened to me was part of a national movement against whistleblowers and political opponents.

<u>October 18, 2005 - Plourde 4th Level Supervisor Proposed 30-Day Suspension</u>: Colonel Plourde, my 4th level supervisor, summoned me to her office to issue a retaliatory 30-day Suspension. My 1st-, 2nd-, and 3rd-level supervisors had no involvement. Plourde's letter was 5 Pages with 24 Pages of attachments. Plourde's letter stated in part on Page 1, Paragraph 1:

"*You are hereby notified that I propose to suspend you from duty and pay for thirty (30) calendar days for the offenses of Refusal to Cooperate in an Agency Investigation, Insubordination and Failure to Follow Instructions. This action is proposed in order to promote the efficiency of the service and will be effective not earlier than thirty (30) calendar days after your receipt of this notice. This action is being processed in accordance with DCMA Instruction "Maintaining Discipline," September 2004 revision, and the Labor-Management Agreement between DLA and the DLA Council of Locals and the DCMAE Supplement thereto, dated January 30, 1997. Although this agreement has expired, the terms of this agreement are being followed until the completion of a new nationwide bargaining agreement with AFGE.*"

In the 1st Paragraph, Plourde cited an expired union contract, which was bizarre. From there, Plourde's letter mentioned the surrogate Stacy Scantlebury about 31 times up to Page 4, upon which time Plourde sprung the surprise statement that…

"*This command coordinated the scope of our investigation with the DoD IG to assure that it did not conflict with their ongoing inquiries. They informed us and you that these investigations did not interfere in any way with their investigations. Whether or not my investigation interfered with the DoD IG was a call to be made by the DoD IG, not you.*"

Meyer never mentioned any coordination with DCMA to me and in fact turned me against the DCMA investigation as the evidence clearly shows. Plourde provided no supporting coordination documents showing how DCMA coordinated with DoD IG.

Hence, Plourde's statement "*They* (DoD IG) *informed us and you that these investigations did not interfere in any way with their investigations*" was a deliberate ambush tactic. I was never informed by Dan Meyer, Plourde, Scantlebury, or the DoD IG that there was no interference between the alleged investigations. What Dan Meyer told me is a matter of record herein.

Tactically, Plourde provided 24 pages of mundane supporting documents, including emails from me complaining about retaliation. I had 30 days grace period to respond with my side of the story and counter the charges. I first emailed Dan Meyer to inquire about the alleged "coordinated" activity.

Dan Meyer Deflects Coordination Inquiry - Go to Uldric Fiore

October 19, 2005 4:00 PM: I emailed Dan Meyer, with Charlie Murphy copied, and the proposed 30-Day Suspension statement in part as follows.

Mr. Meyer;

Please refer to Page 4 (about line 10 from the top) of the attached document and inform me how the Command coordinated with DoD IG to assure that the DCMA inquiry did not interfere with ongoing inquiries.

Please provide the documentation in this area and any explanation that you have regarding coordination issues.

Did you inform DCMA that I filed issues with the DoD IG Hotline? If so please provide the documents/information.

Also please explain how me giving up potential witnesses in your investigation would not compromise your investigation.

Also did you explain to DCMA that you did not know the legal basis for their investigation and that they were suppose to provide it to your lawyers?

Did you ask DCMA for legal proof of their investigation prior to you giving them authorization to run the DCMA investigation?

It seems that now you are the approving authority for the DCMA investigation. You have admitted to me yourself that you do not know if the investigation was legal and how your lawyers are baffled as to what authority DCMA has to run the investigations.

October 19, 2005 4:22 PM: Dan Meyer quickly responded to me, stating:

"This needs to be addressed to:

Uldric Fiore, General Counsel

Office of General Counsel

U.S. Department of Defense, Office of the Inspector General

400 Army Navy Drive – Suite 918A

Arlington, VA 22202-4704

He has the details."

I then placed focus on both Uldric Fiore and Dan Meyer, both making an interesting, conflict-of-interest discovery about Dan Meyer.

Dan Meyer – Whistleblowing is "Fucking with the Sovereign"

Documented September 9, 2006 Report to Congress & June 21, 2006 Deposition: On/about November 7, 2005, I called Dan Meyer and tried to get some information and clarity. I documented Meyer's comments at that time and transcribed them later on September 9, 2006, and in a June 21, 2006 deposition. I misplaced my original memo for record.

Meyer's shocking statement was me *"fucking with the sovereign"*. This would tie to Dan Meyer's Wikipedia page, where a *"waiver of sovereign immunity"* is discussed. This would explain, in part, Meyer's actions with Leigh Owens and Bruce Krasker in August and September 2005.

June 21, 2006 – Meyer & "Sovereign": I testified to Meyer's sovereign comments as follows:

Dan Meyer told me and I want, I want it, this is an exact quote he said that I was f'ing with the sovereign okay, and he used the f word, I'm f'ing with the sovereign and I says Dan what does that mean?

"Yeah with the sovereign and I'm there like who is the sovereign, and he says it was that letter, I wrote down somewhere, he said it was that letter that I sent, a e-mail that I sent up to Grassley's office,"... "and another time I remember him saying it's all that stuff I have going on with Grassley and McCain..."

June 21, 2006 - Testified to Jean Lewis: The other part of Meyer's dislike stemmed from the fact that I circumstantially caused the exposure and eventual ouster of Jean Lewis that came from Falsified Trail 2. I also testified that Dan Meyer would not drop the Jean Lewis issues as follows:

"Dan Meyer, during this exact timeframe, that Scantlebury was doing her thing brought up this Jean Lewis situation and it was over two years and I'm there like Dan why are you still talking, I'm, thinking to myself, why are you still talking about this for. Why don't you just drop this Jean Lewis thing."

"And the bottom line is, you know, we get into the, you know, sun rises and sets on Jean Lewis, that's one reason."

June 21, 2006 - Testified to Not Reward a Whistleblower: I also testified that Meyer talked about climate to not reward whistleblowers as follows.

"And also another reason Dan Meyer says the climate is not there to support whistle blowers, in other words they don't want to be seen as is rewarding a whistle blower. So this would be kind of a one way to get rid of Pedeleose."

My June 21, 2006 deposition had some pages, focusing on the "sovereign", Jean Lewis and the climate of not rewarding whistleblowers. My September 9, 2009, report to Congress also documented Meyer's other comments as follows:

I was a *"poster child not to go public with information"*.

Meyer indicated he (Meyer) was *"three feet from the line"* and Uldric Fiore may have gone *"over the line"*. Meyer also said Fiore was *"slippery"*. Meyer indicated it was not until the week prior to August 3, 2006, that the DoD IG realized how bad DCMA had *"dropped the dime"* on the DoD IG. Meaning the "Stay Out of Jail" email trail by Owens, Krasker, and Stephanie Zimtt-Mack.

Uldric Fiore Was Elusive – Non-Responsive

March 7, 2006: I lost my initial emails to Uldric Fiore; however, my follow-on email of March 7, 2006, stated to Fiore, copied to Tom Gimble, Dan Meyer, and Charlie Murphy, stated:

"Mr. Fiore,

(Fourth Request)

Please provide the information requested below. The longer that you personally withhold the documents from me the more proof that I have that you (DoD IG) engaged in reprisal actions against me.

I respectfully request the documents requested below and/or ECD when documents will be provided to me. I do hold personally you as the accountable individual."

Fiore responded on March 8, 2006 to all on distribution stating:

"As I twice previously advised, your POC on your request is the FOIA Office. Since you persist in addressing e-mails on this FOIA matter to me, please be advised that I will simply forward any further e-mails on this matter to the FOIA office without reply to you."

Meyer and Fiore were immediately and consistently nonresponsive. It took about 3 years to piece together the information outlined herein, which included the following.

June 28, 2006 - Uldric Fiore & Nicholas (Chip) Retson – Former Army Colleagues: In a sworn statement, Uldric Fiore admitted that he and Chip Retson were *"former Army colleagues many years ago"*. Both were present at the August 10, 2005, tactical meeting between DCMA and the DoD IG.

This would help explain why Stacy Scantlebury was an AR 15-6 (Army) Investigative Officer. Regardless, I had to move forward with my response to DCMA Deputy Director Steve Bogusz regarding Plourde's retaliatory 30-Day Suspension, as follows.

Response to Steve Bogusz - 5th Level Supervisor – DCMA Deputy Director

November 3, 2005: Since Plourde was my 4th-level supervisor, my rebuttal went to my 5th-level supervisor, Steve Bogusz, Deputy Director, DCMA District East. The rebuttal had a cover letter and two attachments. The first attachment was my initial response dated November 1, 2005 (4 Pages), followed by a Chronological Report (12 Pages).

My response was limited because it was never explained how DCMA allegedly coordinated with DoD IG. Meaning, I could not cross-reference my notes, data, and electronic trails with DCMA and DoD IG notes, documents, and electronic trails. I was at a severe disadvantage.

I informed Bogusz of my work with Senators Grassley and McCain; DCMA violations under 18 USC 1505; my success as a whistleblower (substantiated disclosures); and DCMA investigation conflicts of interest in using AR 15-6, where I stated, in part.

"In particular AR 15-6 states: "Informal procedures are not intended to provide a hearing for persons who may have an interest in the subject of the investigation"."

I went on to say to Steve Bogusz.

"While specific names were mentioned in conjunction with firing of employees (submitted to DoD IG and Senator Grassley's office) it was not exactly known how far up the Chain (District Level, etc.) the unlawful targeting of employees to be fired went."

"The second involved a whistleblower "sting" operation where Mr. Henry Hagel and I would have been forced to reveal whistleblower sources and contacts, thus creating more (known whistleblowers) for management to harass. Mr. Hagel has left Federal Service under duress rather than suffer continual persecution and release whistleblowers sources and contacts."

"Whistleblower protections that would thwart management attempts at reprisal were circumvented by DCMA management arbitrarily changing the subject to a "personnel matter" from a "whistleblower matter". This is a common whistleblower reprisal tactic that allows a concealed venue to reprise against whistleblowers through a seemingly unrelated area."

"The point that Colonel Plourde and DCMA is missing involves the fact that the information Colonel Plourde wanted was already submitted to the DoD IG (and the office of Senator Charles Grassley) in addition to existing DoD IG inquiries. Colonel Plourde and DCMA management was informed of this fact on more than one occasion."

The response goes on with a detailed chronological list of events that have already been detailed herein. Plourde's October 18, 2005, Proposed 30-Day Suspension letter was probably written by those who participated in the tactical weaponized lawfare investigation. My response to Steve Bogusz was probably forwarded to those (Owens, and/or Krasker) who participated in the tactical weaponized investigation, as was Steve Bogusz's response back.

DCMA later admitted, in writing on May 10, 2006 (no rebuttal letter), to MSPB that whistleblower retaliation did occur. Prior to MSPB, I had to go to OSC and experience the "Cerberus" analogy.

OSC Closes Inquiry – No Known Investigation – "Cerberus" Analogy

<u>January 13, 2006 – February 7, 2006 – OSC Closes Investigation</u>: I made my case to OSC after October 18, 2005. I cannot locate the exact file; however, my case was sabotaged by being denied coordination documents. OSC provided a preliminary determination to close my case on January 13, 2006, and I remember responding. OSC formally closed my case on February 7, 2006.

<u>October 24, 2007 Temporarily Prevailed at MSPB</u>: OSC closed my case because OSC did not believe that OSC could "convince the Merit Systems Protection Board (MSPB)" that I was justified not to cooperate in an agency investigation. However, I later convinced 2 of 3 MSPB Judges at the full MSPB Board in Washington, DC, because DCMA admitted that whistleblower retaliation did occur. Meaning, DCMA issued a no rebuttal letter May 10, 2006.

There is no evidence that OSC conducted any investigation into my 30-Day Suspension. I later discovered OSC issues questionnaires for documents. That is why I included Chapter 2 of this book to show that OSC was one-third of the Cerberus analogy. A true OSC investigation would have found what I just presented regarding Dan Meyer's duplicity and a tactical weaponized investigation. This cover-up activity enables further U.S. Government corruption.

Steve Bogusz Approves Final 30-Day Suspension Decision

January 20, 2006: Bogusz tactically approved the 30-Day suspension, effective January 25, 2006, without providing the alleged coordination documents between DCMA and DoD IG.

March 24, 2006 – Admission to Sabotage: DCMA admitted at MSPB Discovery as follows.

"Admit that after Mr. Roy Rogers (acting AFGE 2069 Union President) and I asked Mr. Bogusz to supply the coordination documents between DCMA and the DoD IG on/about November 18, 2005, Mr. Bogusz did not supply the coordination documents (nonresponsive) and went ahead and approved the 30 day suspension.

Response: Admitted"

Bruce Krasker Updates Uldric Fiore - OSC Preliminary Letter Closing Case

January 18, 2006 (Appendix A3-1): A DCMA employee associated with Bruce Krasker sent an email to Uldric Fiore which stated the following:

RE: OSC Letter Preliminary Closing of Mr. Pedeleose's Case

Attachments: KP .pdf

Good Morning,

Attached is the K. Pedeleose letter per Mr. Krasker.

The subject line of the email states "*OSC Letter Preliminary Closing of Mr. Pedeleose's Case*". Implying, Krasker kept Fiore updated on my case. This email was in response to a Freedom of Information Act (FOIA) request, where Fiore printed the email sent by DCMA on January 18, 2006, at 9:38 AM.

Bruce Krasker Directly Provides Trophy to Uldric Fiore

January 23, 2006 (Appendix A3-2): Bruce Krasker emailed Uldric Fiore with the Subject "*KP*" stating:

"*Ric We delivered the Decision to Suspend for 30 days today to Mr. Pedeleose. He was out last week so we reissued it with a new effective date, Jan 25. He refused to sign and we so noted.*"

So now, this concludes the trophy aspect for Fiore and the DoD IG. Now it's time for damage control via another con to Congress as follows.

Tom Gimble & Dan Meyer Testimony (Con) to Congress

Testify to Procedure - Not Actual Behavior, Weaponization, and Lawfare

February 14, 2006: The documented behavior by Meyer and Gimble is specific and proves duplicity in written testimony to Congress. Meaning, my experiences and documentation of Meyer and Gimble do not align with Congressional testimony. Written testimony in part is as follows.

"Statement of Mr. Thomas F. Gimble Acting Inspector General Department of Defense before the Subcommittee on National Security, Emerging Threats, and International Relations House Committee on Government Reform on National Security Whistleblower Protection"

"Mr. Chairman and Members of the Subcommittee:

Thank you for the opportunity to appear this morning to discuss whistleblower protections available to members of the military personnel, Department of Defense (DoD) civilian employees, and employees of DoD contractors. Accompanying me are Ms. Jane Deese, Director of Military Reprisal Investigations, and Mr. Dan Meyer, Director of Civilian Reprisal Investigations.

My comments address three general areas I believe to be of interest to the Subcommittee:

1. Personnel actions involving an individual's security clearance;

2. The general availability of whistleblower protection, and

3. Our procedures for investigating complaints of reprisal for whistleblowing."

Gimble went on to state in part;

"CRI was established in 2003 to provide an alternate means by which DoD civilian appropriated fund employees could seek protection from reprisal. This is done in coordination with the U.S. Special Counsel. CRI was established with the goal of providing limited protection for DoD appropriated fund employees, who also have recourse to OSC, and DoD intelligence and counterintelligence employees, who do not."

"The creation of CRI allows the DoD OIG to further publicize the message that whistleblowers will be protected from reprisal. Additionally, it currently provides resources to investigate a limited number of individual claims of reprisal for whistleblowing."

Simply put, Meyer's and Gimble's behavior in my case misalign with testimony before Congress.

Gimble Replaced Schmitz: Tom Gimble was the acting DoD IG because, as my resume states, Joseph Schmitz was part of a circumstantial exodus caused by me. So, in effect, the DoD IG made no improvement with the removal of Joseph Schmitz. Maybe even have gotten worse.

Claude Kicklighter (the following DoD IG) would actually embarrass Gimble by forcing Gimble to write me a retraction letter (as stated in my resume). Kicklighter would later give Uldric Fiore the "boot", or as described by Charlie Murphy on September 15, 2008:

"Fiore is gone. Kicklighter gave him the boot as he departed, but we do not know why. He didn't tell us. We can make some guesses. I will also tell you that the questions regarding Fiore go way beyond your case. That's all I will say for now."

In short, DoD IG testimony before Congress is a con game to mislead the public from the facts. That's why I placed details in this book, to educate the public and Congress. Following the con game to Congress, DCMA ensured my deposition was sabotaged in my 30-Day Suspension.

Sabotaged Deposition – No Coordination Documents Provided

March 29, 2006 - MSPB Deposition: I made DCMA force my deposition because I wanted to make the point that the deposition was DCMA's idea. Meaning, deposing me was a stupid idea. As expected, the MSPB judge assigned to the case, Lonny Bartholomew, sided with DCMA.

I made it clear that since I did not have the alleged coordination documents between DCMA and DoD IG, my testimony could change. Meaning, I could only testify to what I knew with no comparison to the alleged coordination documents. DCMA went forward regardless.

The deposition worked out great as I expected. I later entered my deposition on the MSPB record. Bruce Krasker soon confirmed, via electronic trail, the intent to sabotage my deposition.

Bruce Krasker Tactically Releases DCMA's "Stay Out of Jail Cards"

March 31, 2006 – (Appendix A2-1 to A2-4): Krasker tactically collected Dan Meyer's (ill-advised) coordination emails from August 4-8, 2005, and tactically released the alleged coordination documents about 2 days after my deposition. This was the DCMA con game on Dan Meyer. These were the same aforesaid "Stay Out of Jail Cards".

Krasker, on March 31, 2006, in rapid succession (3:53 PM, 3:56 PM, 3:57 PM, and 3:58 PM), forwarded some of the coordination documents to Gary Jencson, who took my deposition. Hence, Krasker tactically collected and then tactically released documents. This was electronically time-stamped. Steve Bogus used the same tactic, except with other documents, as follows.

Steve Bogusz Surprise Evidence - Tactical Release of Coordination Documents

April 6, 2006: Steve Bogusz, the deciding official in my 30-Day Suspension, in an undated letter received on April 6, 2006, stated in part.

"RE: FOIA Request No. 06-0139 (Department of Defense Office of the Inspector General)"

"By letter dated March 10, 2006 the Office of the Inspector General of the Department of Defense referred certain documents responsive to your FOIA request to this agency for review and direct response to you. The referral consisted of fifty-nine pages of documents."

"Materials are withheld under exemption (b)(6) when the disclosure of information would constitute a clearly unwarranted invasion of the personal privacy of individuals. Materials are withheld under exemption (b)(7) when the disclosure of information could reasonably be expected to constitute an unwarranted invasion of personal privacy in law enforcement records of individuals. Exemption (b)(7) is also used to protect the identity of government law enforcement personnel named in the files."

Weaponized FOIA Process: The weaponized FOIA process redacted the names of alleged law enforcement personnel who engaged in tactical, weaponized government. Second, it appears Bogusz tactically held the FOIA from March 10, 2006 to April 6, 2006 to ensure it was delivered after my deposition. The absence of a date on the FOIA letter suggests further covert tactics.

This clashes with the events on January 23, 2006 when Bruce Krasker openly emailed Uldric Fiore details of my 30-Day Suspension with the Subject *"KP"*. On January 18, 2006 Theresa Cook (DCMA FOIA, I believe), who works for/with Krasker, emailed Uldric Fiore my January 17, 2006 30-Day Suspension letter. The point is, my privacy does not matter; however, the FOIA process was used in a weaponized government with my demise as a trophy.

Deep State Treasure Trove: The 59-page, undated, FOIA from Bogusz, after my deposition, held a treasure trove of the Deep State operation against whistleblowers. That information was already used herein in Falsified Trail 3 to better explain tactical weaponized government and lawfare.

September 28, 2005: The FOIA showed that Gary Jencson was copied on an email on September 28, 2005 7:20 AM, which led to the October 5, 2005 9:04 AM final email from DoD IG stating it was okay to inform me of coordination. Relevance is that Gary Jencson was litigating the MSPB case against me, while Jencson participated in the case. Meaning, DCMA attorneys participate in weaponized government, litigate the same case, and tactically release documents.

Meaning, Jencson tactically released MSPB discover after my deposition, as did Bogusz. Possibly, both were mailed the same day.

Gary Jencson - Surprise Evidence - Tactical Release of Evidence

April 3, 2006: Jencson's MSPB Discovery documents included some of the same incriminating documents as those from Bogusz regarding the 2005 retaliatory, tactical, weaponized investigation.

Jencson's Discovery also included Declarations and Affidavits from Stacy Scantlebury, Colonel Plourde, and Steve Bogusz. I would use the affidavits to impeach the credibility of Plourde and Bogusz, most notably. This begins the MSPB case litigation.

Tactically Weaponized "Obey First, Grieve Later" Doctrine

The Ultimate Deep State Weapon & Insulation Against Any Law, Any Time

April 28, 2006 - Perfect Weapon: The DCMA case weaponized the "Obey First Grieve Later" doctrine; however, DCMA referred to it as "cooperate first and grieve later". This means an employee should work first, do as they are told, and the grieving can be done later. This is highly understandable in the workplace when "Obey First Grieve Later" is used ethically. However, "Obey First Grieve Later" was tactically weaponized as lawfare in Falsified Trail 3.

The tactical weaponized investigation may have started as a perjury trap, and then led to the "Obey Now Grieve Later" Doctrine as a backup plan. The answer may never be known.

Ultimate Weapon, Ultimate Insulation: "Obey First, Grieve Later" or "Work First, Grieve Later" was the ultimate weapon and ultimate insulation from culpability. DCMA corruptly reasoned that "Obey First, Grieve Later" could pry into any investigation, causing the release of sensitive information to upend lawful investigations or order any level of corruption.

DCMA believed "Obey Now, Grieve Later" could overrule any law at any time. DCMA actually admitted to violations of the law in writing, believing that "Obey First, Grieve Later" was the ultimate weapon. That is one reason DCMA issued the May 10, 2006, no rebuttal letter to MSPB.

DCMA was trying to show that "Obey First, Grieve Later" was the ultimate weapon. This would force Cerberus (OSC, MSPB, and OPM) to risk reputations to protect DCMA against what was a blatant scandal. I, however, responded to and rebutted DCMA's case before the MSPB as follows.

Response to 30-Day Suspension – DCMA Worked Behind My Back

April 28, 2006 – Response to 30-Day Suspension: I integrated the tactical-surprise evidence from Steve Bogusz and Gary Jencson into a case for MSPB to the best extent possible within the time available. I used my documents, what Meyer told me, the FOIA response from Bogusz, the MSPB Discovery response from Jencson, and my March 29, 2006 deposition courtesy of DCMA.

The underlying fact was obvious: DCMA worked behind my back and then used surprise evidence.

Rebuttal to Agency Submittal & Rebuttal to Management Declarations

May 9, 2006: I provided a detailed rebuttal to DCMA of about 19 pages and included my sworn deposition. I included a section on Colonel Plourde titled: *"False, Misleading, and Contradictory Statements"* and a similar section on Steve Bogusz titled *"False, Misleading, and Contradictory Statements, Including Negligent Conduct"*.

In short, I easily impeached the DCMA case and the integrity of senior management officials with what evidence I had. Largely because of management's arrogance and blatant disregard for law and ethics. I would outline my submission here; however, the MSPB full board decision of October 24, 2007, did a far better job of outlining my case. Probably because DCMA never rebutted what I said.

Meaning, DCMA would openly and arrogantly admit to retaliation.

Death Knell - No Rebuttal Letter – May 10, 2006

May 10, 2006: Gary Jencson wrote a 3-sentence response to my case, confirming my allegations as 1st-hand, stipulated facts. The DCMA case death knell response stated.

"*Dear Judge Bartholomew:*

I have reviewed the appellant's "Response to Charges" and determined that rebuttal evidence is not necessary. As such, the agency will not submit rebuttal evidence in this appeal. The agency will file a brief closing argument on or before May 24, 2006."

To my understanding, DCMA did ask Dan Meyer to be deposed in my case. I spoke with Meyer at that time and Meyer was very nervous and refused to be deposed. On June 28, 2006 Henry Shelley stated in part, Dan Meyer was "*really, really worried about that*". Meaning a MSPB hearing. However, DCMA had an eclipsing case strategy.

"Obey Now, Grieve Later" & "Work First, Grieve Later" Eclipses All Law

DCMA could have asked Colonel Plourde to rebut my allegations; however, it did not. The most likely reason for the no rebuttal was the case strategy. Meaning, the DCMA case rested on the "Obey Now, Grieve Later" or "Work First, Grieve Later" doctrine, eclipsing all law regardless of how criminal DCMA acted, whistleblower retaliation or not, the "Obey Now, Grieve Later" or "Work First, Grieve Later" doctrine eclipses all other laws and doctrines. A very typical DCMA arrogant, and unethical, strategy.

The DCMA strategy stood a good chance based on the known "Cerberus" analogy outlined herein. Meaning, Chapter 2 of this book proves that OSC, MSPB, and OPM are as corrupt as DCMA, and that such any unethical and arrogant strategy would prevail. DCMA even planned to use Dan Meyer as a witness to testify about DCMA covert actions against me.

Dan Meyer – "Whistleblower Advocate" Against Whistleblowers

April 11, 2006: DCMA planned to use a purported "whistleblower advocate" against a whistleblower. Meaning, DCMA's witness list stated the following in part.

"Rebuttal Witness - Daniel P. Meyer, Chief, Civilian Reprisal Investigations, DoD IG. Mr. Meyer will be called only if necessary for rebuttal. Mr. Meyer is expected to testify that the DoD IG was informed of the agency investigation and that the agency investigation did not interfere with any then-pending DoD IG investigations. Mr. Meyer will also testify regarding his communications with the agency in this matter."

Senator Grassley, through Charlie Murphy, placed high hopes in Dan Meyer as a whistleblower advocate. I knew Dan Meyer would be useless as of April 22, 2004, thinking Meyer would do nothing. I never figured Meyer would aggressively work against me. Meyer's duplicity did get attention as follows. Especially when DCMA announced Meyer as a witness against me.

Senator Grassley's Letter to DoD IG Regarding Meyer as a DCMA Witness

& DoD IGs Continued Con Against Senator Grassley

May 5, 2006: Senator Grassley sent a list of questions to the DoD IG on April 21, 2006. Uldric Fiore responded in part as follows.

"The Principal Deputy Inspector General, Mr. Thomas F. Gimble, asked that I (Uldric Fiore) *respond to your April 21, 2006 letter concerning the potential testimony of Mr. Dan Meyer, Director of Civilian Reprisal Investigations (CRI), at a Merit Systems Protection Board (MSPB) hearing involving an appeal by a Department of Defense (DoD) whistleblower. Although not named in your letter, the proceeding in question involves a Mr. Kenneth Pedeleose, an employee of the Defense Contract Management Agency (DCMA) in Atlanta, GA."*

Repeating the Cover Story to Senator Grassley: Fiore responded to Senator Grassley using the same DoD IG and DCMA cover story (pretext) about the alleged coordination of investigations in 2005. Meaning, Uldric Fiore ran the same con on Senator Grassley that Dan Meyer ran on Charlie Murphy. This may account for the June 5, 2008 investigation against Fiore. However, one odd account from Fiore that I can never recall happening is as follows.

"In the discovery phase of the MSPB proceeding, Mr. Pedeleose sought to take Mr. Meyer's deposition, and to have the DCMA attorney take Mr. Meyer's deposition, both of which the DCMA attorney successfully resisted. The DCMA attorney believed, however, that Mr. Pedeleose was likely to make allegations at the then pending hearing that the DCMA inquiry did or would encroach on Mr. Meyer's reprisal investigation or that Mr. Meyer had breached confidentiality. To address such allegations if raised, the DCMA attorney coordinated with the OI G Office of the General Counsel to have Mr. Meyer available as a potential rebuttal witness."

Fiore's comments to Senator Grassley seemed like double-talk and incoherent. It was clear that I asked Meyer and Fiore for coordination documents and was continually stonewalled. So again, Fiore engaged in more duplicity with Senator Grassley. Meaning, Fiore should have stated how I was stonewalled on the coordination documents. I did make allegations against Meyer and DoD IG.

Uncontested Allegations Against Dan Meyer, DoD IG, & DCMA

I made uncontested allegations against Dan Meyer, DoD IG, and DCMA in my March 29, 2006 deposition that were stipulated to on May 10, 2006 by DCMA in a written letter. Meaning, DCMA provided no rebuttal and accepted the following, plus many other allegations, as first-hand facts.

I believe the Inspector General's Office -- and this is another thing we need to discuss about the facts of the case was engaged in an act of reprisal against me.

So in answer to your question: Yes, I believe that the Inspector General's Office engaged in an act of reprisal against me, they assisted the Agency. This is my belief.

"And I says, "Dan, is what they're doing over here lawful? Is this a lawful investigation?" He said, "We have absolutely no idea. We have never seen this before." Okay. He also had concerns"

Furthermore, DCMA stipulated on May 10, 2006 that my April 28, 2006: *"Response to Charges (Statement of Facts, Issues, and Affirmative Defenses)"* was not going to be rebutted. Meaning, the following information and allegations became first hand facts.

"Clear up to February 27, 2006 I was still unclear about the coordination between DCMA and the DoD IG. Even the e-mail from Dan Meyer does not go into the detail, that I later found out about how the DoD IG and DCMA conspired and retaliated against me.

Relevance to My Case: I believe that the DoD IG was so ashamed of what they had done they made every effort to keep me in the dark and hid their actions. I would discover the full scope of the alleged coordination until April 6, 2006. I should have been told when the coordination began and all issues would have been resolved."

"Aside from Mr. Meyers adverse actions towards me. I did try several times to confirm that the DCMA alleged investigation was lawful and in good faith. When I received the alleged coordination documents on April 6, 2006, it was obvious that the DCMA alleged investigation was in bad faith and was a cover for retaliation."

"Dan Meyer actively assisted DCMA with tactical information on how to thwart Congressional involvement. Mr. Meyer Stated (AA3): "Though it is perhaps beyond my portfolio, be careful of the Congressional end of this case-which has been quiet/or a while. Grassley and McCain are interested in the issues Pedeleose is perceived as advancing, so you may want to make sure your liaison is in the loop when the Colonel's investigation goes ahead.""

"I received a 30 day suspension resulting from the actions of Mr. Dan Meyer who circumvented Congressional protection that I would have had from my involvement in Congressional oversight reviews (See S7 and S8)."

I also made allegations against Uldric Fiore as follows at MSPB on April 28, 2006:

"January 23, 2006 in a communication between Mr. Bruce Krasker and Mr. Uldric Fiore the Subject of the e-mail was simply "KP". The fact that Mr. Krasker sent the e-mail to Mr. Fiore after the alleged investigation had concluded indicates that there was a conspiracy between DCMA and the DoD IG. Mr. Fiore is a senior attorney and official of the DoD IG. The involvement of Mr. Fiore in disciplinary action against me indicates that the reprisal (disciplinary action) was always the goal. Mr. Fiore had no need to know the information otherwise.

This type of disparate treatment indicates that I was singled out by name by high level officials. In some instances only my initials (KP) were used."

"*Political Motives (Ms. L. Jean Lewis)- One Reason DoD IG for DoD IG Retaliation.*" This relates to Falsified Trail 2, where I was walked out the gate, and Jean Lewis, who was political in the 1990s, was discovered. Meaning DoD IG blamed me, and in fact, I did give Jean Lewis's name.

"*Dan Meyer (DoD IG) Informs Leigh Owens of IG Disclosures*". I made allegations that Dan Meyer informed Leigh Owens of IG disclosures. DCMA issued a formal letter on May 10, 2006, stating that there was no rebuttal evidence, meaning that what I said about Dan Meyer was stipulated by DCMA.

Senator Grassley's concern to the DoD IG about Dan Meyer even being asked to testify is why DCMA and the DoD IG did not tell me on October 5, 2005, about the alleged coordination. Had I been told in 2005 that DoD IG and DCMA were allegedly coordinating, it would have upset the tactical, weaponized retaliation and lawfare against me.

The Longer Deep State Trail via Surprise Evidence: The eventual tactic was to use surprise evidence, then let the "Cerberus" aspects of OSC, MSPB, and OPM cover everything up. That worked for DCMA and DoD IG, although it was a long road that took from June 21, 2005 to February 12, 2009, to reach fruition. That long trail would identify the Deep State in action.

The following shows that the DCMA gambit of relying on OSC and MSPB cover-ups did pay off initially. However, it took two tries at MSPB, where, in the end, MSPB sold out what little, if any, integrity it had, along with the DOJ and the Federal Court of Appeals. The following is the cover-up trail.

"Cerberus" Cover-up Analogy (Federal Machinery) Goes to Work

Initial MSPB Decision – MSPB Judge Lonny Bartholomew

June 14, 2006: The initial MSPB decision came from MSPB Judge Lonny Bartholomew. Bartholomew ruled entirely in favor of DCMA, despite overwhelming evidence that I was singled out, along with evidence of fraudulent and covert acts committed by DCMA and the DoD IG. DCMA even admitted to retaliation and collusion with the DoD IG by failing to rebut my case and by placing my deposition on the record without rebuttal.

Bartholomew's decision was sickening to read; it ignored whistleblower protections and condoned fraudulent acts by management officials. Bartholomew's decision lived up to the expected, discredited, reputation of MSPB. This was likened to the weaponized "Federal Machinery" proposed during the Nixon administration, outlined in Chapter 2 herein. Nixon would have loved and cherished the MSPB along with the OSC and OPM as the embodiment of weaponized "Federal Machinery."

Tactical Reason for Hearing on Written Records: Prior to Bartholomew, I was aware that MSPB proceedings and hearings were clown shows at best, resembling administrative "love fests" between MSPB and government agencies. Prehearing conferences with Bartholomew were no exception and were exemplified in Bartholomew's decision. Likewise, the number of false statements from management officials made it impossible for me to counter them during a live hearing, given my knowledge of MSPB bias.

Meaning, a Hearing on Written Records was a tactical, and necessary, opportunity to curb judicial bias and more adequately handle and quantify false statements from management at my convenience.

I appealed the case (Petition for Review (PFR)) to the full MSPB board on July 5, 2006, using the same evidence provided to Judge Bartholomew. While the PFR was pending, an investigation was initiated into the retaliatory, weaponized investigation (Falsified Trail 3) of 2005.

National Security Agency (NSA) Investigation

June 8, 2006: NSA investigator Rod Biggs contacted me as a result of my complaint to the Federal Bureau of Investigation, the Integrity Committee of the President's Council on Integrity & Efficiency, on February 6, 2006. I stated in part.

"The working relationship and resulting ethical breaches between the DoD IG and DCMA are so close that DCMA has actually disclosed the relationship in disciplinary action against me. The Most recent is a 30-day suspension from duty and pay effective January 25, 2006; through and including February 24, 2006."

"In short, disclosures to the DoD IG hotline about DCMA management misconduct were routed directly to DCMA management staff and attorneys. Status of pending cases that directly involve the DCMA management staff were also discussed."

"DoD IG Personnel involved in these actions (to best of my knowledge and/or documentation) include:

Mr. Leonard Trahan Director Defense Hotline.

Mr. Uldric Fiore Legal Counsel DoD IG

Mr. Dan Meyer Director, DoD IG Civilian Reprisal Investigations

There may be more DoD IG officials involved in this matter; however, these are the DoD IG officials of which I am aware of at this time."

Chronologically, my February 6, 2006 complaint was forwarded to the DoD IG, and on April 26, 2006, DoD IG Principal Deputy Inspector General Richard Race contacted NSA IG Joel Brenner. Race then sent a May 17, 2006 letter to Brenner, stating, in part.

"Reference is made to our phone conversation 26 April '06 regarding this matter. Thank you very much for assisting us. The attached transmittal from the Integrity Committee (IC) of the President's Council on Integrity and Efficiency is forwarded to you for action, as we discussed in our phone call. As many of our components are named or touched upon by the Complainant, we are conflicted in the handling of this case."

DoD IG referred the matter to an outside agency (NSA) because it determined that investigating DoD IG would create a conflict of interest.

June 28, 2006 Statements & Meyer Emails to Grassley: The value of the NSA IG investigation was the quotes used herein regarding the June 28, 2006, and June 21, 2006, sworn statements. The NSA investigation also included emails from Dan Meyer to Charlie Murphy, used to explain the con and duplicity by Dan Meyer. However, the NSA willfully chose to ignore the evidence and sworn statements and cover up the DCMA and DoD IG retaliation as follows.

NSA “Whitewash – “Deep State” Cover-up

November 1, 2006: The NSA “whitewash” and cover-up is one reason I provided a detailed email trail of information to prove my case and allegations. Meaning, the words and behavior of others to make the case. This helps counter the following NSA vitriol conclusion, stated in part.

“Current matter. DoDIG CRI is currently investigating a reprisal complaint submitted by Mr. Pedeleose which is separate and apart from the instant matter. In order to avoid future conflict allegations, we recommend that DoDIG consider transferring this other reprisal complaint to the U. S. Office of Special Counsel.

Future Interaction. We concur with MSPB Judge Bartholomew's view that Mr. Pedeleose is "obsessed with a self-indulged perception of pervasive agency malice." Mr. Pedeleose appears to have alleged wrongdoing by nearly every Government entity with which he has interacted. His written materials evidence that he has firmly convinced himself that he is the target of a far-reaching and malevolent Government conspiracy, and that each and every interaction with a Government official warrants their inclusion in what he terms "'the facts of his case." In view of this situation, we recommend that any further DoDlG interaction with Mr. Pedeleose, no matter how minor, involve DoDIG counsel and be conducted entirely on the record."

NSA advised DoD IG to “lawyer up”. It is to my understanding that DoD IG attorneys, and possibly Dan Meyer, may have consulted attorneys. Meaning, DoD IG interactions with me have left attorneys consulting attorneys. I decided a relentless shakeup and pursuit was needed to provide further transparency and deeper “Chink the Armor” of the Deep State.

“Chink in the Armor” of the Deep State

After I submitted Falsified Trail 3 to the full MSPB in 2006 and after the NSA whitewash, I began a relentless pursuit to dig deeper into the tactical, weaponized investigation in 2005. The pursuit began in 2007. The events were documented in chronological order as follows, interspersed with other notable events of 2007, starting with terminated employee 2.

“Chink in the Armor” Part 1

Case Settled for Terminated Employee 2 – Cash in the Travel Budget

July 26, 2007: The employee, who was terminated on June 14, 2005, via letter in the mail, received a substantial cash settlement from DCMA on July 26, 2007. I began the case as a “first responder” and pushed the case prior to litigation. The employee then retained an Atlanta, GA, law firm immediately prior to the EEO hearing.

The point being, that case was a “Chink in the Armor” of the Deep State. Meaning, a victory that I aggressively drove to fruition as a first responder. That “relentless” pursuit was successful, and I deployed the tactic again with another “Chink in the Armor” of the Deep State as follows.

Dan Meyer – Tactical Backdating Weaponized Investigation – March 18, 2005

May 31, 2007: Attached to the September 6, 2005, e-mail from Meyer to Krasker was a list of questions with the "*time starting on March 18, 2005*". March 18, 2005, was a ruse to deflect attention from DCMA's investigation of the same issues as the DoD IG was investigating. All the events started in June 2005 forward, meaning the March 18, 2005 date was an avenue for my relentless pursuit of the tactical weaponized investigation and lawfare (Falsified Trail 3).

My relentless inquiries began on May 31, 2007, and led to a retraction letter dated September 10, 2007, signed by DoD IG Principal Deputy Thomas Gimble, which retracted an August 27, 2007, letter also signed by Thomas Gimble. This was outlined in Chapter 1, my resume.

More specifically, the June 5, 2008, IG report stated the retraction letter was a "*result of [the DoD complainant's] relentless requests for information...*" I was the "DoD complainant". The IG report gave a sample of the "Thirty Fourth Request" within the "relentless" requests. From memory, over 50 requests were sent nearly every workday by a combination of fax and e-mail.

Dan Meyer Was Rattled: The relentless pursuit rattled Dan Meyer to the point where Meyer unleashed regrets and tactics to cover up Falsified Trail 3 as follows.

"Chink in the Armor" Part 2 – Regret Email by Dan Meyer
"Bad Decision" Dealing with Krasker (DCMA)

July 27, 2007 (Appendix A1-15): The day after "Chink in the Armor" Part 1 (July 26, 2007), Meyer regretted meeting with Krasker on August 10, 2005, stating in part on July 27, 2007.

"*The meeting was risk, it could have sparked more issues, I expressed reservations about going, was given the opportunity not to attend, but decided that it was worth supporting OGC* (Office of General Counsel) *in the spirit of making amends. Relations between my floor and your corner were a little saggy at that point. So I went. Bad decision on my part. In retrospect, I should have left you all alone with Krasker...*"

Meyer learned the hard lesson of dealing with Bruce Krasker and DCMA. DCMA cannot be trusted, and I would advise anyone not to trust DCMA in any way. Meyer then spoke of "top cover".

Dan Meyer – Tactical "Top Cover"

July 27, 2007 (Appendix A1-15): Meyer e-mailed DoD IG officials stating: *"I had no contact with DCMA Boston, except through OGC. That is why I was invited to Ric's meeting with them, because OGC was 'providing me top cover"*.

"Top cover" refers to a concealment tactic in which others knew, or should have known, what Meyer was doing. Meaning, Meyer was tactically distancing from culpability in one sense, while Meyer was directly emailing Leigh Owens, as the aforesaid email trails have shown. Regardless of DoD IG's "top cover," Meyer was responsible for Meyer's problems and Meyer's actions. Meyer knew what Meyer did, and what Meyer did was documented in a "pile of paper".

Dan Meyer - Tactical Cover-up Regarding the "Pile of Paper" Anxiety

July 27, 2007 (Appendix A1-15): Meyer tactically informed DoD IG members.

"But do note that DCMA has given KP evidence (in the Atlanta MSPB case) that KP indicates will prove that OGC was conducting the conversations with Krasker and his people. So your work product is going to be matched up against that pile of paper. I am getting the same feeling that I have had before – we, OIG (Office of Inspector General)*, are drafting documents which may contradict previous materials coming out of government offices. We don't know what DCMA has, or what they provided KP, about OGC's discussions with DCMA. We do know what I communicated – NSA IG has reviewed that. This is a very difficult environment in which to be writing a letter."*

Meyer had good reason for concern since DCMA and DoD IG "*work product*" was *"matched up against that pile of paper"* supporting this book. The "*pile of paper*" was supplemented by my interactions with Meyer. FOIA requests and two IG investigations continued to supplement the "*pile of paper*". From there, Meyer made false statements to the DoD IG as follows.

Dan Meyer - False/Contradicting Statements to DoD IG

July 27, 2007 (Appendix A1-15): Meyer stated:

"*I wouldn't have returned Krasker's calls or e-mails if he had contacted me...I had no contact with DCMA Boston, except through OGC."*

However, Meyer e-mailed Bruce Krasker on September 6, 2005, stating: "*Bruce, thanks for narrowing these questions...*" Hence, a false statement by Meyer. Those questions included the March 18, 2005, start date that was the topic of the "relentless" pursuit that rattled Dan Meyer.

Meyer also indicated the following further contact with Krasker.

September 12, 2005 (Appendix A1-13): Meyer emailed Charlie Murphy regarding protection letters from Senator Grassley as follows, stating in part.

"Bruce K is calling you to ask what they are suppose to do with the letters."

Hence, Meyer must have had contact with Krasker (*"Bruce K"*).

The relevance is that Meyer made false statements to DoD IG officials. Meyer's contacts with Krasker may have been more extensive than originally made known. It is still unclear what was actually stated at the August 10, 2005, meeting, meaning more detailed discussion may have taken place. Meyer also admitted to providing tactical advice on "*Congressional interest*".

Dan Meyer - Tactical – "Congressional Interest was not Following"

July 27, 2007 (Appendix A1-15): Meyer included the following tactical comment to DoD IG officials regarding Congressional interest (Senator Grassley via Charlie Murphy).

"*As of August 2005, KP was going to MSPB, we had found no reprisal on the allegations we were looking into, and the Congressional interest was not following KP into his labor activities (which is what led to the August meeting).*"

Relevance is that Meyer successfully conned Senator Grassley, via Charlie Murphy, to abandon Henry Hagel and me, thus greenlighting the tactical, weaponized investigation to continue to the point where DoD IG was "*happy*" to discuss disciplinary action against me (Appendix A1-14). Dan Meyer regretted his actions and suggested cover-up techniques to DoD IG officials in writing.

Meyer also had anxiety over the "*pile of paper*" that DCMA provided to me for Falsified Trail 3. The anxiety was justified because "Chink in the Armor" Part 3 followed in about three months.

"Chink in the Armor" Part 3

Irreparable, Irreversible Damage - Future Cover-ups in the Crosshairs

October 24, 2007: MSPB provided an irreparable, irreversible, "Chink in the Armor," of the Deep State. Meaning, it is ethically impossible to reverse a decision when clear, uncontested, evidence is known by the judges. Any attempt at a cover-up would bring MSPB credibility into the crosshairs. Which is what this book does, in volume, against OSC, MSPB, and OPM.

Specifically, on October 24, 2007 MSPB admitted to a clear understanding of the DCMA retaliation against me. MSPB followed the evidence, understood the evidence, explained the evidence, and then correctly ruled in my favor. It was a foregone conclusion after DCMA placed my March 29, 2006 Sworn Deposition on the record without rebuttal followed by a May 10, 2006 no-rebuttal letter to my Response to Charges.

DCMA then provided written documents, electronic email trails, showing actual whistleblower retaliation in progress. Meaning, DCMA applied the Death Knell to their own case similar to Nixon's White House Tapes.

DCMA's Electronic Trails & Nixon's White House Tapes

DCMA proved there was a Deep State via electronic trails. This was analogous to the Nixon era where Nixon used the electronic trails of the day which were audio recordings. Specifically, the Nixon White House Tapes. Those tapes captured Nixon as well as those who spoke with Nixon. Similar to DCMA, except DCMA used emails as electronic trails.

This means DCMA should have learned the lessons from history. It also means that both Nixon and DCMA were "hoist by one's own petard," or caught in their own traps. The fact that OSC, MSPB, OPM, DOJ and the Federal Court of Appeals unethically rescued DCMA further proves a broken Government. In a way, everything really does tie back a half century to the Nixon era (1970s).

The October 24, 2007 decision of Falsified Trail 3 was a centerpiece, watershed moment, that provided across-the-board transparency into the Deep State. The following explains how MSPB followed the evidence, understood the evidence, explained the evidence, and then correctly ruled in my favor.

MSPB Win at Full MSPB – Contradicts NSA Conclusion - Deep State Transparency

October 24, 2007: By this point, the tactical weaponized government had sustained losses on July 26, 2007 (settlement of terminated employee 2), and the following day, July 27, 2007, regrets by Dan Meyer along with cover-up tactics. The Deep State was losing. A few months later, two of the three MSPB judges (Mary M. Rose, Barbara J. Sapin) reversed Judge Bartholomew's decision, with the following findings stated in part.

1: MSPB - Confirmed Whistle-blowing: "*The appellant submitted a May 16, 2005 report titled "Cover-up in the Department of Defense,". The report was developed by the appellant and other employees who had for a number of years been involved in disclosing to Congress and other authorities details of safety problems and waste in the troubled history of the C-130J program. The appellant's involvement in disclosing problems with the C-130J program was widely known at DCMA. The report identified safety and waste problems with the C-130J program that existed before and after the issuance of a July 23, 2004 report by the IG stating that the IG substantiated the allegation that, at that time, the C-l30J aircraft did not meet contract specifications and therefore could not perform its operational mission. A month after the appellant submitted this report, the appellant helped VanDerbeck, an engineer and a probationary employee, file a complaint with the DoD IG regarding safety issues that she had observed as she worked in the C-130J program. In her June 10, 2005 complaint, VanDerbeck identified 14 alleged violations in the C-130J program. The appellant's e-mail to the IG of VanDerbeck's complaint was copied to Plourde. On June 15, 2005, the appellant received information that in a meeting, Plourde discussed the system safety issues that VanDerbeck was raising and that Plourde was quoted as saying that "since Susan Vanderbeck is a probationary employee all they (DCMA management) have to do is fire her." The appellant e-mailed this information to the IG. The e-mail specifically identified those present at the meeting, Plourde, Henrietta Snow, and Myra Tate, and stated that the appellant suspected that Tate told "Shelton-Thomas, who in turn told Ms. Davis" what Plourde said. The agency terminated VanDerbeck the following day.*"

2: MSPB - Plourde Reacts: MSPB stated: "*On the same day, the appellant sent an e-mail to the IG (DoD) informing the IG that he had confirmation of his earlier e-mail to the IG reporting that Plourde was targeting VanDerbeck for firing because of her whistle-blowing and informing the IG that Plourde was targeting additional employees for firing. The next day, June 21, 2005, Plourde began an investigation into the rumors about terminations.*"

3: MSPB – Illegal Order Conflicts with DoD IG Investigation: MSPB stated: "*The appellant then sent e-mails to DCMA Director Major General Darryl A. Scott, DCMA East Director Keith Ernst, and Daniel P. Meyer of the DoD lG's office alleging that Plourde's Letter of Direction was an illegal order and accusing her of abuse of authority, threatening a federal witness, and witness tampering. The appellant explained in his deposition that he believed that the Scantlebury investigation would interfere with the investigation of the same matters that he believed would be investigated by the IG. The appellant stated "Did I just blatantly not agree cooperate with her [Scantlebury] based on the fact that I had suspicions? No, I turned it over to the Inspector General and I wanted an independent look at this from an outside organization.*""

4: <u>MSPB – DCMA Stipulated to Whistleblower Retaliation</u>: "*Both parties submitted the entire transcript of the appellant's deposition into the record. For that reason, the Board has credited the deposition testimony as it would a stipulation by the parties. We find it noteworthy that both parties submitted many of the same documents into the record.*"

5: <u>MSPB – Scantlebury Never Advised of DoD IG Involvement</u>: MSPB stated: "*Although Scantlebury must have been aware of the e-mail communications with the IG because the IG reviewed the questions that she would be asking the appellant, there is no evidence that Scantlebury showed the appellant those e-mail communications or otherwise informed him that the list of questions had been approved by the IG.*"

On June 23, 2005, I told Scantlebury this was a "Whistleblower Matter". Scantlebury replied: "*I respectfully request that you not include me on e-mail messages such as this. I really have no need to know this information.*" At that point, Scantlebury was directly involved in the case, as MSPB has noted. Meaning, Scantlebury tried to distance herself from culpability.

6: <u>MSPB – Agency Failed to Prove Charges</u>: MSPB stated: "*…the agency failed to prove the charges.*"

7: <u>MSPB – "Obey Now Grieve Later" Does Not Apply</u>: MSPB stated: "*Two considerations underlie the "obey now, grieve later" rule: (1) the agency and its mission may be harmed by the employee's failure to act; and (2) the employee may be mistaken in his belief. Therefore, cases where employees are disciplined for breaking the rule usually involve investigations of potential crimes and serious misconduct…None of these considerations are present in this case. The agency concedes that the Scantlebury investigation did not involve any potential crimes or even misconduct meriting discipline. It was an inquiry into rumor spreading, nothing more. The agency provides no evidence of harm due to the appellant's lack of full cooperation. Further, the e-mails from the IG show that it is uncertain whether the appellant was mistaken in his belief that the investigation, if not illegal, might conflict with the IG's investigation into similar matters.*"

8: <u>MSPB – Information Given to DoD IG</u>: MSPB stated: "*He* (Pedeleose) *informed Plourde and Scantlebury on more than one occasion during the investigation that he had given the information that they sought to the IG.*"

9: <u>MSPB – Plourde and Scantlebury Disingenuous</u>: "*there is no evidence that Plourde or Scantlebury informed the appellant of the steps that the agency had taken to coordinate the two investigations. This failure contrasts with the fact that Scantlebury, with Plourde's knowledge, informed the appellant of the actions that the agency had taken to consult with the U.S. Attorney. Further, this failure appears disingenuous against the backdrop of the appellant's repeated statements of concern to Plourde and Scantlebury about the potential conflict with the IG's investigation. By not conveying the IG's views to the appellant, Plourde and Scantlebury essentially cut off the means by which the appellant could have complied with their investigation and orders without fearing interference with the IG's investigation. Under the circumstances of this case, we find that the agency failed to prove its charges.*"

10: <u>MSPB – No Evidence of Approved Questions</u>: MSPB stated: "*there is no evidence that Ms. Owens, Scantlebury, or Plourde informed the appellant that the list of questions Scantlebury wished to ask had been approved by the IG or that the IG and the agency had agreed upon a means to proceed with both investigations, despite the appellant's repeated protests about the potential conflict between the investigations.*"

11: <u>MSPB – Agency Failed to Prove Charges</u>: MSPB stated: "*we found that the agency did not prove its charges, the strength of the agency's action is weak.*"

12: <u>MSPB – Plourde "wrongdoer" Had Motive</u>: MSPB stated: "*The record also shows that Plourde, who as the proposing official was involved in the agency action, had a motive to retaliate against the appellant. The motive to retaliate can be inferred from the fact that the alleged wrongdoer knew of the allegations of wrongdoing directly.*"

13: <u>MSPB – Plourde Abused Authority</u>: MSPB stated: "*Plourde was aware of the appellant's allegations. She was aware that the appellant assisted VanDerbeck in her whistle-blowing activity, and that, after the agency terminated VanDerbeck, he represented her in her EEO complaint. Plourde knew that the appellant believed that she had violated the law and abused her authority in threatening to fire VanDerbeck.*"

14: <u>MSPB - Plourde Aware of Whistle-blowing</u>: MSPB Stated: "*Plourde was also well aware of the appellant's contribution to Congressional investigations into the C-130J program, investigations which resulted in a report calling for the termination of the C-130J, the program that she was charged with administering. The appellant's participation in those investigations was widely known at DCMA. The IG had cautioned Owens in an e-mail that Senators Grassley and McCain were interested in the issues the appellant was perceived as advancing.*"

15: <u>MSPB – Plourde Shifting Reasons</u>: MSPB stated: "*Plourde's motive to retaliate is also inferred from the shifting reasons that she gave to conduct the investigation. On one hand she said that there was no basis for the rumors and the investigation was because the rumors were having a negative effect on employee morale. Yet, as we quoted above, in her affidavit, Plourde stated "I was concerned that one of my supervisors was inappropriately discussing confidential management information with subordinates and that this conduct was feeding rumors that certain employees were targeted to be fired.*""

16: <u>MSPB – Leak Investigation</u>: MSPB stated: "*Plourde's statement and actions imply that she had a real concern that information that she wanted kept confidential was leaking to employees and that she wanted to get to the ultimate source of that leak.*"

17: <u>MSPB – Force of Plourde's Actions Show Motive</u>: MSPB stated: "*The force of her actions after she traced the rumors to the appellant implies that she had a motive to retaliate against the appellant, who published the allegation of her violation of law and abuse of authority and would not provide her the information that she wanted.*"

18: <u>MSPB – Plourde's Motive to Retaliate</u>: MSPB stated: "*Plourde's motive to retaliate is further evidenced in the fact that she did not inform the appellant that the IG approved the questions for the Scantlebury investigation and what recourse he had if he believed that additional questions would interfere with the IG investigation. The appellant repeatedly told Plourde and Scantlebury that he had given the information they sought to the IG and that he was concerned that their investigation would interfere with that of the IG. Nevertheless, neither Plourde nor Scantlebury told the appellant that they had consulted the IG and worked out a means of coordinating the two investigations*."

19: MSPB – Singled Out: MSPB stated: "*Finally, there is no evidence regarding whether the agency takes similar actions against employees who are not whistleblowers but who are otherwise similarly situated; therefore, we find that the agency has failed to meet its significant statutory burden of proof to show by clear and convincing evidence that it would have disciplined the appellant absent his whistleblowing*."

MSPB had 19 reasons to clear me of the fraudulent and retaliatory charges outlined in the 30-day suspension. This was even before the two aforesaid IG investigations. However, MSPB still had a "Cerberus" part that needed to contain negative information. That came in a dissenting opinion from Neil McPhee as follows.

MSPB Judge Neil McPhee – Supports Weaponized Investigations

Admits Agency was Caught in Their Own Trap

October 24, 2007 - Dissenting Opinion: The MSPB decision included a dissenting opinion from Neil McPhee, who appeared upset that DCMA had been caught in its own trap. McPhee stated in part:

"The evidence in support of the agency 's decision to suspend the appellant is very strong; indeed, the evidence is uncontested."

McPhee reversed the case facts because it was DCMA that issued a formal no-rebuttal to my case on May 10, 2006. Meaning, McPhee reversed the facts. DCMA admitted to whistleblower retaliation. McPhee went on to show that the law does not matter, stating, in part, that.

"If, however, I agreed with the majority that the charges could not be sustained and that the appellant made a protected disclosure that contributed to his suspension, I would assess the agency's arguments in support of its affirmative defense differently from the majority because at the time it acted the agency reasonably believed under prevailing law that it was entitled to discipline the appellant for the conduct described in the charges."

McPhee admits DCMA was caught in their own trap. Whistleblower protection law was on my side. DCMA tactically weaponized an investigation for insulation to skirt the law. DCMA never had a legitimate reason for an investigation, and there was no damage to the government.

MSPB Ignored Deep State Facts – Needs More Aggressive Decision

I am grateful at least two MSPB judges ruled in my favor. However, MSPB acted as if DCMA actually had an honest investigation. Meaning, this book seeks to educate on the real behavior of the Deep State. The Deep State includes deliberate maleficence that needs to be called out. As such, the education on the Deep State cover-ups continues with OPM's support of weaponized government and lawfare as the third part of the Cerberus cover-up analogy.

Linda Springer (OPM) Intervenes Supporting a "Disingenuous" Commander

Condoning Tactical Weaponized Lawfare Traced to Senior Officials

November 28, 2007: Following my successful win at MSPB on October 24, 2007, and despite the fact that DCMA admitted to retaliation and tactically engaged in weaponized government, Linda Springer stated the following to MSPB in part.

"This is notice that the Office of Personnel Management (OPM) is exercising its statutory right under 5U.S.C. §7703(d) to request reconsideration of the Board's decision in the case cited below. I am of the opinion that the Board erred in interpreting a civil service law, rule, or regulation affecting personnel management and that the Board's decision will have a substantial impact on civil service law, rule, regulation, or policy directive.

Kenneth M Pedeleose v. Department of Defense

Docket No. AT-0752-06-0350-1-1, October 24, 2007"

Linda Springer ignored whistleblower protections and ignored the law. DCMA's case against me (Obey Now Grieve Later, Work First Grieve Later) was based on accepted practice and not a law, not a rule, and not a regulation. DCMA even admitted to whistleblower retaliation, and Colonel Plourde was labeled "*disingenuous*" by MSPB. Springer completed the operational "Cerberus" triad of OSC, MSPB, and OPM to contain negative information that could trace wrongdoing (18 U.S.C. 1505) and whistleblower retaliation, to Senior DoD officials.

Linda Springer was also engaged in duplicity, since Springer publicly allayed concerns about OSC Scott Block, as outlined in Chapter 2. This deserves a brief recap as follows.

Linda Springer (OPM) Duplicity Regarding OSC Scott Bloch

December 12, 2003 (OSC Director Scott Bloch): Scott Bloch was a political appointee for President George W. Bush with a statutory term from December 12, 2003–December 11, 2008.

March 22, 2005 – Government Accountability Project (GAP): "*Federal Workers Who Sought Help from U.S. Special Counsel Scott Bloc*". This article stated:

"*The controversy began when Bloch abruptly announced reassignment of twelve attorneys and investigators from Washington, D.C. headquarters to field offices, including a new field office in Detroit, Michigan. The reorganization targeted employees who were either whistleblowers or suspected of being whistleblowers.*"

"*Recently, GAP has also learned that some 1000 cases and whistleblowing disclosures have been dumped without investigation by the OSC, often without even calling the whistleblower. This is an emergency, because plans to gut due process appeal rights at the Merit Systems Protection Board mean aggrieved federal workers will have nowhere to turn except the Special Counsel.*"

Relevance is that 2005 was the date of Plourde's/DCMA tactical weaponized investigation, so DCMA was riding the wave of Scott Bloch/OSC corruption. Meaning, this embolden DCMA to act recklessly and arrogant since OSC was enabling whistleblowing.

June 28, 2005 (OPM Director Linda Springer): Linda Springer was appointed OPM Director with a term to August 13, 2008.

OPM Allegedly Investigating Scott Bloch October 17, 2005: As of October 17, 2005, Linda Springer was purportedly investigating Scott Bloch.

October 20, 2005 – News From OPM: OPM issued a public news release regarding the investigation of Scott Bloch, concluding:

"*Inspector General McFarland has agreed to promptly conduct a thorough investigation and report his findings along with recommended remedial actions, if appropriate, to OPM Director Linda M. Springer and Deputy U.S. Special Counsel Jim Renne.*"

Springer's public statements supported whistleblowers. Springer's Deep State private side actively supported a tactical weaponized government and lawfare using government-funded legal resources. Meaning, the actions of OPM and Linda Springer in my case infer duplicity. I can remember no positive actions coming from Linda Springer or OPM investigations of Scott Bloch.

OPM Opposition to MSPB Decision – Vacate & Alter Official Records

January 22, 2008: OPM's "Brief in Support of Its Petition for Reconsideration" of the October 24, 2007 MSPB decision was a request to vacate and alter an official record against substantial facts and irrefragable evidence stipulated to by DCMA. Meaning, the OPM brief was a cover-up request because DCMA weaponized "Obey Now, Grieve Later", "Work First, Grieve Later".

OPM struggled with the fortress of facts in my favor, as evidenced by OPM's erratic writings. OPM was represented by Kerry B. McTigue (General Counsel), Steven E. Abow (Assistant General Counsel), and Becky C. Ronayne (Attorney-Advisor) for a 17 Page brief. OPM used Neil McPhee's dissenting opinion, which concluded that DCMA was essentially caught in a DCMA trap.

It would add another section to this book to show the numerous illogical, untrue, and obfuscating claims contained in the OPM brief. Hence, OPM summary statements are in part.

"It is worth noting that this kind of quantum expansion of these narrow restrictions is likely to sow confusion in the Federal workplace among managers and employees concerning permissible workplace behavior."

MSPB did not make a "quantum expansion" of anything. MSPB ruled "Obey Now, Grieve Later", "Work First, Grieve Later" was not to be weaponized and that disingenuous commanders like Colonel Plourde would not be tolerated. It was OPM that made the quantum leap in the highly subjective theory of confusion in the workforce by stopping the weaponization of government and disingenuous management. OPM continued as follows.

"OPM does not quarrel with the Board's factual findings on this issue, which comport with those of the dissenter."

Death Knell: OPM or the dissenter, Neil McPhee, could not legally or logically quarrel with facts in the case because DCMA issued a no-rebuttal letter on May 10, 2006, that stipulated in total to my testimony and conclusions that were based on DCMA's data.

"Assuming arguendo that the appellant's disclosure was protected under the Whistleblower Protection Act, the Board nevertheless erred as a matter of law in determining that the agency would not have taken the same action against him but for the disclosure. Simply put, the Board's conclusion that the agency would not have taken the same action is inextricably intertwined with the Board's determination that the agency failed to prove its charge. As we have discussed above, this determination is wrong as a matter of law."

DCMA admitted to whistleblower retaliation by providing written information on an official record of how DCMA worked behind my back to circumvent the Whistleblower Protection Act. On May 10, 2006, DCMA issued a formal letter stating that no rebuttal evidence was presented to my accusations and affirmative defenses, meaning my information was 1st-hand under DCMA's agreement.

"Obey Now, Grieve later" was the backdoor, pretext, and ultimate weapon that OPM focused on rather than the law. OPM continued to state, in part, with a more bizarre statement.

"Accordingly, even if we assume that the appellant's disclosure was protected under the Whistleblower Protection Act, the Board would have to redo its analysis of whether the agency would have taken the same action but for the disclosure, using the legally correct conclusion that the agency proved its charge."

OPM asks the MSPB to alter an official record in which DCMA stipulated whistleblower retaliation. The Agency could not prove its charge because it engaged in whistleblower retaliation. Meaning, May 10, 2006, was an unrecoverable death knell.

"OPM also requests that the Board apply the correct standard and determine that the appellant's June 15, 2005 e-mail to the IG did not constitute a protected disclosure under the WPA."

OPM asks the board to reverse a disclosure to the DoD IG that DCMA stipulated to in the May 10, 2006, no-rebuttal letter. The June 15, 2005 disclosure and others were discussed at length in my March 29, 2006 deposition, and DCMA did not challenge them. Colonel Plourde never rebutted the contents of the June 15, 2005 disclosure because other employees witnessed Plourde's behavior. Plourde made the case against Plourde, and DCMA agreed.

To counter OPM, I was represented by the American Federation of Government Employees (AFGE) with a trained attorney applying the law as follows.

AFGE Supports MSPB Decision – Opposes OPM

DCMA Developed Factual Record Proving Retaliation

March 17, 2008: AFGE provided an attorney to respond to the OPM's January 22, 2008, brief. The AFGE brief was 35 pages, while the OPM brief was 18 pages. Some notable comments in the AFGE brief are as follows.

"OPM's argument merely repeats the Agency's argument below, and is not supported by any changes in the law or facts that warrant reconsideration of this case. Compare OPM Brief, pg. 12 (... OPM does not quarrel with the factual findings on this issue ..."

"OPM fails to address the fact that, as the Board expressly stated in its opinion, the exception created by the Board in this case hinged on Appellant's repeated attempts to ascertain his obligations in DCMA's investigation by contacting DoD IG, and on DoD I G's and DCMA's disingenuous responses to Appellant's attempts."

"Further, in asserting that the Board's decision works a quantum expansion of the exceptions to the "obey now, grieve later" doctrine, OPM fails to acknowledge that the Board placed particular weight on the unrebutted fact that when Appellant subsequently sought advice from DOD IG on whether he should comply with DCMA's investigation, DoD IG gave him the unreasonably vague answer that DoD IG "had no idea" whether the Agency's investigation was lawful."

"Most importantly, OPM chooses to ignore the MSPB's discussion of DCMA's repeated failures to inform Appellant that DoD IG had cleared Plourde 's investigation and Scantlebury's questions. As the MSPB correctly determined, in light of all of the facts presented in this case, the only reasonable explanation for Plourde's persistent refusal to disclose something as simple as the DoD I G's approval of her investigation is that she hoped to maneuver Appellant into a situation where she could discipline him without creating the appearance of illegal retaliation."

AFGE accurately summarized OPM's brief as follows:

"DCMA had the opportunity to, and did, fully develop the factual record below. Thus, DCMA was not unfairly deprived of its ability to defend its decision in this case. OPM's real complaint here seems to be that DCMA is hoist by its own petard. This complaint provides no ground for reconsideration."

DCMA developed the factual record that proved whistleblower retaliation. DCMA forced my deposition and then placed my deposition on the official MSPB record without rebuttal. Then, DCMA placed written documents on the record that proved whistleblower retaliation. A truly arrogant and reckless move that would expose the Deep State of tactical weaponized government. DCMA was caught in its own trap.

In parallel to OPMs efforts to contain the exposure of Deep State, weaponized, lawfare, retaliation against me, that were part of Falsified Trail 3, there were other notable events happening. The first was an IG investigation of Uldric Fiore from the fallout of Falsified Trail 3.

IG Investigation – Uldric Fiore's Official Conduct was Deficient in Three Areas

June 5, 2008: The IG report on Uldric Fiore was initiated by Senator Grassley as follows.

"At the request of the Department of Defense (DoD) Inspector General, we opened an investigation into the conduct of DoD OIG General Counsel Uldric Fiore. The DoD Inspector General had received a letter dated September 25, 2007, from Senator Charles Grassley questioning the following: (1) Fiore's role in drafting a response letter to Senator Grassley concerning a DoD press release that did not include pertinent e-mails and (2) Fiore's actions and involvement in issues concerning a DoD OIG complainant." (Appendix A3-4, Page 1of 3)

I was the *"DoD OIG complainant"* outlined above.

June 5, 2008 Information Already Integrated Herein: The information in the June 5, 2008 IG report has already been integrated into this book wherever the date June 5, 2008, appears. The information augments previous information in my MSPB case to provide a clearer, more accurate, and detailed picture of what tactically transpired in Falsified Trail 3.

The IG report on Fiore concluded by stating: (Appendix A3-4, Page 3 of 3)

"*Fiore's official conduct in matters relating to [the DoD complainant] was deficient in three areas. First, Fiore's involvement in discussions with DCMA officials of disciplinary action against [the complainant] and his failure as a supervisor to limit [an Associate General Counsel's] role in his interactions with DCMA management to the coordination of their respective investigations compromised the independence of the OIG. Second, Fiore's involvement in the [the DoD complainant's] hotline complaint to the DoD OIG which included allegations against him and four other attorneys in his office created an appearance of loss of impartiality. Third, Fiore's involvement in the review of correspondence to [the DoD complainant] which foreclosed further communication with [the complainant] on a matter that related to allegations that [the complainant] had made against him created an appearance of loss of impartiality.*

This report is being forwarded to the DoD Inspector General for whatever action he deems appropriate."

Relevance is, Uldric Fiore was found deficient by investigation. Meaning, Fiore acted inappropriately. This was who OPM was vigorously protecting. This should be no surprise, since Uldric Fiore and Bruce Krasker worked so closely that my 30-day suspension was paraded as a trophy. (Appendix A3-1)

Just 3 Days later, Colonel Plourde would take a victory lap, exodus from our office, apparently for the Pentagon F-35 program.

Plourde's Victory Lap – Victory Dinner

June 11, 2008: Colonel Plourde had a farewell dinner party (what seemed a victory party dinner) that invited approximately 66 Lockheed Martin employees and other participants of Falsified Trail 1, 2, and 3 including Gary Jencson, Leigh Owens, Stacy Scantlebury, Joe Caldwell, Charles (Ben) Chaffman, and Whitney Krause (DCMA Attorney in Warmup Termination 2).

A block of rooms was allegedly reserved for visiting guests. Henrietta Snow held a similar event on or about February 21, 2014, with a $ 50-a-plate dinner. Unknown who Henrietta Snow invited.

Plourde's farewell dinner encompassed the most notable personalities of the Falsified Trails against me. There may have been well over 100 individual names from a variety of organizations, not including groups within the list. The dinner was arranged by another employee (Mark Buckner), who would play an integral role in Volley 4 (Falsified Trails 11, 12, and 13). Buckner's wife also worked for Lockheed Martin.

Shortly after Plourde's farewell (victory) dinner Uldric Fiore was given the "boot".

Uldric Fiore Given the "Boot", Issues "Beyond" My Case

September 15, 2008 (Appendix A3-5): The investigation report on Fiore was dated June 5, 2008. On September 15, 2008, I discovered that Fiore was no longer at DoD IG. I emailed Charlie Murphy's staff to gather more information. Murphy replied, stating in part.

"*You are right. Fiore is gone. Kicklighter* (then DoD IG who replaced Joseph Schmitz) *gave him the boot as he departed, but we do not know why. He didn't tell us. We can make some guesses. I will also tell you that the questions regarding Fiore go way beyond your case. That's all I will say for now.*"

Uldric Fiore was a key participant in Falsified Trail 3 with issues beyond my case. It is unknown exactly when Fiore left the DoD IG; however, circumstantial timing suggests Fiore was given the "boot" as a result of the June 5, 2008 investigative report that was critical of Fiore. Nothing was done to correct the damage inflicted by Fiore in my case (Falsified Trail 3). This was who OPM was protecting.

To maintain the retaliatory and hostile atmosphere, DCMA backfilled with Joe Tessier. Tessier would take up where Plourde, Fiore, and the like left off. Tessier was my 2nd-level supervisor throughout the Volley 3 (Falsified Trails 4, 5, 6, 7, 8, 9, and 10) rapid-fire event. As the following shows, Tessier's reputation preceded him.

The C-5 Team Will Not Tolerate "Backstabbers"

December 13, 2007: Henrietta Snow visited the C-5 Team I was on. Snow was asked whether the rumors were true that Joe Tessier had been offered the position of a 14 (2nd-Level Supervisor) on the C5 team. Snow replied that the interview panel had favorably recommended Tessier. Snow was then told that the C5 team will not tolerate "*backstabbers*".

Tessier's reputation preceded Tessier. On August 18, 2003, and November 29, 2010, there were rumors that Tessier was selected outside the promotion panel's recommendations. Meaning, Tessier should not have been in a management position and was a weapon as the following shows.

Weaponized Chaos & Intimidation

Joe Tessier altered working conditions via weaponized chaos and intimidation against me as follows.

May 8, 2008: Tessier first stifled me by forcing work-related communications through DCMA management, much like the tactic in Falsified Trail 1. Meaning, Tessier was using the DCMA weaponized "playbook" against me. Tessier's May 8, 2008 letter used the same weaponized pattern as Joe Caldwell on May 27, 2003 (Falsified Trail 1) stating in part.

"This Command's managers must be aware of and involved in any issue significant enough to require the attention and involvement of the company's senior management officials."

Meaning, the May 8, 2008 weaponized Memorandum was the bellwether of things to follow where I was cut off from complaining to Lockheed Martin. Things soon got worse as follows.

May 12, 2008: I documented Tessier's actions to then DCMA Director Charlie Williams and other DCMA senior leaders, in an attempt to stifle my involvement in the Lockheed Martin Earned Value Management System (EVMS) (financial and progress tracking of weapon system development) and the Lockheed Martin estimating system. Lockheed Martin had been deficient in these areas for several years. Chapter 4 of this book has greater details. Tessier was not stopped.

June 23, 2008: Prior to Tessier, I issued several Corrective Action Requests (CARs) against the Lockheed Martin estimating system. Tessier pressured and persisted until I dropped the issue.

Tessier was weaponized chaos that altered my working conditions regarding contract oversight of Lockheed Martin.

Senior Management Consistent Shunning & Non-Response to Complaints

In writing this book, and doing multiple reviews of evidence, there was one consistent fact over the decades. Senior DCMA management, at the Director's Level, is silent to complaints of fraud, hostile workplace, or anything that is non-productive at DCMA. Chapter 2 explains this fact. Local commanders share equal blame.

That explains my resume where I continually sought external resolution, with success, and why this book is literally an encyclopedia of weaponization, lawfare, and chaos. Because the weaponization, lawfare, and chaos is condoned and nurtured at the DCMA Headquarters (HQ) level and sent downward. The only thing that even remotely held back the weaponization, lawfare, and chaos is some remote fear of the consequences of violating law. That fear ended on February 12, 2009.

On February 12, 2009, a true watershed moment, DCMA HQ, Joe Tessier and Nanette Nelson (1st Level Supervisor) were greatly enabled to unleash total weaponization, lawfare, and chaos upon me with complete and unbridled impunity.

February 12, 2009 MSPB Vacates October 24, 2007 Decision

MSPB Judges Neil McPhee and Mary Rose vacated the October 24, 2007 MSPB decision that was in my favor on February 12, 2009 against MSPB's own findings. Judge Barbara Sapin had apparently left MSPB, so the MSPB decision was based on only 2 judges. The February 12, 2009 MSPB decision was objective evidence of U.S. Legal and Judicial System corruption as follows.

Disingenuous: MSPB used the word "*disingenuous*" as applied to Scantlebury and Plourde who did not inform me that the DoD IG had cleared questions. There were other officials who could have informed me of alleged cleared questions and did not. They include Dan Meyer, Bruce Krasker, Uldric Fiore and Leigh Owens. Because this was a textbook case of weaponized and tactical whistleblower retaliation and lawfare. This was a plan. It took about 6 months after the 30-Day Suspension notice of October 18, 2005 before I saw any evidence of coordination. Even then the evidence showed tactical planning against me.

Shifting Reasons: Colonel Plourde had "shifting reasons" for the weaponized investigation. Implying Colonel Plourde was lying about motives. Because the investigation itself was a weapon and insulation to maneuver me into disciplinary action.

Nineteen (19) Total Reasons: The October 24, 2007 MSPB decision had 19 reasons in my favor. Meaning, the case had irrefutable evidence in my favor.

Admissions to Retaliation: DCMA made admissions to retaliation and made no rebuttal to my allegations, affirmative defenses (Response to Charges), and my deposition. DCMA's documents proved there was a concerted retaliatory effort between DCMA and DoD IG.

February 12, 2009, was the date Kangaroo courts were confirmed as the "Federal Machinery" outlined in the Nixon administration. U.S. Government oversight was confirmed as a "garbage disposal" for anything ethical. Cover-ups were in the mix, meaning 18 U.S.C. 1505 and 5 USC 2302(b)(8) (whistleblower protection act). MSPB reversed the MSPB findings and vastly expanded the Government Swamp. The February 12, 2009, cover-up made me nauseous. I realized the system was totally corrupted.

DOJ and the Federal Court of Appeals for the Federal Circuit would follow suit and rubber-stamp MSPB's corrupted decision. I did make an effort to stop Judicial corruption.

DOJ & Federal Court of Appeals for the Federal Circuit

April 16, 2009 - Case 2009-3135: I submitted the exact same evidence in the case as existed since 2005, using facts and quotes. My case was linked to actual facts, behavior, etc. I repeated what MSPB accurately stated on October 24, 2007.

May 11, 2009 – DOJ Response to Case 2009-3135: DOJ provided an entry of appearance for Michael N. O'Connell on April 3, 2009. The case was submitted by Michael F. Hertz (Deputy Assistant Attorney General), Jeanne E. Davidson (Director), Todd M. Hughes (Deputy Director), and Michael N. O'Connell (Trial Attorney, Commercial Litigation Branch, Civil Division, DOJ).

DOJ Ran Me Down - Ignored 1st Hand Information: The DOJ informal brief ran me down and did nothing to address the facts of the case. DOJ failed to provide any weight to the fact that DCMA stipulated whistleblower retaliation on May 10, 2006. Meaning, DOJ disingenuously misrepresented 1st hand information stipulated by the DCMA.

May 4, 2009 - DOJ Ran Down Doug Kinan: Doug Kinan, a DCMA employee who had similar experiences as I with DCMA, was also run down by DOJ when Kinan supported my case with an Amicus Brief. Kinan was mentioned in Chapter 2 of this book. DOJ was so unprofessional that the signature block for Todd Hughes of the DOJ was the mark of Zorro, meaning a "Z" for a signature. Meaning, not even the professionalism for a coherent signature.

Federal Court Diverged from 1st Hand Information/Facts – "Garbage Disposal"

August 6, 2009 - Federal Court Ruling on Devoured Facts: As the case progressed through multiple cover-up layers (OPM, MSPB, DOJ), the truth and 1st hand information (stipulations) separated from case facts. OPM and MSPB devoured, twisted, and pulverized facts like a garbage disposal. The DOJ further devoured and pulverized facts. By the time the case got to the Federal Court of Appeals, the 1st hand stipulated facts had been pulverized. Hence, the "garbage disposal" label.

AFGE did not assist me since it was a foregone conclusion that the "Federal Machinery" was covering up. The system was rigged against anything ethical, and it seemed AFGE cut its losses.

October 6, 2009 - Judicial Misconduct: Based on the last names of the judges on the August 6, 2009, decision, the judges' complete names would be: Randall R. Rader, S. Jay Plager, and Alvan A. Schall. I filed judicial misconduct cases F-09-90008, F-09-90009, and F-09-90010 against three 3 Federal judges. With little surprise, Chief Judge Paul R. Michael cleared his judges.

Supreme Court Case 2009-780

The Federal Court decision was so biased that I was easily able to put out a Supreme Court Case. With little surprise, the case was turned down for review on February 22, 2010. The overall, predictable, letdowns formed a pattern with DCMA impunity.

DCMA Gestapo Tactics Disclosure to Congress, DOJ, & DoD

Counter Investigations & DCMA Impunity

September 8, 2005: As DCMA escalated their weaponized investigation for Falsified Trail 3, it raised serious concerns. The harassment was increasing, becoming more specific and targeted. DCMA was acting with impunity. In response, I made a disclosure to Senator Grassley via Charlie Murphy, Gentry Shellnut (DOJ), DoD IG hotline, and Dan Meyer. At the time I did not realize how deep the covert actions went. I stated in part.

"It seems that DCMA is trying to establish their own independent government where they hold themselves as investigator, jury, judge, etc. ...In a manner of speaking DCMA is establishing their own internal force of individuals similar to Germany's WWII Gestapo or SS squads. I do not make that statement lightly and the evidence points in that direction.

Due to the involvement of Mr. Keith Ernst and Ms. Sallie Flavin (see attached PDF file) this seems to be widespread and deeper than I originally thought."

December 13, 2005: I sent a similar email, this time addressed to Thomas Gimble, that also used the word *"Gestapo"* as related to DCMA weaponized investigations. I used the term *"counter investigative operation"* with the email titled *"DCMA Scandal."* Again, I still did not know the depth of the corruption. I had no real transparency at that point in time.

September 9, 2006: Henry Hagel and I sent a 35-page report to congress with the following quotes about DCMA weaponized investigations: "*…an administrative weapon against whistleblowers and to cover for government corruption.*" "*…the unedited story of how investigations are used as retaliatory weapons…*" "*The investigative process was an ideal retaliatory weapon for Colonel Plourde and Mr. Keith Ernst.*" "*…a covert administrative weapon to manipulate (game/con) the system,*" Meaning, as of 2006 weaponized government was discussed.

The point is, as transparency grew the understanding of weaponized government and lawfare came into focus. It's called Lawfare.

It's Called Lawfare

20 Attorneys & 7 Director/Command Level Officials

The number of attorneys and senior officials at Director and Command levels in Falsified Trail 3 is telling in and of itself as follows (titles are included on Index of names for Falsified Trail 3).

DCMA Attorneys (7 Known): Bruce Krasker, Leigh Owens, Stephanie Zimmit-Mack, Gill Bass, Nicholas Retson, Gary Jencson, Donald Srail.

DoD IG Attorneys (4 Known): Uldric Fiore, Ray O'Connor, Mark Boyll, Michael Child.

DOJ Attorneys (6 Known): Charysse Alexander, Jeanne Davidson, Todd Hughes, Michael O'Connel, Michael Hertz, Tony West. (Tony West opposed Kinan Amicus Brief.)

OPM Attorneys (3 Known): Kerry McTigue, Steven Abow, Becky Ronayne

Directors & Command Level (7 Known): Dan Meyer, Keith Ernst, Sallie Flavin, Steve Bogusz, Linda Springer, Leonard Trahan, Colonel Nicole Plourde.

That's why it's called Lawfare. The attorneys work for Director and Command level officials to weaponize legal skills against anyone who tries to expose corruption. It's that clear. The aforesaid group were involved against me for textbook weaponization, lawfare, retaliation, and coverup.

The Court of Appeals for the Federal Circuit was so predictably corrupted, that the DCMA was immediately enabled, with unbridled impunity, to begin retaliation (Volley 3) prior to me filing any Federal Court case as follows.

Meaning, green light to Government Swamp expansion, weaponization, and lawfare.

February 12, 2009 - Watershed Moment to Expand the Government Swamp

The February 12, 2009, MSPB decision proved institutional legal and judicial corruption could be factored into daily retaliatory operations. Meaning, the DCMA saw the "slippery slope" of February 12, 2009, and took full advantage of weaponization and lawfare with unbridled impunity. The DCMA needed far less resources than was used in Falsified Trail 3. The Volley 3 Index of Names is as follows.

Volley 3 - Falsified Trails 4, 5, 6, 7, 8, 9, and 10 Index of Names

(March 3, 2009 – February 16, 2010)

Cleo Anderson [FT(4,5,6,7,8,9,10)]	DCMA Attorney
Nanette Nelson [FT(4,5,6,7,8,9,10)]	DCMA First Level Supervisor C-5 Engineering Team
Joe Tessier [FT(6,7,8,9,10)]	DCMA Second Level Supervisor C-5 Team
Lou Gentile [FT(10)]	DCMA C-5 Quality Assurance Supervisor
Colonel Casey Blake [(4)]	DCMA, Commander
Henrietta Snow [FT(3,10)]	DCMA Deputy Commander, DCMA
Dorcas Smith [FT(10)]	DCMA Human Resources
Debra Mitchell [FT(10)]	DCMA Human Resources
Jeanne Davidson [FT(3,4,5,6)]	DOJ Director
Tony West [FT(3,4,5,6)]	DOJ Assistant Attorney General
Steven Gillingham [FT(4,5,6)]	DOJ Assistant Director
Christopher Bowen [FT(4,5,6)]	DOJ Trial Attorney
Benjamin Mizer [FT(7,8,9,10)]	DOJ Principal Deputy Assistant Attorney General
Robert Kirschman [FT(7,8,9,10)]	DOJ Director
Elizabeth Hosford [FT(7,8,9,10)]	DOJ Assistant Director
Joshua Kurland [FT(7,8,9,10)]	DOJ Trial Attorney

Weaponized Efficiency Guarantee – No Need for Covert Cover

Economy of Scale for the "Slippery Slope" - Expanding the Swamp

Tactical weaponized government and lawfare has an efficiency with a confirmed corrupt system. Meaning, Falsified Trail 3 (Volley 2) had an entourage of about 29 persons to achieve one retaliation (30-Day Suspension) that took the summer of 2005 (June 21, 2005–October 18, 2005) then to February 12, 2009. That is, a ratio of 29 persons to gain one suspension. However, there was collateral damage to other persons (fellow whistleblowers).

This is in contrast to Volley 3, which had an entourage of 16 persons (nearly half Falsified Trail 3) who achieved 7 Falsified Trails, including 2 suspensions, in a one-year span. This was a weaponized lawfare economy of scale.

The point being, a weaponized economy of scale from a "slippery slope" that factors in a corrupted system. Meaning, the weaponization and lawfare were fully enabled, with guaranteed cover-ups, in rapid fire succession. There were 7 Falsified Trails in one year (March 2009-February 2010) that started immediately after February 12, 2009. There was no more need for DCMA to be covert. Caution and covert cover were thrown to the wind.

Open Obstruction – Expanding the Swamp: The lack of covert action and caution by DCMA provided an excellent opportunity to show how the Government Swamp was expanded and enabled by the U.S. Judicial System corruption on February 12, 2009.

DCMA immediately started to openly rewrite my reports, stop me from attending meetings, obstructed my work, and eliminate any settlement of issues, or even the discussion of settling issues. Avenues of potential resolution were closed at all levels. I was a human "punching bag" where the Government Swamp had the upper hand.

The new job was documenting corruption as it unfolded. Basically, all the Falsified Trails meant to me were more data points to show the Government Swamp in action.

Falsified Trail 4 follows and shows how the Government Swamp expanding immediately after February 12, 2009.

Falsified Trail 4: March 3, 2009 Memorandum - Rewrite Reports

Aggressive retaliation and cover-ups of problems began shortly after February 12, 2009. Meaning, I started at the DCMA on/about March 1994 and issued my reports directly to the requester because the DCMA did not want the appearance that I was pressured to favor Lockheed Martin. After February 12, 2009, DCMA had no concerns for the appearance of wrongdoing or open cover-ups. DCMA openly engaged in rewriting my reports as follows.

Lockheed Martin Problems: Chapter 4 of this book will show that Lockheed Martin has had serious problems since 1998. Problems with EVMS (Earned Value Management System, (financial Tracking)) surfaced in 2002 and existed possibly sooner. Beginning in 2006, I served as the EVMS monitor for the C-5 Reliability Enhancement & Re-engining Program (RERP). Joe Tessier entered my chain of command in 2008 and became an instant problem.

Lockheed Martin Withholding Data: In early 2009, and sometime prior, the DCMA employees were suddenly denied access to Lockheed Martin databases to determine the health of software development on the C-5 RERP program. The database was called Product Version Control System (PVCS). Denial of the PVCS data coincided with the negative trend reported in Lockheed Martin's financial records, indicating a lack of control over cost and schedule. On March 3, 2009, I was ordered to remove negative data about Lockheed Martin. Meaning, Falsified Trail 4 had started and the Government Swamp of corruption was expanding.

Direct Order to Remove Negative Data About Lockheed Martin

March 3, 2009: My then first-level supervisor, Nanette Nelson, directed me in writing, via a written Memorandum, to omit negative data from my reports on Lockheed Martin. Nelson stated in part.

"You are reminded that your input is incorporated into the PSR (Program Status Report) *provided to, and relied upon, by our customers. Any data or conclusions included in the PSR thereafter represent the agency's opinion or position, not that of any individual contributor. As the agency is accountable for the accuracy and supportability of the report's content, it has a responsibility to assure that the report's conclusions are derived from verifiable facts and sound analysis. My review of your input was conducted in furtherance of that responsibility.*

I am disappointed that you elected to forward copies of your report to the customer without complying with my request to amend it to include additional data and analysis in support of your conclusions. Therefore, you are directed to provide your EVMS reports to me for review prior to inclusion in the final product to the customer. You are not to provide your EVMS reports directly to the customer without prior approval from me."

I complied with Nelson's direction under the weaponized "Obey First, Grieve Later" doctrine. There was no viable avenue for grievance, meaning the grievance avenue was a "Paper Tiger."

The most noticeable part of Nanette Nelson's memorandum was the writing style and aggressive tone that were not characteristic of Nelson. After some questioning, I traced the letters to a DCMA attorney, Cleo Anderson.

"Cleo Anderson Letters" ("Ghostwriting") For Falsified Trails

The March 3, 2009, letter from Nelson was traced to the DCMA HQ attorney Cleo Anderson. The first clue was Nelson's writing style, which was the opposite of that in the "Cleo Anderson Letter". Meaning, Nelson never wrote a letter like Anderson, further meaning Nelson was a surrogate.

I coined the term "*Cleo Anderson Letters*" in early 2009 and follow-on information would confirm letters were *"composed and reviewed by DCMA HR legal counsel at the headquarters level"*. When Nelson would call me into her office I would jokingly say, "*is this another Cleo Anderson letter*." The writing styles were specific and had a legal overtone.

Nelson and Joe Tessier never admitted that Cleo Anderson wrote the threatening and retaliatory letters signed and issued to me; however, Nelson and Tessier never denied it either. Nelson and Tessier would sign the letters in my presence, either by printing the letters or using the ritualistic Manila folder.

Manila Folder Ritual: The Manila folder ritual was a ceremonial display where the Manila folder was slowly opened in my presence, revealing the weaponized document of my destruction (Falsified Trails). Managers would maintain blank expressions and then sign the documents, completing the execution step in my reputation. Following the Manila folder ritual, I would make several copies of the retaliatory letters to document the DCMA corruption that now forms the foundation of this book.

Cleo Anderson Entangled in the Facts of Cases - Lawfare

Cleo Anderson was the replacement for Bruce Krasker and Leigh Owens of Falsified Trail 3. Cleo Anderson's name surfaced continuously up to 2015, meaning Cleo Anderson was entangled in the facts of tactical weaponized government and lawfare. The rapid-fire Falsified Trails wreaked of law-fare and were bizarre to a large extent. Meaning, DCMA had no shame for cover-ups as Falsified Trail 5 shows.

Falsified Trail 5: March 20, 2009 – Mentally Unstable & Stop Attending Meetings

March 4, 2009, 9:34 PM: Following Nanette Nelson's direction to protect Lockheed Martin, I received similar, but more pointed, direction from the Lead Engineer, Gerard Woodlief, on my team, who also worked for Nelson. The issue started with Lockheed Martin denying DCMA data to support audits. I noted this fact in my reports. Woodlief responded in part as follows.

"*...from here on out, I do not want any EVM Reports submitted forward to the PI* (Program Integrator) *that contain controversial statements about the Contractor, or comments that are not specifically related to a direct assessment of the data, as it relates to Cost, Schedule and/or Performance.*

Your latest EVM Report contains negative comments about access to data and meetings that are issues that we need to work outside of the EVM Report, since they do not provide Cost, Schedule and/or Performance Conclusions and/or 'actionable' Recommendations to the Customer."

The point is, it is difficult to assess cost, schedule, or contract performance and make 'actionable' recommendations without objective support data from Lockheed Martin. That is why I mentioned the denial of supporting data by Lockheed Martin.

Woodlief also stopped me from attending meetings and questioned my mental stability.

Stop Attending Meetings – Mentality Stability & Office Safety Questioned

March 16, 2009: In a verbal conversation, Gerard Woodlief stopped me from attending Lockheed Martin status meetings even though I was responsible for issuing reports on Lockheed Martin status as related to the C-5 RERP project. The specific meeting involved Configuration Management (CM), where changes and updates to the C-5 program are discussed.

My need to attend the meeting stems from program changes that would translate to cost and/or schedule. Since I reported on cost and schedule, it is logical that I attend to compare what Lockheed Martin was saying on cost and schedule oversight with planned program changes. Woodlief disagreed and, on March 16, 2009, essentially stopped me from going to CM meetings, which were only about an hour a week.

Following that verbal exchange, Woodlief allegedly placed a bizarre written complaint to Joe Tessier with a copy to Nanette Nelson, Henrietta Snow, and the new commander, Colonel Casey Blake (who replaced Colonel Plourde).

March 20, 2009 - Typed on a Word Processor – Internet Explorer File: The complaint was apparently an e-mail that appeared typed on a word processor. Nelson once stated it was saved as an Internet Explorer File. Unknown why it was not provided as an email other than the fact that it was retaliatory, as were other letters. I had to force Nelson to provide me with a copy.

Nothing Would Come of This: Before I received the alleged complaint, I asked Nelson what was going to happen. Nelson explicitly stated "*nothing*" would become of the complaint.

Fiction Story - Scripted: The wording of the alleged complaint from Woodlief was like a fiction novel of me speaking in a "*loud voice*" and how I was "*yelling*" while Woodlief described himself as '*quietly*' communicating with me, with the word '*quietly*' in single quotes. Meaning, the letter was scripted to portray Woodlief as calm and me as a yelling maniac. I denied all allegations.

Alleged/Presumed Violence: Woodlief depicted me as a crazy person who makes "*loud comments*" in the office and how I was "*adversely affecting the office environment.*" Woodlief concluded the bizarre document by stating about me.

"*Although I am not a Mental Health expert, he seems to be mentally unstable, frustrated and extremely angry with management here, and he now includes me in this group (which is evident from his comments in e-mails that he has sent me).*

Although I have verbally stated this to you and Nanette previously, I would like to formally state that there are times I clearly fear for my safety, as well as the safety of my fellow team members, and that I believe Ken is capable of performing an act of violence at our office (given the right condition, such as a Written Reprimand, Suspension, or Termination)."

Nelson stated "*nothing*" would become of Woodlief's complaint even though Woodlief allegedly feared for his (Woodlief's) safety and the safety of fellow team members. It is also notable that I was given a 30-Day Suspension in 2005 and there was no violent outburst. Only me documenting how corrupted and retaliatory DCMA was.

Passed Around for Laughs: I actually passed around Woodlief's complaint for laughs. Meaning, Woodlief allegedly feared for his safety, with Nelson indicating nothing would come of this. Woodlief's complaint served no other purpose than proving how bizarre the DCMA was.

Research Alleged Complaint: On about August 4, 2010, I went to Nelson and verbally asked if I could talk to Woodlief about the alleged complaint. Nelson indicated she would look into it. Since I was aware that Cleo Anderson was the instigator for retaliatory acts, I sent an e-mail on August 5, 2010, to Anderson to get a straight answer to my question. I wanted Cleo Anderson out front.

On August 16, 2010, Nelson responded with a scathing e-mail (which appeared to be written by Cleo Anderson) denying me the opportunity to talk to Woodlief about the alleged complaint. This confirmed my suspicions that the alleged complaint was falsified and nothing more than fodder for the "Federal Machinery" or nothing more than a falsified building block in a retaliation scheme. I concluded Woodlief wrote the bizarre, alleged complaint only because Nelson said he did, and Woodlief and I had a conversation about stopping my attendance at meetings.

Altered Working Conditions: Tessier, Nelson, and Woodlief altered working conditions to where I was not able to do my job. Meaning, soon after February 12, 2009; I was threatened to alter my reports to remove negative information about Lockheed Martin; I was denied access to meetings; And, I had my mental stability questioned. The result was an expansion of the Government Swamp enabled by the February 12, 2009 MSPB decision. DCMA had lost all self-respect. I scheduled a meeting with Colonel Casey Blake to address the issue. Colonel Blake was less than receptive as the following shows.

Falsified Trail 6: April 2, 2009 - One Day Suspension – Commander's Lawfare

Colonel Blake was a rising Pentagon star with a pending promotion to Brigadier General. Meaning, Blake's promotion seemed foremost in Blake's mind, which would explain Blake's future actions.

Colonel Blake was the last commander I planned on talking to about problems. Since 1994, DCMA commanders exhibited growing disregard for law and ethics, which is why my resume is bolstered with whistleblowing events. Commanders either stayed the same or grew worse since 1994. Blake was the last chance for hope. A brief timeline is as follows.

March 9, 2009 – Contact Colonel Blake: I had already been extensively dealing with Nelson and Tessier on issues with no results. I contacted Colonel Blake for help.

March 11, 2009 – Blake Invokes Owens & Anderson: Colonel Blake's response to me copied in the DCMA attorneys Leigh Owens and Cleo Anderson. This meant Blake was resorting to lawfare. Meaning, Colonel Blake openly brought in Cleo Anderson for protection.

March 12, 2009 – Blake Changes Subject: Blake changed the subject and sent an e-mail stating:

"Nanette/Joe, please meet with Mr. Pendeleose next week wrt his work-related issues."

March 16, 2009 – Direct Order: I made it clear these were not work-related issues. Colonel Blake responded more forcefully with a "direct order" stating:

"Mr. Pedeleose, I undertand your desire to meet with me but I am giving you a direct order to try and resolve your issues with Ms. Nelson and Mr. Tessier. I will not be meeting with you on the 18th."

Colonel Blake cancelled the March 18, 2009, meeting with me.

Colonel Blake exceeded shunning me. Colonel Blake was avoiding me to any extent possible. The inclusion of Cleo Anderson and Leigh Owens seemed a cry for help from Blake to the point where Cleo Anderson had to redact Colonel Blake's words in Falsified Trail 6.

March 16, 2009 - Redact Blake's Words: Cleo Anderson printed a March 16, 2009, email, apparently from Blake, that was used in a retaliation package of Falsified Trail 6. The email printed by Cleo Anderson was stamped as follows.

" (REDACTED -ATTY/CLIENT PRIVILEGE)"

At this point it was obvious Cleo Anderson was the new Leigh Owens. Cleo Anderson would eventually use Attorney Client Privilege 13 times to protect Colonel Blake who was shortly thereafter promoted to Brigadier General. My new opponent would be Nanette Nelson who was the retaliation surrogate as follows.

Proposed One-Day Suspension – Alleged Rude Behavior

April 2, 2009: I received an undated Proposed One-Day Suspension from Nanette Nelson. The retaliatory charge stated in part.

"Since January 2009, you have directed a tirade of offensive electronic correspondence to your chain of command at DCMA (Lockheed Martin Marietta) as well as senior executive officials both inside and outside of DCMA. The statements in your e-mails were unsubstantiated, inflammatory, and undermined your chain of command's authority."

Common Office Practice: Nelson's charges were false. Meaning, what I stated to management officials was a common office practice to reduce office litigation. An MSPB Judge (Richard Vitaris) would actually agree in a follow-on decision. To prove this point I was given a $1,500 cash award (December 31, 2008) for even more pointed comments to management. The 2009 comments in the Proposed Suspension were mild as follows.

Nothing I can Trust: I had stated that Colonel Blake has "*shown me nothing in a commander I can trust. I do not trust you* (Colonel Blake)." This statement was true. Colonel Blake demonstrated no qualities of commander I can trust.

Dirty Retaliatory Work: I stated that Nanette Nelson has done "*dirty (retaliatory) work for*" Joe Tessier. This was true and confirmed by the "Cleo Anderson Letters" Nelson was handing out. The "Cleo Anderson Letters" were not in Nelson's writing style and not within Nelson's demeanor. I also stated Nanette Nelson was "*lying about*" her (Nelson) motives, which I believe to be true.

The aforesaid comments and those in the suspension notice were toned down common office practice allowed by the DCMA to avoid litigation. However, Tessier approved the suspension.

Joe Tessier Approves One-Day Suspension

June 17, 2009: Tessier worked in concert with Nelson to approve the one-day suspension. Tessier's Memorandum titled Notice of Decision to Suspend was 2 pages and represented the "Cleo Anderson Letter" style. Meaning, running me down and building management up. It was textbook whistleblower retaliation since I was forced to make disclosures against Nelson. Litigation would start later in 2009 because I was still confronting the 30-day suspension (Falsified Trail 3) at the Federal Court and Supreme Court levels.

Part of my affirmative defense in litigating the One-Day Suspension was to show that the alleged rude behavior was a common office practice to help avoid litigation in my office. Examples are as follows.

Common Office Practice by the DCMA to Avoid Litigation

The following are examples of permitted behavior and comments to the DCMA management prior to MSPB reinstating my 30-day suspension (February 12, 2009). Meaning, there was no longer a need to avoid litigation because the DCMA would win at any litigation due to predictable Cerberus style cover-ups and judicial corruption. Prior acceptable comments are as follows.

January 28, 2008: E-mail to Marie Greening (then the DCMA Aeronautical Systems Director) and my senior chain of command stating:

"Based on the conduct by Colonel Plourde thus far, I am forced to draw the conclusion that Colonel Plourde was "enlisted" (hired by reputation) to terminate me from employment, and to cover up problems at this facility."

"Based on the events of 2005, Colonel Plourde has already attained a reputation for retaliation. I was the recipient of Colonel Plourde's headstrong and persistent torment and psychological abuse towards me. I have witnessed Colonel Plourde's tormenting demeanor, and antics, in action, and draw the conclusion that Colonel Plourde was sent here on a mission."

Marie Greening thanked me for the alleged rude and disrespectful comments, stating in part.

"Thank you for your written clarification of the comments you made at the all hands meeting at DCMA LMM."

April 28, 2008: E-mail to Joe Tessier and senior management:

"Colonel Plourde personally and blatantly violated the chain of command in 2005 when she jumped over three layers of command to retaliate against me. Thus, the chain of command use is in question from multiple aspects. I see a similarity in aggressive and inappropriate management style in your actions."

"I have seen similar beginnings as yours from prior management staff and sincerely hope that you will abandon that non productive path. I will hold those above you accountable for your actions against me. I am tired of senior management sitting by with supposedly clean hands while lower level management staff create torment for me and set me up for failure."

May 5, 2008: E-mail to Tessier, copy to Marie Greening, Nelson, then DCMA Director Keith Ernst, Henrietta Snow, and other DCMA senior management:

"My interpretation of your comments and demeanor on May 1, 2008 are that you remain intransigent and unyielding in your retaliatory position against me. This is typical retaliatory behavior that I hoped DCMA management would abandon. Obviously you wish to continue your harassment against me and attempts to drive me to failure."

"I guess that you want me to go to these meetings and cower before the LM Aero management staff as if they were some sort of omnipotent beings or gods. However since your motives are retaliatory I will figure that you will try and frame me if I speak to one of those executives."

"My demise from management will be channeled through you while those above you remain with allegedly "clean hands". For the record anything you do will be directly attributed to those above you. The fact that you were promoted so high with a "personal" problem in your past indicates that you have been chosen for other tasks."

June 24, 2008: E-mail to Charlie Williams (then Agency Director) and Colonel Blake:

"As a result of Mr. Tessier's ongoing retaliatory and fraudulent conduct against me and Ms. Greening's disingenuous attitude in resolving issues, I am forced to forward for your attention and action."

"This situation can be resolved in under five minutes. Ms. Greening has proved that Mr. Tessier is the instrument of fraud that she will use to destroy me as a whistleblower."

June 25, 2008 – "Cult Like Mentality": E-mail to Colonel Blake and DCMA Director Williams:

"*To make the issue short, DoD has a cult like mentality when it comes to supporting corruption and retaliation.*"…"*I have seen and experienced the practice of placing hostile managers in my chain of command and then senior managers allowing and/or assisting the hostile manager to administratively tear the organization and whistleblower apart. Allowing Mr. Tessier to go on the attack while his superiors sit back and do nothing is a practice that I will object to.*"

December 13, 2007 "Backstabbers": After hearing Joe Tessier would be C-5 Team Group Chief, one employee openly stated with Henrietta Snow and others present: *"I informed Ms. Snow that the C5 team will not tolerate "backstabbers".*

Employee "Venting" Was Allowed: The point is, alleged rude conduct was employee venting to avoid and slow litigation. This was done under a hostile workplace and altered working conditions. As Chapter 1 and Chapter 2 shows, DCMA has no concern for efficiency of the Federal Service.

December 31, 2008 - Cash Award $1,500: I received a $1,500 cash award after making the aforementioned comments. Hence, prior to February 12, 2009, MSPB ruling, the DCMA management up to the DCMA Directors level allowed alleged rude and disrespectful comments to avoid litigation.

$10,000 Per Manager/Supervisor: To my understanding, in/around 2004, DCMA was spending $10,000 per manager/supervisor to try to install professionalism to any degree and stem litigation and complaints by employees against DCMA. No improvement was noted.

Falsified Trail 7, Letter of Warning and Instruction (LOWI), that follows, was where Nanette Nelson helped alter Lockheed Martin statements. Meaning, this was a further expansion of the Government Swamp from just rewriting my reports and stopping me from attending meetings.

Falsified Trail 7: September 29, 2009 - LOWI – Rewrites with Lockheed Martin

After April 2009, it was fruitless to resist Blake, Tessier, Nelson, and Woodlief. I acquiesced by letting Lockheed Martin write my reports. Meaning, whatever Lockheed Martin said was included verbatim in my report without challenge. Behind the scenes, I communicated with criminal investigators to try and keep some honesty in the process since the DCMA was institutionally corrupted. Most disclosures were by email, and in one instance, I presented an inventory list of potential subjects for criminal investigation. This process continued up to my retirement in December 2020. Allowing Lockheed Martin to write government reports worked well until August 2009.

Lockheed Martin Potential Cost Mischarging of Contracts

August 31, 2009: I interviewed a Lockheed Martin manager for a monthly cost and schedule review (EVMS) of the C5 RERP Program focusing on R&M (Reliability & Maintainability). I typed out my notes in electronic form and forwarded them back to Lockheed Martin for review and any corrections. Lockheed Martin would alter as Lockheed Martin saw fit, and I would not challenge, regardless of what Lockheed Martin stated. The following are rough notes I sent to Lockheed Martin.

"Cost Control Measures: LM Aero is minimizing cost by not charging to the contract at this time. In the beginning of the contract DT&E (Developmental Test & Evaluation) was scheduled to go directly into OT&E (Operational Test & Evaluation). However with the new schedule there will be a familiarization period (Fam Demo) thus R&M is covered under the ICS (Interim Contractor Support) *contract for this period. That is, the ICS contract bridges R&M from DT&E to OT&E. Once Fam Demo is complete R&M will begin charging to OT&E."*

September 1, 2009 – Lockheed Martin Responds: Lockheed Martin responded with the following wording to my rough notes.

"*Cost Control Measures: LM Aero is minimizing cost by not charging to the SDD* (System Design & Development) *contract at this time. In the beginning of the contract, the program was to transition directly from DT&E (Developmental Test & Evaluation) into QOT&E (Qualification Operational Test & Evaluation). However, the current plan and schedule includes a 9-month Familiarization/Demonstration (Fam/Demo) period at Dover AFB prior to the start of QOT&E. The Fam/Demo efforts are covered under a separate Interim Contractor Support (ICS) contract, and C-5M R&M efforts are covered under the ICS contract for this period. That is, the ICS contract bridges R&M and other LM IPTs* (Integrated Product Teams) *from DT&E to QOT&E. R&M will resume charging against SDD as soon as QOT&E begins for the tasking previously described.*"

The Lockheed Martin write-up had the appearance of cost mischarging. Meaning, the development contract was out of money (overrunning), while the ICS contract (logistical support) had plenty of money, so Lockheed Martin switched development costs to the ICS (logistics) contract. There was possible legitimacy to the Lockheed Martin statement in the transition out of the development phase of the contract to the logistics contract, so it wasn't too alarming.

I figured Lockheed Martin's statement would pass Nelson's review since Lockheed Martin wrote the statement. I was wrong. Nelson called me into her office and said we need to be sure which contract Lockheed Martin is charging and why. I was perplexed by the remark because Lockheed Martin was clear that there were two contracts and how they planned to charge the contracts.

My confusion annoyed Nelson to the point where Nelson went to talk to Lockheed Martin.

September 8, 2009: Lockheed Martin emailed Nelson and copied me, stating:

"Ms. Nelson,

As we discussed by phone, please see the recommended redlined wording for "Cost Control Measures" in the attached document.

Please let me know if you have any additional questions."

The attached document red lined (altered) Lockheed Martin's original statement to the following"

"Cost Control Measures: LM Aero R&M is not charging to the SDD contract at this time since there are no further R&M related contractual SDD tasks to be performed until QOT&E begins. R&M will resume charging against SDD as soon as QOT&E begins for the tasking previously described. QOT&E is scheduled to begin on October 1, 2009."

Nelson's actions caused Lockheed Martin to remove mention of the second contract.

September 9, 2009: I was perplexed by Lockheed Martin's write-up and emailed Nelson. stating.

"Nanette,

Please let me know what you want me to change, or leave as is.

Personally, I liked the previous wording since it was more direct and gave insight into LM Aero charging patterns.

For the record I do take exception to any changes in the report however this is a team effort.

If you are going to direct changes to the report please be specific.

September 9, 2009: Nelson responded back the same day to me, stating:

"Please see Ricks revision and revise your report accordingly."

Disclosure Against Nanette Nelson

September 9, 2009: I made a detailed disclosure against Nelson with the same aforesaid information trail. The allegation stated in part.

"Allegation: With the vehement nature in which Nanette Nelson wanted the report watered down I would suspect that LM Aero in the future, if not now, is mischarging development cost into sustainment contract. That is cost that could be attributed to the development contract (that is out of money) will be charged to sustainment contract (which has money)."

Shortly after the disclosure I received Falsified Trail 7 as follows.

Falsified Trail 7 – Letter of Warning and Instruction (LOWI)

September 29, 2009: Nelson's actions to me were another "Cleo Anderson Letter" stating in part.

This letter serves as a warning and instruction concerning your performance and conduct as an employee of the Federal service. This letter is being issued in accordance with Article 26 of the Collective Bargaining Agreement dated April 2006.

On September 8, 2009, I directed you to provide clarification on information contained in your monthly EVMS report. Specifically, I asked you to clarify whether Lockheed Martin is charging to SDD for some areas that are not covered by the ICS contract. I explained to you that your report must clearly reflect what is being charged to which particular contract and why. We discussed your response, and I explained that additional information was still needed to clarify a statement contained in your report. You told me that you would not seek clarification, and therefore I had to follow-up with the contractor and obtain the necessary clarification. Based on the contractor's revised comments, on September 9, 2009, I again asked you to revise your report accordingly. In response, you demanded that I send you an email explicitly directing you to revise your report.

False Statements: I did not say I would not contact Lockheed Martin; I stated I was confused because what Lockheed Martin had originally written on September 1, 2009, explained how the contracts were being charged to. Meaning, Nelson made a false statement because when Nelson finished talking to Lockheed Martin, there was only one contract mentioned. Nelson's actions confused the issue. I made a memo for the record on November 8, 2009, to detail these facts.

Falsified Trail 7 was a tipping point because Nelson went overboard with the false statement, since it was Nelson who actually caused the report to be watered down. The other issue was the obvious "Cleo Anderson Letters." This forced Colonel Blake back into the fray via the union.

Composed & Reviewed Lawfare at Headquarters (HQ) Level

The September 29, 2009, LOWI was so intricately written that it was obvious Nelson was not the author. The LOWI clearly went against facts because Nelson's actions watered down the Lockheed Martin statement.

I contacted the union (AFGE) for assistance. The union official noticed that the LOWI had a legal "flavor" to it and took the suspicions to Colonel Blake.

October 15, 2009: AFGE confronted Colonel Blake with the September 29, 2009, LOWI from Nelson. AFGE representative documented the following:

"On 9 Oct 2009, I met with Col Blake to confirm he was scheduling a meeting with Ken Pedeleose to discuss the letter of warning and instruction given to Mr. Pedeleose on 29 Sep 2009. During our conversation I brought it to his attention the letter appeared to have been composed by someone having a legal background. Col Blake concurred with my question by informing me the letter was composed and reviewed by DCMA HR (Human Resources) *legal counsel at the headquarters level."*

The point is, Nanette Nelson was a surrogate, and letters were "Ghostwritten" by legal counsel. AFGE continued inquiries and documented the following.

October 16, 2009: AFGE further documented the involvement of Cleo Anderson as follows.

"On 16 Oct 2009, Col Blake and I met to discuss what action he was going to take regarding the Letter of Warning and Instruction given to you on 23 Sep 2009. Col Blake informed me at the beginning of the meeting with some compromise he would recommend the letter be kept in the supervisor's file for a period of six months. During this meeting he also stated that people (unidentified by name) were afraid of Mr. Pedeleose. It seemed for a minute I had succeed in reducing the time for the letter to remain in the file to six months. Col Blake then called the supervisor Ms Nelson to confirm this agreed time frame with her in a conference call. Ms Nelson confirmed she had been in contact with a Cleo Anderson, Legal who advised the letter should remain in the supervisor's file for one year. At this point my meeting with Col Blake ended. Some fifteen to thirty minutes later Col Blake showed me a draft of his proposed memorandum to Mr. Pedeleose regarding the withdrawal of the letter in this memorandum Col Blake had inserted the time frame of one year for retention in the supervisor's file. I questioned this point of time and he informed me he would take the advice of legal for one year."

This further confirms the involvement of Cleo Anderson and shows that the Deep State events, similar to Falsified Trail 3, were continuing. This was transparency to the "Cleo Anderson Letters" that were the new, weaponized lawfare against me.

Colonel Blake was also aware of my whistleblowing as follows…

Colonel Blake was Aware of My Whistleblowing & Court Cases

& Well Aware of "Cerberus" Effect

November 13, 2009: AFGE further confirmed Colonel Blake was well aware of my whistleblowing and court issues as follows. The November 10, 2009, meeting notes below were documented on November 13, 2009, as follows.

"Prior to the scheduled meeting with Mr. Pedeleose and Col Blake to discuss Mr. Pedeleose request in resolving future personnel issues with his supervisor Nanette Nelson and his Group Chief Joe Tessier, Col Blake informed me he was quite aware of Mr. Pedeleose and his appeal with the courts over his whistle blowing efforts several years ago and that the outcome will probably not result in his favor. During this conversation Col Blake continued to address personnel issues that were in the past and in my opinion had no purpose in discussions regarding the present personnel issues being discussed. After several discussions with Management I have come to the conclusion there is a form of retaliation against Mr. Pedeleose in this CMO (Contract Management Office), *if there isn't why is management constantly seeking legal and HR advise to answer the most simple personnel issues a supervisor would have and should have learned in a basic supervisor's course. In closing I want to state, "attendance at COHORT* (Group) *training is not the avenue to take to learn basic management skills" courses such as the Army and the Air Force's supervisor's training are courses where supervisor's should be establishing their skills and not COHORT training."*

Colonel Blake was well aware of my whistleblowing and well aware of the "Cerberus" effect. Meaning, cover-up with the result not in my favor. Blake was documented as stating that the "*appeal with the courts over his* (Pedeleose) *whistle blowing efforts several years ago and that the outcome will probably not result in his* (Pedeleose) *favor"*. This is more than likely why Colonel Blake enlisted Leigh Owens and Cleo Anderson on March 11, 2009. Meaning, Blake wanted insulation. With the end result being more weaponization and lawfare.

Regardless, it is confirmed by conversation, "Cleo Anderson Letters", email and Memorandums of Record, that Cleo Anderson is involved. Same playbook as Falsified Trail 3 but with new participants. This raises the issue to the institutional weaponization and lawfare level.

However, the November 13, 2009 Memorandum for Record made a statement that is the lead-in for Falsified Trail 8. The statement is as follows and traces to a plan to rattle management.

"Prior to the scheduled meeting with Mr. Pedeleose and Col Blake to discuss Mr. Pedeleose request in resolving future personnel issues with his supervisor Nanette Nelson and his Group Chief Joe Tessier".

Rattle Management: After Falsified Trail 3, I rattled DoD IG and Dan Meyer by relentless emails to find the origins of the March 18, 2005 date. It worked because Dan Meyer issued the aforesaid regret email on July 27, 2007, and Tom Gimble issued a retraction letter. Knowing the DCMA management was falsifying against me, I chose to rattle management by wanting to settle the issue. It worked. Tessier was rattled, and Nelson issued another "Cleo Anderson Letter".

Falsified Trail 8: November 18, 2009 – Memorandum - Shun Resolution

October 22, 2009 – Limit Time to Falsify Cases: I sent an e-mail to Nelson and Tessier titled "*Resolving Future Issues*". The requests were designed to limit management's shunning of me and to limit management's tactical time in retaliation. Meaning, management shunning and delays are efforts to buy time to falsify cases and present surprise evidence against me. Falsified Trails 1 & 3 are prime examples thus far. Excerpts from my October 22, 2009, e-mail are as follows.

"*In accordance with Colonel Blake's leadership philosophy, I respectfully submit the following. In my meeting with Colonel Blake on October 20, 2009 I informed him that I would be writing my concerns and requests and would be using his leadership philosophy. I also informed Colonel Blake that even if we do resolve the issues below at our level, I requested that he be informed of my concerns and any potential resolution.*

I propose the following:

A: At any time that management believes that I am not performing my duties adequately, I request to be notified immediately at that time not to exceed a 24 hour period after the incident in question. Written notification in e-mail is preferred.

B: At anytime management or any employee believes that I am allegedly out of line including raising my voice, or any other action deemed to be inappropriate, I request to be notified immediately. Upon such notification I will cease communications with individuals in question and we can seek external resolution (notifying union officials, etc.) and document all concerns.

C: At any time management has questions regarding my reports, I request that the questions and/or comments please be made in writing (e-mail) so that adequate attention can be given along with a documentation trail. I will make attempts to resolve by either answering myself or securing answers from the contractor, LM Aero.

D: Any issue of interest or concern to management regarding me, my performance, my demeanor, etc., needs to be raised with me immediately not to exceed 24 hours after incident."

"*The reason I make these requests is to hopefully resolve issues at a low level to avoid formal complaints such as whistleblower retaliation, etc.*"

As expected, Tessier and Nelson did not respond to good management practices that invoked Colonel Blake's management philosophy. There was no counteroffer or acknowledgement to resolve issues. I was shunned by Tessier and Nelson because my requests would stop Falsified Trails (weaponization and lawfare) and stop surprise evidence manufactured behind-the-scenes. I knew it was management pattern and practice to take time and covertly falsify against me. By immediately notifying me, the time for behind-the-scenes falsification was eliminated.

When I had had enough of the shunning, I approached the union for assistance.

October 29, 2009 – Force Response from Management: AFGE contacted Colonel Blake, stating.

"The following email was submitted by Ken to Nanette and Joe as of today's date there has been no response to his written request. On 26 Oct while Joe was in B95 I inquired of him had he read Ken's request, his immediate response to me "he (Ken) will not make demands of management" immediately I detected with this response he (Joe) seems to have an attitude problem. Therefore I request a meeting with you again along with Ken when you have the available time. However before we meet Ken does deserve the respect of an answer."

The union effort forced a response indicative of what DCMA would write to falsify a case.

November 18, 2009 – No Communication – No Resolution: I was summoned to Nanette Nelson's office and issued another retaliatory "Cleo Anderson Letter" which stated the following.

"Ken

This serves as a response to your email of October 22, 2009, in which you appear to request that your chain of command follow a particular protocol-conceived by you--when there is disagreement with your performance or conduct.

I am obligated to follow the April 2006 Collective Bargaining Agreement in dealings with bargaining unit employees. As you well know, if you are dissatisfied with a management action, I encourage you to take the recourse available to you under the CBA and DCMA policy, and applicable federal laws and regulations.

Your "demands" for special treatment and constant communication outlined in your email October 22, 2009 are not conducive to a productive working environment.

As you are aware, federal employees are expected to comply with the directives of their supervisors. As I have clearly explained to you in several communications within the last year (the most recent being the September 29, 2009 Letter of Warning and Instruction), 1 expect you to carry out your job duties effectively and in a more cooperative manner.

As a reminder, failure to comply with supervisory direction may lead to a formal performance-based and/or disciplinary action."

NANNETE R. NELSON

C-5 Engineering Team Supervisor"

The DCMA proved consistent retaliatory actions. There was no meeting or discussion other than to issue the retaliatory letter, which, in the minds of DCMA, represented disciplinary action. Meaning, I was disciplined for merely asking to resolve issues. This was Falsified Trail 8.

What happened during Falsified Trail 8 was that DCMA had already started Falsified Trail 9, and Falsified Trail 10 started on November 18, 2009. Meaning, DCMA already had retaliations in the "pipeline" (already being falsified). Falsified Trail 9 starts the proof of continued weaponization, lawfare, and falsification. Meaning, I was likened to the Fort Hood shooter.

Falsified Trail 9: January 20, 2010 – LOWI - The Fort Hood Shooter

January 20, 2010 – Falsified Employee Complaint: The following are parts of my Memo for Record regarding my year end performance appraisal for 2009 performance year.

"During my performance appraisal on January 20, 2010 which began at 1:00 Nanette Nelson made comments about my cooperation and team work. The comments I wrote down as Nanette Nelson spoke were as follows: "Cooperation &Teamwork Improve tact and diplomacy among team members - However gave no negative examples.""

"Nanette Nelson did admit that the lowering of my performance rating from Outstanding to Fully Successful was related to the comments employees were making about me. When I tried to get Nanette Nelson to be specific about the comments made about me or who made the comments Nanette Nelson refused."

"When I began inferring that it is unfair for me not to know what it was I did wrong then Nanette Nelson said that she was going to save this for after the performance appraisal however now is the time to show it. Nanette Nelson went to her computer and printed a letter with the date January 20, 2009 [sic] (I suspect she meant to print 2010), got the letter off of the computer, sat down across the table and issued me the attached letter. I did ask Nanette nelson of Cleo Anderson (DCMA Attorney) wrote the letter and Nanette Nelson would not confirm."

The LOWI (Received January 20, 2010), printed then signed by Nanette Nelson, stated in part.

"An employee at our facility has complained of communications that you made recently. The employee informed me that during work hours (not at lunch or on a break) you showed this employee a letter containing offensive, derogatory content directed toward DCMA management. The employee stated that you have repeatedly been the source of disparaging and unprofessional statements directed at management. The employee also stated that on numerous occasions you have tried to persuade them, over the employee's objection, to support your belief that management cannot be trusted."

After reading the LOWI, I indicated I would not sign my performance appraisal until I spoke with the union. Nelson did give me a copy of the performance appraisal; however asked Joe Tessier if it was all right to do so. My complaints to Joe Tessier also fell on deaf ears, and Tessier indicated that the name of the employee would not be released.

I told Joe Tessier that one of the aggravating parts about the letters I get from management is that each time I get one, I have to sit down and count the multiple false statements in the letters. Joe Tessier said that everything I need is in the letter and that the name of the employee would not be released.

I ended the conversation with Joe Tessier by stating that I have never seen a situation like this where I cannot even determine what I allegedly did wrong to have any idea of not repeating it.

Not Allowed to Know Anything

When I asked Nelson about the alleged complaint, I was not allowed to know anything as follows.

1. Not allowed to know the name of the alleged employee.

2. Not allowed to know any specifics of the alleged complaint.

3. Not allowed to know when the alleged complaint was made.

4. Not allowed to know the dates of the instances in question.

5. Not allowed to know any specifics of an alleged "letter" referenced in the alleged complaint.

6. Not allowed to know "communications" medium (verbal, email) was used.

7. Not allowed to know what constituted alleged "offensive" or "derogatory".

8. Not allowed to know what alleged "disparaging" or "unprofessional" statements were.

9. Not allowed to rebut allegations.

August 9, 2007 - Nelson Violated Policy: The DCMA August 9, 2007 Directors Policy Statement on Harassment states in part: "*All complaints will be immediately and thoroughly investigated*" and to "*immediately correct it if it does occur*". Nelson did no investigation, I am aware of, and could not investigate a charge she could not explain. Nelson only handed me the alleged complaint which in fact was hearsay on Nelson's behalf. There was no supporting evidence whatsoever. The facts came into focus as time progressed as follows.

Memo for Record with Alleged Harassed Employee

March 30, 2011: One particular employee always migrated to me for help because I was known as a source for objective information and how to deal with management. The employee had a running feud with Gerard Woodlief, as I did in Falsified Trail 5. I documented that the employee *"had immediate recall and said he had complained about Gerard Woodlief and that he brought up the complaint that Gerard Woodlief made about me."*

I asked the employee if I had harassed him, and he stated that *"I had not harassed him"* and that the conversation with Nanette Nelson was about Gerard Woodlief and how Gerard Woodlief was harassing him. I documented this in a Memo for Record. So, at this point, I had supposedly eliminated one employee. However, this employee had serious reliability and credibility issues that I documented on April 22, 2013, October 11, 2012, and November 9, 2005. Meaning, I kept a file on this employee since this employee was highly manipulative.

Continuing Feud with Gerard Woodlief

May 17, 2011: The alleged harassed employee asked me to review notes regarding a complaint against Woodlief due to an ongoing feud. The employee referenced the complaint Woodlief made against me. I indicated that there is no evidence that Woodlief wrote the alleged complaint against me because I was not allowed to talk to Woodlief per Nanette Nelson. The point is, this was part of the scheming by this employee. One scheme centered on the Fort Hood shooter as follows.

Ft. Hood Shooting - Scheme for Transfer to Another Team

October 11, 2012, 07:00 AM: The alleged harassed employee called me to a private meeting, trying to scheme a transfer to another team. The following is my sanitized Memo for Record in part.

The employee wanted to be moved from the C-5 Team. The employee went into a conversation about one of his colleagues who had pictures of assault weapons on his computer screen. The employee was trying to figure out how the assault weapons could fit into a transfer scheme.

My impression was that the employee was developing a scheme to say he was afraid of the other employee and linking it to the other employee's conversations and research into assault weapons. The alleged harassed employee brought up the Columbine shootings. The alleged harassed employee also made reference to the colleague as being related to the Fort Hood shootings.

I went to talk with Mark Buckner (Supervisor) at about 08:40 that morning, and asked Buckner to tell my colleague to stop conversations about assault weapons and research on assault weapons (on the computer screen) in the office. I asked Mark to keep our conversation confidential.

Ft. Hood Shooting Transfer Scheme was Falsified Trial 9

February 5, 2014 – Received OSC FOIA (FO-14-0473) of Employee Alleged Complaint: I was litigating Falsified Trails 7, 8, 9, and 10 (Part 2 of Volley 3), and did a FOIA (FO-14-0473) to OSC to see what the DCMA had provided to OSC regarding me. The documents lined up with the exception of one. The alleged complaint from the employee (November 10, 2009) stated in part.

"Ms. Nanette Nelson, Team Supervisor

I am experiencing emotional and psychological intimidation; my fear of Mr. Ken Pedeleose, Engineer objectives toward management have increased due to the persistent and unrelenting negative comments Pedeleose has made. The most recent incident occurred in September, 2009 and involved the contents of a letter. The dialogue in the letter was written in an offensive manner, and included derogatory statements by Mr. Pedeleose associated with management's inability to manage. This unrelenting exposure to. negative commentaries are adversely affecting my emotionally and my psychologically well-being."

"It is with grave concern, that I am documenting the information I initially discussed with Ms. Nelson and Mr. Joseph Tessier in Ms. Nelson's office on November 06, 2009 and followed with an e-mail to Ms. Nelson regarding my fear that Mr. Pedeleose may execute an equally disastrous act as the one recently committed at Fort Hood, Texas. Your support in resolving this issue is requested.

I am requesting relocation from my current work station in L-10 Building as a result of the above."

Took me 4 years to get the complaint. The complaint was not in the writing style or word usage the employee would use. I know because the employee asked me to review work products and complaints about others. The complaint seemed manufactured to make it appear to be written by the employee. On receipt, I forwarded it to the alleged harassed employee.

Confront the Alleged Harassed Employee About Falsified Trail 9

February 5, 2014 7:10PM: The same day I received the OSC FOIA containing the November 10, 2009, alleged complaint, I forwarded it to the alleged harassed employee, stating:

I need your response on the attached preferably tonight.

Have you ever seen the attached document before?

Is this your signature on the attached? Did you sign this document? (See attached).

If you did sign it was it you that wrote it or did someone else write it for you?

I later called the employee at about 8:06 PM that same night (February 5, 2014). My Memo for Record on February 6, 2014 indicated that management placed various things in front of him to sign.

February 18, 2014: The alleged harassed employee eventually responded back stating,

"Ken, how did you obtain a copy of the attached document?

I have seen the attached document, I question the signature on the attached document, and someone else wrote this document.

I would like to speak wiht you tomorrow."

Fortunately, I kept good notes that documented the Fort Hood shooting transfer scheme. It may never be known who falsified the complaint or if the signature was falsified. Meaning, employee, management, or a combination of both. The one clear point is that it is typical DCMA schemes and falsification. I was very familiar with the alleged harassed employee because I reviewed the employee's work products and was entrusted to help with the employees' personnel case as follows.

Alleged Harassed Employee Contacted Me 27 Times for Assistance

The alleged harassed employee contacted me 27 times for assistance, and I even helped the employee with his personnel case of April 22, 2013. This does not include verbal requests.

Dates Contacted Include 17 Contacts (June 2009 – May 17, 2011): June 29, 2009 (10:52AM, 12:22PM, 1:26PM, 1:43PM); July 6, 2009; July 13, 2009 (10:15AM, 1:18PM); July 21, 2009; July 29, 2009 (7:48AM, 8:39AM, 9:11AM); September 22, 2009; December 14, 2009; March 22, 2011; March 30, 2011; May 17, 2011 (9:24AM, 4:28PM);

Personnel Case Contacts 10 Contacts (April 2013 – November 2013): April 22, 2013; May 2, 2013; September 27, 2013 (6:53AM, 6:57 AM); September 30, 2013; October 9, 2013; October 22, 2013; October 23, 2013; October 29, 2013; and November 25, 2013.

From that point, the DCMA went to the finale of falsification, of Volley 3, Falsified Trail 10.

Falsified Trail 10: February 16, 2010 - 14-Day Suspension – Full of Rage

February 16, 2010: Part 2 of Volley 3 was the finale for the DCMA retaliation and built on past Falsified Trails. The proposed suspension notice from Nanette Nelson stated in part:

"You are hereby notified that I propose to suspend you from duty and pay for fourteen days for misconduct, specifically, Insolent and Intimidating Behavior Toward Management Officials. This action is proposed to promote the efficiency of the service and will be effective not earlier than fourteen (14) calendar days after you receive this notice."

Nelson attached the following Falsified Trails to the suspension letter.

Notice of Proposed Suspension-April 2,2009	(Falsified Trail 6)
Notice of Decision to Suspend -June 17, 2009	(Falsified Trail 6)
Letter of Warning -September 29, 2009	(Falsified Trail 7)
Memorandum For Record (Gentile) -November 18, 2009	(Falsified Trail 10)
Memorandum (Nelson) -November 18, 2009	(Falsified Trail 8)
Memorandum For Record (Tessier) -November 18, 2009	(Falsified Trail 10)
Letter of Instruction -January 20, 2010	(Falsified Trail 9)

November 18, 2009 - Alleged Violence: The centerpiece of Falsified Trial 10 was retaliatory statements by Joe Tessier and another supervisor on my team, Loe Gentile. The statements by Tessier and Gentile followed the same falsified pattern as prior complaints in Falsified Trail 2 (walk out the gate by Lockheed Martin armed guards), and Falsified Trail 5 (alleged complaint by Gerard Woodlief questioning my mental stability). The alleged complaints by Tessier and Gentile seemed written and coached by the same person.

Coaching & Self-Portrayal Aspects of Alleged Complaints – Calm & Quietly

The most notable part of the retaliatory statements is the management self-portrayal as follows.

March 20, 2009: Gerard Woodlief stated in (Falsified Trail 5) in part: *"I went to Ken's cubicle and 'quietly' asked him what value did he feel that he, as the EVM Engineer, was adding for our team"*. Woodlief placed emphasis on the word "'*quietly*'" by using single quotes.

November 18, 2009: Joe Tessier stated in part: *"I calmly explained that my reason..."*

November 18, 2009: Lou Gentile stated in part: *"Speaking in a calm voice..."*

Meaning, the alleged complaints seemed coached. Most notably, the November 18, 2009, alleged complaints from Tessier and Gentile were in the same format, and I remember that at one point I had to ask for legible copies. Gentile's alleged statement was grainy, as if it had been faxed multiple times.

The alleged statements were typed on a page and not emailed which reduced traceability. In short, falsifications, scams, con games, price gouging and cover-ups are what this book exposes. It's what I have witnessed. That helps explain 3 months of revisions and reviews as follows.

Time Delay of 90 Days – Nearly 3 Months – Surprise Evidence

Tessier and Gentile's Memo for Records were dated November 18, 2009. The first I saw and heard of these alleged Memo's for Records was about 90 days or nearly 3 months later (February 16, 2010). These events below were not even discussed during my performance appraisal.

November 18, 2009: Tessier described me as "*explosive behavior*", "*full of anger*", "*face was red*", "*loud and demanding*", "*more agitated than any other time in the past*", "*unstable temperament*", and "*emotional display*".

Gentile alleged my "*fit of rage*" and grandstanded, with unsupported comments of fears of being "*hit*".

Despite these vivid and negative portrayals, the Agency (DCMA) waited nearly three (3) months to bring to my attention the alleged concerns of Gentile and Tessier.

Denied Allegations: I denied the allegations in total, and in fact, the statements from Tessier and Gentile were the best contradictions to Tessier and Gentile as will be shown.

Nannette Nelson had 3 Specific Opportunities to Avoid Surprise Evidence

1st Opportunity - Prior to Performance Appraisal: The first opportunity for the DCMA, Nelson, or anyone to address my alleged behavior (alleged fit of rage) was the time from November 18, 2009, to January 19, 2010. Meaning, prior to my 2009-year end performance appraisal. Nothing was done by the DCMA, Nelson, Tessier, Henrietta Snow, or anyone during this time frame to even mention the alleged incidents on November 18, 2009.

2nd Opportunity - During 2009 Year End Performance Appraisal: During my 2009 year-end performance appraisal (January 20, 2009), there was nothing mentioned whatsoever about my alleged rage on November 18, 2009.

3rd Opportunity January 21, 2010 – February 2, 2010: After my 2009-year-end performance appraisal, there was another time window to bring the charges. Meaning, the whistleblowing that occurred on February 3, 2010, as outlined in a February 4, 2010, email to Nelson that will be discussed soon. That timeline suggests retaliation based on the knowledge and timing of the disclosure to Nelson.

The point is, there were 3 months to bring the charges against me or at least address the issues to a resolution. The delays in bringing my behavior to my attention relate back to Falsified Trail 8, where I tried to resolve issues. Had Tessier and/or Nelson acted professionally, the issues would have been addressed on the spot, rather than springing the issues as surprise evidence.

Instead, Tessier and Nelson allowed me to make a case further supporting retaliation and outlining bizarre management actions as follows.

Alleged Rage Sent to a Program Management Meeting

Tessier Stated "fit of rage", "explosive behavior", "full of anger" – Needed at Meeting:

On November 18, 2009, Tessier demonized me as having "*explosive behavior*", "*full of anger*", "*face was very red*", "*loud and demanding*", "*more agitated than any other time in the past*", "*unstable temperament*", and "*emotional display*". However, Tessier immediately (no delay) sent me to a meeting. Tessier stated, "*I need your support for this event*" and my response was (per Tessier) "*OK where do you need me to be*".

This was a major contradiction in Tessier's story and confirms falsification against me. If I were "*full of anger*", "*face was very red*", "*loud and demanding*", etc., Tessier would not send me to a meeting and if I were in that violent mental state, someone at the meeting would have said something.

Tessier Denied Leave

Tessier Denied Me Leave: Tessier stated, "*I* (Pedeleose) *want to go home.*" Tessier replied: "*yes, I* (Tessier) *do mind, I need your support…*". Tessier had no concern about my demeanor on the alleged day of occurrence and denied me leave when I asked to go home. If I were in a "*fit of rage*" and "*full of anger*", etc., Tessier would have let me go home and approved leave.

No Threats or Vulgar Language

Tessier & Gentile Quotes Do Not Match Alleged Demeanor: Anyone in a "*fit of rage*", with "*explosive behavior*", and "*full of anger*" would make threats and or use vulgar language. None was present in this case or even mentioned or quoted. Tessier acknowledged I said: "*I* (Pedeleose) *want to go home.*" "*I* (Pedeleose) *have to go home now.*" "*OK where do you need me* (Pedeleose) *to be*?" Lou Gentile mentioned no vulgar or profanity language at all by me.

Five-Story Building and Nobody Heard Anything

Only Tessier and Gentile witnessed my alleged "*fit of rage*" and "*full of anger*" demeanor. In a five-story building with hundreds of people around, no one else saw or heard anything.

Fully Successful Performance Rating

January 20, 2010: I was rated fully successful. My performance rating mentioned nothing negative about anything in 2009. The 2009 performance appraisal on January 20, 2010, outlined three (3) rating categories as Outstanding ratings and two (2) rating categories as Fully Successful.

The point is, charges were patently falsified using only the false and self-contradicting statements by Joe Tessier and Lou Gentile. The following sworn statement shows where the falsification took place.

Sham & Hearsay Declaration - 90 Days of "Revisions & Reviews"

April 24, 2014: Deborah Mitchell, the DCMA Director of Labor and Employee Relations (LER), issued a declaration giving insight on falsified charges over 90 days. Mitchell stated in part.

"COMES NOW, Deborah Mitchell, who deposes and, as permitted by 28 U.S.C. § 1746, declares the following to be true:

My name is Deborah Mitchell. I am competent in all respects to testify as to the matters set forth in this declaration. I have personal knowledge of the facts stated herein and know them to be true."

"From 2009 to 2010, one of my staff specialists was Ms. Dorcas Smith. Ms. Smith was assigned to support the Contract Management Offices in the Eastern Region, including DCMA Lockheed Martin Marietta.

Nanette Nelson worked closely with Ms. Smith on the fourteen-day suspension for Kenneth Pedeleose. Ms. Smith's role was to gather all the facts and documents that formed the basis for the disciplinary action, advise Ms. Nelson of the appropriate penalty that was consistent with similar offenses throughout the Agency, and prepare a draft of the suspension letter for Ms. Nelson's review and approval. The draft was also reviewed by the local legal counsel. This process was repeated as necessary."

"According to my records, Ms. Nelson first consulted with Ms. Smith concerning Mr. Pedeleose's altercation in November 2009, and the initial draft of the proposed suspension was presented to Ms. Cleo Anderson, the local counsel, in December 2009. After further revisions and reviews, the proposal was completed and issued to Mr. Pedeleose on February 16, 2010. Ms. Smith then followed a similar consulting and review process with the deciding official, Ms. Henrietta Snow."

"Revisions & Reviews": Everything in Falsified Trail 10 allegedly happened on/before November 18, 2009. The alleged harassment of the unknown employee happened on November 10, 2009, and was mentioned in Nelson's February 16, 2010, Notice of Proposed Suspension as follows.

"I also received a harassment complaint from another employee in November, and I issued you a Letter of Instruction concerning that issue on January 20, 2010."

Falsified Trail 6 (One Day Suspension) was decided on June 17, 2009.

There was no legitimate need, even with holidays, for 90 days (nearly 3 months) of revisions and reviews other than to falsify the case or to hold the suspension for a retaliatory move as a weapon.

Something else happened because the February 16, 2010, suspension letter was on about 3 ½ pages.

90 Days – Nearly Three (3) Months - For A 3 ½ Page Letter

The February 16, 2010, Proposed 14 Day Suspension letter was only 3 ½ pages long. The header section (DoD and DCMA emblems) took up about 25% of the first page. No significant writing took place until 1/3 down the first page. The letter included copied information from the union contract (Collective Bargaining Agreement). Probably 1/4 of the Proposed Suspension Letter or more was boilerplate, meaning general information such as filing responses, etc.

After the blank spots are removed, the letter is a little over 3 pages long of meaningful writing. That allows a writing rate of about one (1) page per month for a very simple subject matter. The overall point is that something else happened. Possibly, the nexus to whistleblowing which is as follows. Meaning, whistleblowing was the real motive.

Nexus to Whistleblowing – "Hand Grenade" Counter Case Accusation

Truth in Negotiations Act (TINA) Violation

One possibility for the revisions and reviews excuse was the possibility of a counter case that was ready to throw like a "Hand Grenade", pull the pin, and 8 seconds later, an impact. This is based on the following.

November 18, 2009 – File a Complaint: Lou Gentile made a remark in his alleged Memo for Record stating:

Mr. Pedelease told me that he would file a complaint against me, his supervisor, and the group chief.

DCMA's response to a potential complaint would be to falsify Memos for the Record in DCMA's favor. However, I dropped the issue on November 18, 2009. Then another issue arose, which had its origins back in October 2009.

Truth In Negotiations Act (TINA) Violations to Inflate Cost

October 8, 2009 (Meeting October 9, 2009): By October 2009, my disclosures were serialized against DCMA and Lockheed Martin. Disclosure 22 was an email inventory list of potential criminal issues against Lockheed Martin. On my day off (October 9, 2009), I met with a criminal investigator to discuss what on the inventory list would be of interest. Item 8 was discussed at length and as follows.

"Standard Hours/LM Aero is maintaining 2 sets of Records: It was discovered during September-October 2009 that LM Aero is giving proposals to Government that are based on outdated information. This was C-5 RERP LRIP Lot 4. LM Aero used estimate from development actuals and then LM Aero tried to conceal the fact that LM Aero was using detailed standard hours to reduce cost. This would result in significant windfall profits for LM Aero."

The criminal investigator indicated this was a TINA violation. At that point, I began to incorporate TINA violations in my reports since it represented what Lockheed Martin was doing.

Common Practice to Remove Me from Critical Meetings

The removal from meetings would correlate to the fact that I discovered TINA violations. The timeline is as follows.

November 18, 2009: The November 18, 2009, meeting was the same meeting Lockheed Martin was showing internal data to manage the C-5 RERP Program. I saw Lockheed Martin's proposal, which had older data that, when used, inflated the cost. By that time, I had already met with the criminal investigator. The point is, Tessier and Gentile removed me from the meeting as Lockheed Martin was explaining the basis of what would be a TINA violation. Prior to November 18, 2009, Nelson confirmed in a November 12, 2009, email that I would be attending the main meeting. I was still removed despite the fact that Nelson, the supervisor, placed me at the main meeting.

Knew I Would Be Removed: I left without hesitation on November 18, 2009, because I knew I would be removed. It was common practice to sideline me at these type meetings to cover-up for Lockheed Martin. I cannot recall one main meeting I ever attended in full, which was called IBR (Integrated Baseline Review) for EVMS. Always sidelined, sometimes along with DCAA.

Incorporated TINA Violations into Technical Reports (Cost Analysis)

I incorporated TINA violations into my C-5 RERP Low-Rate Production Lot 4 report (January 28, 2010), since I already confirmed with a criminal investigator. This was Disclosure 25. Nelson and another DCMA engineer interrogated me based on my mention of TINA as follows.

February 4, 2010 - Nelson Notified of Disclosures (Nexus): I informed Nelson that I spoke with OSI (Airforce Office of Special Investigation) and also verbally disclosed it to Nelson on February 3, 2010. I stated in an email in part:

"As I indicated yesterday, I did speak with OSI about the Lot 4 proposal and was given the term TINA (Truth In Negotiations Act). I had simply started my allegations as LM Aero engaging in fraud and price gouging. I was able to link to specific violations of law."

"I am under no obligation to share my communication with OSI or any other investigator with you, and only did so to give you the opportunity to know where I was coming from."

"All I have to do is provide a reason to believe wrongdoing occurred. I am not required to prove the entire case or even confirm violations of TINA or confirm violations of any other laws. It is obvious by your ongoing hostile attitude towards me, that you are engaged in whistleblower retaliation and efforts to stop my reports from leaving the office. Fortunately I am able to address both issues outside the office."

At the time I notified Nanette Nelson verbally of the allegations to OSI, Nelson rocked back in her chain and Nelson said *"I guess its over."*

Nexus - Retaliation Follows After Nelson Discovers Whistleblowing

February 16, 2010: About seven (7) working days after Nelson was aware I made disclosures, Nelson retaliated with a proposed 14-day suspension. This would suggest that whistleblowing was the nexus. Regardless of the theory or timeline, I was retaliated against. My report that mentioned TINA was rewritten by Tessier as follows.

March 8 & 10, 2010 (Disclosure 25) – Tessier Goaded & Rewrote TINA from Report: On March 8, 2010, I placed a complaint against Tessier to Henrietta Snow, stating the following in part.

"On about Thursday, March 4, 2010 at 1330 hours I was approached by Nanette Nelson who stated that Joe and her (Nelson) needed to meet with me on my technical report. The report was my technical report (TSN) on LRIP Lot 4."

"I asked what are the problems and Joe only stated generalities with no specifics. I informed Joe that he was free to make any changes he chooses and that I really did not care what he changed."

I also informed Nelson and Tessier that if they wanted to, we could go back to my desk and *"they could dictate changes and I would type in the changes on my computer."* Tessier simply rewrote my report, and I made the changes. I later made Disclosure 25 (March 10, 2010) against Tessier.

This issue ultimately feeds into the capstone case, Chapter 5, of this book.

April 21, 2010 – 14-Day Suspension Approved: Henrietta Snow was the deciding official and approved the 14-Day Suspension. I was not surprised at Henrietta Snow's actions.

However, follow-on events gave Nanette Nelson the "Deer in the Headlights" expression that would remove Nelson as a surrogate used in the weaponization and lawfare against me.

Meaning, Nelson appeared to be the victim of a con in similar fashion as Charlie Murphy was conned by Dan Meyer in Falsified Trail 3. This would explain the "Cleo Anderson Letters" that were not in Nanette Nelson's writing style and the fact that the weaponized retaliatory letters used in lawfare against me were composed and reviewed at the DCMA HR (Human Resources) Legal Counsel level as previously mentioned.

The point being, Falsified Trail 3 involved about 20 government attorneys along with 7 senior DoD and DCMA officials. So, the risk was assumed by senior management officials. After that successful lawfare venture, the U.S. Legal and Judicial system was guaranteed corrupted on February 12, 2009 with the MSPB decision (cover-up).

Then along came Nanette Nelson who was a new supervisor and easily conned into being a surrogate for weaponization and lawfare. Nelson was further doomed with Joe Tessier as Nelson's immediate supervisor. DCMA went rapid fire weaponization and lawfare with 7 falsified trails in less than a year (March 2009-February 2010. Nelson took the brunt and Tessier had no concern anyway.

Unfortunately for DCMA, Nanette Nelson would suddenly stop being a surrogate as follows.

Nelson's "Deer Caught in the Headlights" Expression – Lawfare Drop Off

March 29, 2010 10:38 AM: I sent an e-mail to Nanette Nelson that stated in part.

"*Nanette,*

Attached is request for official time regarding a case that I will be submitting to the Merit Systems Protection Board (MSPB).

This is in response to the one day suspension I received on June 17, 2009 (See Attached). I allege whistleblower retaliation."

March 29, 2010 11:28 AM: Nelson responded back (possible "Cleo Anderson letter") stating:

"*Ken,*

I will be glad to consider your request for official time. However, I'm unaware of a basis upon which you can appeal a one-day suspension to the MSPB more than nine months after the suspension went into effect. You are welcome to provide me additional information in this regard and I will promptly revisit your request."

March 29, 2010 12:23 PM: I responded to Nelson and attached a copy of the March 12, 2010 letter from OSC and stated in part:

"*Nanette,*

In response to your question, I provide the attached letter from the Office of Special Counsel (OSC). The answer you need is called an "individual right of action" and I am well within the time limits to file at MSPB.

Since you engaged in a Prohibited Personnel Practice (PPP) (whistleblower retaliation in this case) I have a right to appeal the matter before the Merit Systems Protection Board (MSPB) under the individual right of action. All of the legal statutes are identified on the attached letter so you may review them.

Please let me know if this answers your question?"

Very shortly, if not immediately, after I sent the March 29, 2010 12:23 PM e-mail I thought it best to walk to Nelson's office and clear the issue up. I accomplished a great deal more.

"Deer Caught in the Headlights": Nelson was behind her desk, and I asked if I could talk to her. Nelson seemed concerned and somewhat confused. I informed Nelson that she (Nelson) was the target of a Prohibited Personnel Practice regarding the retaliatory letters she had signed. I emphasized to Nelson that she (Nelson) "signed" the letters.

At that point, Nelson exhibited a "deer caught in the headlights" expression. Nelson realized what Nelson had done. Meaning, from March 3, 2009, to February 16, 2010, Nelson helped DCMA rapidly fire 7 Falsified Trails (4, 5, 6, 7, 8, 9, & 10) against me. Nelson was terrified and her expression showed it. Then Henrietta Snow wanted to weaponize training and use Nanette Nelson again.

Weaponized Training - Nelson No Longer a Surrogate for DCMA

January 20, 2011 – Memo for Record: I was forcefully summoned to a meeting by Henrietta Snow (then third-level supervisor) with Nanette Nelson and a union official in attendance. The meeting partly focused on my whistleblowing and how management should make fraud referrals, not employees. I took this as a veiled threat and a cover-up since DCMA management protects Lockheed Martin, as this book herein demonstrates.

Weaponized Training: The second half of the meeting singled me out for a series of weaponized retaliatory training classes to be forced onto my Individual Development Plan (IDP) as a punitive measure to tactically and undeservedly damage my reputation. Nelson needed my permission to access my IDP. I refused Nelson access to my IDP. Nelson abruptly dropped the issue.

Hence, Nelson learned her lesson. This proves I still had management's attention. It also proves that management would not go forward without a weaponized surrogate for retaliatory lawfare against me. Nelson was then out of the picture as a surrogate.

March 29, 2010 - Nelson No Longer a Surrogate: After March 29, 2010, Nanette Nelson was no longer a "heat shield", insulation, surrogate, or a pawn for management. The adverse letters abruptly stopped and even weaponized training was ended as far as Nelson was involved. This was a welcome lull in the retaliations that allowed me to work the cases for the One-day suspension and the 14-day suspension as follows.

One-Day Suspension (Falsified Trail 6) "Cerberus" Cover-up

The case facts for the One-Day suspension (Falsified Trail 6) were already included and mentioned. The following is the timeline for the eventual "Cerberus" (Federal Machinery) cover-up.

November 13, 2009 – OSC Receives Case: Received acknowledgement letter from OSC.

February 23, 2010 – OSC Preliminary Letter Closing Case: As was typical with OSC, I received the standard form letters eventually closing my case regardless of the evidence in my favor.

March 12, 2010 – OSC Closed My Case: OSC closed my case stating I can go to MSPB. This was near the point where Nanette Nelson experienced the "Deer in the Headlights" expression.

Submitted Case to MSPB: At some point I submitted my case to MSPB and Judge Richard Vitaris was assigned to my case. Judge Vitaris recognized the absurdity of the DCMA case and suggested mediation. DCMA and I agreed to mediation.

Unhinged MSPB Mediation Hellscape

October 15, 2010: I attended mediation and was accompanied by a union representative since I wanted a witness against further falsified charges. The MSPB Judge assigned was Lynn Yovino. The joint mediation session started out without incident, and I was hopeful of a resolution. The mediation started at about 9:30 AM and lasted until approximately 11:00 AM.

At some point after 9:30, Yovino separated the parties into different rooms. When Yovino came to talk to me, there was immediate hostility toward me. Yovino asked me what I wanted. I informed Yovino that the suspension was to be removed from the record and the lost salary returned to me.

Yovino then asked the question again in an irritated tone and became more unhinged. I then became confused. Yovino then spoke about training for management officials.

For several minutes, I tried to reason with Yovino to no avail. When the alleged mediation ended about 11:00 AM, I told Yovino what I thought of MSPB. As I tried to stand, my legs were weakened, and I could barely walk. I almost handed my keys to the Union official I was with because I was so mentally shaken. I did recover on the walk to my vehicle and did drive home.

Yovino's demeanor was nothing new in MSPB's bullying of appellants. That is why I always used hearings on written records. MSPB judges are hostile and adverse to the law. I was going to complain about Yovino and thought it best to drop the issue. Because Judge Vitaris seemed in my favor.

The hearing with Judge Vitaris continued. At one teleconference, Judge Vitaris mentioned that there was a meeting with MSPB judges where the 30-day suspension (Falsified Trail 3) was used as a discussion point. Even MSPB recognized issues with Falsified Trail 3.

October 30, 2010 – Submit Case to MSPB with Serialized Disclosures: I submitted my MSPB case for Falsified Trail 6 to MSPB Judge Vitaris. Disclosures had to be serialized for understanding and expediency since DCMA and Lockheed Martin had engaged in so much illicit behavior.

MSPB Initial Ruling in My Favor – Reversed Falsified Trail 6

December 14, 2010: Vitaris ruled in my favor, reversing the one-day suspension. Stating in part.

"The appellant's disclosures fall into three broad categories: (1) allegations of fraud, waste, and abuse by Lockheed Martin in its military aviation construction projects; (2) the agency's failure to act upon and/or affirmative covering up of Lockheed Martin's misdeeds; and (3) the appellant's past alleged whistleblowing activity."

"The agency chose not to seriously challenge whether the appellant's disclosures were protected for a reason: The appellant's position as an Industrial Engineer for the DCAA (should be DCMA), *supervising the Defense contracts with Lockheed Martin, afforded him personal knowledge of the information that formed the basis for his disclosures... He has, moreover, a track record of substantiated whistleblowing activity which he has provided in support of his argument that he had a reasonable belief for the 19 disclosures asserted in this case."*

"For the most part, the appellant's beliefs regarding the first category of alleged protected disclosures -fraud, waste, and abuse by Lockheed Martin - are based upon the appellant's first hand knowledge as an Industrial Engineer, his experience, and the documentary evidence he submitted to the Board."

"The second category -disclosures that the appellant's superiors censored his reports and covered up for Lockheed Martin -are based upon the appellant's first-hand knowledge. Finally, the disclosures in the third category -the appellant's record of past whistleblowing activity -have previously been substantiated by IG reports or otherwise and the appellant provided the relevant documentary evidence to that effect."

"For the reasons stated above, I find that the appellant had a reasonable belief as to the truth of alleged protected disclosures 1, 2, 3, 4, 5, 7, 8, 10, 11, 12, 13, 15, and 16."

The agency notes that the appellant only served the agency with copies of disclosures 2, 4, 6, 8, and 10, of which only disclosures 2, 4, 8 and 10 are protected disclosures.

"Protected disclosures 2, 4, 8, and 10 must be found to be a contributing factor to the appellant's one-day suspension as a matter of law under the so-called "knowledge/timing" test."

I find that the agency has failed to produce a firm belief in my mind it would have taken disciplinary action against the appellant if he were not a whistleblower.

The evidence does clearly show that whistleblowing was a contributing factor. However, Judge Vitaris did miss a critical point regarding vicarious liability (holding higher level officials accountable).

Vicarious Liability - Retaliations Emanate High in the Chain of Command

Vicarious Liability: Judge Vitaris did not recognize the fact of Nelson being a surrogate in the case as the following shows. Vitaris stated in part.

"Disclosure 14 alleges that Colonel Casey Blake directed his subordinates to ensure the rewriting of reports to delete information critical of Lockheed Martin. Several of the appellant's earlier disclosures concerned these rewrites. Here the appellant contends that the "real retaliation" came from Colonel Blake, who is much higher in the chain of command. The appellant states he came to this conclusion based upon information from his union steward, Mr. Jim Lockhart, that Colonel Blake had told him that the agency's legal counsel had· been involved in drafting a letter of warning for the appellant regarding his reports. I do not believe a disinterested observer would reasonably conclude that Colonel Blake had abused his authority or been involved in retaliation based upon this double hearsay evidence."

Surrogates as Weapons & Insulation: Vitaris ignored the surrogate aspect of retaliation. Meaning, Colonel Blake in Falsified Trail 6 was culpable since Blake should have stopped Nelson's retaliation. Instead, Nelson's "Deer in the Headlights" fear stopped Nelson after the fact.

Deliberate Non-Trace to High Levels: Systemic evidence trails show OSC, MSPB, and OPM ("Cerberus") stop the tracing of illicit acts to high levels in the DoD chain of command. I have heard this before, and Falsified Trails 3 & 6 prove this fact, as does Attorney Client Privilege.

Cleo Anderson - Weaponized Attorney Client Privilege 13 Times

Altered Evidence to Protect Command & HQ Levels

Cleo Anderson claimed Attorney Client Privilege 13 times total for the following calendar dates during MSPB discovery: June 8, 2010; June 14, 2010; and June 16, 2010. One example follows.

"Describe how altered e-mails got from Colonel Casey Blake back to Nanette Nelson. Specifically, Enclosure (A) is e-mail text only of an e-mail sent from me to Colonel Blake. The e-mail header information has been removed. My interrogatory question is to please outline in detail how that email sent on March 16, 2009 made its way back from Colonel Blake to Nanette Nelson and into a package of information supporting a one-day suspension against me. I am asking for the trail/chain of events.

Response: The Agency objects to this Interrogatory and states that its response would violate the attorney-client and work product privileges."

Meaning, Cleo Anderson altered evidence to protect Colonel Blake and senior management, leaving Nanette Nelson as the surrogate. Regardless, I prevailed on Falsified Trail 6. However, Nixon's "Federal Machinery" termed "Cerberus" analogy herein would undo the win to avoid any traceability to senior management and ensure a whistleblower would not win.

Nixon's "Federal Machinery" Strategy in Action – "Cerberus" Analogy

September 30, 2011 – MSPB Overturns Decision: MSPB Judges Susan Tsui Grundmann, Anne M. Wagner, and Mary Rose overturned the decision in my favor. A typical MSPB cover-up explains why I included Chapter 2 of this book to show why MSPB was discredited as of 2002. Then, the DOJ and Federal Court of Appeals rubberstamped for MSPB, as the following shows.

January 20, 2012 - Federal Court Case 2012-3027 – DOJ Informal Brief: DOJ attorneys Tony West (Assistant Attorney General); Jeanne E. Davidson (Director), Steven Gillingham (Assistant Director); and Christopher A. Bowen (Trial Attorney) submitted an informal brief and West and Davidson didn't bother to even sign. The brief was the usual running me (whistleblower) down.

April 12, 2012 – Federal Court Decision Case 2012-3027: Federal Circuit Judges Prost, Mayer, and Wallach rubberstamped the DOJ, which had rubberstamped MSPB, proving that Nixon's "Federal Machinery" lives on as a "garbage disposal" for ethics and cover-up for senior officials.

OSC, MSPB, OPM, DOJ, and Federal Judges have proven a "garbage disposal" for honesty in government. Meaning, soft-on-crime (enabling) actions and decisions of OSC, MSPB, OPM, DOJ, and Federal Judges are contributors to adverse national issues such as the national debt, national security problems, etc. Falsified Trail 10 followed the same predictable fate.

Fourteen-Day Suspension (Falsified Trail 10) "Cerberus" Cover-up "Federal Machinery" "Rubberstamp" Mode

Falsified Trail 10 included Falsified Trails 7, 8, and 9, which have already been explained in detail as retaliatory and unsupported. The "Cerberus" "Federal Machinery" "rubberstamp" mode follows.

October 25, 2013 – OSC Preliminary Dismiss of Case: OSC provided the usual form letter that began the dismissal of my case. I responded to OSC as follows.

November 3, 2013 – Letter to OSC Director Carolyn Lerner: I issued a complaint against Tony Cardillo, OSC Chief of Dallas Field Office (DFO), and Anne Gullick (OSC Attorney), to OSC Director Carolyn Lerner, stating in part.

"Following the 14 day suspension I began preparing a case to OSC. I took my time to do a proper legal analysis and place case facts in the format that MSPB uses. I prepared a well outlined and integrated case that was contained in a five inch (5") binder totaling 924 pages."

"The OSC Complaints Examining Unit (CEU) understood the legal analysis (facts as compared to law) and recommended mediation in the case even prior to investigation."

"In fact, all Anne Gullick did was restate the Agency case and bolster it with false and bias information. Tony Cardillo did nothing to stop Anne Gullick."

"One of the most blatant false statements from Anne Gullick is where Anne Gullick states on Page 2 of Enclosure 2 "Not wanting to disrupt the meeting in progress, Mr. Gentile asked you (Pedeleose) step into the hallway for further discussions." This statement is false. I asked Gentile to step into the hallway because Gentile was the disruption, not me."

I cannot recall a response from Carolyn Lerner. The point is, OSC was in a rhythm of restating the Agency case and moving on. There was no investigation, I am aware of.

<u>November 18, 2013 – 130 Page Response</u>: In addition to information already provided to OSC, I responded to OSC, copy to Carolyn Lerner, with a 130-page response including a 26 Page affidavit and supporting documents. This was a more concise explanation of my case for easy understanding. I also followed up with a FOIA to OSC to see what DCMA provided.

<u>November 26, 2013 – FOIA FO-14-0473 to OSC</u>: OSC responded to a FOIA request that I put in for documents DoD/DCMA sent to OSC. There was an email follow-up on December 2 and 3, 2013 noting since DoD was the originator of documents, DoD would have to approve release.

<u>December 5, 2013 – OSC Closes Case</u>: Tony Cardillo responded to my November 18, 2013, response and ignored my evidence. Cardillo continued to run me down and concluded in part:

"...we conclude that your agency can establish by clear and convincing evidence that it would have suspended you for 14 days absent your protected activity. Accordingly, we plan to take no further action and are closing our file in this matter."

Gullick, Cardillo and Lerner proved OSC was a cover-up operation and an extension of Scott Bloch and the national, discredited reputation OSC has had since 2002, as outlined in Chapter 2.

<u>February 5, 2014 – Received FOIA FO-14-0473</u>: I received the FOIA from OSC, and there was only one document that I had not seen. That document was dated November 10, 2009 (Falsified Trail 9) regarding the alleged complaint that I was similar to the Ft. Hood shooter. That information has already been integrated herein. DCMA did provide OSC a critical document not provided to me.

No Investigation by OSC at Any Time – OSC Rhythm of "Dumped" Cases

The FOIA gave no indication of an investigation by OSC at any time. There only seems to be a gathering of documents. In fact, in any case I sent to OSC, I can remember no instance where management was bothered at all or even knew OSC was running an alleged investigation. OSC gathered documents and issued form letters dismissing cases.

<u>March 22, 2005 – OSC "Dumped" Cases</u>: This ties back to Chapter 2, where GAP (Government Accountability Project) stated in part.

"Recently, GAP has also learned that some 1000 cases and whistleblowing disclosures have been dumped without investigation by the OSC, often without even calling the whistleblower. This is an

emergency, because plans to gut due process appeal rights at the Merit Systems Protection Board mean aggrieved federal workers will have nowhere to turn except the Special Counsel."

The point is, DCMA factored in OSC and MSPB corruption by rapid firing Falsified Trails at me. I was fortunate I had two IG investigations due to my links to Senator Grassley, which assisted me in at least documenting institutional weaponized corruption. Nevertheless, the cover-ups continued.

"Cerberus" Contain Negative Information - Cover-up Rhythm

May 5, 2014 – Declaration & Cover Letter: I submitted a 27 Page Declaration to MSPB along with 274 pages of supporting documents.

July 28, 2014 – MSPB Judge Vitaris Denied Corrective Action: Judge Vitaris ruled in DCMA's favor against overwhelming evidence in my favor, which was already presented herein for Falsified Trails 7, 8, 9, and 10. DCMA's rapid-fire strategy worked.

Vitaris' acquiescence to corruption proved the typical MSPB "Cerberus" containment machine. The November 10, 2009, complaint (Falsified Trail 9) was never entered onto the record that I have ever seen or remembered. So, the Vitaris decision was obviously flawed at that point alone.

August 25, 2014 – Petition for Review (PFR) Full Board: I submitted the same case to the MSPB full board.

January 22, 2015 – Full MSPB Board: The MSPB full board rhythm again covered for DCMA. This included MSPB Judges Sesan Tsui Grundman, Anne M. Wagner, and Mark A. Robins.

March 30, 2015 – Submit case to Federal Court Docket 2015-3090: I appealed the case to the Federal court.

May 7, 2015 – DOJ Informal Brief Case 2015-3090: DOJ did the usual job of weaponizing DOJ and running me down. No surprise there.

August 10, 2015 - Federal Court of Appeals – Case 2015-3090: Federal Judges Prost, Newman, and Taranto continued the cover-up and ruled against me. No surprise there either.

This is How It Gets Started to Enable and Expand the Government Swamp

Via Institutional Weaponization and Lawfare

Falsified Trails 1 through 10 may seem like local disagreements between management and me. However, the Falsified Trails enabled the Government Swamp to expand. Chapter 4 will show the results in more detail. I was able to document, and did have small successes, however overall, I was extremely hindered. Meaning, the Falsified trails stopped me from doing my job and severed my working relationship with Congress.

It is notable that the weaponization and lawfare against me began in 2003 and now continues into 2015. Over a decade later. Cleo Anderson was involved in 2009 and continued in 2015. This forms the allegation of institutional weaponization and lawfare where one commander, management official and/or attorney is replaced by another over the decades with the same adverse mentality. The current trend is half-century overall with Ernie Fitzgerald as the starting point (1970).

DCMA recognized the corruption rhythm trend and worked with new surrogates by the name of Mark Buckner and Isaiah Waindi to replace Joe Tessier and Nanette Nelson. Cleo Anderson would have a continued role, along with a newcomer to the weaponization, lawfare, and retaliation scene, Debbie Elwell.

The Index of Names in Volley 4 was as follows.

Volley 4 - Falsified Trails 11, 12, and 13 Index of Names

(March 10, 2015 – September 30, 2015)

Cleo Anderson [FT(11,12,13)]	DCMA Attorney
Mark Buckner [FT(11,13)]	DCMA Second Level Supervisor, Engineering Director
Myra Tate [FT(11)]	DCMA Third Level Supervisor, Deputy Commander
Isaiah Waindi [FT(12,13)]	DCMA First level Supervisor C-5 Team
Debbie Elwell [FT(12,13)]	DCMA Personnel Human Resources
Kimberly Turner [FT(13)]	DCMA FOIA
David Wray [FT(13)]	DCMA FOIA
Scott Faucet [FT(12,13)]	DCMA Investigator
Lt. General Wendy Massiello	DCMA Director
Captain Michael Murphy	DCMA Director East
Ray Burick	Lockheed Martin Vice President C-5 Program
Diane Stefani	Lockheed Martin Human Resources Director (Marietta)
Brad Kent	Lockheed Martin C-5 Manager
Ann Holland	Lockheed Martin Business/Finance
Denise Joyce	Lockheed Martin Pricing and Estimating

Other Management Officials: Other management officials mentioned in this Chapter are as follows.

Vice Admiral David Lewis	DCMA Director
Jason Rawson	DCMA, Second Level Supervisor (Engineering Director)
Colonel Lance French	DCMA Commander
Colonel Sheri Bennington	DCMA Commander
Colonel John Drohan	DCMA Commander

There was no DOJ members listed since I gave up at this point on the U.S. Legal and Judicial System. I considered the U.S. Legal and Judicial System too corrupted. No sense in wasting time when there were a foregone conclusion and a rigged system. Another win by DCMA would only widen and deepen the Government Swamp to further corruption.

The system was so openly corrupted and weaponized by Falsified Trail 11 that even Lockheed Martin increased in participation. Meaning, Lockheed Martin Human Resources was involved.

Falsified Trail 11 follows.

Falsified Trail 11: March 10, 2015 - Weaponized Training – "Personal Matter"

January 20, 2011 - October 11, 2011 – Mark Buckner as New Supervisor: As of January 20, 2011, Nanette Nelson was still my supervisor. At some time before October 11, 2012, Mark Buckner became my supervisor because I made a memo mentioning Buckner as my supervisor.

Falsified Trail Delay: Buckner delayed the Falsified Trails because Buckner's wife worked for Lockheed Martin. Meaning, Buckner probably didn't want attention because Buckner expected a promotion to GM-14 (second level supervisor), which Buckner eventually received.

Buckner once indicated that the only reason he (Buckner) was a supervisor (1st Level) was because his wife was on the Lockheed Martin C-130 Team and Buckner was on the DCMA C-5 Team. I was on the DCMA team for oversight of Lockheed Martin EVMS/Business management, where Buckner's wife worked. Meaning, there was still a conflict of interest, although not alarming.

System Audit Oversight of Lockheed Martin EVMS – Buckner's Wife

2010 – 2015 EVMS System Oversight: I was on the team overseeing Lockheed Martin's EVMS from the system level. This oversight covered the entire facility from C-130 to C5 programs. There are two sign-in sheets that prove I would oversee Buckner's wife's work on EVMS. The dates are March 17, 2010, to June 10, 2015. I kept quiet and non-confrontational since challenging Lockheed Martin was hazardous to my career. The system audits were "check-the-box" (for show).

Quashing Audits & Private Meetings with Lockheed Martin

May 22, 2013 Buckner's 1st Private Meeting: Mark Buckner's first known private meeting was with Denise Joyce (Lockheed Martin Manager) on about May 22, 2013. Buckner informed me on May 31, 2013: *"I have concluded that Ms. Joyce's discussion with me will remain private."* This was due to problems with the Lockheed Martin Bill of Materials (BOM). Meaning, discrepancies in the material to assemble and modify aircraft, spare parts, etc.

Quashed Audit in 2013 – "Stand Fast": I planned to audit the Lockheed Martin material estimating system in response to $584,610 of wrongful charges from Lockheed Martin during November 18, 2011. On July 17, 2013, Buckner quashed the audit and directed me to "*stand fast*". I documented Buckner's and DCMA's management action in a detailed August 31, 2013, report to Congress. Buckner seemed to be the surrogate in quashing the audit.

August 31, 2013 Report – Quashed Audits: The most notable event by Buckner and DCMA management was quashing an audit of Lockheed Martin's Bill of Materials (BOM). I had found serious problems in the 2013 timeframe, and I was considered the local expert on traceability of, and problems with, Lockheed Martin BOMs. August 31, 2013, was a formal disclosure, and my first-hand account of events was written from documents at the time. Overall, this book shows how weaponization and lawfare altered my working conditions and expanded the Government Swamp.

The next audit event ended up as weaponized training imposed upon me by Mark Buckner.

Program Office Request for Audit of EVMS Schedule - One Artifact Audit

October 2014 Approximate: Following Falsified Trail 6, I was letting Lockheed Martin write their own reports on EVMS. Meaning, I did not challenge Lockheed Martin since doing so would invoke more wrath upon me. My working conditions were altered and my career survival hinged on me not openly challenging Lockheed Martin. Behind-the-scenes I documented cover-ups with criminal disclosures, Memos for the Record, etc. However, Lockheed Martin's EVMS (financial tracking, scheduling) was noticeably deficient. In response, the C5 program office asked if I could look at how Lockheed Martin maintained the schedule. Meaning, this audit was not of my choosing.

To avoid management wrath by challenging Lockheed Martin, I compromised with an audit of one document or artifact. Meaning, one document from Lockheed Martin and the audit was passed.

One Document/Artifact Audit of Lockheed Martin EVMS Schedule System

October 29, 2014 – December 2, 2014: My audit of Lockheed Martin EVMS schedule adherence hinged on one document (artifact). Meaning, if Lockheed Martin gave me anything, I would approve Lockheed Martin's EVMS schedule. Any audit needs at least one artifact.

Lockheed Martin had a conference room where various reports (potential artifacts) were pinned to the wall. My Lockheed Martin counterpart, Brad Kent, showed me a document where Lockheed Martin tracked the schedule. I asked for a copy of the document, which may have been one page and maybe a few support pages. The document was already on the wall. I needed at least one artifact because I was going to pass Lockheed Martin on the audit regardless.

Brad Kent indicated that a Lockheed Martin Vice President (Ray Burick) would have to approve me receiving the document. I was concerned since I had a detailed file on Ray Burick aggressively covering up Lockheed Martin problems with EVMS going back to 2006.

Multiple Requests for One Document: From November 4, 2014, onward, I was denied access to even one document. The email trail is consolidated in the October 29, 2014 – December 2, 2014 files. On October 29, 2014 Brad Kent responded to my request for one document by stating in part.

"Stacy and I were attempting to think of other ways to provide a metric that offers a trend of our IMS (Integrated Master Schedule) *performance instead of looking at BEI* (Baseline Execution Index) *alone. In retrospect, LM believes that SPI* (Schedule Performance Index) *is much more meaningful than BEI primarily in that the BEI calculation assumes each task has the same weight. For the SPI calculation, each task has its own independent weight and also includes vendor schedule data. The metrics that Stacy and I showed you are based on tasks only and there is no task weighting involved. The charts that we showed you are internal LM metrics but I would like to follow up with you in person to discuss further options."*

Received Nothing: The point is, it didn't really matter if Lockheed Martin used BEI, SPI, or something else; Lockheed Martin was continually behind schedule. I believed BEI to be of more value at the time to see how Lockheed Martin was completing tasks versus just an overall schedule metric (SPI). In the end, I received nothing, and Lockheed Martin remained behind schedule.

On December 1, 2014, Brad Kent stated:

"Ken,

I suggest that you have a talk with Mark Buckner as Ray Burick met with Mark on Nov 19th."

I was stonewalled for nearly 30 days while Burick met with Buckner on a "personal matter".

Ray Burick Private "Personal Matter" Meeting with Mark Buckner

November 17, 2014: Burick emailed Buckner stating.

Mark,

Good Morning.

If possible, I would like to get together with you this week for a discussion regarding a personal matter. Diane Stefani (Marietta Site HR Director) will attend with me.

Would like to meet as soon as convenient. Is there a good day/time for you Mark.

Thanks,

Ray

Multiple Conflicts: Ray Burick (Lockheed Martin Vice President) went directly to Mark Buckner. The normal course for a Vice President is to communicate with the DCMA Commander on site, as happened in Falsified Trail 1 between Sandra Shoemaker and Colonel Wright. Additionally, Burick was discussing a *"personal matter"* with Mark Buckner, whose wife worked for Lockheed Martin, where I was overseeing Buckner's wife's work.

Further, and worse yet, Burick, in writing, indicated he will be accompanied by Diane Stefani (Lockheed Martin HR Director). Hence, multiple conflicts and no prior or follow-on meeting communications with me. I was being aggressively shunned.

Ray Burick Forwards E-mails to Mark Buckner

November 19, 2014: On November 19, 2014 Ray Burick forwarded internal Lockheed Martin email communications to Mark Buckner stating Lockheed Martin's side of the issue. I forced the internal emails from Buckner via union grievance and received the emails on April 6, 2015. The first is from my Lockheed Martin counter-part Brad Kent who copied in other Lockheed Martin executives.

From: Kent, Bradley

Sent: Thursday, November 06, 2014 10:24 AM

To: Burick, Ray A

Cc: Sprouse, Jim; Brotherton, William R; Hammer, Mark L; Holland, Anne M

"Ray,

I want to bring to your attention negative comments that were directed against you during a local DCMA meeting held in L-10 on November 5, 2014..."

"Specifically, he (Pedeleose) *wanted answers to who from LM management had made the decision to not provide him with some LM internal charts that I had showed him a few weeks before. I*

responded that I had made the decision to not provide him the data plots. During the ensuing discussion Ken made the statement that the "Lockheed Vice President has lied to me." He specifically was directing this at you. I again stated that I was the one who had made the decision not to provide the data. Ken again responded with the same statement that the" Lockheed Vice President has lied to me."

First, Brad Kent definitely stated to me that Ray Burick would have to release the information. I would not have approached Ray Burick otherwise. Also, I did not refer to Ray Burick as a Vice President; I referred to him as "Ray" or "Ray Burick." I cannot recall saying Burick lied, although Ray Burick previously stated in a general way that Lockheed Martin would be more open with information.

However, another Lockheed Martin employee responded on Sunday night stating the following.

From: Holland, Anne M

Sent: Sunday, November 09, 2014 11:36 PM

To: Kent, Bradley; Burick, Ray A

Cc: Sprouse, Jim; Brotherton, William R; Hammer, Mark L

Subject: RE: DCMA Comments at CMC/WxR Meeting on 5 November 2014

"I concur with Brad's synopsis below.

On the subject of the specific documents that Ken was requesting, I have in my notes that Ken continually reiterated, "That a LM VP broke his promise and was not giving DCMA everything they were asking for.""

Kent and Holland disagree on what was said. Regarding "everything," I only asked for one document that was already printed. Then, Brad Kent made a false statement as follows.

From: Kent, Bradley

Sent: Thursday, November 13, 2014, 1:56 PM

To: Burick, Ray A

Cc: Hammer, Mark L; Burick, Ray A

Subject: RE: LM Response to Ken Pedeleose's Schedule Health Metric Questions

"Ray,

I did NOT have any conversation with Ken Pedeleose on this issue after our DCMA meeting last week and do NOT agree with his first statement in the below email."

The first statement by me was:

"Ray,

When I last spoke to Brad Kent about the issue below he indicated that the decision had been elevated to you (VP Level).

I know that earlier this year you indicated that LM Aero would be open with information. Now there seems to be a reversal of that position.

DCMA respectfully requests a response to the question below as to why existing data is being denied to confirm health of C-5 CWR (Color Weather Radar) *program."*

Lockheed Martin EVMS Was Deficient Since 2002: Chapter 4 of this book shows that Lockheed Martin had multiple EVMS deficiencies since 2002. Meaning, what Burick and Kent were doing in withholding data was no surprise. Additionally, Chapter 4 will show that Lockheed Martin could not perform on contracts as early as 1998. The Stonewall timeline continues in 2014.

December 1, 2014 – Contact Colonel Drohan & Myra Tate: I sent email after email with no response, and was only told a meeting had happened between Burick and Buckner. I contacted the office Commander, Colonel Drohan, and Deputy Commander Myra Tate, stating in part.

"The e-mail trail below is the exact reason that I became a whistleblower and the exact reason why the IG and other investigators continually visit this facility.

I made a simple request to LM Aero for information that can prove any actual adherence to EV implementation at the program level. I was given nothing."

Drohan and Tate remained silent.

December 2, 2014 1:35PM: I sent another email to Buckner, with a copy to Brad Kent, stating in part.

"Mark,

I am still waiting for someone to tell me what the meeting (which was apparently about my simple data request to LM Aero) was about?

Could someone help me out here?"

December 2, 2014 2:49PM – Meeting Scheduled: Mark Buckner never responded to my email; however, sent me a meeting request. The meeting was for December 3, 2014, from 3:30-4:00. With the statement: *"Meeting to discuss EV"*. I did attend the meeting on December 3, 2025.

The meeting with Buckner was useless. The next option was a complaint against management. I was disgusted after a decade of weaponization, lawfare, and retaliations.

Relevance is, I was stonewalled and shunned from Lockheed Martin to command levels in DCMA (Drohan & Tate) as if there was something to hide. There was even a private meeting where Ray Burick brought in the Lockheed Martin Human Resources Director. One explanation to all the chaos is the following.

C-5 Reliability Enhancement and Re-engining Program (RERP)

Hotline Evaluation DoD IG Audit Report 2015-039

November 18, 2014: On May 29, 2013 a DoD IG hotline complaint was issued against the Lockheed Martin C-5 RERP by someone other than myself. Six allegations were made, with four substantiated, as follows:

1: Government failed to discourage repeated tender of nonconforming components. (Substantiated)

2: Government delegated inherently Government functions to Lockheed Martin. (Substantiated)

3: Government failed to approve and document Lockheed Martin flights. (Undetermined)

4: Government accepted non-conformances that were corrected at additional cost to the government. (Substantiated)

5: DCMA failed to comply with the DCMA Instruction for the corrective action process. (Substantiated)

6: Government failed to ensure that Lockheed Martin used U.S. Airforce service guidance. (Not Substantiated)

The aforesaid substantiated DoD IG complaint dovetailed with what I was saying about Lockheed Martin. Meaning, DCMA was protecting and covering up for Lockheed Martin. Chapter 4 will provide further reasons for DCMA to cover-up for Lockheed Martin.

Prior to meeting with Buckner, I made disclosures as follows. Buckner had lost my confidence.

December 3, 2014, 8:31AM– Criminal Disclosure: I made the following disclosure to Colonel Drohan, Myra Tate, Mark Buckner, with a copy to local criminal investigators and Edward Kell (then DoD IG), who issued the aforementioned IG audit. I stated in part.

"The most recent suspected criminal act involves Ray Burick (LM Aero C-5 VP) meeting with Mark Buckner on about November 19, 2014 after I asked Brad Kent and Ray Burick for even one shred of proof that LM Aero is managing in any way the C-5 Color Weather Radar program. Ray Burick never responded to my requests for even a limited look into LM Aero records to support the health of the Color Weather Radar program."

December 3, 2014 10:08AM– Criminal Disclosure: This disclosure outlines my files on Ray Burick going back to July 24, 2006 to August 23, 2006 where I stated in part.

"In an earlier e-mail this morning (with limited distribution) I promised to express my concerns about LM Aero VP Ray Burick currently withholding information regarding health of Color Weather Radar program. I have had a file on Ray Burick going back to 2006."

The disclosure goes into detail about how Ray Burick would drill down to find what documents I was given by Lockheed Martin in my audits and then cut that source off. Meaning, the government had reduced insight into how Lockheed Martin managed programs and schedule projections. This reduced insight corresponds to other identified financial tracking problems (See Chapter 4). All of which link to increased cost caused by weaponized government and lawfare, along with criminal vulnerability.

Shunning & Hostile Workplace - EEO Case Against Drohan, Tate, & Buckner

December 4, 2014 – EEO Case (250 Page Case File 9Y-15-0138): I filed an EEO case via email and copied Colonel Drohan, Myra Tate, and Mark Buckner, citing violations of the August 9, 2007 DCMA Director's Policy Statement on Harassment, which states in part.

"All supervisors and managers are responsible for making sure that our work-place is a positive and safe environment for all of our employees, free from any and all discrimination, harassment, intimidation and shunning behaviors. Managers and supervisors will be held accountable if these behaviors are allowed."

The extended shunning behaviors by Colonel Drohan, Myra Tate, and Mark Buckner had an adverse effect on me. Several emails were sent by me, merely asking for a response. I received nothing. At the December 3, 2014, meeting with Buckner, I left more disgusted than before.

Mark Buckner's One-Sided "Legal Brief" Meeting Minutes

December 10, 2014, 12:55PM: Mark Buckner issued meeting minutes that appeared to be written by an attorney, similar to a legal brief. Seemed a "Cleo Anderson Letter" preparing for litigation. That would explain the long delay from December 3, 2014, to December 10, 2014. I followed up with a rebuttal on December 10, 2014, 3:34 PM. This was a typical DCMA back-and-forth exchange where I had to undue false and one-sided statements. Typical DCMA behavior.

Pushed the EEO Case (9Y-15-0138) Against Drohan, Tate & Buckner

January 6, 2015 – Buckner Interviewed: The DCMA EEO counselor interviewed Mark Buckner. In the final EEO file I could find no interview for Colonel Drohan or Myra Tate.

January 14, 2015: I notified Drohan, Tate, and Buckner of the following in part.

"I am going to have to file a formal EEO complaint regarding the recent actions taken by you that centered on private meetings with Ray Burick regarding me personally. This is only half the case with the other half being criminal. This was entirely your (DCMA) choice to go this route and was done in response to the shunning and silence by Colonel Drohan and Myra Tate who should have done something to resolve the issue."

Meaning, systemic shunning had a severely negative effect on me and altered working conditions.

February 20, 2015 – Request for Hearing Case 9Y-15-0138: I requested a hearing before an EEOC judge. DCMA was copied on the request and responded back with the Case file that started on December 4, 2014. The file was 250 Pages.

Mark Buckner responded with weaponized training as follows.

Buckner Retaliates with Weaponized Training

March 10-11, 2015: Buckner's response to the EEO case was weaponized training to discredit me. Myra Tate and Cleo Anderson's names were on some emails. Buckner stated March 10, 2015.

"Ken

In an effort to enhance your training and skills development, I am directing you to take the following interpersonal skills course on April 27-29. Course information is as follows:

Course administered by Management Concepts

Title - Interpersonal Skills: Developing Effective Relationships

Location - Atlanta, GA"

Complaining was met with more shunning, so in response, I filed a union grievance as follows.

Weaponized Training Grievance to Obtain Documents

March, 23, 2015 – Union Grievance: The grievance stated in part.

"Employee Grievance on management failure to respond to provide justification for admonishment as related to "Directed Training"."

"I was subjected to adverse action (admonishment followed by "Directed Training" with several individuals involved in the process behind the scenes) without just cause and management has failed to respond with their reasons and justification for the adverse actions or what happened behind the scenes regarding the "Directed Training". Inferring that I am deficient "unprofessional" for no reason, having "Private" discussions with contractor managers, and then formally directing me to training while routing that action through "command suite, GC and HR" (wide distribution) indicates that some type of documentation exists and the admonishment was not private."

Buckner pretext to the weaponized training is as follows.

Mark Buckner's Pretext for Weaponized Training was Weaponized Data

(November 19, 2014 – March 10, 2015)

April 6, 2015 – 68 Page Pretext: Buckner's response to the grievance was the November 19, 2014, private meeting with Burick about 110 days prior to the weaponized training of March 10, 2015. Meaning, I finally got some behind-the-scenes data that I would not have gotten otherwise. Much like the time I rattled Dan Meyer into the regret email of July 27, 2007.

Nearly 110 Days of Delay: A disinterested observer would conclude that Buckner's response that the weaponized, punitive, training was tied to an event that happened nearly 110 days or over 3 months earlier was absurd. Buckner could have easily scheduled the weaponized punitive training within a few weeks at the latest. Easily in January 2015. Meaning, Buckner retaliated for the EEO case, and to protect Colonel Drohan and Myra Tate, as the most likely event. Regardless, the behind-the-scenes electronic trails (emails) with Ray Burick, Brad Kent, and Ann Holland provided valuable insight into Lockheed Martin actions against me personally as already shown, and integrated, herein.

Nevertheless, the original weaponized punitive training scheduled for Atlanta, GA (close to my office) was cancelled on April 20, 2015. Buckner then feverishly sought another class as if Buckner's life depended on it. That weaponized class was in Washington, DC. The weaponization comes from the fact that directed punitive training damages my reputation.

<u>May 27, 2015 – Washington, DC ($2,405)</u>: Buckner was so feverish to enroll me in weaponized punitive training that Buckner approved a training class in Washington, DC that was guaranteed to run. The class cost $949 tuition plus $1,456 per Diem for a total of $2,405.

Conclusion – No Concern for the Warfighter, Tax Payer, or Public Safety

Altered Working Conditions to Enable Corruption

As the Falsified Trails extend, and the Government Swamp widens, with more data gathered, the overall point emerges that DCMA does not manage contracts. DCMA does not have the concerns of the taxpayers in mind. And DCMA does not have the safety of military equipment to the warfighters in mind. DCMA factors in weaponization and lawfare continually.

DCMA has systematically covered up issues using DoD and DCMA attorneys as weapons. DCMA continuously covers up for contractor. This is an evidence-based allegation that DCMA has provided the evidence trail, and associated behavior, to justify.

Falsified Trail 11 even shows that training is feverishly weaponized as if Mark Buckner's life depended on my attending the weaponized training.

Chapter 2 of this book outlined an April 16, 2004, Climate Review in my office that stated in part.

"*Issues that remain unresolved fester and lead to poor morale and performance, turnover, and eventually litigation. All are present at DCMA-LMM.*"

DCMA is an organization that has multitudes of festering issues. The Falsified Trails in this book are some examples. Chapter 4 has more issues related to cost and price gouging by Lockheed Martin. The data points are cumulative showing DCMA is a hostile workplace with altered working conditions contrary to national security.

The point is, notice the workplace conversations documented in the electronic trails and allegations along with management responses and management behavior. Conversations about criminal and illicit acts are common and the management staff takes the comments in stride or retaliates. That's the way DCMA was managed. Meaning self-respect was lost. Issues that could have been resolved in minutes were escalated and documented at high levels. That aspect of management was concerning and prompted me to document another disclosure.

Falsified Trail 12 follows…

Falsified Trail 12: July 27, 2015 LOWI – Reported Conflicts of Interest

March 16, 2015 11:07AM: Knowing the past issues at the facility that I reported, documented, and substantiated, as well as the shunning to simple recent issues in 2015, I was again forced to elevate concerns. I submitted a written DoD IG Hotline complaint against Mark Buckner Serial Number 20150316110400316. Colonel Drohan, Myra Tate, and Mark Buckner forced issues outside the office and outside DCMA.

The complaint centered on Buckner's conflict of interest where his wife worked at the same facility. Mark Buckner was basically overseeing his wife's work at Lockheed Martin which was a basic conflict of interest. The quashing of past audits was a concern with Mark Buckner. However, the shunning when I went up against Ray Burick for one document on an EVMS audit was very concerning. Buckner did not support me at all. Buckner had protected Lockheed Martin too much.

I ended the Hotline Complaint with the following prediction.

"Do not expect DCMA LMM, or DCMA Headquarters, to do an objective investigation or take any action against Mark Buckner. Colonel Drohan and Myra Tate are well aware of what has transpired and I expect they will cover-up the situation up. DCMA is institutionally "in bed" with the contractor and Mark Buckner is part of that DCMA management team. To say again, I do 100% expect DCMA LMM management up to and including Lt. General Wendy Masiello to cover-up for Mark Buckner."

Meaning, I 100% expected a cover-up and a total cover-up was what happened. That was the benefit of me working at DCMA for so long. What I predicted did happen later in the year.

The point is, Drohan, Tate, and Buckner forced the situation outside of our office. The second point is that DCMA would use a DCMA investigator (Scott Faucett) who worked at the DCMA HQ level to cover-up for Drohan, Tate, and Buckner. DCMA FOIA office would later heavily redact Scott Faucett's Report of Investigation (DMR 15-053) in FOIA 15-172. Buckner would later leave his position, so the DCMA cover-up worked for a while. Details will follow shortly.

March 16, 2015, 12:37PM – OSI Investigators: I also forwarded to local criminal investigators, who stated.

"Thanks for the courtesy notice Ken. Do you mind if I forward to Steve Holtz, DCMA Fraud Counsel?"

I responded: *"Go ahead. I am forwarding to Lt. Gen Masiello anyway in a few minutes."*

This was another example where investigations against DCMA are forwarded back to DCMA for investigation. Working conditions were altered and the government swamp was widened.

Complaint to DCMA Director Lt. General Wendy Masiello Re: Mark Buckner

March 16, 2015 1:02PM: I continued my complaints about Mark Buckner to then DCMA Director Lt. Gen Wendy Masiello. I copied Buckner, Drohan, Tate, Isaiah Waindi (1st Level Supervisor), and Captain Michael Murphy (Commander, DCMA District East). I stated in part.

"Myra Tate must have read my mind this morning and at the last minute Myra Tate suddenly and unexpectedly developed an open door policy. That "door" was closed and locked when I sent e-mail after e-mail about Mark Buckner and the private meetings he has had with Lockheed Martin officials regarding me. That goes back to 2013."

"Most notably with the private meetings and private discussions that Mark Buckner carries on with Lockheed Martin about me (Pedeleose, DoD Whistleblower). Colonel Drohan and Myra Tate sat back for months and did nothing while I suffered with Buckner's abuse while he had private discussions with Lockheed Martin about me and quashed audits. Forced to think I could come up with one conclusion."

"Candice Buckner is Mark Buckner's wife and works at this Lockheed Martin facility on the C-130 team."

"In closing, I am tired of being harassed and the fact that Candice Buckner works for Lockheed Martin is a logical explanation for Mark Buckner's actions. Aside from that, the original allegations that DCMA LMM is "in bed" with the contractor still holds true. It is an either or situation if not both."

Two days later, another DCMA conflict of interest arose with DCMA EEO as follows.

False Statements at EEO Briefing to the Workforce

March 18, 2015: Debra Simmon (DCMA EEO) gave an EEO briefing in my office. The briefing forced another complaint to DCMA Director Masiello and my chain of command as follows, stating in part.

"We just finished an EEQ briefing by Debra Simmon of the DCMA EEO office.

Ms. Simmon made a seriously false statement to the work force that needs to be corrected.

Ms. Simmon made the statement that when an employee makes a complaint against another employee the complaining employee may remain anonymous.

That statement is totally false. If the employee being complained about challenges the allegation then management is forced to release the name and circumstances.

I tried to bring this point to Ms. Simmon and Ms. Simmon hurriedly shuttled away and ignored me drowning me out with her microphone.

I tried to relay the point to Ms. Simmon that there is a process known as discovery whereby employees can force the information to be provided as to who made the complaint and specifics of the complaint."

Debra Simmon gave the workforce false impressions of the EEO process. This was deliberate when Simmon turned and walked away from me. I told Simmon *"that's wrong"*. Colonel Drohan later issued a retraction as follows.

March 23, 2015 – Drohan Corrects Simmon: Colonel Drohan sent an email that stated in part.

"Last week Ms. Debra Simmon provided our workforce an excellent briefing on various aspects of the EEO process. During the briefing, a concern was raised that EEO complaints do not remain anonymous. To ensure there is no confusion, I want to clarify this point: anonymity, if requested by the Complainant, can be preserved for complaints at the counseling or pre-complaint stage. But anonymity does not apply once a formal complaint is filed."

Debra Simmon was wrong. However, the issue went much deeper since it is tactically wise, while being unethical, for DCMA to investigate DCMA and clear DCMA as follows.

Final Agency Decision (FAD) False Statement by DCMA EEO

March 23, 2015 9:05AM: Debra Simmon also made the statement that DCMA EEO uses outside parties (organizations) to write or evaluate EEO cases know as FAD. This gave the impression that DCMA EEO is separated from the process. Fortunately, I had DCMA FAD dated February 5, 2015 for the case against Mark Buckner (Case Number 9Y-15-0138). I decided to test the FAD statement by Simmon and contacted Clinton Covert (DCMA Acting EEO Director). I stated in part.

"Attached is the Final Agency Decision (FAD) in my recent EEO complaint.

Per an EEO briefing last week Debra Simmon indicated that Final Agency Decisions are not done by the "Agency" and are so to speak "farmed out" for outside organizations to do the analysis.

Question: Regarding the attached, what organization by name including specific individuals did the analysis and wrote the attached document. I need to know by name who reviewed my EEO case and the specific name of the organization and persons or persons involved in that review for the attached. I need contact information for those persons."

Clinton Covert responded at 12:56 PM the same day stating.

"Please note that the attached letter dated February 5, 2015 informs you that I have reviewed all of the information in your EEO complaint that was filed on January 20,2015. The letter also provides the rationale for dismissing your complaint in accordance with the provisions set forth in 29 CFR Part 1614.107. Please refer to the attached letter as it also outlines your appeal options. Thank you."

Relevance is, DCMA was not sending the EEO cases out for independent opinion. DCMA was doing the reviews in-house, giving the DCMA workforce a false impression of impartiality.

Colonel Drohan Supports Punitive Weaponized Training

April 21, 2015 – Continue Conflicts: Colonel Drohan had the opportunity to resolve the issues between myself and Mark Buckner by simply removing the word "directed" from the Interpersonal Skills Course (weaponized training). Drohan refused, stating in part.

"On April 20, 2015, I held a Step 2 grievance meeting with you and Mr. Pedeleose. During this meeting, Mr. Pedeleose stated that the training would not be effective as he is being directed to attend. Mr. Pedeleose also stated that his manner of communication is affected by his perception that he works in a hostile environment, and he has no confidence in the leadership of the organization." (Simply put, altered working conditions.)

"Given Mr. Pedeleose's own acknowledgement that his communications are not always well-received, it remains critical for him to learn more about resolving conflict and the nuances of working with different individuals. The Interpersonal Skills training course appears very well-suited to address this goal. Further, while I believe that Mr. Pedeleose sincerely believes his own concerns, his allegations concerning the integrity and intentions of the leadership at this CMO are simply false and continue to impede his ability to establish effective communication with leadership."

Drohan's response seemed like another "Cleo Anderson letter." Drohan was part of the problem and shunning. Drohan allowed the word "directed" to remain, thus supporting weaponized training. Drohan was partially correct in that I have no confidence in DCMA leadership.

Meaning, trying the find the end of corruption in DoD and DCMA is like trying to find the end of the universe. It may never be done, but Drohan provided an avenue to be explored. I started the following day at 8:22 AM as follows.

How Far to Protect Conflict of Interest - DCMA Investigates DCMA Again

<u>April 22, 2015 8:22AM</u>: I sent an email to Lt. Gen. Wendy Masiello and Captain Murphy with copy to Drohan, Tate, Buckner, Waindi and union leadership stating the following in part.

"It is a direct conflict of interest, of the most blatant type, for Mr. Buckner to have his wife work at Lockheed Martin (same facility) where Mark Buckner (Engineering Director) controls audits and actions against Lockheed Martin. There has never been a more clear conflict of interest. The salary of Candice Buckner at Lockheed Martin has to be a significant source of income for the Buckner family that Mark Buckner would protect at any cost. Mark Buckner would want to silence me (whistleblower) from disclosing problems at Lockheed Martin and Mark Buckner is doing just that. Mark Buckner is protecting his financial interest. No reasonable manager would ever push for a "Directed Training" class the way Mark Buckner has without a strong motive. Especially when the recipient of the training believes and positively knows there is no problem."

"Request: This is no longer a grievance. This is a whistleblower retaliation issue. I respectfully request to change the term "Directed Training" to "Voluntary Training"."

"If you respond to the negative, or do not respond at all, I will conclude that it is the intent of DCMA Director to have whistleblower disclosures handled outside the Agency through Congressional channels or by whatever media is available to address criminal and unethical activity at this Agency. At instances of my choosing I will forward complaints to you through Congressional channels."

"Please respond by COB May 1, 2015. If you need more time please let me know."

The email was longer and was a continuation of the March 10, 2015, email by Buckner that started the weaponized training. There was a response.

<u>April 30, 2015 7:10PM – Captain Murphy Responds</u>: Murphy responded in what appeared to be another "Cleo Anderson Letter". Had a legal tone. Part of the response is below.

"I am responding to your April 22,2015 email (below)"

"This issue has previously been addressed by the DCMA East Region Counsel in a Conflict of Interest Opinion. However, given that the opinion was written in August 2014, it would be appropriate for the Agency to ensure that there has not been any change in circumstances which would give rise to a conflict of interest. As such, the Agency will review the matter again."

Meaning, DCMA was going to investigate DCMA again. I responded back as follows.

May 4, 2015 6:44AM: I was off Friday and responded Monday morning to all (Murphy, Masiello, Drohan, Tate, Buckner, Waindi, and union officials), stating in part.

"What means the most to me is that you did respond. Whether it be to the positive or to the negative a response does mean quite a lot. I would hope that Colonel Drohan and Myra Tate would use you as an example.

Regarding Mark Buckner, it is a definite conflict of interest for Mark Buckner to be in the position he is in and I believe that Mark Buckner himself realizes this. When the selection process was moving forward I asked Mark Buckner how it was going. I remember specifically that Mark Buckner told me that his name was not referred. Shortly after, Mark Buckner was announced as the DCMA LMM Engineering Director. Maybe Mark Buckner thought no one would not notice."

"I will most likely report the issue of Mark and Candice Buckner to Congressional levels since I know 100% it is a conflict of interest and there is no defense for it. In reality there is nothing to look at; the conflict of interest is clear. The salary that Candice Buckner brings to into the home of Mark Buckner would be substantial."

Consistent & Sustained Pattern: The past, and the following, shows DCMA investigated DCMA, and DCMA determined, DCMA had no problems. This is another reason for the expanding Government Swamp and altered working conditions. Meaning, the more I look at the evidence, the more convinced I am. There is a consistent and sustained pattern of maleficence that has expanded the Government Swamp. I'm just documenting it in this book.

DCMA Investigates DCMA - Conflict of Interest Investigates Conflict of Interest

April 27, 2012 Organization Chart - Conflict of Interest: During May 2015, I was contacted by DCMA investigator Scott Faucett. Faucett works for DCMA HQ. As of April 27, 2012, Faucett's office fell under the direct purview of the DCMA Director on the same level as the DCMA Office of General Counsel. Meaning, DCMA was in a conflict of interest to investigate a conflict of interest. I was disappointed, but not surprised. I played along.

May 19, 2015: My first email contact with Scott Faucett was scheduling a conference room for a private phone discussion. During that discussion, Faucett indicated he would send me questions that I had to handwrite answers to. That was odd and unlike any investigation I had seen. Prior investigations had recorded sworn statements taken in person. I thought handwritten statements were unprofessional and were designed to limit responses.

Significant Documentation to Investigator Scott Faucett

May 20, 2015 – June 10, 2015 – 32 Exhibits to Faucett: To support my allegations against Mark Buckner and DCMA, I provided Faucett 32 Exhibits (scanned documents, emails, notes, etc.) to objectively prove my position. The exhibits were considered part of my May 26, 2015 statement for evidence tracking purposes although the Exhibits were sent out in batches as follows.

Exhibits	1 – 17	Sent May 20, 2015
Exhibits	18 – 27	Sent May 21, 2015
Exhibits	28 – 29	Sent May 26, 2015
Exhibits	30 – 31	Sent May 28, 2015
Exhibits	32	Sent June 10, 2015

May 26, 2015 – 23 Page Statement: I responded to Faucett's question in a typed statement. The entire package was 23 Pages. I wasn't sure when Faucett would investigate, although my statement was submitted on May 26, 2015, and the majority of the Exhibits were submitted by May 28, 2015.

Scott Faucett Investigated When I Was Out of Office for Weaponized Training

June 3, 2015 – June 5, 2015 – Weaponized Training: Tuesday, June 2, 2015, was a travel day, and the weaponized Interpersonal Skills course was June 3-5, 2015 (Wednesday-Friday). Monday, I may have been in the office, but I do not recall. It appears from witness statements that Mark Buckner may have been interviewed by Faucett on Monday, June 1, 2015. Buckner was in a different building about a mile from me, so I would not have noticed Faucett's presence.

June 11, 2015: I was talking with my colleagues, and the subject of an investigation came up. My colleagues indicated that I was out of the office, and an investigator entered and asked questions. My colleagues indicated they knew it was about me because I left, and the investigator walked in.

I contacted Scott Faucett, stating the following in part.

"It has come to my attention that during the week of June 1, 2015 you visited Marietta, GA, DCMA LMM and conducted interviews.

This was undoubtedly part of your investigation that I provided you a written statement on.

I need the following:

1: Estimated completion date for your investigation or date investigation completed.

2: Copy of investigation report (no redactions) with notes, statements, etc. from witnesses and/or that gathered outside of witness statements/interviews."

Faucett responded the same day, stating in part.

"Pursuant to your email message dated June 11, 2015; please note that the DCMA-DMR investigative file was forwarded to General Counsel (GC) for review. GC will provide an opinion concerning the conflict of interest concerns addressed in your complaint to the Director, DCMA (dated April 22, 2015). DCMA-DMR cannot predict/estimate a completion date as this file is under review by GC."

July 16, 2015: I contacted Lt. Gen. Masiello and Captain Murphy, along with Tate, Buckner, Waindi, and the new commander, Colonel Sheri Bennington, and asked for the decision from the DCMA General Counsel.

July 17, 2015 4:58PM: Captain Murphy responds to all, excluding Lt. Gen Masiello, late on Friday, stating in part.

"As you provided below, DCMA GC reviewed the DCMA-DMR After Action Report (AAR) regarding your allegations of conflict of interest levied against Mr. Mark Buckner, the DCMAE-LMM Director of Engineering. The investigation resulted in a finding that the allegations were unsubstantiated. Subsequently, Central Region counsel completed a written conflict of interest analysis based on the facts garnered in the investigation and found no conflict of interest."

July 20, 2015 6:29AM: I respond to all, and copied Masiello back in stating in part.

"I noticed you left off Lt. General Masiello so I added her back into this communication.

I plan on more than just a FOIA. I plan an allegation of cover-up.

I was actually going to make the cover-up allegation without asking the results of the investigation however I thought it best to ask."

"There was less than 1% chance that the issue would not be covered-up. Now I am 100% certain."

DCMA investigated DCMA and DCMA covered up for DCMA. No surprise there. Also, no surprise the lawfare followed.

Falsified Trail 12 - Letter of Warning and Instruction (LOWI)

July 27, 2015

July 27, 2015: Isaih Waindi, then first-level supervisor, quickly threatened me to stop digging into the cover-up of Mark Buckner's conflict of interest. Waindi stated in part.

"This letter serves as a warning and instruction concerning your conduct as a Federal employee. This letter is being issued in accordance with Article 26 of the Collective Bargaining Agreement dated April 2006."

"In your July 20, 2015 response to Captain Murphy's email, you accused the Agency of a cover-up. You wrote: "I was actually going to make the cover-up allegations without asking the results of the investigation however I thought it best to ask. There was less than 1 % chance that the issue would not be covered up." You unreasonably accused the Agency of covering up conflict of interest allegations without first obtaining objective facts."

"In recent months, you have consistently engaged in this behavior. In December 2014, Mark Buckner (then your first-line supervisor) met with you to address your unprofessional communication with

Lockheed Martin company employees. In February 2015, you engaged in a severe outburst during the CMO's EEO training and you verbally attacked our guest speaker, Ms. Debra Simmon. As your new first-line supervisor, at that time I talked with you, and I reiterated the importance of your actions and words and the need for you to address your frustration in an appropriate manner. Also, in June 2015, you attended a training course on Interpersonal Skills that sought to teach you proper communication techniques."

The issues of Mark Buckner, Ray Burick, and Debra Simmon have already been addressed. I did not verbally attack Simmon. I told Simmon she was "wrong" and then followed up to prove that Simmon was wrong. Simmon walked away from me as I was explaining why Simmon was wrong. Meaning, at the time I had to go external to Simmon for resolution, the issue was no longer a misunderstanding. It was deliberate by Simmon.

Waindi admitted to me directly that others wrote the LOWI as follows.

Cleo Anderson & Debbie Elwell Letter

July 27, 2015: I made a memo for the record immediately after I spoke with Waindi, stating in part.

"This morning July 27, 2015 at slightly after 0900 hours Isaiah Waindi handed me the attached letter of warning and instruction and followed with threats about how I cannot make allegations against DCMA directors. The conversation centered on the attached "Email to Captain Murphy LG Masiello July 20 2015". Isaiah indicated that I should not have made allegations of a cover-up without knowledge of facts. I explained to Isaiah that I had proof in that I gave Scott Faucet (investigator) a 23 page statement with 32 exhibits."

"I asked Isaiah if he wrote the July 27, 2015 letter of warning and instruction and initially he indicated that he issued the letter. At some point later (when I pressured the issue) Isaiah indicated that the letter was written by DCMA attorney Cleo Anderson and Labor Employee Relations (LER) Debbie Elwell was also involved."

Meaning, Isaiah Waindi was a surrogate acting like Nanette Nelson in the prior Falsified Trails.

Cleo Anderson and Debbie Elwell are part of DCMA HQ. Meaning, at this point, after a review of past Falsified Trails, DCMA attorneys and LER/Human Resources (HR) are standard parts of the retaliation, weaponization, and lawfare process. Meaning, lawfare to silence me. The retaliation surfaced at DCMA HQ in Falsified Trail 1 when DCMA Director Keith Ernst cheered on retaliation. The retaliatory trend has had multiple appearances of attorneys and LER/HR since then, with Falsified Trail 3 as the Flagship case which traced high into the DoD chain of command.

Isaiah Waindi implicated Cleo Anderson and Debbie Elwell in carrying on the DCMA HQ institutional weaponized campaign against me. Meaning, from 2003 to 2015 I was still a target.

Conclusion – DCMA Investigating DCMA

Conflict of Interest Investigates Another Conflict of Interest

Falsified Trail 12 followed the same pattern as other Falsified Trails, with the twist that DCMA now investigates DCMA to clear DCMA. An internal loop of corruption enabling further corruption and further expanding the Government Swamp.

The internal closed loop of corruption also has DCMA HQ involved. Meaning, Cleo Anderson and Debbie Elwell are from DCMA HQ and take an open role in the weaponization and lawfare.

Weaponization, lawfare, retaliation, and the enabling of corruption emanate at HQ levels. Falsified Trail 3 made this point abundantly clear. This corruption loop worked so well that DCMA openly began the DCMA IG as follows. Meaning conflicts of interest are on open display.

May 16, 2018 - DCMA IG: The conflicts of interest went unchallenged in lawfare and weaponized government to the point that DCMA initiated its own IG in 2017. That was outlined in a May 16, 2018, DCMA article that stated in part.

"*The DoD IG just returns the referral to us* (DCMA) *as either an information referral or an action referral.*" The article went on to state that in the last four years, only one of DCMAs' allegations was investigated by the DoD IG.

The DCMA IG was an advertised threat to the DCMA workforce as an omen that whistleblowing against the military-industrial complex would be investigated by DCMA. Meaning DCMA will know or have good clues who the whistleblowers are. That is one reason issues are not resolved. Meaning, allegations of wrongdoing are sent back to the wrongdoers for evaluation. A very vicious circle that widens the Government Swamp and enables institutional corruption.

When that process runs its course, another conflict of interest takes over, which is the FOIA (Freedom of Information Act) process which has also been weaponized by DCMA for cover-ups.

Falsified Trail 13: September 30, 2015 - 14 Day Suspension - Coverup

Cover-up the Path to Conclusions: Falsified Trail 13 now moves down the line to the next level of DCMA cover-up, which is to conceal the path and evidence trail Scott Faucett and DCMA used to develop the conclusion that allegations against Mark Buckner were unsubstantiated and the case was closed. Meaning, the conclusion was known; however, the path and evidence to the conclusion were a mystery and unknown. This is where the FOIA weaponized cover-up takes over.

Investigating the DCMA Investigator Scott Faucett

August 4, 2015: Scott Faucett had completely lost my trust so I contacted Faucett's colleagues for more information. Brian Sullivan responded back and indicated the case file was "DCMA-DMR 15-0053". Sullivan was Faucett's supervisor as identified in a September 1, 2015 email.

August 4, 2015 – FOIA to Congress: I submitted a FOIA request for DCMA-DMR 15-0053 to Senator Johnny Isakson to put emphasis on my request. I suspected DCMA would be intransigent.

August 7, 2015: I received a response from Senator Isakson's office as follows.

"According to the response we received from Department of Defense, your information should be submitted to the point of contact provided in letter and not through our office."

It was obvious DCMA was concerned at this point and did not want outside attention to what would become a cover-up. Meaning, run a con on Senator Isakson like the prior con on Senator Grassley.

August 10, 2015 – FOIA Request: I submitted a FOIA request for Scott Faucett's unredacted investigation DCMA-DMR 15-0053. I stated in part.

"I request the following information without redactions or editing regarding case file DCMA-DMR 15-0053. I understand that birthdates and social security numbers need to be redacted however all other information such as names, positions, titles, documents, etc. should remain clear and transparent."

There is no need to include the documents or e-mails I (Ken Pedeleose) gave to Scott Faucett. That should reduce the volume of information.

1: Investigative Report DCMA-DMR 15-0053: Please provide a copy of the complete final Investigative Report (not just a summary) that was done by Mr. Scott Faucett or others regarding the investigation done (by Mr. Faucett) or others during the timeframe of May 2015 -July 2015 at DCMA LMM at Marietta, GA. The investigation centered on conflict of interest of Mark Buckner with his wife Candice Buckner (who is a contractor (Lockheed Martin) employee) and other issues.

Limited Scope – Limited Timeframe - Recent FOIA

The FOIA request was for a limited timeframe (May-July 2015). Limited scope, meaning a focus on one person, Mark Buckner, at one facility. The FOIA was recent, meaning it was an investigation completed a few weeks earlier. The FOIA was internal to DCMA. Being an alleged "investigation", the file should be well organized from the evidence trail to the conclusion, all scanned into an electronic file. Meaning, DCMA routinely scans information into electronic files.

DCMA FOIA Response – 6,000 Pages - $1,413 – 12 Hour Record Search

August 17, 2015: I received a shocking response from Kimberly Turner, FOIA/Privacy Analyst, DCMA, that stated in part.

"The DCMA FOIA office has received your attached FOIA request regarding DCMA investigation DMR 15-053. We have assigned control number 15-172 to your FOIA request for administrative purposes. Please refer to that control number in any future correspondence regarding this FOIA."

"It has been determined that there are approximately 6000 pages of records that may be responsive to you lengthy request. As a requester that fits into the "other" category, you are entitled to the first two (2) hours of search and the first 100 pages of reproduction free. All additional hours to search and reproduce the records for review must be paid for by the requester at a rate of $44.00 per professional hour and $.15 per page. It is estimated that the entire search for all records being requested will take approximately 12 professional hours, equaling $528 and based on the 6000 pages, the reproduction cost for you to receive the records will be approximately $885 for a total of $1413.00."

This was the first point of many to follow that showed DCMA had something to hide. Scott Faucett's alleged investigation started in May 2015 and was completed in early June 2015. That was 2 months at most. It would have been impossible to review 6,000 pages in that limited timeframe.

The need for 6,000 pages to determine if Buckner's wife worked at Lockheed Martin is ridiculous.

Also, the week of June 1–4, 2015, Scott Faucett was taking written statements in my office. Meaning, the written statements were gathered in one place.

The NSA IG investigation of 2006 that included the June 28, 2006, sworn statements was approximately 509 Pages and was electronically scanned. No need to copy. The DCMA used scanned files as a common practice. Meaning, I received other larger FOIAs with no problems.

It is unknown where the "12 professional hours" would come from since Faucett would have the files readily available. Meaning, the FOIA process was now a cover-up to stop transparency.

Search for Facts of $1,413 Cost

(Email Trail August 17, 2015 – September 1, 2015)

August 17, 2015 – September 1, 2015 Email Trail: There was a lengthy email trail from August 17, 2015, to September 1, 2015, trying to figure out the need for $1,413. The email trail is attached to (an extension of) the September 1, 2015, trail where Kim Turner stated in part, September 1, 2015:

"Specifically, as noted by the investigator, the investigation is comprised of several voluminous components which include the following: (1) an Investigative Report (total of thirteen (13) pages); (2) various witness statements (totaling 163 pages); (3) contractual documents, including solicitations, contracts and modifications (totaling over 4,000 pages); and (4) an assortment of miscellaneous documents (totaling forty-five (45) pages), including an Investigative Action Report and certain financial materials. To search for these materials, including a page-by-page search for items responsive to your request, the investigator reports that he logged a total of 5.50 hours.

To make a complete response to your FOIA original request, based upon the additional information provided, we estimate total fees for search and duplication to be no more than $950.00. Such estimate considers that you are receiving two hours of search time and the first one hundred (100) pages of duplication at no cost. Thus, to continue with processing of your original request, we need from you a willingness to pay up to, and including, $950.00. Moreover, we would need a preliminary payment of $500.00 from you to continue with work required to fully respond to your FOIA."

The response of an investigator needing 5.5 hours to search a recently completed file was bizarre and unrealistic, as was the alleged need for 4,000 pages of contractual documents. Modifications and solicitations. Nevertheless, I concluded the email trail on September 1, 2015, as follows.

<u>September 1, 2015, 11:12AM</u>: I responded to Kim Turner, stating in part.

"I will reduce my request to (1) Investigative Report (total of thirteen (13) pages); (2) various witness statements (totaling 163 pages)."

"You may omit my (Pedeleose) witness statement which is approximately 23 pages. I do want the complete 13 page investigative report and other witness statements without redactions."

"In advance I will say that if I see any redactions other than birthdates or social security numbers I will state cover-up. If I am extorted for 5.5 hours of investigative time I will state cover-up."

The point is, Kimberly Turner's response was so over-the-top it represented the typical DCMA cover-up. I can say this from the many FOIAs I have received over the years. Most notably, the NSA FOIA was over 500 pages, where I quoted multiple times from the statements of June 28, 2006. From there, the shunning and silencing of me started as follows.

Kim Turner (FOIA Office) No Response/Shunning

<u>September 2, 2015 – September 8, 2015</u>: I sent follow-ups to the September 1, 2015, email to Kim Turner on September 2, 2015, and September 8, 2015. Kim Turner did not respond. This was the shunning part of the retaliation I received in Falsified Trails 1, 3, and 11 as examples. During the non-response, Kim Turner and whoever worked with Turner carefully crafted and polished an email to my supervisor to essentially get me to back off my FOIA request.

Kim Turner to David Wray – Friday Afternoon Polished Email Relay Tactic
(See Attachment at End of Book)

<u>September 11, 2015, 1:49 PM (Attachment Page 2 of 7)</u>: Rather than respond to my September 1, 2015, email, Turner shunned me and then crafted a polished email to David Wray (her supervisor) and copied a DCMA attorney, William Bailey Jr. The email was stamped:

"[ATTORNEY-CLIENT PRIVILEGED MATERIAL] (DO NOT DISCLOSE)"

The email to David Wray (Turner's supervisor) (Attachment Page 2 of 7) stated:

"I am forwarding the below email string from a FOIA requester, Mr. Ken Pedeleose, a DCMA Atlanta employee, to you because it raises some concerns that may need to be addressed. I am also copying

DCMA legal counsel on this message in the hope that counsel can also provide legal assistance concerning this matter.

In his September 2nd email, the requester comments "if DCMA still insists on extorting money from me," regarding the fees we estimated based on his request for approximately 6,000 pages of records. Then in his September 8th email, he states "Extorting money is not part of that framework. These e-mail exchanges prove that a cover-up is in work." Such allegations are disturbing and highly irregular from a FOIA requester.

Mr. Pedeleose's statements are not accurate and raise unsupported integrity issues. The requester even raises conflict of interest issues without any factual basis. We are continuing to follow the spirit and the letter of the law regarding application of the FOIA to his request.

As my direct supervisor, please take whatever action, if any, which you deem appropriate based upon the claims raised in the string of email messages below from Mr. Pedeleose. We will continue to process Mr. Pedeleose's FOIA request under statutory requirements.

We look forward to any input you may have on this matter."

Turner's email to Wray had the stench of a Falsified Trail, including the "Attorney-Client Privileged Material" stamp. Meaning it was written, or coached, by an attorney and was highly refined. The shunning was a DCMA tactic to enflame the situation and shift blame to me.

The Friday afternoon email "Relay" used the weekend to clear guilty consciences. Like lighting a bomb fuse and then running to gain distance, and cover, from the fallout. The email "Relay" closes the loop as follows.

David Wray's Immediate Relay to Isaih Waindi – Late Friday Lawfare

(See Attachment Near End of Book)

September 11, 2015 3:05PM (Attachment Page 1 of 7): David Wray, in short order, relayed Turner's email directly to my supervisor Isaih Waindi. Like a Relay in Baseball. A planned move to take me out stating in part.

"I am writing to make you aware of concerns raised by Ms. Kim Turner, the Freedom of Information Act (FOIA) and government information specialist who works for me, about correspondence she has received from an employee at DCMA Lockeed Martin Marietta, Mr. Ken Pedeleose. Ms. Turner has been diligently assisting Mr. Pedeleose with a complex FOIA request. His recent request for records pertaining to an investigation resulted in approximately 6,000 pages of material responsive to his request. FOIA requires that requesters pay .15 per page for the cost of providing copies of material (usually for anything more than 100 pages). The law also requires that the requester pay for the employee's time to conduct the search for the records at a rate of $44 per hour (the first two hours are free). The law does not exempt from payment a requester who may have called for the investigation, in the first place.

When informed of the cost associated with the search for and reproduction of the 6,000 pages responsive to his request, Mr. Pedeleose essentially accused Ms. Turner of attempting to extort money from him. He has repeated this charge and says he has deliberately chosen that word. I assure you that Ms. Turner is doing nothing of the sort. She is providing excellent customer service and doing so while adhering to the legal requirements of the Freedom of Information Act -- in other words, she is doing her job. As Ms. Turner's supervisor, I am unwilling let this questioning of her integrity and professionalism go unanswered. Ms. Turner is the ONLY full-time FOIA specialist at DCMA, and his is not the only complex FOIA request she has to handle.

I request that you review the email chain below and consider what action or counselling may be in order."

Wray's email to Waindi was also highly polished. Like an attorney who was writing a preemptive document in a case to impress a judge with all the necessary elements making me out a villain.

Waindi's response resembled another "Cleo Anderson Letter" as follows.

Falsified Trail 13 – Proposed 14 Day Suspension

September 30, 2015: Isaih Waindi issued a Proposed 14-day Suspension that stated in part.

"This is official notification that I propose to suspend you from your position as an Industrial Engineer, GS-0896-1 2, for fourteen (14) calendar days based on your failure to follow instructions. This action is being proposed to promote the efficiency of the service, and if sustained by the deciding official, will be effective not earlier than fourteen (14) calendar days from the date you receive this proposal notice. This proposed action is being taken in accordance with Title 5, United States Code, Chapter 75 (5 USC 75); Title 5, Code of Federal Regulations, Part 752 (5 CFR 752); the DCMA Instruction on Maintaining Discipline; and Article 29 of the Collective Bargaining Agreement between DCMA and AFGE Council 170."

The Proposed Suspension went on to state the July 27, 2015, LOWI regarding the cover-up where DCMA investigated DCMA. Waindi went on to state in part.

"On September 11, 2015, while I was out of the country on leave, an email was sent to me by David Wray, DCMA Director of Communication. Mr. Wray's email informed me of concerns elevated to him by Kim Turner, the Agency's Freedom of Information Act (FOIA) and Privacy Analyst. The email thread shows that on August 10, 2015, you initiated a FOIA request to DCMA. Ms. Turner was responsible for processing your request, and on August 17, 2015, she emailed you to explain the FOIA process and the potential cost involved in responding to your request. You responded to Ms. Turner on at 4:05 p.m. on August 17, 7:06 a.m. on August 18, and 10:11 a.m. on August 20. In your August 17 email to Ms. Turner, you wrote: "I am very disturbed on the e-mail below and blanket statements made and it seems that this is being made cost prohibitive so that I will back off." In your August 20 email to Ms. Turner, you wrote: "In the absence of a response I will conclude you are refusing to respond to my request knowing that this investigation was due to my actions and I am entitled to a copy of the documents."

Waindi went on to make Kimberly Turner out to be the victim and me out to be the aggressor. As I suspected, Cleo Anderson and DCMA HQ were involved as follows.

Cleo Anderson and Debbie Elwell: Waindi did state that Cleo Anderson and Debbie Elwell were involved in the suspension. I documented this on October 29, 2015, in a Memo for the Record when

I spoke with Mark Buckner. The involvement of Cleo Anderson is standard news in the Falsified Trails. Debbie Elwell was a newcomer in 2015.

Waindi admitted (September 30, 2015) to being "out of the country" when David Wray emailed. Meaning Waindi wouldn't have the time anyway to cherry-pick statements and write the letter.

Response to Mark Buckner Regarding Proposed 14-Day Suspension

October 19, 2015: Mark Buckner was the deciding official in the 14-day suspension, which is ironic since the cover-up was about Buckner's conflict of interest. Meaning, Buckner was in a conflict of interest deciding a conflict of interest. I stated to Mark Buckner in part.

"I had a nine page write-up that was nearing completion to send to you and then I had a second thought. This case is about your conflict of interest in that I made disclosures regarding your conflict of interest by being married to a Lockheed Martin employee (your wife Candice Buckner) while silencing me as a whistleblower and stopping my audits. The case culminated with a 23 page statement and 32 Exhibits to Mr. Scott Faucet (alleged DCMA investigator)."

"Alleged Independence (DCMA Investigating DCMA): When a DCMA alleged investigator (Mr. Scott Faucett) first contacted me, Mr. Faucett indicated he was "independent". DCMA investigating DCMA is not independent."

"Talk to Witnesses Unfamiliar With Allegations: Scott Faucett indicated he was going to talk to a lot of people in the office. Talking to people with no knowledge of facts was concerning and does not rebut my allegations."

"Handwrite Statements (Limit My Response): Scott Faucett indicated that I had to "handwrite" my statements to him. I took this as a tactic to slow me down."

"Did Not Accept My Statement -Refused to Discuss With Me: I gave Scott Faucett a 23 page type written statement and 32 exhibits proving my point about your conflict of interest and office climate. Scott Faucett originally said he would review my statement, call me back and swear me in to make the statement formal. Scott Faucett never called me back."

"Does Not Take 6,000 Pages to Verify Mark Buckner's Wife Works at LM: Any reasonable person would conclude that it does not take 6,000 Pages to determine if Mark Buckner's wife (Candice Buckner) works at Lockheed Martin."

I realized nothing I said would stop the 14-Day Suspension and I was correct.

Mark Buckner Approved the Weaponized (Retaliatory) 14-Day Suspension

October 28, 2015: Buckner approved the retaliatory 14-Day Suspension dated on October 28, 2015 although given to me on October 29, 2015. My October 29, 2015 Memo for Record stated in part as follows.

"Mr. Buckner first stated he got "assistance from GC and LER". (General Counsel and Labor Employee Relations)

I pressed the issue as to if Cleo Anderson was involved and Mr. Buckner indicated that he did not know if Cleo Anderson was involved.

I continued to press the issue and then Mr. Buckner admitted that "Debbie Elwell coordinated with Cleo Anderson".

Mr. Waindi admitted in earlier conversations that Cleo Anderson and Debbie Elwell were involved in the proposed suspension letter dated September 30, 2015."

Buckner had zero shame in covering up the investigation into his wife. DCMA thrives on conflicts of interest. However, someone or some organization recognized Buckner's conflict of interest.

Mark Buckner Removed from Position for Appearance of Conflict of Interest

November 15, 2017 – Mandatory Meeting: A meeting notice was sent out to Mark Buckner's Engineering group that read: *"MANDATORY// Engineering and Analysis Special Meeting"*

The mandatory meeting was to inform Mark Buckner's Engineering and Analysis Group that Buckner was being removed due to the appearance of a conflict of interest. My memo for the record to investigators stated in part.

"Just discovered that Mark Buckner (DCMA LMM Engineering Director, my second level supervisor) is being removed from office for conflict of interest where his wife works for Lockheed Martin at the same facility. I made a DoD IG complaint that probably assisted in that regard to finally end the Mark Buckner problem. Mark Buckner is being moved to some position at DCMA Atlanta."

I remembered during the meeting that Myra Tate (who led the Mandatory meeting) indicated that "work arounds" were discussed for Buckner. Meaning, there was a known conflict of interest.

Parallel Issue - Stopping Corrective Action Requests (CARs)

November 8, 2017: Attached to my November 15, 2017, email was a disclosure of how CARs of Lockheed Martin problems were being stopped. This was similar to Falsified Trail 4 of March 3, 2009. I went on to state in my Memo for Record in part.

"For the last few weeks Lockheed Martin (LM) has withheld information from our C5 software folks who have active software surveillance on the C-5 program. What was later discovered was that for some time LM was Withholding information from DCMA employees on the C-130 program."

"I have heard for some time (several weeks) that the commander structure in this office beginning with Ms. Tate will resist writing CARs on LM. The stated reason is that it will cause LM to spend money fixing their problems. Hence, with no CARs LM can save money although the tax payers and people who fly on aircraft produced or modified at this facility will take the risk. In simple terms, cover-up."

This was hearsay; however, it fits a DCMA systemic trend similar to Buckner. I made the aforesaid disclosure based on how disturbed my colleagues were. Notwithstanding, the story of Mark Buckner's exodus was smoothed over by the office Commander Colonel Lance French as follows.

Smoothed Over Story on Mark Buckner's Exodus

Process Development Office (PDO) Exacerbating Problems Across DCMA

November 27, 2017: Colonel French smoothed over the Buckner exodus story as follows.

"Effective 26 Nov 17, Mr. Mark Buckner assumed a position with the Process Development Office where he will be responsible for developing and maintaining functionally integrated policy for Contract Administration Services and mission processes. In his new position, he will report directly to the PDO Director and have an opportunity to engage with the agency senior leadership team to impact strategic planning and mission process improvement, in addition to developing new business capability processes, business rules, and integration with automated infrastructure tools."

Meaning, Buckner was circumstantially sidelined with stories that clashed between what Colonel French stated and what Myra Tate stated on November 15, 2017. The concerning point is Buckner was now involved in process development (PDO). This would mean that problems caused by Buckner at one facility would now be spread across DCMA.

I suspected this a cover story since on August 24, 2004 Ben Chaffman (then Deputy Commander) announced on he will be leaving to participate on a *"DCMA Product Assurance IPT"* (Integrated Product Team) to improve *"Product Assurance support to customers in the System Design and Development phase of the program life cycle."* This occurred after Substantiated Allegation 4 (July 23, 2004) where DCMA and the Air Force conditionally accepted $2.6 billion of C-130Js that did not meet commercial specifications or operational requirements.

Like Mark Buckner, Chaffman was now in a position to further exacerbate problems from just a local level to across DCMA level.

To summarize, positions with grandiose titles were potential cover stories for sidelined DCMA officials. Meaning, "Throw Under the Bus" and then put in a position to inflict further damage. This was suspicion. However, I believe that my suspicions were true, based on DCMA modus operandi and the fact that DCMA has demonstrated no ability to manage DoD contracts. In fact, DCMA cannot even manage DCMA's own contracts (Chapter 4). Regardless, I made a Memo for Record.

December 4, 2017: I made a memo for the record that stated.

"The e-mail below from Colonel French conflicts with what Ms. Myra Tate stated about Mark Buckner's removal as Engineering Director of DCMA LMM. Ms. Tate indicated on Wednesday November 15, 2017 in a special meeting that Mr. Mark Buckner was removed due to "appearance" of conflict of interest with his wife Ms. Candice Buckner who works in Lockheed Martin. Ms. Tate indicated that a disqualification letter was issued to allow Mr. Buckner to remain in his position. Essentially Mr. Buckner could not due his duties as Engineering Director."

Colonel French and Myra Tate contradicted each other, although they were in sync with the fact that Mark Buckner was leaving. Soon after that fiasco, discussions on FOIA 15-172 fiasco resumed.

Investigation Report Cover-up - FOIA 15-172 for DMR 15-0053

January 17, 2018: Received an email from the DCMA FOIA Department that stated in part.

"I am the new FOIA Analyst for the Defense Contract Management Agency (DCMA). This correspondence is in regards to the below Freedom of Information Act (FOIA) request below. Defense Contract Management Agency (DCMA) assigned control number 15-172 to your request for administrative purposes.

In good faith, DCMA conducted a search for responsive records and found a large volume of documents that may contain responsive information relating to your request. As required under the FOIA, DCMA must initiate a line-by -line review of those materials.

A significant time has passed since you first initiated and modified your FOIA request during calendar year 2015. Furthermore, lacking any other alternative, in order to substantively respond to your request, the DCMA FOIA Office would need to again undertake a significant review process for records and potential additional records pertaining to DCMA FOIA 15-172."

Excessive Cost Removed: It was noticeable that the excessive cost for the document search had suddenly disappeared. Meaning, the excessive search cost of "*12 professional hours, equaling $528 based on the 6000 pages*", was a weaponized lawfare ruse.

FOIA Submitted August 10, 2015 – Received Redacted February 26, 2018

February 26, 2018: The FOIA letter was dated February 26, 2018 and was received March 5, 2018. Attachment Pages 3 to 7 is some of the investigation report. The cover letter stated in part.

"This correspondence responds to your Freedom of Information Act (FOIA) request directed to Defense Contract Management Agency (DCMA) on August 10, 2015. You submitted your request, specifically seeking administrative records prepared as part of an investigation into allegations of criminal misconduct which purportedly occurred at the Defense Contract Management Agency, Lockheed Martin Marietta (DCMA-LMM) during the time frame of May through July, 2015. DCMA assigned control number 15-172 to your request for administrative purposes."

FOIA Received Nearly 2 ½ Years Later with Heavy Redactions – No Fee

It took about 931 days (nearly 2 ½ years) for approximately 165 pages (some duplicates) of witness statements and a 13-page investigation report for FOIA 15-172 (Mark Buckner's conflict of interest). The FOIA was from Bruce A. Cole, DCMA Director, Strategic Communication. The Attachment at the end of this book has sample FOIA Pages. There was no fee ($) charged.

The investigation was completed and signed on June 9, 2015, in a 13 Page report. The 165 Pages of witness questionnaires had handwritten answers. There was a total of 178 pages. The FOIA was heavily redacted, indicating DCMA was still worried about a simple personnel issue.

I have seen multiple investigations such as DCIS (Defense Criminal Investigative Service), DoD IG, NSA, Department of Interior (DOI) IG, EEO, and the weaponized Falsified Trail 3. Scott Faucett's alleged "investigation" fit the cover-up pattern perfectly and was highly suspect.

Faucett waited until I left the office before he (Faucett) entered. Faucett could have easily spoken with me and gone through my evidence. Instead, Faucett went behind my back. Even my colleagues saw through it when Faucett entered the office when I had left for the weaponized training.

Faucett's alleged investigation, with handwritten answers, was the worst. Even Stacy Scantlebury in Falsified Trail 3 spoke with people, asked questions, and typed statements to sign. DCMA's heavily redacted FOIA showed concern and worry about Mark Buckner's conflict of interest.

Analysis of the FOIA for Investigation Report DCMA-DMR 2015-0053

Heavily Redacted Conflict of Interest FOIA – With no $528 Fee

Pages 3 to 7 of the Attachment to this book are samples of the FOIA (15-172) Report of Investigation (DCMA-DMR Case No. 2015-0053) by Scott Faucett with the following being noted.

Heavily Redacted for a Simple Issue: The FOIA was heavily redacted for a simple issue. Meaning, the investigation of a conflict of interest with Mark Buckner overseeing his wife's work at Lockheed Martin. This is not national security sensitive or counter terrorism tactics. It's a simple local and single conflict of interest issue that the DCMA has expended significant government resources and time to cover-up.

Criminal Investigations: Page 3 of Attachment to this book stated: *"it was discovered that the U.S. Air Force Office of Special Investigations (OSI)* (Criminal Investigators) *had already set in motion a comprehensive investigative review into several audit issues involving LM* (Lockheed Martin)*."*

Meaning, criminal investigations took place. Probably due my August 31, 2013 report to Congress (disclosure) titled: "*Restoring Financial Accountability & Cost Savings in the Department of Defense.*" I did meet with investigators on this issue and was aware that DCAA forensic auditors were involved.

OSC Discussions – Run Pedeleose Down: The DCMA investigation (Page 6 of Attachment) ran me down by building up OSC, stating: *"OSC is the premier authority relevant to whistleblower retaliations."* Further stating that my complaints to OSC had been *"thoroughly examined by OSC's General Counsel (GC) and the OSC Dallas Field Office Chief."*

Chapters 2 and 3 in this book show OSC as an enabler of the Deep State and has expanded the Government Swamp. OSC would dismiss complaints without investigation. OSC and MSPB were discredited as of 2002. Meaning, this book provides transparency on the Deep State operations to overcome the DCMA's self-serving, biased, investigations, lawfare, and weaponization.

No Fee for FOIA: The most obvious part of the DCMA weaponization and lawfare is that the "*12 professional hours, equaling $528*" had suddenly disappeared and the FOIA was provided albeit nearly 2 ½ years later. I had provided no funds to DCMA since I was well aware there was weaponization and lawfare that I, at the time, referred to as retaliation and a cover-up.

November 15, 2017: There was a sudden meeting where Myra Tate explained that Mark Buckner was being removed from his position for the appearance of a conflict of interest. This further called the DCMA investigation of Mark Buckner into question.

November 27, 2017: Colonel French smoothed over the Buckner exodus story as follows.

"Effective 26 Nov 17, Mr. Mark Buckner assumed a position with the Process Development Office where he will be responsible for developing and maintaining functionally integrated policy for Contract Administration Services and mission processes."

The point is, the evidence contradicts the DCMA investigation of Mark Buckner. As is typical of DCMA, there is always an objective evidence trail proving that DCMA, as an organization, is uncredible and disingenuous. Five of the six chapters of this book are the evidentiary findings to support those conclusions. The only saving grace for DCMA is the overall U.S. Legal and Judicial System that has expanded the Government Swamp. It worked yet again for DCMA as follows.

The U.S. Legal System is Too Corrupted to Litigate Falsified Trail 13

I never pursued the second 14-day suspension (Falsified Trail 13) along with Falsified Trails 11 & 12 because of widespread institutionalized corruption in U.S.G. Prior experience and evidence prove without a doubt that "Federal Machinery" will grind up any case like a "garbage disposal" and send it down the "sewer" to the ever-expanding Government Swamp.

The incestuously corrupted U.S. Legal and Judicial System uses "Case Law" from corrupted legal decisions that have replaced law and ethics.

If Falsified Trail 13 was litigated it would have expanded the Government Swamp further by adding more weaponized case law to be used in further lawfare. Meaning, I was guaranteed a loss before I ever started. I saw zero ethics in the U.S. Legal and Judicial System and have the same opinion as I write this book.

The April 21, 2002, MPRI report on the DoD IG stated: "*Few whistleblowers now prevail before the MSPB because the governing statute, the Whistleblower Protection Act, has been steadily eroded by restrictive interpretations that make it most difficult to sustain a winning case.*"

The U.S. legal system's corruption is responsible for the Government Swamp and institutional corruption. If the U.S. Legal and Judicial System were legitimate, the Swamp and institutional corruption would not exist.

I physically received the FOIA response on/about March 5, 2018. The files were heavily redacted, so I put in an appeal for an unredacted copy, which was my original request in 2015. That email trail follows, and as usual, DCMA landed in more controversy, supporting the allegation of continued cover-ups. That evidence trail is as follows.

FOIA Appeal Cover-up

March 5, 2018 – FOIA Appeal: I stated to DCMA FOIA office (Kevin Strakal).

I received and downloaded the files.

Thank you very much for your hard work in completing this.

I will say that I must file an appeal to this FOIA because of the heavy redaction.

I understand Birth dates and places of birth however the rest of the redaction is unacceptable and I must file an appeal.

That said, I have 2 questions if you do not mind responding.

1: Do you need an explanation only of why the FOIA is unacceptable or do you want the FOIA documents attached as well in the appeal. (There are a lot of documents and I need to be sure.)

2: What specific involvement does Ms. Kim Turner (mentioned on the attached) have in this process? I thought you had replaced Ms. Turner or Ms. Turner was no longer with DCMA.

Responses to these questions are greatly appreciated.

March 6, 2018: Kevin Strakal responded, stating in part.

"I received your email, thank you. I have forwarded your appeal to the personnel who will be handling your request."

My questions were never answered. My follow-up below proves what I know about the DCMA.

Follow-up to Vice Admiral (VADM) David Lewis (Then DCMA Director)

September 25, 2018: I heard nothing on the FOIA 15-172 appeal and contacted VADM David Lewis (DCMA Director), copying David Wray, Kimberly Turner, and my local DCMA management staff. I stated in part.

"I work at DCMA LMM in Marietta, GA. Colonel Lance French is my commanding officer.

From memory you indicated when you arrived at DCMA that you need to know problems before you can fix them. While I can identify many problems at DCMA I am focusing on just one in this e-mail.

Specifically, this is a complaint regarding Freedom of Information Act (FOIA) 15-172. The FOIA involves a serious Conflict of Interest (COI) against my prior second level supervisor (Mr. Mark Buckner). Summary is as follows:"

"Mr. Buckner was married to a Lockheed Martin employee Ms. Candice Buckner. On/about some point in late 2014 Mr. Buckner was promoted to my second level supervisor. At that point Mr. Buckner began an aggressive campaign against me as a DoD whistleblower."

"During this time I continually asked how Mr. Buckner could be promoted to second level supervisor with his wife working at Lockheed Martin (same facility. I experienced over 3 years of delays and stonewalling from DCMA FOIA which is the reason for this e-mail and complaint."

"I request a complete investigation report on Mr. Buckner (the attached FOIA 15-172) with no redactions other than personal information which may include birth dates and social security numbers. I expect names and other information to remain. There was also 160 or so pages of witness statements associated with the FOIA that I need. I believe that 3 years to process a FOIA that consists of 13 pages along with 160 or so pages of witness statements is concerning and is registered as a complaint against the DCMA FOIA office. Three years is excessive."

September 26, 2018: David Wray responded, stating in part:

"I am Ms. Turner's supervisor. I am also the DCMA Initial Denial Authority for FOIA requests. I am responding for the director in that capacity.

I have to agree with you that three years is too long to take to reply to a FOIA request."

"I have full faith and confidence in Ms. Turner, who is a FOIA expert and now serves as DCMA FOIA Officer, and her staff to process Agency FOIA requests as effectively and efficiently as possible given constrained resources and the volume and complexity of requests we receive."

"Having filed the initial complaint against Mr. Buckner does not make this part of your job performance. Consequently, you should be using your personal email for FOIA-related inquiries and I have copied your personal email on this reply. In the future, the DCMA FOIA office will only reply to you at your personal email. The DoD FOIA office has instructed all agencies to enforce this policy."

After 10+ Years (Decade) & Still No FOIA 15-172 for DMR 15-0053

No FOIA response has been received as of early 2026. I doubt I will ever get a response since FOIA 15-172 for investigative report DMR 15-0053 centers on DCMA investigating DCMA, and now DCMA must report on how DCMA investigated DCMA, most notably after Mark Buckner was removed for the appearance of a conflict of interest. This is why I added the FOIA process as part of weaponized government and lawfare. Meaning, FOIA covers-up facts so that no true or accurate conclusions can be reached. An added weapon of the "Federal Machinery" lawfare.

An unredacted FOIA (investigation report) would have cleaned up the issue once and for all.

The aforesaid FOIA debacle aftermath surfaced on January 17, 2018. However, my security clearance was revoked nearly a week earlier. This was too much of a coincidence for my liking.

Security Clearance Revoked – January 9, 2018

January 9, 2018: The Consolidated Adjudication Facility (CAF) (DoD security clearances) issued me a letter through DCMA stating in part:

"*...a preliminary decision has been made by the Department of Defense (DoD) Consolidated Adjudications Facility (CAF) to revoke your eligibility for access to classified information and/or assignment of duties that have been designated national security sensitive.*"

I received the January 9, 2018, letter on/January 22, 2018 by Colonel Lance French personally.

From January 22, 2018, to about April 22, 2018, I responded to the security clearance revocation from CAF. This was termed a Statement of Reasons (SOR) why my security clearance should be restored. I prepared the SOR in two parts as follows.

Part 1 - Statement of Reasons (SOR) – 83 Page Report

April 23, 2018: I responded with an 83 Page report titled: *"Response to Mitigate CAF Statement of Reasons (SOR) Standalone Report For: Kenneth M. Pedeleose"*. The 83 Page report was the rough outline for this book. Even with extensions, there was limited time to respond based on the volume of false allegations, lawfare, and retaliations against me.

Part 2 – Ten (10) Attachments/Artifacts, Two Character References

April 23, 2018: The attachments focus on the DoD campaign against whistleblowers and transition to positive statements about me, awards, me being a Subject Matter Expert (SME), etc. Attachments are as follows and include multiple documents/artifacts in many cases.

Attachment 1: Anti-Whistleblower Climate (1 Page write-up, 13 Pages support documents)

Attachment 2: Well-Known Whistleblower (1 Page write-up, 28 Pages news media articles)

Attachment 3: Character References as Subject Matter Expert (SME) for investigations. Letters, emails, and notes regarding my support for investigations. (1 Page writeup, 9 support documents)

Attachment 4: Charleston Naval Shipyard (CNSY) Awards (1 page write-up, 20 pages of awards)

Attachment 5: Asked for/Mentioned By Name (1 Page writeup, 9 Pages support documents)

Attachment 6: Sustained High Performance Ratings at DCMA (1 Page writeup, 17 Pages of Performance Ratings)

Attachment 7: DCMA Multiple Historic/Cash Awards (1 Page write-up, 32 pages of awards)

Attachment 8: Instructor/SME at DCMA (1 page write-up, 24 support documents)

Attachment 9: Supreme Court Case 2009-780 response to Falsified Trail 3

Attachment 10: Congressional Report "Cover-up In the Department of Defense" May 16, 2005, 52 Pages

Character References: There were two-character references for me personally, although many of the attachments were documents of my positive character, and accomplishments.

The main SOR and attachments were dated April 23, 2018 although the attachments had multiple dates over decades of my positive performance.

Security Clearances Unaffected After Falsified Trails Proved as Bogus

2014: There were prior instances where my security clearance was investigated but not revoked. This occurred in early 2014 with letters dated January 28, 2014; April 8, 2014; May 27, 2014. By 2014 Falsified Trails 1–10 was already "fired" at me. I kept my security clearance by proving the Falsified Trails as bogus information. This was in a personal interview with an OPM investigator.

The process was started again after Volley 4 of the Falsified Trails. The end result proves that the Falsified Trails were nothing but attempts to execute my reputation. Weaponization and lawfare by more simple terms.

Security Clearance Reinstated – June 27, 2019

June 27, 2019 – Letter 1: My security clearance was reinstated with the following stated in part.

"The attached letter to the above named Subject advises of the final determination by the Department of Defense, Consolidated Adjudications Facility (DoD CAF) regarding the Subject's security clearance and eligibility to occupy a national security sensitive position. Mr. Kenneth M. Pedeleose has been granted clearance eligibility, effective June 27, 2019."

June 27, 2019 – Letter 2: A second letter stated the following:

"The DoD CAF reviewed and considered Mr. Pedeleose's response to the Statement of Reasons (SOR), dated April 23, 2018. Although the DoD CAF acknowledges that Mr. Pedeleose made allegations of whistleblower retaliation in his response to the SOR, the adjudication of Mr. Pedeleose's eligibility was based solely on the evaluation of security eligibility criteria. The DoD CAF was unable to resolve his claims of reprisal for whistleblowing because the DoD CAF did not have complete report of the investigation concerning the alleged whistleblowing and retaliation. Therefore, the DoD CAF could not make a reasonable determination that retaliation for whistleblowing played any role in the proposed adverse security action."

I successfully repelled the DCMA lawfare and weaponized government. Meaning, the Falsified Trails were just that: a bunch of lawfare, distorted and falsified information. The goal was met. I understand the CAF could not determine if the revocation of my security clearance was retaliation.

Reinstatement of my security clearance was just as rewarding, in addition to the fact that I was a DCMA SME about a year before my security clearance was revoked.

Subject Matter Expert (SME) As of February 27, 2017

It should be obvious in this book that DCMA deteriorated and atrophied due to institutional corruption. Meaning, cover-ups were DCMA's mainstay. The end result was DCMA HQ reaching out to the field personnel for assistance when it came time for actual work to be accomplished.

January 20, 2017 10:36 AM – Initial Letter: DCMA sent out an email to DCMA Engineering & Analysis (E&A) teams that stated in part.

"We have received a HQ request for assistance in developing the ENGR233 - Technical Support to Indirect Costs (TSI) Workshop (Overhead Cost Analysis)*, to launch in Q4FY17. The intent is for HQ to teach up to four (4) ENGR 233 classes. After CY18, HQ probably will teach one or 2 classes annually, depending on the demand.*

Although HQ has received a good amount of TSI artifacts from the field last year, they still need help defining the TSI process and the associated artifacts for the workshop; especially in these areas:

Reviewing the FPRP Business Bases

Reviewing CERs (Cost Estimating Relationships)

Reviewing IR&D project listings (Independent Research & Development)

Obtaining additional contractor information needed to complete the analysis

Evaluating the data to come up with recommendations

"HQ is seeking five (5) SMEs to attend a week-long ENGR233 Course Development event, scheduled for the week of 27 Feb 2017 with travel days on Sunday, 26 Feb and Friday, 3 Mar (will finish at noon)."

The aforesaid processes were standard DCMA practice when I arrived in 1994. Over the years, DCMA deteriorated to the point where the TSI skills were lost. I recall one DCMA Management Review Team (MRT) visit on/about 2013 to 2014 was surprised I had the aforesaid skills in TSI.

January 20, 2017 10:38 AM – "Send Ken": Mark Buckner, with all the alleged and falsified negative allegations about me, contacted my then first-level supervisor 2 minutes later and stated.

"I want to send Ken with the expectation that he will bring back a trip report.
What say you?"

My supervisor approached me, explained the situation, and indicated that I could take a few days and think about the new assignment. I immediately said I did not need a few days and to please submit my name.

I filled out the necessary questions and forwarded the response on January 24, 2017.

January 25, 2017 – Accepted as SME for Course Development: The following day I was selected as one of five SMEs throughout the entire DCMA organization. The email stated in part.

"Thank you so much for volunteering to support the Engineering Division (TDE) with the course development of ENGR233. We've submitted your names to Workforce Development to make arrangements for your travel orders."

February 27 – March 3, 2017 Designated SME: After the first meeting to write the TSI course, I was provided a certificate for being an SME that stated in part.

"For your exceptional support as a Subject Matter Expert (SME) developing the Technical Support to Indirect Costs (TSI) Workshop, Feb 27 -Mar 3,2017. Your expertise and insight into the TSI process and technical analysis will significantly contribute to the success of this workshop. This innovative course will provide real-world scenarios that the Technical Specialist will encounter."

Asked to Teach Course on Direct Cost Analysis

On the last day of the first visit, I was asked to also teach the course on direct cost analysis that was titled Technical Support to Negotiations (TSN), also termed Technical Pricing Support (TPS). Meaning, I was a SME for Indirect (Overhead) Cost Analysis and Direct Cost Analysis.

SME Instructor from 2017 – Retirement in 2020

I remained an SME instructor from 2017 to retirement (end of 2020). In mid-2019, DCMA began discussions to transfer the TSN course (Direct Cost Analysis) to Defense Acquisition University (DAU). Even prior to that point, I saw a deterioration in the TSN training to the point where I was glad, I was self-taught. Meaning, the course deteriorated from what I was teaching and what I thought should be taught.

SME Artifacts of Success

April 23, 2018: My success as an SME, which doubles as character references/artifacts, can be found in Attachment 8 of my SOR for security clearance.

February 27, 2017 - Travel Artifacts: My first travel orders as an SME were for the February 27, 2017, development for the TSI class (submitted February 8, 2017). Other travel orders through 2019 were in that package. Courses were starting to go online, most notably after COVID in 2020.

Being an SME contradicted DCMA's claim of me being a problem and greatly enhanced the reinstatement of my security clearance. Being an SME further substantiates that I can technically prove what I am saying. However, even as an SME DCMA continued to retaliate, as I was denied even a temporary promotion.

Denial of Temporary Promotion - November 20, 2018

In 2018, a temporary promotion opened that was a perfect match for my skills. Meaning, I was an SME teaching a lot of what the temporary promotion covered. The other duties were also within my skill set because I had mapped and studied the safety and development issues on the C-130J and the development issues on the C-5 program. I worked on C-130 and C-5 programs at various times starting in 1994.

The selecting official for the temporary promotion was Jason Rawson, who replaced Mark Buckner. Apparently, Rawson was selected by Myra Tate. Rawson may have been previously promoted to a project that eventually failed, known as the Integrated Workload Management System (IWMS) (a way to electronically manage contracts). IWMS is outlined in Chapter 4 of this book as a DCMA debacle where it was noted that DCMA could not manage DCMA contracts.

The timeline for denial of the promotion is as follows.

Rawson's Excuses to Deny Temporary Promotion

September 18-19, 2018 – Rawson's Security Clearance Excuse: One of Rawson's excuses for potential denial of a temporary promotion was due to my security clearance, which I was working to reinstate. I sent an email to Colonel French (then commander) to try and get clarification. I stated to Colonel French, copy to my supervisor Richard Bolden, and Myra Tate the following in part.

"I just finished meeting with Mr. Rawson. We had a productive discussion about the lead position that may be available.

During our discussion Mr. Rawson mentioned that the pending security clearance investigation that you and I spoke about earlier this year (January 2018) may have a negative effect on me being selected for even a temporary lead position.

My question to you is, will the pending security investigation preclude me from being selected to the lead position for ALEA if it comes available?

I ask because the impression I got from Mr. Rawson is that I will be at odds to DCMA meaning DCMA has issued several adverse actions against me and as such it will be going against DCMAs position of me if I am selected for the lead position.

Put another way, DCMA has spent quite the effort demonizing my reputation and now if I get promoted to even a temporary position that would make DCMA look "two faced" for lack of more pleasant terms and undermine all the work DCMA has placed in demonizing me."

I cannot recall if Colonel French ever gave a response. Rawson gave the excuse of leadership at another point that I can remember. It was obvious Rawson was not interested in my credentials. Only denying me even a temporary promotion. Regardless, I provided my resume, which was toned down from Chapter 1 of this book.

Resume to Jason Rawson

<u>November 5, 2018 8:41AM</u>: I sent my resume to Rawson. There were actually two temporary promotions and I more strongly applied for the one on my team where I was a SME. My resume was unique in that I combined EVMS, TSN, TSI, and aircraft issues in one package. Meaning my resume covered a wide universe of tasks, including being an SME.

Rawson acknowledged receipt of my resume at 9:32 AM (same day) and stated in part.

"Our prior discussion still stands regarding the security investigation being a potentially prohibitive factor for promotion opportunities. Let me know if there's more you'd like to discuss with me regarding that, though a discussion with the Commander might be in order."

I responded back to Rawson at 10:36 AM (same day), stating in part.

"In your e-mail below you indicated "potentially prohibitive factor". "Potentially" does not indicate an absolute certainty.

I also ask, who was your source for indicating "potentially prohibitive factor" in addition to specific law, rule, or regulation."

Email to DCMA Director Vice Admiral (VADM) David Lewis

<u>November 6, 2018 8:32 AM</u>: I sent a lengthy email to DCMA Director VADM David Lewis asking about the security clearance since locally I could not get answers. The usual shunning and non-response took place locally. I copied my chain of command and union officials on the email.

<u>November 15, 2018, 11:03 AM</u>: I got an email back from Hugh Wiley, who was DCMA's Director of Security and Counterintelligence, that stated in part.

"Until such a decision is rendered, from a security perspective, you currently retain the same rights and privileges as any other DCMA employee when applying for positions with the Federal Government. Should you apply and be selected for another position within DCMA, you will be required to meet the security eligibility requirements of the new position prior to appointment."

No Need for Secret Security Clearance Anyway

Throughout my entire Federal Career, there was only one time I had a need for a security clearance. That was at the Charleston Naval Shipyard, where I had to review a document that was labeled "Confidential." That would have been well before 1994. At DCMA, I have never had the need for a Secret clearance. Meaning, the money and time spent on the Secret clearance were wasted.

I cannot explain why I had or needed a secret clearance. Regardless, I was not selected for even a temporary promotion.

Jason Rawson Announces Selectees

November 20, 2018 12:28PM: Jason Rawson announced the selectees for the temporary promotion. I was not selected. However, Rawson met with me prior to the announcement and I did a Memo for Record as follows.

November 20, 2018 12:41PM Memo for Record: I documented the Memo for Record as follows.

"At about a little before 1200 noon today (November 20, 2018) Jason Rawson came over to talk to me and indicated that I would not be considered for the 2 lead positions (GS13) on the Engineering staff. I indicated that may not be bad and that it would keep me out of close proximity from him (Jason) and management. Close proximity to management staff would make it easier for me to be fired."

"I told Jason that I did not believe him in his motivation or reasoning. Jason indicated that I was the only one he was talking to personally. Jason indicated that my security clearance issues were not a factor. Jason indicated that he spoke with Cleo Anderson about my security clearance."

"Jason indicated that he was concerned about me thinking my colleagues needed improvement. (The conversation we had a few weeks ago was about how Richard Bolden said he had to shadow some on his team to see what they were doing. Jason indicated that Richard Bolden stated that to him as well.) I indicated that those were my comments to him and that I was an Agency SME working with DCMA HQ, DAU, and training several persons at the Agency."

It may have been for the best that I was not selected because management wants to be surrounded by a certain type of employee, which leads to the following.

Comments from Those Temporarily Promoted

When Jason Rawson announced who was promoted, I struggled for words to diplomatically explain that nothing had changed at DCMA. One of the lead engineers promoted provided revealing e-mail communications that put my feelings into words and proved my point as follows. The engineer that was temporarily promoted stated the following in two emails.

November 29, 2018: "*There are certain subjects that I never had a chance to work with before, so I would like to learn from our SMEs, please help me out. Please, include me in your email communication in the projects you're working on, so I can be up to speed of what's going on.*"

December 11, 2018: "*As a lead engineer, I'd like to know what's going on. That way I can fill up my management with updates whenever they have any TSN related questions. However, I just want to make it clear that I'll be just monitoring and provide any inputs whenever and wherever suitable. I still leave the work and decisions to my SMEs.*"

Meaning, lead engineers update management. At DCMA, I have seen no value or benefit from lead engineers. Most notably, I was an SME teaching the subjects that the so-called "Lead Engineers" should have been teaching. Same for DCMA HQ, which went to the field for SMEs.

Fear & Avoid Close Proximity

I abandoned hope and pursuit of future promotions and started on retirement. Talking to DCMA management was like talking to a mafia boss who had the system bought off. I figured that if I ever got a promotion, I would be retaliated against and quickly fired. I needed to confirm that DCMA was as corrupted as I thought it was. On November 26, 2018, I made one last attempt to see if DCMA had any shred of integrity left.

Does DCMA Have Any Integrity Left

November 26, 2018, 9:12AM – Email to DCMA Director: I emailed DCMA Director VADM David Lewis without copying anyone else. That meant if anyone else responded, I would know VADM Lewis forwarded my message. Prior to that point, VADM Lewis indicated interest in fixing DCMA, so I wanted to see if Lewis was sincere. I stated in part.

"*Past DCMA Directors have done nothing to stop the retaliations and as it appears nothing will be happening anytime soon, if ever.*

The past 2 months, which involved conversations with Mr. Rawson who is acting on DCMA's behalf, have proved to me that DCMA has not forgot or forgiven my past whistleblowing to members of Congress.

There was a temporary GS-13 position (attached) that I am a DCMA Subject Matter Expert (SME) for. I was denied even a temporary promotion even though I am a DCMA SME.

Stated another way, my fear is that if I put in for the positions below I will be retaliated against most definitely if I get the positions.

I am highly disappointed that I have to feel this way about DCMA and even more disappointed that DCMA is not producing a constructive work environment without fear of reprisals."

VADM Lewis responded at 10:03AM (same day) with the following statement.

"*If you want to apply for the open positions, do so. Only you are holding yourself back from making the application.*

I do not (cannot) respond to e-mails from employees on issues that are under active investigation or complaint."

Seems the Director was aware of my situation. Meaning, an extension of Keith Ernst (past DCMA Director) although VADM Lewis at least responded to me, adding to my cache of data.

"House Party" Attitude

The DCMA is a perpetual "House Party" for corruption and cronies, and a "House Party" to increase retirement salary. DCMA management provided the evidence for that analogy and the DCMA management behavior provided the evidence for this book. Overall, I was not sorry to see any DCMA Director, DCMA Commander, DCMA Deputy Director or DCMA Deputy Commander leave. I had no trust in any DCMA management official from the second level supervisor upward. First level supervisors' integrity and trust were on a case-by-case basis. I was fed up with DCMA as follows.

Personal Request to Supervisor

November 26, 2018: I made the following personal request to my supervisor stated in part.

"*I respectfully request that you please not ask me to train locally in front of a group here at DCMA LMM. That is in our local office. Not even our team.*"

"*To be even more blunt I am not angry I just believe that the promotions below are essentially a "spit" in my face and to go in front of a group after that experience is humiliating to me.*"

"*I know the reason I did not get the promotion and not one was related to my credentials, leadership, or professionalism.*"

"*I also have no intentions of putting in for the positions recently announced. No sense in getting "spit" on twice or leaving myself open for more adverse actions if I am accepted.*"

The additional "spit" in my face came from the fact that one of those promoted, I actually had to help issue a report. That is documented on February 4, 2016, and March 8, 2016. In effect, I had a prior trainee promoted over me for retaliatory reasons against me. Jason Rawson was of the age where Rawson could have been my son. All of this lends credence to the following.

Conclusion & Extrapolate for National Debt (Chapter 4)

The 13 Falsified Trials against me spanned over a decade, 2003 – 2015. Ernie Fitzgerald indicated that he had to battle the Pentagon for 35 years (1970 (fired by Nixon) to 2005 (forced out)). As noted herein, Fitzgerald was in Time Magazine on October 17, 2005, talking about his eviscerated position, and I received a proposed 30-day suspension the following day (October 18, 2005).

The point being, the DoD vendettas on behalf of the military-industrial complex are not short-lived. The DoD 35-year vendetta against Ernie Fitzgerald proved that. My situation is analogous to Fitzgerald's, although on a smaller scale in the DoD military-industrial complex. DoD vendettas are enabled by a corrupted government, meaning the Cerberus analogy of OSC, MSPB, and OPM supported by DOJ. I have lost all confidence in the U.S. Justice and so-called "Legal System."

Extrapolation to National Debt: It is highly plausible, knowing the roots of corruption back to 1970, with what is mentioned herein, other news media articles not documented herein, etc., that all the national debt can be extrapolated from 1970 to now.

Meaning, my resume success (Chapter 1); the generalized ill behavior of Government "Oversight" organizations (weaponized government and lawfare) (Chapter 2); and the actual retaliatory and specific practices of DoD and DCMA (weaponization and lawfare) (Chapter 3) can be extrapolated to the national debt.

Meaning, Chapter 1, Chapter 2, and Chapter 3 are the precursors to the national debt due to corrupted management, gross mismanagement, waste, fraud, abuse of authority, weaponization, lawfare, cover-ups, and lack of corrective action.

Chapter 4 follows…

CHAPTER 4: Cost of Weaponized Government & Lawfare

Based on evidence and extrapolation herein, a conservative estimate is that 30%-50% of the national debt can be attributed to the Deep State, "Federal Machinery", Cerberus analogy (OSC, MSPB, OPM), and the military-industrial complex using Lawfare. Meaning, I was stifled from really going after price gouging to allow affordable equipment and parts to the U.S. Military.

The trail to understanding the 30% - 50% estimate starts with the original military-industrial complex scam that weaponized commercial price gouging.

Commercial Designation 50%-100% Price Increase

The military-industrial complex understood that Federal Acquisition Regulations (FAR) processes protected government efficiency and taxpayer interests. To skirt FAR safeguards, the military-industrial complex "streamlined" a scam within FAR that weaponized and enabled price gouging. To understand this "streamline" scam, it is necessary to understand the difference between commercial acquisition and traditional acquisition as follows.

Commercial Pricing Analysis (Public Transparency) FAR Part 12: Commercial purchases of goods and services fall under FAR 12. Meaning, price reasonableness (protecting taxpayers) is based on publicly available information about the goods and services. Price is what the public pays or what the market price is. FAR Part 15 determines price reasonableness differently.

Traditional (DoD) Cost Transparency FAR 15: Specialized military equipment has no public price trail and falls under FAR Part 15. DoD analyzes certified cost and pricing data to determine the contractor's cost of goods and services being proposed and then develops a price that includes a fair profit, contractor allowable cost, and applicable rates and factors. The current name is Truthful Cost or Pricing Data Act, previously called Truth in Negotiation Act (TINA).

Meaning, DoD uses contractor data to determine the cost that the contractor incurs to produce goods and services, and then adds a fair profit atop that cost, along with DoD audited rates and factors, to determine the final price. I was involved in that process for approximately 26 ½ years.

The end of Chapter 3 of this book explained how I was an SME in TSN and TSI. Meaning, I was well-versed in the intricate internal analysis of contractor data for both direct and indirect costs. Within the cost analysis for FAR 15 is the intricate fact that DoD, in a way, "adopts" defense contractors and compensates for losses by DoD contractors. A brief explanation is as follows.

"Adopt" Defense Contractors: The "adoption" point involves DoD contractors having all their corporate costs covered in exchange for providing certified cost and pricing data and being truthful about it under the law. One example of "adoption" fallout occurred during 2003.

April 22, 2003 - "Adoption Fallout": During 2003, there was a stock market decline, and as such, Lockheed Martin corporate pension plans were no longer overfunded. Lockheed Martin had to contribute to their pension plan as required by law, and the cost was passed to the U.S. Government. In this case $454,725,000 additional was spread over Lockheed Martin DoD contracts, such as C-130, C-5, F-22, F-16, F-35, F-117, etc., that the U.S. Government (taxpayers) had to pay.

The "adoption" and FAR all fit into an intricate DoD cost and pricing process that the military-industrial complex and Deep State would circumvent, to a chain reaction of price gouging.

Deep State Interference to Government Efficiency & Transparency

(Everything is Interlinked – Chain Reactions to Interference)

Chapter 4 thus far summarizes the intricate and internal path to government efficiency and affordability that determines the actual cost of DoD contractors to produce military equipment, goods, and services. Meaning, transparency to contractor data.

Chapters 1, 2, & 3 show how the Deep State, Federal Machinery, Cerberus analogy (OSC, MSPB, OPM), and military-industrial complex did everything from the "foot in the aisle" trip-ups to direct interference to stop me and enable price gouging against the taxpayers.

Weaving all this together, Lockheed Martin is loosely speaking "adopted" by the U.S. Government under FAR 15. Meaning, the Government has access to Lockheed Martin data to develop fair and reasonable prices via transparency. This access controls price gouging and provides cost transparency. To circumvent FAR 15 the military-industrial complex enacted a "streamlining" scheme, under Acquisition Reform (Federal Acquisition Streamlining Act (FASA), that would enhance price gouging, and no cost transparency, using FAR 12.

The overall point being, the military-industrial complex made the Lockheed Martin C-130J a FAR 12 (commercial acquisition) and allowed Lockheed Martin to remain "adopted" by the U.S. Government. Meaning, it was a win-win for Lockheed Martin, with the price-gouging amenities and cover of FAR 12, knowing the C-130J was not available in the public marketplace, and with the "adoption" safety net of FAR 15.

This is a perfect fit knowing the covert antics of the military-industrial complex and the history since the Nixon Administration of the 1970s. This book explains that in detail.

The following case study shows the military-industrial complex knew early on that the Lockheed Martin C-130J was doomed to failure from multiple points. The military-industrial complex fed false stories to the public about C-130J success while the C-130J, and Lockheed Martin, was deteriorating behind the scenes.

Exposing this cover-up triggered Falsified Trail 3 against me that was tactically well organized and staffed with 20 government attorneys and 7 senior government officials. Falsified Trails 1 & 2 were not well organized although were the precursors to Falsified Trail 3 for similar reasons.

The C-130J Case Study follows.

C-130J Case Study – Weaponizing Commercial Price Gouging

50% to 100% Price Increase – Defund Oversight

The Lockheed Martin C-130J timeline begins with the weaponization of the acquisition process.

Federal Acquisition Streamlining Act (FASA) of 1994: The major DoD opportunity to enable cover-ups and price gouging began with acquisition reform, or more specifically, FASA. FASA was touted to decrease acquisition costs through streamlining, innovation and teaming. However, FASA actually enabled mismanagement, price gouging, and cover-ups due to reduced transparency.

Meaning, rules cannot be broken if there are no rules to begin with. FASA eliminated rules through streamlining and green-lighted corruption. The C-130J was a product of FASA.

In 1994, Lockheed Martin proposed the C-130J as a commercial program under FASA without pre-arranged customers. By being commercial (FAR Part 12), Lockheed Martin did not have to provide certified cost or pricing data as would have been required under FAR Part 15.

Defund Oversight and Remove Transparency: The C130J commercial venture was somewhat analogous to the defund police movement in that the contract was streamlined to remove detailed oversight that would have occurred under FAR Part 15. Meaning, minimal money is saved on oversight (eliminate transparency), while billions of dollars were expended without oversight. Worse yet, DoD was aware that the C-130J commercial venture was doomed from the start.

DoD Was Aware C-130J was a Risk - Would Fail – "Draft" Report Issued

June 3, 1994 (C-130J 1994 Pentagon Draft Report): A Pentagon C-130J Draft report outlined concerns with the C-130J program even prior to development. The report was a "Draft" because the "Draft" designation in DoD was a cover-up technique. Meaning, no formal documentation is kept. Like it never happened. Some excerpts are as follows:

Overoptimistic Development Projections: The Pentagon report stated, *"development cost for the C-130J appears to be overly optimistic at $350 million."* There were two factors that led to this conclusion, including "*aggressive flight test schedule*" and "*insufficient manpower loading*". The Pentagon report stated the "*development of the C-130J could be as high as $538 million.*"

The Pentagon report also noted Lockheed Martin planned to "*charge development costs over and above the stated $350 million to Independent Research and Development (IR&D). Charging these costs to IR&D would increase overhead rates applicable to future government contracts.*" The following briefly explains what IR&D is and IR&D financial ramifications.

IR&D Benefit for DoD Contractors: IR&D allows DoD contractors to research, develop, and financially charge development costs for new innovative processes and products, to overhead accounts, that will have benefit to U.S. Government. This is a benefit of DoD "adopting" defense contractors. However, Lockheed Martin went commercial (private venture) on the C-130J.

In short, Lockheed Martin planned to transfer the cost of a private C-130J commercial development to other Lockheed Martin DoD contracts, including C-5, F-22, and other Lockheed Martin DoD contracts. The analogy would be Boeing developing the commercial Dreamliner aircraft and charging the development cost to the military C-17 aircraft overhead cost.

DoD was also aware that Lockheed Martin had no development plan for the C-130J.

No Development Plan – Level of Effort (LOE): The Pentagon knew approximately 34 percent of "*C-130J cost accounts are measured using the level of effort (LOE) earned value method. This type of LOE is most directly related to passage of time and is not a good indicator of actual performance.*"

Meaning, put people in a room for a given amount of time and hope everything works out.

Flight Test Program: Lockheed Martin "*proposed 946 hour flight test program*" and later stated "*an additional 778 hours of flight testing may be required.*" In addition, the Pentagon stated:

"*Four recent commercial programs which incorporated new engines, integrated avionics, and glass cockpits averaged 1636 flight test hours.*"

"*Federal Aviation Administration (FAA) requirements have added approximately 25,000 lines of code to the software development effort. This software in currently in the requirements analysis phase while the remaining software has just begun prototype coding. These facts will extend the software development effort at least five months.*"

DoD was well aware that the commercial C-130J was projected to fail based on initial evidence and when compared to other commercial programs. The development cost estimates further reinforced the potential failure of the C-130J.

Development Cost Estimates: Lockheed Martin manhour (MH) estimates for the C-130J project development were all the same for minimum, most likely, and maximum at 1,667,000 MH. The DoD estimates (possibly done by the DCMA) were listed as 2,246,811 MH (minimum), 3,495,267 MH (most likely), and 4,308,633 MH (maximum). This was an indication of potential cost overruns. This was even before the C-130J model specifications were analyzed.

March 22, 1995 – "Carte Blanche" C-130J Model Specifications: The following details a review of the C-130J drawings. The comment was stated in part by a then-DCMA supervisor.

"*I have reviewed the C-130J Model Spec (ER/S-7100M/J-0l, 12 Dec 94) as requested by Col. Boylan at a previous staff meeting and have highlighted the following "holes" that I feel give the contractor carte blanche:*"

"*First, the spec does not invoke a top drawing. And, therefore, does not invoke the airplane drawing tree. So, we cannot go by drawings or the referenced specifications - commercial or otherwise - to make a conformance determination. A complete airplane specification should invoke the top airplane drawing and all the referenced drawings and specifications.*"

"*Workmanship requirement is described in ambiguous terms that are subject to interpretation.*"

"*Maintenance and Repair requirements are acknowledged, but neither specified nor guaranteed.*"

The C-130J was controversial from the start, and Lockheed Martin's ethics compounded the issue.

June 30, 1995 - Plead Guilty and Still Denies Access to Records: Lockheed Martin pleaded guilty to conspiring to violate the Foreign Corrupt Practices Act by making payments to a foreign government official and by knowingly falsifying books and records.

To prove trustworthiness, Lockheed Martin agreed to allow Access to Records as part of an Administrative Agreement; however, it continually denied access to C-130J records as the DCMA management stood idly by. Some Quotes from the Administrative Agreement are as follows:

"*On January 27, 1995, in the United States District Court for the Northern District of Georgia, Lockheed entered into a Plea Agreement and pleaded guilty to conspiring to violate the Foreign Corrupt Practices Act by making payments to a foreign government official and by knowingly falsifying books and records regarding the government official's status as a consultant...The court sentenced Lockheed to a criminal fine of $21,800,000. The Plea Agreement specifically acknowledged that Lockheed fully cooperated with the government during the course of the investigation.*"

The Plea Agreement also had a specific section titled "Access to Records," which states in part.

"*In addition to any other right the Air Force may have by statute, regulation, or contract, the Air Force or its duly authorized representative may examine Lockheed Martin's books, records, and other company documents and supporting materials for the purpose of verifying and evaluating: (a) Lockheed Martin's compliance with the terms of this agreement; (b) Lockheed Martin's business conduct in its dealings with all of its customers, including the Government; (c) Lockheed Martin's compliance with Federal laws, regulations, and procurement policies and with accepted business practices; and (d) Lockheed Martin's compliance with the requirements of Government contracts or subcontracts.*"

Regardless, Lockheed Martin denied access to records under the guise of C-130J commerciality and the government did not enforce access to records. C-130J commerciality was a perfect weapon, and based on the government pushing C-130J commerciality, it was a deliberate weapon as follows.

September 19, 1995 - C-130J Made Commercial: The C-130J was made commercial, about 2 ½ months after Lockheed Martin pleaded guilty to conspiring to violate the Foreign Corrupt Practices Act. The C-130J was designated a Commercial Program even though it was not available in the commercial marketplace. This enabled Lockheed Martin to legally conceal data and have no transparency into their contracting and development issues.

DoD (Paul G. Kaminski, Under Secretary of Defense, Acquisition and Technology) made the C-130J commercial under the guise of acquisition reform.

Price Escalation 50% - 100%

C-130J commercialization was supposed to save money, but it dramatically escalated in price. The following chart was copied from the May 16, 2005, report to Congress and shows the C-130J price escalation as follows.

C-130H 1995-1996:	$30.160 Million
C-130J (First aircraft October 1995):	$33.9 Million

C-130J (October 9, 1996, FY 96 – FY 01 Contract): $44.2 Million - $57.8 Million

C-130J (December 22, 2000): $59.6 Million - $63.9 Million

C-130J (March 14, 2003 Contract) $66.5 Million - $69.9 Million

Note: The June 3, 1994, report stated: "*$350 million would be amortized over the first 120 aircraft ($2.9 million per aircraft)*". Meaning, $2.9 Million per aircraft does not double cost.

"One Page Catalog"

August 8, 1996: Under a commercial contract, Lockheed Martin was required to have a catalog of prices. Lockheed Martin met this requirement by writing the C-130J price on a single sheet of paper. This was known as a "One Page Catalog," and one such "catalog" had C-130J prices of $51.6 - $53.9 million each. This seemed a mockery of the commercialization process that was further propagated by the government's proposed and unsupportable C-130J savings.

Proposed C-130J Savings – "Gross Exaggerations and Distortions of Facts"

July 17, 1997: The Divisional Administrative Contracting Officer (DACO) described the C-130J proposed savings as follows:

"*The great bulk of the "would cost" data presented by Mr. Taylor is the product of fantasy and invention, utterly unsupportable. Worse, I think Mr. Taylor's calculations represent a purposeful and self-serving attempt to deceive the Air Force, the Department of Defense, and the public regarding the merits of the C-130J acquisition... These numbers, however, represent gross exaggerations and distortions of fact*".

The May 16, 2005, report to Congress documented the estimated savings deterioration over time.

December 1995: $15 billion in estimated savings.

September 16, 1996: $7.357 billion in estimated savings.

July 16, 1997: $3.5 billion in estimated savings.

One available draft analysis dated July 16, 1997 (related to the July 17, 1997 report) stated in part:

"*My staff, as well as DCAA, feels this savings estimate is grossly overstated, and the "Would Cost Approach" used to substantiate this position misrepresents the savings the US Government will achieve through the application of commercial practices.*"

Most notable is the fact that the Air Force indicated $2,400,000 in Development Cost Savings while Lockheed Martin claimed $900 million for development costs, further noting.

"*The proposed savings to the Government of $2.4 billion cannot be substantiated. We have been provided information by LMASC* (Lockheed Martin) *showing an estimate of $900 million for development; however, this information cannot be confirmed since the contractor is no longer required to submit cost and pricing data on a commercial contract.*"

Also noted was Testing Cost Savings of $1,149,300,000, which stated:

"*The Testing Savings you identified was based on using Air Force historical costs associated with various Aircraft Development and Production Programs (i.e. C-17, C-141, etc.) and then estimated the cost expected to be incurred with the C-130J as if had been a "typical" Air Force Development and Production Program.*"

Relevance is, the C-130J was a modification program with the airframe already developed and the addition of new engines and avionics. The other programs were new aircraft development.

The point is, savings discussions are debatable, up to insulting intelligence, when the cost doubles. This instituted a need for workforce "brainwashing."

Acquisition Reform "Brainwashing" – Abandon Facts for Beliefs

May 5, 1998 - Acquisition Reform Day III: I lost other documentation for Acquisition Reform Days I and II; however, I found III. Basically, Government employees were forced to endure a "brainwashing" session where Acquisition Reform was touted as a success despite the fact that the C-130J pilot program for Acquisition was rapidly proving a failure with no sustainable savings.

The hope was that Government employees would abandon facts for beliefs that Acquisition Reform was working. However, at the same time, Lockheed Martin was deteriorating from within.

Program & Functional Reviews Failing

June 22, 1998 - Lockheed Acknowledges Poor Management: William Bullock (President, Lockheed Martin Marietta Plant) issued a memorandum to his Operating Council stating in part.

"*Our current program and functional reviews are not capable of providing what we need*".

This was one of two data points in 1998 showing that Lockheed Martin had deteriorated internally. The second data point was July 24, 1998, when the Air Force had to rescope contracts based on what Lockheed Martin could provide versus what the Air Force needed. That will be discussed soon. In short, Lockheed Martin had the persona of a top manufacturing entity while Lockheed Martin deteriorated behind the scenes. This prompted a C-130J performance cover-up.

C-130J Performance Cover-up – C-130J Grossly Overrun

June 23, 1998: The DACO voiced concerns about the subjective manner in which the DCMA rated Lockheed Martin's C-130J contract performance. The DACO, who was excluded, stated in part.

"...the C-130J development program in total is grossly overrun...", "...total program cost performance has, in fact, been abysmal."

"*LMASC* (Lockheed Martin) *personnel from the PM on down have repeatedly voiced their repugnance towards customer involvement in the program in any shape. They refuse to provide data, lie and evade customer questions, and have only with the greatest reluctance worked with us in Quality and Engineering Surveillance matters. To date they have abundantly refused to inventory GFP* (Government Furnished Property) *and GFE* (Government Furnished Equipment) *supplied them on the contract and have been aggressive in their resistance to customer-sponsored initiatives.*"

The DCMA covered up for Lockheed Martin since 1998 at the least. Dissenting voices were silenced, ignored, or excluded from meetings. As shown herein, I experienced weaponization and lawfare as a whistleblowing leader. The next step was to falsify cost savings.

Multiply C-130J Savings by 1 ½

August 13, 1998: C-130J savings estimates were unsupportable and outrageous. An e-mail from DCAA stated that Lockheed Martin wanted the government to give them what the government savings would be, and Lockheed Martin would *"...multiply it by 1 and ½"*.

The show's blasé mentality toward proper reporting and deliberate attempts to misrepresent C-130J cost savings. In fact, the C-130J was dragging down other programs at this time in 1998.

C-130J Negative Cost Effects on F-22 via Overhead Rate Linkage

September 11, 1998: C-130J failure was financially affecting F-22 through the linkage of overhead rates since the C-130J and F-22 shared the same rate structure. The DACO stated in part.

"If "0" C-130Js were produced, all other things being equal, the cost of the F-22 would increase by $464,495,000 over the years 2000 – 2002. The F-22 program would be in its Low Rate Initial Production (LRIP) Phase during this time, producing a limited number of aircraft per year. There will be some EMD (Engineering Manufacturing & Development) *overlay during this time, but for all practical purposes, we can allocate overhead increases on the planes to be produced per year."*

Meaning, the C-130J program business base absorbed some overhead cost at the Marietta facility. With the C-130J program faltering due to slow sales, other programs, including the F-22, would have to absorb more overhead costs. Variable overheads can be cut; however, some fixed overheads cannot be cut. This is an offshoot of the financial linkages between DoD programs.

C-130J "Paper Airplane" Certification

September 15, 1998: The misrepresentation of facts on the C-130J continued by having the Federal Aviation Administration (FAA) certify a "*paper airplane*" (382J) because there is "*...currently no existing aircraft matching this configuration*". The e-mail stated: *"The C-130J is not covered under FAA Certification."*

Meaning, the C-130J military version was not really commercial. The next step was an exclusive meeting and a catered lunch to help sell the C-130J.

C-130J Exclusive Meeting & Darleen Druyun "Catered Lunch"

October 21, 1998 – Exclusive Meeting: Lockheed Martin requested an exclusive meeting with DoD officials that removed the DCMA and DCAA from sensitive cost discussions at the time of the downfall of the C-130J. A Lockheed Martin executive wrote, *"we are not trying to hide anything, merely attempting to preserve the commerciality of the program"*.

"We believe the facts will show that the commercial item contract is a very good deal for the USG, and we hope that the program issues discussions will result in a win/win way forward for the USAF and Lockheed Martin."

Lockheed Martin didn't hide the exclusive meeting and tried to state the C-130J was a "good deal for the USG" despite the fact that the program was in collapse and dragging down the F-22.

October 30, 1998 – Darleen Druyun (Air Force Principal Deputy Assistant Secretary) Visit: Darleen Druyun visited the Lockheed Martin, Marietta, GA, facility for a review of the C-130J program. My understanding was that the Druyun visit was in regard to C-130J problems and slumping sales of the C-130J. The October 30, 1998, visit agenda did list some limited local higher-level DCMA and DCAA personnel.

Catered Lunch: The October 30, 1998 meeting agenda included a catered lunch for: Ms. Druyun along with Brigadier General (select) Chedister (PEO Airlift and Training) along with Lockheed Martin senior executives J.A. (Mickey) Blackwell (President and Chief Operating Officer); W.B. (Bill) Bullock (President) and T.A. Terry Graham (Executive Vice President and Chief Operating Officer). The catered lunch appeared to be private based on the following note on the October 30, 1998 agenda stating.

"*(note: All other attendees will have lunch in the Executive Dining Room)*"

Lean Manufacturing Introduction: Following the catered lunch, the agenda showed a "*Lean Introduction*" followed by a shop floor tour for "*Lean Manufacturing Implementation*". The tour carts showed Druyun, Chedister, Blackwell, and Bullock in the same tour cart.

A private catered lunch may raise some attention; however, it would be considered trivial had it not been for the following two peripheral events of July 28, 1999, and October 24, 1999.

"Breakfast With Key Staffers" – "Spit In My Face Weekly"

July 28, 1999 (C-130J/F-22, DoD Cover-up Strategy): The Raptor Action Group Update outlined a formal damage control (cover-up) plan of specific tactics to head off negative publicity towards the F-22 and ensure a consistent public message. It also seemed to have application to C-130J and other programs. Items of interest include:

"breakfast with key staffers"; *"assure consistent message"; "cost is on track"*; *"Release Public Affairs Guidance outlining distinction between educating public and lobbying"*; *"Rapid response to negative stories/editorials"*, etc.

The aforesaid appeared as cover-up tactics for problems on the F-22, C-130J, and other programs. The tactics were needed due to the following, which had some links to the October 30, 1998, meeting, as related to an October 24, 1999, news media report as follows.

October 24, 1999 – Lockheed Under Fire by Air Force for Poor Management, Arrogance:

This was an article by Tony Capaccio, Bloomberg News, mentioned in the Fort Worth Star-Telegram, describing the interaction between Darleen Druyun and Lockheed Martin. Some interesting quotes from the article are as follows.

"*Air Force Principal Deputy Assistant Secretary Darleen Druyun directed her most pointed criticism at Lockheed's Space & Strategic Missiles unit, which accounted for more than a quarter of the company's $26 billion in 1998 sales.*"

"Druyun described the space division as being "at the bottom of the heap of all the sectors I deal with - - they have arrogance plus," according to the company officials' notes that ended up on a Yahoo message board on the Internet."

"Druyun's strongest comments were directed at the space unit's former management. "Senior manager (sic) spit in my face weekly," Druyun was quoted as saying. "Quality in Space on a scale of 1 to 10 is 4. They are more interested in profit than quality," according to the e-mail. "Subcontractor management in Space is the worst, especially Denver," referring to the Colorado-based Astronautics unit."

"Druyun's assessments weren't all negative. She is quoted in the e-mail as praising a Lockheed Martin productivity initiative called Lean Manufacturing."

"You have excellent 'leanness on the F-22 (fighter jet), C-130J (transport) and F-16 (fighter)," the email quotes Druyun as saying. In contrast, Lockheed Martin's candidate for the multibillion Joint Strike Fighter competition with Boeing is "not lean."

Relevance is, news media articles are normally a good source of information. However, in the case of Lockheed Martin's "Lean Manufacturing", the C-130J is clearly called into question. By October 30, 1999, the C-130J program was anything but "lean," meaning not efficient. The C-130J cost had escalated and was starting to drag down adjacent programs such as the F-22 fighter, which shared the same overhead rate structure. The liquidated damages followed after that.

C-130J Liquidated Damages & More "Brainwashing"

December 1, 1999: Less than 2 months after Druyun said the C-130J was lean, the C-130J continued to decline with the United Kingdom (UK) getting liquidated damages as follows.

"The UK Ministry of Defense is to receive liquidated damages worth an estimated $79 million to compensate for Lockheed Martin's late delivery of the Royal Air Forces (RAF's) new C-130J transport aircraft."

This prompted more "brainwashing" as follows.

January 24, 2000 – Brainwashing for Acquisition Reform: By 2000, Acquisition Reform was a disaster based on the C-130J alone. Undersecretary of Defense J.S. Gansler issued a memo titled:

"Acquisition and Logistics Reform Week – May 22-26, 2000, "Embracing Change for the 21st Century Warfighter"

Meaning, regardless of the C-130J disaster, DoD was still pushing Acquisition Reform. At this juncture, I was disgusted and took action as follows.

Disclosure on C-130J Public Safety Threat and Cost Risk

April 5, 2000 (C-130J, Turned Over to DCIS): After witnessing multiple cover-ups at the Lockheed Martin, Marietta, GA, facility, I formally presented an in-person witness interview to the Defense Criminal Investigative Service (DCIS) for investigation regarding the C-130J. I believed the C-130J to be a public safety threat. The witness interview was 5 pages long with about 1,000 pages of support data in 3 binders. The investigator summed up my disclosure as follows.

"Pedeleose informed Reporting Agent (RA) of several problems with C-130J program he thought could result in substantial and specific danger to public health or safety."

From there DoD continued with touting the C-130J as success.

C-130J - Acquisition Reform Success Story

September 22, 2000: I kept a document dated 9/22/00 that outlined the C-130J as an acquisition reform success story despite the fact that the C-130J program was near collapse and was dragging down the F-22 by increased overheads caused by the diminishing business base of C-130Js.

Relevance is, success stories about the C-130J were not true; however, they kept coming despite facts that the C-130J was in trouble. I considered this to be falsifying to the public and Congress. That's why I became a whistleblower and why my resume in Chapter 1 appears the way it does.

Padlock C-130Js

May 30, 2001: I did a memorandum of record documenting the following in part.

"It was discussed that C-130Js were being inspected and would need to be padlocked to preclude Lockheed from cannibalizing parts."

Lockheed Martin was switching parts (equipment) between aircraft to make it appear that all C-130Js produced were operational. This was called the equipment rotation program because vendors could not produce all the parts for the C-130J. Hence, after a C-130J flight test, parts (equipment) were removed to flight test another C-130J aircraft. Gave the appearance of success.

90 Page Congressional Disclosure – Senator Charles Grassley Took Action

July 26, 2002: In 2001, I began writing a report to Congress addressing the administrative mayhem, cover-ups, and criminal vulnerability I saw at the Lockheed Martin facility in Marietta, GA. This was after I exhausted existing remedies and saw no other alternatives. Even the DCIS investigation I supported on April 5, 2000, was stalled.

The decision to go public was based on the protection achieved in public places to report the appalling and sickening things I saw. My resume (Chapter 1) has more details, along with other now contemporaneous reports to Congress I authored. Other employees signed on to the Congressional disclosures based on the year issued.

Congressional Responses to July 26, 2002 Report: From July 26, 2002, to August 9, 2002, 59 copies of the July 26, 2002, report were issued to members of Congress, including President Bush and Secretary of Defense Rumsfeld. I received voice messages from members of Congress stating the report was being forwarded. President Bush also sent a letter stating the report was forwarded.

Senator Charles Grassley – Only Member of Congress for Aggressive Action: The only member of Congress to take aggressive action was Senator Charles Grassley. I worked with Senator Grassley's staffer, Charlie Murphy, in late 2002 until Dan Meyer, in Falsified Trail 3, severed that relationship in 2005.

This explains why Dan Meyer focused so heavily on Charlie Murphy of Senator Grassley's staff to remove any avenue for remedy. As the following shows, the responses from Georgia representatives to Congress were abysmal.

Senator Zell Miller, August 15, 2002: Senator Zell Miller of Georgia was first to be mailed the July 26, 2002, report to Congress. Senator Zell Miller responded on August 15, 2002, stating in part:

"*Thank you for contacting my office regarding your concerns with the Defense Contract Management Agency. I appreciate you sending me the attached technical report and I read it with interest.*

I have enclosed your report, for it would be best for you to send the report to the Inspector General in the Department of Defense at the below address. The Inspector General has the authority to investigate the issues outlined in your testimony.

It was good to hear from you, and I encourage you to contact my office on issues of importance to you."

"*With kindest regards, I am Sincerely, Zell Miller*"

Senator Zell Miller proved useless in the fight against corruption, as did Congressman Bob Barr.

Congressman Bob Barr October 21, 2002: Congressman Bob Barr of Georgia was sent the July 26, 2002 report on July 27, 2002. On October 21, 2002, Congressman Barr responded in part.

"*I have reviewed your letter and I want to thank you for keeping me informed about issues which are important to you. Please be assured that I will keep your views in mind when, and if, this issue comes before me in the House of Representatives. If you would like to discuss the matter further, I would like to invite you to several town hall meetings I will be hosting over the next several weeks...*

As always, if I can ever be of any assistance, please do not hesitate to contact me.

With kind regards, I am very truly yours, BOB BARR"

Congressman Barr proved equally useless as Senator Zell Miller.

Senator Grassley - The "Only Game in Town"

The responses I have received from Congress over the years show why the U.S. Government is in the position it is in. The C-130J responses were just the first example. Past Congresses and past presidents overall have not taken aggressive action against corruption. In and of itself, inaction enables corruption against the U.S. Government. That is one reason I wrote this book. To provide an education, and a first-hand account, of real events at the working level so the public understands facts and the Congress and President can move forward informed.

Senator Grassley was once called by a reporter the "only game in town." Senator Grassley was the only Senator to work at length with whistleblowers. Senator McCain's involvement was brief but welcome. That being in contrast to Senator Zell Miller, Congressman Bob Barr and others who say idly by.

C-130J Recap

50%-100% Cost Increase, Plummeting Quality, Substantiated Allegation 4

July 23, 2004 (DoD IG Report on C-130J, (D-2004-102)): The DoD IG issued a report on the C-130J stating: *"We substantiated the allegation that the C-130J aircraft does not meet contract specifications and therefore cannot perform its operational mission. The Air Force conditionally accepted 50 C-130J aircraft at a cost of $2.6 billion even though none of the aircraft met commercial contract specifications or operational requirements."*

The C-130J became Substantiated Allegation 4. My adversaries were the military-industrial complex, who continually stated the C-130J was an Acquisition Reform success story when, in fact, the C-130J was a disaster. Only one Senator took aggressive action.

Additionally, Lockheed Martin never really recovered from Acquisition Reform in the 1990s. This was compounded by DCMA, whereby DCMA continually ran interference for Lockheed Martin as Chapter 3 has shown. Meaning, that this book is structured to present the enabling of corruption (Chapter 2 and Chapter 3) leading to enhanced price gouging and corporate deterioration (Chapter 4) caused by weaponized government and lawfare (coverups).

By the end of this book, if not much sooner, it should be clear why the Pentagon cannot pass an audit. It's because of weaponization and lawfare. I use myself as the example along with DCMA electronic, written, trails and DCMA behavior.

The report continues by explaining the link to national debt by explaining the price gouging techniques on the C-5 Program Depot Maintenance (PDM) (C-5 Overhaul). The C-5 PDM ran in parallel with the C-130J and basically experienced the same decline in 1998 as did the C-130J.

Single Item Pricing - 80% Cost Increase (Part 1 - 1998)

C-5 PDM Beginning - 1998: C-5 PDM began in early 1998. Defense Supply Center Richmond (DSCR) under DLA (Defense Logistics Agency) had program management responsibilities, and the DCMA Lockheed Martin (my office with me as a team member) assisted with pricing and technical support. The overall end customer was Warner Robins Air Logistics Center (WR-ALC).

Single Item Pricing - 80% Price Gouging: From the onset, Lockheed Martin tried to use single item pricing versus Economic Order Quantity (EOQ). Lockheed Martin was provided with prior usage data to purchase in EOQ to save money, but strongly resisted. Single-item pricing can escalate costs as much as 80% and will be explained shortly.

Rescope Contract to Meet Lockheed Martin Capability for Spare Parts
June 1998 Lockheed Martin Collapse

June 23, 1998: Six months into the effort, Lockheed Martin could not perform on a spare parts contract. Rear Admiral D.H. Stone, DSCR Commander, stated to Lockheed Martin, Mickey Blackwell, President, in part:

"*I believe DLA, the Air Force, and Lockheed Martin shared high expectations for this contract. To date, Lockheed Martin's performance is not meeting those expectations. In order to fulfill the PDM mission, WR-ALC and DSCR are expending significant organic resources in labor-intensive work-arounds to overcome the shortcomings in Lockheed Martin's performance. Our staffs are aware of the issues and have been working them. Recently, we have seen a positive change in direction by Lockheed Martin with a focusing of efforts towards solving the work stoppage items. The contract, however, was intended to prevent work stoppage situations.*

At my deputy's request, your staff has proposed a plan of actions to improve performance and meet the intent of the contract. It is our assessment that, even if perfectly executed, the plan will not meet the customers expectations. I have been advised by my headquarters and local staff that I am at a point where I must consider taking some formal action to bring the contract in line with Lockheed Martin's ability to deliver."

July 24, 1998 – Rescope Contract to What Lockheed Martin Can Provide: About one month later Rear Admiral Stone sent another letter to Blackwell, stating in part.

"*After receiving your response to my letter regarding Lockheed Martin's performance on the C-5 contract and the meeting with Mr. Bullock, it is clear that the time has come to rescope the contract. It is unfortunate that this need arises not from a change in customer requirements, but in order to align the contract with Lockheed Martin's demonstrated support capability of the C-5 PDM line at WR-ALC...*

Over the next few weeks, we intend to work closely with Lockheed Martin and the Air Force to definitize the letter contract to include the continuation of support in those areas that we feel Lockheed Martin has the capability of showing success."

The point is, Lockheed Martin could not perform on a simple spare parts contract. This was a parallel time to the C-130J commercial contract, where problems were also identified in 1998.

June 22, 1998: William Bullock (President, Lockheed Martin Marietta Plant) issued a memorandum to his Operating Council, indicating, "*Our current program and functional reviews are not capable of providing what we need*". Thus, admitting internally that process controls and measurement systems had problems.

Relevance is, at nearly the exact mid-point (June-July) in 1998, Lockheed Martin acknowledged poor management internally on June 22, 1998. The following day (June 23, 1998), Rear Admiral Stone issued a scathing letter regarding Lockheed Martin's poor performance on a simple spare parts contract.

About a month later (July 24, 1998), the C-5 PDM spare parts contract was rescoped to what Lockheed Martin could provide versus what the customer/DoD needed. However, the controversy did not end.

September 8, 1998 – Overstock Position Back to June 15, 1998: One data point that was never researched at the time indicated DLA – DSCR was in an overstock position on parts that could have been used on the C-5 PDM contract. However, parts were still purchased from Lockheed Martin. The original e-mail was dated June 15, 1998. The e-mail was forwarded between Lockheed Martin employees on September 8, 1998, and later provided to the DCMA.

The overstock position on parts only added to the controversy. This helps support the DoD's waste of money if the June 15, 1998 email information is correct.

C-5 PDM (Part 1) - Single Unit Overpricing (Price Gouging)
Government Stuck Together & Negotiated EOQ Pricing – 80% Savings

March 22, 1999: The single unit pricing on the C-5 PDM in 1998 was projected to be approximately 80% overestimated (price gouging). Government employees, in this case, did stick together and fought back against the tactical price gouging. In short, when items are purchased in units of 1 each, versus EOQ based on historical use, the price can be escalated near 80%. Information is as follows for both cost and price (after profit).

	Proposed Single Unit	Negotiated EOQ	Savings Estimate	% Saved Approx
Cost	$39,555,632	$7,963,457	$31,592,175	80%
Price	$43,511,195	$8,632,387	$34,878,808	80%

The savings on the C-5 PDM were calculated at over $31 million (cost, prior to profit). Tactical price gouging would have cost taxpayers $39,555,632; however, ethics, determination, and contract visibility provided a negotiated cost of $7,963,457 (80% cost reduction). These were real and measurable savings due to contract visibility. Affordability increases with transparency.

It should also be noted that during the C-5 PDM in 1998, I submitted a DoD IG Hotline complaint that yielded another disturbing data point that would trace further into the future.

Hotline Complaint on C-5 PDM Closed Partially Substantiated

June 12, 1998: I contacted the DoD IG Hotline regarding Lockheed Martin's pricing practices and deception on the C-5 PDM. The DoD IG complaint (Serial #69535) was closed partially substantiated on January 11, 1999. The IG never even assigned an investigator.

The interesting point is that the month of June 1998 keeps surfacing for both C-130J and C-5 PDM. This would seem to be a turning point downward (watershed moment) for DoD and Lockheed Martin. Meaning, Acquisition Reform actually drove DoD to a worse condition. Acquisition Reform was actually an enabling point for corruption that prompted my earlier whistleblowing.

Closed Loop (Factored In) Corruption

March 6, 2000 - DoD IG Transfer ("Farm Out") Investigations: Case #69535 (closed partially substantiated) was investigated by DCAA and not the DoD IG. A follow-on FOIA on this issue confirmed on March 6, 2000 (3/6/2000), the following from DoD IG, stating in part:

"*I we tasked this to DCAA & they gave us a ROI* (Report of Investigation) *that partially substantiated the allegations. We* (DoD IG) *closed the case as partially substantiated on 11 Jan 99.*"

Relevance is, DoD IG doesn't investigate the majority of cases and, in fact, sends the cases back to the wrongdoers or other Agencies for evaluation. This deliberate negligence enables institutional corruption to be factored in as follows.

November 1998 (C-5 PDM): Colonel Evans (then DCMA Commander) made an unsolicited remark to the DCMA Team I was on to the effect, "*Don't bother to call the Congress or the Senate these people will do nothing for you*". When asked if Colonel Evans meant the C-130J or the C-5 PDM, Colonel Evans responded the C-5. The main issue is not the remark but the management's knowledge of the 1998 Hotline call (Case 69535). Colonel Evans eventually went to work for Lockheed Martin, to my understanding.

Corruption is arrogantly factored in, arrogantly displayed with impunity, enabled and is deliberate with malice, as the following shows.

May 16, 2018 the DCMA IG – Corruption Circles: The trend of DoD IG farming out investigations was again spoken of on May 16, 2018, in an open article to the DCMA employees about the new DCMA IG, stating in part:

"*The DoD IG just returns the referral to us* (DCMA) *as either an information referral or an action referral.*" The article went on to state that in the last four years, only one of the DCMA's allegations was investigated by the DoD IG.

Allegations against the DCMA are sent back to the DCMA for the DCMA to investigate the DCMA. This circular self-contained corruption scandal inbreds upon itself. That is why I was forced to make a criminal disclosure, in person, on February 28, 2000, regarding the follow-on C-5 PDM termination claim as follows.

Single Item Pricing - 79%-80% Cost Increase (Part 2 – 2000)

Tactical overpricing occurred even after the parts were manufactured on the C-5 PDM and placed in a termination claim that would arguably be considered a false claim to the government. I eventually made a criminal referral directly to a local DCIS criminal investigator and not the DoD IG Hotline. Here is how the issue got started.

Termination Claim: The 1998 contract was modified to reflect what Lockheed Martin could provide. However, there were parts in manufacturing that apparently could not be stopped. Lockheed Martin, in 1999, proposed a Termination Claim to recover the cost. The Lockheed Martin Termination Claim stated the following regarding cost traceability on November 10, 1999.

"*The LMAS* (Lockheed Martin) *Accounting system DOES NOT contain a separate record of actual costs associated with each C5 PDM In-house Manufactured part. There are incomplete manufacturing records by detail part number. However, these records do not reconcile directly to the accounting records by part number. These manufacturing records are available for audit. Due to the fact that actuals for part number are not available, a unit cost for each non-negotiated in-house manufactured part has been developed using the contractor's Spares Pricing System".*

Relevance is, costs were apparently captured in aggregate while and after the parts were made. Lockheed Martin made the claim that the parts were manufactured one at a time. However, the manufacturing records indicated the parts were made in groups. The bottom line is, this was the false claim to the government previously mentioned in my resume (Substantiated Allegation 1).

Show Lockheed Martin the Criminal Case

February 2, 2000: As time progressed, it was more evident that Lockheed Martin was engaged in fraud (a false claim to the government). The decision was made to show Lockheed Martin the government information that would form the basis of a criminal complaint. It was not called criminal at that point, but the evidence suggested criminal. There was an email sent by the then DCMA contracting officer that read in part.

"*I have sent an e mail to Ed Owens requesting the Lockheed team meet with us at 1:30 p.m. on Tuesday Feb 8 to present our proposal to them, provided Capt Monaghan approves it first. We are sending her our proposal today and have asked her to review it and provide a reply by Friday and we can go from there.*"

Ed Owens was a Lockheed Martin executive, and I do not remember his position. The meeting did take place, and I was one of the main presenters. The agreement was that Ed Owens would only listen and not be subjected to any questions. The meeting was not of my choosing, although I was the one who had the data to form a criminal complaint, which I later made a few weeks later.

February 17, 2000 – Extension to Review "Problems": The contracting officer for DSCR sent an e-mail indicating Lockheed Martin Logistical Systems (LMLS) wanted an extension to review "problems". The email stated in part.

"I wanted to let everyone know that LMLS (Brenda Cleveland and Steve Wren-senior vp) contacted me and asked if they could have the rest of the week to review the problems we pointed out to Ed Owens last week and and opportunity for another face-to-face sometime next week. Although you all know that I desparately wanted to tell them to go fly a kite, our legal folks thought it was in the government's best interest to entertain this request one last time. I will keep you posted, but anticipate another meeting at your facility sometime late next week or early the following week if that is conducive to your busy schedules."

I tolerated the situation because no money had changed hands as yet, and I was not in charge of the negotiation. In the lull, I closed the loop on the potential criminal case.

February 23, 2000 - Close the Loop on Potential Criminal Case: While waiting for Lockheed Martin to respond, I closed the loop on the potential criminal case, showing parts were not manufactured one at a time, suggesting a potential false claim to the Government. This was Revision 2 to my original report of January 13, 2000. The savings result from overpricing is as follows:

	Proposed	Recommended	Savings Estimate	% Saved Approx
Cost	$2,849,248.81	$594,285.49	$2,254,963.32	79%-80%

Relevance is, that single-item pricing with manufactured parts is the same tactical price gouging as purchasing parts at nearly 80%. Meaning, the single unit price gouging tactic is the same overpricing for both manufactured and purchased parts at nearly 80%. The other point is that Lockheed Martin could not perform on the C-5 PDM contract, although it spent significant effort on price gouging. Lockheed Martin caused Lockheed Martin's problems. The story continues as follows:

February 24, 2000 (Exclusive Meeting): Lockheed Martin's response to viewing the potential criminal complaint was to request an exclusive meeting with management. The e-mail below was originally sent to Tommy Treat (DCMA Contracting Officer) and Robert Murphy. Robert Murphy was a DCMA HQ observer involved as a liaison. Walt Walker was my supervisor. Tommy Treat forwarded the message to the DCMA Marietta team, copied in part as follows.

"Received a msg from LMLS regarding our impending negotiations. They requested we meet in Marietta next Thursday or Friday. Friday morning is much better for me. They also requested that I limit the number of government participants to 2. While I think this number is unreasonable, I don't disagree that maybe initially you, me and possibly Walt should meet with them and then, if necessary, call in support as needed. I am going to offer an "observation" invite to Bob Murphy and Debbie Minter (my replacement) as well."

My response to the exclusive meeting was to initiate a criminal complaint.

Physically Call Criminal Investigator into the Office

February 28, 2000: I called a criminal investigator directly into the facility that same morning, outside the local DCMA command suite. I made no attempt to remain anonymous. I presented the C-5 PDM fraud case to a Special Investigator who opened an investigation immediately and notified the DCMA management. This would become Substantiated Allegation 1 in my resume.

Single Unit Tactic for Pricing or Manufacturing is Still 80%

80% Price Gouging – 80% Overestimating

The single unit tactic for purchasing parts and/or manufactured parts equates to the same thing, which is 80% Overestimating or 80% Price Gouging. As my resume, Chapter 1, indicated, the DCMA engaged in Criminal Vulnerability, and the DoD IG tried to cover up the fact that the DCMA continued to negotiate a contract on data known to be false and purposely overstated. However, well in advance of those conclusions, I recognized local in-person disclosures led to success.

In summary, thus far, the C-130J escalated 50%-100% depending on the year and C-130J version due to Acquisition Reform, which weaponized commercial pricing. The single-unit tactic escalated the cost by 80% for both purchase parts and manufactured parts. These events were originally part of Acquisition Reform. However, DCMA would enable more criminal vulnerability.

Chapter 3 Criminal Vulnerability Enabling (Weaponization & Lawfare)

It was Acquisition Reform for the C-130J and C-5 PDM that caused my initial whistleblowing. The corruption, enabling, and criminal vulnerability was easy to spot. My whistleblowing made me a target for weaponization and lawfare as Chapter 3 has shown in detail. Meaning, Chapter 3 shows how DCMA and DoD IG stifled me from doing my job and severed my Congressional support from Senator Grassley. OSC, MSPB, OPM and DOJ would cover-up for DCMA. In response, DCMA escalated Falsified Trails (weaponization and lawfare).

As previously stated in Chapter 2 (May 4, 1988) Ernie Fitzgerald was put "*under a general who was charged with "keeping Fitzgerald busy" and "not letting him work with Congress*".

The point is, the evidence and tactics in Chapter 2 and Chapter 3 enabled Lockheed Martin to price gouge the government because I was distracted with weaponization and lawfare that altered my working conditions. Same with Ernie Fitzgerald.

Meaning, this enabled more price gouging tactics by Lockheed Martin known as Judgment Estimating that I was precluded from pursuing in 2008 due to weaponization and lawfare.

Judgement Estimating – 24%-69% Cost Increase

By 2007, Lockheed Martin's estimating system was under criticism for several years. One trend was Lockheed Martin using Judgement Estimating. Meaning, Judgement Estimating was based on what one person thought something should cost, normally measured in hours and then converted to dollars.

The question was: How accurate was Lockheed Martin in estimating labor for fixed price contracts using personal judgment (Judgement Estimating)? Proposal estimates eventually translate from labor (hour) cost to final contract price ($). The history on this analysis is as follows.

August 16, 2007 - 24% to 69% Overestimated: I issued nine Corrective Action Requests (CARs) on nine different Lockheed Martin cost proposals in one day. Regardless of the deficiency found, the issue remained how accurate the estimates were that used Judgement Estimating. To provide a fair analysis, Judgement estimates had the opportunity to prove accuracy as follows.

Proposed – Negotiated – Actual Comparison: To determine estimating accuracy, Lockheed Martin was asked to provide the proposed labor amount, negotiated labor amounts, and what the contract actually used for labor for the proposals. This was the most accurate comparison available.

The result was 24% - 69% overestimated on labor for contracts that were 90% - 100% complete at that time. Knowing that Lockheed Martin had multiple deficiencies in proposals, the amount would range possibly in the hundreds of millions of dollars over the decades. Even with the best forensic accountants, it would be impossible to determine the total amount of loss to the U.S. Government.

Project Abandon Due to Altered Working Conditions

August 12, 2008 – Closed CARs & Never Pursued: Joe Tessier, who was noted many times in Chapter 3 herein, created such a hostile work environment that I was forced to drop the project. Tessier created such an administrative "run & shoot" hostile workplace that I could not even do my regular job, let alone focus on improvements to Lockheed Martin estimating. The year 2009 was even worse. The following are examples of Tessier's hostility that altered my working conditions.

Altered Working Conditions Enabling Price Gouging

May 8, 2008 – Stifle Communications: Joe Tessier stated in writing.

"*To eliminate any uncertainty on the issue, you are directed that all work related communication with Lockheed's senior leadership, including Mr. Rhyant, must be coordinated in advance with DCMA Lockheed Martin Marietta management. This Command's managers must be aware of and involved in any issue significant enough to require the attention and involvement of the company's senior management officials.*"

The fact is, any communications with the DCMA management would be stifled and resisted. The goal of the DCMA management was to cover up problems with Lockheed Martin.

May 12, 2008 – Complaint to DCMA Director: Based on Tessier's attempts to silence me, I emailed then the DCMA Director Charlie Williams and the DCMA Deputy Director Marie Greening, as well as my local senior leadership, including Colonel Plourde and Henrietta Snow. Stating in part.

"While I am kind in dealing with LM Aero estimating issues at the present time, the truth is I believe that such problems are a cover for price gouging and criminal activity. Disarray in and of itself is a cover. A bad estimating system is wasteful to the point where LM Aero can charge anything they want. It is like having an open door to a bank vault where Defense contractors can take what they want. This is a burden shift from fraud to abuse, waste, and negligence in that contractors can just take what they want.

Mr. Tessier is engaging in intimidation tactics. I am responding to this as a retaliation due to my ongoing complaints about LM Aero and DCMA activity, some of which has risen to the criminal level."

This was the trend in 2008, and as Chapter 3 shows, the 2009 trend was even worse. The hostile work atmosphere was sickening and did alter working conditions.

Disclosure Planned in 2009: I planned on writing a Congressional disclosure similar to this book in 2009. I was stopped by the blitz of Falsified Trails that began after the MSPB covered up for the DCMA on February 12, 2009. From that point, I went into survival mode.

The following are some events prior to Tessier that the DCMA also did not pursue and actually regretted getting started to begin with.

Deteriorating Estimating Systems

December 3, 2003 Estimating System Deterioration: As of 2003 there were questions and meetings with Lockheed Martin accounting problems. One question was tracking actual cost as follows:

"Why Lockheed Martin cannot track actuals? I am currently working a proposal in which Lockheed has to estimate actuals."

"How is the Lockheed estimating system approved? The proposals I have continually used supervisors judgement on major development programs. Much of the estimates are based on Level of Effort (LOE) which is a time based parameter (Passage of Time) versus performance based."

"How does the DACO ensure that the proper base is applied to factors."

"How is the accounting system approved? Do they just sample? Do they do a complete test? How is the money accounted for?"

The point is, Lockheed Martin's estimating problems that led to price gouging went back several years. The issue resurfaced in 2006 as follows.

Estimating System Compliance Review

December 18, 2006: The Lockheed Martin estimating system deteriorated to the point where a local (Marietta, GA) review was conducted. The review focused on the details of how Lockheed Martin estimated with the following parameters of BOEs (Basis of Estimates):

- Major Programs and TINA Compliant Contracts
- 1,019 Labor Only Basis of Estimates (BOEs) for C-130J, C-5, P-3, and Facilities
- Excluded F-22 and Navy Spares
- 11 Engineers from 4 DCMA commands
- October 2005 through October 2006

The results were as follows:

Non-Compliant Rate 69%: A total of 69% of BOEs (Lockheed Martin individual labor estimates) were non-compliant with Lockheed Martin's purported estimating system. A total of 53% of the BOEs had more than one non-compliance.

Judgement Estimating 70%: This shows Judgement estimating traces back prior to 2007. Basically, no objective audit traceability. Relevance is, Lockheed Martin's estimating system was deficient on its face for a while.

The blame extended beyond Tessier to the DCMA Director's level, since the DCMA Directors failed to control Tessier and showed no concern for corruption, price gouging, etc. Same for the following.

Material Estimating - Discrete Vs Allocated – $584,610

November 18, 2011 - $584,610: This issue involved the estimating of materials, where Lockheed Martin explained as follows.

"This Proposal is submitted to provide a credit update to Lot 5 C-5 RERP Material and Fabrication to remove allocated material cost that were inadvertently bid as discrete material. The effect of this correction is a reduction to the Bill of Material of $433,102 and a fully burdened price reduction of $584,610."

Meaning, Lockheed Martin bid overhead (allocated, Miscellaneous small parts like nuts, bolts, rivets, etc.) parts along with large discrete (high value) parts. On August 31, 2013, I documented where I tried to audit Lockheed Martin's material estimating system, and the audit was quashed. This is the theme of this book. The other point is how far into the future did Lockheed Martin's estimating problems (price gouging) continue into the future. The answer is quite far regarding Estimating Factors and touches upon the DFARS (Defense Federal Acquisition Regulation Supplement).

The next issue involves Estimating Factor Documentations/Descriptions (EFDs).

Estimating Factors - 49% to 60% Cost Increase

EFs or EFDs are add-on amounts (factors added to other estimated costs) supposedly to cover other contractor costs. The EFs or EFDs are analogous to the add-on cost on phone or cable TV bills above base amounts. Roughly like an add-on tax that has limited cost transparency, as follows.

August 2017 – December 2017 (EFD2017 Date): An estimating factor review occurred during 2017, outlining the following major issues with Lockheed Martin estimating EFs/EFDs.

"*Visibility of cost information, including cost data through LMA SAP (*System Application & Product) *system, was very difficult to obtain and in some cases the EF review team was not able to obtain the necessary information to determine the cost as fair and reasonable (see program office for further details). As the review team understands the resource challenges imposed with a special review teams on-site, the team has concerns the local Government teams will not receive the visibility nor the responsiveness necessary to conduct proper oversight on a universe of 140+ EFs which will hinder the ability to recommend positions to facilitate a DCMA lead negotiation strategy.*"

"*LMA's failure to provide detailed breakdown of heads and hours, limits the EF review team's assessment of hours/heads, and does not allow for the determination if the heads/hours as incurred, and as proposed, represent a fair and reasonable estimate.*"

"*In further review of the Excel working files, the EF review team noticed there was insufficient written basis of estimate included in the proposal packages that would provide "sufficient details for the Government to reasonably make an informed judgment regarding the acceptability of the Contractor's estimating practices". DFARS 252.215-7002(d)(2)(ii).*"

"*Lack of written basis of estimates with adequate methodology and rationale documented, makes the EF proposals inadequate for evaluation and signals concerns with the estimating systems as it relates to the DFARS criteria for an adequate estimating system.*"

The point being, Lockheed Martin's EFDs were deficient.

December 18, 2018: My office had an "urgent" request to evaluate several Lockheed Martin EFDs. As an SME, I informed my management and fellow employees of the following.

"*The approaches I have seen thus far to evaluating the EFDs are not in accordance with the way the EFDs should be evaluated. I have stated previously that I (as a DCMA instructor) cannot teach one thing and then do something different in actual practice.*"

January 8, 2019: The EFD discussion continued and I again stated to management and employees;

"*I cannot go against the prescribed way to evaluate factors such as those we are reviewing. That is I cannot teach one way and then turn around and do the opposite.*"

The point was, the EFDs were deficient. The objective deficiency is quantified as follows.

Lockheed Martin Disclaimer - "Include But Are Not Limited To"

The Lockheed Martin justification for EFs/EFDs contains a disclaimer stating:

"*The activities for this EF include, but are not limited to, the following.*"

What this means is that Lockheed Martin EFDs (factors) that inflate cost proposals use fluid numbers that are not traceable. Meaning, Lockheed Martin can provide data to evaluate the factors, and then, following the evaluation, Lockheed Martin can use the EFDs wherever Lockheed Martin pleases. Further, this means the EFDs are moving targets. Fluid numbers that continually change.

However, I did do a deep dive for one set of factors (CERs, Cost Estimating Relationships) for F-35 Special Tooling as follows. CERs are addon factors similar to EFs or EFDs.

F-35 Special Tooling - Lot 11 - Production Non-Recurring (PNR) 49% - 60% Overestimated for 332 Special Tools

July 27, 2016, F-35 Special Tooling Report: The Lockheed Martin F-35 Special Tooling proposal for non-recurring (one-time) cost is a great example of how CERs tactically inflate cost using a factor. My July 27, 2016, report effectively dismantled the Lockheed Martin F-35 CER.

My analysis involved each of the specific elements that made up the CER. This is aside from the statement of "*included but not limited to*" which rendered the proposal defective. Issues and explanations of the Lockheed Martin F-35 PNR Special Tooling proposal are in part as follows.

Special Tooling Defined: Special Tooling is defined as tooling for a specific end item. In this case the F-35. This means F-35 Special Tooling is only for the F-35 program and the F-35 only. As compared to Standard Tooling.

Standard (Capital) Tooling: Standard Tooling or Capital Tooling are the general tools that can be used or transferred between programs. Multiple uses across many programs and processes.

Relevance is that the money source, meaning F-35 special tooling, is directly charged to the F-35 contract. Standard or Capital Tooling has a different money source, more related to tooling across multiple programs. Standard tooling is more related to overhead cost.

Estimating Non-Recurring (One-Time) Cost for F-35 Lot 11 (25,600 Labor Hours): The Lockheed Martin F-35 proposal estimated non-recurring costs (one-time) for Lot 11. Basically, the F-35 production was in a steady state recurring ("Cookie Cutter Mode" as an analogy), meaning far past the development stage. As such, non-recurring costs should be near zero due to the maturity of the F-35 program.

However, Lockheed Martin estimated 25,600 labor hours, which was actually revised down from 29,037 labor hours. Using a wrap rate of $250/hour, the cost would be about $6,400,000. The estimate gets worse because non-recurring was limited from program onset.

Limited Non-Recurring Labor Due to Outsourcing of Tooling: Lockheed Martin's non-recurring labor was limited even in the design phase. Lockheed Martin does tool requirements (non-recurring) and then forwards the tool requirements to the tool designer (vendor, subcontractor). The designed tool is then subcontracted out to a vendor to make the tool.

Hence, even in the design phase, Lockheed Martin had limited involvement other than technical requirements. Essentially, the design work (Technical Requirements) is done (complete) at this point for non-recurring cost in Lot 11, thus non-recurring cost is reduced. The subcontractor aspect of F-35 tooling further limits non-recurring labor for Lockheed Martin.

Lockheed Martin's non-recurring involvement would be roughly preparing paperwork for the subcontractor, responding to questions, and making sure the subcontractor does their job. There may be some labor hours needed; however, nothing requiring 25,600 hours.

Build to Print: Of the 332 F-35 Special tools, 257 would be considered as build to print, meaning the design work is already completed. The need for non-recurring labor hours would be limited to retrieving tool specifications for outsourcing once increased production need is determined.

Included But Not Limited To: The Lockheed Martin F-35 proposal had the statement: "*The following tasks are included but not limited to this BOE.*" Hence, the extent of data in the factor was unknown. These factors were known as CERs, which were similar to EFs or EFDs.

Relevance is that the F-35 Special Tooling had no real basis, meaning there was no cost traceability with the statement "*are included but not limited to*". However, Lockheed Martin did provide some tasks that gave some insight and transparency to how defective the proposal was.

Insight to Defective Proposal – Aggregate Cost: Lockheed Martin did provide some insight to various labor tasks that were divided into 5 categories of aggregate costs. Some categories were obviously not Special Tooling or Non-Recurring. The list is as follows:

1: Build Plan & Planning Activities

2: Build to Packages (BTP) Project Tooling

3: Tool Trial Run (TTR) Management

4: Standard Tooling

5: Numerical Control (NC) Programming

It was obvious Category 4 (Standard Tooling) was not part of Special Tooling, so about 20% off the top was not relevant. Meaning overpricing since Standard Tooling goes across all or many programs. Standard Tooling and Special Tooling are different cost categories from different pools of money.

The remaining 4 Categories had several sub-categories that were an intermix of recurring and non-recurring issues. The main issue of non-recurring costs is overseeing vendors which is what I used as an estimate to keep the process moving, despite the fact that the proposal could be deemed defective.

Estimate 1 to 3 Engineers for a Year Each Phase: Rather than zeroing out the proposal, I reviewed the major tasks and estimated on a Level of Effort (LOE) basis so negotiations could move forward. Meaning, I estimated one to three engineers for each phase, working an entire year on F-35 PNR Lot

11 Special Tooling alone. Knowing that the tooling was already designed and was outsourced to a vendor (someone else making the tools). The work phases are as follows.

Phase 1: Prepare for PNR 11 (Determine Tool Need, Forward to Contract Out Work)

Phase 2: Respond to Vendor/Outsource Questions

Phase 3: Tool Try and Set Up.

It should be noted that there was some inclusion of smaller tasks that were also reduced however the vast majority was engineering labor. The proposed and reduced estimate is as follows.

Proposed (Hours)	Proposed R1 (Hours)	DCMA Low (Hours)	DCMA High (Hours)
29,037	25,600	10,270	13,088

In short, Lockheed Martin estimated 25,600 labor hours, which seemed to be Lockheed Martin's total F-35 Engineering labor. Meaning, Lockheed estimated for all tooling, standard and special, and basically all tooling tasks. I estimated the amounts based on true non-recurring work with vendors and came up with a low position of 10,270 hours and a high position of 13,088 hours. Basically, I allotted a number of engineers for each phase over the course of a year, which was extremely generous. Meaning, that was all the engineers did for that year. Nothing else.

49% - 60% Overestimated: My low position generated about a 60% reduction (10,270/25,600). My high position is about a 49% reduction (13,088/25,600). Relevance is, for a proposal that was objectively defective from the onset, my estimate was extremely generous.

Using a $250/hour wrap rate, my estimate would be $2,567,500 to $3,272,000 versus Lockheed Martin's estimate of $6,400,000. This was actually a small proposal; however, the principle can extrapolate to larger proposals and/or other proposals.

Also calculated into the reduction were the labels attached to the special tooling as follows.

$500 Estimated - Adding Labels to Special Tooling: The Lockheed Martin proposal included 664 hours (about $166,000 using a $250 wrap rate) to attach identification labels to the special tooling. Lockheed Martin estimated 2 labor hours per tool or about $500 per label (using $250 wrap rate). It was later discovered that the vendors, not Lockheed Martin, applied the labels.

I allowed Lockheed Martin about half an hour (low estimate) to research the information needed on the label and send it to the vendor. This was due to the fact that special tooling needed a serial number for each tool and was logged into a database.

I notified the F-35 Joint Program Office (JPO) of this fact and my DCMA engineering counterpart at Ft Worth (on July 18, 2016), where I was used as the SME for the finding of Vendors versus Lockheed Martin applying the identification labels.

Relevance is, CERs/EFs/EFDs (factors) are contaminated and not traceable allowing tactical overpricing of 49%-60%. The Lockheed Martin disclaimer "*The following tasks are included but not limited to this BOE*" absolve Lockheed Martin of culpability.

While working the F-35 project I had restrictions on communications to F-35 JPO (Joint Program Office). Meaning, I was still being stifled to contain negative information as follows.

November 3, 2016 - Making up Regulations: This is the only known cost proposal I worked for the F-35. While working the F-35 proposal ((TSN) Technical Support to Negotiations) I was placed on communication restriction with F-35 JPO (government office) documented as follows.

"*Since my arrival in DCMA in 1994 I noted times where regulations were manufactured. One recent regulation involves my dealings with TSNs and supporting DCMA LMM Pricing. I was working F-35 TSN and was told that if I had a question for F-35 Program Office I would ask question to Priscilla Driscoll and Priscilla would send to F-35 and then F-35 would respond to Priscilla and then Priscilla would send to me. This alleged regulation was manufactured. This needs to stop.*"

Relevance is, the DCMA manufactures regulations to protect Lockheed Martin. The aforesaid regulation may have been manufactured for my benefit, as was the Letter of Direction from Joe Caldwell in Falsified Trail 1 and those from Joe Tessier in 2008. I did have one private conversation with JPO during the F-35 TSN when others failed to dial in. Left me and JPO alone on the call.

I notified JPO of issues Lockheed Martin was having with special tooling for F-35 and how a CAR was written by the DCMA. Apparently, Lockheed Martin duct-taped special tooling together, although I never verified. The JPO was concerned and indicated that such incidents affect Lockheed Martin's award fee. There was also another issue (that I forgot) that happened on the same call.

I informed JPO not to use my name when contacting the DCMA about the CAR because the DCMA will figuratively "*go through the roof*" meaning get angry or upset. JPO did not use my name in questioning DCMA; however, I was questioned very aggressively after JPO contacted the DCMA.

The point is, regulations are manufactured by DCMA to protect Lockheed Martin and contain negative information that may have a negative effect on Lockheed Martin. In the case of JPO, it was a regulation for me not to communicate alone with government offices, meaning JPO.

So now the list of overpricing (price gouging) techniques now includes 49%-60%. Past price gouging in Chapter 4 was 80% and some for 24%-69%. Notwithstanding the C-130J, which increased the price by 50%-100%.

The following includes price gouging techniques in the 31% range using elaborate tactical math for C-5 Contractor Logistics Support (CLS). Some past rumored profits may be 120%, and other issues, could be traced back to the Falsified Trails where my involvement was stifled. However, this was a difficult and very large cost proposal that needed technical review so it was transferred to me.

Elaborate Math (Cost Model & Analogy) – 31% Cost Increase

Tactical overpricing outlined herein has been one-dimensional thus far. However, Lockheed Martin also uses elaborate tactical math overpricing (price gouging) that follows more complicated mathematical trails. For purposes of expediency, I will explain in general terms since the technical math traces to expose the elaborate math trails are complicated. The history is as follows.

Start of C-5 CLS Warner Robins Air Logistics Center (ALC) 2016: My office, and the DCMA in general, had pricing evaluation teams (sometimes referred to as Centers of Excellence) that were supposed to evaluate contractor proposals. To my understanding, the 2016 C-5 CLS proposal was shuttled around, possibly through the Centers of Excellence, until it found its way to my desk.

The C-5 CLS proposal was for logistics support, repair of C-5, mostly large, expensive, and technically complex aircraft components known as Line Replaceable Units (LRUs), although some portions were for consumable or disposable parts. Lockheed Martin was the prime contractor.

The C-5 CLS proposal supported Warner Robins, GA, ALC, and had about 695 BOEs (Basis of Estimates), probably explaining why the proposal was shuttled around and given to me to work. Another reason may be the problems with prior contract negotiations, which were documented on June 1, 2016, by a senior DoD executive who stated to the negotiation team in part.

"*The DoDIG has been expending a lot of energy lately in challenging CLS arrangements ... our metrics, our performance oversight, our strategy itself, and what we're paying in comparison to what the contractor is actually doing.*"

The aforesaid remark actually came after I assisted with the negotiation. One issue was profit.

120% Profit - Altered Working Conditions: One discussion in the analysis to follow focused on how Lockheed Martin made 120% profit on the prior contract, which is probably why Warner Robins sought outside help, which eventually led to me. I wondered why the DCMA wasn't involved in prior C-5 CLS proposals. "Farmed out" and altered working conditions were the answer.

"Farmed Out" – Altered Working Conditions: Looking back, I remembered a prior C-5 proposal evaluation that "farmed out" in small segments for various employees to work. This was directed by my management (Nanette Nelson), and I was involved in "farming out" the sections to less experienced employees. The "farm out" process did alter working conditions and negated the ability to identify patterns. This was a subset of the prior hostile and abusive work environments in Chapter 3. Meaning, altered working conditions did effect cost and enable price gouging.

However, now I was reviewing the entire proposal without interference. I was able to "de-confuse" the proposal on my terms and see how the entire proposal was structured versus individual snippets.

"De-Confused" C-5 CLS Proposal – Pattern Recognition – Domino Effect: The C-5 CLS proposal had about 695 BOEs (individual estimates) with recognizable patterns. To de-confuse, I sorted like BOEs into piles. This took some initial time but had a big payoff. The payoff was the domino effect, whereby an analysis of one BOE in the group translated to all BOEs in the group

BOE Groups: When sorting (de-confusing) was complete, I discovered Lockheed Martin had copied 17 BOEs 40 times over with minor changes only to each BOE. There was a stray group of 3 BOEs copied 5 times over with minor changes. The process was coined "BOE Groups".

Domino Effect: My evaluation went from 695 separate BOE evaluations down to 17 BOE Group evaluations, plus some small 15 evaluations. Of the 17 BOE Group evaluations, 3 BOE Groups accounted for the majority of the labor hours requiring evaluation. Hence, I de-confused from 695 evaluations to 3 BOE Group evaluations for the majority of the cost. I did review all BOE Groups.

Working alone, and with Warner Robins ALC support, I was able to isolate patterns and consolidate work. BOE Grouping was the single major point that "de-confused" the proposal. I will take a large credit; not all credit for what followed. I was instrumental in the success, and I believe that had others done that evaluation, the result would not have been the same. Sorting the BOEs did take patience.

November 5, 2015 - 31% Savings on Cost Basis: There were 2 major problems identified within the 3 large BOE Groups as follows:

Cost Model – Elaborate Math-Based: Lockheed Martin had used an in-house cost model that essentially doubled a significant amount of labor depending on the BOE reviewed. This clashed with the fact that C-5 flight hours had only increased 17%. The relevance is that the cost model nearly doubled (2X) when there should have been only a 17% increase in cost (multiply by 1.17). The cost model was tested and found to give inflated costs.

Inaccurate Analogy Between Consumables and LRUs: The second major issue was an elaborate mathematical analogy between consumables (disposable) parts and LRUs (large aircraft repairable parts). Simply put, there is no analogy between consumables (disposable parts) and LRUs (major aircraft components) that can be repaired.

In short, Lockheed Martin used a web of elaborate math to escalate contract costs. My analysis, and working alone with Warner Robins support, yielded major savings that I will take credit for as the initial catalyst to "de-confuse" a complicated cost proposal. Savings are as follows.

August 12, 2016 Price Negotiation Memorandum (PNM): The contract started at $119,934,961 (September 22, 2015) proposed cost for 5 years. It was discovered that the 5-year contract was too big to negotiate at once and was negotiated at a smaller 20-month version of $43,053,974 (May 26, 2016). The final negotiated cost was $29,586,163 after the price gouging was removed.

Savings on cost basis are $43,053,974 - $29,586,163 = $13,467,811 About 31% savings.

Relevance is, the tactical elaborate math escalated proposed amounts about 31%. There was some duplication in the proposal; however, the bulk was tactical, elaborate math to inflate cost. From that point the remainder of the Option Years had to be analyzed and negotiated. Lockheed Martin used a different strategy (Linear Regression) to overprice (price gouge). On July 5, 2017 I was asked for by name to do my part on the analysis which was key to the negotiation. Meaning, I did an analysis and educated others on Lockheed Martin price gouging techniques. I set the example.

Elaborate Math (Linear Regression) – 31% Cost Increase

Part 1 of C-5 CLS negotiated the Base Year contract and Option Year 1. Part 2 of C-5 CLS was for Option Years 2, 3, & 4. For Part 2, Lockheed Martin switched to a new tactical math approach to escalate the proposed cost (price gouge) using linear regression.

December 19, 2017 - Linear Regression: Lockheed Martin tried to assert there was a linear change as the number of parts increased on a proposal for repair. This is not true. I issued an 80-page report to counter Lockheed Martin's tactical math that inflated the proposed cost based on the linear math theory. The following statement best summarizes the facts of repair parts on C-5 aircraft and possibly any military aircraft or equipment.

"*...the majority of the failures are already anchored within the 150 part group with the majority of parts experiencing 1 or less failures. Hence the 150 part group already has the majority of the most highly ranked failure ("bad actor") parts meaning anything else added would be a low failure part or a consumable part.*"

Meaning, only certain parts fail with regularity on the C-5 aircraft, which defeats the linear regression theory. The proposal already had 150 parts that were the "bad actor" (high failure rate) parts. So, if the number of parts did increase, the added parts would have low failure rates, meaning negligible cost. I had to expend effort in an 80-page report to prove this point, plus other inaccurate assertions by Lockheed Martin. I again prevailed with about the same savings as CLS part 1.

September 7, 2018 - 31% Savings: The overall savings of overcoming linear regression were nearly the same as those of CLS Part 1, as follows.

May 22, 2018 - $76,231,839: The Lockheed Martin proposed amount for C-5 CLS II (Option Years 2, 3, & 4) was $76,231,839.

August 1, 2018 – $39,688,756: The first Air Force calculated proposal was $39,688,756. From memory, there may have been some descoping (eliminate work) of the Lockheed Martin proposal.

August 16, 2018 - $28,036,826: The Air Force objective cost was $28,036,826.

August 24, 2018 - $27,364,664: The final negotiated amount was $27,364,664.

Savings on cost basis are $39,688,756 - $27,364,664 = $12,324,092 About 31% savings.

Relevance is, tactical elaborate math and similarly linear regression in this case, escalates proposed costs (price gouges) by about 31%. The next issue is Independent Research and Development (IRAD), which are discrete issues, meaning not on a percentage basis.

Independent Research & Development (IR&D/IRAD) C-130J - $8,337,307

Defense contractors like Lockheed Martin are geared toward development projects, meaning an experienced staff already exists. The U.S. Government recognizes this opportunity and allows U.S. Defense contractors to charge research costs and some development to overhead accounts to overall save the U.S. Government money. This is called IR&D. Falsified Trail 1 involved IRAD.

The catch is, IR&D costs are charged to overhead accounts where the cost is absorbed by other programs on the same corporate rate structure. For Lockheed Martin in Marietta, GA, that would include C-130, F-22, C-5, spare parts, etc. The following example is dated; however, the same principle applies to more recent times.

C-130J IRAD Commercial Case Study: As previously stated, the C-130J was a commercial contract with limited visibility, financially intermixed through overhead costs with F-22, C-5, etc., contracts at the Marietta, GA facility. C-130J development was supposed to be amortized in the C-130J sale price at a proposed $2.9 million for the first 120 C-130Js. However, Lockheed Martin tried to spread C-130J development cost to overhead accounts for the F-22, C-5, and other non-commercial (DoD-specific) contracts at Lockheed Martin through IRAD. The following are some examples of potential abuse of the IRAD process. I challenged the costs; however, I do not know the end result. The system was too corrupted. Examples are as follows.

December 10, 2003 - Global Air Traffic Management (GATM) $1,061,975 – Roughly speaking, GATM is a program that allows military aircraft to fly in the same airspace as civilian aircraft. This would be a classic IRAD candidate, with the exception that there was the appearance that this GATM was for the development of the C-130J mission computer, which is a commercial contract.

GATM was the center of Falsified Trail 1. Lockheed Martin was highly protective of GATM data, which greatly raised my suspicions. I challenged $1,061,975 of the cost. It should be noted that IRAD costs are charged on a yearly basis as work progresses, and this was for the years 1999 and 2000. Meaning, a greater amount of cost may be involved.

March 18, 1999 - C-130J Cargo Handling $140,468 – CFY1997: I deemed this an IRAD mischarge since C-130J was a commercial contract for Contractor Fiscal Year (CFY) 1997.

March, 18, 1999 - Propeller Design, Fab., and Calibration $311,925 – CFY1997: I deemed this another mischarge of IRAD since C-130J was a commercial contract.

March 18, 1999 - C27J Risk Reduction (Foreign Offset) $6,822,939 – Date CFY1997: I deemed this a mischarge of IRAD since C-130J was a commercial contract. However, this went one step further in that the C-27J was being developed as a foreign cost offset for a foreign government. The foreign cost offset is loosely explained as a foreign government purchasing Lockheed Martin C-130Js, and in turn, Lockheed Martin would develop the C-27J. Meaning, Lockheed Martin is funding a foreign competitor and charging development cost to other contracts (F-22, C-5, etc.) via overhead.

Total Questioned Charges: $6,822,939 + $311,925 + $140,468 + $1,061,975 = $8,337,307

"Blank Check" Charging - Up To 12X Airforce Cost

PWL (Post Wash Lube) is basically a grease job on a C-5 aircraft. The main point is that Lockheed Martin was allowed a "Blank Check," charging above the estimated amounts. This is part of the Capstone example of Chapter 5 of this book. The brief explanation is as follows.

"Blank Check" Charging - Over & Above Work: "Blank Check" charging is a descriptive or analogous term linked to Over & Above work, which means work outside the scope of the contract. Documenting Over & Above work is known as Modification Inspection Reports (MIRs), which also includes Modification Deficiency Reports (MDRs). Basically, repairs that are either needed (such as safety of flight issues) or are optional. PWL is one such example.

July 23, 2013 – PWL 1st Contact: The C-5 Program Office was concerned with Lockheed Martin's estimates versus charging on PWL. On July 23, 2013, it was stated that the "*maintenance guys at Dover* (AFB)" took "*24-30 hours*" to prep and complete PWL. The following Lockheed Martin PWL hours billed on a "Blank Check" basis (meaning above estimates) was as follows.

Task	Estimate	Hours Billed – "Blank Check" Billing
Post Wash Lube	-	189.3 Hours
Post Wash Lube	39 Hours	203.2 Hours
Post Wash Lube	39 Hours	59 Hours
Post Wash Lube	38 Hours	224.1 Hours

January 28, 2014 – Draft PWL Report – "Blank Check" Audit Quashed: I was only allowed to issue a Draft Copy report by my then supervisor, Mark Buckner, on PWL. Most likely because I again probed into the "Belly of the Beast" for apparent cost mischarging corruption and made discoveries.

Cost Mischarging: There was the appearance with circumstantial evidence Lockheed Martin was using the "Blank Checks" (bill whatever Lockheed Martin wanted) to cover for cost overruns on the C-5 RERP. I included this in my January 28, 2014 report with peripheral support evidence. This also feeds into the C-5 RERP Claim Capstone Case in Chapter 5. The chart below is what Lockheed Martin estimated and what Lockheed Martin "Billed".

Task	Estimate	Hours Billed – "Blank Check" Billing
Post Wash Lube	38 Hours	224.2 Hours
Post Wash Lube	39 Hours	59.0 Hours
Post Wash Lube	39 Hours	371.6 Hours
Post Wash Lube	39 Hours	477.7 Hours
Post Wash Lube	39 Hours	380.5 Hours
Post Wash Lube	30 Hours	73.2 Hours

The data showed Lockheed Martin, in some cases, took 12 times longer for PWL than the Air Force would do for 24-30 hours. From a cost perspective, the Air Force cost is $7,500 (30 Hours X $250/Hour) compared to a Lockheed Martin cost of $119,425 (477.7 Hours X $250/Hour). That is using the Lockheed Martin wrap rate of $250/hour, with the Air Force rate more than likely being much lower.

Meaning, Lockheed Martin billed over $100,000 to grease a C-5 while the Air Force cost was likely $7,500 or maybe less. This supports the theme of massive contributions to the National Debt.

I had made disclosures about 9 years prior on a similar "Blank Check" charging as follows.

February 1, 2005 – Fraud Disclosure: I observed others complain about Over & Above work cost charging for years. One of my earlier disclosures stated contracting officers are:

"*allowing Lockheed to charge to the C-5 Modernization contract with no fixed price estimate of work or knowledge of how much Lockheed is charging to the contract.*"

Meaning, Lockheed Martin was allowed uncontrolled charging ("Blank Check" analogy) for Over & Above work well prior to 2013 and 2014.

January 16, 2014 – Fraud Disclosure: I made another fraud disclosure on the MDR issue (PWL) since my then supervisor, Mark Buckner, would only allow a Draft report to be issued aside from the obvious overcharging, which I believe was contract mischarging. For completeness, 2014 also saw another disclosure, from a person other than me, as follows.

C-5 RERP DoD IG Substantiated Allegations

November 18, 2014 (DoD IG Audit Report 2015-039): On May 29, 2013 a DoD IG hotline complaint was issued against the Lockheed Martin C-5 RERP by someone other than myself. The complaint may have been delayed due to a hostile work environment reported on October 9, 2014 dated back to May 28, 2013 incident. Regardless, six allegations were made, with four substantiated, as follows:

1: Government failed to discourage repeated tendering of nonconforming components. (Substantiated)

2: Government delegated inherently Government functions to Lockheed Martin. (Substantiated)

3: Government failed to approve and document Lockheed Martin flights. (Undetermined)

4: Government accepted non-conformances that were corrected at additional cost to the government. (Substantiated)

5: The DCMA failed to comply with the DCMA Instruction for the corrective action process. (Substantiated)

6: Government failed to ensure that Lockheed Martin used U.S. Air Force service guidance. (Not Substantiated)

Aside from this, overhead rates were also victims of the altered working conditions and deterioration of Lockheed Martin accounting.

Project Business Base & Overhead Rates –
23.9%-38.5% Cost Increase

Plant Wide Actuals & Accurate Business Base to Project Overhead Rates: On about 2001 I saw the decline in Lockheed Martin data and infrastructure to support and project overhead rate analysis. As already stated herein, other declines actually began in 1998. This was technically known as Forward Pricing Rates (FPR), used to project future and anticipated cost of DoD goods and services. Good historical data is needed to make accurate projections.

In the 1990s, Lockheed Martin could provide a complete summary account of Plant Wide Actuals for each program with a detailed breakout of direct labor hours for production, manufacturing, quality assurance, engineering branch, engineering shop, integrated logistics support (ILS), business management, production support, flight ops, etc. This was the Business Base for overhead rates.

Plant Wide Actuals provided summarized data for each of the aforesaid departments' direct labor hours. From there accurate analysis could be done on past data. Then, the projection of future business base could be performed for use on future overhead rates (FPR) to price out future DoD contracts. Similarly, providing an amount for Congress to budget in the DoD.

Simply stated, accurate past data is needed as a starting point to project future overhead rates. Prior to 2001, the history was determinable and available. After 2001, the data ended with a decay in Lockheed Martin infrastructure that ran in parallel to the half-century decay outlined herein. The following are the results of one of the last FPRs I did where good data was available.

August 31, 2000 - C-130J Overhead Rates 23.9% - 38.5%: One of my last analyses indicated Lockheed Martin rates were off 23%-38.5%. Meaning, the overhead rates were too high and the government was paying 23%-38.5% too much on overhead cost for the C-130J.

This relates to Lockheed Martin's loss of infrastructure and financial discipline, which dates back to 1998, as previously stated in Chapter 4. The DCMA has also lost infrastructure in the form of skills to calculate contractor overhead rates. That is why I was made a SME to teach analysis of contractor overhead rates beginning 2017. Also, the DCMA mismanaged the DCMA contracts.

The DCMA Mismanaged the DCMA Contracts

August 16, 2018 – Integrated Workload Management System (IWMS) Mismanaged: POGO issued an investigative report titled: "*Pentagon's Contracting Gurus Mismanaged Their Own Contracts*" by Daniel Van Schooten.

A few years prior to the POGO article, I was aware that the IWMS project was staffed by my DCMA colleagues, some of whom I knew. I was unaware of the project management skills of the selected the DCMA employees. My understanding is that the IWMS project was 90% telework, meaning the DCMA employees worked at home 90% of the time.

In/about 2018, I heard a rumor that the IWMS project lost $75 million, and no one knew where it went. I was not surprised since this was typical DCMA.

At some point after August 16, 2018, I was told that the DCMA was again criticized for poor performance. I asked what the issue was and discovered POGO did a report on the IWMS project. Sample quotes from the POGO article as follows.

"*The Pentagon's contracting gurus repeatedly made massive, preventable mistakes while managing contracts for a critical software project of their own, violating federal budget law along the way, according to scathing internal reports and other records obtained by the Project On Government Oversight. Ironically, the purpose of the mismanaged system is to help manage the rest of the Pentagon's contracts.*

At various points, the internal documents POGO obtained state that some of the agency's foul-ups on the project indicate "a serious systemic problem within the organization" and raise "serious concern over contracting practices and processes within DCMA." The draft final report states that many senior leaders set the agency's procurement staff "and DCMA up for failure."

The project, called the Integrated Workload Management System, is a software system created to help review, implement, and track defense contracts. By the time the agency abruptly stopped all development work on the system in May 2017, it had awarded over $46.6 million in contracts related to the project over the course of three fiscal years (an agency spokesperson says the agency kept contract costs down to $44.9 million). At least $17 million of this was unauthorized-a violation of a budget law called the Antideficiency Act. Penalties for such a violation can include a prison sentence, though that is rare; however, the investigation found evidence that one employee had "willful intent to violate" the law."

Relevance is, the DCMA is grossly deficient and negligent in managing DoD contracts as this book has shown. The POGO article spoke of "*$37 million in suspected separate Anti deficiency Act violations-on top of the confirmed $17 million in violations found by the independent investigation.*" It is unknown where the rumored $75 million loss fits in other than hearsay and rumor; however, I would not quickly discount the $75 million.

Cup Holders - Coffee Pots - Coffee Cups - Toilets ($802 - $22,105)

The following is a list of spare parts horror stories found in 2017 and 2018. Unknown if they still continue however with gross mismanagement and price gouging, the trend probably endures.

July 11, 2017 - $1,407.03 Cup Holders: Lockheed Martin sold the cup holders for $1,407.03 although apparently paid $888/unit. This shows the impact of rates, factors, and profit which total in the 30%+ range. The Army Depot had a price of $464/unit and some other activities may have a price of $700/unit.

August 31, 2017 - $802.78 Coffee Pot: The price for the coffee pot was based on Lockheed Martin apparently reducing the height by 2 inches to fit on the C-130J.

June 26, 2018 - $22,105.78 Toilets: This amount may be for the entire toilet versus just the seat although unknown if this toilet comes with the seat or the toilet seat is purchased separately.

Regardless there is an extended price of $88,423.12 when 4 toilets were purchased.

October 30, 2018 - $1,280 Coffee Cups (Washington CNN Zachary Cohen): Senator Grassley questioned the Air Force on the $1,280 coffee cups. The article stated that the "*Air Force has spent $326,785 on nearly 400 cups since 2016 – an average of $817.*"

Factored Cost - Relevance and Impact: The data raises interesting traceability on overhead rates and factors (EFs, EFDs, CERs) with the $1,407.03 cup holders as the example. The added factors can escalate the amounts in the 49%+ range. This may be a few hundred dollars for the cup holders; however, for large DoD purchases, the added rates (EFs, EFDs, CERs) may go into the millions or even billions over the years, or decades, depending on the purchase size.

Meaning, escalated rates and factors for the price gouging effect have a ripple effect in direct contract price.

Extrapolating History to Current State of Affairs: This book covers a half-century of information on the Deep State, Federal Machinery, price gouging, etc., which means there is an extension past Lockheed Martin. Ernie Fitzgerald has shown that point. The following is an extension that explains how past problems extrapolate to the current state of affairs using Boeing as an example.

Boeing 2024 News - Link to - 1990s McDonnell Douglas

Boeing 2024 Guilty Plea – Conspiracy to Defraud: In 2024, Boeing made the news by pleading guilty to one charge of conspiracy to defraud the U.S. for the role in two fatal 737 MAX crashes. Other issues surround an aircraft door blowing out. These events should not be surprising because the past history of Boeing parallels Lockheed Martin and McDonnell Douglas.

The closest proximity to current Boeing events would be Boeing and McDonnell Douglas, which merged in about 1997. The information trail starts as follows.

March 16, 1992 (Ernest Fitzgerald Report on C-17): A report from Ernie Fitzgerald outlined several deficiencies at the McDonnell Douglas, Long Beach, California, facility regarding the C-17. The following is a sample list of issues.

"*no priced bill of material for the C-17 available...*" There were complaints about this going back to 1988.

"*The factory appeared ill-disciplined, sloppy, with obviously poor methods and quality practices – in short, almost unmanaged.*" Ernie Fitzgerald also noted a "*...pattern of non-enforcement of contractual requirements...*"

Command Influence: Ernie Fitzgerald's report also mentioned an incident where 3 senior Air Force officials visited the C-17 facility to assist in getting McDonnell Douglas Corporation a progress payment on the C-17. Among the officials was "*Ms. Darlene Druyen*" [sic].

Following Druyun's visit with other senior Air Force officers, the progress payment was justified with the following wording: "*This payment is made in light of the urgent and pressing financial need of the McDonnell Douglas Corporation and the potential adverse impact to the C-17 program.*" Relevance is that command influence can play a part in getting corporations' money.

Following Fitzgerald's report, the DoD IG would do their own investigations and publish their own findings on the C-17 program, affirming the C-17 had serious issues, and expand on the issues.

January 14, 1993 - DoD IG Report on McDonnell Douglas: The DoD IG report was titled, "*Government Actions Concerning McDonnell Douglas Corporation Financial Condition During 1990*". This report identified specific practices used by government officials on the C-17 to create false appearances of success and cover-up inappropriate actions. Sample quotes are as follows.

"Improper contracting actions reduced contractor financial risk on the C-17 program by $1.6 billion and created a false appearance of success to facilitate both the contractor obtaining additional financing through commercial sources and issuance of debt securities, and the Air Force securing additional funding from Congress."

"The improper actions substantially increased Government program risk, provided premature payments to the contractor, negatively impacted first aircraft delivery, and contractually obligated the Government to award a subsequent Lot III production contract." The Lot III production contract was important as *"additional source of funding"* to the contractor and provided a *"false indication of program success"*.

"Established Government oversight and internal management control processes"..., "were impaired by Air Force officials." "These officials provided incomplete and misleading information, and, in some cases, relied on intimidation and abuse of their positions of responsibility to cause improper actions to be taken."

"The SPD (System Program Director)*; the Deputy Comptroller, Air Force Systems Command; and the Deputy Chief of Staff for Contracting, Air Force Systems Command improperly interfered with the process for administration of Government progress payments. They provided unsubstantiated and misleading information to senior acquisition officials and cognizant contract administration personnel at the Defense Plant Representative Office (DPRO) to cause premature contract payments."*

"...we identified contracting actions that appeared to be "rushed" primarily to ensure continuing cash flow to the MDC (McDonnell Douglas Corporation) *and to show improvement in its financial condition."*

"The actions taken by senior Air Force officials resulted in improper financial assistance to the contractor and covered up the need to establish an executable program schedule."

"Additionally, the contractor acted, partly with the support and approval of Air Force officials, to suppress negative financial information concerning losses on the program."

"The SPD, with the assistance of the Deputy Comptroller of the Air Force Systems Command, used his rank and position to direct or influence a wide range of improper actions. He was subsequently praised for his performance and promoted by the Air Force." When the actions of the SPD were challenged by the Inspector General the *"Air Force summarily decided no further review of these matters was warranted."*

"Conversely, the DPRO Commander, an Air Force Colonel, acted to protect the government interest and was criticized for not being a "team player."

C-17 Mirrors C-130J: McDonnell Douglas was a mirror image of the C-130J. Examples are the use of rank and position for cover-ups, and not being labeled a "team player" as a start. After I made my February 28, 2000 criminal (fraud) disclosure on the C-5 PDM, my supervisor openly wrote on my performance appraisal (July 26, 2000), *"Needs improvement in the area of teaming & team work."* Meaning, weaponized government using adverse performance evaluations as weapons.

Half Century Extrapolation: Corruption has been institutionalized in DoD for half a century. Ernie Fitzgerald's situation dated back to 1970. My situation with the Falsified Trails went from 2003 to 2015 and included the denial of even temporary promotions after that. Meaning, it is possible to extrapolate data herein to the national debt, further meaning that trying to find the corruption in government is like trying to find the end of the universe.

Lack of Corrective Action Enables Further Corruption

Senior officials on the C-17 program were recommended for disciplinary action in the January 14, 1993, DoD IG Report. Among them was Darleen Druyun. The list of senior officials recommended for disciplinary action includes:

Ms. Darleen Druyun (Former Deputy Chief of Staff for Contracting at the Air Force Systems Command)

Lieutenant General Barry (Former C-17 Program Executive Officer)

Major General Butchko (Former C-17 System Program Director)

Brigadier General Nauseef (Former Deputy Comptroller for the Air Force Systems Command)

C-17 Deputy Director for Contracting (No Name provided)

It is unknown if anyone was truly disciplined; however, Druyun continued her career.

Darleen Druyun Continues Career: Darleen Druyun would later be upgraded to the position of Principal Deputy Assistant Secretary (Acquisition & Management) (Air Force). About a decade after the McDonnell Douglas incident, Darleen Druyun would plead guilty to a conflict of interest.

April 20, 2004 - Druyun Pleads Guilty: Darleen Druyun pleaded guilty to a conflict-of-interest charge when she accepted a $250,000 a year job with Boeing.

The point is, nothing changed, status quo. As such, NASA (National Aeronautics and Space Administration) is the next example with astronauts stuck in space and the NASA DoD IG.

NASA History & Astronauts Stranded in Space

Astronauts Stuck in Space: In 2024, the NASA astronauts stranded in space were an issue, as apparently related to Boeing. However, NASA issues go deeper as follows.

January 22, 2007 - NASA IG Robert Cobb: An IG investigation on January 22, 2007, focused on, among other issues, an abusive work environment by NASA IG Robert Cobb. The investigation indicated that IG Cobb used profanity calling the staff member's work a "*fucking piece of shit*"; Special Agents in the field as "*knuckle draggers*"; And referring to staff as "*fuck sticks*".

One account stated: "*morale among NASA OIG staff was "horrible.""* The report stated "*IG Cobb confirmed use of the F-word in his office*".

The report also indicated "*investigators organized the case into 79 separate allegations.*"

The point is, DCMA, DoD IG, NASA, Boeing, Lockheed Martin, etc., all seem to follow the same pattern. Meaning, the overall system is enabled by institutional corrupted government and a laughable, and enabling. U.S. Legal and Judicial System. Past damage is not easily undone. Cronies may be left in place, damage carries forward, and infrastructure is damaged. I talk from experience and documentation on that point as shown herein.

The next two sections are the segue to the capstone case. Meaning, a detailed look at the collapse of financial reporting and tracking for major DoD development programs.

Systemic management and performance issues are as follows.

Systemic Management & Performance Issues - 1998 Onward

1998 Start of Systemic Issues Enabled by Acquisition Reform: The year 1998 was the start of systemic issues for Lockheed Martin. Acquisition Reform of the 1990s started the downfall and enabled the cover-up. As previously shown, on June 22, 1998 Lockheed Martin, Bill Bullock, stated in part: *"Our current program and functional reviews are not capable of providing what we need."* The next month, July 24, 1998, a Lockheed Martin contract was rescoped (adjusted) *"to align with Lockheed Martin's demonstrated support capability"* not because of a change in customer requirements. The systemic issues were most noticeable in Lockheed Martin's EVMS.

Lockheed Martin's EVMS issues and inability to perform on contracts were embedded in Falsified Trails 4 through 11. EVMS is used on complex development projects as a management tool to track progress on cost and schedule using a comparison of budgeted work against actual work completed. EVMS is based on data, and if the data is inaccurate, the EVMS output will be inaccurate.

EVMS is analogous to the computer phrase; garbage in, garbage out. Meaning that if the estimating system is defective, therefore, the EVMS output will be defective. This is in addition to adding EVMS parameters correctly and tracking the completion of work correctly. As this book shows, Lockheed Martin is deficient in all areas.

Falsified Trail 11 showed that Lockheed Martin could not provide one document to prove schedule tracking. The following explains why.

May 9, 2002 – First Documented EVMS Problem: A then fellow employee and colleague, Myra Tate, began questioning Lockheed Martin EVMS system processes during Joint Surveillance, which means Lockheed Martin and the DCMA oversee Lockheed Martin together as a team. Problems arose, and Tate informed 2nd-level supervisor Joe Caldwell, along with others, of the following.

"*I can not get LM Aero to commit to the Joint Surveillance Agreement. It seems the agreement has gone to being merely a check mark for getting it done with not much action thereafter. Whenever I try to set a meeting date, they are non-responsive. Those meetings that I have conducted have been very difficult to schedule.*"

This was the first data point I remember about Lockheed Martin EVMS problems. Myra Tate was Deputy Commander during Volley 4 of the Falsified Trails 11, 12 & 13. However, Myra Tate was an employee, not management, in 2002. Meaning, once in management there is an assimilation that takes place as evident in the Falsified Trails.

June 4, 2002, Continuance of EVMS Systemic Issues: Myra Tate continued addressing Lockheed Martin EVMS problems with Joe Caldwell, stating the following.

"The biggest problem has been with the C-5 program...this problem is not just limited to C-5. It has been a challenge scheduling these meetings with all the managers; there appears to be a lack of committment on the part of LM Aero. I strongly suggest that we develop a surveillance schedule."

Lockheed Martin was resistant to being audited or even to Joint Surveillance as early as 2002. This forced the prospect of a Corrective Action Request (CAR).

August 13, 2002 Draft EVMS Corrective Action Request: Myra Tate forwarded me a copy of the Draft CAR to Lockheed Martin on October 1, 2002. Unknown if the CAR was ever issued. The Draft CAR outlined an OTB (Over Target Baseline), which means the original plan (baseline) exceeded cost estimates (went over budget). The Draft CAR stated in part.

"*LMAS* (Lockheed Martin) *has not demonstrated compliance with the prescribed EVMS Criteria and continues to experience systemic problems with baseline maintenance and control and cost estimating namely in the development of EAC* (Estimate at Completion). *As a result, unexpected cost growth continues to affect large dollar value programs. There are six EV programs at the Marietta site, three of which are deemed significant based on dollar value, the F-22 EMD* (Engineering Manufacturing and Development), *C-5 AMP* (Avionics Modernization Program), *and C-5 RERP* (C-5 Reliability Enhancement and Re-Engining Program). *The C-5 RERP only recently began EV reporting. The remaining two programs are high visibility programs, which have experienced several baseline changes as well as OTBs since inception.*

There is no evidence of sound risk management practices and estimating practices in place to preclude any of the cost growth currently being experienced on the EV reporting programs."

Meaning, Lockheed Martin could not perform on contracts. The remedy, by then Deputy Commander Ben Chaffman, was to relieve Myra Tate of EVMS duties.

September 24, 2002 3:40PM– Relieved of EVMS Duties: A little over a month after Myra Tate proposed a Draft Car on Lockheed Martin EVMS, Myra Tate was relieved of her EVMS duties. The reason for the removal of duties by Ben Chaffman was that Tate was doing the duties above her grade level. It is notable that Tate had done the EVMS duties for nearly 2 years (19 months). Tate forwarded me her lengthy Memorandum for Record, which stated as a purpose:

"*Discussion of meeting held to relieve Myra Tate of her EV System Surveillance duties*"

Relevance is, Myra Tate and I were on the same page as employees documenting complaints about management. I just took the documentation to a new level and went to Congress with problems.

Notably, Myra Tate's Memorandum for Record (MFR) indicated Tate was relieved of duties "*At approximately 12:30 p.m. on Sep 24, 2002*". Tate forwarded her MFR to management and union officials on September 24, 2002, at 3:40 PM, and immediately, within the same minute, forwarded me the MFR. Tate did inform me of plans for litigation, meaning an EEO case.

Shaking Up Management: Myra Tate also informed me, near the time her (Tate) EVMS duties were removed, that whatever I was doing was shaking up management. This was most likely due to the July 26, 2002, report to Congress that did make it back to the DCMA. Relevance is, Myra Tate and I were on the same page as fellow employees prior to Tate moving into management.

Myra Tate Settlement June 19, 2003: As an employee, Myra Tate kept me informed of her (Tate) litigation after EVMS duties were removed. The DCMA later provided me with Myra Tate's settlement agreement dated June 19, 2003.

Continuing the 2002 timeline, Myra Tate identified locally what was obvious on a larger scale and involved the F-22.

September 26, 2002 – Colonel Wright F-22 Joint Estimate Review Team (JERT): The F-22 was experiencing cost problems, and the commanding officer (Colonel Wright, 4th-level supervisor) was doing a review of what was obvious locally. Colonel Wright stated in an e-mail in part:

"*I wanted to let you know that the USAF has made the decision, which was endorsed by Gen Harrington* (then DCMA Director) *that I would be the Government Team Lead for the F-22 JERT (read Should Cost Review). This will require me to be full time on the team between now and approximately the middle part of January 03.*"

Relevance is that about two days after Myra Tate's duties were removed, the commanding officer (Colonel Wright, part of Falsified Trails 1 & 2) was on a special F-22 review team. This was shortly after my first Congressional report of July 26, 2002, which was shaking up management, meaning a lot of documented problems existed in 2002 and prior. There was no resolution, only cover-ups.

January 16, 2003 – EVMS Monitor Moves to Management: I documented that the responsibility for EVMS monitoring had been shifted to the management GS-14 level (2nd-level supervisor). I copied that fact to DoD IG auditor Tom Bartoszek, who was working on allegations from my July 26, 2002, disclosure to Congress. I stated the following in part to Bartosek.

"*Just heard yesterday that the EVMS monitor has moved up to the GS-14 level. It was taken from Ms. Myra Tate (GS-12 Engineer) (I provided you info how she was relieved shortly after writing a corrective action request (CAR) against Lockheed Martin.)*" From there, it was shifted to a GS-13 (lead engineer) and then to Joe Caldwell (2nd-level supervisor).

Relevance is, management was now doing employee work on EVMS. There may be many theories; however, a management staff "shaken up" by a Congressional report may have wanted to contain negative information. One way of containing negative information is the issuance of "Draft" CARs that also give the "all is well" appearance, allowing false certifications such as ISO 9000.

Draft CARs to Conceal Problems & Enable Certification

June 30, 2003 – ISO 9000 False Certification from "Draft" CARs: The issue of the Draft CAR Myra Tate was going to issue is deeper and more far-reaching than it appears. The focus is on the word "Draft". When a Draft report or CAR is forwarded, it is not logged and largely ignored as if it never happened, or was never finalized. The chain of events regarding Draft CARs starts with the June 30, 2003, Substantiated Allegation 2 in my resume (Chapter 1), which stated in part:

"*Although officials at Warner Robins Air Logistics Center repeatedly requested LMAS officials to address the EFI* (Electronic Flight Indicator) *performance problems, no formal action was taken and failures continued to increase and aircraft began to be grounded. DCMA decided that formal action was needed and issued a draft, unsigned Level III CAR on September 24, 2000, to LMAS to expedite repair of the EFI units.*"

In short, Draft CARs bury problems. In this case, which was multiple C-130s grounded, as the June 30, 2003, substantiated allegation states in part as follows. "*As a result, more than 1,100 EFI failures occurred and 16 C-130H aircraft were grounded. In addition, confusion concerning DCMA policy continues and future logistics problems from poor planning and oversight may occur.*"

April 5, 2001 – Disclosure on Draft CARs: This issue seems isolated; however, the Draft CARs facilitated Lockheed Martin to be certified in ISO 9000 because the Draft CARs were not logged and thus not part of the ISO 9000 review. On April 5, 2001, I made the following disclosure on DoD IG Case 79529, which was a precursor to the June 30, 2003, substantiated disclosure. I stated in part on April 5, 2001.

"*Below is my compalint and additional information I submitted on case 79529. (That was the case where I explained how Corrective Action Requests {CARs) are being covered up at this facility, along with other things .) Well in any good investment one should expect dividends, interest, capital gains, etc. This project (cover-up) was no exception.*

Yesterday and today (4/4/01 and 4/5/01) I attended a British Standards Institute (BSI) audit of LMAC. Basically LMAC has to be recertified in ISO 9000 periodically. During the management briefing (4/4/01) LMAC (Ms. Janet Nash) presented to BSI (Mr. Peter Tilford) that they had received no Level III CARs this year. A truly outstanding event, in my opinion."

October 23, 2003: The Draft CAR issue surfaced again on October 23, 2003, when Colonel Evans (past commander) went to work for Lockheed Martin. I was working with Senator Boxer's staff at that time and forwarded the April 5, 2001, aforesaid disclosure on October 23, 2003, stating in part.

"*This is an old e-mail that I found where the benefits of (Colonel Evans) not issuing Corrective Action against Lockheed showed up. That is under ISO 9000 (quality system) the contractor (Lockheed) would have to show how they corrected problems from the customer (government) complaints. The fact that Colonel Evans did not issue corrective action against Lockheed did provide benefits to Lockheed during certification. That is Lockheed looks good during certification time by not having any complaints from the customer. Colonel Evans was the one representing the government (customer).*"

Relevance is, Draft reports and Draft CARs do document problems; however, they are covered up due to the "Draft" designation, which implies the problems were not formally followed up on. In this case, Lockheed Martin achieved ISO 9000 certification (basically bragging rights), although problems existed that may have precluded ISO Certification.

August 31, 2018: Joe Tessier worked with the DCMA HQ on OASIS (On-Line Aerospace Supplier Information System), which is only applicable to organizations that have AS9100 on contract and certified to the current version. The relevance and concern are my documented history of Joe Tessier and the fact that the DCMA assisted in covering up problems so Lockheed Martin can get BSI certification. The point being, cover-ups to enable certifications where problems exist.

"Draft" Reports - "Don't Write It Down" - Manufactured Regulations

As a brief summary, June 3, 1994, was a Draft report on the C-130J; August 13, 2002, Draft CAR by Myra Tate; April 5, 2001, and October 23, 2003, Draft CARs disclosures that enabled Lockheed Martin ISO 9000 certifications; January 28, 2014, Draft report on MDRs by Mark Buckner. On November 3, 2016, the special, manufactured, regulations for me for the F-35 were published. The 13 Falsified Trails also help conceal information by altering working conditions. The next issue is to just "*Don't Write It Down*".

July 15, 2004 "Don't Write It Down": In 2004, there was an e-mail trail titled "*Don't Write It Down - Cover-up*". This followed a training class that mirrored the "Draft" CARs and reports. The July 15, 2004, disclosure stated in part.

"*I just left a class on Predictive Analysis which took place on July 13-15, 2004. One of the instructors from DCMA Mr. Larry Ciangiolo (DCMA) casually mentioned a remark made which apparently came from one of the program managers on the THAD program. (Apparently some type of missile, I am not sure.)*

The remark was that the Program Manager indicated to the people under him to "Don't write it down". This was in apparent reference to problems being discovered on the program and an attempt to cover-up issues."

"*Consider this e-mail as my note to you of on going cover-ups in the Department of Defense and the fact that I write issues down. That simple remark (Don't write it down), and others like it are a pre-cursor to cover-up actions.*"

The "don't write it down" comment enables further corruption and eliminates objective evidence trails. As noted herein, I wrote down, documented, and kept detailed notes on the DCMA and DoD to leave a complete evidence trail of issues back to root causes. I cared enough to do this due to my concern about witnessing the maleficence by the DCMA and DoD management.

Continuing with EVMS, the problems continued to surface. However, I was now in a position to document EVMS problems directly.

Documented EVMS Cover-up – Cost & Schedule Tracking

May 2006 Approximate: In May 2006, I began EVMS duties for C-5 RERP, assisting another employee who was the lead. This was after the 30-day suspension for Falsified Trail 3. I was now directly involved in EVMS. Management was mistaken if they thought a 30-Day suspension (Falsified Trail 3) would snap me in line. I continued to document to have a clear record.

Shortly after I arrived on the project, Lockheed Martin management, primarily Ray Burick, started to withhold data as follows, similar to Falsified Trail 1.

Schedule Tracking Data Withheld – Ray Burick in 2006

July 24, 2006 1:46 PM: The EVMS report I issued had a set of statistics that measured overall progress of developmental C-5 RERP aircraft (known as SDD, System Design & Development). The monthly statistics came from Lockheed Martin data. The DCMA program integrator, Lou Gentile, forwarded the DCMA daily status report to government offices and Lockheed Martin senior officials.

July 24, 2006 2:52 PM: Blair Marks, a Lockheed Martin senior manager, emailed Gentile asking:

"*Lou,*

Out of curiosity, how are you making the progress measurement you described as follows:

DCMA Engineering has been tracking overall (top level) progress on SDD #2 (111) and SDD #3 (55). Statistics are as follows: SDD #2 (111) has progressed 6% during the month of July 2006 (data date July 20,2006) versus 5% increase progress during entire month of June 2006. Thus progress has increased. SDD #3 (55) has also progressed 6% for the month of July 2006 (data date July 20, 2006) versus 4% progress during entire month of June 2006. It seems that progress is increasing at a faster pace than before for both SDD #2 and SDD #3. With another week to go in July 2006 progress should be far better than past months."

The statement above regarding SDD aircraft was my EVMS input. The Lockheed Martin data was showing progress slower than expected. When projected out, the data indicated first flight for the SDD aircraft would not be met. Meaning, Lockheed Martin data for the first flight conflicted with Lockheed Martin data for the actual schedule progress.

<u>July 24, 2006 5:15 PM</u>: Gentile emailed my colleague and me and asked:

"Can you help me answer the question below? I should probably know the answer already but I can't think of it at the moment. I sure it has to do with our analysis of EV data..."

<u>July 25, 2006 7:43 AM</u>: My colleague responded to Gentile and provided the name of the Lockheed Martin employee who provided the data.

<u>August 21, 2006</u>: I went to my Lockheed Martin contact for a schedule, asking for the progress of the SDD aircraft. The response was as follows.

Ken,

I would like to request that you get these charts through the Program Office. (Mr. Ray Burick)

Following this comment, I contacted Ray Burick for the data (August 21–23, 2006) along with others in DCMA and Lockheed Martin. Burick was illusive and mentioned some type of weekly review. The long story short is I was denied the data by Ray Burick. Probably because Lockheed Martin's Data conflicted with what was outlined in the schedule. The point being, Ray Burick was instrumental in Falsified Trail 11 and Lockheed Martin had schedule problems from 2006 to 2014.

<u>August 23, 2006 – Complaint Against Ray Burick</u>: I emailed Blair Marks and the Senior Lockheed Martin program manager on C-5 RERP (George Schultz), stating in part.

"Monday of this week (August 21, 2006) Mr. Ray Burick has begun withholding information from me regarding schedule on the C-5M Program regarding Ships 55 and 111."

"To make a long story short, I had some confidence that the C-5M program (prior to Mr. Burick's shut down of information) may be a success. That confidence is now shaken. Mr. Burick has (per my records) not responded to my request below.

If Lockheed Martin has nothing to hide on the C-5M program then information flow should be open and there should be transparency. If Lockheed Martin does have something to hide then I suspect that Mr. Burick's intransigent attitude will be supported by senior leadership of LMAC."

I cannot remember the data being provided again. This was a duplicate of the 2014 Falsified Trail 11 as related to Ray Burick.

Standard Communication: Alleged rude and disrespectful comments were common when I stated to Lockheed Martin: *"If Lockheed Martin does have something to hide then I suspect that Mr. Burick's intransigent attitude will be supported by senior leadership of LMAC* (Lockheed Martin)*."* Meaning, prior to February 12, 2009 alleged rude and disrespectful comments were common. DCMA and Lockheed Martin had serious issues and took allegations in stride until corruption in the U.S. Legal system was confirmed on February 12, 2009. Then the enabled cover-ups accelerated.

The following shows that Lockheed Martin had other systemic EVMS problems.

EVMS System Level Non-Compliance – 2007 Onward

November 19, 2007: The DCMA documented the following result of an August 20-31, 2007, Post Acceptance Review for Cause (RFC), in part stating.

"The DCMA EVM Center, fulfilling its role and responsibilities as the DoD Executive Agent for EVMS, has reviewed the overall processes and contents of the LMAC EVMS and recommends the Divisional Administrative Contracting Officer (DACO) not accept the LMAC EVMS as being compliant with the 32 guidelines of the ANSl-748-98 Standard without significant corrective action. At this time the probability of LMAC successfully implementing a corrective action plan is good. The DCMA findings indicate that the supplier has not overcome internal issues associated with organization, work authorization, scheduling, managerial analysis, subcontract management, and material management. Also, in large part, the system description and associated processes failed to meet the intent of the guidelines due to interpretive inaccuries and incompleteness."

"The DCMA EVM Center has thoroughly documented the results of the RFC process showing that LMAC had not demonstrated compliance at the time of the review. One hundred thirty one (131) Level 1 Discrepancy Reports (DR) were generated during the review. The findings associated with each DR raise concerns regarding LMAC's management processes and practices and their ability to assess emerging issues of cost, schedule, and technical performance in a timely manner. These concerns also bring into question the accuracy and validity of the performance measurement data that is being used to manage DoD Programs."

Hence, Lockheed Martin continued EVMS problems past 2002. As a side note, on June 22, 1998 William Bullock issued a memorandum to his Operating Council indicating; "*Our current program and functional reviews are not capable of providing what we need*". Thus, admitting internally that process controls and measurement systems had problems. The issue surrounding the antics of Ray Burick in withholding data are well documented. From there, the Falsified Trails took center stage as follows.

Falsified Trails 4 – 11 Take Effect – Cover-up EVMS Problems

Chapter 3 of this book had details of Falsified Trails 1 – 13. Of those, Falsified Trails 4 through 11 were centered largely on Lockheed Martin EVMS issues, although Lockheed Martin had problems past EVMS. For expediency, and to save space in this section, the reader may review Falsified Trails 4 thru 11. Meaning, there is no sense in repeating what has already been stated. However, I did make a DoD IG complaint that was not outlined in Falsified Trails 4 through 11 as follows.

March 4, 2009 1:08 PM – DoD IG Disclosure: I made a disclosure directly to Gordon Heddell then DoD IG Director. I copied Colonel Blake, Nanette Nelson, Henrietta Snow, Joe Tessier, and then C-5 Government Program Manager John Artuso, stating in part.

"I am obligated by law (as well as my own personnel ethics) to disclose issues that I believe to be of a waste, fraud, or abuse issue. I hold Colonel Casey Blake accountable for the issues I am raising below. (The precedent is called vicarious liability. When the manager knows of a problem and allows it to continue then the manager is of equal blame.)

Contrary to what Ms. Nelson has stated on her attached letter, I was pressured to change my report and I advised Ms. Nelson that I was responsible for defending the conclusions in the report. The letter contains false statements designed to make me look bad. In fact, the more I read Ms. Nelson's letter (knowing that she had input to write it) the more concerned I become.

At present LM Aero is denying access to software personnel and I am denied access to LRIP data. I am developing workarounds however that does not resolve the issue. Colonel Blake has allowed a small issue to escalate (all I wanted to do was report accurate data and document for future reference) so I must be on to something that needs to be hidden at this facility."

Relevance is, I cannot remember a response to this disclosure from management or the DoD IG. I also notified the C-5 Program management government office as follows.

March 4, 2009 3:48 PM: I forwarded a copy of Nanette Nelson's Memorandum regarding rewrites of my reports to the C-5 RERP Program officials at Wright Patterson AFB, including Program Manager John Artuso, along with Nanette Nelson, and Joe Tessier. I stated the following.

"I am no longer able to provide you direct copies of my EVMS reports. My reports are being censored by management in accordance with the attached letter of direction.

I have sent separate letter to Mr. Artuso and DoD IG identifying my concerns with the altering of my reports."

As is typical, no corrective action or concern was heard. It is typical that at a time of problems, the DCMA management stifles the message rather than solves the problem. However, a DoD IG report did surface in July 2010.

DoD IG Report on DCMA Earned Value Management Center

July 28, 2010 – DoD IG Report 2010-6-002 – Focusing on 2008: The DoD IG Oversight Review Report was titled "Report on Allegation of Unsatisfactory Conditions Regarding Actions by the Defense Contract Management Agency, Earned Value Management Center". The DoD IG report stated in part.

"We substantiated the alleged unsatisfactory conditions. During two reviews of a DoD contractor in 2008, the Earned Value Management Center failed to (1) allow the Defense Contract Audit Agency (DCAA) sufficient time to perform an audit of the contractor's system, (2) adequately resolve the DCAA findings, and (3) demonstrate independence and objectivity in fulfilling its oversight responsibilities.

In addition to the substantiated allegations, we found that the Earned Value Management Center did not issue compliance review reports as required, or recommend suspending or withdrawing approval of the contractor's system for continued noncompliances with earned value management guidelines."

Relevance is, my experiences with the DCMA EVMS were not isolated. The DoD IG report shows the DCMA is a problematic organization. The EVMS system issues continue into 2019.

EVMS Audit - Significant Deficiencies Identified - 2019

February 22, 2019: The DCMA EVMS Center sent a letter to Lockheed Martin stating in part.

"The pupose of this initial determination is inform you that a Focused Review of LM Aero's Earned Value Management System (EVMS) was conducted by the Defense Contract Management Agency (DCMA) EVMS Center during November 26-29, 2018.

Based on my review of this report's findings and recommendations, I have determined there appear to be three significant deficiencies in your EVMS. Defense Federal Acquisition Regulation Supplement (DFARS) 252.234-7002(b)(1), EVMS, states:

"(b) System criteria. In the performance of this contract, the Contractor shall use-

(]) An Earned Value Management System (EVMS) that complies with the EVMS guidelines in the American National Standards Institute/Electronic Industries Alliance Standard 748, Earned Value Management Systems (ANSIIEIA- 748) "

LM Aero was noncompliant with ANSI/EIA-748, EVMS Guidelines 3, 6, and 27 resulting in significant deficiencies."

Relevance is that problems existed since 2002, and it is unknown how long problems existed prior to that. The problems still continued past 2019.

EVMS Audit Significant Deficiencies Identified - 2020

April 27, 2020: The DCMA EVMS Center sent another letter to Lockheed Martin stating in part.

"The purpose of this initial determination is inform you that a Review for Cause (RFC) of LM Aero's Earned Value Management System (EVMS) was conducted by the Defense Contract Management Agency (DCMA) EVMS Center from March 3, 2020 through March 12, 2020."

"Based on my review of the EVMS RFC Initial Report, dated April 16, 2020, I have determined that there are three potential significant deficiencies in your EVMS."

"LM Aero was noncompliant with ANSI/EIA-748, EVMS Guidelines 12, 16 and 29 resulting in potential significant deficiencies."

Relevance is, Lockheed Martin was deficient in EVMS and other financial areas for nearly 20 years, I am aware of. Suspensions, disciplinary actions, and threats against me didn't change Lockheed Martin's financial and estimating deficiencies. It only added to my cache of data. By this point in time, I was planning retirement because I could not effectively do my job from multiple standpoints. The major issue was that Lockheed Martin's proposals were untraceable as follows.

The "Last Email" 2019 – Lockheed Martin Proposals Untraceable

About a year prior to my retirement, I could no longer trace costs in Lockheed Martin proposals. On November 6, 2019, I issued what I termed the "Last Email" on the last proposal I worked on prior to the Capstone case of the C-5 RERP Claim. The history of the last email started in July 2019.

July 31, 2019 – Start of the Last Email: The issue began with Lockheed Martin's proposal on IDR (I forget the acronym) being untraceable. The correct process was supposed to be placing the proposed cost in a BOE (Basis of Estimate) for evaluation. When evaluated and agreed upon, the BOE (proposed cost) amount would go into a Lockheed Martin pricing model for final cost and acceptance. In this case, it appeared Lockheed Martin (LM) went straight to the price model to develop a cost similar to an extended warranty on the C-130J aircraft. I stated in part.

"*During the walkthrough of the in-house repair parts it became apparent what LM had done which confirms what I originally thought. In short, LM took direct labor hours and entered them into pricing models without including them in a BOE. Adding further loss of confidence, LM captured direct labor hours in aggregate basically thwarting audit. When I expressed my confusion LM indicated I needed to read through multiple files, gather the excel spread sheets and then LM would take a day and walk me through the process.*

In summary, LM captured labor hours in aggregate, and worked through various excel spread sheets to develop a flight factor of what was over $1,500 per flight hour. Hence the direct labor was never categorized in a BOE and the factor somehow made its way into PC tops (or pro Pricer) (one of those) to achieve a final cost."

The point is, I could not trace the cost to the final amount of $1,500 per flight hour extended warranty. The Excel spreadsheets were a maze of numbers and led to nothing. The confusion kept up for several months until, on November 6, 2019, I issued the final e-mail.

November 6, 2019 – The "Last Email": Conversations with the government program office continued and culminated with me eventually explaining what I have stated in this section of the book. I focused on how Lockheed Martin may have achieved 120% profit on one contract (C-5 ICS previously mentioned). I stated in part:

"*As promised here is my response to your e-mail request. I titled some of the attachments "Pattern Elaborate Over Estimating" because LM takes the reader down an elaborate maze of excel spread sheets and goes through analogies (mostly illogical) to escalate price and gain profit through over-estimating direct labor. This is how the 120% profit was achieved although it was discussed and I never personally calculated it.*"

"*DCMA analyzed the proposal and discovered that LM was using an in-house cost model known as "Envision". The problem with Envision was that it grossly overestimated amount of repairs and when the labor was calculated to accomplish the repairs there was a significant increase. In short, Reference A BOE Group 1 (beginning on/about Page 7) identifies Escalation amounts of 90%, 216%, 242%, 240%, and 241%. This means that the labors was escalated from minimum of 90% to a maximum of 242%. LM was using this prior to DCMA being involved which means that labor over-estimating was occurring rampantly. This would account for one side of the 120% profit."*

"To be precise there was a 17% increase in flight hours although labor was escalated 90%-242%. This was illogical on its face. LM later caved in and adjusted their numbers significantly downward."

"The other side of the 120% profit would be accomplished from LM overestimating by applying the analogy factors from Line Replaceable Units (LRUs) (large aircraft components) to consumable (disposable) parts... Essentially, and to provide an analogy, say one would want to estimate the yearly cost to maintain a simple peddle bicycle. What LM would do is estimate the cost of an expensive sports car (maintenance, insurance, etc.) and say the bicycle would need the same attention and cost as the expensive sports car."

"This is why I became concerned when LM issued a defective proposal that placed cost directly into the pricing model versus the BOE. I lost traceability and knew that LM would use some elaborate method to inflate labor cost for more profit. When I lost traceability I notified of the defective IDR proposal."

The gist of this discussion, and the "Last E-mail", is that this book herein builds up to this point where I lost traceability. It can be traced back half a century to the days of Ernie Fitzgerald, although my data covers 26 ½ years (March 1994 – December 2020).

I documented intently for over a quarter of a century (26 ½ Years) because the DCMA was a shocking, abusive, corrupt, and toxic place to work. The documentation is now contemporaneous. I predict ruination because the public is being misled and headed towards involuntary, administrative, "shock therapy" with the national debt. Meaning, the national debt and institutional corruption will have a negative effect on the U.S. way of life if not controlled and remedied.

Hopefully, my documentation trail and proposed remedy, will reverse, lessen the impact, or at least provide the reasons for expected financial ruination. I do predict financial impact from cover-ups and institutional corruption.

National security is also a concern from potential impacts to the intel community where, as one example, Dan Meyer (of Falsified Trail 3) may be, or have been, residing.

The only remaining question is how widespread all of this will be and if remedy will occur in time.

This book is a disclosure to the U.S. Congress, and U.S. President, since past efforts to gain attention, resolution, or remedy, have been ignored or covered up. Weaponization and lawfare were enablers of institutional corruption, and the Government Swamp, as was the enabling caused by the U.S. Legal and Judicial System most notably after the February 12, 2009 decision outlined herein, Chapter 3.

Chapter 5 is the Capstone Case and the last criminal disclosure I made against Lockheed Martin. DCMA was involved from the cover-up aspect. The Capstone Case occurred near the same time frame as the "Last Email." Chapter 5 is the capstone example because it is a prime example that incorporates all the ill attributes, maleficence, and cover-up tactics outlined thus far in this book.

Prior to Chapter 5 is the following brief recap of Chapters 1 through 4.

CHAPTER 1 – 4 Summary

Altered Working Conditions Enabling Price Gouging

The information thus far in this book is the precursor to the C-5 RERP claim of 2018. Meaning, the DCMA and DoD continually covered up for Lockheed Martin, which included altering working conditions, enabling further corruption, and the inability to perform on contracts.

Chapter 1 was my success, which shows I was extremely effective at what I did. I garnered adverse attention at high levels. Meaning, I was a threat to corruption.

Chapter 2 was the overall anti-whistleblower climate and altered working conditions throughout DoD and the government. OSC, MSPB, and OPM were weaponized and worked incessantly to contain negative information from escaping ("Cerberus" Analogy). Meaning, discredit anyone coming forward exposing what was wrong with the government. The oversight organizations of the DCMA, DCAA, and DoD IG had abusive and altered work environments. News media reports and investigations confirmed these facts and are included in Chapter 2.

Chapter 3 was pure weaponization and retaliation against me. Meaning, DCMA weaponized every aspect possible against me. The following is the partial weaponization list.

Weaponized Authority	Falsified Trails 1-13
Weaponized Personnel Actions	Falsified Trails 1-13
Weaponized Attorneys	Falsified Trails 1, 3-13
Weaponized Surrogates	Falsified Trails 1, 3-13
Weaponized Investigations	Falsified Trails 2, 3 & 12
Weaponized Doctrine (Obey First, Grieve Later)	Falsified Trail 3
Weaponized Conflicts of Interest	Falsified Trails 3, 11, 13
Weaponized FOIA	Falsified Trails 2 & 13
Weaponized Office Conflicts Between Employees	Falsified Trails 5 & 9
Weaponized Shunning	Falsified Trails 1, 6, 8, 11
Weaponized Electronic Trails (Email Relays)	Falsified Trails 1, 3, 6, 11, 12, & 13
Weaponized Training	Falsified Trail 11 and 2011 attempt
Weaponized Human Resources/Labor Relations	Falsified Trails 3, 6, 10, 12, & 13
Weaponized Status & Access to Other Agencies	Falsified Trail 3
Weaponized Cover-ups by OSC, MSPB, OPM	Falsified Trails 3, 6, 10, 13 (Abandon Case)
Weaponized Security Clearances	Chapter 3, Revoked Security Clearance

I was smothered by weaponization and lawfare. I could not do my job other than document for the future and make disclosures. Taxpayers were vulnerable, and I was a taxpayer and a victim.

The U.S Legal and Judicial system enabled the weaponization, lawfare, and Government Swamp.

Chapter 4 shows how DoD Weaponized Price Gouging on the "Commercial" C-130J using Acquisition Reform and commercialization as a weapon and enabler. The price gouging during Acquisition Reform only developed an appetite for further price gouging and cover-ups. Lockheed Martin experienced multiple problems with EVMS and multiple overpricing situations.

The following are summary tables (samples) of what I managed to overcome; knowing what I overcame was only a small part of what I could have accomplished.

Year	Savings	Chapter	Summary Title
February 23, 2000	$2,254,963	4	Single Item Purchase (79%-80% Over)
August 12, 2016	$13,467,811	4	Price Gouging Elaborate Math (31% Over)
September 7, 2018	$12,324,092	4	Price Gouging Elaborate Math (31% Over)
November 11, 2011	$584,610	4	Material Estimating Glitch

Warner Robins was criticized by DoD IG for allowing Lockheed Martin to gain high profits, which I understand were in the 120% range. So, I was given leeway to proceed and was asked for by name on July 5, 2017, by Warner Robins for the September 7, 2018 project.

Other Calculated Savings include, Independent Research and Development (IRAD) and Potential Savings on a percentage (%) basis are as follows.

Year	Savings	Chapter	Summary Title
March 18, 1999	$140,468	4	C-130J Cargo Handling (IRAD)
March 18, 1999	$311,925	4	C-130J Propeller (IRAD)
March 18, 1999	$6,822,939	4	C-27J IRAD Foreign Offset
December 10, 2003	$1,061,975	4	Global Air Traffic Management – C-130J
August 31, 2000	-	4	23.9% - 38.5% Overhead Rate Overestimating
August 16, 2007	-	4	24%-69% Judgement Overestimating
July 23, 2013	-	4	Up to 12X Cost of Air Force Work
July 27, 2016	-	4	49%-60% Factor Overestimating – F-35

<u>30% - 50% Price Gouging Average</u>: The Deep State, "Federal Machinery", enabled 30% - 50% price gouging (overestimating) as an average, which enabled the Capstone Case (disclosure) to follow. This all feeds into the national debt and causes an affordability problem for military equipment. All of this inbred and evolved over half a century starting with the Nixon Administration (1970).

The Capstone Case (disclosure) for the C-5 RERP was a product of the aforesaid meaning years of decay, altered working conditions, "blank check" cost charging, retaliations, "Federal Machinery", Lawfare, Weaponization of Government, hostile and altered working conditions, criminal vulnerability, etc., documented herein. Simply put, the stage was set for disaster and corruption.

The following is the Capstone Case (disclosure) for the C-5 RERP. Chapter 5.

CHAPTER 5: Capstone Case – Criminal Disclosure for $143,529,290 Claim

Armed Services Board of Contract Appeals (ASBCA) Number 62209

The capstone disclosure was a culmination of issues contained in this book, showing the result of deterioration, maleficence, gross mismanagement, weaponization and lawfare in one project. This was my final disclosure prior to retirement in December 2020. Multiple disclosures started on November 21, 2019 (OSI), December 2, 2019 (Congressman Tom Graves), December 17, 2019 (Senator David Perdue), and December 16, 2019, to the DCMA management.

Disclosure Words to Senior DCMA Management: My December 16, 2019 disclosure included the key words from this book such as "FOIA 15-172", "Obey Now Grieve Later" Doctrine, "private" meetings, "silence" to my requests, "non-response" to my requests, "hostile" towards me, "DoD Inspector General and GAO reports," "alleged criminal activity," "false claim," "cover-up," and the like. I coped my entire chain of command up to DCMA director VADM David Lewis plus many others. About 14 names in all. I can remember no response and definitely no resolution. DCMA exhibited the standard no concern. Hence, the reason I wrote this book.

The disclosures all center on C-5 RERP Contract FA8625-07-C-6471, eventually sent to the ASBCA, Case Number 62209, for $143,529,290. The C-5 RERP Claim focused on cost issues, hence the $143,529,290 amount. In short, the ASBCA Claim by Lockheed Martin was the topics within this book rolled into one actual case. To my understanding (rumor) there may have been other Claims over the years although ASBCA Claim 62209 may have been among the largest.

November 21, 2019 Disclosure Data: The disclosure on the C-5 RERP Claim was related to cost issues and the issues that fed cost issues. This included the tactic to limit the C-17 Program production run using the C-5 RERP.

Limiting C-17 Production Run via C5 RERP

November 22, 2002: On or about this date, a Lockheed Martin presentation was attached to a November 22, 2002, email, which stated in part: *"C-5 Modernization Key to Limiting C-17 Production Run"*

This relates to the C-5 Claim proposal because it suggests a motive against a rival aircraft producer. Meaning, Lockheed Martin was in state of decay since June 22, 1998 (Chapter 4) and even earlier with Acquisition Reform on the C-130J. The state of decay and lack of manufacturing discipline in Lockheed Martin meant it could not economically modernize the C-5 aircraft. To compensate, Lockheed Martin lowballed their earlier proposal on C-5 RERP to seemingly draw the government in. The November 21, 2019, disclosure stated in part.

"In the case of LM claim, LM overestimated learning and underestimated the T1 starting point. That coupled with other reckless business decisions caused the C-5 RERP production line to implode. The data also supports possibilities that LM underestimated the C-5 RERP to limit C-17 production and gain lucrative follow-on contracts."

The lucrative contracts would be spare parts where Lockheed Martin overestimates by 31%, as outlined in Chapter 4. The lowball estimate is further supported by the following data based on hours. The T1 (start point for production) is calculated first as follows by Lockheed Martin:

Calculate T1 – Start Point for Production (95,000 Hours)

May 16, 2007 – November 17, 2007: Lockheed Martin reduced estimates for C-5 RERP T1, start point, aircraft as follows.

Development Aircraft Used for T1 (Production Start Point):	111,547 Hours
Loss of Learning & Items Unique to Delivery:	15,085 Hours
Total of First C-5 RERP Production Aircraft:	126,632 Hours

The first production aircraft start point (T1) is 126,632 Hours and was expensive, although was based on actual historical data. Lockheed Martin reduced the 126,632 hours using unsupported judgments to subtract from the cost as follows.

Continuous Improvements to Lower Cost:	(20,043 Hours)
Other Impacts, 10% judgment of Development Aircraft:	(11,154 Hours)
Total Unsupported Decrement	(31,197 Hours)

Total T1 for First Aircraft is: 126,632 Hours – 31,197 Hours = 95,435

Lockheed Martin then subtracted off 435 hours "management challenge" based on Judgment Estimating, bringing the final estimate as follows:

95,435 Hours – 435 Hours = 95,000 Hours (Unsupported reduction hours: 31,197+435=31,632)

The point is, Lockheed Martin grossly underestimated the start point using judgment that would account for any loss in the claim of $143,529,290 for the 21 C-5s in the claim. Math is as follows.

31,632 Hours X $250/Hour Wrap rate X 21 C-5s in the Claim = $166,068,000 absent learning

Meaning, the learning curve would reduce the $166,068,00 closer to $143,529,290.

October 5, 2009 Data: The November 21, 2019 disclosure stated in part.

"Throughout the RERP modification LM held data away from USG view. However, some data did slip through. One such document dated October 5, 2009 (Reference (I1)) indicated that LM was planning on a first unit (T1) cost of 88,000 hours versus the 95,000 hours presented to the USG. As was previously shown the 95 ,000 hours was based on judgement and unsupported conclusions of which no benefits materialized."

Meaning, Lockheed Martin withheld data continually forcing me to draw conclusions and accept Lockheed Martin's position with what data I could gather. There was also the adverse effect, and obstruction, of Falsified Trails 1 thru 10 including threats to my career, which interfered with my analysis. This helped enable further corruption. The point being, problems were compounded by altered working conditions and cover-ups. However, I did document what I found.

"Baked in Cost" of Modification to Older C-5 Aircraft

Lockheed Martin claimed the C-5s being modernized in the production phase were not in good condition and needed additional work. However, the development & test aircraft, used to project future production costs, were from the same pool of older C-5 aircraft and were also in poor condition. Meaning, the additional cost of the older aircraft is included ("baked in") within the actual cost of the prior aircraft. Also, the C-5 RERP was to upgrade the C-5s anyway. The next step was the learning estimate. Immediate problems were recognized.

Employee Learning & Improvement Estimate – Potentially Falsified

Learning involves production workers becoming more efficient over time. Meaning, as workers learn, and familiarize with the project, the time to do a task lessens.

Learning curves are measured in percentages. A percentage of 80% means there is a lot of room for progress and quick learning. Cost will drop fast. A learning curve of 95% or 98% means the cost will not drop as fast because there is efficiency, not much learning left. The difference is multiplying future cost by .80 (big cost drop) or multiplying by .95 (small cost drop).

November 21, 2019 Disclosure: When Lockheed Martin estimated the C-5 RERP, a learning curve of 85% was developed from prior data, which was used. The disclosure stated the following in part.

"LM data points from the SDD program (144,328 hours, 123,346 hours, and 111 ,547 hours used to form the 85% learning curve for C-5 RERP (Reference (D1)) show a high "R-Squared" (R^2) or goodness of fit of .9994 (knowing that an R^2 of "1" indicates perfect fit of data to the curve). This implies the data was backed into as if it were a created (massaged or potentially falsified)."

Meaning, there was too perfect a fit (not believable) for Lockheed Martin developmental aircraft data.

C-5 Modernization (RERP) Problems as Early As 2011

March 11, 2011: The following is from a March 11, 2011, Memorandum attached to a March 15, 2011, e-mail regarding Low-Rate Initial Production (LRIP). The memorandum stated in part.

"MEMORANDUM FOR: DCMA LMM Senior Leadership Team (SLT), C-5 Program Offices at Air Force Materiel Command (WR-ALC/GRS, ASC /WLS), and Logistics and Requirements Directorates at Air Mobility Command (AMC/A4 and AMC/A5)" "SUBJECT: Minutes of Government Only Meeting between AFMC, AMC, and DCMA"

"DATE OF MEETING: 14 February 2011"

"PURPOSE: To determine the way-ahead for successful execution of the C-5M LRIP Modification program by discussing significant issues impacting the ability to execute Contract Administration Services. The topics of discussion included LRIP Statement of Work (SOW), Clause Hl06 Rapid Repair and Response (R3), Foreign Object Debris (FOD) inspection requirements, 781 write-ups, AFMC 202, Mandatory Program Guidance, Use of C-5A versus C-5M technical orders, and Timely Response to Contract Deficiency Reports (CDR)/DD Form 1716. Action items were generated and assigned to responsible parties along with milestone dates for completion."

Statement of Work (SOW) – No "Teeth" for Enforcement

March 11, 2011: The overarching concern with SOW is summarized in part as follows.

"Lack of detail in the contract and SOW hinder the effective enforcement of quality standards for products and services. Hence, this negatively impacts DCMA's ability to execute contract administration services relative to quality and engineering surveillance."

Meaning, the contract had no "teeth" (provisions) for enforcement. The government was powerless to ensure a quality product for the warfighters. This would be an offshoot of the problems already identified in this book. Something analogous or similar to the C-130J commercial contract that was mentioned in Chapter 4. From there, Lockheed Martin was given a "blank check" charging.

Rapid Repair and Response (R3) - "Blank Check" Charging

(Over & Above (O&A) Work)

March 11, 2011: The R3 part of the contract is work that is "Over and Above" what is called for on the contract. Meaning, outside of the contract scope. Basically, items found broken or worn on the aircraft need repair. These items are documented on Modification Deficiency Reports (MDRs) or Modification Inspection Reports (MIRs). Documentation of things broken on the C-5 outside the contract scope. The overarching concern with R3 is summarized in part as follows.

"Overarching Concern: The current R3 clause is in conflict with Cost Accounting Standard (CAS) 401 as cited by DCAA audit findings (see attached). The R3 Clause says "the contractor shall not be bound by the work request estimate, but the cumulative actual cost of labor and materials shall not exceed the NTE amount established in the applicable R3 CLINs". DCAA attempted to audit the R3 Clause and found the "contractor confirmed it could not provide any supporting documentation to demonstrate that for hours proposed at less than 100 hours, cost are tracked per individual MIR." As a result of this finding DCAA has indicated that they cannot compelete an audit of the contract, making contract close out a near insurmountable challenge. Several individuals pointed out that LMA possessed the required data but no CDRL existed requiring the data available internally to the contractor be made available to DCMA or DCAA for audit purposes. DCMA proposed terminating DCMA involvement in the R3 process entirely given lack of audit enforcement and the significant manpower effort required by DCMA to process, review and approve R3 MDR/MIRs. Additional concerns were raised that the R3 clause does not require all aircraft maintenance work be accomplished IAW with C-5M tech orders and that the work be properly documented in 781 series forms or AFTO Form 95 to ensure accurate migration of the necessary data into the G081 system. These two issues, if not fixed, will result in AMC being unable to accept the aircraft after DD-250 until all documents are reviewed by AMC maintenance personnel, appropriate AFMC I 07/202 waivers are obtained, and GO81 historical maintenance documentation is completed to a level compliant with TO 00-20-1.

Meaning, Lockheed Martin can charge whatever they want; Lockheed Martin is not responsible for justifying the cost; And the government cannot audit the cost. In fact, Lockheed Martin would later ask the government to justify costs. "Blank Checks" in simpler terms. Issues continued as follows.

USG Funded Lockheed Martin Cost Overruns (Rework)

November 21, 2019 - DODIG-2015-039 C5 RERP November 18, 2014: On November 18, 2014, the DoD IG issued report 2015-039, which in part outlines the fact that USG-funded rework by Lockheed Martin without equitable adjustment. Six allegations were made, with four substantiated, as follows:

1: Government failed to discourage repeated tender of nonconforming components. (Substantiated)

2: Government delegated inherently Government functions to Lockheed Martin. (Substantiated)

3: Government failed to approve and document Lockheed Martin flights. (Undetermined)

4: Government accepted non-conformances that were corrected to additional cost to government. (Substantiated)

5: DCMA failed to comply with the DCMA Instruction for the corrective action process. (Substantiated)

6: Government failed to ensure that Lockheed Martin used U.S. Air Force service guidance. (Not Substantiated)

Meaning, Lockheed Martin owes the U.S. Government money and not the other way around. Also, meaning, the U.S. Government was lenient with Lockheed Martin, and the DCMA and SPO protected Lockheed Martin versus what Lockheed Martin stated in C-5 Claim ASBCA 62209.

Nun-McCurdy Breach & Still Perfect Learning Curve Fit of .9994

November 21, 2019 Disclosure - Nunn-McCurdy Breach October 16, 2007: The Nunn-McCurdy Breach meant the C-5 RERP program overran budget. This is also notable since Lockheed Martin had a goodness of fit (R^2) of the aforesaid .9994 (nearly perfect) learning curve, meaning how could a troubled program with a Nunn McCurdy Breech (cost overrun) achieve such a near-perfect learning curve example. The October 16, 2007 attachment to the disclosure stated in part.

"Costs of the C-5 have risen in the range of 15 percent to 25 percent, according to Air Force Secretary Michael W. Wynne. The Air Force declared the program to be in breach of the Nunn-McCurdy amendment immediately before the Air Force and Lockheed Martin officials briefed a U.S. Senate committee on the status of a major C-5 modification program on October 7, 2007."

February 28, 1980 – EVMS Certified: With the October 16, 2007 file was the EVMS certification date of February 28, 1980. Then called Cost/Schedule Control System. Meaning, about 27 years (1980-2007) since EVMS was certified. This helps explain the EVMS problems in Chapter 4 herein.

December 28, 2001 – September 27, 2001 Cost Escalation: The Nunn-McCurdy Breach file of October 16, 2007, showed cost escalation of C-5 RERP SDD, which started December 28, 2001 ($881,813,003) and after about 44 contracts mods rose to $1,076,271,015 on September 27, 2007.

The point is, the causation for the near-perfect correlation of .9994 would be highly unlikely for a development program in addition to other serious issues. The next item is that Lockheed Martin systems are not auditable.

Lockheed Martin Systems "Not Auditable"

November 21, 2019 - January 19, 2010: This was a technical report, and disclosure, where I documented:

"*LM Aero has denied government access to their internal systems stating that the systems are not auditable, even though LM Aero (through DCMA observation) bases their financial solvency and financial security on the internal systems.*"

This is one data point in a chain of other data points. One notable event was Falsified Trail 11, where Lockheed Martin could not provide even one page of documents for the EVMS schedule during 2014. Another data point is as follows regarding "one-pager" documents.

Denial of Documents for C-5 RERP Schedule Adjustments

November 21, 2019 - November 10, 2010 - Deny Documents: DCMA asked for the "one-pagers" Lockheed Martin was using to manage the C-5 RERP. Lockheed Martin responded in part, as follows.

"Outside of the current forums including the official IMS (Integrated Master Schedule) *submittals and bi weekly reviews (Tues/Thurs 730 meetings) where this info is discussed, we will be unable to provide additional internal working documents."*

Meaning, Lockheed Martin denied transparency into program management. The overall point being, this book has gone to length to demonstrate why Lockheed Martin would not provide transparency into operating procedures which trace problems back to 1998.

Time Studies (Excessive Cost) – Over & Above (O&A) Work

November 21, 2019 - February 18, 2010 Disclosure: The first C-5 RERP Aircraft arrived on or about August 18, 2009. By February 18, 2010 (about six months later), the DCMA had identified "*excessive cost of over and above work and possible cost overcharging.*"

Accordingly, the DCMA planned time studies and observations to determine the root cause of the excessive cost. The DCMA then requested Lockheed Martin to notify the DCMA when MDR (O&A) work began. Lockheed Martin was non-responsive to the DCMA request for notification to witness MDR (O&A) work.

Two facts emerge from this disclosure. First, within about six months of the first aircraft arrival, the DCMA identified excessive cost and possible cost overcharging on MDRs (O&A). Second, Lockheed Martin was non-responsive to the DCMA requests. As the following shows, Lockheed Martin did not know how many MDRs were duplicates, cancelled, etc.

Lockheed Martin Could Not Track MDRs (O&A Work)

November 21, 2019 - July 15, 2014: BY 2014 the Air Force wanted to limit MDRs to Lockheed Martin. I evaluated the proposal and asked Lockheed Martin the following.

"Question 1: Say the 400 MDRs is accepted. What happens if there is a duplicate MDR or one written by mistake. Does that add toward the 400 MDR number or will LM say that even if it is a duplicate or cancelled MDR it will be added to the 400 MDR count."

Lockheed Martin responded as follows;

"For question 1, the answer is TBD. If LM submits an REA (Request for Equitable Adjustment)*, that will be negotiated later post Lot completion."*

"Question 2: Taken that the original number of MDRs is 650, how many of the 650 MDRs were cancelled, duplicate, written by mistake, etc."

Lockheed Martin responded as follows;

"Question 2, Dan Woodall (DCMA employee) *should be able to get you that data."*

The point is, Lockheed Martin expected DCMA to make the case for Lockheed Martin.

Excessive MDR Cost Sample

November 21, 2019 - DCAA Report May 31, 2017 & May 11, 2017: DCAA sampled CAT (Category) II MDR (O&A) work and concluded excessive costs by Lockheed Martin on CAT II MDR (O&A) work. The analysis indicated in part on May 11, 2017:

"Out of the 92 MDRs provided by DCAA, 9 are classified as Cat 1 or Cat 3 and should be removed from the sample set. Cat 1 and Cat 3 MDRs are contractor responsibility and not considered O&A. In all cases, the 9 MDRs began as a Cat 2, but were later changed to a Cat 1 or Cat 3 for various reasons."

"Of the remaining 83 MDRs, DCMA determined 49 of the MDRs (59%) had excessive charging of labor hours of 10 labor hours or more.

DCMA determined that 11 of the 83 MDRs (13%) had excessive charging of labor hours of 100 labor hours or more. These 11 MDRs averaged 170 labor hours in excess.

Twenty (20) of the 83 MDRs had insufficient information listed in QADS (Quality Assurance Document System) *or SFM* (Shop Floor Manager) *to make a reasonable estimate of the labor hours. In all cases for these 20 MDRs, the type of work performed was complex and extensive."*

"*DCMA believes the hours charged for MDR classified as Cat 2 are not reasonable in over half the MDRs reviewed. From this sample set, DCMA has determined LM Aero has a deficiency in regards to accurately charging labor hours.*"

On May 30, 2017, Lockheed Martin responded in part, stating.

"Given the subjective nature of the estimates, this may lead to an overstatement of the differences between such estimates and LM's actual C-5 RERP O&A cost data."

The point is, a complete loss of cost discipline and concern initiated by "blank check" charging. Lockheed Martin simply dismissed the DCMA audit of MDR (O&A) cost. It was notable that other data was unsupportable and untraceable as follows.

Data Untraceable, Unsupportable, Questionable – 3 Systems Ago

November 21, 2019 - October 16-17, 2019: During fact-finding of the C-5 RERP claim proposal, DCAA asked Lockheed Martin a question on October 16, 2019, stating in part.

"On October 8, 2019, we had a meeting between LM-DCAA-DCMA. In the meeting, LM personnel informed that LM cannot duplicate the data from a system that was 3 systems' generations ago. Please explain this in more detail. What do you mean? What type of data LM cannot duplicate? What is the name of the system that is 3 systems' generations ago?"

Lockheed Martin could not trace the data and responded on October 17, 2019 as follows.

"The USG team asked us previously to provide relevant actuals for the C5 AMP and C5 RERP SDD contracts, which preceded the C5 RERP LRIP contract that is the subject of this action. The actuals for both SDD and AMP contracts are summarized in data item #4 from the claim data package. Data item #4 is the Basis of Estimate (BOE) for the Build & Delivery portion of the RERP LRIP NTE proposal. In that BOE, LM Aero provided SDD actuals with the workorders and ADAR instructions for the three SDD aircraft as those hours are in LM Aero's cost ledger. Also in that BOE, there is a table summarizing the actual installation labor hours experienced under the AMP contract; however, because the labor performed under the AMP contract was done by our LM Greenville team, the labor hours incurred were against LM Greenville's cost ledger at the time and were provided to LM Aero by LM Greenville.

We've contacted the LM Greenville team based on your questions at the last face-to-face meeting and asked if they could revalidate the AMP hours in their system today. Their short answer to us was "no" because of the age of that data and several financial system changes since the AMP program. Today, I've asked the finance team in Greenville for some more detail, such as the system names, etc., and will let you know how they respond.

My only other recommendation is to check any DCAA/DCMA/SPO records from the evaluation of the C5 RERP proposal to determine if the USG validate the AMP data in 2007 when it was originally provided. I am not sure if that would have been covered by a DCAA assist audit or other technical review."

Single Point Failure - Rebase-line Agreement - Violating Contract Agreement

November 21, 2019 - November 6, 2012: The November 21, 2019 disclosure and my technical report December 12, 2019 outlined single point failures for the C-5 RERP claim which included contract mod P00178 (November 6, 2012). This was an equitable adjustment to release the government from any liability. P00178 states in part:

"This Supplemental Agreement constitutes a full and equitable adjustment between the Government and the Contractor arising out of or in connection with all C-5 RERP Production Schedule impacts, including the pylon sheer plate, improperly manufactured tower fitting, LM Aero manufacturing manning needs, etc., to the date of this Supplemental Agreement execution except for the issues associated with the Bucket Engineering Change Proposal (ECP) 12- 0012A, that LM Aero is preparing. The "Bucket ECP" will address the cost impact of those issues; however the Contractor will not seek any further adjustments to the C-5 RERP Production Schedule. Once fully executed, the "Bucket ECP"

(ECP 12-00012A) effort and this Supplemental Agreement (P00178) will constitute a full and equitable adjustment between the Government and the Contractor and release all parties from liability under the contract for further claims or equitable adjustments arising out of or in connection with any past legacy issues, runway closure, the aircraft cut wire, DCMA flight crew availability, and/or DCMA additional inspection requirements in addition to the issues discussed in Paragraph 1 of this contract modification."

Meaning, Lockheed Martin received an equitable adjustment and re-baselined (started over) negating prior data. Lockheed Martin violated P00178 by using a learning curve (86.9%) developed prior to P00178 (November 6, 2012). P00178 negated such data being used after a re-baseline. The point being, there was a new scope of work that would drive a new learning curve. It was not possible to disassociate the new scope of work after it was integrated into the new re-baseline and use an old learning curve. More adjustments were as follows.

Lockheed Martin Received 3 More Adjustments - Affected Scope & Learning

November 21, 2019 – October 15, 2018: Lockheed Martin received 3 more adjustments that effected contract scope. On October 15, 2018 Lockheed Martin outlined the following in part.

"P00310 – Pylon Fuel Leak & CCPs for C-Model Credits – 25 February 2015

P00265 – CCP 13-00054 Removal of Visor Door Actuator 12 March 2015

P00219 – ECP 12-00012A – Bucket ECP – 7 June 2016"

Already Paid – Not the Same Scope for 86.9% Learning Curve: The aforesaid contract mods totaled to 55,574 hours that Lockheed Martin agreed to and that would drive a new learning curve, negating the 86.9% curve. The points being: contract scope adjustments (changes to work) affected learning, negating 86.9% Learning Curve; Lockheed Martin was already paid for disruptions; And Lockheed Martin had "Blank Check" charging. This is aside from sabotage damage to the learning curve.

Sabotage to Production (Aircraft Cut Wires)

November 21, 2019 - January 23, 2012: Cut wires were mentioned in the November 21, 2019 disclosure, December 12, 2019 technical report, and P00178 (November 6, 2012). Lockheed Martin made the following statement in part on October 15, 2018.

"Early in the program Lockheed Martin experienced several production-related issues that required correction during performance. These were shear plate work, tower fittings, and an aircraft that was impacted by cut wires. Taking a conservative approach to this Claim, Lockheed Martin has chosen to treat these issues as its own responsibility and to remove the actual hours attributable to each."

Lockheed Martin can mathematically remove the hours, estimated or actual; however, the hours already caused production disruption to the 86.9% learning curve. Meaning, mathematically, hours can be removed; however, ethically and actually, the disruptions have already affected the new, emerging learning curve. This point is expanded on as follows.

Measured Mile - Elaborate Math – Criminal Vulnerability

The following is a summary that proves the Measured Mile data Lockheed Martin used leads to criminal vulnerability.

Lockheed Martin's T1 (Starting Point) of 2009 Based on Unsupported Judgement: The 85% learning curve was based on data that could not be duplicated (3 systems ago). So, that was in question. The T1 of 95,000 hours was significantly adjusted based on judgment. So, that was in question.

Lockheed Martin Already Received Equitable Adjustments + "Blank Check" Charging: P00178, P00265, P00310, and P00219 gave Lockheed Martin equitable adjustments. The "Blank Check" charging for R3 (Time & materials) meant Lockheed Martin was already paid for disruption cost.

Re-baselining Negated Prior Estimates & Negated Prior Learning Curves: Once the contract mods (P00178, P00265, P00310, and P00219) were implemented, the 86.9% learning curve was over. Meaning there was fresh start (re-baseline) and forget the past data (86.9% learning curve).

Cannot Factor Out Disruptions from Learning: Trying to mathematically factor cost from learning is like trying to factor out ingredients in cake batter. Meaning, once mixed, the ingredients of flour, eggs, and sugar are virtually inseparable. Ingredients can be added prior to baking, but not subtracted out. Same for production operations and learning.

Rewrite Technical Report: The November 21, 2009 disclosure was 73 Pages with some single point failures. This was actually the first technical report prior to be rewritten on December 12, 2019. The December 12, 2019, Technical report was a watered-down report of 69 Pages.

“Watering Down” Report to Favor Lockheed Martin

The reason I made the November 21, 2019, disclosure was that my original report was being rewritten and watered down. The history is as follows.

November 14, 2019, Regarding November 13, 2019, Private Meeting: DCAA kept taking exceptions to me using the term “potential false claim”. My November 14, 2019 Memo for the Record is stated in part as follows. Richard Bolden was my first-level supervisor.

“Met with Richard Bolden yesterday (Wednesday November 13, 2019) regarding the private meeting requested by DCAA regarding the Lockheed Martin (LM) C-5 RERP Claim audit and DCAA pressure on DCMA (that was targeted at me) to water down my report.”

“Private meeting was apparently yesterday November 13, 2019 on about 9:30 AM. Meeting attendees included (per understanding from Mr. Richard Bolden who was in attendance): Jonathan Vaughn (DCAA), Kelly Berkowitz (DCAA), Jason Rawson (DCMA 2nd level supervisor DCMA LMM Engineering), Denise Jones (DCMA 2nd level supervisor DCMA Contracts), Marguerite Antoine (DCMA contracts supervisor), David Van Dingenen (DCAA), members of Program Office (Wright Patterson AFB, members unknown), and AFMC (Air Force Material Command) *Fraud counsel (members unknown).”*

“I concluded the conversation with Mr. Bolden late yesterday afternoon in that an extension would be necessary so that my report can be re-written to placate to DCAA. At one point we discussed just sending the report to DCAA ahead of time so DCAA can write-out anything deemed negative to Lockheed Martin. The process at this time is to placate to DCAA not issue an accurate report. Mr. Bolden indicated that it would take him a while to rewrite my report to meet DCCA (Should be DCAA) *requests. Extension may be as far in the future as December 12, 2019 to ensure the DCMA report is written to DCAA satisfaction.”*

The aforesaid Memo for Record was attached to an email trail that went back to November 5, 2019. Meaning, I was documenting an email trail because I knew a cover-up was in the works. I actually contacted Colonel French (Commander 4th Level Supervisor) and Myra Tate (3rd Level Supervisor) on November 6, 2019 (attached to November 14, 2019 Memo for Record. That is why I stated the following at the conclusion of my November 14, 2019, Memo for the Record.

“I do not blame Mr. Bolden for the actions of rewriting the reprot because the system is institutionally corrupted with both Colonel Lance Frence (should be French) *and Ms. Myra Tate turning a blind eye and a deaf ear to alleged contract fraud by Lockheed Martin and DCAA pressuring to re-write the report. I am powerless to stop the corruption and Mr. Bolden would not do this absent pressure to do so and a DCMA management staff that has turned a blind eye to corruption for several years.”*

This is the reason I included DCAA in Chapter 2 of this book. Because DCAA is a problematic entity, as is the DCMA. On February 24, 2004, Senator Grassley stated in a letter to Joseph Schmitz regarding the DCMA and DCAA: *“Those two entities have a long-standing reputation for turning a blind eye to contractor rip-offs.”* Hence, 15 years later, nothing changed.

DCAA Claims Attorney-Client Privilege

<u>November 6, 2019</u>: May 2nd level supervisor, Jason Rawson, who made an appearance in Chapter 3 of this book, was involved in the capstone as well for the C-5 RERP Claim, where he was contacted by DCAA. Rawson stated in an email, in part, and quoted DCAA as follows at various parts.

"After reading the DCAA email further, I see that they requested both the DCAA auditors and the DCMA technical specialists not be included in the discussion regarding concerns over the report. For that reason, I am not forwarding the entire email chain from DCAA. However, it's unreasonable for DCAA to think we wouldn't address their concerns directly with our team, so I have copied the relevant text from their email unedited below. Please take a look and keep these concerns in mind as the tech report gets finalized."

"Based on weekly status meetings with the assigned DCMA engineer, we have the perception that the DCMA technical report may be providing conclusions (including a history of the C-5 aircraft program) that are beyond the scope of our DCAA request."

"Another DCAA concern is the potential use of certain language that may take away from the integrity of the Government's position. We have been told in our weekly status meetings that the DCMA technical report will make references to "false claim", "falsification of information", etc. and other similar accusatory language that implicates the contractor has committed fraud or falsified information (with insinuation of the "intent" aspect) in support of its claim."

"Based on our DCAA experience with dealing with such claims whereby the contractor was unable to support the reasonableness of its claimed amounts, we have seen DCMA technical reports reflect the contractor's claim as being without merit (and therefore question the claim, in its entirety, in regards to reasonabless), but not report such conclusions as "false claim", "falsification of information", etc. (conclusions that are generally reached in a court based on evidence gathered by investigators, not DCAA or DCMA)."

"Based on guidance we obtained from our DCAA Office of General Counsel (subject to the attorney-client privilege), DCAA would not prepare a fraud referral based on the DCMA technical report because it is a DCMA product. We were told that DCAA may notify DCMA that it is at its discretion whether to prepare a fraud referral (which we did during our weekly status meeting with DCMA on October 29, 2019)."

The DCAA (apparently higher DCAA management) didn't want to hear the negative history for the C-5 RERP program. Hence, the exclusion of the DCAA auditors and DCMA technical specialists (mainly me). The detailed history was also a concern, as was the mention of fraud references. Most disturbing was the use of the attorney-client privilege. It is unknown why the attorney-client privilege would be used, or needed, by a government office like DCAA.

Jason Rawson only gave select portions of the email. Nevertheless, on November 21, 2019, I made a disclosure of my complete unedited report, which was 73 pages long. I began laying the groundwork for the disclosure as follows.

Criminal Disclosure on C-5 RERP Claim

October 31, 2019: The October 31, 2019 email trail actually began October 29, 2019 and culminated on October 31, 2019 with the following response from investigators stated in part.

"We received your email and from what we understand, you are conducting a technical analysis in support of a Defense Contract Audit Agency (DCAA) audit of a $143M claim Lockheed Martin Aeronautics Company submitted to the USG pertaining to the C-5 RERP. We are aware of the claim, the DCAA audit and that DCM A's technical analysis in support of that audit has revealed some irregularities. DCAA already reported that information to us. Yes, we are interested in understanding those irregularities and whether they possibly relate to fraudulent activity and/or ongoing cases. However, we prefer to wait until your assessment is complete prior to discussing. Once your assessment is complete, and it is approved, we will review and reach out to you for an interview."

Investigators were already aware of the issues, and apparently, DCAA had already provided some insight. This may be the reason why Rawson indicated the DCAA wanted the DCAA auditors removed from the email trail. Regardless, I made the disclosure on November 21, 2019, and informed my management that I planned to do so on November 6, 2019 (attached to November 14, 2019, Memo for Record), stating in part to Colonel French and Myra Tate on November 6, 2019.

"I am working a C-5 Claim audit and have found suspected fraud. I have already been in contact with investigators.

At about the same time I contacted investigators DCAA requested a private meeting with DCMA management.

Mr. Rawson indicated that he would provide the e-mail from DCAA although he later backed off of his request."

"Please provide assistance as I suspect force will be necessary to dislodge Mr. Rawson from his negative response."

I recall no response to this email and made no resistance to the rewrite of my report. As was typical, I did the only thing within my power, which was document against DCMA.

The overarching point is, for years I was forced to confront, and workaround, DCMA management regarding potential fraud by Lockheed Martin. While management sat idly by, other than retaliating against me, I built my resume with a multitude of substantiated disclosures. From there, evidence has grown into a book, if not an encyclopedia of DoD and Government corruption, weaponization and lawfare. Ernie Fitzgerald experienced the same things at the Pentagon except Fitzgerald was harassed for 35 years.

Getting back to the C-5 RERP Claim, my report was rewritten as follows.

Report Rewritten & Watered Down

December 12, 2019: My report was rewritten and watered down. November 15, 2019, DCAA granted an extension stating in part.

"We hereby grant your office's request for an extension to the revised due date of November 20, 2019 (from the original due date of October 15, 2019) to a revised due date of December 12, 2019."

The report was reduced from 73 pages to 69 pages. The case was made, however, watered down from what I originally had. I supported the investigation and retired at the end of December 2020. Then came the Notice of Deposition from Lockheed Martin to me.

Notice of Deposition by Lockheed Martin - Offer to Testify

March 10, 2022 - Deposition Request: I was called by the DCMA attorney, Cleo Anderson, on or about March 17, 2022, and informed that a deposition was requested by Lockheed Martin in the C-5 RERP Claim. I was surprised and remember thinking how stupid it was for Lockheed Martin to depose me. I remember Cleo Anderson describing me as a "strong witness."

Cleo Anderson informed me that I can decline since I am no longer a federal employee; however, a judge may order the deposition. I concluded that if Lockheed Martin, or their attorneys representing Lockheed Martin, were that stupid to depose me, I would agree to the deposition. Cleo Anderson then forwarded my concurrence to the government attorneys in the C-5 Claim.

March 17, 2022: I began email correspondence with the government attorneys defending the Government against the C-5 Claim. The government attorneys were Lawrence Anderson, Kyle Gilbertson, and Caryl Potter.

In our first conversation, I made it clear I was a successful government whistleblower. Following that, there seemed to be a 50/50 split as if the attorney for Lockheed Martin would proceed with me or back off. My deposition was scheduled for April 12, 2022 and was via videoconference.

Lockheed Martin Deposition High Points – April 12, 2022

April 12, 2022: My deposition covered my whistleblowing, the Lockheed Martin Claim, and my December 12, 2019, Technical Report. The following are highlights of my deposition.

Contemporaneous (Historical) Documents Discussion – Knew This Day Was Coming: I made it clear that if I misspeak my anchor document is my report. In this case, December 12, 2019. Meaning I wrote down in detail what my thought process was. I did that exactly for the purpose of the C-5 Claim being litigated. I stated at the beginning of my deposition.

"So if I misspeak, that is my real deposition, those 69 pages. So I'm telling you up front when I wrote that, I knew this day would be coming. That is why I wrote it down in detail. That is why I have all the supporting documents.

I have played these games with depositions in the past. Trust me, I have been through a lot of them. If you give me the opportunity to explain my history, I will do that. But right now, you continue with what you want to do."

From there, I proceeded to my whistleblowing history. This was the test to see if the deposition would continue, or be ended, and my ability to make substantiated cases.

April 12, 2022 – Whistleblowing Discussion: After the supporting documents' discussion, I went into the whistleblowing discussion, stating in part.

"There have been an assortment of Merit Systems Protection Board cases, EEOC, Equal Employment Opportunity cases, Department of Defense Inspector General's Office cases, NSA, National Security Agency investigation cases, and just to bring it up, a lot of that has been from my background as a whistleblower.

Those are the ones that I could remember. One of them was actually a Department of the Interior investigation. So we have Inspector General's Office for the Department of Defense, the DODIG. Then we have the DOI, Department of the Interior Inspector General, because I made allegations against the Department of Defense Inspector General's Office, and they couldn't investigate themselves.

And then another one that was with the National Security Agency of which again more allegations against the Inspector General's Office of which the NSA came in, National Security Agency, and did that. So there's been a few of them."

From there, I spoke about Ernie Fitzgerald, how my security clearance was revoked, walking out the gate by Lockheed Martin armed guards, and my involvement with Senator Charles Grassley, stating in part.

"I was working with Senator Charles Grassley at that time. I was working somewhat with the news media. I had been working with criminal investigators, false claims against Lockheed Martin. So the bottom line is I was labeled a legitimate threat to the government.

Your case right now that you have in front of you is an offshoot of that whistleblower battle at the facility. Now, does that help answer your question?"

From there, I went to talk about my arrival at the facility.

"I got to that facility in 1994. I'm talking about Lockheed Martin. Okay. Back then they called themselves Lockheed Martin. Today I believe they call themselves Lockheed Martin Aeronautical Companies.

The bottom line is I got there. When I arrived, the facility was a mess. There were criminal investigators walking the halls. There were people making allegations against management, this, that and the other."

The whistleblowing discussion culminated in my discussion of criminal vulnerability.

"And they also stated that criminal vulnerability, the government management staff knew of the fraud and they did nothing about it. Okay. So criminal vulnerability, government management knows about it. They are not doing anything about it."

I made it clear who I was and what I was capable of. Nevertheless, the attorney for Lockheed Martin continued. Samples of deposition are as follows.

Lockheed Martin Started to Manage 2 Years After Start of LRIP

(Low-Rate Initial Production)

April 12, 2022: Lockheed Martin started managing the C-5 RERP two years into LRIP. The individual mentioned below, Jim, is actually Jim Sprouse. I stated in part.

"Believe it or not, this program started around August of 2009. This is another issue that I will testify to that I remember at the facility."

"Believe it or not, when they started to manage this process, it was in 2011. Because Lockheed Martin had a lot of problems on their shop floor."

"And what happened was we had an individual come over, his name was Jim, I forget his last name, I think his first name was Jim or James, and basically we set up what was called the deliver now conference room to overcome all of the problems that Lockheed Martin had."

"For example, miscellaneous small parts, Lockheed Martin people would come in the room and they would say we haven't got any miscellaneous small parts to work this, nuts, screws, washers, this, that and the other. So the bins on the floor were empty. That was causing Lockheed Martin a problem."

"He would literally call in the people that worked on the aircraft and pretty much walk them through. Tell me what your problem is. Tell me how we are going to fix this problem."

Another notable area was the baseline as follows.

Asked to Provide a Baseline

April 12, 2022: One portion of the deposition focused on the baseline and how DCAA asked me to provide a baseline. I stated in part.

"That was one of their questions early on, provide a recommendation for a reasonable baseline. And the bottom line is a reasonable baseline to what?"

"And there was no way possible to do that with the Lockheed Martin data the way it was. Their data that they gave us was suspect to begin with."

"Besides that, let's just say that I did provide a baseline. Let's just say I did do that. Okay. You would go in with a bunch of MDRs that still you couldn't even tie back to that baseline that you said would interfere with you."

"And besides that, DCAA, if you must know, they were the ones that went in and pressured my supervisor and my management staff for me to rewrite my report. So let's not talk about how pristine DCAA is."

The point is, Lockheed Martin data was suspect, meaning no baseline existed to begin with that I could see. And DCAA went to my management to water down my report. I offered the following.

Measured Mile is Elaborate Math (Scam)

April 12, 2022: One of my deposition responses is as follows regarding the Measured Mile.

"Because I have seen Lockheed Martin use elaborate math scams before, and this right here fell in to that exact same practice."

"The answer is when Lockheed uses it, yes. In this proposal, in this claim right here you can talk about six decades, and if you or the government attorneys, and I don't know if they are still on the line, if you want me to come up and talk to the judge about it and go down through my report, rather than you cherry picking your data, then I will go down through the report and I will show them that Lockheed Martin's Measured Mile analysis is a math scam, it is without merit, and it is unsupportable."

The term "elaborate math" was in the November 21, 2019, disclosure and the December 12, 2019, report. Prior, pattern & practice, examples of elaborate math scams were part of Chapter 4.

The next issue was a causal link to MDRs (Over & Above) as follows.

No Causal Link – New & Intermixed Scope of Work – Multiple Variables

April 12, 2022: Other quotes in my deposition are as follows, as related to the causal link.

"But the bottom line is you can't – you can't go back and unring the bell if that stuff interferes with people, interferes with the learning curve, such as ECPs (Engineering Change Proposals)*, rework, changes from conditions, work force changes, maybe you got new people coming on to the system.*

You cannot wash that away from a person's mind through an accounting measure. You are talking about learning curves and –"

The attorney interrupted and asked… *"How would you have -- how would you have Lockheed Martin account for those things then?"*

I responded as follows: *"Okay. The first thing is I'm not sure that Lockheed Martin can account for them. Okay. And by the way, this is Lockheed Martin's responsibility, not mine, because they never provide a causal link.*

I would like to see the causal link between their learning curves, which is your Measured Mile analysis, and the MDRs. And you are going to factor out, you know, certain things and you are going to look at it, and, you know, we will factor this out, and oh, by the way, this is how much money that you owe us.

You cannot factor it out of the learning curve. Again, any time you want me up in front of a judge, you let me know. Give me the word, you or the government."

The point is, if Lockheed Martin were in a long-term contract with long-established learning curves like the early C-130H line or a factory that manufactures artillery shells (repetitive operation), then the Measured Mile may apply. Here, there were multiple variables with a new and intermixed scope of work. Not possible to factor out any loss of learning. Meaning, just say so as follows.

Because Lockheed Martin "Says It, So It Must Be So"

April 12, 2022: The attorney for Lockheed Martin responded to causal link as follows.

"See here on page 8 of Exhibit 2, here's a statement from Lockheed Martin where it says: A contributor to the high volume of O & A changes on the RERP contract was such over inspection and increasing of the requirements for over-and-above work or O & A work beyond the anticipated standards to support flight worthiness.

Why wouldn't you consider that a causal link?"

I responded in part: *"…but the point is saying it doesn't mean that it happened because you are making this one statement and it's like oh, well, Lockheed says it, so it must be so."*

The real point is that Lockheed Martin never proved any loss of money as follows.

Lockheed Martin Never Lost Money – Just Didn't Meeting Learning Goal

Lockheed Martin was provided a "Blank Check" charging for Over & Above work and four adjustments. Lockheed Martin simply stated they didn't meet a learning goal of 86.9% that was unrelated after the baseline adjustment. Meaning, Lockheed Martin never admitted they lost money, they simply stated they did not meet learning curve objectives.

Lockheed Martin Already Received Equitable Adjustments + "Blank Check" Charging: P00178, P00265, P00310, and P00219 gave Lockheed Martin equitable adjustments. The "Blank Check" charging for R3 (Time & materials) meant Lockheed Martin was already covered for disruption cost.

Re-baselining Negated Prior Estimates & Negated Prior Learning Curves: Once the contract mods P00178, P00265, P00310, and P00219 were implemented, the prior 86.9% learning curve estimate was over. The C-5 RERP basically started fresh at that point negating all past events and negating past estimating parameters.

Offered to Testify

April 12, 2022: I offered to testify at the ASBCA hearing as follows.

"So again, if you want me up in front of a judge to talk about six decades of Measured Mile analysis, all you have to do is ask."

"And I will gladly sit in front of a judge. I will explain to the judge with my 69 pages, rather than having you sit here and cherry pick their data."

"Again, any time you want me up in front of a judge, you let me know. Give me the word, you or the government."

After my deposition, I communicated with Government attorneys as follows.

Post Deposition Communications with Government Attorneys
"Out of the Stadium" - "Work in Progress"

June 8, 2022: I finished reviewing my deposition with only very minor corrections. The communications with government attorney Lawrence Anderson were, in part, as follows.

"In my humble opinion you hit the ball out of the stadium. I don't think Lockheed would dare take a chance calling you as a witness at the hearing, but if the Lockheed attorneys do indicate such a desire, we'll tell you immediately."

I responded in part: *"The one issue I would like to know is how government plans to win case."*

Anderson stated, *"Ken, that's a work in progress. The journey itself is the goal."*

The deposition made a solid case against Lockheed Martin. That is why I wrote the November 21, 2019, disclosure and December 12, 2019, documents with such detail, with over 80 attachments. Meaning, details should be addressed if the issue arises to a legal level. Basically, I use that method in all my reports as the documents will become historical records. The prehearing contact followed.

Prehearing Contact with Government Attorneys

October 7, 2022: I contacted Lawrence Anderson and stated in part.

"Just wondering what ever happened with the $143 Million claim from Lockheed Martin ..

Was it settled, dismissed, ...?

I remember the hearing was for October 2022 and curious about the status."

Anderson responded in part.

"We have a 19 day hearing starting October 11 and going through Nov 4. Once the hearing is over, briefing will take at least four to six months. Then, we will await a decision .....which will likely take one to three years. The decision will be public for you to see on the ASBCA website (all the decisions are published on line for free download on the site)."

The point is, in my deposition, I made it clear I was available as a witness in front of the judge. I also contacted the government attorneys prior to the hearing. Doubtful Lockheed Martin would ever call me. I had hoped the government attorneys would use me as a witness. I made no attempt to force myself on the issue; however, I made it clear during my deposition that I was willing to testify. I also had contact just prior to the hearing, so I was in communication.

Here is what happened.

Lockheed Martin Wins $131,888,860 Decision

April 22-23, 2024 – Decision for Appeal 62209: The ASBCA started with the following statements.

"This appeal involves a contract for Lockheed Martin Aeronautics Company (Lockheed Martin) to modernize and install new engines for 49 C-5 Galaxy aircraft owned by the United States Air Force. Lockheed Martin alleges that the Air Force and the Defense Contract Management Agency (DCMA) directed it to perform excessive and disruptive "over and above" (O&A) work to repair pre-existing (or "legacy") defects on the aircraft and seeks to recover $131,888,860 for the additional work. The Air Force asserts Lockheed Martin failed to prove its entitlement to this amount and its calculation of damages is unreasonable. Additionally, the Air Force contends Lockheed Martin's claim is barred by the Contract Disputes Act's statute of limitations and releases contained in bilateral modifications to the contract. We sustain the appeal."

The point is, the Air Force was correct regarding bilateral agreements as follows.

Contract Mods Negated Claim

November 6, 2012: The Air Force was correct that Lockheed Martin was barred from bringing the action against the Air Force because Lockheed Martin agreed to a re-baseline in writing (POO178 November 6, 2012), as well as other funding (equitable adjustments) from P00265, P00310, and P00219, not to mention "Blank Check" (Time & Materials).

Contract Mod (P00178) stated in part.

"Once fully executed, the "Bucket ECP" (ECP 12-00012A) effort and this Supplemental Agreement (P00178) will constitute a full and equitable adjustment between the Government and the Contractor and release all parties from liability under the contract for further claims or equitable adjustments arising out of or in connection with any past legacy issues, runway closure, the aircraft cut wire, DCMA flight crew availability, and/or DCMA additional inspection requirements in addition to the issues discussed in Paragraph 1 of this contract modification."

Meaning, the Air Force and Lockheed Martin were mutually released, bilateral, from liability. The next issue involves the Government attorneys.

13-Day Hearing - No Witnesses by Government

April 23, 2024 -: ASBCA 62209 Decision concluded with the following statement.

"Using the measured mile method and its government-audited and approved labor rates and factors, Lockheed Martin calculated its damages to be $131,888,860 (findings 275-97). Lockheed Martin's data and methods were corroborated by Mr. Gaudion's report (findings 274, 284, 286), a DCAA audit (findings 280, 283), and unrebutted witness testimony from Lockheed Martin finance personnel (see findings 289-97). Based on the record and the aforementioned findings, Lockheed Martin has met its burden of establishing a prima facie case with respect to quantum. While the Air Force contends that Lockheed Martin has failed to prove quantum by a preponderance of the evidence (gov't br. at 16-21), it does not provide any valid basis refuting the evidence presented by Lockheed Martin, and thus it has failed to defeat Lockheed Martin's prima facie case of quantum recovery. BAE Sys., 16-1 BCA 36,404 at 177,507. In fact, during the course of the 13-day hearing, the Air Force never even called a single expert witness to contest any of Lockheed Martin's quantum evidence, including Mr. Gaudion's report. Accordingly, we hold that Lockheed Martin is entitled to recover $131,888,860 for impacts to the RERP effort for Lots 3 through 5 caused by O&A work."

The point is, there was a 13-day hearing and the Air Force/Government did not call even one expert witness despite the fact that I offered to be a witness at the hearing and contacted the government attorneys prior to the hearing on October 7, 2022 and during my deposition it was discussed that I was a Subject Matter Expert (SME).

It also seemed that the only government official, Kathryn Sowers (Air Force's Systems Development Manager), was a witness for Lockheed Martin. Although it was unclear who called Sowers or if testimony was copied from Sower's deposition, if a deposition was taken. Regardless, the ASBCA openly criticized the Government attorneys for not calling witnesses.

The "Measured Mile" analysis ranks high on the criminal vulnerability scale with regards to elaborate math scams. Meaning, a price gouging scam by the Military-Industrial Complex most notably the way it was used by Lockheed Martin. I was ready to openly confront at the hearing and, neither side, Lockheed Martin or the Government, did not call me as a witness. I would also question the decision by ASBCA on the grounds of bilateral modifications to the contract to compensate Lockheed Martin.

The next issues are the billing structure and enabling price gouging.

Analysis of Claim ASBCA 62209 (Part 1 – Billing Structure)

(930% to 1009% - Multiply Direct Costs by Factor of 9.3X - 10.09X)

October 15, 2018 Claim: The original bill cost for Contract FA8625-07-C-6471, C-5 RERP Claim, are as follows with comparisons to "Direct Production" amount of $14,227,798. The following is for the original Claim (Bill) amount of $143,529,290 and includes the final amount of $131,888,860 for comparison to Direct Production cost. (Note. Original Claim was also off $1 in addition.)

Departments and Expenses	Dollars	% Direct Production
Direct Production Cost	$ 14,227,798	
Other Costs (Factored/Rate Based)	$ 11,556,021	81% (.81X)
Total Labor Expense	$ 25,783,819	
Total Other Expense[1]	$ 117,745,472	
Total Price (original Claim)	$ 143,529,290	1009% (10.09X)
Total Amount Per ASBCA	$ 131,888,860	930% (9.3X)

Note 1: Includes Fringe & Overhead, Other Costs, Program Office, Fee/Profit, G&A, etc.

The prior chart shows some high billed percentages compared to the Direct Production (touch labor work). This would be a culmination point for the figures outlined in Chapter 4 of this book. Meaning, the overcharges such as elaborate math (31%), untraceable CERs/EFDs (49%-60%), etc., show up in the final cost. During the ASBCA 62209 hearing, the amount was somehow reduced to $131,888,860 or a factor of about 9.3X (131,888,860/14,227,978) as compared to Direct Production Cost.

Other Costs (Factored/Rate Based) $11,556,021: These costs were Factored/Rate Based, meaning mathematically derived. The original calculated amount was hours converted to costs ($). Most likely estimated using the catch phrase "*include but not limited to*" as described in Chapter 4 regarding CERs and EFDs. In this case the percentage against production cost is .81. Meaning, for each dollar of actual touch labor there is a corresponding cost of $.81 support cost that may be untraceable. This is separate from overhead, but like a direct overhead, or direct support, charge.

In short, Part 1 of the Capstone Case shows how cost is escalated in an actual "bill" (Claim) to the U.S. Government. Meaning, how final "price" is escalated to an amount of 9.3X to 10.09 times Direct Production "cost". Chapter 4 showed price gouging amounts of 31%, 24%-69%, 49%-60%, 79%-80% and the like escalate cost in the price billed to the U.S. Government.

Additionally, there was an enabling effect to criminal vulnerability and tactical price gouging as outlined in Chapter 2 and Chapter 3. Meaning, working conditions were altered (obstruction) to reduce protection for U.S. Government interests. This enables price gouging and criminal vulnerability. The next point is that the C-5 Claim shouldn't have happened to begin with.

C-5 Claim ASBCA 62209 (Part 2 - Enabled)

Shouldn't Have Happened to Begin With

The capstone case was a classic example of what I experienced in 26 ½ years at the DCMA, dealing with Lockheed Martin. That is why this book was presented in a structured way. First, I explained who I was with my resume (Chapter 1). How I protected Government interests. Meaning, I should have been supported by the DCMA management staff. Instead, my DCMA management opposed me. This enabled the C-5 Claim and criminal vulnerability.

Chapter 2, isolated the DoD, the DCMA, the DCAA, the DoD IG, the OSC, the MSPB, the OPM, and the Court of Appeals for the Federal Circuit, to show the history of cover-ups and working against the U.S. government's interests and efficiency. Meaning, enablers to criminal vulnerability and tactical price gouging via extensive evidence trails and timelines outlined herein. This enabled the C-5 Claim and criminal vulnerability.

Chapter 3, my consequences for protecting government interests was 13 Falsified Trails against me. Executing my personal and professional reputation and severing my working relationship with Senator Grassley. This enabled the C-5 Claim and criminal vulnerability.

Chapter 4, specific cost examples of tactical price gouging (elaborate math) and the like, could be responsible for as much as 30% - 50% of the national debt, as a minimum. I was precluded from seeking corrective action against Lockheed Martin and DCMA management allowed no firm action to correct Lockheed Martin. This enabled the C-5 Claim and criminal vulnerability.

Chapter 5, is an example of the entire system at work, where I was peripherally involved and then unwisely invited in by Lockheed Martin in ASBCA Case 62209. Meaning, I could have made a difference due to Lockheed Martin's unwise choices; however, the U.S. Government attorneys did not call me as a witness in 13 days of hearings. This enabled the C-5 Claim and criminal vulnerability.

The ASBCA judges share blame by allowing a case where Lockheed Martin was given prior equitable adjustments (bilateral contract Modifications) releasing the Government from liability. Meaning, the capstone case was the perfect case where both the Government attorneys and ASCBA shared equal blame within the same case. This approved the C-5 Claim enabling more criminal vulnerability.

The Evidence Trail Speaks for Itself – One, or a Few, Against Many

Weaponization and lawfare have compromised government oversight and cost efficiency proving there is a Deep State. The 2025 and 2026 conversation in the U.S. Government is DOGE, weaponization, lawfare, price gouging, national debt, and affordability. This book is my testimony. I am a direct witness and victim of Deep State, weaponized government and lawfare traced to the national debt. Meaning, my resume would show that one or a few people can prevail against a large group. This is evident in the Substantiate Allegations where the status quo (large group) was challenged by a few, supported by one Senator, Charles Grassley, and prevailed against the Deep State and Military-Industrial Complex. Chapter 6 is the suggested remedy to extend this success.

CHAPTER 6: Remedy to Shrink the Government Swamp

Restorative Justice & Attitude Adjustments for Management

The judge in this case is the President of the United States. The jury is the U.S. Senate and House of Representatives. I am a victim and taxpayer who is appalled at what I have witnessed in DoD and government overall. I have lost all confidence in the U.S. Legal and Judicial System.

U.S. presidents have pardoned various individuals over the years and have used executive powers because the U.S. Legal and Judicial System is failing. Hence, the need for restorative justice. This book shows such a systemic and institutional failure where personnel actions, authority, attorneys, and surrogates are prime weapons in lawfare. Now it's time for the remedy.

The remedy starts with restorative justice for victims and attitude adjustments to management. This will put affordability within reach because, as this book shows, weaponization and lawfare negatively affect cost and even a few people, with the proper Government support, can make a difference.

Senior Management – Senior Leadership - Attorneys

This book shows that senior management, senior leadership, and attorneys are not interested in national security; Not interested in efficiency of Federal Service; Not interested in cost efficiency; Not interested in affordability; And treat Federal Funds with less respect than Monopoly Money. The system has unraveled for over half a century. This attitude needs adjustment. Meaning, senior management, senior leadership, and attorneys are the problem, not the solution. Society should not be fooled by the ultra-professional façade.

Ultra-Professional Façade – Serial Killer Analogy

Maleficence in government, weaponization, lawfare, cover-ups, and enabling of corruption by the U.S. Legal System was vicious, vindictive, institutional, relentless, well-organized, and well-connected like organized crime. The actions were concealed by management's ultra-professional façade to outsiders. This ultra-professional façade was historically analogous to serial killers.

Serial killers such as John Wayne Gacy (Killer Clown), Dennis Rader (BTK Killer), Robert Hansen (Butcher Baker), David Berkowitz (Son of Sam and .44 Caliber Killer), and Rodney Alcala (Dating Game Killer) existed at length in society, mocking law enforcement and society, prior to capture.

John Wayne Gacy was respected. Dennis Rader was a church leader. Rodney Alcala, in or about 1978, won a date on a national television show called "The Dating Game". Alcala's span of crimes ranged from 1968 to 1979, with 8 confirmed victims and 130 victims possible. Meaning, Alcala was on national television amidst a murder spree. Hence, understanding and overcoming the ultra-professional demeanor façade is paramount to remedy.

Supporting employees is the first step because employees are the best source of documentation and witnesses to facts.

Support and Protect Employees – Shrink the Government Swamp

Employees are the key to understanding and exposing institutional corruption, price gouging, lawfare, and weaponized government. First-level supervisors' integrity is on a case-by-case basis. Second level supervisors upward, the integrity is zero to counterproductive and adverse. Meaning, everything from the "foot-in-the-aisle" interference to blatant cover-ups and Falsified Trails. The evidence herein shows this fact. There seems to be an assimilation into institutional corruption, part of the Deep State, once management officials become part of second level supervision.

Understand Deep State Assimilation During Remedy Phase

Myra Tate was the example of assimilation into the Deep State weaponized government. As fellow employees, Myra Tate and I were in agreement on management. Meaning, Tate kept me informed on issues of concern. Such as, September 24, 2002 when Myra Tate had her EVMS duties removed by then Deputy Commander Ben Chaffman. And, October 1, 2002 when Myra Tate forwarded the August 13, 2002 Draft CAR regarding Lockheed Martin EVMS problems. Then, after the July 26, 2002 report to Congress, Tate informed me that I was shaking up management.

Myra Tate made first level supervisor about the time of her EEO settlement which was on or about June 19, 2003. Tate kept me informed of her litigation against DCMA. Then, I was walked out the gate by Lockheed Martin armed guards on August 14, 2003. Myra Tate, as a first level supervisor, on or about October 27, 2003 explained what happened during the investigation of my infamous walk out the gate by Lockheed Martin armed guards. I documented that conversation with Myra Tate in an October 28, 2003 email to the DoD IG.

After Substantiated Allegation 4 (July 23, 2004, the C-130J) Ben Chaffman announced his exodus on August 24, 2004. Henrietta Snow moved into the Deputy Commander position. At some point later Myra Tate became second-level supervisor and changed. Tate's biggest change was being promoted to Deputy Commander upon Henrietta Snow retiring on or about February 21, 2014. Meaning, 2014 was the start of Volley 4 (Falsified Trails 11, 12, and 13). During Falsified Trails 11, 12, and 13 Myra Tate acted much like Ben Chaffman or Henrietta Snow watching me being tormented and retaliated against while shunning me.

The point is, Myra Tate and I were in agreement on management util Myra Tate made second-level supervisor. When Myra Tate was promoted to third-level supervisor, Tate was no better than the past Deputy Commanders. Tate was fully assimilated into the Deep State. As Deputy Commander, Myra Tate could have resolved the issues and, instead, did nothing. This observation is critical.

The Deep State, weaponized government and lawfare have assimilated to such dimensions, that whoever exposes the Deep State will be demonized. This would include judges. That is why I was forced to write this book with such detail and put it in the hands of the public. That way, with the Deep State working practices more intently understood, remedy would be easily facilitated. The Government Swamp could be more easily drained. The Deep State is already public conversation; however in-depth statistics were lacking. This book provides extreme detail in an encyclopedia form. Hopefully, remedy will take hold before "belt tightening" is needed.

Offset "Belt Tightening" and Ruination – Achieve Affordability

Drain the Swamp in 5 Minutes or Expand the Swamp by Doing Nothing

Affordability is not possible unless weaponization and lawfare are remedied. Meaning, as the debt grows, "belt tightening" and panels to limit health care and public services will emerge. The goal of this book is to objectively offset that dilemma. Simply put, the Congress and the President have the power to start draining the Government Swamp in as little as 5 minutes by reversing such things as Falsified Trails in this book. Meaning, send a quick message that events outlined in this book will not be tolerated. That potential watershed moment will be explained in more detail within this remedy section. Doing nothing will expand the Government Swamp.

Pragmatist - Speaking Truth to Power Led to Weaponization & Lawfare

Over a quarter century prior to 2025 I saw the path the U.S. Government was on with waste, fraud, and abuse. I tried to speak truth to power at that time and was met with weaponization and lawfare. Those experiences allowed me to from the link of weaponized government and lawfare which form the foundation of this book. Meaning, I became a pragmatist to understand how things really work.

Be a pragmatist when using the remedy and do what works to achieve the end goal of government efficiency and affordability. Don't fall for the ultra-professional demeanor façade and con game; otherwise, more victims will follow. The following is the first, quickest, cost and time effective, and easiest step to restore government integrity and quickly drain the Swamp. Meaning, embarrassment via administrative "shock therapy". Restorative justice and attitude adjustments by other terms. Thomas Gimble is the example.

Embarrassment and "Shock Therapy" (Attitude Adjustment)

Chapter 1 of this book outlines the situation of Thomas Gimble. Gimble was directed to issue a simple retraction letter. John Crane stated in part in the June 5, 2008, IG report.

"*Should he* (Gimble) *have been upset? That's up to Tom Gimble, that he felt humiliated by it, that he felt that it made him look bad, that he felt it would give [the DoD complainant] extra ammunition.*" (I (Pedeleose) was the "DoD complainant")

Crane further stated: "*And he* (Gimble) *said that he* (Gimble) *would rather retire than to sign a retraction letter. And I said, 'Once again, that's a matter that you need to raise with General Kicklighter.'*"

Gimble was right, the retraction letter was "*extra ammunition*" in the fight against institutional corruption, lawfare, and maleficence. The "*ammunition*" was Gimble being "*humiliated*", "*made him look bad*", and Gimble "*would rather retire than to sign a retraction letter*".

Gimble was directed to write a retraction letter by then DoD IG Director Claude Kicklighter. There was no long debate; no drawn-out, corrupted, legal proceeding; there were quick, timely results. Issues were resolved based on what was right. Gimble was just an example. Meaning, embarrassment and "Shock Therapy" does work and is a cost-effective remedy.

Immediately Shrink the Government Swamp: Restorative justice by embarrassment and shock therapy, as what happened to Thomas Gimble, will have an immediate effect to shrink the Government Swamp.

Restorative justice (making victims whole) will provide instant adjustment to management attitudes; Instant shrinking of the Government Swamp; Instant understanding that weaponization and lawfare will not be tolerated; and place the government on the path to affordability. The personnel proclivities and any embarrassment of subordinate management are at risk for those who engage in wrongdoing.

The President has the power to do this and in fact even lower-level officials can enact immediate remedy. In short, expunge adverse records of victims of weaponization, lawfare, and retaliation. The Congress can codify laws to force restorative justice. Zero tolerance and retroactive action can make major attitude adjustments to weaponization and lawfare.

Zero Tolerance for Abuse of Authority in Personnel Cases

There should be zero tolerance for abuse of authority by management officials and no discretion by judges to overlook abuse of authority in personnel actions. Personnel actions are a major weapon in lawfare, institutional corruption, and weaponization. The Falsified Trails herein include multiple examples of abuse of authority and tactics outlined as follows.

1: Entrapment

2: Discrimination

3: Retaliation

4: Weaponized Investigations and Lawfare

5: Disparate Treatment and Manufactured Regulations for Certain Employees

6: Shunning

7: Shifting/Changing Reasons for Adverse Personnel Actions.

8: Outlandish Charges (Such as drinking non-alcoholic sparkling cider from the bottle.)

9: Punitive or Weaponized Training

10: Delays in Providing Evidence in Cases - Surprise Evidence

11: Any Disingenuous Behavior by Management

12: Altered Evidence Including Altered Emails

13: Conflicts of Interest within or by Management

14: Hostile Workplace Affects

15: Con Games

16: Perjury Traps

17: The DCMA Liaisons to Spread False Information to Congress

18: Any Attempt to Circumvent Law

19: Singling Out Employees

20: Lying or Falsification by Management

21: Suborning Perjury

22: Kernel of Thought – Planting Ideas to Mislead and Deceive

This is a sample list of the adverse actions in the Falsified Trails against me. In personnel cases against employees, there should be no complexities or abuse of authority. Zero tolerance.

Legal & Judicial System Remedy - The Law & Zero Tolerance

The U.S. Legal and Judicial System is the main route for weaponization and lawfare. As such there needs to be strict laws restricting judges. Meaning, eliminate judicial discretion to look the other way on corrupt acts by management. Force judges to look at the law and not the case law that is riddled with weaponization and lawfare. Proposed remedy is as follows.

Zero Tolerance for Surprise Evidence

Falsified Trail 3 was the textbook case of surprise evidence. Any case that includes surprise evidence should be immediately dismissed by senior agency officials or judges in the case. No exceptions. Surprise evidence is an indicator of malice by agencies or management officials.

Codified Retroactive Laws and Retroactive Remedy – Anti-Manipulation Law

Retroactive laws and retroactive remedies will show management that, regardless of the timeframe, if management is caught weaponizing government or using lawfare, the decision can be overridden by Congress or the President in the interest of the Federal Service, national security and the interest of taxpayers. Like the contaminated water at Camp Lejeune (1953-1987) resolved several decades after the event.

The retroactive aspect will loom over management as a reminder that unethical manipulation of laws can be reversed at any time with retroactive removal of all mention of past personnel cases from decisions. This will enforce honesty throughout history and endure time. Zero tolerance helps support that aspect and cleans up the U.S. Legal and Judicial System.

Codified Law - No Discretion by Judges

Judicial discretion can be as unethical and damaging as management's abuse of discretion. In the so-called "legal" and "quasi-judicial" (MSPB) cases, the manipulations can be staggering, where minds wander into the obscure within institutionally corrupted government. Judges' discretion needs to be zeroed out, and they must follow the zero-tolerance guidelines.

Codified Ban on Case Law to Decide Cases

April 21, 2002: The MPRI report, Chapter 2, made a finding about OSC and MSPB, stating in part.

"These forums (MSPB & OSC) *have become increasingly discredited as a viable source of legal relief for aggrieved whistleblowers. Few whistleblowers now prevail before the MSPB because the governing statute, the Whistleblower Protection Act, has been steadily eroded by restrictive interpretations that make it most difficult to sustain a winning case."*

Meaning, case law is watered down, hence the law is no longer effective. The remedy is to force judges, with no discretion allowed, to review each case under the laws of Congress, not watered-down opinions. The same holds true for the OPM, which has abused statutory authority as follows.

Eliminate/Revoke OPM Statutory Right to Reconsideration of MSPB Rulings

In Falsified Trail 3, Linda Springer, then OPM Director, stated in part on November 28, 2007;
"This is notice that the Office of Personnel Management (OPM) is exercising its statutory right under 5U.S.C. §7703(d) to request reconsideration of the Board's decision in the case cited below. I am of the opinion that the Board erred in interpreting a civil service law, rule, or regulation..."

This was the first step in covering up the DoD IG and Senior DCMA Management involvement in Falsified Trail 3. From there, the further enabling of corruption came when the DCMA, starting with Nanette Nelson, commenced with rewriting reports after February 12, 2009.

The remedy is to revoke OPM's statutory right to intervein in MSPB decisions. Linda Springer and OPM have shown that such intervention has enabled further weaponization, lawfare, and corruption in the U.S. Government. In Falsified Trail 3, the "Obey First, Grieve Later" doctrine was neither a government law, rule, or regulation; hence, the OPM should not have been involved at all.

Remedy to Eliminate Government Attorney Weaponization & Lawfare

Management and Attorney Contact Logs

DoD management has institutionally weaponized direct access to government attorneys. Falsified Trail 3 is the Flagship example. The direct access by management needs to be eliminated. Government attorneys should support employees and management equally.

Attorney Access Log Book: A log book of government management contact with government attorneys needs to be made available for transparency. This would ensure government attorneys remain honest and not entangled in the facts of personnel cases. This book has multiple instances where attorneys are entangled in the facts of weaponization and lawfare cases against me. Meaning, government attorneys are the true source of weaponization and lawfare.

Written Request & Explain Why Attorneys are Needed: Knowing why government management contacted government attorneys, and making the managers request in writing government attorney assistance, will reduce weaponization and lawfare. In my case, government attorneys were available to management at the flick of the wrist or a phone call. That ease of access enabled weaponization and lawfare. From there, the attorney-client privilege in government cases needs to be eliminated.

No Attorney-Client Privilege with Government Attorneys

In Falsified Trail 6, the DCMA attorney, Cleo Anderson, claimed Attorney-Client Privilege 13 times. In Falsified Trail 13, Kim Turner (DCMA FOIA) sent a September 11, 2015, email stamped "Attorney-Client Privileged Material" that started disciplinary action against me. The key word was "Material" implying an attorney probably wrote or coached the weaponized email. The Attachment in this book shows the email sent by Kim Turner, and later forwarded to my supervisor Isaiah Waindi by David Wray (Kim Turner's supervisor).

In the capstone case (Chapter 5), Jason Rawson (then 2nd level supervisor) was sent an email from DCAA (November 6, 2019), where the DCAA claimed Attorney Client Privilege.

Attorney-client privilege is a weapon and should be barred by law in government operations for personnel actions or <u>any issues</u> involving Government management officials. Meaning, the Attorney-Client Privilege can be a harboring place for unethical activity, weaponization and lawfare.

Government Attorneys as Witnesses – Entangled in Facts of Cases

Government attorneys are weaponized and entangled in the facts of personnel cases as shown in Chapter 3. Government attorneys should protect government integrity and the efficiency of the Federal Service, not protect or enable corruption and weaponization.

Forcing government attorneys to testify in cases would ensure government attorney skills are used to protect the integrity of the Federal service and support a zero-tolerance approach to corruption.

Management Clears Schedules for Independent Investigations

Vicarious Liability with no Plausible Deniability

Government Directors, senior managers, and supervisors need to clear schedules to be witnesses in cases and for independent investigations. The "too busy"; willful ignorance; or plausible deniability defense should not be accepted. This will provide motivation to abandon weaponized government and lawfare through forced accountability. Meaning, management officials will be brought into the facts of the case and forced to respond with facts.

Vicarious liability would apply anyway since senior managers are responsible for the actions of subordinates. Meaning, the senior managers either knew, or should have known, any maleficence within their command. In my case, I used electronic trails (emails) to specifically inform senior DCMA and DoD IG officials of maleficence. This eliminated willful ignorance.

<u>5-Minute Resolutions</u>: The 5-minute resolutions are relevant because a professional management staff could have resolved all of the issues in the Falsified Trails within 5 minutes. Instead, issues festered into an inventory list that exists herein of corruption, weaponized government, and lawfare. Meaning, management will be motivated by law to resolve issues, versus weaponization and lawfare.

No Private Management Affidavits Via Weaponized Government Attorneys

Sham Affidavits & Sham Declarations

A noticeable fact herein is that management affidavits and declarations appear to be written by the same person, meaning written or coached by a government attorney. The following are examples in Falsified Trail 3.

April 26, 2006 Affidavit of Steven T. Bogusz

April 27, 2006 Declaration of Nicole H. Plourde

April 28, 2006 Affidavit of Stacy Scantlebury

Written by Same Person – Date Sequenced: The above affidavits and declarations follow the same format and appear written by the same person. Meaning, coached or written by a government attorney for a favorable decision by a judge. Furthermore, the aforesaid affidavits and declarations followed in sequence as if the attorneys spent the day with each individual, Bogusz, Plourde, and Scantlebury, in that order, well after the proposed 30-Day suspension of October 18, 2005.

Sham Declarations and Sham Affidavits: The process of submitting sham affidavits and sham declarations immediately prior to a hearing opens the door to last minute manipulations to coverup for prior weaponization, lawfare, retaliation, etc. Meaning, put in the last-minute words to sway the judge to cover-up case facts. Examples herein are as follows.

November 18, 2009 – Colorful Fiction Story: Falsified Trail 10 saw similarities in the memo and memorandum for record by Joe Tessier and Lou Gentile. Both were dated the same day (November 18, 2009) and appeared coached by a fiction writer. Meaning, Tessier and Gentile colorfully stated I was in a fit of rage; however, I lacked corresponding actions (throwing items, cussing/swearing, threats, etc.). Like a fiction story with no surrounding facts discovered about 3 months after the fact.

March 20, 2009 – Word Processor: Gerard Woodlief, then lead engineer, allegedly placed a complaint about me to Joe Tessier, copy to Nanette Nelson, Henrietta Snow, and Colonel Casey Blake. That complaint appeared to be written on a word processor, although it was presented as an email. Nelson handed me the complaint and essentially walked away. Meaning, the alleged complaint was not real and had no basis in fact and no need for concern. Just a weaponized data point in time.

February 20, 2007 and May 10, 2005: The "verbal lashing" of an employee prior to Falsified Trail 3 involved a declaration done behind the scenes, about 21 months after the fact, more than likely with a DCMA attorney. Meaning, other individuals participated in the EEO investigation with sworn statements in the EEO case file. Except for the February 20, 2007, statement, which was done behind the scenes.

The February 20, 2007, statement helped identify a May 10, 2005, altered document that was touted as an apology email. The May 10, 2005, email was clearly altered.

Deborah Mitchell – April 24, 2014: The most classic and textbook sham declaration would be from Deborah Mitchell in Falsified Trail 10 of February 16, 2010. Mitchell's declaration was over 4 years and 2 months late (February 16, 2010 to April 24, 2014).

Worse yet, Mitchell testified for the actions of other persons on her staff. Meaning, the declaration was hearsay. Then there was a baffling, and incriminating, near 3 months of "*revisions and reviews*" in the case from November 18, 2009 to February 16, 2010.

Remedy - Independent Investigations and Document Gathering: Falsification, lawfare and weaponization are enhanced by behind-the-scenes efforts. To stop, or at least curtail these unethical actions, investigations need to be conducted by independent investigators near the time of the infraction. All documents gathered and sworn statements taken by independent investigators. Not government attorneys with a vested interest in the agency. Also, provide all documents to the employee during the proposed action. No surprise evidence as in Falsified Trail 3.

If there is a case to be made, the government agency can make it. Just make it honestly, not in Falsified Trails or behind-the-scenes. Meaning, truly unruly employees leave a wide trail of evidence, like I have documented with the management and legal staff in this book.

Human Resources (HR), Labor Relations (LR) and Agency Attorneys

Involve Employees Prior to Disciplinary Action – Stop Case Fabrication

The Falsified Trails herein identified that HR, LR, and Agency attorneys are an extension of retaliatory management, weaponization and lawfare working against employees. This needs to end. Human Resources and Labor Relations should interview the employee to obtain the employee's side of the story before disciplinary action proceeds. This would help reduce the fabrication of cases.

Eliminate and Identify Ghost Writing – Eliminate "Cleo Anderson Letters"

Ghost writing, such as "Cleo Anderson Letters" of the Falsified Trails, also needs to end. This was an extension of weaponized attorney skills leading to Falsified Trails. If supervisors or managers had to write the letters, there would be more low-level resolution versus high-level litigation.

No Self-Investigations for Agencies

The DCMA needs to be barred from using internal investigators to investigate and clear the DCMA. The DCMA now has an established IG, and in the past, the DCMA has had internal investigators assigned at the Director's and Headquarters level. In Falsified Trail 13, the DCMA investigator investigated the DCMA and then cleared the DCMA with clear evidence of conflict of interest.

It is a clear conflict of interest for an organization to do self-investigations and should be banned.

Eliminate DoD IG Outsourcing Investigations to Agencies/Wrongdoers

May 16, 2018, DCMA IG: The DCMA stated, in part, as follows. *"The DoD IG just returns the referral to us (DCMA) as either an information referral or an action referral."*

The article went on to state that over the last four years, only one of the DCMAs' allegations had been investigated by the DoD IG. This conflict of interest must end. This includes DCMA being advised of cases. Meaning, DCMAs' modus operandi is to use DoD IG insight to engage in weaponization and lawfare against whistleblowers as this book shows. The DoD IG should do investigations and not forward back to Agencies or the wrongdoers.

Independent Investigations in Whistleblower Retaliation Cases

Case Made Up Front – All Documents, Transcripts, and Evidence Provided Upfront

Each management official should be investigated in person by independent investigators with recorded sworn statements and transcripts provided to employees. No government attorneys present. Documents can be gathered at that time. Management can present the case against the employee. Employees should also be investigated in person, and documents gathered.

Since the management staff is the aggressor and initiator in retaliation cases, no leeway should be given in document collection. Management and leadership can make the case if there is a case to be made.

Nothing will stop management from making or proceeding with cases against unruly employees, since at the time of adverse personnel action, management should have had the case made anyway. Meaning, a truly unruly employee provides a wide trail to follow, much like the management trail herein. There will be no need to falsify or exaggerate anything. Unruly employees will self-destruct on their own volition.

Vicarious Liability – Anti-Surrogate Law

Weaponized surrogates such as Joe Caldwell (Falsified Trail 1) and Nanette Nelson (Falsified Trails 4, 5, 6, 7, 8, 9, 10) should not be blamed alone. Especially when Keith Ernst cheers on retaliation (Falsified Trail 1) and openly participates in Falsified Trail 3. The effective remedy would be for each adverse personnel action to have a direct link to the senior levels. In the DCMA, that would be the Director. Vicarious liability would apply anyway and should be at the forefront at the start.

The transparency of having senior managers take responsibility for weaponization and lawfare versus hiding behind surrogates would be a major attitude adjustment for the good to drain the Government Swamp. This would be followed by de-weaponizing the FOIA process.

Stop Weaponization of FOIA (Freedom of Information Act)

The DCMA has weaponized the FOIA process similar to the DCMA investigators. This was for Falsified Trail 2 and 13. Both FOIAs were redacted. For Falsified Trail 13, I placed a FOIA in 2015 (DCMA FOIA 15-172). FOIA 15-172 was heavily redacted regarding the DCMA Report of Investigation (DMR 15-053). I then requested a clean copy of the FOIA and gave a reminder in September 2018.

<u>September 25, 2018</u>: I heard nothing on the FOIA 15-172 appeal for an unredacted FOIA. I then contacted VADM David Lewis (then DCMA Director), copying David Wray, Kimberly Turner, and my local DCMA management staff. To this date (early 2026), FOIA 15-172 has not been received. That would be over 10 years. This indicates FOIA is a weapon for cover-up.

At the end of Chapter 6 is an evidentiary Attachment to understand how the FOIA and investigation process was weaponized into lawfare (Falsified Trail 13). Meaning, the investigation centered on a simple Conflict of Interest (COI) issue. The heavy redaction, of a simple issue, confirms a cover-up.

Obey First, Grieve Later Doctrine - Not for Weaponization Purposes

Falsified Trail 3 openly weaponized the "Obey First, Grieve Later" doctrine. Only with institutional corruption and weaponization would such a tactic be used. As corruption and the Government Swamp expands, the idea would probably spread. Meaning, it should be made clear that the "Obey First, Grieve Later" or "Work First, Grieve Later" doctrine would never be an absolute law. It would be clear to management that any abuse of any doctrine would have reverse consequences.

Case Riders (Misconduct by Judges) Attached in Case Decision

Lead and supervisory judges can capriciously cover up judicial misconduct, thereby enabling further corruption and weaponization by management officials and other judges. Meaning the judge (enabler) remains in the clear. If the U.S. Legal and Judicial System worked there would be no Government Swamp.

The remedy is a visible attachment to each case, with judicial misconduct allegations attached to the decision itself, outlining the alleged misconduct. The readers of the decision can then make independent decisions and understand judicial enabling of institutional corruption, weaponization, and lawfare. It was Falsified Trail 3 that exposed the U.S. Judicial system to such criticism. Meaning, Falsified Trail 3 was an irrefragable, perfect, case of weaponization and lawfare against me, an extremely effective whistleblower. That Legal and Judicial cover-up leads to the following.

Investigate the Actions of Dan Meyer on the Whistleblowing Community

"Pentagon's Key Whistleblower Counselor Moves to Intel Community"

After Dan Meyer severed my communications with Senator Grassley, my voice was silenced, and I essentially became a "punching bag" for management. Reports were rewritten, cover-ups became institutional, and the like. However, Dan Meyer continued in government and was more highly enabled after MSPB covered up Meyer's actions on February 12, 2009, along with the NSA report on PCIE on November 1, 2006. Meaning, detailed cover-ups took place (Cerberus Analogy).

On July 29, 2013, an article from Government Executive arose with the title: *"Pentagon's Key Whistleblower Counselor Moves to Intel Community"*. The article stated in part.

"Dan Meyer, for more than a decade the major whistleblowers counselor working out of the Pentagon inspector general's office, assumed a new post at an undisclosed location to provide interagency coordination for President Obama's new policy protecting whistleblowing by national security employees.

The shift comes amid headlines about controversial leakers such as defrocked National Security Agency contractor Edward Snowden and Army Private Bradley Manning, whose court martial for disclosing thousands of agency documents to Wikileaks is reaching a climax.

The 48-year-old Meyer is an attorney and Navy veteran who himself blew a whistle to Congress exposing misdirection in a probe of a 1989 explosion aboard the U.S.S. Iowa."

Meyer seemed shaken by the fallout of the U.S.S. Iowa incident. Meaning, Meyer seemed affected by the torment of being a whistleblower. I remember Meyer saying that he was glad he didn't get any money from a book that was written, apparently, about the incident.

Meyer also brought up Whitewater, which was political for L. Jean Lewis, meaning politics was in the mix. I continued conversing with Meyer so as not to alienate Meyer, Senator Grassley, and Charlie Murphy. I expected nothing from Meyer, and anything I got would be more than what I expected. However, Dan Meyer's hidden talents against whistleblowers may have gotten recognition.

June 7, 2013 – Glenn Greenwald on Security and Liberty: There was an article by Glenn Greenwald prior to July 29, 2013, Government Executive article that was titled:

"On whistleblowers and government threats of investigation" Subtitled: *"No healthy democracy can endure when the most consequential acts of those in power remain secret and unaccountable"*

"Ever since the Nixon administration broke into the office of Daniel Ellsberg's psychoanalyst's office, the tactic of the US government has been to attack and demonize whistleblowers as a means of distracting attention from their own exposed wrongdoing and destroying the credibility of the messenger so that everyone tunes out the message."

The gist seemed to be that whistleblowers needed support.

The timeline would be, on or about June 7, 2013, it appeared the Obama administration was concerned about whistleblowers. Shortly after, on or about July 29, 2013, there was an announcement that Dan Meyer was to be transferred to the intel community to seemingly help whistleblowers.

The point is, and knowing that I lost track of Dan Meyer after 2007, it would appear that the Obama administration and the Intelligence community were quietly leading whistleblowers to a reputation "slaughter." This was based on my experiences with Dan Meyer in Falsified Trail 3 and my testimony on June 21, 2006, where I testified that Meyer indicated I was fucking with the sovereign.

The question is; Did the Obama Administration use Dan Meyer as a weapon against the Intel Community? Falsified Trail 3 is already a matter of record and well documented for my concerns.

Meaning, it appeared that Dan Meyer was a weapon if, in fact, Meyer acted as he did in my case. Gathering those details of Dan Meyer's further interactions with whistleblowers after Falsified Trail 3 needs to be a matter for detailed and honest investigation with transparency. Knowing the cover-ups in weaponized government and lawfare, transparency would be a challenge. That's why I wrote this book with painstaking detail and transparency. Largely to help others with transparency.

The Hopes of Senator Grassley – The "Only Game in Town"

I was once told by a reporter that Senator Grassley was the *"only game in town"* with regard to a member of Congress working directly with whistleblowers. This proved true by my experience with Senator Grassley's staffer, Charlie Murphy. As the *"only game in town,"* I recommend to Senator Grassley and any other member of Congress the following.

Senator Grassley placed high hopes on Joseph Schmitz, L. Jean Lewis, and Dan Meyer. All let Senator Grassley down as shown herein. There may be more letdowns for Senator Grassley, although I am not sure. Senator Grassley or any member of Congress should place no hope in any management official as an immediate internal fix to institutional weaponized government, lawfare and institutional government corruption.

Watch behavior continually and don't turn your back (Senator Grassley). Expect betrayal, evaluate cases on the national good, national security, and use common sense, not emotions. Deal with deceit swiftly, decisively, and retroactively. Use restorative justice. Know and understand that government and DoD management is not on the side of integrity, not on the side of the efficiency of the federal service, not on the side of affordability, and not on the side of the taxpayers. Change will come from the top, meaning the U.S. Congress and the U.S. President to solve U.S. problems and drain the Government Swamp.

Place trust in employees. History has shown that employees are an accurate and best source of data that can expose institutional corruption and weaponized government. I assembled this book to prove that fact. Let this book be the encyclopedia to understand how government really works.

The next remedies focus on establishing an effective workforce and workforce practices, along with eliminating other cover-up techniques and practices. Meaning, the remedy is now progressing from attitude adjustments on management weaponization and lawfare to more concrete aspects of achieving affordability, eliminating price gouging by DoD contractors, etc.

Advanced College Degrees are Not the Remedy

Common Sense – Problem Solving – Patience – Pattern Recognition – Ethics –

and Technical Writing Skills are the Answer

The common perceived remedy to problems is to increase the education level of those hired. That actually works in reverse and worsens the problem. Those who hold Master's Degrees and higher education past the Master's Degrees are normally seeking stepping stones to advance. Meaning, not much interest in really mastering skills, and knowledge, to deeply understand the job, and after a year on the job, a promotion is expected.

I spent 26 ½ years in one position and mastered that skill. My resume shows that. I appreciated my job, knew I was doing needed work, and was obstructed by management in doing my job to full capacity. My education ended with a Bachelor of Science in Industrial and Systems Engineering. A similar degree to Ernie Fitzgerald, although Fitzgerald was a registered professional engineer.

The Systems Engineering part of my degree helped me focus on the overall system. Meaning, the interaction of all parts to achieve an end goal. That experience and skillset helped me assemble this book into an evidentiary and forensic file that can tackle today's problems in government with weaponization and lawfare up to affordability.

The success I have achieved has come through common sense, problem-solving skills, patience, pattern recognition, and ethics. Some education is required, along with report and technical writing skills, to convey an idea. Higher education only clouds the issue and leads to cronyism.

Terminate Acquisition Demonstration Project (Weaponized Cronyism)

"Flexibility" is the Weaponized Path to the Government Swamp & Lawfare

The Defense Acquisition University (DAU) describes the DoD Civilian Acquisition Workforce Personnel Demonstration Project (AcqDemo) stated in part as follows.

"The purpose of the project is to demonstrate that the effectiveness of DoD acquisition can be enhanced by allowing greater managerial control over personnel processes and functions and, at the same time, expand the opportunities available to employees through a more responsive and flexible personnel system. This demonstration project will provide managers, at the lowest practical level, the authority, control, and flexibility they need to achieve quality acquisition processes and quality products. This project not only provides a system that retains, recognizes, and rewards employees for their contribution, but also supports their personal and professional growth."

The AcqDemo project is a scam that weaponizes cronyism to the maximum extent in management via "flexibility." AcqDemo may still exist in the U.S. Government, at the management and HQ level. Many of the problems identified in this book are rooted in cronyism and flexibility. As such, I have zero trust, and zero confidence, in second-level supervisors and above. First level supervisors are case-by-case basis for trust, confidence, and integrity. That is objectively supported by the documented facts herein. Meaning, AcqDemo is a catalyst for corrupted government.

Congress and the President should immediately terminate AcqDemo without hesitation.

End the "Head in the Sand", Blind Eye to Corruption

The thought that employees can ignore corruption needs to end. Known in slang as burying the "head in the sand." Those who ignore corruption, management, or employees, need to be held accountable in similar ways as the wrongdoers.

Teach Scam Identification in Training Courses – Not Just Basics

Training for those employees who evaluate cost proposals should include training to spot scams, such as elaborate math that is used to price-gouge and inflate cost proposals. This includes aspects of untraceable costs, such as the statement *"includes but is not limited to"* when evaluating rates and factors such as CERs and EFDs. This is in addition to routine training on the techniques, such as learning curves, comparison to actual cost, etc. This helps reduce price gouging for costs buried deeper in price proposals and contractor estimating systems.

Ground Level Traceability Upward Financial Analysis - Plantwide Actuals

End the Workarounds

Lockheed Martin in the 1990s had the financial systems and tracking to facilitate ground-level upward analysis of costs. This was called Plantwide Actuals, meaning the entire facility costs (on an hourly basis for cost buildup) were available in one printout/file. That ability disappeared on or about 2000. The impact was mainly felt on the analysis of overhead rates. The DCMA does teach a workaround method for overhead rates. The remedy is that DoD contractors should be able to quickly provide plant-wide actual costs in a concise report. This allows greater cost control and monitoring.

The DCMA Employee Work Product Direct to Customers,

Eliminate Management Censoring & Rewriting of Reports

The DCMA has abused its management authority to rewrite reports to cover-up for Lockheed Martin and obstruct transparency. There are multiple examples provided herein, which include Falsified Trail 4 and 7 (Chapter 3), as well as the Capstone Case (Chapter 5), as examples. Draft reports and Draft CARs are other examples. Some customers of the DCMA may actually want honest reports and honest dialogue to make informed decisions, achieve affordability, and limit award fees (incentives) for poor performing contractors.

The remedy would be for the customer to request direct reports from the DCMA employees to the end user (customer) without pressure or rewrites from the DCMA management to protect DoD contractors like Lockheed Martin. The DCMA management could also provide the management rewritten report for comparison in parallel to the employee's report. Meaning, the option is always open to DCMA customers to use the DCMA management censored reports for cover-ups.

The DCMA has left a trail of report censoring, and facilitating cover-ups as demonstrated herein. Employees providing direct reports to customers will provide transparency into how reports are altered to protect DoD contractors and conceal embarrassing problems. This parallel process would also identify DoD Program Offices within the military-industrial complex who cover-up for DoD contractors.

Customers, aside from the DCMA, Can Write CARs on DoD Contractors

The DCMA has a monopoly on writing Corrective Action Requests (CARs) on DoD contractors, and the DCMA historically chooses to cover up for DoD contractors. The remedy would be for outside customers to write CARs on DoD contractors. This would help augment transparency much like aforesaid employees issuing reports directly to customers.

Eliminate Draft Reports and Draft Cars

The DCMA has used the "Draft" designation on CARs and reports to cover-up for Lockheed Martin which include; June 3, 1994 Draft report on the C-130J; August 13, 2002 Draft CAR; April 5, 2001 and October 23, 2003 Draft CARs that enabled Lockheed Martin ISO 9000 certifications; January 28, 2014 Draft report on MDRs. Draft reports and draft CARs need to be banned, and problems formally documented or issued in writing.

Criminal Vulnerability - Time and Materials Contracts & Agreements

ASBCA Case 62209 had, at its core, Time-and-Materials (Blank Checks) charging by Lockheed Martin. Meaning, Lockheed Martin was not bound by estimates to do work. This opened the door widely to criminal vulnerability. Time and material contracts need to end or be strictly controlled.

Criminal Vulnerability – Review of Policy & Management Actions

There should be a complete review of all DoD and the DCMA policy and practices that can enable criminal vulnerability. This includes emphasis on the involvement of any individual involved in the Falsified Trials against me. As an example, Joe Tessier and Stacy Scantlebury may have been involved in the DCMA HQ policy and the DCMA senior leadership at the DCMA HQ level.

Joe Tessier on the DCMA OASIS (On-Line Aerospace Supplier Information System) initial date August 31, 2018, and Stacy Scantlebury, where it was identified on June 29, 2010, that Scantlebury had been promoted to the DCMA, Investment and Development Human Capital Directorate.

Both Tessier and Scantlebury were tactically involved in Falsified Trails against me, where their actions were so disturbing that I developed this book. In total, all the DoD and DCMA policies and regulations need to be reviewed and corrected to address Criminal Vulnerability. These comments are based on behavior, and the results of the behavior, that negatively affect the U.S. Government.

Basically, any management official on the Index of Names herein should have their actions traced. I was very disturbed by what I have seen and fear my observations may not be isolated.

Independent Ombudsman with Oversight Empowerment

Organizations like the DCMA cannot be trusted under any circumstances for self-management. An independent Ombudsman or similar position must be available on an ongoing basis to investigate allegations of abuse by management officials. Meaning, an Ombudsman or similar position onsite at HQ levels for immediate access by employees to report and correct management officials and government attorneys immediately. Simply put, immediate, onsite, transparency and resolution.

Eliminate the "Measured Mile" Appeal Process Using Learning Curves

Limit ASBCA Discretion

ASBCA Claim 62209 demonstrated that Lockheed Martin used an elaborate math scam in a potential false claim using learning curves. As shown in Chapter 4, Lockheed Martin is well adapted and skilled in the use of elaborate math in price gouging. The Lockheed Martin ASBCA claim was unsupported, however nevertheless prevailed. Chapter 5 has the details.

The point being, learning curves are not absolute facts and are estimation tools only that are influenced by new work. Meaning the scope and volume of work changed. It was clear that the work scope changed significantly after 2012, making learning curves prior to 2012 null and void in ASBCA Claim 62209. Simply put, a re-baseline took place nullifying past estimates.

In short, ASBCA needs to be heavily monitored. ASBCA needs to understand DoD contractors like Lockheed Martin are well adapted at elaborate math and price gouging techniques. ASBCA Claim 62209 by Lockheed Martin is a textbook example to eliminate the "Measured Mile" analysis.

No Discretion by Government Attorneys in ASBCA and Similar Cases

The April 23, 2024, ASBCA62209 decision stated in part at the end: *"In fact, during the course of the 13-day hearing, the Air Force never even called a single expert witness to contest any of Lockheed Martin's quantum evidence, including Mr. Gaudion's report. Accordingly, we hold that Lockheed Martin is entitled to recover $131,888,860..."*

I volunteered to be a witness, and agreed to a deposition. The Air Force attorneys never called me. The blasé attitude toward any fraud or criminal vulnerability in government needs to be end.

Eliminate Manipulating and Conning Congressional Staffers

Dan Meyer, in Falsified Trail 3, gave the textbook example of the manipulation and conning of Senate Staffer Charlie Murphy. The electronic trail proves as much. For that reason, there should be no unfettered access of management officials to Congressional staffers. Another example is as follows.

July 28, 1999: The Raptor Action Group Update outlined a formal damage control (cover-up) plan of specific tactics to head off negative publicity towards the F-22 and ensure a consistent public message. It also seemed to have application to C-130J and other programs. Items of interest include:

"Breakfast with key staffers"; *"Assure consistent message"; "cost is on track"*; *"Release Public Affairs Guidance outlining distinction between educating public and lobbying"*; *"Rapid response to negative stories/editorials",* etc.

The point is, end behind-the-scenes manipulation of Congressional staffers and the public.

Eliminate Faith in Congressional Training Acts and Leadership Programs

The Defense Acquisition Workforce Improvement Act (DAWIA), as implemented by the Defense Acquisition University (DAU), was apparently designed to instill ethics and training in the Defense Acquisition process. DAWIA is an introduction only to DoD acquisition. Meaning, I was glad I was self-taught and had problem-solving skills and common sense because if I had to rely on DAU and DAWIA, I would be lost. Similar to leadership programs that the DCMA sponsors. The DCMA leadership, promotion, and managerial development programs are a joke and range from cronyism to snack breaks.

Meaning, just because Congress takes action or there are alleged training and development programs, there is no assurance of success. There must be follow-up and enforcement.

Increase Documentation – Decrease Manufactured Regulations

On July 15, 2004 DCMA had training that mentioned "don't write it down". Similar training to use the phone to avoid documentation was provided at other times. On November 3, 2016 I documented where DCMA manufactured regulations for the F-35, where I have to route questions to DoD F-5 Joint Program Office (JPO) through other employees to stop the release of negative information.

The point being, the DCMA has left a long tactical evidentiary trail of concealing problems, enabling fraud, and facilitating price gouging. DCMA needs to increase documentation and decrease manufactured regulations. This will set the stage for the highly necessitated lifestyle change for weaponized government and lawfare as follows.

Congressional Appropriations Based on Need and Should Cost

Not Backed into With Price

In the 1990s I heard the rumor that Lockheed Martin would look at Congressional appropriations and then back into the amount with a price for C-130Js. Meaning, there was an amount of money available, and Lockheed would conveniently have a price proposal to acquire that money. Prior to commercialization on the C-130J in 1994 there was some cost discipline. After 1998, as shown in Chapter 4, the cost discipline had ended and the corruption incestuously inbred upon itself.

The point being, this book has shown how to evaluate cost so Congress and the President can more adequately make appropriations for need, based on what things should cost, and not the price. There are techniques that can be used. In order to use those techniques effectively there must be a life style change to eliminate weaponized government and lawfare.

Life Style Change for Weaponized Government & Lawfare

Government Swamp lifestyles have weaponized every aspect of management possible, necessitating a lifestyle change. Meaning, the following are the current weaponized, including lawfare, lifestyles and tactics funded by taxpayers and factored into routine operations.

Weaponized Personnel Actions (Prime Weapon)	Falsified Trails 1-13
Weaponized Authority	Falsified Trails 1-13
Weaponized Attorneys, Attorney Client Privilege	Falsified Trails 1, 3-13
Weaponized Surrogates	Falsified Trails 1, 3-13
Weaponized Investigations and Coverups	Falsified Trails 2, 3, and 13
Weaponized Doctrine (Obey First, Grieve Later)	Falsified Trail 3
Weaponized Conflicts of Interest	Falsified Trails 3, 11, 13
Weaponized FOIA	Falsified Trails 2 and 13
Weaponized Office Conflicts Between Employees	Falsified Trails 5 and 9
Weaponized Shunning	Falsified Trails 1, 6, 8, 11
Weaponized Electronic Trails (Email Relays)	Falsified Trails 1, 3, 6, 11, 12, and 13
Weaponized Training	Falsified Trail 11 and 2011 attempt
Weaponized Human Resources/Labor Relations	Falsified Trails 3, 6, 10, 12, and 13
Weaponized Lockheed Martin Armed Guards	Falsified Trail 2 (Swatting)
Weaponized Lockheed Martin Human Resources	Falsified Trail 11
Weaponized Status and Access to Other Agencies	Falsified Trail 3
Weaponized Cover-ups by OSC, MSPB, OPM	Falsified Trails 3, 6, 10, 13 (Abandon Case)
Weaponized Kernels of Thought and Con Games	Falsified Trail 3 (Planting Ideas/Thoughts)
Weaponized Security Clearances	Chapter 3, Revoked Security Clearance
Weaponized Hostile and Abusive Workplace	Institutional and Overarching

Meaning, every aspect of government management and oversight was tactically weaponized. Weaponization and lawfare needs to end and retroactive action taken to adjust management attitudes and make the victims whole with restorative justice. The aforesaid plan in Chapter 6 is a start.

This Book Explains Why…Using a Half Century of Evidence

This book explains why the Pentagon has problems passing audits. There should also be no doubt why the Lockheed Martin F-22 Raptor and the Lockheed Martin F-35 Lightning are the highest priced fighters on the planet. There also should be no surprise at the Fat Leonard scandal, Boeing door blow out, Boeing guilty plea to defraud the U.S. for two fatal 737 MAX crashes, September 11, 2001 terrorist attacks, fall of Enron & WorldCom, Valerie Plame case, Minnesota fraud scandals that could top $9 Billion, etc.

Meaning, corruption and incompetence are institutional and trace back over half a century with the Cerberus style cover-ups of OSC, MSPB, OPM and DOJ along with the U.S. Legal and Judicial System providing no corrective action. Thus, enabling institutional corruption and incompetence to inbreed on itself. DCMA's repetitive use of weaponization and lawfare extrapolated my thoughts to these conclusions.

The next issue explains the transparency, or the "how," for these conclusions and transparency.

This Book Explains How…Using Electronic Trails, Evidence, & Behavior

My success against corruption in Chapter 1; Management behavior outlined in Chapter 2; Electronic trails and management behavior outlined in Chapter 3: Gross mismanagement and corruption Chapter 4; The Capstone Case Chapter 5; And, the Attachment and Appendix to this book all provide transparency into the Deep State weaponization, lawfare, and price gouging. Meaning, an explanation as to how the U.S. Government is in the current state it is and why the national debt soars. This leads to questions as follows.

Question for the U.S. Congress and The U.S. President

Is this the management that should have carte blanche access to weaponize resources?

Or is it more pragmatic to use the proven rational approach where employees are protected against weaponized government, where Congress and the President followed institutional weaponization, lawfare, and corruption to the root source and forced remedies (restorative justice) for the victims, and action against the wrongdoers, for the public good and in the interests of the U.S. Government.

The cases of institutional weaponized government, corruption, and lawfare existed for a half a century. The prime example is Ernie Fitzgerald, who was forced to administratively battle the Pentagon (DoD) for 35 years (1970–2005).

The U.S. Congress and U.S. President have the power and authority to be apex predators to hunt out institutional corruption, weaponization, and lawfare to extinction prior to financial ruination traced to the U.S. national debt. This will help affordability.

Institutional corruption and institutional weaponization of government exist because the U.S. justice system has become a weapon and enabler, favoring corruption. Meaning, the U.S. Justice system is on a water level with corruption, weaponization, and lawfare. The U.S. Legal and Judicial System has enabled the Government Swamp to a vast expansion. Soft on crime policy at the Federal level is another term. This book has gone to the belly of the beast (heart of the problem) to prove that fact.

The best and quickest remedy is to let employees protect the government, and its integrity, with the full support from the President and Congress. Restorative justice will pave the way to affordability and draining the Government Swamp. This could be accomplished in minutes with executive action and later codified into law by Congress.

The remedy can be as easy as embarrassment, as shown by the reaction of Thomas Gimble to a simple Retraction Letter. Presidents have pardoned criminals in prison, so resolving something as simple as personnel actions caused by weaponization and lawfare should present no problem. Same for Congress, whom allegedly claim to protect government interests, save money, and increase affordability.

The overall goal is to end institutional corruption, weaponization, and lawfare. This book is a contribution using contemporaneous facts and documentation to restore financial accountability, affordability and ethics in government. The evidence of the Deep State operational level helps prove the points herein.

Closing the Loop on Repetitive Weaponization & Lawfare

Page 6 of the Attachment to this book included the following statement.

"...the judicial system is akin to a "kangaroo court" and same amounted to predictable judicial misconduct in order to spare the Executive Branch of Government further embarrassment."

That phrase outlines the theme of this book with supporting evidence. Meaning, the repetitive weaponization and lawfare onslaught against me. Thirteen Falsified Trails in all against me personally. President Nixon started the onslaught against Fitzgerald in the 1970's. Watergate stopped Nixon, although Nixon's ideas lived on and were revived in the Bush administration in 2003. DCMA improved the weaponization and lawfare process with weaponized electronic trails (emails) used in the lawfare process.

The Nixon White House Tapes were analogous to DCMA's electronic trails (emails). Meaning, both used variations of electronic recorded documentation that outlined clearly, and objectively, where the problems were. Traceability and transparency followed. Those problems were centered in weaponization and lawfare at the senior levels of government. Nixon was just the start. DCMA and DoD refined Nixon's ideas during the Bush administration.

Ernie Fitzgerald was a victim of Nixon in 1970, and then during 2005, for Falsified Trail 3, Nixon style tactics were used again, this time on Fitzgerald and me. Proves a definite trend whereby this book outlines facts that already existed for a half century and assembled the facts in a convenient location. An encyclopedia of sorts that linked weaponization and lawfare effects the national debt to the amount of 30%-50%, conservative estimate.

Since this book is based on documentation, it is fitting to provide examples of that documentation. The following are samples of the documents referenced in this book. The actual documents would go well into the thousands of pages. The attachment is first followed by the Appendix.

Attachment - Weaponization & Lawfare - Falsified Trail 13

Lawfare – Attorney-Client Privileged Material

Attachment Pages 1 & 2

September 11, 2015 Emails - Attachment Pages 1 & 2 – Falsified Trail 13: This is an example of a weaponized email where there is a clear indication that an attorney was involved. Meaning, both emails were stamped as follows.

"[ATTORNEY-CLIENT PRIVILEGED MATERIAL] (DO NOT DISCLOSE)"

There was no legitimate reason for the "ATTORNEY-CLIENT PRIVILEGED MATERIAL" designation. The only plausible explanation was that an attorney wrote, or coached, the emails and had Kim Turner and David Wray send the emails as surrogates in a retaliatory weaponized lawfare effort against me. The September 11, 2015 emails was lawfare that led to a 14-Day suspension for me. Additionally, the word "MATERIAL" does indicate an attorney wrote the email for someone else to send.

Legal Polishing: The emails are well polished with refined wording. Made to fit a case that an attorney would litigate. The emails were sent quickly (relayed) on a Friday afternoon with the end goal being my supervisor, Isaiah Waindi. I was given a 14-Day suspension.

Weaponized FOIA Cover-up – Conflict of Interest Investigation

Attachment Pages 3 to 7

June 9, 2015: This was the FOIA from an investigation report tied to Falsified Trail 13. The subject of the investigation was very simple. Is there a conflict of interest with Mark Buckner (my then 2nd supervisor) where his wife worked for the contractor Lockheed Martin. Meaning, Mark Buckner was overseeing his wife's work at Lockheed Martin. The investigation concluded there was no conflict of interest (unsubstantiated) and the case closed. The point being, the amount of redaction does indicate a cover-up for a very simple subject.

Waindi, Isaiah

From:	Wray, David J.
Sent:	Friday, September 11, 2015 3:05 PM
To:	Waindi, Isaiah
Cc:	Wray, David J.; Turner, Kimberly J.
Subject:	FW: 15-172 - Fee information for FOIA For DCMA-DMR 15-0053 (Third Request) [ATTORNEY-CLIENT PRIVILEGED MATERIAL] (DO NOT DISCLOSE)
Signed By:	david.wray@[redacted]

Mr. Waindi,

I am writing to make you aware of concerns raised by Ms. Kim Turner, the Freedom of Information Act (FOIA) and government information specialist who works for me, about correspondence she has received from an employee at DCMA Lockeed Martin Marietta, Mr. Ken Pedeleose. Ms. Turner has been diligently assisting Mr. Pedeleose with a complex FOIA request. His recent request for records pertaining to an investigation resulted in approximately 6,000 pages of material responsive to his request. FOIA requires that requestors pay . 15 per page for the cost of providing copies of material (usually for anything more than 100 pages). The law also requires that the requestor pay for the employee's time to conduct the search for the records at a rate of $44 per hour (the first two hours are free). The law does not exempt from payment a requestor who may have called for the investigation, in the first place.

When informed of the cost associated with the search for and reproduction of the 6,000 pages responsive to his request, Mr. Pedeleose essentially accused Ms. Turner of attempting to extort money from him. He has repeated this charge and says he has deliberately chosen that word. I assure you that Ms. Turner is doing nothing of the sort. She is providing excellent customer service and doing so while adhering to the legal requirements of the Freedom of Information Act -- in other words, she is doing her job. As Ms. Turner's supervisor, I am unwilling let this questioning of her integrity and professionalism go unanswered. Ms. Turner is the ONLY full-time FOIA specialist at DCMA, and his is not the only complex FOIA request she has to handle.

I request that you review the email chain below and consider what action or counselling may be in order.

Thank you for your time.

R,

Dave

David J. Wray
Director of Communication
Defense Contract Management Agency

Attachment Page 1 of 7

(6)

-----Original Message-----
From: DCMA FOIA
Sent: Friday, September 11, 2015 1:49 PM
To: Wray, David J.
Cc: Bailey, William J. JR
Subject: FW: 15-172 - Fee information for FOIA For DCMA-DMR 15-0053 (Third Request) [ATTORNEY-CLIENT PRIVILEGED MATERIAL] (DO NOT DISCLOSE)

Dave,

I am forwarding the below email string from a FOIA requester, Mr. Ken Pedeleose, a DCMA Atlanta employee, to you because it raises some concerns that may need to be addressed. I am also copying DCMA legal counsel on this message in the hope that counsel can also provide legal assistance concerning this matter.

In his September 2nd email, the requester comments "if DCMA still insists on extorting money from me," regarding the fees we estimated based on his request for approximately 6,000 pages of records. Then in his September 8th email, he states "Extorting money is not part of that framework. These e-mail exchanges prove that a cover-up is in work." Such allegations are disturbing and highly irregular from a FOIA requester.

Mr. Pedeleose's statements are not accurate and raise unsupported integrity issues. The requester even raises conflict of interest issues without any factual basis. We are continuing to follow the spirit and the letter of the law regarding application of the FOIA to his request.

As my direct supervisor, please take whatever action, if any, which you deem appropriate based upon the claims raised in the string of email messages below from Mr. Pedeleose. We will continue to process Mr. Pedeleose's FOIA request under statutory requirements.

We look forward to any input you may have on this matter.

V/R,

Kim

Kimberly Turner
FOIA/Privacy Analyst
DCMA-DSP

Attachment Page 2 of 7

DEFENSE CONTRACT MANAGEMENT AGENCY
3901 A. AVENUE, BUILDING 10500
FORT LEE, VA 23801-1809

DCMA-DMR (Chicago Field Office) June 9, 2015

MEMORANDUM FOR DIRECTOR, DCMA

SUBJECT: After Action Report: DCMA-DMR Case No. 2015-0053

STATUS: Unsubstantiated and closed (Ref: 1 and Ref: 2)

Ref: (1) DCMA-HQ Generated Case: Conflict of Interest (COI)/Ethics Violations
Ref: (2) DCMA-HQ Generated Case; Claims of Whistleblower Retaliation

The purpose of this correspondence is to document the results of an independent investigative review in order to document every independent action taken in accord to each allegation/issue that had been reported. As such, this After Action Report is a compilation of multiple source allegations/issues dealing with complex contractual and managerial concerns addressing the original complaint: ranging from mismanagement, whistleblower reprisal actions to COI concerns. Note that this complaint had been generated by a (b)(6), (b)(7)(C), (k)(2) employee, (b)(6), (b)(7)(C), (k)(2). Same had directly contacted the Director, DCMA (via email messaging) alleging that several senior level (b)(6), (b)(7)(C), (k)(2) officials are attempting to silence (b)(6) whistleblower activities; which in turn is alleged to affect this Agency's ability to function effectively. The crux of this complaint stems from the fact that (b)(6), (b)(7)(C), (k)(2) had been directed by management to attend an interpersonal skills course; as (b)(6), (b)(7)(C), (k)(2) contends that this directive was retaliatory in nature. In addition, (b)(6), (b)(7)(C), (k)(2) alleges that the (b)(6), (b)(7)(C), (k)(2). is involved with some type of blatant COI issue as (b)(6), (b)(7)(C), (k)(2) also works for Lockheed Martin (LM); at the same facility. These claims relate to (b)(6), (b)(7)(C), (k)(2) concern that (b)(6), (b)(7)(C), (k)(2) controls audits and actions against LM as the salary of (b)(6), (b)(7)(C), (k)(2) (LM employee) is a significant factor relevant to the (b)(6), (b)(7)(C), (k)(2) family income; which would be protected at any cost by (b)(6), (b)(7)(C), (k)(2). Therefore, the allegation that (b)(6), (b)(7)(C), (k)(2) has been attempting to stifle (b)(6), (b)(7)(C), (k)(2) as a whistleblower is an ongoing issue as (b)(6), (b)(7)(C), (k)(2) states that (b)(6) is a major player in disclosing problems at LM. Furthermore, as a tie-in with this referral to the Director, (b)(6), (b)(7)(C), (k)(2) alleged that the (b)(6), (b)(7)(C), (k)(2) and the (b)(6), (b)(7)(C), (k)(2) had somehow conspired, and/or colluded in some manner to continually stifle (b)(6), (b)(7)(C), (k)(2) as a whistleblower at every turn.

Investigators Note:

As this investigation moved forward, it was discovered that the U.S. Air Force Office of Special Investigations (OSI) had already set in motion a comprehensive investigative review into several audit issues involving LM. OSI review and notes will be documented within this brief under Ref. (2), OSI Investigation/Quashing of Audit Concerns.

Attachment Page 3 of 7

"Test of Openness" Memo; OSI Investigative Notes-BOM Issues; Level III CAR's 50153, 40291, and 50012; C-130 and C-5 contracts/MODS. Credible witness facts, documents, reports, and statements were procured from the (b)(6), (b)(7)(C), (k)(2) senior management group and applicable (b)(6), (b)(7)(C), (k)(2) line personnel; to include persons of interest from LM (28 in all).

Over 5,784 pieces of evidence have been examined, to include 87 hard copy exhibits and procurement of 28 independent statements (as described above). Attached for perusal is the DCMA-DMR Exhibit List; referenced exhibits shall be provided upon request.

Analyses/Investigative Review:

In response to Allegation/Issue I: In an effort to confirm/dispel any wrongdoing, and/or COI activity; reporting investigator completed a comprehensive review of the matters in question. Initial investigation revealed that COI concerns had already been addressed as this matter was presented to (b)(6), (b)(7)(C), (k)(2) senior management; dating back to August 2014. Originally, DCMAE-General Counsel (GC) had drafted an opinion directly related to the (b)(6), (b)(7) situation. The concern focused on (b)(6), (b)(7)(C), (k)(2) position relevant to whether or not (b)(6) working situation has created an impermissible conflict of interest (statutory, lack of impartiality, or an appearance of a conflict of interest) due to (b)(6), (b)(7)(C), (k)(2) employment at LM as a (b)(6), (b)(7)(C), (k)(2) of some type for the C-130 Program. A final COI opinion had been completed on September 8, 2014. To note, DCMAE-GC's opinion (dated Sept. 8, 2014) is a (b)(5), (b)(6), (b)(7)(C), (k)(5), (k)(2)

(b)(5), (b)(6), (b)(7)(C), (k)(5), (k)(2) implemented the Plan of Action in December CY2014. (b)(6), (b)(7)(C) provided a copy of the Plan of Action to DCMA-DMR; same had been disseminated to the appropriate (b)(6), (b)(7)(C), (k)(2) chain of command that will be charged with its implementation – Plan of Action is in place.

Attachment Page 4 of 7

Analyses/Investigative Review:

In response to Allegation/Issue II: The scope of examination included an in-depth review of the type of allegations directly associated with (b)(6), (b)(7)(C), (k)(2) complaint alleging that (b)(6), (b)(7)(C), (k)(2) senior management had, and/or are continuing to retaliate against [redacted] for past/current whistleblower activities. As previously noted: in order to incorporate each document and witness identification into one identifier, same have already been addressed in the first header block of this brief as same are all encompassing to each allegation/issue raised.

Foremost; this investigation revealed that the personal submission of documentation provided by (b)(6), (b)(7)(C), (k)(2) noted multiple instances of whistleblower retaliation claims as same were addressed through the U.S. Office of Special Counsel (OSC), Department of Justice (DOJ), and the Joint Chiefs of Staff (each agency concern will be addressed separately in this brief). In each instance, documented results into their investigation/review of these claims validated that the criteria/elements necessary to pursue whistleblower reprisal relief had not been disclosed, and/or met – case files were closed. (b)(6), (b)(7)(C), (k)(2) openly condemned OSC, DOJ, and Joint Chiefs of Staff as not competent in their assessment of his complaints. Variances to each claim of reprisal had been submitted by (b)(6), (b)(7)(C), (k)(2) which addressed MRSB suspensions, OSC disciplinary reprisal reviews, criminal acts, etc. as all were linked to allegations surrounding whistleblower reprisal actions. Note that OSC is the governing authority relevant to whistleblower actions/reprisal concerns.

As with this case; the criteria/elements necessary to pursue these allegations had not been met. (b)(5), (d)(5) [redacted] Based on the totality of facts/information procured during this investigation; to include past claims submitted by (b)(6), (b)(7)(C), (k)(2), DCMA-DMR could not conclude that retaliatory action had taken place due to (b)(6), (b)(7)(C), (k)(2) protected activity; as reported by same. (b)(6), (b)(7)(C), (k)(2) claim/allegations had not met the threshold for this action to proceed. (b)(5), (d)(5) [redacted] Related whistleblower issues brought up by (b)(6), (b)(7)(C), (k)(2) as direct links to current issues are listed below. As a final note; (b)(6), (b)(7)(C), (k)(2) stated that (b)(6), (b)(7)(C), (k)(2) had admitted to criminal activity during a meeting with same over/ whistleblower related activities. It had been discovered that this alleged reference was due to the effective communication training issue. This claim stems from an email message in which (b)(6), (b)(7)(C), (k)(2) claimed that (b)(6), (b)(7)(C), (k)(2) had some sort of criminal intent to retaliate against same for past whistleblower activities. DCMA-DMR had not disclosed any criminal intent on the part of (b)(6), (b)(7)(C), (k)(2) [redacted] [redacted] ever admitted to criminal activity as it related to (b)(6), (b)(7)(C), (k)(2) whistleblower activities.

OSC Decisions:

Further investigation revealed that (b)(6), (b)(7)(C), (k)(2) had filed formal whistleblower reprisal complaints through OSC – File Numbers MA-12-1338 and MA-10-0395. Note that OSC is the premier authority relevant to whistleblower retaliations. OSC's primary mission is to safeguard the merit system by protecting federal employees from prohibited practices, especially reprisal for whistleblowing. These particular complaints had been thoroughly examined by OSC's General Counsel (GC) and the OSC Dallas Field Office Chief. To clarify, OSC's whistleblower retaliation investigations are a streamlined process which focuses on prohibited practices as defined in 5 U.S.C. § 2302 (b) (8). As such, specific criteria/elements necessary to build upon such an allegation are examined; the same criteria/elements described within DCMA-DMR's review are incorporated into their investigative plan of action as well. Based on information and investigative review, (b)(5), (b)(6), (b)(7)(C), (d)(5), (k)(2)

DOJ Rulings:

DOJ investigation revealed that (b)(6), (b)(7)(C), (k)(2) had filed an informal brief via the U.S. Courts of Appeal for the Federal Circuit Court: Docket No. 2015-3090. To note, (b)(6), (b)(7)(C), (k)(2) concerns focused on his claim that the agency (DCMA) had suspended (b)(6) in CY2014 in retaliation for whistleblowing activities. (b)(6), (b)(7)(C), (k)(2) claimed that this particular action was linked somehow to the current retaliatory action of sending him to directed training. Within this brief, (b)(6), (b)(7)(C), (k)(2) contended that the decision of the full Merit System Protection Board (MSPB) was capricious and politically biased against (b)(6) as are the claims for this current issue. (b)(5), (d)(5) As such, the DOJ Principle Deputy Assistant Attorney General respectfully requested that the court affirm the MSPB's judgment sustaining the agencies (DCMA) decision; opinion rendered on May 7, 2015. As a response, (b)(6), (b)(7)(C), (k)(2) wrote back to the U.S. Courts of Appeal for the Federal Circuit Court and highlighted his displeasure with DOJ's opinion. (b)(6), (b)(7)(C), (k)(2) expressed that the judicial system is akin to a "kangaroo court" and same amounted to predictable judicial misconduct in order to spare the Executive Branch of Government further embarrassment. No further action taken by DOJ.

Joint Chiefs of Staff Review:

The Joint Chiefs of Staff review disclosed that (b)(6), (b)(7)(C), (k)(2) had forwarded a whistleblower disclosure report referencing audits that were alleged to have been undermined: forwarded to General Martin **DEMPSEY** – Joint Chiefs of Staff (dated September 10, 2013).

(b) (5), (d)(5)

In an effort not to taint OSI's ongoing investigation, contact with OSI Special Agent (SA) (b) (6), (b) (7)(C), (d)(2) had been established; lead investigator in relation to the LM BOM audit issues. (b) (5), (b) (6), (b) (7)(C), (d)(5), (d)(2)

(b) (5), (b) (6), (b) (7)(C), (d)(5), (d)(2) As a vetting action to this claim; DCMA-DMR also conducted a comprehensive review into this matter and concluded that the quashing of audits was not a criminal act as related to the reprisal issues now being investigated. The decision to audit the contractors MMAS via DCAA intervention is a prudent business decision as unexpected increases in cost relevant to BOM issues may come to fruition. DCMA-DMR confirmed these facts (b) (5), (d)(5) no further action is warranted

Attachment Page 7 of 7 FOR OFFICIAL USE ONLY

Illustrative Appendix of Weaponization & Lawfare

Appendix 1: Electronic Weaponized Trails to the Deep State

Appendix 1, 2, and 3 are document samples used to write this book. These Appendix provide more transparency and proof of actual written communications outlined herein. Focusing on Falsified Trail 3.

Appendix 1 provides greater transparency as to how I was labeled extremely effective and the weaponized communications that followed. The weaponized communications traced into high level DCMA and DoD IG officials. The evidence trail is as follows:

United States Senate

COMMITTEE ON FINANCE

WASHINGTON, DC 20510-6200

February 24, 2004

Mr. Joe Schmitz
Inspector General
Department of Defense
400 Army Navy Drive
Arlington, VA 22202

Dear Mr. Schmitz:

I am writing to raise questions about your recent review and audit of allegations that Lockheed Martin was overcharging on spare parts for the Air Force C-5 aircraft.

I was both surprised and disappointed to learn today that your office had released the report - Audit Report No. D-2004-054, dated February 23, 2004. After a very preliminary review of the draft audit report on February 10, 2004, my staff informed me that your report was **weak and incomplete.** Following the briefing on February 10th, my staff raised a number of important questions bearing on this matter. These questions were passed to your office. One of the questions pertains to allegations that your audit results rest squarely on **"false information"** - "false information" that first surfaced in a report issued by your office on November 28, 2001 and clearly known to your auditors. Until all these issues are laid to rest, I will continue to have questions about the integrity of your audit process.

Here are the facts in this case - as I understand them:

In late 2002, several whistleblowers at an aircraft plant in Georgia contacted my office with a formal complaint. They continue to allege that Lockheed Martin is overcharging the government on a 1997 contract for the Air Force C-5 aircraft program. They provided extensive documentation to support their claim. I turned over all that material to you, asking that it be carefully examined. That review is now complete. The results of your review are presented in the above-mentioned audit report.

One of the parts that was the focus of your review is the "Clip Strut Support Vapor Barrier" - part number NSN 5340-00-140-8526. It is a one inch bracket associated with the TF-39 engine that powers the C-5 airplane. This part is an excellent case in point.

The original contract proposal for this part, which was offered by Lockheed Martin in November 1999, was $5,217.91 per bracket. On February 23, 2000, the government - the Defense Contract Management Agency (DCMA), rejected that offer and instead recommended that the part be purchased at a unit cost of $258.90. The government's "should cost" figure was $4,959.01 below the unit cost sought by Lockheed Martin.

A1-1: February 24, 2004 Page 1

While contract negotiations over these parts dragged on, Lockheed Martin actually manufactured a total of 219 of the angle brackets. Payment records indicate that the government purchased these 219 brackets in September 2000 for **$1.05 per bracket**. That is a preliminary figure, however. The auditors report that the $1.05 unit price does not include "legitimate contract costs, such as overhead, profits, and tooling set-up expenses." These added costs are the subject of ongoing negotiations and will be tacked on to the unit price when the contract is finally **"definitized."** Until that process is complete, the auditors report that the price of the bracket is **"in limbo."** Under normal circumstances, the auditors say, the final unit price would rise to $258.90 - **the government's best estimate of what the part should cost**. However, the auditors caution that the $258.90 estimate is now four years old and could be way out of date. They say that the final price could go up or down relative to that figure.

The whistleblowers contend that the audit's reliance on the $258.90 estimate is a fatal error. They allege that the $258.90 figure is based on "false information," and they further allege that the auditors know that. To back-up their claim, they cite the **"Criminal Vulnerability Report, #2002-01"** prepared by the Defense Criminal Investigative Service (DCIS) on November 28, 2001. That report clearly states: **"The in-house manufactured part portion of Lockheed Martin's proposal included false information."** This is a very serious charge, indeed. This issue is not addressed and resolved in the audit report.

The audit concludes that the whistleblowers' allegations of overcharging cannot be substantiated at this time. Your auditors close with this warning: **"DCMA and DCAA [Defense Contract Audit Agency] need to maintain vigilance until the price for the remaining parts is negotiated."** In my mind, Mr. Schmitz, that conclusion is truly weak. Those two entities have a long-standing reputation for turning a blind eye to contractor rip offs. They are not known for being vicious junk yard dogs when it comes to protecting the taxpayers' money. Please don't depend on them to be vigilant. I am depending on you to watchdog them. Toward that end, I need answers to the following questions: 1) Does the finding of "false information" in the Criminal Vulnerability Report #2002-01 refer to any of the parts covered by your audit, including NSN 5340-00-140-8526?; 2) Why do your auditors accept the government's $258.90 unit prices as legitimate?; 3) How do they know that is really a fair price?; 4) Why would your auditors think it was a good idea to buy into Lockheed Martin's huge overhead costs? ; and 5) Why not recommend that this part be purchased in the market place at a lower cost from an independent contractor that doesn't have Lockheed Martin's overhead expense? Under the IG Act, each IG is expected to make recommendations in a case like this, yet I find no specific recommendations in this report. Why?

Your consideration of these matters would be appreciated.

Sincerely,

Chuck Grassley

Charles E. Grassley
Senator

A1-1: February 24, 2004 Page 2

<u>A1-1: February 24, 2004</u>. This is the scathing letter from Senator Grassley to Joseph Schmitz after the DoD IG covered up the fact that DCMA knowingly continued to negotiate a contract on data known to be false and purposely overstated. Grassley states in part.

"Those two entities (DCMA & DCAA) *have a long- standing reputation for turning a blind eye to contractor rip offs. They are not known for being vicious junk yard dogs when it comes to protecting taxpayers' money."*

The point is, DoD IG auditors tried to cover-up for DCMA and my insight to Senator Grassley via Charlie Murphy exposed the cover-up.

Pedeleose, Ken

om:	Meyer Daniel P., OIG DoD <DMEYER@DODIG.OSD.MIL>
ent:	Friday, March 19, 2004 9:53 AM
To:	Pedeleose, Ken
Subject:	FW: update

I have to admit, Ken, that you are extremely effective -- I have never seen Congressional staff this active on an intake.

Working away on your case,

Dan

-----Original Message-----
From: Lewis, L Jean, OIG DoD
Sent: Friday, March 19, 2004 9:52 AM
To: Meyer Daniel P., OIG DoD
Subject: FW: update

fyi...

-----Original Message-----
om: Murphy, Charles (Grassley) [mailto:Charles_Murphy@grassley.senate.gov]
ent: Friday, March 19, 2004 9:10 AM
To: Pedeleose, Ken
Cc: jlewis@dodig.osd.mil; Crane, John R., OIG DoD
Subject: update

Ken, I met with the DOD IG audit group on Wednesday. I walked them thru the problem from our perspective, focusing of course on the DCIS documents. My bottom line: the DOD IG audit report is tainted. The write up on page 5 on the C-5 engine bracket contains false information. They knew that, and failed to address and resolve that problem. They should have put that information in the proper perspective. They responded by saying that they hung their hat on the word "paid." And the government paid $1.05 for the part. I responded by saying that was a narrow view. As the DOD IG, they are supposed evaluate information and propose corrective action and alternative approaches when money is being wasted in foolish ways. They have so much talent in the audit department, and they hang their hat on the word "paid." It seems like the audit department has a bad case of tunnel vision. They also said that the $258.90 figure was developed by you. "You proposed that figure." is that true? My feeling is that figure is also way out of sync with reality when the bare bones price is 90 cents. They said no negotiations are in progress and no figure is on the table. They assured me that Senator Grassley's concerns would be addressed in the C-130J report due in draft next week. I closed by saying that I would withhold further judgment until I see the C-130 report and I reserve the right to review the workpapers. charlie

1

A1-2: March 19, 2004

<u>A1-2: March 19, 2004</u>. Dan Meyer, who was instrumental in Falsified Trail 3, was copied into the events between myself and Charlie Murphy of Senator Grassley's staff of the aforesaid DoD IG cover-up. Meyer responded to an investigation by Murphy stating in part.

"*I have to admit, Ken, that you are extremely effective -- I have never seen Congressional staff this active on an intake.*"

Hence, Meyer knew I had the attention of Senator Grassley and was extremely effective.

Additionally, in Murphy's email I was asked about the amount of $258.90 for a C-5 engine cowling (aerodynamic protective cover) bracket for the C-5 engines. I proposed that amount based on Lockheed Martin records. The main issue was duplicative set-up times. Murphy misunderstood the DoD IG comments on the Air Force paying $1.05 for the part. The $1.05 was material cost. Doubtful a part that holds the cover of a C-5 engine would cost $1.05.

Pedeleose, Ken

From:	Meyer Daniel P., OIG DoD <DMEYER@DODIG.OSD.MIL>
Sent:	Thursday, April 22, 2004 8:14 AM
To:	Pedeleose, Ken
Subject:	Re: Climate Review

More like 'referee' Ken, or better yet, a coach aiding competing athletes.
I'll be bold here an tell you I think our former COS came close to compromising our role in your case. She was too emotionally involved, perhaps due to her own issues with Whitewater. The IG Act requires me to be independent and neutral, like a referee - if you have been fouled under the court rules - Title 5 - I'll blow the whistle and recommend penalties.

This doesn't mean I don't understand the pressure you are under. Mt whistle blowing led to two 30 million dollar lawsuits, took me 15 years to resolve them.

Sent from my BlackBerry Wireless Handheld

-----Original Message-----
From: Pedeleose, Ken <Ken.Pedeleose@dcma.mil>
To: Meyer Daniel P., OIG DoD <DMEYER@DODIG.OSD.MIL>
Sent: Thu Apr 22 07:40:47 2004
Subject: RE: Climate Review

Dan,

I won't single you out as DoD is largely at fault, however you are calling this thing like a "fight" commentator looking to see who scores the "knockout punch" on the other. I blame the DoD climate for this. That is why I changed my tactics from a back alley brawl to an open, in the news media issue

That way the world can see how DoD reacts and supports fraud and let's the little guy take up the fight for the big shots like Rumsfeld and Schmitz who should be taking the side of what is right. Instead everyone is looking to see "who wins", and who inflicts the most pain and misery on the other.
Like the Roman games, gladiators, run the gauntlet, etc. The real issue may one day revert to who sat on the side lines and watched the mahem.

I remember when I was in high school and there was a city park next to the school building. If two kids got in a fight there was crowd of on lookers giving advice to their friends in the fight. Stuff like "you got'em now", "good hit", "punch em in the face", etc. It seems that you and DoD are taking that attitude with me. If the agency scores a big hit and "busts me wide open" then you and DoD can say good try Ken. Ken here is where you went wrong....Better luck next time.

Thanks,

Ken Pedeleose
-----Original Message-----
From: Meyer Daniel P., OIG DoD [mailto:DMEYER@DODIG.OSD.MIL]
Sent: Wednesday, April 21, 2004 5:39 PM

1

A1-3: April 22, 2004

A1-3: April 22, 2004. Soon after Meyer arrived it was obvious that Meyer was not going to do anything for whistleblowers. I challenged Meyer on that fact at which time Meyer referred to himself as a *"coach"*. This confirmed Meyer was at the least a zero for whistleblower support.

United States Senate

COMMITTEE ON FINANCE

WASHINGTON, DC 20510-6200

April 26, 2004

To whom it may concern:

I am writing to you regarding Mr. Ken Pedeleose, Industrial Engineer, at the Defense Contract Management Agency (DCMA).

Mr. Pedeleose is continuing to assist the Finance Committee in its oversight investigation of spare parts overpricing on Air Force contracts.

Federal law provides individuals, who are assisting a Congressional investigation, with complete protection from retaliation. In this regard, Federal law specifies:

> **"Whoever corruptly, or by threats or force, or by any threatening letter or communication influences, obstructs, or impedes or endeavors to influence, obstruct, or impede the due and proper administration of the law under which any pending proceeding is being had before any department or agency of the United States, or the due and proper exercise of the power or inquiry under which any inquiry or investigation is being had by either House, or any committee of either House or any joint committee of the Congress – shall be fined under this title or imprisoned not more than five years, or both"**

See 18 U.S.C. 1505 (partial citation)

I have instructed Mr. Pedeleose to contact me if he has any concerns about possible retaliation. If you have any questions as to this letter, please contact Mr. Charles Murphy at 202-224-3744.

Your full cooperation in this matter would be appreciated.

Sincerely,

Chuck Grassley

Charles E. Grassley
Chairman

Copy to:
Director, DCMA, BG Darryl Scott

A1-4: April 26, 2004

A1-4: April 26, 2004. Charlie Murphy became concerned with the level of corruption discovered in 2004 and provided me a protection letter from Senator Grassley.

08/16/2005 11:23 FAX 202 225 1684 SEN GRASSLEY 001

United States Senate

COMMITTEE ON FINANCE

WASHINGTON, DC 20510-6200

August 16, 2005

To Whom It May Concern:

I am writing to you regarding Mr. Henry R. Hagel, Aerospace Engineer, at the Defense Contract Management Agency (DCMA).

Mr. Hagel is continuing to provide assistance, technical knowledge, insight and information to the DOD IG and Mr. Ken Pedeleose on the problems associated with the C-130J. This includes technical reports along with Mr. Pedeleose to Senator Charles E. Grassley to support the continuing investigation of the C-130J including spare parts pricing and other financial aspects of Lockheed Martin and its products.

Federal law provides individuals, who are assisting a Congressional investigation, with complete protection from retaliation. In this regard, Federal law specifies:

"Whoever corruptly, or by threats or force, or by any threatening letter or communication influences, obstructs, or impedes or endeavors to influence, obstruct, or impede the due and proper administration of the law under which any pending proceeding is being had before any department or agency of the United States, or the due and proper exercise of the power or inquiry under which any inquiry or investigation is being had by either House, or any committee of either House or any joint committee of the Congress – shall be fined under this title or imprisoned not more than five years, or both"

See 18 U.S.C. 1505 (partial citation)

I have instructed Mr. Hagel to contact me if he has any concerns about possible retaliation. If you have any questions as to this letter, please contact Mr. Charles Murphy at 202-224-3744.

Your full cooperation in this matter would be appreciated.

Sincerely,

Chuck Grassley

Charles E. Grassley
Chairman

Copy to:
Director, DCMA, BG Darryl Scott

A1-5: August 16, 2005

A1-5: August 16, 2005. Henry Hagel (fellow whistle-blower) was also provided a protection letter similar to mine. Hagel and I worked in tandem on the fraud, corruption, and safety violations on C-5 and C-130 programs.

Hagel was the eyes and ears on the C-130J program while I was on the C-5 program. The letter states in part that *"Mr. Hagel is continuing to provide assistance, technical knowledge, insight and information to the DoD IG and Mr. Ken Pedeleose on the problems associated with the C-130J"*.

The protection letters were provided to the DCMA director. Dan Meyer was also aware.

OIG DoD

From: Meyer Daniel P., OIG DoD
Sent: Friday, July 27, 2007 10:10 AM
To: [redacted] OIG DoD
Subject: FW: Pedeleose's Third Congressional, this time to McCain : ~~FOUO~~

Attachments: Lessons learned AC4011_121202.doc

Lessons learned AC4011_121202....

Looking at the e-mails around the date, March 18th 2005 ---

perhaps this informed the decision to pick the date?

-----Original Message-----
From: Meyer Daniel P., OIG DoD
Sent: Tuesday, March 22, 2005 10:08 AM
To: [redacted], OIG DoD; Ugone, Mary L., OIG DoD
Cc: Trahan, Leonard C., OIG DoD
Subject: Pedeleose's Third Congressional, this time to McCain : ~~FOUO~~

~~FOR OFFICIAL USE ONLY~~ This e-mail contains unclassified information that may be withheld from the public because disclosure would cause foreseeable harm to an interest protected by one or more of the Freedom of Information Act (FOIA) Exemptions 2 through 9 identified in 5 USC 552(b).

Ken Pedeleose is drafting a third Congressional to McCain, this one regarding the F22-Raptor. This document lies at the heart of his disclosure.

He is also teaming up with Doug Kinan, so I am forwarding this also to Len so that we can make sure we are well-situated should Congressional 3 go to Grassley (hence Murphy), as well.

There are no additional reprisal actions attached to this; I am now midstream in the depositions of Lockheed and DCMA management in the reprisal complaint CRI inherited from MRI/COS.

As in all cases, my goal is separate the source's thoughts on "disclosure" from the "reprisal", so as to leave appropriate authorities such as Audit, DCIS, etc. free to do their work in deciding whether specific and credible information exists to prompt further investigation.

Getting the whistleblower to "let go" the issue is the hardest part of the interaction,

Dan Meyer

Dan Meyer, Director - Civilian Reprisal Investigations

b(6)
b(7)(C)

1

DoD IG 8

A1-6: March 22, 2005

<u>A1-6: March 22, 2005</u>. This email was forwarded as part of a FOIA request. Attached to the July 27, 2007 email is a March 22, 2005 email that showed how Dan Meyer was working behind the scenes against me. Dan Meyer stated in part.

Subject: "*Pedeleose's Third Congressional, this time to McCain*"

"*Ken Pedeleose is drafting a third Congressional to McCain, this one regarding the F22-Raptor. This document lies at the heart of his disclosure*".

"*He is also teaming with Doug Kinan* (another whistleblower)*, so I am forwarding this also to Len* (Leonard Trahan, then DoD IG Hotline Director) *so that we can make sure we are well-situated should Congressional 3 go to Grassley (hence Murphy), as well*".

This showed Myer was concerned about Charlie Murphy of Senator Grassley's staff.

I misplaced the email attachment to Meyer however the disclosure was in the May 16, 2005 report to congress that stated in part.

"An April 2004 report indicated that F-22 software was released 75% functional and software from vendors is unfinished. Other examples include an F-22 aircraft dropped to the ground during assembly nearly crushing those underneath. In another instance holes could not be drilled properly during assembly operations".

Meyer would then continue working with DCMA behind my back.

This would also help support the fact as to why the F-22 is among the highest priced fighters ever built. Meaning, manufacturing that has issues and lack of cost discipline outlined herein.

OIG DoD

From: Meyer Daniel P., OIG DoD
Sent: Thursday, August 04, 2005 10:48 AM
To: 'Owens, Leigh'
Cc: Gimble, Thomas, OIG DoD; Boyll, Mark, OIG DoD; Crane, John R., OIG DoD
Subject: Moving Forward : ~~FOUO~~

Sensitivity: Private

~~FOR OFFICIAL USE ONLY~~

Leigh --

Mark Boyll, our acting GC, stopped by with some suggestions from our legal team. I'd like your input on this, my goal being to enable the Colonel as much as possible in an AR 15-6 investigation. Our attorneys came up with three options, less appealing to more appealing:

(1) Give you my concerns with five of Stacy's questions, and ask that they not be used in the AR 15-6 investigation. I am not a fan of this option, because if I were Stacy I would consider these five questions essential. But on CRI's side of the coin, those five questions may endanger a source in the VanDerbeck case.

(2) Second idea, OIG DoD could initiate an investigation of Mr. Pedeleose's non-reprisal allegations that an unlawful termination plan (the so-called "hit list") was being implemented. We would then ask DCMA to not proceed in deference to our investigation. I think this is a little heavy handed.

(3) Third idea, using my recent NSA work as a model. The Colonel could request a Joint Investigation. I could deputize Stacy (for lack of a better word) and she could report to me, the findings could be run through OIG DoD, and DCMA would benefit from the neutrality and impartiality of an IG. We could bring DCMA's IG into the equation as well. Mark did recommend that we establish the reporting protocol up front - so I could be assured that any sourcing information in the VanDerbeck case will remain confidential.

Given Senators McCain and Grassley's interest in this case, this may provide a way for the IG community to aid the Colonel and provide the external credibility which will be desirable as events move out of Georgia and up towards Washington. Something to mull over.

Get back to me when you get into the office.

Best regards,

Dan Meyer

b(6)
b(7)(C)

1

DoD IG 74

A1-7: August 4, 2005

A1-7: August 4, 2005. On the morning of August 4, 2005 Meyer sent a string of emails turning me against the DCMA weaponized investigation. This was outlined in Falsified Trail 3 of Chapter 3. A summary of Meyer's comments turning me against the DCMA investigation is as follows:

August 4, 2005 8:51 AM (Meyer to Pedeleose): "*Our attorneys are meeting on this right now – started 0830. I* (Meyer) *have routed the non-reprisal complaint alleging criminal activities. You can also take that to your local office of the FBI, if you want to.*"

August 4, 2005 8:53 AM (Meyer to Pedeleose): "*Ask Scantlebury for the letter of authority adopting AR 15-6 as the standard for investigations within DCMA. Odd that they did not cite the Air Force regulation.*"

August 4, 2005 8:55 AM (Meyer to Murphy, Hagel, Pedeleose): *"Charlie - a letter with Henry's name would be a good idea; his contribution over the past 18 months should also be highlighted. Henry, you might want to do a draft for Charlie using Ken's letter."*

August 4, 2005 8:57 AM (Meyer to Pedeleose): "*Plourde is Air Force, right? or Army. What about you and Henry – are you DCMA employees (my hunch), or Army civilian employees detailed to DCMA? Our attorneys are intrigued as to why AR 15-6 is being cited.*"

August 4, 2005 9:55 AM (Meyer to Pedeleose): "*And ask her* (Scantlebury) *for the organizing Air Force or Department of Defense regulations for Colonel Plourde's office, giving Colonel Plourde the authority to authorize an administrative investigation.*"

Less Than an Hour Later Dan Meyer Leaves No Doubt I was Conned

August 4, 2005 10:48 AM (A1-7) (Meyer to DCMA and DoD IG): Meyer emails Leigh Owens (DCMA), along with DoD IG officials Thomas Gimble, Mark Boyll, and John Crane and states in part (A1-7).

"*I'd like your input on this, my goal being to enable the Colonel as much as possible in an AR 15-6 investigation. Our attorneys came up with three options, less appealing to more appealing:*"

Option 3 was to "*deputize Stacy*".

"*Given Senators McCain and Grassley's interest in this case, this may provide a way for the IG community to aid the Colonel and provide external credibility which will be desirable as events move out of Georgia and up towards Washington. Something to mull over.*

The point is, Meyer ran a con on me, Henry Hagel, and Charlie Murphy of Senator Grassley's staff. Meyer would inform Murphy that he (Meyer) urged me to cooperate. The email trail proves otherwise. Also, Meyer wanted to use the DoD IG to give Colonel Plourde's weaponized investigation "*credibility which will be desirable as events move out of Georgia and up towards Washington*".

Meaning, I was conned and turned against the DCMA investigation on the morning of August 4, 2005 from 8:51 AM to 9:55 AM. Less than an hour later on August 4, 2005 at 10:48 AM Dan Meyer worked to bolster the DCMA weaponized investigation. In short, there were multiple weapons at play. The weaponized investigation and direct access (communications) behind my back along with the overall con job and duplicity.

Appendix 2 will show that DCMA would run a con on Dan Meyer.

the same. You would be the only one with the best information on how to deconflict the two inquiries, so I would think DCMA called you for a date, or might have sent you an email?

Please advise.

Associate General Counsel
Office of Legal Counsel
Office of the Inspector General
Department of Defense
(703) 604-[redacted]/604-[redacted](Fax)
[redacted]@dodig.mil

-----Original Message-----
From: Meyer Daniel P., OIG DoD
Sent: Thursday, July 26, 2007 3:20 PM
To: [redacted], OIG DoD
Subject: FW: E-mails from Mr. Pedeleose : ~~LRS~~
Sensitivity: Private

[redacted] this refreshed my memory; it was DCMA who called your office. What sort of inquiry are you conducting? Internal to OGC?

From: Fiore, Uldric, OIG DoD
Sent: Monday, August 08, 2005 6:03 PM
To: Schmitz, Joseph E., OIG DoD
Cc: Race, Richard T., OIG DoD; Gimble, Thomas, OIG DoD
Subject: RE: E-mails from Mr. Pedeleose : ~~LRS~~
Sensitivity: Private

Sir -

Fully concur that you need not respond/acknowledge e-mails (same rational as with [redacted] [redacted].

DCMA's Acting GC called in and asked to meet with us with the Boston Regional Counsel who will be flying in on Wed. We (including) Dan Meyer will meet with them Wed. afternoon.

Ric

Uldric L. Fiore, Jr.

General Counsel and

Assistant Inspector General (Office of Legal Counsel)

Office of the Inspector General

Department of Defense

703-604-[redacted] / FAX 703-604-[redacted]

b(6)
b(7)(C)

2

DoD IG 27

A1-8: August 8, 2005

A1-8: August 8, 2005: This was a response from Uldric Fiore to Joseph Schmitz (Then DoD IG) to an email titled *"Emails from Mr. Pedeleose"*. Fiore states in part.

"...you need not respond/acknowledge e-mails same rational as with (Name Redacted).

DCMA's Acting GC (probably Chip Retson) *called in and asked to meet with us with the Boston Regional Counsel* (Probably Bruce Krasker) *who will be flying in on Wed. We (including) Dan Meyer will meet with them Wed. afternoon."*

Meaning, whistleblowers are shunned but it's ok for DoD IG officials to meet with DCMA attorneys, against whistleblowers, in what turned out as weaponization and lawfare (Falsified Trail 3).

FOIA_06-0139 (2).TXT

Thanks for all your efforts here.

Tommy Treat is retired, but still in the area. I will find a number for him and let you know.

Leigh

Sent from my BlackBerry Wireless Handheld

-----Original Message-----
From: Meyer Daniel P., OIG DoD <DMEYER@DODIG.OSD.MIL>
To: Owens, Leigh <Leigh.Owens@dcma.mil>
Sent: Wed Aug 10 13:27:02 2005
Subject: Got the box. : FOUO

FOR OFFICIAL USE ONLY
This e-mail contains unclassified information that may be withheld from the public because disclosure would cause foreseeable harm to an interest protected by one or more
of the Freedom of Information Act (FOIA) Exemptions 2 through 9 identified in 5 USC 552(b).

Thanks; this material on VanDerbeck will help narrow the questions for Harvey Leake and Henrietta Snow on September 12th.

On the Pedeleose case, our attorneys are meeting with the DCMA Acting General Counsel today at 2PM; the Director of the Hotline and I will sit in; sorry it has taken so long, but I think they will have some solution for us by the end of the day. Though it is perhaps beyond my portfolio, be careful of the Congressional end of this case - which has been quiet for a while. Grassley and McCain are interested in the issues Pedeleose is perceived as advancing, so you may want to make sure your liaison is in the loop when the Colonel's investigation goes ahead.

Deposition of Walter Walker was exceedingly professional, and very helpful. I think I can share with you that of the 21 alleged reprisals, I am down to looking at 1 - that is 1, Leigh.

I am deciding whether I need to take a statement from a "Tommy Treat", and his availability would help me decide. I am more concerned about thoroughness at this point, as I think this report may garner national attention. Is Mr. Treat still with DCMA? Retired? Can we line him up by phone?

Thanks for the patience,

Dan Meyer

Dan Meyer, Director - Civilian Reprisal Investigations

U.S. Department of Defense, Office of the Inspector General
Page 35

A1-9: August 10, 2005

EXHIBIT 3

b6 b7c

A1-9: August 10, 2005. Dan Meyer emails Leigh Owens and states in part. *"Grassley and McCain are interested in the issues Pedeleose is perceived as advancing, so you may want to make sure your liaison is in the loop when the Colonel's investigation goes ahead."*

Meaning, Meyer gives Owens (DCMA) a warning about Grassley and McCain. DCMA provided me this email to show how tight DCMA was working with Dan Meyer against whistleblowers. Meyer would later regret dealing with DCMA. This was DCMA's Exhibit 3, in Falsified Trail 3.

CHAIRMAN
COMMITTEE ON INDIAN AFFAIRS
COMMITTEE ON ARMED SERVICES
COMMITTEE ON COMMERCE, SCIENCE, AND TRANSPORTATION

United States Senate

(202) 224-2235

5353 NORTH 16TH STREET
SUITE 105
PHOENIX, AZ 85016
(602) 952-2410

4703 SOUTH LAKESHORE DRIVE
SUITE 1
TEMPE, AZ 85282
(480) 897-6289

407 WEST CONGRESS STREET
SUITE 103
TUCSON, AZ 85701
(520) 670-6334

TELEPHONE FOR HEARING IMPAIRED
(602) 952-0170

June 22, 2005

VIA FACSIMILE AND FIRST CLASS MAIL

Mr. Robert J. Stevens
President and Chief Executive Officer
Lockheed Martin Corporation
6801 Rockledge Drive
Bethesda, MD 20817

Re: C-130J

Dear Mr. Stevens:

Thank you for your letter of April 21, 2005. Your letter addressed some of my concerns raised during our February 15, 2005 meeting, but did not address my main concern and request to produce the cost and pricing data of the C-130J program so as to determine whether the contractor costs and the prices negotiated and eventually paid are fair and reasonable.

In anticipation of an AirLand Subcommittee hearing regarding the Defense Department's recent decision to complete the C-130J multi-year procurement contract - essentially reversing its previous decision during the Department's fiscal year 2006 budget process - I renew my request to you to provide me the following information:

1. Please provide the Incurred Costs and information for each C-130J Production Lot, including but not limited to the following:

   a. Realized profit or loss for each production lot and explanation if loss was incurred.

   b. Laydown of cost/price growth post award, broken out by major category.

   c. Number of C-130J aircraft produced for the Air Force, Foreign Military Sales (FMS), and commercial customers for each year.

   d. All plans for the number of C-130J aircraft to be produced for Air Force, FMS, and commercial customers for past and future years.

PRINTED ON RECYCLED PAPER

A1-10: June 22, 2005 Page 1

2. Please provide the total Research and Development (R&D) and or nonrecurring costs for the C-130J program, including but not limited to the following:

a. Total of any unrecovered R&D or nonrecurring costs.

b. Plan to recover any R&D or nonrecurring costs and years.

c. R&D and nonrecurring costs allocated to FMS customers and years allocated.

d. Any Independent Research & Development (IR&D) costs associated with C-130J program and years the costs were charged.

3. In April 2005, Air Force officials testified that terminating the C-130J program would probably result in substantial increases in overhead costs in the F/A-22 "Raptor" program. Please explain in detail the rationale why the cost of the F/A-22 program would increase significantly and what the costs would be to the F/A-22 program if the C-130J program were terminated. Additionally, please explain the determination of overhead rates across each weapon system.

Costs should be segregated by major cost category and include all direct costs and indirect costs, whether amortized or pooled, and applicable rates to include the basis for indirect cost rates. Also, please provide the cost data requested at (1) both the prime and by major sub levels and (2) sufficient to determine that the government paid a reasonable value as determined by government audit agencies.

Please provide this information in writing by Thursday, July 7, 2005. Thank you in advance for your cooperation.

Sincerely,

John McCain
Chairman
Subcommittee on AirLand

JSM/cjp

A1-10: June 22, 2005 Page 2

A1-10: June 22, 2005. I was in the loop with Senator McCain's investigation challenging Lockheed Martin on the C-130J.

Lockheed Martin Corporation
6801 Rockledge Drive Bethesda, MD 20817
Telephone 301-897-6642 Facsimile 301-897-6611

LOCKHEED MARTIN

Robert J. Stevens
Chairman, President and Chief Executive Officer

July 7, 2005

The Honorable John McCain
Chairman
Air-Land Subcommittee
Committee on Armed Services
United States Senate
Washington, D.C. 20510

Dear Mr. Chairman:

Attached is a response, prepared by my staff, to the questions presented in your letter of June 22, 2005. I share your determination to ensure that the men and women who serve in the United States Armed Forces receive the full benefit and capabilities they deserve from the investments made by Congress to modernize and equip our Armed Forces. The Lockheed Martin Corporation firmly believes the C-130J meets that standard, and we are proud of the C-130J's contributions to military operations in Iraq, Afghanistan and the global war on terrorism.

In addition to the attached response to your questions, Lockheed Martin understands the USG's desire to move away from commercial contracting into a more standard contracting environment and is in support of several initiatives to this end. The C-130J Program is currently cooperating with the USAF on an 'alpha' contracting approach in responding to two Requests for Proposals, one for initial aircraft support and one for mid-term/long-term sustainment of the aircraft. The end result is expected to be two FAR Part 15 contracts with full cost and price visibility. In addition, the USAF has also initiated the conversion of the current multi-year contract to a more traditional USG contract effective for aircraft procured in FY06 through FY08. As part of that conversion, Lockheed Martin has cooperated fully in allowing a government team (including USG audit agencies) access to the C-130J profitability and cost records. It is the Corporation's intent to continue to partner with the USG in establishing and converting these contracts to satisfy the desire for full cost and pricing visibility into the C-130J Program.

Mr. Chairman, I wish to reaffirm my commitment that we will work to resolve any concerns you have about our performance on this program. Again, I look forward to our next meeting.

Respectfully,

Robert J. Stevens

Attachment

A1-11: July 7, 2005

A1-11: July 7, 2005. This document shows I was in the review loop with the documents Lockheed Martin provided to Senator McCain. I reviewed and provided a response of about 2 ½ pages on July 25, 2005. I made the mistake of copying in Dan Meyer. I stated in part.

"I would consider the July 7, 2005 response to Senator McCain's request for information as non-responsive. This stems from the fact that my past experience with Lockheed data indicates that a

request for Cost and Pricing Data would involve significantly detailed financial data. The Lockheed response resembled more of a sales pitch than a response to a request for data".

"The current pricing and estimating climate within Lockheed is abysmal at best. I have heard it (problems) is spread across Lockheed and not just at this facility. Challenging the contractor is a lost art since those who challenge the contractor are fired, shunned, ignored, or sidelined."

"The most egregious chart in the Lockheed submittal Page 8 of 9 (21 April 2005). This is a "curve" with just 2 data points (A-400M and C-17). I would equate this to statistical cherry picking and an attempt to artificially increase the price of the C-130J."

The point being, there were about 25 pages of supporting documents that were useless.

The follow-on point (next page) is while I was protecting taxpayer interests by working with Congress, Senator McCain, DCMA was working behind my back with the Assistant United States Attorney (AUSA/DOJ).

08/25/2005 15:51 FAX 404 581 6181 U S ATTORNEY'S OFFICE 002

U.S. Department of Justice

United States Attorney
Northern District of Georgia

Suite 600 Richard Russell Building Telephone (404)581-6000
75 Spring Street, S.W. Fax (404)581-6181
Atlanta, Georgia 30303

August 25, 2005

VIA FACSIMILE & MAIL
Leigh. S. Owens
Defense Contract Management Agency
2300 Lake Park Drive, Suite 300
Smyrna, GA 30080-4091

Re: Administrative matter

Dear Ms. Owens:

I received your letter of August 16, 2005, attached hereto, in which you requested written confirmation of my previous oral opinion on whether our office would pursue criminal prosecution of a particular matter. On July 19, 2005, you and Gill Bass described a matter to me that involved one employee, Ken Pedeleose, allegedly advising another employee that she was about to be fired. You asked whether the United States Attorney's Office would consider such a matter for criminal prosecution. I advised that we would not, and that in my opinion, it was appropriate to use Kalkines warnings in the administrative investigation. If the facts as described above vary in substance from my summary, please advise me immediately, as my conclusion could change.

Sincerely,

DAVID E. NAHMIAS
UNITED STATES ATTORNEY
Charysse L Alexander
by Gail Sevsler

CHARYSSE L. ALEXANDER
CHIEF, PUBLIC CORRUPTION &
GOVERNMENT FRAUD

Attachment

2

A1-12: August 25, 2005

A1 -12: August 25, 2005. DCMA attorney Leigh Owens weaponized her DCMA status with AUSA Charysse Alexander to obtain a declination letter to threaten me. It worked, however Alexander stated that DCMA was interested in one employee *"Ken Pedeleose"*. The letter by Charysse Alexander was a lawfare weapon used by Leigh Owens, DCMA and DOD IG against me.

DOCID: 3270653

From: Meyer Daniel P., OIG DoD [mailto:DMEYER@dodig.osd.mil]
Sent: Thursday, September 15, 2005 10:34 AM
To: Murphy, Charles (Grassley)
Subject: Re: question

I have been working on a solution with Dina Rasor, my fear is that Ken will
cook off before I can bring the resources together. Fitzgerald is willing
to bring him in to his shop.

Sent from my BlackBerry Wireless Handheld

-----Original Message-----
From: Murphy, Charles (Grassley) <Charles_Murphy@grassley.senate.gov>
To: Meyer Daniel P., OIG DoD <DMEYER@dodig.osd.mil>
Sent: Thu Sep 15 09:40:28 2005
Subject: RE: question

Ken is calling me at home which honks me off. Ernie must have given him my home number. He is spinning out of control. I can tell. He is getting nutty. I want him to work this with you. You have to look at it and make a determination. I am not telling you what to do or looking for some particular outcome. You just have to figure out what's right - all things considered. I am not convinced this guy has a solid case. Let me know how you want to proceed, charlie

-----Original Message-----
From: Meyer Daniel P., OIG DoD [mailto:DMEYER@dodig.osd.mil]
Sent: Monday, September 12, 2005 5:43 PM
To: Murphy, Charles (Grassley)
Subject: Re: question

Just got out of the Lockheed facility. Contrary to my advice, Ken and Henry
have given DCMA your letters, and invoked them to say they don't have to cooperate with the administrative investigation into the wrongful employment
practices. I think they are both on thin ice - Bruce K is calling you to
ask what they are suppose to do with the letters. I am on record having coordinated their questions under the IG Act (requiring agencies to not interfere with our investigations). They limited the time frame involved,
and struck questions not related to the Ms. Gerry Sands who was allegedly
targeted for wrongful removal).

Plourde also had Gordon England down last week, so she is shoring up the Pentagon flank.

I am back in DC tomorrow AM. Nephew graduated from Infantry Basic last Saturday, has picked up one of two available Special Forces slots.

Sent from my BlackBerry Wireless Handheld

A1-13: September 12-15, 2005 (6)
DoD IG 77

A1-13: September 12-15, 2005. September 12, 2005 was one date Dan Meyer conned Charlie Murphy. Meyer told Murphy that he (Meyer) coordinated with DCMA on the investigation. However, Meyer never informed me of that fact. Meyer also named dropped Gordon England (then Acting Deputy Secretary of Defense) stating in part.

"Plourde also had Gordon England down last week, so she is shoring up the Pentagon flank."

Charlie Murphy responded on September 15, 2005 (Appendix A1-13) that I (Pedeleose) was *"Spinning out of control"* and *"getting nutty."* Meyer then knew the *"Congressional interest"* was neutralized. My support was lost and DoD IG was *"happy"* to move forward against me.

It was obvious by earlier emails Meyer misled me and now misled Charlie Murphy of Senator Grassley's staff.

Re: Investigation : FOUO Page 1 of 4

[redacted] OIG DoD

From: [redacted], OIG DoD
Sent: Friday, September 16, 2005 2:57 PM
To: [redacted]
Cc: Fiore, Uldric, OIG DoD
Subject: RE: Investigation : ~~FOUO~~

FOR OFFICIAL USE ONLY

Understood. When we met with [redacted] and [redacted] we discussed possible charges against the individual and whether a charge for failure to cooperate should be considered. I'd be happy to discuss that with you at the appropriate time.

Associate General Counsel
Office of Legal Counsel, DODIG
Tel: 703-604-[redacted]
Fax: 703-604-[redacted]

CAUTION: This message may contain information protected by the attorney-client, attorney work product,deliberative process or other privilege. Do not disseminate without prior approval of the Office of Legal Counsel, Office of the Inspector General, DoD.

From: Owens, Leigh [mailto:Leigh.Owens@dcma.mil]
Sent: Friday, September 16, 2005 2:50 PM
To: ROConnor@DODIG.OSD.MIL
Subject: Re: Investigation : FOUO

He refused to be interviewed. Read a statement to Ms. Scantlebury threatening to have her prosecuted for making false statements, and using Government resources in furtherance of an ilegal investigation. We will probably give him one more opportunity to cooperate via an email from Ms. Scantlebury. If he continues to refuse we will proceed with a disciplinary action.

Leigh

Sent from my BlackBerry Wireless Handheld

-----Original Message-----
From: OConnor, Raymond V., OIG DoD <ROConnor@DODIG.OSD.MIL>
To: Owens, Leigh <Leigh.Owens@dcma.mil>
Sent: Fri Sep 16 14:36:44 2005
Subject: RE: Investigation : ~~FOUO~~

522

FOR OFFICIAL USE ONLY

We did see the info. Was wondering if he has been interviewed and if any adverse action is being considered at this time.

A1-14: September 16, 2005 7

A1-14: September 16, 2005. When the *"Congressional interest"* (Charlie Murphy, Senator Grassley) quit supporting me, the DoD IG felt comfortable openly stating in part.

"*... we discussed possible charges against the individual and whether a charge for failure to cooperate should be considered. I'd be happy to discuss that with you at the appropriate time.*"

Meaning, the DoD IG took advantage of the situation and moved against me in concert with DCMA. However, I took advantage of the documents and electronic trails DCMA provided me to make a case against DCMA and DoD IG. That case is included in this book as well as the July 27, 2007 email of regret by Dan Meyer, which is as follows.

OIG DoD

From: Meyer Daniel P., OIG DoD
Sent: Friday, July 27, 2007 8:01 AM
To: , OIG DoD; 'Donald.Hortsman@dodig.mil'
Subject: Response to Ken Pedeleose

Sensitivity: Private

Date idea came up at the meeting - in early August. I had no contact with DCMA Boston, except through OGC. That is why I was invited to Ric's meeting with them, because OGC was 'providing me top cover."

Mark suggested a date at the meeting. I arbitrarily threw out the idea of January 1st There was some discussion, and I think Mark suggested the date chosen. Then DCMA left to go back to Boston. Three weeks later, they sent me the questions through . You are telling me that the date is on that correspondance. It's there because Krasker left the meeting with the date proposed by OGC, and accepted it in their return correspondance.

I wouldn't have returned Krasker's calls or e-mails if he had contacted me, . As of August of 2005, KP was going to MSPB, we had found no reprisal on the allegations we were looking into, and the Congressional interest was not following KP into his labor activities (which is what led to the August meeting). So this case was over, moving on. The meeting was a risk, it could have sparked more issues, I expressed reservations about going, was given the opportunity to not attend, but decided that it was worth supporting OGC in the spirit of making amends. Relations between my floor and your corner were a little saggy at that point. So I went. Bad decision on my part. In retrospect. I should have left you all alone with Krasker.

That's about all I remember. But do note that DCMA has given KP evidence (in the Atlanta MSPB case) that KP indicates will prove that OGC was conducting the conversations with Krasker and his people. So your work product is going to be matched against that pile of paper. I am getting the same feeling that I have had before - we, OIG, are drafting documents which may contradict previous materials coming out of government offices. We don't know what DCMA has, or what they provided KP, about OGC's discussions with DCMA. We do know what I communicated - NSA IG has reviewed that.

This is a very difficult environment in which to be writing. a letter.

Sent from my BlackBerry Wireless Handheld

----- Original Message -----
From: , OIG DoD
To: Meyer Daniel P., OIG DoD
Sent: Fri Jul 27 06:25:00 2007
Subject: RE: E-mails from Mr. Pedeleose : ~~LES~~

Dan:

No internal inquiry from OGC.
Kicklighter and insists he wil

But, back to the issue at hand, I understand that DCMA sent questions to OGC for your review, but the date was already in the questions Ray received. How did DCMA come up with the date of 3/18? Wouldn't Krasker have called you to discuss, or Leigh Owens? says that he was not contacted on that, and would not have had an idea what date to use, Ric b(5)

1

DoD IG 26 b(6) b(7)(

A1-15: July 27, 2007

A1-15: July 27, 2007. Dan Meyer issued a regret email with warnings that concisely outlined the tactics used against me in 2005. The tactics and key words are as follows.

"*As of August 2005, KP was going to MSPB, we had found no reprisal into the allegations we were looking into, and the Congressional interest was not following KP into his labor activities (which is what led to the August meeting).*"

Meyer realized that Congressional interest was not following and the "coast is clear" to retaliate against me. The retaliation included an August 10, 2005 tactical meeting at DoD IG offices between

Dan Meyer, Uldric Fiore, and DCMA attorneys Chip Retson and Bruce Krasker among others where Dan Meyer had *"top cover"* from OGC (DoD IG Office of General Counsel (OGC)). Meaning, others covered for Dan Meyer during the weaponized retaliation against me.

Meyer's biggest regret was meeting with Bruce Krasker (DCMA attorney). Meyer stated: *"In retrospect. I should have left you* (DoD IG) *all alone with Krasker."* Appendix 2 outlines how Krasker and Leigh Owens ran the con on Dan Meyer outlined in a *"pile of paper"*.

Meyer stated: *"But do note that DCMA has given KP evidence (in the Atlanta MSPB case) that KP indicates will prove that OGC was conducting the conversations with Krasker and his people. So your work product is going to be matched against that pile of paper. I am getting the same feeling that I have had before - we, OIG* (Office of Inspector General)*, are drafting documents which may contradict previous materials coming out of government offices. We don't know what DCMA has, or what they provided KP, about OGC's discussions with DCMA."*

"This is a very difficult environment in which to be writing, a letter."

Appendix 2 will show that it was Dan Meyer that left the best *"pile of paper"* trail with DCMA. In fact, DCMA is largely responsible for the *"pile of paper"* used to help write this book and prove the Deep State, weaponization and lawfare does exist.

Nevertheless, Tom Gimble of the DoD IG should have taken Meyer's advice and not write letters.

INSPECTOR GENERAL
DEPARTMENT OF DEFENSE
400 ARMY NAVY DRIVE
ARLINGTON, VIRGINIA 22202-4704

SEP 1 0 2007

Mr. Kenneth Pedeleose
5252 Barrett Parkway, SW #13
Marietta, GA 30064

Dear Mr. Pedeleose:

I am writing to you to retract the letter I sent dated August 27, 2007, regarding your series of requests initiated on May 31, 2007, that you sent to Mr. Claude M. Kicklighter, the Inspector General of the Department of Defense, that contain allegations against members of the Inspector General staff along with requests for information.

Mr. Kicklighter will be on a fact finding mission to Southwest Asia that starts on September 4, 2007, and which is expected to last until the latter half of October. Upon his return, Mr. Kicklighter will review information regarding your concerns and make a determination about any future course of action.

Your information requests will continue to be considered under the Freedom of Information Act (FOIA).

Sincerely,

Thomas F. Gimble
Principal Deputy

cc:
General Counsel, DCMA

A1-16: September 10, 2007

A1-16: September 10, 2007. Tom Gimble did not heed Meyer's warning and wrote a letter on August 27, 2007. About two weeks later then DoD IG Director Claud Kicklighter forced Gimble to write a retraction letter. Gimble reluctantly did so on September 10, 2007 and also realized it would give me *"extra ammunition"* (per June 5, 2008 IG investigation). The existing *"ammunition"* was the *"pile of paper"* Meyer spoke of that is outlined in Appendix 2.

Appendix 2: The "Pile of Paper" Con on Dan Meyer

The DCMA con on Dan Myer left a clear electronic email trail by Meyer's DCMA contact Leigh Owens. Leigh Owens tactically forwarded Meyer's emails to Bruce Krasker directly, or sometimes through another DCMA attorney Stephanie Zimmt-Mack who would forward to Bruce Krasker.

Krasker tactically held the emails as surprise evidence against me at MSPB. Specifically, my deposition was March 29, 2006 with DCMA attorneys Gary Jencson and Donald Srail. About two days after my deposition (March 31, 2006), Krasker quickly released the behind-the-scenes emails to Gary Jencson from 3:53PM to 3:58PM. This sabotaged my deposition because the behind-the-scenes, weaponized, evidence was denied to me.

Meaning, I could not make the connections to a more solid case against DCMA. Although DCMA admitted to whistleblower retaliation anyway. The electronic trails are as follows:

3/31/2006 3:53 pm

Jencson, Gary E.

From: Krasker, Bruce
Sent: Friday, March 31, 2006 3:53 PM
To: Jencson, Gary E.
Subject: FW: : FOUO
Sensitivity: Private

More IG contact

Bruce Krasker
Counsel
Defense Contract Management Agency East
495 Summer Street
Boston, MA 02210
(617) 753-4269
(617) 753-3037 (fax)
Bruce.Krasker@dcma.mil

From: Owens, Leigh
Sent: Thursday, August 04, 2005 1:10 PM
To: Zimmt-Mack, Stephanie; Krasker, Bruce
Subject: FW: : FOUO
Sensitivity: Private

FYI

Leigh S. Owens
Counsel
DCMA Atlanta
(678) 503-6041
DSN: 697-6041

If you are pleased with my service, please tell others.
If you are not, please tell me!
Either way, the DCMA Atlanta Office of Counsel values your feedback; please complete this SHORT Customer Comment Card
http://ice.disa.mil/index.cfm?fa=card&site_id=182&service_provider_id=88204&service_category_id=1

From: Meyer Daniel P., OIG DoD [mailto:DMEYER@DODIG.OSD.MIL]
Sent: Thursday, August 04, 2005 1:09 PM
To: Owens, Leigh
Subject: RE: : FOUO
Sensitivity: Private

4/03/2006

A2-1: August 4, 2005 (1:09PM & 1:10PM) Page 1

There are a couple of e-mails after this one -- see the latest. I understand re: inherent rights; but I am also sensitive to the fact that at least one of the sources Stacy is trying to identify may be the source on the VanDerbeck case. Would rather not have a fifth DCMA reprisal complaint; trying to go the other way, with fewer rather than more cases.

her matters, Senator Grassley is probably going to weigh in on Henry Hagel's case; not sure whether the letter is going to ... chmitz or to DCMA.

Dan Meyer

Dan Meyer, Director - Civilian Reprisal Investigations
U.S. Department of Defense, Office of the Inspector General
400 Army Navy Drive - Suite 918A
Arlington, VA 22202-4704

Tele: (703) 604.8807/W
Facs: (703) 602.6002/W

---

rom: Owens, Leigh [mailto:Leigh.Owens@dcma.mil]
ent: Thursday, August 04, 2005 12:51 PM
o: Meyer Daniel P., OIG DoD
ubject: RE: : FOUO
ensitivity: Private

)an,

think it is the inherent right of a Commander to ask questions, and gather information concerning issues occurring in or impacting ... nmand. I think that Col. Plourde could have called each one of these folks, Messrs Hagel and Pedeleose included, into her ... and directed them to answer her questions concerning the source of the inaccurate rumors and the scope of their ubsequent dissemination. Sensitive to the fact that some members of her command would question the objectivity of any review he conducted herself, she decided to ask for someone outside of the command to do the fact gathering on the issue. I believe hat they act on a delegation of her authority. AR 15-6 serves solely as a guideline for conducting this kind of fact-gathering.

his morning Col. Plourde and I were informed by the C-5 team leadership that they have been approached by yet another mployee, Mr. Johnny Carter, expressing anxiety that he is on a hit list for disciplinary action/removal. Apparently he sits next to Ir. Pedeleose, and has heard his names mentioned in Mr. Pedeleose's telephone conversation concerning such a list. This is the iird of our employees who is dealing with the anxiety of these unfounded rumors.

eigh S. Owens
ounsel
CMA Atlanta
78) 503-6041
SN: 697-6041

you are pleased with my service, please tell others.
you are not, please tell me!
ther way, the DCMA Atlanta Office of Counsel values your feedback; please complete this SHORT Customer Comment Card
tp://ice.disa.mil/index.cfm?fa=card&site_id=182&service_provider_id=88204&service_category_id=1

---

om: Meyer Daniel P., OIG DoD [mailto:DMEYER@DODIG.OSD.MIL]
nt: Thursday, August 04, 2005 10:07 AM

4/03/2006

A2-1: August 4, 2005 (1:09PM & 1:10PM) Page 2

A2-1: August 4, 2005 (1:09PM & 1:10PM). Dan Meyer sends an email to Leigh Owens at 1:09PM and Leigh Owens the next minute forwards it to DCMA attorneys Stephanie Zimmit-Mack and Bruce Krasker at 1:10PM with the phrase "FYI" (apparently For Your Information). Krasker holds the email for over 7 months then forwards the email about 2 days after my deposition to Gary Jencson (DCMA Attorney representing DCMA at MSPB).

3/31/2006 3:56 PM

Jencson, Gary E.

From: Krasker, Bruce
Sent: Friday, March 31, 2006 3:56 PM
To: Jencson, Gary E.
Subject: FW: Urgent: Interview : FOUO

More

Bruce Krasker
Counsel
Defense Contract Management Agency East
495 Summer Street
Boston, MA 02210
(617) 753-4269
(617) 753-3037 (fax)
Bruce.Krasker@dcma.mil

From: Zimmt-Mack, Stephanie
Sent: Friday, August 05, 2005 8:08 AM
To: Krasker, Bruce
Subject: FW: Urgent: Interview : FOUO

From: Owens, Leigh
Sent: Thursday, August 04, 2005 2:01 PM
To: Zimmt-Mack, Stephanie
Subject: FW: Urgent: Interview : FOUO

Leigh S. Owens
Counsel
DCMA Atlanta
(678) 503-6041
DSN: 697-6041

If you are pleased with my service, please tell others.
If you are not, please tell me!
Either way, the DCMA Atlanta Office of Counsel values your feedback; please complete this SHORT Customer Comment Card
http://ice.disa.mil/index.cfm?fa=card&site_id=182&service_provider_id=88204&service_category_id=1

From: Meyer Daniel P., OIG DoD [mailto:DMEYER@DODIG.OSD.MIL]

Page 2 of 5

Sent: Thursday, August 04, 2005 2:01 PM
To: Owens, Leigh
Subject: RE: Urgent: Interview : FOUO

Mr. Pedeleose used to send these directly to the DoD Hotline; I have been routinely hitting "Forward" to the Hotline, without reading the e-mails. The Hotline will handle his non-reprisal complaint alleging violations of federal merit system principles according to its protocol. I am still not convinced this is not an outgrowth of his union duties and responsibilities, hence the desire to find a way to parse it away from the VanDerBeck complaint and its investigation.

Your observation about appearances is very important,

Dan Meyer, Director - Civilian Reprisal Investigations
U.S. Department of Defense, Office of the Inspector General
400 Army Navy Drive - Suite 918A
Arlington, VA 22202-4704

Tele: (703) 604.8807/W
Facs: (703) 602.6002/W

-----Original Message-----
From: Owens, Leigh [mailto:Leigh.Owens@dcma.mil]
Sent: Thursday, August 04, 2005 1:55 PM
To: Meyer Daniel P., OIG DoD
Subject: FW: Urgent: Interview
Importance: High

Dan,

I do note that you were an addressee on Mr. Pedeleose's email below. Gerry Sawyer's supervisor had to have a conversation with Gerry to ...er that she had not done anything wrong in cooperating with Ms. Scantlebury. While Mr. Pedeleose may not have intended it this way, ...atement that he is referring her name to the IG for review to determine if she has compromised an investigation might be perceived as an attempt at intimidation designed to discourage any further cooperation. This puts our employees in a position where they are reluctant to come to management to determine whether or not the rumors they hear in the workplace are accurate, for fear of being accused of interfering with some ongoing investigation they do not know exists.

Leigh S. Owens
Counsel
DCMA Atlanta
(678) 503-6041
DSN: 697-6041

If you are pleased with my service, please tell others.
If you are not, please tell me!
Either way, the DCMA Atlanta Office of Counsel values your feedback; please complete this SHORT Customer Comment Card
http://ics.disa.mil/index.cfm?fa=card&site_id=182&service_provider_id=88204&service_category_id=1

-----Original Message-----
From: Scantlebury, Stacy
Sent: Thursday, August 04, 2005 1:42 PM
To: Owens, Leigh
Subject: FW: Urgent: Interview
Importance: High

FYI

S. Scantlebury

-----Original Message-----

4/03/2006 **A2-2: August 4, 2005 (2:01PM & 2:01PM) Page 2**

A2-2: August 4, 2005 (2:01PM & 2:01PM). Dan Meyer sends an email to Leigh Owens at 2:01PM and Owens forwards it to DCMA attorney Stephanie Zimmit-Mack the same minute 2:01PM with no words. Zimmit-Mack forwards to Krasker the next day August 5, 2005. Krasker holds the email for over 7 months then forwards the email about 2 days after my deposition to Gary Jencson.

The aforementioned emails seemed the point of origin for the con on Dan Meyer because Leigh Owens would later forward more of Meyer's earlier emails to Krasker as follows.

3/31/2006 3:57 PM

Jencson, Gary E.

From: Krasker, Bruce
Sent: Friday, March 31, 2006 3:57 PM
To: Jencson, Gary E.
Subject: FW: Urgent: Interview : FOUO

Dan Meyer says he urged KP to cooperate...

Bruce Krasker
Counsel
Defense Contract Management Agency East
495 Summer Street
Boston, MA 02210
(617) 753-4269
(617) 753-3037 (fax)
Bruce.Krasker@dcma.mil

From: Owens, Leigh
Sent: Monday, August 08, 2005 1:09 PM
To: Krasker, Bruce
Subject: FW: Urgent: Interview : FOUO

Leigh S. Owens
Counsel
DCMA Atlanta
(678) 503-6041
DSN: 697-6041

If you are pleased with my service, please tell others.
If you are not, please tell me!
Either way, the DCMA Atlanta Office of Counsel values your feedback; please complete this SHORT Customer Comment Card
http://ice.disa.mil/index.cfm?fa=card&site_id=182&service_provider_id=88204&service_category_id=1

From: Owens, Leigh
Sent: Wednesday, August 03, 2005 11:29 AM
To: 'Meyer Daniel P., OIG DoD'
Subject: RE: Urgent: Interview : FOUO

Thank you. We are awaiting your input based upon the recommendations of your counsel.

A2-3: August 8, 2005 1:09PM Page 1

Leigh S. Owens
Counsel
DCMA Atlanta
) 503-6041
DSN: 697-6041

If you are pleased with my service, please tell others.
If you are not, please tell me!
Either way, the DCMA Atlanta Office of Counsel values your feedback; please complete this SHORT Customer Comment Card
http://ice.disa.mil/index.cfm?fa=card&site_id=182&service_provider_id=88204&service_category_id=1

From: Meyer Daniel P., OIG DoD [mailto:DMEYER@DODIG.OSD.MIL]
Sent: Wednesday, August 03, 2005 11:27 AM
To: Owens, Leigh
Subject: FW: Urgent: Interview : FOUO
Importance: High

The narrow questions I have put to our attorneys is how two investigations can proceed, and what does a witness in one (ours) say to your investigator if disclosing information will affect the OIG DoD investigation.

I have urged Pedeleose and Hagel to cooperate, and to answer questions that they feel will compromise the OIG DoD nvestigation by referring the matter to us; we can then decide, and not have two witnesses setting OIG policy (which is my fear).

Our attorneys are still looking at other angles, but I want to arrange this so the Colonel can move forward on matters within her urisdiction.

n Meyer

Dan Meyer, Director - Civilian Reprisal Investigations
J.S. Department of Defense, Office of the Inspector General
400 Army Navy Drive - Suite 918A
Arlington, VA 22202-4704

Tele: (703) 604.8807/W
Facs: (703) 602.6002/W

---

rom: Pedeleose, Ken [mailto:Ken.Pedeleose@dcma.mil]
ent: Wednesday, August 03, 2005 8:06 AM
o: Hagel, Henry; Scantlebury, Stacy
c: Meyer Daniel P., OIG DoD; Leake, Harvey; Conforto, Robert T.; Tate, Myra C.; Snow, Henrietta; Plourde, Nicole, Col USAF; homas, Joe; Sawyer, Gerry; Bogusz, Steven; Scott, Darryl A., Maj. Gen. (DCMA DIR); Ernst, Keith (East Director); Flavin, Sallie DCMA DEP. DIR)
ubject: RE: Urgent: Interview
mportance: High

Ir. Hagel,

are excellent questions.

Is. Scantlebury,

4/03/2006 **A2-3: August 8, 2005 1:09PM Page 2**

<u>A2-3: August 8, 2005 1:09PM</u>: Leigh Owens forwards an August 3, 2005 email by Meyer on August 8, 2005 at 1:09PM directly to Bruce Krasker with no words. Krasker holds the email for over 7 months then forwards the email about 2 days after my deposition to Gary Jencson.

3/31/2006 3:58PM

Jencson, Gary E.

From:	Krasker, Bruce
ent:	Friday, March 31, 2006 3:58 PM
To:	Jencson, Gary E.
Subject:	FW:
Attachments:	ScantleburyQuestions.doc

This is list of questions to Meyer

Bruce Krasker

Counsel
Defense Contract Management Agency East
495 Summer Street
Boston, MA 02210
(617) 753-4269
(617) 753-3037 (fax)
Bruce.Krasker@dcma.mil

From:	Owens, Leigh
Sent:	Monday, August 08, 2005 1:10 PM
To:	Krasker, Bruce
Subject:	FW:

Leigh S. Owens
Counsel
DCMA Atlanta
(678) 503-6041
DSN: 697-6041

If you are pleased with my service, please tell others.
If you are not, please tell me!
Either way, the DCMA Atlanta Office of Counsel values your feedback; please complete this SHORT Customer Comment Card
http://ice.disa.mil/index.cfm?fa=card&site_id=182&service_provider_id=88204&service_category_id=1

From: Owens, Leigh
Sent: Wednesday, August 03, 2005 4:27 PM
To: 'Meyer Daniel P., OIG DoD'
Subject:

Mr. Meyer,

Please find attached a list of the questions Ms. Scantlebury intends to ask Messrs. Hagel and Pedeleose when they are interviewed. The agency would, of course, ask follow on questions logically arising from the responses provided. In the interest of moving this matter forward, I think it would be more efficient to have your office review the questions and give us some guidance on the appropriate scope of our inquiry on the front end of the process.

1

A2-4: August 8, 2005 1:10PM Page 1

ScantleburyQuestions.doc (33 K...

Leigh Owens , Counsel
DCMA Atlanta
(678) 503-6041
DSN: 697-6041

If you are pleased with my service, please tell others.
If you are not, please tell me!
Either way, the DCMA Atlanta Office of Counsel values your feedback; please complete this SHORT Customer Comment Card
http://ice.disa.mil/index.cfm?fa=card&site_id=182&service_provider_id=88204&service_category_id=1

A2-4: August 8, 2005 1:10PM Page 2

2

A2-4: August 8, 2005 1:10PM: Leigh Owens takes another August 3, 2005 email with Meyer and forwards it on August 8, 2005 at 1:10PM directly to Bruce Krasker with no words. Krasker holds the email over 7 months then forwards the email about 2 days after my deposition to Gary Jencson.

The point is, Owens and Krasker ran a con on Dan Meyer. That helps support Dan Meyer's statement: "*I* (Meyer) *should have left you* (DoD IG officials) *all alone with Krasker".* Meyer enabled the con on Meyer by merely communicating with DCMA.

The next education in dealing with DCMA belongs to Uldric Fiore who directly communicated with Krasker on the "KP" (Ken Pedeleose) trophy.

Appendix 3: Fiore's Trophy and the "Boot" that Followed

The weaponized lawfare retaliation against me in Falsified Trail 3 had leaders. DCMA had Bruce Krasker closely followed by Leigh Owens. DoD IG had Uldric Fiore and Dan Meyer although Meyer was the catalyst that enabled the weaponization and lawfare of Falsified Trail 3. Without Dan Meyer Falsified Trail 3 had no chance of success.

Attention now shifts to Uldric Fiore who is educated in the perils of dealing with DCMA and Bruce Krasker to have my suspension as his (Fiore's) trophy.

Fiore, Uldric, OIG DoD

From: Cook, Theresa [Theresa.Cook@dcma.mil]
Sent: Wednesday, January 18, 2006 9:38 AM
To: Uldric.Fiore@dodig.mil
Subject: RE: OSC Letter Preliminary Closing of Mr. Pedeleose's Case
Attachments: KP.pdf

Good Morning,

Attached is the K. Pedeleose letter per Mr. Krasker.

Theresa

Theresa Cook
Paralegal Specialist
DCMAE-GC
(617)753-4353
theresa.cook@dcma.mil
(617)753-3037

530

A3-1: January 18, 2006 Page 1 of 2 AA 15

DEFENSE CONTRACT MANAGEMENT AGENCY
DEFENSE CONTRACT MANAGEMENT AGENCY EAST
495 SUMMER STREET
BOSTON, MA 02210-2184

IN REPLY REFER TO:

DCMAE-CC January 17, 2006

MEMORANDUM FOR Mr. Kenneth M. Pedeleose, DCMAE-RHSB

SUBJECT: Notice of Decision - Suspension

You are hereby notified of the decision to suspend you from duty and pay for thirty (30) calendar days, effective January 22, 2006 through and including February 18, 2006, for the offenses of refusal to cooperate with an agency investigation, insubordination and failure to follow instructions. This action is taken in conformity with the DCMA Instruction "Maintaining Discipline," September 2004 revision, and the Labor-Management Agreement between DLA and the DLA Council of Locals and the DCMAE Supplement thereto, dated January 30, 1997."

A Notice of Proposed Suspension dated October 18, 2005 and delivered to you on October 19, 2005 proposed your suspension for thirty (30) calendar days for the offenses described in the notice. You replied to that notice with letters dated November 1, 2005 and November 3, 2005. Your written reply also included a 12-page Chronological Report with a total of 205 pages of supporting documentation attached. You have also presented a number of questions about the authority for the underlying investigation. I have read and carefully considered your written replies and questions, your Chronological Report and the documentation attached thereto. The following comments are made regarding your replies:

a. You have raised the issue of "whistleblower reprisal" based upon your assistance to the Senate oversight investigations of the C-130J program and the DoDIG investigations of the C-130J contract cancellations. You allege that DCMA Management was attempting to undermine your efforts to assist in these matters. However, I find no evidence that Colonel Plourde or DCMA Management was motivated by reprisal or interfered or intended to interfere with your assistance with any Senate or DoDIG investigations relating to the C-130J program. The purpose of the investigation initiated by Col Plourde on June 21, 2005 was to identify the source of the rumor then circulating among the employees within her command that management had a list of particular employees that it (management) intended to terminate from employment. This rumor had been communicated to at least one employee, Ms. Gerry Sawyer, who was sufficiently upset by the information to tender her resignation rather than face a potential removal from service. It was Col Plourde's belief that this rumor was false in that neither she nor her Deputy had established such a list, and it was her observation that the rumor was having a negative impact on employee morale. Accordingly, it was Col Plourde's intent only to locate the source of the rumor in order to dispel the same. The fact that Col Plourde's investigation occurred in the same timeframe as some of your contacts with the Senate and/or the

531

AA 16

A3-1: January 18, 2006 Page 2 of 2

A3-1: January 18, 2006: Bruce Krasker has Paralegal Specialist Theresa Cook forward Uldric Fiore the 30-Day Suspension letter for me. Meaning, Fiore was still in the loop for the lawfare and using the 30-Day suspension as a trophy.

An interesting note is the Subject line which stated *"OSC Letter Preliminary Closing of Mr. Pedeleose's Case"*. This implies at some point DCMA and maybe Fiore were closely monitoring the actions of OSC. The initials "KP" for the Attachment meant I was a common topic of discussion.

Also interesting is Page 1of the 30-Day suspension letter which stated in part: *"It was Colonel Plourde's belief that this rumor was false"* (Regarding employees targeted to be fired). The key word is *"belief"*. The point is, two employees were already fired by Henrietta Snow (3rd Level Supervisor) with Colonel Plourde's (4th Level Supervisor) approval. First and second level supervisors were not involved in the terminations (removal from Federal Service).

The fact is, Plourde decimated the whistleblowing network in my office with help from the DoD IG and Henrietta Snow. This is a fact documented in this book, not conjecture.

KP Page 1 of 1

Fiore, Uldric, OIG DoD

From: Krasker, Bruce [Bruce.Krasker@dcma.mil]
Sent: Monday, January 23, 2006 3:10 PM
To: Uldric.Fiore@dodig.mil
Subject: KP

Ric

We delivered the Decision to Suspend for 30 days today to Mr. Pedeleose. He was out last week so we reissued it with a new effective date, Jan 25. He refused to sign and we so noted.

Bruce Krasker
Counsel
Defense Contract Management Agency East
495 Summer Street
Boston, MA 02210
(617) 753-4269
(617) 753-3037 (fax)
Bruce.Krasker@dcma.mil

AA 22

A3-2: January 23, 2006 536A

A3-2: January 23, 2006: Krasker directly emails and updates Fiore regarding my suspension. Meaning, Fiore kept in close written contact with Krasker and the status of my suspension (Fiore's trophy).

that, that process would not in any way interfere with his confidentiality responsibilities and ultimately, you know, explained that, what Mr. Jencson working through us explained that what he wanted was to make sure Mr. Meyer was available as a rebuttal witness in the event that Mr. Pedeleose made allegations against him.

MR. BIGGS: Umm hum.

MR. FIORE: In the process because that was inconsistent with his understanding of what Mr. Meyer's role had been.

MR. BIGGS: Okay.

MR. FIORE: And that eventually was resolved also and Mr. Meyer was available, Mr. Pedeleose had a rather contentious telephone conference with the administrative judge to the point where Mr. Pedeleose withdrew his request for a hearing. I think it was made clear that he was not impressing Mr. the administrative judge favorably with his appearance by telephone, an appearance in person probably would not have been any more productive.

MR. BIGGS: Okay. Tim do you have anything to

A3-3: June 28, 2006

DoD IG 324

<u>A3-3: June 28, 2006</u>: Proof that Uldric Fiore was directly involved well after the lawfare in 2005 is also provided in Fiore's sworn statement of June 28, 2006, where Fiore states in part:

"Mr. Pedeleose had a rather contentious telephone conversation with the administrative judge to the point where Mr. Pedeleose withdrew his request for a hearing."

First, Fiore was not party to any conversations I had with the administrative (MSPB) judge. Meaning, someone in DCMA (probably DCMA attorneys Gary Jencson, Donald Srail or Bruce Krasker) informed Fiore of the contentious conversation.

Second, I never withdrew my request for a hearing. I opted for a hearing on written records. I expected an in-person hearing would be an administrative "love fest" between DCMA and the MSPB judge. The hearing on written records leveled the playing field and help offset judicial bias on the release and presentation of facts. Gave the MSPB judge less opportunity to bully me, and a better opportunity for me to show how corrupted the MSPB is against irrefragable data.

Third, Dan Meyer refused to participate in the MSPB hearing, because I spoke with Dan Meyer who was very shaken.

The point is, Fiore received personal updates. Only question is who informed Fiore.

In the end Fiore was the topic of investigation. The reason that the Department of the Interior Inspector General had to investigate DoD IG was that I placed DoD IG under investigation. It was surprising that DoD IG did not investigate DoD IG. Because DCMA investigates DCMA and clears DCMA of wrong doing. DCMA is far better at using a closed loop of corruption. Probably DCMA has more practical weaponization and lawfare experience and is less visible on the hierarchical scale. DCMA also factors in Legal and Judicial System corruption.

Meaning, after 13 Falsified Trails it could be said DCMA is professional and highly skilled at weaponization and lawfare. There are 5 Chapters in this book with DCMA emerging as the focal point.

Anyway, Fiore didn't fare well with an independent investigation that wasn't covered up.

United States Department of the Interior
Office of Inspector General

REPORT OF INVESTIGATION

Case Title Fiore, Uldric	Case Number [Exemption 2]
Reporting Office Washington, D.C.	Report Date June 5, 2008
Report Subject Closing Report	

SYNOPSIS

At the request of the Department of Defense (DoD) Inspector General, we opened an investigation into the conduct of DoD OIG General Counsel Uldric Fiore. The DoD Inspector General had received a letter dated September 25, 2007, from Senator Charles Grassley questioning the following: (1) Fiore's role in drafting a response letter to Senator Grassley concerning a DoD press release that did not include pertinent e-mails and (2) Fiore's actions and involvement in issues concerning a DoD OIG complainant.

An August 2004 press release by the DoD contained inaccurate information concerning the status of a DoD Office of Inspector General (OIG) investigation of Jack Shaw, former Deputy Under Secretary of Defense for International Technology Security. Senator Charles Grassley requested that the DoD Inspector General at the time, Joseph Schmitz, outline his involvement in drafting this press release, and Fiore assisted him in preparing this response. A previous investigation by the DoD OIG found that the response letter to Senator Grassley drafted by Fiore contained inaccuracies and omissions and failed to adequately inform Senator Grassley of Schmitz's knowledge and involvement in drafting the inaccurate press release. Specifically, the response letter misleadingly states that Schmitz had neither involvement in the drafting of the final press release nor knowledge of the final published version. In addition, pertinent e-mails were not included in the response to Senator Grassley, as requested.

When we examined the issue of the missing e-mails, including reviewing thousands of pages of documents and conducting countless personal interviews, we ultimately narrowed our investigative focus to the difference in personal recollections of Fiore and L. Jerry Hansen, former Assistant Inspector General for Inspections and Policy, DoD OIG. [Exemption 5].

Our investigation also revealed that Fiore's conduct and involvement regarding the DoD OIG complainant may have compromised the independence of the DoD OIG, creating an appearance of the loss of impartiality. Specifically, we found that Fiore: (1) engaged in, along with his staff,

Reporting Official/Title [Exemptions 6 & 7C]/Special Agent	Signature
Approving Official/Title Alan Boehm/Director	Signature
Authentication Number: [Exemption 2]	

questionable discussions with the complainant's employer, the Defense Contract Management Agency (DCMA), regarding potential discipline of the complainant; (2) was improperly involved in reviewing a complaint from the same individual; and (3) improperly participated in responding to this complainant regarding issues in which he (Fiore) was personally involved.

This report is being forwarded to the DoD Inspector General for whatever action he deems appropriate.

BACKGROUND

On December 21, 2006, Senator Grassley sent a letter to Thomas Gimble, former acting Inspector General, DoD OIG, outlining concerns regarding Uldric Fiore, General Counsel, DoD OIG (**Attachment 1**). Specifically, Senator Grassley questioned Fiore's involvement in drafting a letter to Grassley's staff responding to allegations against former Inspector General Joseph Schmitz. Senator Grassley mentioned Fiore's failure to provide pertinent e-mails with the response letter. Subsequently, the DoD OIG opened an investigation into this issue.

On September 25, 2007, Senator Grassley sent a follow-up letter to Inspector General Claude Kicklighter, DoD OIG, requesting an independent investigation into some of the allegations outlined in the December 21, 2006 letter as well as new allegations questioning Fiore's actions and involvement in issues pertaining to a DoD OIG complainant (**Attachment 2**).

[Exemptions 5, 6, & 7C] Senator Grassley requested an independent investigation into other issues.

Shortly after receiving this letter, the DoD Inspector General requested that the Department of the Interior (DOI) OIG conduct an independent investigation into Senator Grassley's ongoing concerns regarding Fiore.

Agent's Note: *The DoD OIG never released a final report on its investigation of the press release issue due to the DOI OIG opening a new case. [Exemptions 5, 6, & 7C]* ***(Attachment 3)****.*

Fiore's Involvement in Drafting Response Letter to Senator Grassley

On March 13, 2004, the Deputy Senior Advisor for Programs, Ministry of Communications, Coalition Provisional Authority, Baghdad, Iraq, made allegations that Jack Shaw, Deputy Under Secretary of Defense for International Technology Security, also Director of the International Armament and Technology Trade Directorate (IATTD), assisted in steering contracts in Iraq to close friends (**Attachment 4**). In his capacity as Director of IATTD, Shaw reported to DoD Inspector General Joseph Schmitz, under a Memorandum of Understanding (**Attachment 5**).

Shortly after these allegations surfaced, the Defense Criminal Investigative Service, DoD OIG, opened a criminal investigation on Shaw, and a U.S. Attorney agreed to provide prosecutive support. However, the investigation was later turned over to the FBI due to the appearance of a conflict of interest created by the Memorandum of Understanding between Shaw and the DoD OIG (**Attachment 6**).

After the *LA Times* published an article on the allegations against Shaw in July 2004, Shaw agreed to resign from his DoD position if his name was cleared of any wrongdoing (**Attachment 7**). DoD issued a press release on August 10, 2004, which stated the following, in part: "The allegations were examined by the DoD IG criminal investigators in Baghdad and a criminal investigation was never opened....Shaw is not now, nor has he ever been, under

Case Number: [Exemption 2]

ADDENDUM

The following is the conclusion of the DOI OIG OGC's opinion on Fiore's actions regarding [the DoD complainant]:

> Fiore's official conduct in matters relating to [the DoD complainant] was deficient in three areas. First, Fiore's involvement in discussions with DCMA officials of disciplinary action against [the complainant] and his failure as a supervisor to limit [an Associate General Counsel's] role in his interactions with DCMA management to the coordination of their respective investigations compromised the independence of the OIG. Second, Fiore's involvement in the [the DoD complainant's] hotline complaint to the DoD OIG which included allegations against him and four other attorneys in his office created an appearance of loss of impartiality. Third, Fiore's involvement in the review of correspondence to [the DoD complainant] which foreclosed further communication with [the complainant] on a matter that related to allegations that [the complainant] had made against him created an appearance of loss of impartiality.

For OGC's full opinion, please see **Attachment 101.**

SUBJECT

Uldric Fiore, General Counsel, DoD OIG

DISPOSITION

This report is being forwarded to the DoD Inspector General for whatever action he deems appropriate.

ATTACHMENTS

1. Letter from Senator Grassley, dated December 21, 2006.
2. Letter from Senator Grassley, dated September 25, 2007.
3. [Exemptions 5, 6, & 7C]
4. Report of Investigation: Defense Criminal Investigative Service, dated August 16, 2004.
5. Memorandum of Understanding regarding Jack Shaw's endeavors on August 4, 2003.
6. Transmittal Memorandum, dated June 9, 2004.
7. *Los Angeles Times* Article, dated July 7, 2004.
8. Press Release No. 765-04, dated August 10, 2004.
9. Letter from PCIE Integrity Committee, dated December 20, 2005.
10. Letter from PCIE Integrity Committee, dated August 3, 2006.
11. Report of Investigation: U.S. Postal Service OIG, dated June 9, 2006.
12. Letter from Senator Grassley, dated July 7, 2005.
13. Disqualification for Fiore, dated October 28, 2005.
14. E-mails between Inspector General Schmitz and Uldric Fiore from April 29, 2002 to April 26, 2005.

29 **A3-4: June 5, 2008 Page 3 of 3**

A3-4: June 5, 2008: Fiore's wide trail of antics warranted investigation. The Case Title was *"Fiore, Uldric."* The investigation focused on Fiore's involvement with me (Pedeleose, "the DoD complainant") and another person, Jack Shaw. The conclusion stated in part (Page 3 of 3).

"*Fiore's official conduct in matters relating to [the DoD complainant] was deficient in three areas. First, Fiore's involvement in discussions with DCMA officials of disciplinary action against [the complainant] and his failure as a supervisor to limit [an Associate General Counsel's] role in his interactions with DCMA management to the coordination of their respective investigations compromised the independence of the OIG. Second, Fiore's involvement in the [the DoD complainant's] hotline complaint to the DoD OIG which included allegations against him and four other attorneys in his office created an appearance of loss of impartiality. Third, Fiore's involvement in the review of correspondence to [the DoD complainant] which foreclosed further communication with [the complainant] on a matter that related to allegations that [the complainant] had made against him created an appearance of loss of impartiality.*

This report is being forwarded to the DoD Inspector General for whatever action he deems appropriate."

As the following circumstantially shows, Fiore was "booted".

Pedeleose, Ken

From: Murphy, Charles (Grassley) [Charles_Murphy@grassley.senate.gov]
Sent: Monday, September 15, 2008 3:50 PM
To: Pedeleose, Ken; Edwards, Tom (Judiciary-Rep)
Subject: Re: Uldric Fiore

You are right. Fiore is gone. Kicklighter gave him the boot as he departed, but we do not know why. He didn't tell us. We can make some guesses. I will also tell you that the questions regarding Fiore go way beyond your case. That's all I will say for now.

From: Pedeleose, Ken
To: Murphy, Charles (Grassley)
Sent: Mon Sep 15 11:57:44 2008
Subject: Uldric Fiore

Charlie,

I was just told that Uldric Fiore has been moved back to the Army from the DoD IG.

Can you provide any more information and enlightenment in this area since Fiore was a part of my case?

I would guess that the DoD IG (Kicklighter from my understanding) would not have moved Fiore for a doing a good job.

My case was won because I had good documentation against the DoD IG and caught them with some surprising information provided by DCMA (Colonel Plourde). Colonel Plourde did wonders for exposing the DoD IG with her incriminating statement about how DCMA coordinated the scope of their (DCMA) (alleged) investihation with the DoD IG. That sent the DoD IG into defensive mode that uncovered some damaging facts.

Notwithstanding that, and the fact that I won my case, I am still under threat from the 30 day suspension because my case is out for appeal. I can still lose. Also of concern to me are 2 more situations:

1: Those whistleblowers who were not as fortunate as me and not aware that Fiore and others may have been operating behind the scenes.

2: The other members of the DoD IG that remain (to my understanding). These individuals include Dan Meyer and Leonard Trahan that were parts of my case.

Please provide as much information as you can regarding Fiore. I am interested in anything that will be done to undue the damage that Fiore has inflicted on me and the damage inflicted on other innocent employees.

Thanks,

Ken

A3-5: September 15, 2008

3/17/2009

A3-5: September 15, 2008: It seems the action by the DoD IG regarding Uldric Fiore was the "boot". The communication started when I asked Charlie Murphy about Uldric Fiore leaving the DoD IG. Murphy stated to me in the email:

"You are right. Fiore is gone. Kicklighter gave him the boot as he departed, but we do not know why. He didn't tell us. We can make some guesses. I will also tell you that the questions regarding Fiore go way beyond your case. That's all I will say for now."

The point is, Fiore got the "boot" (removed) more than likely because of my complaint however that is speculation.

Summary

These appendices were provided as brief examples of how this book was assembled over the years into an evidentiary file. An encyclopedia of weaponization and lawfare that trace to the national debt. Essentially well documented memoirs courtesy of my adversaries in DoD and DCMA who willingly chose electronic and written trail weaponization and lawfare. These Appendices are only a few samples.

A professional management staff would have resolved every personnel issue within this book in a matter of minutes. Instead, the management staff chose a path of weaponization, lawfare, and retaliation to try and drive me from government. All those efforts did was give me the evidence to write this book. I must have been correct in what I was saying for decades since weaponization, lawfare, and affordability became common topics in 2025.

Meaning the perfect book (encyclopedia) for 2026 and beyond to show, and remind, how the U.S. Government Swamp was formed and expanded to such a degree.

I harbor no ill will or malice towards any person, persons, or organization mentioned herein. The reader may draw their own conclusions as the data is specific and documented in detail in the words, mentality, and behavior of others. Thus, rendering personal opinions inconsequential.

This book was written for the efficiency of the Federal Service, reducing the national debt, and for national security since many of the evidentiary findings of this book will have a detrimental effect on national security.

www.ingramcontent.com/pod-product-compliance
Lightning Source LLC
LaVergne TN
LVHW080011210926
848481LV00011B/2989
* 9 7 9 8 2 3 3 9 2 2 6 1 9 *